Lyman Abbott

An Illustrated Commentary on the Gospel According to Matthew

For family use and reference, and for the great body of Christian workers of all denominations. Vol. 1

Lyman Abbott

An Illustrated Commentary on the Gospel According to Matthew
For family use and reference, and for the great body of Christian workers of all denominations. Vol. 1

ISBN/EAN: 9783337028107

Printed in Europe, USA, Canada, Australia, Japan

Cover: Foto ©Lupo / pixelio.de

More available books at **www.hansebooks.com**

CHRIST TEACHING IN THE SYNAGOGUE. *From Alexander Bida.*

AN

Illustrated Commentary

ON

THE GOSPEL ACCORDING TO

Matthew.

FOR FAMILY USE AND REFERENCE, AND FOR THE GREAT BODY
OF CHRISTIAN WORKERS OF ALL DENOMINATIONS.

By REV. LYMAN ABBOTT,
AUTHOR OF "LIFE OF CHRIST," "DICTIONARY OF RELIGIOUS KNOWLEDGE," ETC.

VOLUME I.

A. S. BARNES & COMPANY,
NEW YORK, CHICAGO, AND NEW ORLEANS.
1878.

BY THE EDITOR OF THIS WORK.

A SERIES OF POPULAR COMMENTARIES
ON THE NEW TESTAMENT.

IN EIGHT VOLUMES.

Volume I. MATTHEW. With Notes and Comments, Maps and Illustrations; also an Introduction to the Study of the New Testament, a condensed life of Christ, and a tabular Harmony of the Gospels. 8vo, cloth, beveled.

" II. MARK AND LUKE. (Ready.)

" III. JOHN. (In Press.)

" IV. THE ACTS OF THE APOSTLES. With Notes, Comments, Maps and Illustrations; also an Introductory Treatise, Chronological Table and Gazetteer. 8vo, cloth, beveled.

(The remaining volumes of the Series in preparation.)

Entered according to Act of Congress, in the year 1875, by
A. S. BARNES & COMPANY,
In the Office of the Librarian of Congress, at Washington.

PREFACE.

THE object of this Commentary is to aid in their Christian work those who are endeavoring to promote the knowledge of the principles which Jesus Christ came to propound and establish—clergymen, Christian parents, Sunday-School teachers, Bible-women, lay-preachers. Intended for Christian workers, it aims to give the results rather than the processes of scholarship, the conclusions rather than the controversies of scholars; intended for laymen as well as for clergymen, it accompanies the English version of the New Testament, in all references to the original Greek gives the English equivalent, and translates all quotations from the French, German, Latin and Greek authors.

The introduction on pages 31–34, contains a statement of those principles of interpretation which appear to me to be essential to the correct understanding of the Word of God. This Commentary is the result of a conscientious endeavor to apply those principles to the elucidation of the New Testament.

It is founded on a careful examination of the latest and best text; such variations as are of practical or doctrinal importance are indicated in the notes. It is founded on the original Greek; wherever that is inadequately rendered in our English version, a new translation is afforded by the notes. The general purpose of the writer or speaker, and the general scope of the incident or teaching, is indicated in a Preliminary Note to the passage, or in an analysis, a paraphrase, or a general summary at the close. Special topics, such as The Baptism, The Temptation, The Trial, and The Crucifixion of Jesus are treated separately in preliminary or supplementary notes. This volume contains thirty such excursus. The results of recent researches in Biblical archæology have been embodied, so as to make the Commentary serve in part the purpose of a Bible Dictionary. A free use is made of illustrations, from antiques, photographs, original drawings, and other trustworthy sources. They are never employed for mere ornament, but always to aid in depicting the life of Palestine, which remains in many respects substantially unchanged by the lapse of time. Since the Commentary is prepared, not for devotional reading, but for practical workers, little space has been devoted to hortatory remarks or practical or spiritual reflections. But I have uniformly sought to interpret the letter by the spirit, and to suggest rather than to supply moral and spiritual reflections, a paragraph of hints is affixed to each section or topic, embodying what appears to me to be the essential religious lessons of the incident or the teaching; sometimes a note is appended elucidating them more fully. The best thoughts of the best thinkers, both exegetical and homiletical, are freely quoted, especially such as are not likely to be accessible to most American readers; in all such cases the thought is credited to the author. Parallel and contrasted passages of Scripture are brought together in the notes; in addition, full Scripture references are appended to the text. These are taken substantially from Bagster's large edition of the English version of the Polyglot Bible, but they have been carefully examined and verified in preparing for the press, and some modifications have been made. For the convenience of that large class of Christian workers who are limited in their means, I have endeavored to make this Commentary, as far as practicable, a complete apparatus for the study of the New Testament. When finished it will be fully furnished with maps;—there are four in this volume; a Gazetteer gives a condensed account of all the principal places in Palestine, mentioned in our Lord's life; and an introduction traces the history of the New Testament from the days of Christ to the present, giving some account of the evidence and nature of inspiration, the growth of the canon, the character and history of the manuscripts, the English version, the nature of the Gospels and their relation to each other, a brief life of Christ, and a complete tabular harmony of the four Gospels.

The want of all who use the Bible in Christian work is the same. The *wish* is often for a demonstration that the Scripture sustains the reader's peculiar theological tenets, but the *want* is always for a clearer and better knowledge of Scripture teaching, whether it sanctions or overturns previous opinions. I am not conscious that this work is written in the interest of any theological or ecclesiastical system. In those cases in which the best scholars are disagreed in their interpretation, the different views and the reasons which lead me to my own conclusions have been given, I trust, in no controversial spirit. For the sole object of this work is to ascertain and make clear the meaning of the Word of God, irrespective of systems, whether ecclesiastical or doctrinal.

No work is more delightful than that which throws us into fellowship with great minds; of all work the most delightful is that which brings us into association with the mind of God. This is the fellowship to which the student of the Bible aspires. I can have for those who use this work no higher hope than that they may find in its employment some of the happiness which I have found in its preparation, and that it may serve them as t has served me, as a guide to the Word of God, and through that Word to a better acquaintance with God himself.

CORNWALL-ON-HUDSON, *May,* 1875.
LYMAN ABBOTT.

TABLE OF CONTENTS.

INTRODUCTION.

	PAGE
Nature of the New Testament	11
Origin and Authority	13
Evidences of Inspiration	14
Limits of Inspiration	16
New Testament Canon	17
The Text	25
Our English Version	28
Principles of Interpretation	31
Relation of the Gospels to each other	34
Origin of the Gospels	36
Harmony of the Gospels	38
Life of Christ	40
Tabular Harmony of the Gospels	44

THE GOSPEL OF MATTHEW.

Introduction to the Gospel of Matthew	49
Map of Palestine	50
Gazetteer	51
Supplementary Notes in Matthew—	
Names of Jesus	57
Birth of Jesus	64
Baptism of Jesus	72
Temptation of Jesus	77
The Sermon on the Mount	83
Christ's Principles respecting Retaliation	96
Christ's Teaching respecting Care	108
Judging our Fellow-men	109
Demoniacal Possession	123
The Publicans	126

	PAGE
THE TWELVE APOSTLES: THEIR LIVES AND CHARACTER	147
JOHN'S EMBASSY TO JESUS	152
BRETHREN OF OUR LORD	187
THE FOUNDATION OF CHRIST'S CHURCH	201
LESSONS OF THE TRANSFIGURATION	210
CHRIST'S LAW OF DIVORCE	224
CHRIST'S BLESSING OF LITTLE CHILDREN	226
CHRIST'S DISCOURSE ON THE LAST DAYS	253
MARRIAGE CEREMONIES IN THE EAST	268
THE LORD'S SUPPER	283
THE LESSONS OF GETHSEMANE	293
THE TRIAL OF JESUS BEFORE THE SANHEDRIM	297
THE DENIAL OF PETER	301
LESSONS FROM PETER'S DENIAL	304
CHARACTER AND CAREER OF JUDAS ISCARIOT	307
THE CRUCIFIXION	312
THE NATURE OF CRUCIFIXION	315
THE RESURRECTION OF JESUS	330

LIST OF ILLUSTRATIONS.

CHRIST TEACHING IN THE SYNAGOGUE. Frontispiece.	PAGE
BETHLEHEM. Looking west from the Convent of the Nativity	57
FISHERMAN CASTING HIS NET. Near Magdala	81
THE POSTURE AT MEAL	127
ANCIENT BOTTLE	130
STAFF AND SCRIP	138
GRAIN BASKET; TRAVELLING BASKET	198
ANCIENT KEY	203
TETADRACHM OR STATER	212
DENARIUS—A PENNY	242
PHYLACTERY IN USE	247
FRINGED GARMENT	247
THE TEMPLE OF HEROD	257
THE CLOAK	261
AN EASTERN MILL	266
A MODERN MARRIAGE PROCESSION IN JERUSALEM	269
ASSYRIAN LAMPS	270
LAMP AND TRIMMER	271
A SHEKEL	281
RECLINING AT MEAL	283
ROMAN WINE CUPS	285
EGYPTIAN CUPS	285
GARDEN OF GETHSEMANE: JERUSALEM IN THE BACKGROUND	290
THE MACHÆRA	295
INTERIOR COURTYARD OF ORIENTAL HOUSE	303
PLAN OF ORIENTAL HOUSE	303
SCOURGES	311
SCARLET ROBE	313
CROWN OF THORNS	312
THE REED	312
GOLGOTHA	314
THE THREE CROSSES	315
HYSSOP	318
TWO CENTURIONS	320
ROAD FROM BETHANY TO JERUSALEM	333

MAPS AND PLANS.

SKETCH MAP ILLUSTRATING THE JOURNEYINGS OF OUR LORD	41
MAP OF JERUSALEM IN THE TIMES OF CHRIST	278

THE STUDY OF THE NEW TESTAMENT.

THE New Testament consists of twenty-seven distinct documents, written by nine, perhaps ten, different authors. They were written without concert of action, at different times, for different purposes, and addressed to different readers. They differ also in character and style; some of them are historic, some of them philosophic and didactic, one is poetic and prophetic. They were all composed during the first century after Christ, in the Greek language—unless Matthew's Gospel was first written in Hebrew—and the manuscript copies have long since perished. Thus our English New Testament is a translation from a Greek original, which is itself a copy of copies, the original being no longer in existence. I propose in this Introduction to trace the history of the New Testament from its origin to the present day; to point out the central principle which unites these documents in one harmonious book; to state the reasons which have led the Christian Church to regard them as in a peculiar sense inspired by God; to give briefly the evidences which satisfy the Church that these books were really written by the authors whose names they bear; to describe the difficulties which Christian scholars have encountered in ascertaining what was the text of the original manuscripts, and how they have overcome those difficulties; and to narrate the history of our present English translation, indicate some of its defects, and the principles adopted in this Commentary in the endeavor to afford the Christian student aid in its interpretation. I propose then further to describe the characteristics of the Gospels, and their relations to each other; to point out the seeming discrepancies and real harmony in their accounts; to indicate the principal features in the earthly life of Jesus Christ; and finally to furnish a table of the Evangelical narratives, arranged in parallel columns, so as to enable the student to fill out and complete this sketch in detail.

PART I. THE NEW TESTAMENT.

I. Its Nature.—The word Testament means covenant or agreement. It is generally so translated.[1] This meaning lingers in the phrase "last will and testament." The will of a deceased is his last testament because it is his last covenant, the last agreement which he can make, one which often has to be accepted and finally executed by his heirs. It appears very clearly in the institution of the Lord's Supper. In the hospitable East a meal was the customary method of at once celebrating and sealing a treaty or compact, as is smoking the pipe of peace among the North American Indians, or the payment of a sum to bind the bargain in our more commercial age and nation. Christ, therefore, immediately before his death, arranged for a supper with his disciples, as a method of both

---

[1] As in Acts 3 : 25; Gal. 3 :15, 17; 4 : 24; and in many places in Hebrews.

sealing and celebrating his compact or covenant with his Church; and taking the cup of wine, he pledged his disciples in it with the words, "This cup is the new testament (*i. e.*, the new covenant) in my blood, which is shed for you."[1] Thus every recurring communion season emphasizes the meaning of this word Testament, and repeats the solemn ratification of the compact between Christ and his people.

The New Testament, then, is God's own covenant or agreement with man.[2] The opening chapter of Matthew intimates the character of this covenant. The angel, in announcing the advent of the Son of God, says to Joseph, "Thou shalt call his name Jesus, for he shall save his people from their sins." The closing chapter of the Book of Revelation intimates the answer to the question, Who are his people? "Whosoever will, let him take of the water of life freely." The New Testament, then, is God's promise to save from the present and future punishment of sin all those who come to Him for such salvation. It is not a book of rules for the government of conduct; that is, it is not a new law. It is not a book of philosophy, respecting either human or divine nature; that is, it is not a new theology. It is simply what its name implies, a new covenant on God's part to save from sin those who come to him, in child-like trust, for such salvation. This is a very simple truth; but it is fundamental to a right interpretation of the book.

The New Testament may be regarded as consisting of three kinds of books, (1) historic, (2) philosophic and didactic, (3) prophetic; though each of these elements is to be found in all the books.

1. The four Gospels and the Book of Acts are mainly historic. The first afford us our only information concerning the life and teachings of Jesus Christ; the second gives an account of the results, in the early church, of the work of the Divine Spirit, whom Christ, at the time of his death, promised to send to the disciples after his ascension. These five books constitute the foundation on which the superstructure of the New Testament is built; the historical basis for the new covenant which Paul in his Epistles analyzes and interprets, and the fulfilment of which John, in the Book of Revelation, pictorially describes.

2. The Epistles, most of which were written by Paul, are philosophic and didactic. They explain the necessity for such a covenant as the New Testament, its nature, the conditions on which we can avail ourselves of it, the consequences of rejecting it, the results of accepting it, in spiritual life, in the individual and the community, in the present world and the hereafter; they contain wise counsels to Christians how best to promote the general acceptance of this covenant by Jew and Gentile; and with vehement rhetoric they urge its acceptance upon the reader. These Epistles, of which I shall write more fully in the introduction to the volume which contains them, differ in character, scope, and purpose. Some of them were written as circular letters to the church at large, some of them to individual churches, some of them to personal friends. They contain, therefore, some personal allusions and practical advice, which are only indirectly applicable to our own time, and some counsels in respect to church organization and church work, which are not, however, to be interpreted as ecclesiastical laws, but as illustrations of those principles of organic action which will render the church efficient in proclaiming the privileges of the new covenant to others.

3. The only purely prophetic book of the New Testament is the Book of Revelation. Its object is to disclose the final fulfillment of the new covenant or agreement of God in

---

[1] Luke 22 : 20.
[2] This covenant is distinctly stated in Jer. 31 : 31-34, quoted in Hebrews 8 : 8-12. The difference between the old covenant and the new is indicated by comparing the language of the third commandment, "Showing mercy unto thousands of them that love me and keep my commandments" (Exod. 20 : 6), with that of Paul, "God who is rich in mercy, for his great love wherewith he loved us, even when we were dead in sins, hath quickened us together with Christ." Ephes. 2 : 4, 5.

the second coming of Jesus Christ, the complete and final overthrow of sin and suffering, and the manifest and perfect triumph of God and godliness throughout the universe.

Thus it will be seen that the New Testament is not a mere collection of independent and disconnected treatises, but a harmonious whole, in which the new agreement or promise of God is first set forth in the life and death of Jesus Christ and the work of the Holy Spirit; second, explained and enforced by the arguments of Paul and his apostolic contemporaries; and finally disclosed in its fulfillment in the vision of John the prophet-apostle.

II. Its Origin and Authority.—If the New Testament is a new covenant, there must be a covenantor. If it is a promise that God will do for man what man cannot do for himself, it must in a peculiar sense come from God, or it is not what it pretends to be. For example, if we suppose the declaration, "He shall save his people from their sins," was directly authorized by God, it is a divine promise on which we can with assurance rely; if not, it only expresses the opinion which a Roman tax-gatherer of the first century entertained upon the subject, and is of no particular value. In other words, the divine origin and authority of the book is involved in its nature, and indeed in its very title. If it were a book of moral philosophy, *i. e.*, if its object were to tell us how to conduct ourselves in this life, or if it were a book of theological philosophy, *i. e.*, if its object were to teach, either by analogies drawn from nature, or by appeals to our own intuition, truths about God and our own souls, it might be uninspired and still valuable. But if it is an agreement on God's part to save his people from their sins, it must be inspired by God; otherwise it is not a divine covenant to do, but only a human opinion concerning what God is likely to do. If it is not inspired it is no New Testament.

Accordingly we find throughout the book the claim, or rather the quiet assumption, of that divine origin and authority which is implied in its very title.

Jesus Christ himself, at twelve years of age, declares to his mother that he has come to earth to do his Father's business;[1] he is repeatedly said by the Evangelists to be acting under the influence of the Divine Spirit;[2] he declares to the Jews in Jerusalem that he speaks to the world those truths which he has received from his Father;[3] he declares to his disciples that the Father dwells in him, and that the words which he speaks he speaks not of himself, but from the Father which sent him and dwells in him;[4] and in solemn prayer he reasserts that the words of truth which he has taught them the Father gave to him for that purpose.[5] He promises to his disciples before his death that he will not leave them alone, but will come unto them and dwell in them;[6] that the Holy Ghost shall be their teacher and shall quicken their remembrance of their Master's teaching;[7] and after his resurrection, when he gives them their final commission, he promises to be with them in all their work, even to the end of the world.[8] The opening chapter of the Book of Acts records the beginning of the fulfillment of these promises in the visible manifestation of the presence of the Spirit of God. In the first apostolic sermon Peter refers to a prophetic promise of inspiration contained in the Old Testament, and declares that the day of its fulfillment has arrived;[9] and the subsequent portions of the Book of Acts contain on almost every page accounts of its further fulfilment.[10] Throughout the Epistles the writers assume to speak, not their own opinions, but the truths which they have been taught of God. They not only declare in general terms that all Scripture is given by inspiration of God, and that holy men of God spake as they were moved by the

---

[1] Luke 2 : 49..... [2] Matt. 3 : 16; Luke 2 : 40; 4 : 14, 18; John 3 : 34; Acts 1 : 2; 10 : 38; Romans 1 : 4.....
[3] John 8 : 28...... [4] John 14 : 10, 24.... [5] John 17 : 8...... [6] John 14 : 17-19...... [7] John 14 : 26; 16 : 7, 13-15. Compare Matt. 10 : 19, 20; Luke 12 : 12...... [8] Matt. 28 : 20. Compare Acts 1 : 4, 5, 8...... [9] Acts 2 : 4, 16-18, 33......
[10] Acts 4 : 8, 31; 6 : 10; 7 : 55; 8 : 29; 10 : 19, 20; 13 : 2, 4, 9-11, 52; 15 : 28; 16 : 6; 19 : 6; 20 : 22, 23, 28.

Holy Ghost'—these declarations apply primarily only to the Old Testament—but they also declare of their own ministry and of the Gospel of the New Testament, that it is the "power of God," the "word of God," the "word of the Lord," "the glorious Gospel of the blessed God," "the commandments of the Lord," the "word of Christ," a "more sure word of prophecy" even than the Old Testament, spoken "in demonstration of the Spirit," in "words which the Holy Spirit teacheth," and preached "with the Holy Ghost sent down from heaven."² If this claim be not true, the book not only ceases to be trustworthy as a promise or covenant of God, it also ceases to be trustworthy as a moral or spiritual guide. For, if the writers of the New Testament were not thus guided and impelled by the Spirit of God, if they were not the authorized bearers of a Divine promise to man, then they were either impostors or visionaries, the perpetrators of a fraud or the victims of a delusion. And neither impostors nor visionaries are safe and trustworthy spiritual guides.

III. Evidences of its Inspiration.—The claim of the New Testament writers that they speak by the authority of God, and under the impulse and inspiration of the Spirit of God, has been generally regarded as well founded by the great majority of those who have studied their writings and the history of the effects which they have produced upon the human race. It is impossible to do more here than summarize very briefly some of the principal considerations which have led to this conclusion.

1. It is the fundamental doctrine of Christianity, confirmed by the history and experience of the Christian Church, that God dwells in the hearts of his children, that he guides, comforts, and strengthens them, that the soul was not made to live alone, but in constant communication with God, and that the influence of the Spirit of God, thus vouchsafed to the spirit of man, is always adapted to his needs. Thus the doctrine of the special inspiration of the sacred penmen is only part of the more general doctrine of the inspiration of all who will accept the divine guidance.

2. The history of the human race shows that there is a need of some more definite and explicit instruction concerning moral and spiritual truth and life than is afforded by the analogies of nature or the intuitions of uninstructed conscience. Without it no people have attained a high state of intellectual, political, or social civilization, still less a high state of moral and spiritual culture.³ Without an inspired book the human race is without any adequate knowledge of God or the future life, without any reliable assurance of pardon for past sin or provision of escape from future sin, and without any trustworthy and immutable standard of human duty or ideal of human character.

3. This need, interpreted by the universal craving for inspired oracles, writings, or priests, is supplied by the Bible. This book or series of books reveals a paternal God, whose love satisfies the filial yearning of the soul for a heavenly Father; it reveals a future life, which satisfies both the requirements of justice and the aspirations after immortality; it not only promises divine pardon on the condition of repentance and faith, but upon such an historical basis that its assurances do actually afford peace of mind to the believer, as no other religion does; it promises, on like conditions, divine help in change of life and character, and the help afforded in innumerable instances, in moral and

---

¹ 2 Tim. 3:16; 2 Peter 1:21...... ² 1 Cor. 1:18; 2:4, 12, 13; 14:37; Col. 3:16; 1 Thess. 2:13; 1 Tim. 1:11; 1 Peter 1:12, 25; 2 Peter 1:19. Compare, also, Acts 10:36; 20:24; Rom. 15:29; 16:25, 26; 2 Cor. 4:4; 6:4; Gal. 1:11, 12, 16; Ephes. 3:9; 6:17; Col. 1:26; Heb. 2:4; 1 Tim. 6:3; 1 John 4:6. It can hardly be necessary to refer the reader to passages in the Book of Revelation, since that is an unmeaning dream except it be regarded as an inspired vision.

³ Let him who doubts this statement, and cites the Greeks and Romans as exceptions, study Pressensé's *The Religions before Christ*, or even Gibbon's or Lecky's descriptions of Roman and Grecian civilization. Or let the reader compare Paul's description of Roman morals, in Romans, chapters I and II, with any of the ancient historians, for they fully justify it.

spiritual changes, not only in individuals but in entire communities, is the best evidence of the origin and trustworthiness of these promises; it affords in the law of love a perfect and an inflexible standard of character, applicable to all ages, classes, and conditions of men; and it affords in the life of Jesus Christ a perfect ideal of human life and character, which all can follow and which none have ever surpassed.

4. The supreme excellence of the precepts and principles of the Bible negative the hypothesis that they were the uninspired productions of the men who transcribed them. It is easier to believe that the Ten Commandments were inspired by God than to believe that they were wrought out by a man whose sole training was derived from a Hebrew slave mother, an Egyptian court, and the life of a Midianitish shepherd; easier to believe that the Sermon on the Mount, and the 14th, 15th, and 16th chapters of John, were inspired by God, than to believe that they were the intellectual production of a Galilean carpenter. The lives which then, and ever since, those have lived who have received the Bible as the Word of God, when compared with the lives of the heathen who have not received its influences, afford also a perpetual evidence that those precepts and principles are of superhuman origin, and possess a superhuman inspiring power.

5. The unity of the Bible indicates that one Supreme intellect directed the various writers by whom its books were composed. It consists of sixty-six separate treatises, written by between forty and fifty different writers, living centuries apart, speaking different languages, subjects of different governments, brought up under different civilizations. Over fifteen hundred years elapsed between the writings of Moses and those of John. All forms of literature—law, history, biography, poetry, oratory, and philosophy—are contained in the Bible. Yet the same substantial truths are taught by all these various writers, and the moral and spiritual unity of the Bible is such that probably few of its readers ever realize that it is, humanly speaking, the product of so many individual minds. Unity of design in the Scriptures proves that there was one designer, as the unity in the architectural design of the cathedral, which is the construction of many different hands, proves the supervising skill of the architect who planned and directed its construction.

6. The fulfilment in the New Testament of prophecies recorded in the Old Testament, and the fulfilment in later times of prophecies recorded in the New Testament, prove that at least those portions which are prophetic were the work of Him who sees the end from the beginning, and afford a sign and seal of the inspiration of the other portions of the sacred writings.

7. The miracles authenticate the divine authority of those who wrought them. Christianity as a system of truth and duty does not, indeed, depend upon the miracles. But to those who accept the New Testament as an authentic narration of actual events, the miracles demonstrate that Christianity possesses the divine sanction, since they could have been wrought only by divine power. To this authentication of their authority frequent reference is made by the writers of the New Testament.[1]

8. The testimony of those writers is in itself not a demonstration of their inspiration, but it is an evidence thereof. That they claim to be inspired, and that Christ promised them such inspiration, we have already seen. If this claim is unfounded we must believe either that they were impostors, pretending to an inspiration which they knew they did not possess, or visionaries, believing themselves to possess an inspiration which they did not in fact possess. The heroism and self-sacrifice of their lives prove that they were not impostors; the excellence of their doctrine proves that they were not visionaries. In brief, to the great body of thoughtful men it will always seem more natural to believe that the writers of the Bible wrote and spoke under the special influence of the Spirit of

---

[1] Mark 16:20; John 10:25; Rom. 15:18, 19; Heb. 2:4.

God, than to suppose that they belong in the same category with either Mohammed or Joe Smith.

9. Finally, if the New Testament be not inspired, Christianity is not a divine covenant, but only a human system of theology and ethics. There is no trustworthy revelation concerning the nature and will of God, no assurance of divine pardon for sin, no provision of divine grace for the tempted. And in fact those philosophies which reject the Bible as the inspired Word of God teach that God is unknowable, or that there is no other God than nature, that his will cannot be ascertained, or is only manifested in natural law, physical and social, and that there is no forgiveness of sins, but that every man must bear in his own person the penalty of his transgressions, and work out by the force of his own will his own redemption.

IV. Limits of Inspiration.—The word Inspiration means literally "in-breathing." The doctrine that the New Testament is inspired of God is the doctrine that the penmen in writing it acted under an influence from God, which conferred upon their minds and hearts a power greater than their own, or, as stated by Peter, that "holy men of God spake as they were moved by the Holy Ghost."[1] The manner in which this Divine influence acted upon their minds, and the extent to which it affected them and their writings, is nowhere distinctly stated in Scripture. There are various theological theories upon this subject, which I do not think it necessary to recount here. They may all be reduced to two general classes—the doctrines respectively of verbal inspiration and of moral inspiration.

By *verbal inspiration* is meant the immediate communication by God to the writers, of every word which they wrote. "I believe," says Tregelles, "the sixty-six books of the Old Testament and New Testament, to be verbally the Word of God, as absolutely as were the Ten Commandments written by the finger of God upon the two tables of stone."[2] So Hooker[3] says of the prophets, "they neither spake nor wrote any word of their own, but uttered syllable by syllable as the Spirit put it into their mouths." That certain passages may have been written thus, as it were, by Divine dictation, the writers being mere amanuenses, is possibly true; that the chief portions of the New Testament were thus written, is, I think, clearly not true.

This method does not accord with God's general principles of action, which are to work *in* us and *with* us, helping our infirmities, not to relieve us of all responsibility and do the work in our stead. It does not accord with the claims of the sacred writers, who indeed, nowhere distinctly define the limits of inspiration, but who do very distinctly imply the existence of a human element, of personal thought and study in the writing.[4] It does not accord with those variations in style, expression, thought, and even teaching, which give individuality to each of the sacred books, which make the three Gospels so different in style, that of John so different from the other three in subject-matter, and the Epistles of James and of Paul so different in the phases of truth which they respectively exhibit. It does not accord with the verbal, and even more than verbal discrepancies which are notable where two or more writers narrate the same event. Many such instances are afforded by a comparison of the parallel accounts of the three Synoptic Gospels. In the four variant reports of the inscription on the cross[5] is a striking illustration of a discrepancy which is just such as we should expect from independent historians, who to a large extent relied upon their own memory, or upon the recollection of others, but is utterly irreconcilable with the theory that they recorded as amanuenses what the Holy

---

[1] 2 Peter 1 : 21. The true rendition of this passage. "holy men spake from God," intensifies its meaning, but does not otherwise modify it...... [2] Quoted in McWhorter's Hand Book of the New Testament, page 23...... [3] Quoted in Lee on Inspiration, page 35...... [4] See for example Luke 1 : 3 ; 2 Pet. 1 : 21...... [5] Matt. 27 : 37 ; Mark 15 : 26 ; Luke 23 : 38 ; John 19 : 19.

Spirit dictated to them.[1] This theory does not accord with the subsequent history of the New Testament. For we have not the original words in which the books were written; with the exception of a few scholars, the great majority of Bible readers are dependent upon a confessedly uninspired translation of a confessedly uninspired copy. Finally, the apostle distinctly declares that the letter killeth, while the Spirit maketh alive; and a theory of verbal inspiration, *i. e.* of the inspiration of the words and letters, so far from quickening the spiritual impulse to a reverent study of the essential truths of the Bible, produces a directly opposite effect, and is neither productive of Scriptural scholarship nor true spiritual culture.

By *moral inspiration* is meant such a divine quickening of the natural faculties of the sacred writers, that, while they used their own memory, reason, and religious and intellectual culture, they were protected from all such errors as would impair the value of their writings as instruments for religious instruction and spiritual impulse, or, in other words, that they were inspired just so far as was necessary to make their writings "profitable for doctrine, for reproof, for correction, for instruction in righteousness." Minor errors in science, in chronology, in dates, diversities in forms and methods of expression, partial and fragmentary utterances,[2] immaterial discrepancies and apparent inconsistencies in different narrations of the same event, do nothing to shake the faith of those who hold this theory of inspiration. It allows, too, the opinion that the inspiration of different books is of a different kind, and that the same degree of authority is not to be attached to the books of Ruth and Esther as to the Ten Commandments, the purely personal epistle to Philemon as to the general epistle to the Romans, or to such a direction as that of 2 Tim. 4 : 13, as to the precepts of the Sermon on the Mount. This is the doctrine of inspiration which throughout this Commentary I have assumed to be the correct one. The evidences of its correctness will appear in the notes themselves.

At the same time there are passages in which the language, as well as the idea, appears to me to have been supernaturally inspired. This is especially the case in many instances in the Evangelical reports of our Lord's discourses, where a peculiar significance is involved in the words used by our Lord and preserved by his reporters—a significance which is often lost in our English translation.[3]

I believe, then, that the New Testament is God's covenant with man; that it is not an outgrowth of human thought, but comes from God; that he has chosen to impart it through imperfect men, as he chooses imperfect men to proclaim and to interpret it; that in writing this New Covenant they had all the divine guidance and impulse necessary to make it a safe and sufficient guide to man in moral and spiritual life; and that their authority to speak for God is attested by the miracles they wrought, by the fulfillment of the prophecies they recorded, by the superhuman excellence of the doctrines and the life they inculcated, but yet more by the divine fulfillment of the compact which in God's name they professed to record, and in the beneficent effects, temporal and spiritual, which have resulted in the case of all individuals and of all communities which have accepted it and complied with its conditions.

V. The New Testament Canon.—The word Canon means literally a carpenter's rule. Hence, by an easy transition, it is used to signify a rule or test in language, art, or religion. As applied to Scripture it may mean either the rules or principles by which the right of any book to be in the Bible is determined, or the authority of such book or books as a rule of faith and practice. It is in the latter sense that the word is now generally used. The term "Canonical books" means the books which afford an

---

[1] See for examples the arrest of Christ, the trial, and Peter's denials. Matt., chap. 26, and notes...... [2] Such as Romans 13:8, 9..... [3] See for example Notes on Matt. 5 : 19, 44; 6 : 25; 7 : 1-5. The instances are very numerous; these may serve to illustrate my meaning.

authoritative rule, in contrast with those which are uninspired and hence afford only human instruction. The history of the formation of the New Testament and the principles which determine what books belong to it and are authoritative, constitute therefore the theme of this section. What evidence have we that the New Testament which we now possess includes the inspired productions of the Apostles and excludes spurious imitations? in other words, what evidence is there that we have the true canon or rule? The evidence is of two kinds: external or historical, and internal or spiritual.

I. *External or Historical Evidence.*—To the question, When, where, and by whom were the books of the New Testament collected into one volume? no answer can be given. The New Testament was not formed; it grew. The external evidence of its authenticity and authority is to be found in a history of that growth, and of the testimony of writers immediately succeeding the apostolic age.

The Gospels bear the evidence in themselves that they were written for the information of the disciples of Jesus Christ, especially for those who had not directly received the Master's instructions, and who had not access to the verbal teaching of eye and ear witnesses.[1] The Epistles were written, either to local churches or to particular individuals, to impart, in a more systematic form, the precepts and principles of Christianity, to correct particular errors, or to afford instruction or inspiration needed in particular churches. Both apostles and churches anticipated the speedy second coming of Jesus Christ, and there is nothing to indicate that either recognized in these separate treatises a contribution to a permanent and universal book. But that the writers claimed to speak by authority of God, and in a peculiar sense under his inspiration, we have already seen.[2] The writers of the New Testament were, moreover, all immediate disciples of Jesus Christ, excepting Paul, who claimed to have received instruction directly from the risen Lord, and to be therefore not less an apostle than the twelve.[3] The epistles thus received by the church from the immediate disciples of the Lord would be naturally held as a sacred possession. They were read publicly in the church services;[4] churches exchanged their epistles one with another;[5] they were unmistakably regarded by both writers and recipients as authoritative;[6] and in one significant passage Peter expressly classifies the writings of Paul with the Old Testament Scriptures.[7] Thus, toward the close of the first century the materials for the New Testament had been accumulated. Each church possessed, in addition to a copy of the Old Testament in common with the Jewish Synagogue, a letter or a gospel, or two or three letters, obtained by a system of exchange, while no church probably possessed the entire New Testament collection. It existed, but in fragments, and divided among the different churches.[*]

The apostles died, leaving these writings as a legacy to the infant churches. As tradition grew more and more remote, and direct counsel from the apostles in the solution of questions of ritual, government, discipline, and doctrine was no longer attainable, these writings appreciated in value, and the authority of the letter was established by the death of the writer. Meanwhile, with the growth of the church, heresies sprang up. The heretics were often unprincipled. They sometimes mutilated the apostolic writings, sometimes denied their authenticity and authority, sometimes endeavored to palm off upon the churches spurious doctrines, with the sanction of a forged apostle's name. These practices, of which we get some hints even in the New Testament,[9] and some indications in very early corruptions of the text, increased after the death of the inspired

---

[1] Luke 1:1-4; John 20:30, 31 .... [2] See under Section III...... [3] 1 Cor. 9:1; 15:8; Gal. 1:15, 16; 2:2; Ephes. 3:3...... [4] 1 Thess. 5:27...... [5] Col. 4:16...... [6] Acts 15:23-31; 2 Cor. 10:1-10; Rev., chap. 2:3 ..... [7] 2 Pet. 3:16.

[*] Mr. Norton, Genuineness of the Gospels, estimates that as many as 60,000 copies of the Gospels were in circulation by the end of the second century, by which time, however, the N. T. canon had been substantially organized...... [9] 2 Tim. 1:15; Titus 1:10-14; Rev. 22:18, 19.

writers. Thus at once the value of the genuine writings, and the evident necessity of a critical examination into all doubtful gospels and epistles, increased. Thus, too, in the controversies which ensued, and which reached their climax in the conflict between Arius and Athanasius (A. D. 325-336), quotations from the inspired writings of the Evangelists and Apostles grew more frequent. These quotations rendered necessary a larger interchange of the original documents. Each church, dissatisfied with a second-hand report of an apostolic writing, sought and obtained a copy of the original, and thus gradually book was added to book, every claimant to inspired authority was subjected to a searching examination, the false were thrown out and the true alone accepted, until at length, by the close of the second century, the New Testament, substantially as we now have it, had grown into a book whose authenticity and authority all parties in the Christian church alike acknowledged.[1] Thus the canon of the New Testament is established, not by the judgment of a single man, whose authority to select it would be difficult to establish, not by the judgment of an ecclesiastical council, which might labor under the just suspicion of ecclesiastical prejudice, but by the general consent of thousands of local churches, and an innumerable body of individual Christians, whose combined judgment must ever be free from all possible suspicion of local prejudice or personal interest, and from any just charge of theological prepossessions. The evidence of the canonicity of the New Testament—that is, the evidence that we have in the New Testament the books written by the immediate disciples of our Lord, and only such—is to be found, not in the opinions of individual scholars, or the decrees of early councils, but in the abundant reference to these books in the controversial writings of the three or four centuries which immediately followed the apostolic age. Without attempting to give this evidence in detail, which would be foreign to my purpose, I shall give such a summary of it as will afford the reader an idea of its character and the student a suggestion for more elaborate investigation.[2]

1. *Clement of Rome.* Of his history little is known. He was Bishop of Rome at the end of the first century, is probably referred to by Paul in Philippians 4 : 3 as one of his "fellow workers," and was certainly a disciple of the apostles. Of the various works attributed to him, only the so-called 1st Epistle to the Corinthians is certainly known to be his. In this epistle, certainly published during the first century, and very probably as early as 64-70 A. D., he quotes, "as the words of the Lord Jesus," expressions in substance identical and in phraseology similar to those reported in the Gospels of Matthew and Luke; in a similar manner embodies sentiments and expressions found in James, 1 Peter, and several of Paul's Epistles; while his quotations from or similarities of expres-

---

[1] "With the exception of the Epistle to the Hebrews, the two shorter Epistles to St. John, the second Epistle of St. Peter, the Epistles of St. James and St. Jude, and the Apocalypse, all the other books of the New Testament were acknowledged as apostolic and authoritative throughout the church at the close of the second century."—*Westcott on the Canon of the New Testament*, p. 306.

[2] To comprise in a few pages the results of discussions which fill hundreds of volumes, which have been conducted on both sides too often with unseemly acerbity, in which not unfrequently strong assertion has served for proof, and special pleading for critical scholarship, which depends on an examination and analysis of the literature of the first three centuries, its own authenticity sometimes involved in doubt, has been a matter of no small difficulty. It was possible to accomplish such a condensation only (1) by giving results and discussions; (2) omitting all authors whose works are really involved in any reasonable doubt, such as Ignatius and Barnabas; (3) passing by without notice, though not without careful examination, the objections of rationalistic critics to the conclusions of Christian scholarship. Whatever on a fair examination has seemed to me *doubtful* I have omitted; there is enough that is certain. The English student who wishes to examine the subject more thoroughly is referred to Westcott, *History of the Canon of the N. T.*, Scrivener's *Plain Intro. to the Criticism of the N. T.*, Davidson's *Intro. to the N. T.*, Hone's *Intro. to the Scriptures*, and Smith's *Bible Dict.*, art. *Canon*, prepared by Dr. Westcott. A popular statement of results is given by Edward Case Bissell in *The Historic Origin of the Bible*, and a condensed statement of the argument in a little tract by Tischendorf, entitled "*When were our Gospels Written?*" The most complete rationalistic argument against the canonicity of the N. T. in the English language is given by the anonymous work *Supernatural Religion*.

sion to the Epistle to the Hebrews is so great that by some its authorship is attributed to him. In addition, his doctrinal statements accord with, and are apparently derived from, the writings of the apostles.

2. *Polycarp*, Bishop of Smyrna, born probably A. D. 70–80, martyred A. D. 166. One short epistle of his, to the Philippians, is extant, concerning the genuineness of which there is no reasonable question. It contains far more references to the writings of the New Testament than any other work of the first age; and still, with one exception,[1] all the phrases which Polycarp employs are woven into the texture of his letter, without any sign of quotation. "In other cases it is possible to assign verbal coincidences to accident; but Polycarp's use of Scriptural language is so frequent that it is wholly unreasonable to doubt that he was acquainted with the chief parts of our canon."[2] His testimony to the genuineness and the then recognized value of the books of the New Testament is the greater because (1) it is incidental and indirect, and therefore demonstrates that the facts and doctrines referred to were already generally accepted in the church, and indicates that the books from which he apparently quotes were widely and popularly known, and regarded as an authority; and (2) because he was personally a disciple of the apostles, especially of John, and was by the apostles ordained to the office of bishop or pastor of the church at Smyrna. His character seems to have resembled that of John in piety and loveliness; he was esteemed even by his ecclesiastical opponents, and loved devotedly by his own disciples; by Jerome he is called the most eminent man of Asia. His quotations from the first epistle of Peter and the epistles of Paul are especially abundant.[3]

3. *Papias.* Of his history little is known with certainty. He appears to have been born toward the close of the first century, and to have been contemporary with Polycarp, but there is no adequate evidence that he ever saw any of the apostles. He refers explicitly to a Gospel of Matthew, which he says was originally written in Hebrew, to a Gospel of Mark, whom he describes as writing as the interpreter of Peter, and also to 1 Peter, 1 John, and the Book of Revelation. He does not refer to Paul's epistles, which Westcott explains by the supposition that he belonged to the Judaizing portion of the church; "in such a man any positive reference to the teachings of St. Paul would have been unnatural."

4. *Justin Martyr.* His birth is uncertain, probably toward the close of the first century. In his early life a Platonist, he was converted to Christianity A. D. 119–132, and wrote A. D. 140–147. His extant works are arguments for the truth of Christianity, which he mainly rests on the facts of Christ's life. Nearly all the principal events in that life may be gathered from his writings, which are founded on what he entitles "the Memoirs of the Apostles." These he describes as containing a record of all things concerning Jesus Christ, and as read customarily in the public services of the churches on the same footing as the prophets, *i. e.*, as inspired and authoritative; in one passage he says that "they are called Gospels." That the "Memoirs" thus described are our four Gospels seems to me unquestionable, though the fact has been questioned. All Justin Martyr's facts not directly traceable to the Gospels, as we have them, are said not to exceed six in number, and there is but one inconsistent with them, which may possibly be accounted for by a variation of manuscript. Besides the Gospels his writings show an

---

[1] The exception is as follows: The blessed and glorious Paul wrote letters to you (the Philippians), into which if ye look diligently ye will be able to be built up into the faith given to you.

[2] Westcott on the *Canon of the New Testament.*

[3] The apostolic fathers—under which general title are included such as were contemporary with any of the apostles (A. D. 70–130)—whose works are now extant, namely, Clement of Rome, Ignatius(?), Polycarp, and Barnabas(?), and possibly Hermias, contain references more or less distinct to the three Synoptic Gospels, the Epistles to the Romans, 1st and 2d Corinthians, Galatians, Ephesians, Philippians, 1st and 2d Timothy, Hebrews, James, 1 Peter, and 1 John. The allusions to Thessalonians, Colossians, Titus, Philemon, and 2d Peter are very uncertain. The reader will find a full and classified account of these references in McClintock and Strong's Cyclopedia, article *Apostolic Fathers.*

acquaintance with all the remaining books of the New Testament except the epistles of James, Peter, Jude, and John, and those to Philemon and Titus. He refers by name to the book of Revelation.[1]

5. *The Canon of Muratori.* This is a Latin manuscript, which derives its name from its discoverer. It is an imperfect copy of a Greek original, written either in Africa or Rome, both the beginning and the end being lost. It claims to have been originally written during the second century, and scholars regard the claim as sustained by internal evidence. Hence "it may be regarded as a summary of the opinion of the Western church on the Canon shortly after the middle of the second century;"[2] that is, when men were still living who had seen and possibly conversed with the apostles. It commences with a fragment of a sentence evidently referring to Mark's Gospel. It goes on to state that the Gospel of St. Luke stands third in the canon, and the Gospel of St. John, a disciple of the Lord, fourth. That the lost fragment refers to Matthew is probable, since four Gospels are distinctly recognized. In the list which follows all the books included in our present canon are embraced, except the Epistles of James and Peter and that to the Hebrews, and possibly 3d John. Two epistles of John are referred to, but it is not improbable that the 2d and 3d are included in one epistle, in this list. According to Westcott, the chasms found in the text of this writing afford the probable explanation of the omission of epistles which are known to have been in use in the churches at the time when the list is believed to have been prepared. An apocryphal "Apocalypse of Peter" is also mentioned, with the remark that some do not choose that it shall be used in the churches. It is a noteworthy and important fact that this Canon of Muratori does not give the writer's individual opinion, but the general consent and judgment of the Christian church of the age, that is, of the second century.

6. *Irenæus,* born 120–140, a disciple of Polycarp, became bishop of Lyons A. D. 177, died probably about A. D. 200. His only extant work is a treatise against heresy. In this work "he maintains the co-ordinate authority of the Old and New Testaments; finds a characteristic reason, in the four quarters of the globe, why there should be just four Gospels, and no more; assigns the authorship of these Gospels to those whose names they now bear; quotes as Scripture the Acts, twelve Epistles of Paul (omitting Philemon), the Apocalypse (or book of Revelation), 1st and 2d John, 1 Peter, and is said by Eusebius to refer, in a work now lost, to the Epistle to the Hebrews."[3] He does not profess to give a complete list of canonical writings; hence his omissions prove nothing against the authority of the books not referred to, while his references are sufficient to prove that in his day the greater portion, if not the whole, of our New Testament was recognized as authority in the church. This testimony is the more significant because it comes from a disciple of a disciple of one of the New Testament writers.

7. *Clement of Alexandria* was a contemporary of Irenæus, and his life covers about A. D. 165–220. His birthplace is thought to have been Athens; the major part of his life was spent at Alexandria. A Christian in faith, he devoted himself to the study of philosophy, with apparently a supreme love for truth, which he was ready to welcome in whatever school he found it. In his writings he treats the Law and the Gospel of equal authority, refers to them as "the Scriptures of the Lord," as though they constituted one recognized collection, and makes unmistakable references to and quotations from the four Gospels, the Acts, all of Paul's Epistles, except that to Philemon, the Epistle to the Hebrews (which he imputes to Paul), 1 John, 1 Peter, Jude, and the Book of Revelation.

---

[1] For a full list of his works, genuine and doubtful, see *Dictionary of Greek and Roman Biographies,* article *Justinus Martyr;* for a full account of the bearing of his writings on the authority of the Gospels, see Westcott on the *Canon of the N. T.*

[2] Westcott. Even the anonymous author of "Supernatural Religion" concedes to this canon as early a date as the third century. .... [3] Bissell's *Historic Origin of the Bible.*

But he also, as well as Irenæus, cites as "divine writings" some works now universally regarded as apocryphal, thus indicating that the final collection of the New Testament writings into one recognized volume was not completed.

8. *Tertullian*, born at Carthage about A.D. 160; the time of his death is uncertain, probably about A.D. 240. In middle life he abandoned the orthodox party and became identified with the Montanists, a sect of enthusiasts and ascetics. He was a voluminous author. His writings recognize the Old and New Testament Scriptures as one "divine instrument," the integrity of which he defends against heretics. He gives no complete catalogue of the New Testament books of his day, but incidentally refers to the four Gospels, the Acts, thirteen Epistles of Paul (including Philemon), 1 Peter, 1 John, Jude, and the Book of Revelation. Certain apocryphal books recognized by Tertullian he characterizes as unauthentic.

Origen, A.D. 186-254, a pupil of Clement of Alexandria. His scholarship not only was remarkable for that age, but would be so in any age. He was a voluminous writer, especially upon Biblical topics; he prepared two editions of the Old Testament, together with commentaries upon it. His independence was such that he was excommunicated and exiled from Alexandria for holding and promulgating opinions which were regarded as not orthodox by his ecclesiastical superiors. His courage, his intellectual independence, and the thoroughness of his scholarship are now generally acknowledged. He distinctly recognizes the four Gospels, 1 Peter, the Book of Revelation, and one of John's Epistles, and refers in general terms to Paul's Epistles, and to the Epistle to the Hebrews, the authorship of which he says is not certainly known. In addition, his quotations from the New Testament are so voluminous that Tregelles asserts that at least two-thirds of it may be found in his extant writings, simply in the form of citations.

The Heretics. The writings of the heretics of the first three centuries are among the not least significant testimonies to the genuineness of the New Testament books. Sometimes they write to disprove the authority of these books, sometimes they quote from them in support of the heretical doctrine; but in either case their quotations afford indubitable evidence that the books referred to were generally accepted as authoritative by the Christian church. *Simon Magus*[1] and his followers not only recognized the facts in the life of Jesus Christ as recorded by the four Gospels, but also the peculiar weight attached by the church to the writings of the apostles. *Cerinthus* (probably beginning of second century) recognized the facts as reported by the four Gospels respecting Jesus Christ, though he denied the supernatural birth, and taught that the Divinity entered Jesus at his baptism and departed previous to his crucifixion. *Basilides*, probably a younger contemporary of Cerinthus, living in the age immediately succeeding the apostles, refers more or less explicitly to Matthew, Luke, John, Romans, Corinthians, Ephesians, and Colossians. *Marcion* (A.D. 130), published a canon of books on which he founded his system of modified or reconstructed Christianity. It includes a revised edition of St. Luke and ten Epistles of Paul, excluding the Pastoral Epistle and that to the Hebrews. He set the others aside, however, not because their authorship was in doubt, but because, according to him, the apostolic writers themselves had but an imperfect apprehension of the truth. Finally *Celsus* (second century), and *Porphyry* (third century), distinguished opponents of Christianity, refer in their attacks upon it to the writings of the disciples of Jesus Christ, in such a way as to leave no doubt that the substantial facts reported in the four Gospels, and the substantial doctrines taught in the Epistles, were recognized by both friend and foe, as constituting the historical and doctrinal system of the Christian church.

Versions and Collections. The *Peshito* Version, in the Syriac tongue, is still the recognized

[1] Acts 8: 9-24.

authority among the various sects of Syrian Christians, who claim to have derived it from the church at Antioch, which sent out Paul and Barnabas on their first missionary journey. It almost certainly dates as far back as the second century, possibly is of still earlier date. It contains in its earliest forms the four Gospels, Acts, fourteen Epistles of Paul, including the Epistle to the Hebrews, James, 1 Peter and 1 John, and perhaps the Book of Revelation. An ancient *Latin Version* was almost certainly in common use in the second century, which, according to Westcott, included the books embraced in the Muratorian Canon, *i. e.*, the four Gospels, Acts, thirteen Epistles of Paul (excluding the Epistle to the Hebrews), three Epistles of John, 1 Peter, Jude, and the Book of Revelation. *Eusebius*, by order of Constantine, prepared (A.D. 332), fifty copies of the Scriptures for public use in Constantinople. The New Testament as prepared by him, embraced all the books of our present New Testament, except the Book of Revelation. Finally, the *Council of Carthage* (about A.D. 397), officially declared what were the books of the Canonical Scripture to be read in the churches. In their list the books of the New Testament are exactly those which are generally received at present. And it must be remembered that their action, like that of Eusebius, was not in the nature of an individual and authoritative decision of a doubtful question, but only an official declaration of the judgment which had been reached by the universal consent of the Christian church.

Summary. The result of this investigation into the historical evidences of the canonicity of the books of the New Testament may be thus briefly stated. It is to be presumed, in the absence of evidence to the contrary, that books are the product of the authors whose names they bear. This reasonable presumption is greatly strengthened when they have borne that name for years and even centuries without question. In the fourth century the books of the New Testament, as we now possess them, were universally attributed to the authors whose names they bear, except the Epistle to the Hebrews, which is, in fact, an anonymous work.[1] In the absence of evidence to the contrary this universal opinion is to be presumed correct. But its correctness is not merely a reasonable presumption. The extant writings of a series of authors, extending from the days of the apostles to the fourth century, form an unbroken testimony to the genuineness of the collection. If the New Testament were destroyed, every important fact in the life of Christ, every important doctrine in the writings of the Apostles, and a considerable part of the words of both Evangelists and Apostles could be gathered from the extant writings of these unconscious and unintentional witnesses. They embrace representatives of every section of the Christendom of the first centuries—Europe, Asiatic Greece, Syria, Alexandria, Africa. They include orthodox and heretics, friends and foes of Christianity. Among them are to be found the ripest scholars, the most critical students, the ablest, most courageous, and most independent thinkers of their times. Many of them wrote before the church had become organized into a hierarchy, or Christianity into a system of recognized theology, and therefore before there was any considerable ecclesiastical or theological temptation to misstatement or misinterpretation. Their testimony is not, indeed, entirely unanimous; some of them accept, as canonical, single books which are now rejected, and others reject, as uncanonical, single books which are now accepted; but there is a substantial accord in their testimony; not a single doubt is raised by any author, friendly or inimical, as to the authorship of the four Gospels,[2] and none as to any of the more important Epistles, excepting, perhaps, the Epistle to the Hebrews; and if every book not supported by their nearly unanimous testimony were laid aside, the substantial teaching of the New Testament would not be affected. It is true that the earlier authors

---

[1] There is nothing in the Epistle to indicate the authorship; the title "The Epistle of Paul the Apostle to the Hebrews" is no part of the original document.

[2] Dr. Peabody says that they were never doubted till the last century. "Christianity and Science," p. 24. See Sec. I. for some other evidences of genuineness of the Gospels, in their language, their geographical accuracy, and their undesigned coincidences.

do not cite the New Testament writers by name. But this might naturally be expected. The author of to-day, in writing of the well-known events of the Civil War, would refer to the fact without citing his authority, while in referring to the more distant events of the American Revolution, he would refer to Sparks, or Hildreth, or Bancroft; so the Apostolic Fathers, assuming that their readers are acquainted with the facts and the doctrines of which they write, abound in references to the facts recorded in the four Gospels, and the doctrines contained in apostolic writings, and even in quotations of words, phrases, sentences, and metaphors from the sacred books, without accompanying them with citations, while the writers of the succeeding ages refer by name to the authors from whom they quote. It is true that no list of the sacred writings appears till toward the close of the second century. But this might naturally be expected. For the New Testament was not written as a book, nor with any conference between the writers of its different documents, but by different writers to different churches and for different purposes. A list of contents could not therefore be made until, by a mutual interchange of these documents, the collection itself grew into a book. This testimony of the ancient fathers is confirmed by that of the ancient manuscripts. While of Plato and Herodotus we have less than thirty manuscripts, and not one of them one thousand years old, we have forty-seven of the New Testament which are more than one thousand years old, four of which certainly date from the fifth century or earlier, and one, the Sinaitic, which is believed by one of the ablest scholars of the age to date from A.D. 325. These manuscripts, though some of them are imperfect, unite in confirming the authorship and authenticity of our New Testament books.[1]

Finally, it must not be forgotten that this testimony has not only been weighed carefully by a large number of Christian scholars, but has also been severely scrutinized by a large number of rationalistic critics. As no ancient book has run the gauntlet of so much hostile criticism, so none is sustained by evidence so irrefragable. The most elaborate analyses of this evidence have been made by hostile critics. As interpreted by them it shows that the writings of the early fathers abound in quotations from certain widely-diffused and generally accepted Gospels and Epistles; that these quotations embody the facts and doctrines of our New Testament, not infrequently in nearly its exact words; that in the middle of the second century Gospels by Matthew, Mark and Luke were in existence; that before the middle of the third century our New Testament, substantially as we now possess it, was generally recognized and accepted in the churches. Unless our Gospels and Epistles existed from the days of the Apostles, these quotations were made from books most of which are not now extant and some are even hypothetical; the Gospels of Matthew, Mark and Luke, referred to by Papias and Marcion, were not our Gospels, but other productions which have perished so utterly that not a trace of them is left in manuscript or quotation; and all our Gospels and many of our Epistles were forged in lieu of the genuine and now lost books, and were accepted by the age which produced them, with a faith so unquestioning and so universal, that no one, heretic or orthodox, in African, Alexandrian, Syrian, or Roman Church, questioned the authorship of any Gospel or any important Epistle. And even this skepticism concedes, what the most hostile criticism cannot deny, that in the present Gospels we have the substantial facts concerning the life and death of Christ, and in the Epistles the substantial teaching of the Apostles, or, in the words of one of the most eminent leaders in infidel belief,[2] "whatever else may be taken away from us by rational criticism, Christ is still left—a unique figure not more unlike all his precursors than all his followers, even those who had the direct benefit of his personal teaching."

In view of this examination it is perfectly safe to say that, while the canonicity of all

---

[1] See below Section V, the text...... [2] John Stuart Mill, "Three Essays on Religion."

the books of the New Testament does not rest upon the same evidence, while some are involved in an uncertainty which does not attach to the others,[1] the genuineness of the collection as a whole is better established than that of any book or collection of books of ancient times—better than that of Homer in Greek, Virgil in Latin, or Shakespeare in English literature.

II. THE INTERNAL AND SPIRITUAL EVIDENCE of the canonicity of the New Testament books consists in a simple comparison of those books with those which are now universally regarded as apocryphal and spurious. The limitations of my space forbid me from giving such a comparison, nor is it necessary. The contrast is so marked that no school, Protestant, Papal, or Rationalistic, attaches any value to the Apocryphal New Testament, and the contrast would be valuable only because it would indicate the nature of those mythical Gospels and spurious Epistles which really were the production of the sub-apostolic age, and with which modern skepticism desires to confound those of our New Testament. The reader who desires to trace the argument, the nature of which I here merely indicate, will find the material in *The Apocryphal New Testament*, or, less perfectly, in the articles *Epistles Spurious*, and *Gospels Spurious*, in McClintock and Strong's Cyclopedia.

VI. The Text.—The books of the New Testament were originally written on papyrus paper, with pens made of reeds, and ink composed of lamp-black or burnt ivory. The material was not such as could be expected to survive a century of use, and in the first centuries there were no adequate libraries or archives where they could be preserved. They were probably written and used in the early churches, as the Old Testament Scriptures still are in the Jewish synagogues, in the form of scrolls; but the form in which the most ancient manuscripts of the New Testament now extant are found is that of the modern book, generally folios or quartos. The earliest manuscripts now extant were written on parchment, *i. e.*, the skins of sheep and goats, or vellum, *i. e.*, the skins of abortive or at least sucking calves. The famous Sinaitic manuscript was manufactured of the skins of antelopes. It was not until the tenth century that paper came into use, manufactured from cotton rags; and not till the twelfth century that paper was made from linen rags. The monks in the middle ages devoted much of their time to copying the books of the Old and New Testament, oftentimes with elaborate and rich illuminations. The libraries of the monasteries afforded a safe repository for these sacred treasures of art and literature, in an age when only superstitious reverence could have preserved them from vandalism. Thus there are now scattered throughout Europe these manuscript copies of the Scriptures, a few complete, more copies of single books, or of incomplete collections of books. There are said to be preserved now more than 2,000 of these manuscripts, bearing date from the fourth to the fifteenth century, and the ablest scholars have devoted their best energies to a careful comparison of them, for the purpose of ascertaining what is the original reading. Among scholars whose judgments are generally regarded as most trustworthy are Griesbach, Lachmann, Tregelles, and Tischendorf; to their opinions on questions of text the reader will find constant references in this Commentary. For the American scholar there is no better method of ascertaining the correct text than that which is afforded by Dean Alford's "Greek Testament." This contains the text which he himself regards as the correct one, with an accompanying statement of the different readings afforded by the various manuscripts of recognized critical value.

The difficulty of determining the original reading is of two kinds. There is first a difficulty in deciphering the manuscript. The more ancient and therefore the more valuable manuscripts, are written not only without division into chapters and verses, but without accents, or breathings, or punctuation, or any indication of the separation between

---

[1] The canonicity of each book will be considered separately in the introduction to it.

the words. The introduction of chapters and verses dates from about the fifth century; they were employed probably for convenience of public service, and also for reference. The introduction of punctuation bears about the same date. That the reader may apprehend the difficulty of deciphering a manuscript without these divisions of a later date, we place side by side an ancient manuscript version of John 1 : 1, 2, with the Greek version from Bagster's Greek Testament :

* * * καὶ ὁ λόγος ἦν πρὸς τὸν θεόν, καὶ θεὸς ἦν ὁ λόγος. οὗτος ἦν ἐν ἀρχῇ πρὸς τὸν

The accompanying reproduction in English of a style and combination of letters answering to the ancient Greek manuscript, will give the English reader a partial idea of its character and the difficulty of deciphering it, enhanced as it is by variations in the form of the letters and obscurity in the manuscripts:

```
        * * * *   ANDTHEWORDWAS
     WITHGDANDGDWASTHEWORD
     HEWASINTHEBEGINNINGWITHGD
     ALLWEREMADEBYHIMANDWITH
     OUTHIMWASMADENOTONETHING·
     THATWASMADEINHIMLIFEWAS·
     ANDTHELIFEWASTHELIGHTOFMN
     ANDTHELIGHTINDARKNESSSHIN
     ETHANDTHEDARKNESSDIDNOTITCOMPRE
     HEND·  THEREWASAMNSE
   NTFROMGODWHOSENAMEWAS
     IOHN·THISPERSONCAME
     ASAWITNESSTHATHEMIGHTTESTI
     FYCONCERNINGTHELIGHTTHATA
     LLMIGHTBELIEVETHROUGHHIM·
```

The difficulty of deciphering is not, however, the only nor the principal one. These various manuscripts present varieties of readings. A few of these varieties consist in what was probably a deliberate addition or a mutilation of the text for doctrinal reasons; in other instances an addition which one copyist has made, perhaps in the margin, perhaps parenthetically, in order to explain the original text, has been by subsequent copyists incorporated in it. The great majority of variations, however, are insignificant and unimportant, and are the result, simply, of a natural error in transcribing. Of the first kind of alteration 1 John 5 : 7 is an illustration : " For there are three that bear record in heaven, the Father, the Word, and the Holy Ghost, and these three are one." This is now known to be an interpolation, added to the Greek text as late as the sixteenth century. Of the second, the statement in John 5 : 4 is an example : " For an angel went down at a certain season into the pool," etc. This was probably added by the copyist for the purpose of explaining why the impotent folk gathered about the pool of Bethesda. So, in some of the ancient manuscripts, Barabbas is called Jesus Barabbas, the name Jesus having been perhaps omitted by subsequent copyists from a sentiment of reverence. Such modifications are, however, very rare. Out of nearly one hundred and twenty thousand variations[1] very few affect the sense, and fewer still have any bearing on the doctrinal and practical teachings of the Bible. Nearly all are merely differences in orthography (as in the English, *favor* and *favour*), or, in the order of words (as, *then went there out to meet him*, and *then there went out to meet him*), or in the names of the same person (as *Cephas* and *Peter*), or similar variations incident to manual transcription.

In ascertaining which of various readings is the correct one, resource is had to two kinds of evidences, external and internal. The external evidence is derived from an examination of the manuscripts themselves. Where the more ancient manuscripts are uniform in their reading, their testimony is generally considered conclusive; where they are not so, recourse is had to internal evidences, that is, to a consideration of the question which reading is inherently most probable. For example: John 5 : 4 is wanting in some of the best manuscripts and is found in others; thus the external evidence is somewhat conflicting. But it is easy to understand how a copyist might have inserted this verse as an explanation of the account, while it is not easy to understand how it should have become expunged from the record if it was originally there, since the angelic interference thus described would not seem strange to the writers of the first centuries. Thus internal evidence is against the genuineness of the passage.

The manuscripts differ not only in the matter of which they are composed, but also in the form of the letters. In the Uncial manuscripts, which are the oldest, the letters are all capitals; in the Cursive manuscripts, which seem to have come into existence in the tenth century, the letters run together, often with no capitals except in the case of initial letters. Sometimes the original writing has been almost or altogether obliterated, and the parchment has been used for other writing. This has been subsequently removed and the original restored. Such manuscripts are called *palimpsest manuscripts;* that is, manuscripts re-written. When the text is accompanied by a version, the manuscripts are termed *codices belingues* or double-tongued. The age of the manuscript can be determined with substantial accuracy by the materials of which it is composed, the form of the letters and words, the presence or absence of punctuation, and other marks of division. The following are the most important Uncial manuscripts. For convenience of reference they are lettered by scholars as here, though in the notes I refer to them by name and not by letter.

A. Alexandrine Manuscript (*Codex Alexandrinus*), now in the British Museum. It is on parchment, in four volumes, three of which contain the Old and one the New Testament. The first twenty-four chapters of Matthew are wanting. It is now generally agreed that it was written in Alexandria, and during the fifth century.

B. Vatican Manuscript (*Codex Vaticanus*), in the Vatican Library at Rome. It is on vellum, contains the Old and New Testaments, but Timothy, Titus, Philemon, the Book of Revelation, and Hebrews 9 : 14 to the end are wanting. It is thought to have been written in Egypt during the fourth century. No really satisfactory edition of this manuscript has ever been published.

C. The Ephraem Manuscript (*Codex Ephraemi*), in the Imperial Library at Paris. It is a palimpsest manuscript consisting of the works of Ephraem, the Syrian, written over fragments of manuscripts of the Old and New Testaments. It is believed to have been written in Alexandria in the fifth century. It contains only portions of the New Testament.

D. Cambridge Manuscript (*Codex Cambridgiensis*), called also *Codex Bezæ*, because presented by Beza in 1581. It is in the University Library at Cambridge, is on parch-

---

[1] The estimates are very various; in the whole Bible they have been estimated as high as 800,000.

ment, and contains the four Gospels, the Acts, and a fragment of the Catholic Epistles, together with a Latin version. Its origin is uncertain, and its value is a matter of dispute; it is now generally attributed to the fifth or sixth century.

א. Sinaitic Manuscript (*Codex Sinaiticus*) in the Imperial Library at St. Petersburg. It derives its name from the fact that it was discovered by a singular accident by Tischendorf in 1859 in the convent of Mt. Sinai. His first hint of its existence was afforded by the fact that fragments of it were brought to him (in 1844) by the ignorant monks in a basket of rubbish with which to kindle his fire! It contains part of the Old Testament and the whole of the New. It is one of the oldest and the most valued of the manuscripts. Tischendorf attributes it to the fourth century.

There are Uncial Manuscripts and a great number of cursive manuscripts. Some of them of considerable value. The English reader will find a good account of them in Kitto's *Cyclopedia*, article *Manuscripts*. See also Alford's *Greek Testament* and Bissell's *Historic Origin of the Bible*. Our English New Testament is translated from a Greek text printed from very late Greek manuscripts, in the sixteenth century. This text, since it is the basis of our English version, is known as the Received Text or *Textus Receptus*.[1] The discovery of ancient manuscripts since that time, the careful and critical collation and comparison of them, and the development of critical scholarship, by this very process, has led to the discovery of errors in the Received Text, and to the elucidation of a text which probably much more nearly conforms to the originals of the sacred writers. In this Commentary I have generally followed the text of Alford's *Greek Testament* wherever any variation in the reading affects the sense. In all such cases I have indicated the variation in the notes, and wherever there is any material question respecting the reading I have also indicated that fact, with a brief reference both to the different manuscripts and to the opinions of the leading critical scholars.

These differences in the text, the reader must not forget, are for the most part of very minor importance. There are a few passages of some significance, as John 8 : 1-11, and Mark 16 : 9-20, the genuineness of which is involved in doubt. But for the most part the variations are verbal and trivial. "So great, in fact," says Mr. Bissell,[2] "is the harmony of teaching in all these documents, though we compare the earliest with the latest, that while three of the most important *Uncials* had not been discovered when our present English translation was made, and one that was known to exist was inaccessible (the Vatican), and only a single specimen of the less valuable of these most ancient witnesses was used (the Cambridge Manuscript), yet no person would hazard the opinion that in our English Bibles we have not, for substance, the teaching of the best documents brought to light during the last two hundred and fifty years." The slight variations in the readings, and the careful and critical examination to which they have given rise, enhance our assurance, that in all substantial respects we have the text of the original documents, whose character is testified to by so many and so independent witnesses.

VII. Our English Version.—From a very early time the endeavor has been made by the church to supply the Bible in the vernacular tongue. A Greek version of the Old Testament Scriptures was in popular use in Palestine in the days of Christ, and the quotations from the Old Testament by Christ and the Apostles are generally from this version. It is known as the Septuagint, a word meaning seventy; the name is derived

---

[1] The "Received Greek Text" (*Textus Receptus*) on the continent of Europe, is that of the Elzevir edition of 1633 and 1634. In England and America the "Received Text" is Mill's reprint, with a few typographical errors corrected, of Stephen's edition of 1550, often differing from the Elzevir edition. The groundlessness of its pretensions to be accepted as the Received Text of the New Testament, is shown by a writer in the *Edinburgh Review* for July, 1851.—Dr. T. I. Conant, in *Abbott's Religious Dictionary*.

[2] *Historic Origin of the Bible*.

from an ancient though now discredited account of its origin. According to this legend, the Septuagint was prepared under the authority of Ptolemy Philadelphus (B.C. 309-247), by seventy-two scholars, who were commissioned for the purpose by Eleazar, the high-priest at Jerusalem, and were by the king shut up in the island of Pharos at Alexandria, till their task, which required just seventy-two days, was completed. That the translation was made in the third century before Christ, and at Alexandria, is probable; the rest of the story is apocryphal. The Septuagint is rejected by the Jews and regarded by Christian scholars as imperfect. But, notwithstanding its errors, it is of inestimable value, not only in the study and interpretation of the Old Testament, but also in throwing light upon the proper rendering of the Greek of the New Testament.

Next in importance to the Septuagint, which contains, of course, only the Old Testament, is the Vulgate, an ancient Latin version of both Old and New Testaments. This translation was prepared by Jerome, A.D. 385-405, and since the seventh century has been adopted in the Romish Church as the authentic text of Scripture. By the Council of Trent it was ordained that this version alone should be esteemed as the authorized text, and that no one should dare to reject it under any pretence whatever. There are two principal editions of this version, called respectively, from the popes under whom they were prepared, the Sixtine and the Clementine. The latter is the standard in the Romish Church at the present day, and is the basis of the Roman Catholic English version of the Bible. This is commonly known as the Douay Version, from the fact that the Old Testament translation was prepared in the sixteenth century at Douay, in France. The New Testament translation was first published at Rheims, and is known as the Rhemish version. The translation is not from the original Greek and Hebrew, but from the Vulgate. It thus perpetuates the errors which the imperfect scholarship of the fifth century had not discovered and corrected; while the literalness of the translation renders it sometimes quite unintelligible. The best Roman Catholic scholars concede the imperfections of the Douay and Rhemish versions, and the superiority of the Authorized or King James' version.[1]

The history of this version[2] carries us back to the beginnings of English history. An attempt was made to translate portions of the Bible into the English, or rather Anglo-Saxon, as early as the seventh century, by the venerable Bede; and another, in the ninth century, by Alfred the Great; but all these attempts were fragmentary and imperfect. They were, for the most part, loose paraphrases—poems founded on Bible narratives, or abridgments; and down to the year 1360, the Psalter was the only book of the Scriptures literally translated into the English language. About this time Wycklitfe, lamenting the degeneracy of the Church and the irreligion of the people, commenced and completed a translation of the New Testament from the Vulgate or Latin version. For this offence he was cited to appear before the Court of Rome, and probably nothing saved him from condemnation except his failing health and early death in 1324. Although before the days of printing, his translation seems to have been extensively circulated; one hundred and seventy manuscript copies, more or less, are still extant, some of them bearing the names of their royal owners. It is said that the yeomen were so anxious to obtain the word of God, that they often gave a load of hay for a few chapters. One and a half centuries later, William Tyndale published the first part of the Holy Scriptures ever printed in the

---

[1] In Smith's *Bible Dictionary*, article *Versions Authorized*, the reader will find a list of passages indicating the nature of the imperfections in this translation. They are chiefly of three kinds: (1) A few that are due to theological bias, such as the substitution of "do penance" for "repentance;" (2) Some that are due to the use of obsolete or un-English words, as "azymes," "pasche," "longanimity;" (3) Some that are due to the avowed principle that the Scriptures were not intended for the common people—a principle which manifests itself occasionally in a translation that is absolutely unmeaning, as in the rendition of Ephes. 6:12, "Against the spirituals of wickedness in the celestials."

[2] The following epitome is taken chiefly from my *Dictionary of Religious Knowledge*.

English language. They were printed at Hamburg, Cologne, and subsequently at Worms; for Rome had still the control of England, and the first edition was so effectually destroyed, that only two copies of it are known to exist. The priests, however, overreached themselves; for they bought up Tyndale's Testaments at a high price, and publicly burned them, but by the operation unwittingly put Tyndale out of debt, and gave him the means to issue a larger and better edition. By treachery he was betrayed into the hands of the priests and put to death; but his work lives to-day as the basis of our English Bible. Almost simultaneously with his death was published the whole Bible, translated by Myles Coverdale, and soon after the (so-called) Matthew's Bible, published under that name by John Rogers, the martyr. The accession of Bloody Mary drove the Reformers from England, and gave rise to the Genevan Bible, so entitled from the fact that it was prepared and published at Geneva. After her death the leading dignitaries in the English Church, under Queen Elizabeth, took measures for the publication of an official translation, which went by the name of the Bishops' Bible. And toward the close of the sixteenth century, yielding to the pressure which had become too great to be longer resisted, the Roman Catholic authorities prepared and published the Douay and Rhenish versions already alluded to.

These various versions were, in God's providence, only preparations for the great work of rendering the Bible in an authorized manner into the English tongue. On the accession of James I., fifty-four of the first scholars of the kingdom, without regard to sect or party, eminent alike for learning and for piety, were appointed to make a new translation. They were engaged in the work for seven years—A. D. 1604–1611. Three years were occupied in individual investigations; three more in systematic and united work. Only forty-seven of the fifty-four scholars were actually engaged. They were divided into six classes—two at Westminster, two at Oxford, and two at Cambridge. The books of the Bible were divided among these classes. Each member of each class translated all the books intrusted to the class. Then the whole class met; and, after thorough revision, adopted a common text. Then that text was transmitted in succession to each of the other classes for revision. Then the text of the whole Bible, approved by the entire six classes, was submitted to the final revision of six elected delegates, with six consulting assistants, and their approved manuscript was placed in the skilful hands of Dr. Smith, distinguished for his knowledge of ancient languages, to examine and prepare it for the press. In their work, not only the former English versions, but the Hebrew, Chaldee, Greek, Syriac, Latin, Spanish, French, Italian, and Dutch, were all consulted; and among the commission were not only men eminent for Biblical learning, but men distinguished as linguists, naturalists, antiquarians, and historians. A single significant circumstance indicates how desirous the translators were to bring the reader into contact with the very letter of the originals. Every word which had no direct representation in the original Hebrew or Greek was printed in italics, that it might be seen what the translators had supplied; and in the marginal readings was added further information where the minds of the translators were in doubt. Thus it will be seen that the English version of the Scriptures is really the fruit of a century of study; to which should be added the reflection that it was prepared at a time when the Reformation was yet fresh, and the Reformers, scarcely free from the trammels of Rome, had not yet begun to divide into different denominations. There probably had never been an era in the history of the Church so favorable for the preparation of an unsectarian translation of the Scriptures as that in which the King James version was prepared.

Still, though a remarkable translation, it is not claimed by any to have been inspired or to be infallible. The state of the original text was imperfect; the knowledge of the Greek and Hebrew grammars was less accurate and thorough than it is now; the same

Greek and Hebrew word is not infrequently rendered by different English words, and the English language itself has undergone changes which require in the translation some modifications.[1] These facts have at various times induced individual scholars to attempt further revisions of the whole or of parts of the Bible; and at length a voluntary commission has been organized, including representatives from the different Evangelical churches of England and America, and embracing the ablest Biblical scholars of both lands, to prepare a new and revised translation of the Bible. Their avowed purpose is, however, to accept the Authorized Version as a basis, and to introduce as few alterations in the translation as is consistent with fidelity to the original. These committees, for there are two, one on the Old Testament and one on the New Testament, are now engaged upon their work. The notes in this Commentary accompany the Authorized or King James Version.

VIII. Principles of Interpretation.—The Bible is not a substitute for thought; it is a stimulant to thinking. Its office is not merely to reveal necessary truth to the unlearned, but also to stir to the highest activity the faculties of all men. It is the storehouse of divine truth, whence the centuries gather their supply. It is the widow's cruse of oil, which, forever drawn upon, never grows less. Thus it abounds with apothegms, proverbs, germinant philosophies enwrapped in single seed texts, which yield their fruitfulness only to the careful and conscientious student. It treats of experiences which transcend thought; it deals with themes which lie beyond the utmost vision of the imagination. Its supreme teachings are hidden alike from the careless and superficial reader, and from the prejudiced and dogmatic controversialist; and are revealed only to the humble, earnest, and thoughtful student. For the assistance of such students, I embody here certain essential principles of interpretation, as they have been evolved in my own study of the New Testament, and have been applied and employed in its interpretation.

1. I have sought to secure the best Greek text. In general, I have followed that of Alford's New Testament; but wherever there appeared, on careful study, any adequate reason for varying from his conclusion, I have done so. Generally the external evidences should outweigh the internal; that is, we are generally to accept as the true text that which is indicated by the most ancient Greek manuscripts; rarely, if ever, may we justly set aside their concurrent testimony, because the reading they afford is difficult to interpret or to reconcile with other passages of Scripture.

2. I have sought, by a careful study of the original, to ascertain the exact literal meaning of the words. When that has been doubtful the translations of the best scholars, in Latin, German, and English, have been compared. In determining the exact meaning of a doubtful Greek word the New Testament usage is always, and the Septuagint usage is generally to be preferred to that of the classical writers. I have founded the notes on the English version, but my studies on the original Greek; and wherever a new translation seemed likely to convey more adequately or more freshly the meaning of the original, it has been given in the notes.

3. The original text and its meaning being understood, the student is next to master the general scope of the address or document which he is studying, and the aim of the speaker or writer. Texts are not to be taken out of their connection—still less to be woven into new connections and relations—to afford a basis for a doctrine, a ritual, or a discipline. The rule of legal interpretation is, in this respect, fundamental to a true interpretation of the Scripture, viz., that the parts of a document, law, or instrument are to be construed with reference to the significance of the whole. In many cases the neglect, on the part of Bible students, to put themselves *en rapport* with the sacred writer involves the writing

---

[1] For a full account of the errors in our English version and the necessity for a new or revised translation, see *The Revision of the New Testament*, combining three papers by Lightfoot, Trench, and Ellicott respectively.

in needless obscurity. Thus the key to the famous parable of the laborers in the vineyard, in Matt., ch. 20, is given by the question of Peter in the preceding chapter, to which it is an answer; and the still more difficult parable of the unjust steward, in Luke, ch. 16, is relieved of much if not of all its difficulty, by observing the fact stated in verse 14, "the Pharisees also, which were covetous, heard all these things: and they derided him." This hint that the parable is aimed at covetousness is the key to its right interpretation.

4. In studying the aim of the speaker or writer we may generally assume that he is to be understood as those to whom he spoke or wrote would have understood him. We are therefore to acquaint ourselves with their customs, their philosophies, their errors, their sins; we are to put ourselves in their place, and to hear and understand as they would have done. It is indeed often true that there is *more* in Scripture than they could have perceived, a fullness of truth which only time could interpret. But this deeper meaning is rarely if ever inconsistent with the less profound truth, which the contemporaries of Christ and the apostles might, and generally would, have apprehended from the discourse or the letter. The failure to apprehend and apply this principle has involved the familiar passage concerning the power of the keys in much of its mystery.[1]

5. Everything in the New Testament is written for a practical or spiritual purpose. It is not a book of abstruse metaphysics; its aim is always the development of a divine life in the soul. It is therefore essential to a correct apprehension of its wording that the student weigh well its practical or spiritual significance. A careful and prayerful pondering of the question, How is this passage to make men better, to bring them nearer to God, or to render their manifestations of the divine life more luminous? will often give the interpretation to passages which remain unsolved enigmas to unspiritual students. The spiritual and the critical study of the Scriptures must go together. The substitution of the critical for the spiritual deprives the New Testament of its soul; the substitution of the spiritual for the critical supplants the doctrine of the Word of God with the imagination of the commentator. Critical study has made great advance in modern times; but I have found no better spiritual interpreters of the New Testament than Chrysostom and Matthew Henry, *i. e.*, none that realize more fully, and employ more constantly, the truth that the words of the New Testament are life. In this Commentary I have devoted little space to drawing doctrinal or ethical conclusions from the text; but I have sought always to ascertain its spiritual purpose, as a necessary condition of interpreting its true meaning.

6. According to the Roman Catholic doctrine the Bible is made for the church, and the church is its interpreter to the people. It is thus like a ship's chart, which the officers, not the passengers, are to consult. Protestant commentators have sometimes practically adopted this view, while theoretically repudiating it. Believing that the Bible is given by God for the people, that it is meant to be their illumination and their inspiration in the divine life, I think it safe to assume that those interpretations which are abstruse, involved, or obscure, those which require peculiar logical and metaphysical acumen, those which do not illumine but darken, do not inspire but deaden, which confuse the mind and benumb the soul, are always to be rejected. And of two interpretations, one of which is characteristically ingenious and the other is characteristically simple, the preference is always, other things being equal, to be given to the latter. Ingenuity in interpretation is a fatal encomium to bestow upon a commentator. Often a knowledge of ancient life is necessary to an understanding of Scripture; often some proficiency in divine truth; still more frequently some attainment in spiritual experience, without which its sublimest declarations are incomprehensible.[2] But these attainments are open to the unlearned many as to the cultured few. Whenever after careful study I have not been

---

[1] See Matt. 16:19, note ..... [2] Matt. 13:11-16; 1 Cor. 2:7-16.

PRINCIPLES OF INTERPRETATION. 33

able to find a simple and natural interpretation, I have contented myself with frankly pointing out the difficulty, stating briefly the principal interpretations of other commentators, and so leaving the passage for the elucidation of the future.

7. A reasonable regard is to be paid to the peculiar idiosyncrasies of the sacred writers and their peculiar circumstances. That Paul should inculcate faith, and James works, and John love; that Matthew should recount the miracles and the ethical instructions of Jesus Christ, and John his spiritual teachings, accords with the free spirit of the Gospel. The truth is divine; its expression is human. Some consideration, therefore, of the temperaments and mental characteristics of the writers, as indicated by their writings, and some allowance therefor is essential to the best elucidation of the truth.[1] From Paul's expression in Rom. 9 : 3, "I could wish myself accursed from Christ for my brethren," a literal interpretation has deduced the doctrine that we ought to be willing to be damned for the glory of God. The interpreter who thus ignores the ardency and warmth of Paul's nature, and his constant use of hyperbole in the endeavor to give utterance to unutterable feeling, loses the truth which is really conveyed, a truth of experience, not of philosophy, the ardent desire for souls which should always characterize the disciple of Jesus Christ. A not less striking illustration of the consequence of ignoring or denying this principle of interpretation is afforded by the doctrine of the Real Presence. This doctrine is founded upon Christ's declaration, This is my body, but with singular if not deliberate inattention to the circumstances under which it was uttered, the symbolic language of the Passover for which it was a substitution, and the fact that Christ often clothed his teaching in poetic forms, or, in other words, was a true poet.

8. Subject to these principles, due consideration is to be paid to the parallel or the contrasted teachings of Scripture. In this Commentary the material for a study of these is afforded by the full marginal references, and by those which are incorporated in the notes. Where the meaning of any writer is in doubt, it is always legitimate to examine other utterances of the same writer, and to interpret what is enigmatical by what is clear. It is also legitimate to examine the utterances of other writers of the same general school or faith, and employ the one in interpreting the other. It is customary, upon this principle, to refer to the debates of the Constitutional Convention, and to the writings of Jefferson, Madison, Hamilton, and their contemporaries, in order to ascertain the meaning of doubtful phrases in the United States Constitution. The substantial harmony of doctrine of the various writers of the New Testament, and the consistency of each writer, is to be presumed, in the absence of evidence to the contrary, and that interpretation is to be preferred which sustains this presumption. For this reason it is true that in many cases Scripture is its own best interpreter. Thus Christ's paradoxical saying in Luke 14 : 26, "If any man come to me and hate not his father and mother * * * he cannot be my disciple," is to be interpreted in the light of the humanizing influence of his general teachings, and his example of filial love to his own mother.

9. But it is not legitimate to deny, limit, or interpret away the plain and unenigmatical declarations of a writer, in order to make them accord with his other utterances, or with the utterances of other writers. This has been often done in the predetermined endeavor to construct a system of theology and ethics out of the Bible. As in science it is the duty of the investigator to accept the plain facts of nature, to harmonize in his system such as he can, and to leave the rest to other investigators, denying nothing because he cannot understand it, so it is the duty of the Bible student to accept the plain facts of Revelation, to interpret in accord such as he can, and to leave such as do not adjust themselves to his system for the study of those that will come after him. It is my simple endeavor in this work to unfold the meaning of the New Testament, passage by passage,

---

[1] See Section IV., on the Limits of Inspiration.

leaving to others to adjust the teachings in one harmonious whole. This is the work of the theologian, not of the commentator. The one constructs, the other simply gathers the materials. If there appear to be unreconciled views in the notes, there are also unreconciled (I do not say irreconcilable) teachings in the Scripture text.

10. Finally, there is no book that has been such a battle ground as the Bible. The great body of those who accept its teachings as adequate authority, agree in respect to the fundamental truths which it teaches; the chief differences in interpretation are between Protestant students and Roman Catholic theologians on the one hand, who deny that it is adequate without the church, and Rationalistic students on the other, who deny that it is authoritative. Still there are passages concerning the interpretation of which there are important and honest differences of opinion between Congregational, Presbyterian, Episcopalian, Baptist, and Methodist students. In respect to all the more important of such passages, where a reasonable room exists for a difference of interpretation, I have endeavored to set forth the different opinions briefly, usually indicating my own conclusion. Whether I have succeeded or not in laying aside denominational bias, it is certain that the student who wishes to get, unmixed, the teachings of the Scripture, must disabuse his mind of theological prepossessions. An unprejudiced mind is as essential to a fruitful study of God's word as a clear lens to the telescopic study of the stars. Next to the prejudices bred of sinful habits and affections, those which spring from a determination to find in the Bible a support for a previously accepted system of doctrine, or a means of assault upon a system prejudged, are the most fatal to a true understanding of the Divine Word. We must approach that Word like little children, in that we must approach it, as they their early studies, with unbiased minds, ready to receive whatever our inspired Instructor has to teach us.

That I have always succeeded in applying these principles I do not claim; to those that would build their religious faith and life upon the Bible, and the Bible only, they are none the less sincerely commended, as the conditions of a successful study and interpretation of the Word of God.

PART II. THE GOSPELS.

I. Relation of the Gospels to Each Other.—The word Gospel is composed of two Anglo-Saxon words, God spel, meaning good news. It is a translation of a Greek word *euaggelion* (εὐαγγέλιον). From a cognate word is derived our English word Evangelist, who is, literally, a messenger or herald of good news. The title, which is commonly given to each of the first four books of the New Testament, is interpreted by, and perhaps derived from, the announcement by the angels to the shepherds of the birth of Jesus Christ: "Behold I bring you good tidings of great joy."[1] The Gospel is, then, the announcement to the world of good news, namely, the advent, incarnation, crucifixion, and resurrection of One whose life is our example, and in whose death is our pardon, and whose perpetual spiritual presence is the source and the assurance of spiritual life, both here and in the hereafter, to all those who accept him. Thus the word Gospel accords with and carries out the idea embodied in the title New Testament, as explained above.[2]

A very marked difference is noticeable between the first three Gospels and the last. This difference is both external and internal.

Matthew and Mark narrate chiefly Christ's ministry in Galilee, with only a brief account of teachings in Perea.[3] Luke narrates also the events and teachings in Galilee, but adds

---

[1] Luke 2:10...... [2] See Part I., Section I...... [3] Matt., ch. 19:—; 20:16; Mark 10:1-31.

several chapters devoted to the report of what I believe to have been his ministry in Perea. But no incident of his ministry in Judea is related by any one of the three. "Had we only their accounts," says Dean Alford, "we could never with any certainty have asserted that he went to Jerusalem during his public life, till his time was come to be delivered up." John's Gospel, on the other hand, is chiefly occupied with a narrative of the ministry in Judea. Only in the sixth chapter does he give any account of Christ's teachings in Galilee; only in a sentence does he refer to a ministry in Perea.[1] The miracles he records as performed in Galilee are, with one exception, not mentioned by the other Evangelists;[2] and the resurrection of Lazarus, the most remarkable of all the miracles, if a comparison can be instituted between them, is narrated only by him. The feeding of the five thousand is indeed narrated by John (ch. 6) in common with the others, but this is apparently only because it was the text to the discourse in the synagogue at Capernaum, which John alone reports. Even in the history of the Passion Week, where all the Evangelists narrate substantially the same events, a characteristic difference is observable. Incidents which we should most expect to find in John's Gospel are omitted. He gives no account of the institution of the Lord's Supper, though fully and exclusively reporting Christ's memorable discourse on that occasion, and makes no reference to the agony in Gethsemane, though he describes both Christ's going thither and his arrest there. A glance at the tabulated Harmony of the Gospels, given at the end of this Introduction, will further indicate to the reader how small a portion of the fourth Gospel is occupied with the narration of events or teachings given by the other Evangelists. I believe the explanation of this fact to be that John, who undoubtedly wrote after the others, had their narratives before him, and wrote to supply elements and incidents which they had omitted. But this view is by no means universally accepted. It is strenuously resisted by Alford.

The difference in internal characteristics, between John and the other Evangelists, is even more remarkable. Matthew, Mark and Luke, are historians, John is a theologian; they write simple historical narratives, he with a definite and an avowed doctrinal purpose; they record most fully our Lord's life, he our Lord's teaching and character; they rarely refer to our Lord's divine character and mission, except either by a reference to the fulfillment of ancient prophecy in him, or by the narration of his own teaching respecting himself,[3] John opens his gospel with what is, perhaps, the most explicit declaration to be found in Scripture of Christ's divinity, lingers reverentially over every utterance in which Christ brings to light this truth, hidden, for the most part, from common apprehension during his earthly life, and closes his account by declaring that, from the various signs wrought by Jesus in the presence of his disciples, he has selected those written in this book, "that ye might believe that Jesus is the Christ, the Son of God; and that believing ye might have life through his name."[4]

The bearing of this contrast between John's Gospel and the other Gospels, on the authority of the former, will be considered hereafter.[5] It must suffice here to state the fact, as one to be constantly borne in mind, in studying the Gospel narratives.

The first three Gospels are commonly known as the Synoptic Gospels, from the fact that, to a large extent, they cover the same ground, so that from a combination and comparison of them, a synopsis of Christ's life, though not a complete or perfect one, may be obtained.

These three Synoptic Gospels, however, by no means duplicate each other. Each contributes its own peculiar element. Referring the student to the sections below on the

---

[1] John 10:40-42..... [2] John 2:1-12; 4:45-54..... [3] Matt. 1:23; 16:16-20; 26:63, 64..... [4] Ch. 21 was probably added by John as an appendix some time after the completion of his Gospel..... [5] See Intro. to John's Gospel.

several Gospels, for a fuller account of their characteristics, we may here sum up the contrasts between them in Bishop Ellicott's brief but admirable note.[1]

"(1.) In regard of the external features and characteristics, we are perhaps warranted in saying that (*a*) the point of view of the first gospel is mainly Israelitic; of the second, Gentile; of the third, universal; of the fourth, Christian: that (*b*) the general aspect, and, so to speak, physiognomy of the first, is mainly Oriental; of the second, Roman; of the third, Greek; of the fourth, spiritual: that (*c*) the style of the first is stately and rhythmical; of the second, terse and precise; of the third, calm and copious; of the fourth, artless and colloquial: that the most striking characteristic of the first is symmetry; of the second, compression; of the third, order; of the fourth, system: that (*e*) the thought and language of the first are both Hebraistic: of the third, both Hellenistic; while in the second the thought is often occidental, though the language is Hebraistic; and, in the fourth, the language Hellenistic, but the thought Hebraistic. (2.) Again, in respect of subject-matter and contents, we may say, perhaps, (*a*) that in the first gospel we have narrative; in the second, memoirs; in the third, history; in the fourth, dramatic portraiture; (*b*) that in the first we have often the record of events in their accomplishment; in the second, events in their detail; in the third, events in their connection; in the fourth, events in relation to the teaching springing from them: that thus (*c*) in the first we more often meet with the notice of impressions; in the second, of facts; in the third, of motives; in the fourth, of words spoken: and that, lastly, (*d*) the record of the first is mainly collective, and often antithetical; of the second, graphic and circumstantial; of the third, didactic and reflective; of the fourth, selective and supplemental. (3.) We may conclude by saying that, in respect of the portraiture of our Lord, the first gospel presents him to us mainly as the Messiah; the second, mainly as the God-man; the third, as the Redeemer; the fourth, as the only-begotten Son of God."

II. Origin of the Gospels.—Whence did the Evangelists derive their information? Matthew and John were eye and ear witnesses of the events and teachings which they recorded. Doubtless their personal recollection, quickened by the Spirit of God, was one chief source whence they derived their histories. But Luke and Mark were not of the Twelve. Moreover, there is, as already observed, a remarkable correspondence in the narratives of the Synoptic Gospels. Of Mark, nine-tenths; of Matthew, a little more than half; of Luke, a little less than half, is common to the other Evangelists. In some cases the parallel passages are almost identical in language; more generally the resemblance is substantial, not verbal. These facts indicate that the Evangelists employed, at least to some extent, the same sources of information, yet wrote independently of each other. To account for the resemblance between them, four hypotheses have been proposed:

1. It has been suggested that the narrators made use of each other's work, and many have endeavored to ascertain which gospel is to be regarded as the first, which is copied from the first, and which is the last, and copied from the other two. But the theory, in its crude form, is in itself most improbable; and the wonder is that so much time and learning have been devoted to it. It assumes that an Evangelist has taken up the work of his predecessor, and, without substantial alteration, has made a few changes in form, a few additions and retrenchments, and then has allowed the whole to go forth under his name.

2. It has been suggested that there may have been a common original gospel, since extinct, from which the three gospels were drawn, each with more or less modification. But if all the Evangelists had agreed to draw from a common original, it must have been widely, if not universally, accepted in the Church; and yet there is no record of its

---

[1] Ellicott's *Life of Christ*, p. 46, note.

existence. If the work was of high authority, it would have been preserved, or at least mentioned; if of lower authority, it could not have become the basis of three canonical gospels. Nor is it easy to see why, if the Evangelists were transcribers, they should have made such remarkable modifications in the work from which they copied.

3. It has been surmised that our Lord spoke in the Greek language; that the Evangelists reported him independently, but reporting the same words, naturally repeated each other in many cases. It is true that the most notable verbal agreements in the Synoptists are in their reports of the sayings of our Lord; but that he spoke in Aramaic, is implied by Mark,[1] and it is almost certain that Aramaic was the language of the common people, to whom he addressed himself. Nor does this hypothesis suggest any explanation of the source whence Mark and Luke derived their knowledge.

4. The fourth hypothesis, the one which is now generally adopted by the most advanced Christian scholars, and which I think the most probable, is that the three Evangelists, in the preparation of their respective Gospels, made use of what is termed an "oral Gospel." This hypothesis—and the reader must bear in mind it is only that— may be thus stated:[2]

The apostles were chosen by Christ to be his companions while he lived, in order to be the personal witnesses of his life, his death, and his resurrection. Almost immediately after his ascension they were scattered abroad. Driven out from Jerusalem by the Providence of God, they went forth, we are told, "preaching the Gospel."[3] This preaching of the Gospel was not with them, as it is with us, the unfolding of a system of truth, or its application to the heart and life of believers. It was just what the original words signify, a heralding of good tidings. The early disciples went forth as witnesses to the fact that the Messiah had come; and their preaching at first consisted chiefly in a simple description of the life, death, and resurrection of their Lord, a simple narration of the mighty works by which he had authenticated his divine mission, and to which the apostles especially were personal witnesses. This historic character of their preaching is illustrated by the few glimpses of it which we obtain in the Book of Acts,[4] and is further indicated by the fact that when the history to which they had been witnesses had become generally accepted, their mission appears to have come to an end. Of them all, John and Peter alone appear in subsequent New Testament history, as either theologians or ecclesiastical organizers. The result of their witness-bearing, taken up and repeated by others, would be, in a brief space of time, a generally accepted belief in respect to the fundamental facts, and the more important teachings of Jesus Christ. But this belief, though widespread, would not be systematized. Different localities and different churches would become possessed of different fragments of the whole, and in forms more or less diverse. When at length, however, the church began to spread from Judea into Greece, and Asia, and Africa, both the churches and the apostles would become sensible of the need of some more permanent record of this oral Gospel, this good news, and the demand and the supply would spring up together. Those less adapted to the work of oral teaching would reduce the current traditions to writing. And gathering their information from this common source, we should expect to find in their accounts a certain similarity in sub-

---

[1] Mark 5:41; 7:34, notes...... [2] For a fuller exposition and defence of it, consult Alford's Greek Testament, *Prolegomena*, and Westcott's *Introduction to the Study of the Gospels*...... [3] Acts 8:4; 11:19-21.

[4] The same cardinal events which are described with the greatest fullness in the written Gospels are noticed with the most minute detail in the speeches in the Acts: the betrayal (2:23); the condemnation by the Sanhedrim (13:27); the failure of the charge (13:28); the condemnation by Pilate (3:13), and by Herod (4:27); the choice of Barabbas (3:14); the urgency of the people and rulers at Jerusalem (13:27, 28); the crucifixion (4:10; 5:30; 10:39); by the hand of Gentiles (4:27, 28); the burial (13:29); the resurrection on the third day (10:40); the manifestation to fore-ordained witnesses (10:41), for many days (13:31), who did eat and drink with him after he rose (10:41); the charge to the apostles (10:42); the ascension to the right hand of God (2:33; 3:21)." —*Westcott on the Study of the Gospels.*

stance, indicative of their common means of information, and certain discrepancies of form, indicative of the differences in the respective writers and in the different phases of the current faith to which they had access. If we were to suppose that this oral tradition was not embodied in written narratives till after the death of the apostles, we might consider the authority of the Gospels questionable. But if, as I believe, our Gospels were all of them written by contemporaries of our Lord, two of them by his life-companions, the third (the Gospel of Mark) partially under the guidance of an apostle (Peter), and all of them under the inspiration of God, there is nothing in this supposition of common origin in an oral Gospel to weaken, in the least, their credibility. Their authenticity is further assured by the consideration that after they were written and were current in the churches, John wrote his Gospel, and could and presumably would have corrected any material errors if they had contained any.

The following considerations render this hypothesis a reasonable and probable one.

It is the customary method of preparing history or biography. The conscientious modern biographer visits the most familiar friends of the subject of his work, gains by conversation with them the various incidents in the life to be described, and the traits in the character to be portrayed, and, even if himself a companion and friend, enlarges and corrects his own knowledge by such an examination of oral tradition. In the absence of evidence to the contrary, this customary method may be presumed to have been pursued by the Evangelists. It best explains the verbal discrepancies and substantial harmony of the three Synoptic Gospels, and accords with their broken, unchronological, and fragmentary character. It accords with Luke's explicit statement of the sources of information whence he derived his own Gospel.[1] The early post-apostolic writers refer to such an oral tradition as one of the sources of information in their own day. Thus Irenæus distinctly states that the great outlines of the Life of Christ were received by the barbarous nations, without written documents, by ancient tradition; and Papias similarly refers to his personal research among the traditions of his own day respecting the apostles and their teachings. The existence and importance of such a body of tradition appears thus to be well authenticated.

I believe, then, with Dean Alford, "that the Synoptic Gospels contain the substance of the apostles' testimony, collected principally from their oral teaching current in the church, partly also from written documents embodying portions of that teaching; that there is, however, no reason from their internal structure to believe, but every reason to disbelieve, that any one of the three Evangelists had access to either of the other two Gospels in its present form;" to which I add that in their use of this "oral Gospel" the Evangelists were aided either by their own personal recollections, as in the cases of Matthew and John, or in part by that and in part by the personal recollections of one or more of the apostles, as in the case of Mark, and perhaps of Luke; that they wrote and published during the lifetime of the apostles, and when therefore any errors, if there had been any, would have received correction; and, finally, that John's Gospel was written some time after the three Synoptic Gospels, with the knowledge of their contents, and in part to supply elements which were wanting in them, and which were necessary to a full comprehension of Christ's character and mission.

III. Harmony of the Gospels.—No one of the Gospels gives a connected and chronological life of Jesus Christ. They are not biographies, but biographical memorabilia; not connected histories, but collections of the teachings and the events in the life of Jesus of Nazareth. No one of them follows a chronological order; no one of them gives a single date. Even the years of Christ's birth and death are left uncertain. Their

---

[1] Luke 1 : 1-4.

records are in these respects exactly what their origin, an oral Gospel, and the inspiration of their writers, moral, not verbal, would lead us to expect.[1]

There are, consequently, numerous discrepancies between the Gospel narratives. These are of several descriptions. Sometimes one Evangelist simply omits events recorded by another. Thus Mark gives no hint of the Sermon on the Mount, and no one of the Synoptists mentions the resurrection of Lazarus. Sometimes the order indicated in one narrative is different from that indicated in another. Thus if we only had Matthew's Gospel we should presume that the healing of the leper was performed immediately after the Sermon on the Mount, while Mark indicates another and a more probable time.[2] Sometimes the discrepancy is only apparent, not real. Thus Luke mentions the ordination of the twelve apostles in connection with the Sermon on the Mount, Matthew gives their names in connection with the subsequent commission to preach the Gospel throughout Galilee. A careless or casual reader might easily imagine the accounts to be discrepant, though they are so only in appearance. Sometimes the difference is simply one of language. Thus the four accounts of the inscription over the cross differ in phraseology, as do the three accounts of the stilling of the tempest in their reports of the language of the disciples in awakening our Lord, and of his language in reply.[3] Sometimes the discrepancy is such as would naturally arise from a difference in the point of view of the observers. Thus the variations in the four accounts of the arrest of Jesus Christ are just such as would naturally arise in reporting such a scene of confusion. Again, the accounts of the birth of Jesus given by Matthew and Luke are entirely different, but not inconsistent, one Evangelist recording one class of incidents, the other a different class. There are a few discrepancies which, with our limited knowledge, it is difficult or perhaps impossible completely to remove. Such is the apparent difference between John and the Synoptists as to the true occasion of the Lord's Supper.[4] There are others which were formerly a serious stumbling-block to the Christian, but in which a fuller knowledge has discovered singular evidences of the truthfulness of Scripture. Such is the seeming geographical discrepancy in the narrative of the miraculous cure of the demoniac, which Matthew describes as performed in the "land of the Gergesenes," and Mark and Luke in the "land of the Gadarenes."[5] A careful comparative study of the four Gospels may not afford a satisfactory solution of all these apparent discrepancies, but it will conduct the conscientious and unprejudiced student to the conclusion of Dean Alford, who gives, indeed, undue weight to these natural variations in the Evangelists' narratives, but who says: "We may be sure that if we knew the real process of the transactions themselves, that knowledge would enable us to give an account of the diversities of narration and arrangement which the Gospels now present to us."

In conducting such an investigation the following principles are to be borne in mind by the student:

1. The true chronological order of Christ's life is not to be found in any one Gospel, but is to be ascertained, if at all, by a comparison of the four accounts. It must often be only a matter of surmise.

2. No one of the Evangelists ordinarily gives a literal report of the language used. The habit of ancient authors was to embody in dramatic forms the substance of the incident narrated. Of this literary habit not only the ancient histories, as Cæsar and Sallust, but the Old Testament also, furnish many examples.[6] Where a modern historian, narrating the stilling of the tempest, would say, "The disciples awoke Christ and reproached

---

[1] See above pages...... [2] See Matt. 8:1, note...... [3] See Mark 4:35-41, notes...... [4] See note on the Lord's Supper, Matt. 26:12, 13, 30...... [5] See for explanation of this discrepancy Matt. 8:28, note.

[6] Thus, "God said, 'Let there be light.'" To whom should he say it? This is evidently simply a dramatic and graphic portraiture of the act of divine creative will. So throughout the O. T. history the conferences are given, not in the manner of a modern historian, but in a dialogue form.

him for his indifference to their danger," the Evangelists put the language of reproach into the disciples' mouths, in forms verbally different, and representing slightly different shades of feeling.

3. Christ often repeated substantially the same teaching, and often, apparently, clothed it in the same words. Certain aphorisms became even characteristic of his teaching. Moreover, to meet the same or similar needs, he repeated, on different occasions, substantially the same miracle of mercy. Thus the denouncing of the Pharisees reported by Matthew, in chap. 23, is in some sense a repetition of the previous philippic reported in Luke, chap. 11, and the feeding of the four thousand in Matt. 15 : 32–39 is in almost all respects a repetition of the previous feeding of the five thousand, reported in chap. 14 : 15–21.

4. Hence we often find the same event or teaching reported by different Evangelists, in phraseology and in chronological connections slightly different ; and we also find teachings and miracles similar, yet not to be confounded, occurring on different occasions; and again we find some cases in which it is not easy to determine whether the two accounts are of the same or of different events. In general we may say that when the differences are merely verbal and chronological it is probable that the event is the same, only the narrative different ; but that when the end or object in view, or the important circumstances, are different, the events are not to be regarded as identical because similar in certain minor or external respects. Thus, to suppose that Christ healed one blind man as he entered Jericho and two as he went out of it, in order to reconcile the discrepant accounts of Luke 18 : 35, etc., and Matt. 20 : 29, etc., is as unreasonable and improbable on the one side, as to suppose that the anointing described in Luke 7 : 36–50 and Matt. 26 : 6–13 are the same, because in both cases performed at a supper table and by a woman.

5. It is possible to determine with tolerable accuracy what were the great eras of Christ's life, what its outlines, what the general course and development of his ministry, and of the opposition which ended in his death. But the chronological order of the specific events and teachings which belong in the several eras must probably always be largely a matter of conjecture.

Applying these principles, we give, for the aid of such as wish to study the life of Christ in its connections, a sketch of that life in outline, and add, at the close of this Introduction, a tabulated harmony of the Gospels, cautioning the student that the latter, in its arrangement in detail of the Gospel narratives, represents only the best conjectures of Bible students.

IV. The Life of Christ.—The life of Christ may be divided into eight eras, as follows : His birth and early education ; the inauguration of his public ministry ; his ministry in Galilee ; his period of retirement ; his ministry in Judea ; his ministry in Perea ; his Passion ; his Resurrection. His birth probably took place four years before the time indicated by our present chronology, *i. e.*, B. C. 4; his baptism at thirty years of age, A. D. 26 ; and his death, after a ministry of between three and four years, A. D. 30.[1]

1. *His birth and education.*—He is born in Bethlehem, whither his mother and reputed father have come from Galilee, on the taking of a census. From Bethlehem he is taken to Egypt, to escape the malice of Herod the Great, and on the king's death is carried to Nazareth in Galilee. Here he dwells till his manhood. Only one incident of his youth is narrated, viz., his disputing with the doctors in the Temple.[2] Matthew (chaps. 1, 2) and Luke (chaps. 1, 2) narrate Christ's birth, each of them incidents apparently unknown to the other.

---

[1] For a fuller sketch of the Life of Christ, from which this epitome is taken, see Abbott's *Dictionary of Religious Knowledge*, article *Jesus*. See also Abbott's *Jesus of Nazareth*...... [2] Luke 2 : 40–52.

2. *The inauguration of his public ministry.*—He first enters upon his life-work by receiving baptism at the hands of John the Baptist, in the Jordan; prepares for it by his mysterious experience of temptation in the wilderness; signalizes it by his attendance on and miracle at the marriage feast in Cana of Galilee, and his expulsion of the traders from the temple at Jerusalem. Here, in conversation with Nicodemus, he reveals privately the truths of atonement and regeneration, which are not publicly preached till much later. But he does not commence the public preaching of the Gospel till the arrest and imprisonment of John the Baptist, some months subsequent, though one miracle and some teaching in Samaria, consequent upon his conversation with the woman at the well, are recorded by John. This era is reported by Matt., chaps. 3, 4 : 1-11; Mark 1 : 1-13; Luke, chaps. 3, 4 : 1-13; and John, chaps. 1 to 4. To this period belong the journeys 1, 2, 3, and 4 on the accompanying map.

SKETCH MAP ILLUSTRATING THE JOURNEYINGS OF OUR LORD.

REFERENCE.

1 and 2. **First Journeys:**
   Nazareth, Bethany, beyond Jordan, Desert of Temptation. Return: Bethany, beyond Jordan, Capernaum, Nazareth.

3. **First Passover:**
   Nazareth, Jerusalem. Return through Judea and Samaria (Sichem, Jacob's Well), Cana, Nazareth.

4. **To Capernaum, &c.:**
   Nazareth, Capernaum (dwelling there).

5. **Feast of Purim:**
   Capernaum, Nazareth, Nain, Bethany, Jerusalem. Return to Capernaum.

6. **In Galilee, &c.:**
   Capernaum, Bethsaida-Julias, Capernaum, Borders of Tyre and Sidon, Coasts of Decapolis, Country of Dalmanutha, Bethsaida-Julias, Cæsarea-Philippi, Mount Tabor, Capernaum.

7. **Feast of Tabernacles:**
   Capernaum, Borders of Samaria, Jerusalem. Return to Perea.

8. **Feast of the Dedication, &c.:**
   Perea, Jerusalem, Bethany, Ephraim, Jericho.

9. **Last Passover:**
   Jericho, Bethany, Jerusalem.

3. *His ministry in Galilee.*—He begins his ministry by preaching a sermon at Nazareth, where he is mobbed, and whence he departs to make Capernaum his home; calls four disciples by the seashore to follow him; then Matthew; then the rest of the twelve. These he ordains, and to them, in the Sermon on the Mount, he explains the fundamental principles of his kingdom. During this ministry he attends the Passover at Jerusalem,

where, by his healing on the Sabbath, the first open opposition to him and his teaching is excited. He then returns to Galilee; his ministry there is one of constantly increasing popularity, though also of increasing opposition, mainly stimulated by emissaries from Judea. He begins to employ parables, as a means of interpreting the nature of the kingdom he had before simply announced. He commissions his apostles to preach it also, and by their aid the Gospel is proclaimed throughout all Galilee. At length the popular enthusiasm reaches its height in a determination to make him king by force; he declares, in the sermon which John alone (chap. 6) has reported, the spiritual character of his kingdom, and the self-sacrifice it entails; the popular feeling, tested by this revelation, proves itself untrustworthy; many that were inclined to follow abandon him, and his public ministry in Galilee comes to an end. This period of Christ's ministry is reported by Matt., chap. 4 : 12 to chap. 15 : 20; Mark, chap. 1 to chap. 7 : 23; and Luke, chap. 4 : 14 to chap. 9 : 17. John reports Christ's journey to Jerusalem to attend the Passover, and his miracle of feeding the five thousand and subsequent sermon thereon, but nothing else of this period of his life.[1] To this period belong the largest number of our Lord's miracles, and his simplest and most fundamental teaching, and most of his longest public discourses, particularly the Sermon on the Mount, the Parables by the sea-shore, and the Sermon or Commission to the twelve.

4. *The period of his retirement.*—After the close of his ministry in Galilee, Christ spends a few brief months in retirement with his disciples, during which time he visits successively the coasts of Tyre and Sidon, the region about Cesarea Philippi, and the eastern coast of the Sea of Galilee. The miracles performed during this time are comparatively few, and are kept, as far as practicable, from public notice; the indications of a constant endeavor to avoid the people are many; and the instructions are chiefly in private, to the twelve, and concerning the principles which are to actuate them in the future conduct of the church. To this period belongs the healing of the Syro-Phœnician woman's daughter, Peter's confession of our Lord's divinity, the Transfiguration, and the feeding of the four thousand. The accounts of it are found in Matthew, chap. 15 : 21 to chap. 19; Mark, chap. 7 : 24 to chap. 9; Luke, chap. 9 : 18–62. John does not refer to any portion of it. This and the previous era include the journeys marked 5 and 6 on the accompanying map, and all the journeys indicated on the Map of the Sea of Gennesaret which accompanies Mark, chap. 1.

5. *The ministry in Judea.*—This lasted for three months, from the feast of Tabernacles in October, to the feast of Dedication in December. It is reported exclusively by John, chap. 7 : 1 to chap. 10 : 39, unless, as may be the case, the parables of the Good Samaritan, and the Pharisee and Publican, and the incident in the house of Martha and Mary [2] belong to the same epoch.

6. *The ministry in Perea.*—This name was given to all that part of Palestine which lay beyond the Jordan. It was occupied by a population partly Jewish, partly heathen. Driven out of Jerusalem I believe that Jesus went into Perea, where he prosecuted his ministry during the winter months, and where he commissioned the seventy to aid him, as before in Galilee he had commissioned the twelve. This is a more probable account of his life than that which supposes his retirement to Galilee and the resumption of his teaching there, after he had turned his back upon it and pronounced his denunciation upon the cities of Chorazin, Bethsaida and Capernaum. According to this view the chief portion of the teachings and events recorded in Luke, chap. 10 to chap. 18 : 34, together with those recorded in Matthew, chap. 19 : 1 to chap. 20 : 16, and Mark 10 : 1–31, belong to this period. From the ministry in Perea Christ was called by the intelligence of the sickness of Lazarus, and after the resurrection of Lazarus, recorded alone by John, chap. 11, retired

---

[1] John, chaps. 5 and 6...... [2] Luke 10 : 25-42; 18 : 9-14.

to Ephraim, where he remained till the time for his Passion had arrived. The journeys marked 7 and 8 on the map, belong to this and the previous era, though I do not agree with the map in supposing that Christ went at this time into Galilee, a supposition which is not supported by evidence.

7. *The Passion week.*—The events of this week are recorded by all the Evangelists. Christ's triumphal entry into the city took place on Sunday. The two following days, Monday and Tuesday, were occupied with the instructions in the Temple, reported most fully by Matthew, ending with a terrible denunciation of the Pharisees, and followed by a prophecy, given to the disciples alone, of the impending destruction of Jerusalem and Judaism. These discourses are much more fully reported by Matthew than by Mark or Luke. Wednesday was spent in retirement at Bethany, at which time, as I think, the supper was given to Christ and he was anointed by Mary, his rebuke of Judas Iscariot at that time being the immediate occasion of the latter's treachery. The Passover supper with the twelve in Jerusalem, took place on Thursday evening, and was followed by the agony in Gethsemane, the arrest, the mock trial, and finally the crucifixion on Friday. Compare for accounts of this week, Matthew, chaps. 21 to 27; Mark, chaps. 11 to 15; Luke, chap. 19 : 29 to chap. 23; John 12 to 19.

8. *The Resurrection.*—The accounts of the resurrection are given by Matthew, chap. 28; Mark, chap. 16; Luke, chap. 24; and John, chaps. 20, 21.

These outlines of Christ's life I believe to be tolerably clear and certain. For the more detailed harmony of the Gospels, and the probable though confessedly conjectural order of the events narrated, the student is referred to the following Harmony, which, however, he must remember is largely conjectural.

TABULAR HARMONY OF THE GOSPELS.

Where the same incident or teaching is treated by more than one of the Synoptic Evangelists in substantially the same manner, the notes are given in full in one Gospel, and only peculiarities of statement or diction are treated in the other. In this table the black-faced type indicates that the reader may expect to find full notes on the passage so marked. The notes on John are full throughout.

I. BIRTH AND EDUCATION. From b.c. 6 to a.d. 8.*

	Location.	Matthew.	Mark.	Luke.	John.
"The Word"					1 : 1-14.
Preface, to Theophilus				1 : 1-4.	
Annunciation of the Baptist's birth	Jerusalem.			1 : 5-25.	
Annunciation of the birth of Jesus	Nazareth.			1 : 26-38.	
Mary visits Elizabeth	Juttah.			1 : 39-56.	
Birth of John the Baptist				1 : 57-80.	
Birth of Jesus Christ	Bethlehem.	1 : 18-25.		2 : 1-7.	
Two Genealogies		1 : 1-17.		3 : 23-38.	
The watching Shepherds	Bethlehem.			2 : 8-20.	
The Circumcision	Jerusalem.			2 : 21.	
Presentation in the Temple				2 : 22-38.	
The wise men from the East	Bethlehem.	2 : 1-12.		2 : 39.	
Flight to Egypt		2 : 13-23.			
Disputing with the Doctors	Jerusalem.			2 : 40-52.	

II. INAUGURATION OF PUBLIC MINISTRY. From Summer, a.d. 26, to Dec., a.d. 27.

	Location.	Matthew.	Mark.	Luke.	John.
Ministry of John the Baptist	Jordan.	3 : 1-12.	1 : 1-8.	3 : 1-18.	1 : 15-31.
Baptism of Jesus Christ	"	3 : 13-17.	1 : 9-11.	3 : 21, 22.	1 : 32-34.
The Temptation	(?)	4 : 1-11.	1 : 12, 13.	4 : 1-13.	
Andrew and another see Jesus	Jordan.				1 : 35-40.
Simon, now Cephas (Peter)	"				1 : 41, 42.
Philip and Nathanael	" (?)				1 : 43-51.
The water made wine	Cana.				2 : 1-11.
Passover 1st and cleansing the Temple	Jerusalem.				2 : 12-22.
Nicodemus	"				2 : 23 to 3 : 21.
Christ's disciples and John baptizing	Jordan.				3 : 22-36.
The woman of Samaria	Samaria.				4 : 1-42.

III. MINISTRY IN GALILEE. From March, a.d. 28, to Summer, a.d. 29.

	Location.	Matthew.	Mark.	Luke.	John.
John the Baptist in prison	Machærus.	4 : 12; 14 : 3.	1 : 14; 6 : 17.	3 : 19, 20.	3 : 24.
Return to Galilee	Galilee.	4 : 12.	1 : 14, 15.		4 : 43-45.
The nobleman's son	"				4 : 46-54.
Capernaum. Four Apostles called	"	4 : 13-22.	1 : 16-20.	5 : 1-11.	
Demoniac healed there	"		1 : 21-28.	4 : 31-37.	
Simon's wife's mother healed	"	8 : 14-17.	1 : 29-34.	4 : 38-41.	
First Circuit round Galilee	"	4 : 23-25.	1 : 35-39.	4 : 42-44.	
Healing a leper	"	8 : 1-4.	1 : 40-45.	5 : 12-16.	
Healing the paralytic	"	9 : 1-8.	2 : 1-12.	5 : 17-26.	
Journey to Jerusalem to 2d Passover	Jerusalem.				5 : 1.
Pool of Bethesda. Power of Christ	"				5 : 2-47.
Plucking ears of corn on Sabbath	Galilee.	12 : 1-8.	2 : 23-28.	6 : 1-5.	
The withered hand. Miracles	"	12 : 9-21.	3 : 1-12.	6 : 6-11.	
Matthew the Publican	"	9 : 9-13.	2 : 13-17.	5 : 27-32.	
"Thy disciples fast not"	"	9 : 14-17.	2 : 18-22.	5 : 33-39.	
Jairus's daughter. Woman healed	"	9 : 18-26.	5 : 21-43.	8 : 40-56.	
Blind men, and demoniac	"	9 : 27-34.			
The Sermon on the Mount	"	5 : 1 to 7 : 29.	3 : 13-19.	6 : 12-49.	
The Centurion's servant	"	8 : 5-13.		7 : 1-10.	4 : 46-54.
The widow's son at Nain	"			7 : 11-17.	
Messengers from John	"	11 : 2-19.		7 : 18-35.	
Woe to the cities of Galilee	"	11 : 20-24.			
Call to the meek and suffering	"	11 : 25-30.			
Anointing the feet of Jesus	"			7 : 36-50.	
Second Circuit round Galilee	"			8 : 1-3.	
Parable of the Sower	"	13 : 1-23.	4 : 1-20.	8 : 4-15.	
" " Can lie under a Bushel	"		4 : 21-25.	8 : 16-18.	
" " Growth of Seed	"		4 : 26-29.		
" " Wheat and Tares	"	13 : 24-30.			
" " Grain of Mustard Seed	"	13 : 31, 32.	4 : 30-32.	13 : 18, 19.	
" " Leaven	"	13 : 33.		13 : 20, 21.	
On teaching by parables	"	13 : 34, 35.	4 : 33, 34.		
Wheat and tares explained	"	13 : 36-43.			
The treasure, the pearl, the net	"	13 : 44-52.			
Conditions of following Christ	"	8 : 19-22.		9 : 57-62.	
Christ stills the storm	"	8 : 23-27.	4 : 35-41.	8 : 22-25.	
Demoniacs in land of Gadarenes	Sea of Galilee.	8 : 28-34.	5 : 1-20.	8 : 26-39.	
Healing of Demoniac and discourse thereon	Galilee.	12 : 22-45.	3 : 20-30.	11 : 14-26.	

* This chronology assumes, with Andrews, that Christ was born b.c. 4. See Matt. 1 : 18, note. It follows Andrews, "Life of our Lord."

TABULAR HARMONY OF THE FOUR GOSPELS.

MINISTRY AT GALILEE—Continued.

	Location.	Matthew.	Mark.	Luke.	John.
His mother and his brethren	Galilee.	12 : 46-50.	3 : 31-35.	8 : 19-21.	....
Reception at Nazareth	"	13 : 53-58.	6 : 1-6.	4 : 14-32.	....
Third Circuit round Galilee	"	9 : 35-38.	6 : 6.	....	....
Sending forth the Twelve	"	10 to 11 : 1.	6 : 7-13.	9 : 1-6.	....
Herod's opinion of Jesus	"	14 : 1, 2	6 : 14-16.	9 : 7-9.	....
Death of John the Baptist	Machærus.	14 : 3-12.	6 : 17-29.	....	....
Approach of Passover (3d)	Galilee.	....	....	....	6 : 4.
Feeding of the five thousand	"	14 : 13-21.	6 : 30-44.	9 : 10-17.	6 : 1-15.
Walking on the sea	"	14 : 22-28.	6 : 45-52.	....	6 : 16-21.
Peter's attempt to walk on the sea	"	14 : 28-32.	....	....	....
Miracles in Gennesaret	"	14 : 34-36.	6 : 53-56.	....	....
The bread of life	"	....	....	....	6 : 22-65.
The unwashen hands	"	15 : 1-20.	7 : 1-23.	....	....

IV. PERIOD OF RETIREMENT. From Summer, A.D. 29, to Fall, A.D. 29.

	Location.	Matthew.	Mark.	Luke.	John.
The Syro-Phœnician woman	Phœnicia.	15 : 21-28.	7 : 24-30.	....	....
Miracles of healing	Galilee.	15 : 29-31.	7 : 31-37.	....	....
Feeding of the four thousand	"	15 : 32-39.	8 : 1-9.	....	....
The sign from heaven	"	16 : 1-4.	8 : 10-13.	....	....
The leaven of the Pharisees	"	16 : 5-12.	8 : 14-21.	....	....
Blind man healed	"	....	8 : 22-26.	....	....
Peter's profession of faith	"	16 : 13-20.	8 : 27-29.	9 : 18-20.	6 : 66-71.
The Passion foretold	"	16 : 21-28.	8 : 30 to 9 : 1.	9 : 21-27.	....
The Transfiguration	"	17 : 1-9.	9 : 2-10.	9 : 28-36.	....
Elijah	"	17 : 10-13.	9 : 11-13.	....	....
The lunatic healed	"	17 : 14-21.	9 : 14-29.	9 : 37-42.	....
The Passion again foretold	"	17 : 22, 23.	9 : 30-32.	9 : 43-45.	....
Fish caught for the tribute	"	17 : 24-27.	....	....	....
The little child	"	18 : 1-5.	9 : 33-37.	9 : 46-48.	....
One casting out devils	"	....	9 : 38-41.	9 : 49, 50.	....
Offences	"	18 : 6-9.	9 : 42-48.	17 : 1, 2.	....
The lost sheep	"	18 : 10-14.	....	....	....
Forgiveness of injuries	"	18 : 15-17.	....	....	....
Binding and loosing	"	18 : 18-20.	....	....	....
Forgiveness. Parable	"	18 : 21-35.	....	....	....
"Salted with fire"	"	....	9 : 49, 50.	....	....
Fire from heaven	Samaria.	....	....	9 : 51-56.	....

V. MINISTRY IN JUDEA. From Oct. to Dec., A.D. 29.

	Location.	Matthew.	Mark.	Luke.	John.
Going to Jerusalem	Jerusalem.	....	....	....	7 : 1-10.
Discussions at Feast of Tabernacles	"	....	....	....	7 : 11-53.
Woman taken in adultery	"	....	....	....	8 : 1-11.
Dispute with the Pharisees	"	....	....	....	8 : 12-59.
The man born blind	"	....	....	....	9 : 1-41.
The good Shepherd	"	....	....	....	10 : 1-21.
Feast of Dedication	"	....	....	....	10 : 22-39.

VI. MINISTRY IN PEREA. From Dec., A.D. 29, to March, A.D. 30.

	Location.	Matthew.	Mark.	Luke.	John.
Beyond Jordan	Perea.	....	....	....	10 : 40-42.
The Seventy disciples		....	....	10 : 1-24.	....
The Good Samaritan		....	....	10 : 25-37.	....
Mary and Martha		....	....	10 : 38-42.	....
Discourses of Jesus: time and occasion uncertain	(The chronology, the harmony, and the location of these events are uncertain. The last hypothesis mentioned [John 10] and the Resurrection of Lazarus [John 11]. See John 10 : 40-42.)	....	....	11 : 37 to 13 : 9.	....
Woman healed on Sabbath		....	....	13 : 10-17.	....
"Are there few that be saved?"		....	....	13 : 22-30.	....
Warning against Herod		....	....	13 : 31-35.	....
Instructions at a Pharisee's house		....	....	14 : 1-24.	....
Following Christ with the Cross		....	....	14 : 25-35.	....
Parables of Lost Sheep, Piece of Money, Prodigal Son, Unjust Steward, Rich Man and Lazarus		....	....	chs. 15, 16.	....
Forgiveness and faith		....	....	17 : 1-10.	....
The ten lepers		....	....	17 : 11-19.	....
How the kingdom cometh		....	....	17 : 20-37.	....
Parable of the Unjust Judge		....	....	18 : 1-8.	....
" " Pharisee and Publican		....	....	18 : 9-14.	....
Divorce		19 : 1-12.	10 : 1-12.	....	....
Infants brought to Jesus		19 : 13-15.	10 : 13-16.	18 : 15-17.	....
The rich man inquiring		19 : 16-26.	10 : 17-27.	18 : 18-27.	....
Promises to the disciples		19 : 27-30.	10 : 28-31.	18 : 28-30.	....
Laborers in the vineyard		20 : 1-16.	....	....	....
Raising of Lazarus	Bethany.	....	....	....	11 : 1-44.
Meeting of the Sanhedrim	Jerusalem.	....	....	....	11 : 45-53.
Christ in Ephraim	Judea.	....	....	....	11 : 54-57.
Death of Christ foretold	"	20 : 17-19.	10 : 32-34.	18 : 31-34.	....
Request of James and John	"	20 : 20-28.	10 : 35-45.	....	....
Blind man at Jericho	Jericho.	20 : 29-34.	10 : 46-52.	18 : 35-43.	....
Zaccheus	"	....	....	19 : 1-10.	....
Parable of the Ten Pounds	"	....	....	19 : 11-28.	....

VII. PASSION WEEK. From Sunday, 2 April, to Friday, 7 April, A.D. 30.

	Location.	Matthew.	Mark.	Luke.	John.
Christ enters Jerusalem	Jerusalem.	21 : 1-11.	11 : 1-10.	19 : 29-44.	12 : 12-19.
Cleansing of the Temple (2d)	"	21 : 12-16.	11 : 15-18.	19 : 45-48.	....
The barren fig-tree	"	21 : 17-22.	11 : 12-14, 20-23.	....	....
Pray, and forgive	"		11 : 24-26.		
"By what authority," etc.	"	21 : 23-27.	11 : 27-33.	20 : 1-8.	....
Parable of the Two Sons	"	21 : 28-32.	....	....	....
" " Wicked Husbandmen	"	21 : 33-46.	12 : 1-12.	20 : 9-19.	....
" " Wedding Garment	"	22 : 1-14.	....	14 : 16-24.	....
The tribute-money	"	22 : 15-22.	12 : 13-17.	20 : 20-26.	....
The state of the risen	"	22 : 23-33.	12 : 18-27.	20 : 27-40.	....
The great Commandment	"	22 : 34-40.	12 : 28-34.	....	....
David's Son and David's Lord	"	22 : 41-46.	12 : 35-37.	20 : 41-44.	....
Against the Pharisees	"	23 : 1-39.	12 : 38-40.	20 : 45-47.	....
The widow's mite	"	....	12 : 41-44.	21 : 1-4.	....
Greeks visit Jesus. Voice from heaven	"	....	....	....	12 : 20-36.
Reflections of John	"	....	....	....	12 : 36-50.
Christ's second coming	"	24 : 1-51.	13 : 1-37.	21 : 5-38.	....
Parable of the Ten Virgins	"	25 : 1-13.	....	....	....
" " Talents	"	25 : 14-30.	....	....	....
The last Judgment	"	25 : 31-46.	....	....	....
The anointing by Mary	Bethany.	26 : 6-13.	14 : 3-9.	7 : 36-50.	12 : 1-9.
Plot against Jesus and Lazarus	Jerusalem.	....	....	....	12 : 10, 11.
Last Passover (4th). Jews conspire	"	26 : 1-5.	14 : 1, 2.	22 : 1, 2.	....
Judas Iscariot	"	26 : 14-16.	14 : 10, 11.	22 : 3-6.	....
Paschal Supper	"	26 : 17-30.	14 : 12-26.	22 : 7-23, 24-30.	13 : 1-35.
Contention of the Apostles	"	....	....		
Peter's fall foretold	"	26 : 31-35.	14 : 27-31.	22 : 31-39.	13 : 36-38.
Last Discourse	"	....	....	....	chs. 14-16.
The prayer of Christ	"	....	....	....	17 : 1-26.
Gethsemane	"	26 : 36-46.	14 : 32-42.	22 : 40-46.	18 : 1.
The betrayal	"	26 : 47-56.	14 : 43-52.	22 : 47-53.	18 : 2-11.
Before Caiaphas. Peter's denial	"	26 : 57, 58, 69-75.	14 : 53, 54, 66-72.	22 : 54-62.	18 : 12-27.
Before the Sanhedrim	"	26 : 59-68.	14 : 55-65.	22 : 63-71.	....
Before Pilate	"	27 : 1, 2, 11-14.	15 : 1-5.	23 : 1-3.	18 : 28.
The Traitor's death	"	27 : 3-10.	....	....	....
Before Herod	"	....	....	23 : 4-11.	....
Accusation and condemnation	"	27 : 15-26.	15 : 6-15.	23 : 13-25.	18 : 29-40; 19 : 1-16.
The daughters of Jerusalem	"	....	....	23 : 26-32.	....
The Crucifixion	"	27 : 27-50.	15 : 16-37.	23 : 33-38.	19 : 16-30.
The penitent thief	"	....	....	23 : 39-43.	....
Darkness and other portents	"	27 : 45-53.	15 : 38-41.	23 : 44-46.	....
The by-standers	"	27 : 54-56.	15 : 39-41.	23 : 47-49.	....
The side pierced	"	....	....	....	19 : 31-37.
The burial	"	27 : 57-61.	15 : 42-47.	23 : 50-56.	19 : 38-42.
The guard of the sepulchre		27 : 62-66; 28 : 11-15.	....	....	....

VIII. THE RESURRECTION. From 9 April to 18 May, A.D. 30.

	Location.	Matthew.	Mark.	Luke.	John.
The Resurrection	Jerusalem.	28 : 1-10.	16 : 1-11.	24 : 1-12.	20 : 1-18.
Disciples going to Emmaus	Jer. Emmaus.	....	16 : 12, 13.	24 : 13-35.	....
Appearances in Jerusalem	Jerusalem.	....	16 : 14-18.	24 : 36-49.	20 : 19-29.
At the Sea of Tiberias	Galilee.	....	....	....	21 : 1-23.
On the Mount in Galilee	"	28 : 16-20.	....	....	....
Unrecorded Works	(?)	....	....	....	20 : 30, 31; 21 : 24, 25.
Ascension	Bethany.	....	16 : 19, 20.	24 : 50-53.	....

The Gospel
according to
MATTHEW
with
NOTES AND COMMENTS.

THE GOSPEL ACCORDING TO MATTHEW.

INTRODUCTION.

By whom written. The testimony of antiquity is unanimous that the Gospel of Matthew was written by the apostle whose name it bears.* Its characteristics are such as one might expect from the writer. He was a publican or tax-gatherer by profession, and was thus trained to orderly and methodical habits of thought; and of all the Gospels his is the most orderly and systematic in its arrangement. He gives more fully than any other writer the public discourses of our Lord. Thus it is that we find in Matthew by far the fullest accounts of the Sermon on the Mount, the apostolic commission, the discourse on blasphemy against the Holy Ghost, that on the duties of the disciples to forgive one another, and the whole series of invectives against the Pharisees, as well as the parables by the sea and those that are prophecies of the destruction of the Jewish nation.†

Original language. But though the authorship of the Gospel was never called in question until the last century, and is as well established as that of any ancient book, it is not certain that we possess this Gospel in its original form. The testimony of the early Church is unanimous that Matthew wrote originally in the Hebrew language; and some confirmation is lent to this opinion by the fact that there are indications that he wrote his Gospel with special reference to exerting his influence upon the Jews, and from the statement of at least one of the fathers that he belonged to the Jewish party in the Christian Church. On the other hand, doubt is thrown over this opinion, both by an examination of the statements of the fathers, and by a consideration of peculiar forms of language employed in the Gospel itself. The question is unsettled, the best scholars not agreeing in their judgment concerning it. If there was a Hebrew original, it disappeared at a very early age. The Greek Gospel which we now possess was, it is almost certain, written in Matthew's lifetime, and it is not at all improbable that he wrote the Gospel in both the Greek and Hebrew languages.

Time of composition. There are no data for determining with accuracy the exact time when it was written. The testimony of the early church, however, is unanimous that it was the first written of the Gospels; and this is confirmed indirectly by the fact that in all copies of the N. T., and in all translations, this Gospel has been placed first. It was probably composed about the middle of the first century.

Object. Whether originally written in the Hebrew language or not, it is reasonably certain that it was written originally for Jewish readers. The ancient opinion that Matthew wrote in Hebrew indicates this, and the inference is confirmed by its character. "We have," says Dean Alford, "fewer interpretations of Jewish customs, laws, and localities than in the two other Gospels. The whole narrative proceeds more upon a Jewish view of matters, and is concerned more to establish that point, which to a Jewish convert would be most important—*that Jesus was the Messiah prophesied in the Old Testament.* Hence the commencement of his genealogy from Abraham and David; hence the frequent notice of the necessity of this or that event happening, *because it was so foretold by the prophets;* hence the constant opposition of our Lord's spiritually ethical teaching to the carnal formalistic ethics of the Scribes and Pharisees."

Characteristics. Of these I have already incidentally spoken. His diction is the Hebraistic Greek of the Septuagint; his external character as a writer is order, method, and simplicity; his view of Jesus Christ is of him as the Messiah-King, come to establish on the earth the Kingdom of God; and of that kingdom he affords the most perfect delineation in his report of the Sermon on the Mount and the Parables by the Sea.

---

* For account of his life see Commentary, p. 111. For some account of this testimony see Intro., pp. 16-19.

† Matt., chaps. 5-7; 10-12: 21-25.

From Monteith's Comprehensive Geography.

GAZETTEER.

Bethany (*house or place of dates*). A well-known village about 2 miles from Jerusalem, on the eastern slope of the Mt. of Olives. Matt. 21:17; 26:6-13; Mark 11:1, 11, 12; 14:3-9; Luke 19:39; 24:50, 51; John 11:1-46; 11:18.

Bethlehem (*house of bread*) a village 5 miles south of Jerusalem and east of the road to Hebron. It occupies part of the summit and sides of a narrow ridge which shoots out eastward from the central chain of the Judean mountains, and breaks down abruptly into deep valleys on the north, south, and east. The village at the present time contains about 500 houses. Gen. 35:19; Ruth 1:19; 1 Sam. 16:4; 2 Sam. 23:15-17; Matt. 2:1-18; Luke 2:1-20.

Bethphage (*house of unripe figs*). A village on the road between Jericho and Jerusalem, and near to Bethany, but whether east or west of it is not known. Matt. 21:1; Mark 11:1; Luke 19:29.

Bethsaida (*house of fish*). A town of Galilee, on the shore of the Lake of Gennesaret. Some scholars suppose two towns of the same name. This is an improbable and unnecessary hypothesis. See note on Mark 6:45. Bethsaida Julias, the only one known to have existed, was on the north shore of the sea, near the mouth of the river Jordan. Matt. 11:21; Mark 6:45; Luke 9:10; 10:13; John 1:44; 12:21.

Cæsarea Philippi. A city about 4 miles east of Dan, the Hazor and Baal-Gad of Josh. 11:10, 17. Its ruins are found in the little village of Banias. Matt. 16:13, note.

Cana (*reedy*). A village in the hill country of Galilee, about 9 miles north of Nazareth, and about 6 or 8 hours from Capernaum. John 2:1-11, notes; 4:46-54; 21:2.

Capernaum. A city on the sea of Galilee, the centre of Christ's missionary operations throughout Galilee. Its site is involved in uncertainty; probably it is to be identified with Tell-Hum, an uninhabited ruin. Matt. 8:5, 14; 9:1, 9; Mark 1:16, 17, 21, 23; Luke 5:27; 7:1, 8; John 6:59.

Chorazin (*district of Zin*). A town of Galilee. The site is uncertain, but recent researches tend to identify it with Kerazeh, two miles north of Tell-Hum. Matt. 11:21; Luke 10:13.

Dalmanutha (*branch*). A village on the western shore of the Sea of Galilee, perhaps identical with Magdala. Mark 8:10, note.

Dead Sea. Called the Salt Sea, The Sea, The Sea of the Plains, *i. e.*, the Arabah, the East Sea, Asphaltic Lake, and Sea of Sodom. The Arabs term it *Bahr Lut*, the "Sea of Lot." It is of an elongated oval shape, broken by a peninsula which projects from the eastern shore, near its southern end, and virtually divides the expanse of the water into two portions. It is about 46 miles long by 10 miles wide in the widest part; its area is about 250 square geographical miles. The northern portion is of great depth, the southern is shallow. The sea, in its present extent, covers what was once the Vale of Siddim.

Decapolis (*of ten cities*). A region in the north-eastern part of Palestine, near the Sea of Galilee. Matt. 4:25, note.

Emmaus. A village, site unknown, 6 or 8 miles from Jerusalem. Luke 24:13-35.

Enon. The place where John baptized. Its location is uncertain. Robinson places it near the north-eastern border of Judea, in the vicinity of Samaria. John 3:23.

Ephraim. A city described as near the wilderness; that is, perhaps, the wild hill country north-east of Jerusalem. John 11:54.

Gadara. A Roman town south-east of Tiberias, giving name to the country of the Gadarenes. Matthew 8:28, note; Mark 5:1; Luke 8:26.

Galilee (*circle*). A name originally confined to a little "circuit" of country round Kadesh-Naphtali, in which were situated twenty towns given by Solomon to Hiram, King of Tyre. In Christ's time, it embraced the whole northern section of Palestine, including the ancient territories of Issachar, Zebulun, Asher, and Naphtali. It extended from the Mediterranean to the Jordan Valley, and from the base of Mt. Carmel and the hills of Samaria, to Phœnicia and the Lebanon range. Remains of splendid synagogues still exist in many of the old towns and villages, showing that from the second to the seventh century the Jews were as prosperous as they were numerous. Josh. 20:7; 1 Kings 9:2; Matt. 4:15; Mark 14:70; Luke 17:11; John 1:46; 7:52. See Matt. 2:22, note.

Galilee, Sea of. Called also Sea of Gennesaret, of Chinnereth or Chinneroth, and the Lake of Tiberias. For map and description, see Mark 1:30, note.

Jericho. An ancient city of the Canaanites, situated in the valley of the Jordan, at the entrance of two passes through the hills,—one to Jerusalem, the other to Ai and Bethel. It is called in Judges 1:16; 3:13, "City of Palm Trees." The N. T. Jericho was 2 miles from the fountain of Elisha, the present *Ain-es-Sultân*. Josh. 2:1-21; 6:1; 2 Sam. 10:5; 1 Kings 16:34; 2 Kings 2:1-22; Ezra 2:34; Neh. 3:2; 7:36; Jer. 39:5; 52:8; Matt. 20:29-34; Mark 10:46-52; Luke 10:30-37; 18:35, 43; 19:1-10.

Jerusalem. A city built on a promontory of rock that juts out from the table-land of Judea.

GAZETTEER.

Deep but narrow gorges separate it from surrounding hills. It is 25 feet above the level of the Mediterranean Sea, and 3600 feet above the valley of the Jordan. A valley divides its rocky foundation into two hills, and the city itself into an upper and lower town. Josh. 18 : 28 ; Judg. 1 : 8 ; 2 Sam. 5 : 6-9 ; 1 Kings 3 : 1 ; 2 Chr. 25 : 23, 24 ; Neh., chaps. 2-6 ; 2 Kings 24 : 10-16 ; 25. For map, see Matt., ch. 26, p. 257.

Jordan. The only considerable river of Palestine. It rises in the Lebanon range, flows for six miles through a marshy plain, enters the waters of Merom, thence descends about nine miles to the Sea of Galilee, falling in that distance about 600 feet ; after quitting this lake at its southern extremity it becomes a headlong torrent, widening in its course, with many a precipitous fall through a strange, lonely valley, occupying in its serpentine course 200 miles in traversing a direct line of not over 60 ; and finally empties into the Dead Sea, 1316 feet below the Mediterranean sea level. From the Sea of Galilee to the Dead Sea, it descends nearly, if not quite, 700 feet. Its width varies from 70 feet, at its entrance into the Sea of Galilee, to 180 yards at its entrance into the Dead Sea. For some of the historical events connected with the Jordan, see Josh. chaps. 3, 4 ; Judg. 8 : 4 ; 10 : 9 ; 2 Sam. 2 : 29 ; 17 : 22 ; 19 : 15-39 ; 2 Kings 2 : 7-14 ; 5 : 10-14 ; 6 : 2-7 ; Matt. 3 : 6, 13 ; Mark 1 : 5, 9.

Judea. This name is now frequently applied to the whole of the Holy Land, more generally designated as Palestine. Properly speaking, however, it only signifies one of the three provinces into which Palestine, west of the Jordan, was divided at the time of Christ—Galilee, Samaria, Judea. The province of Judea comprised the territories of Judah, Benjamin, Simeon, and parts of Dan, from the Jordan to the Mediterranean ; it extended from the wilderness on the south to Shiloh on the north, running up, however, on the sea-coast west of Samaria to a point north of Cæsarea. After the disgrace of Archelaus, A.D. 6, Judea was attached to the Roman province of Syria ; the procurator, subordinate to the Governor of Syria, residing at Cæsarea.

Machærus. See Matt. 11 : 2, note.

Magdala. A town on the Sea of Galilee, identified with the modern *el-Mejdel*, a little north of Tiberias. Matt. 15 : 39 ; Mark 8 : 10, note.

Nain. A city mentioned only in Luke 7 : 11. Its remains lie on the south side of the Little Hermon, two or three hours' distance from Nazareth, on the road to Jerusalem.

Nazareth. A town situated in a beautiful valley about five miles west of Tabor. The modern town is supposed to have been built upon the ancient site ; it has a population of 3120 persons. Matt. 2 : 22, 23, note ; Luke 2 : 39 ; 4 : 16.

Palestine. This name is now universally applied to the country formerly inhabited by the Jewish people, though in the Bible it has other names, as Canaan, Land of the Hebrews, Land of Judea, Land of Promise, Land of Jehovah, and sometimes simply The Land. In size and shape Palestine does not differ widely from the State of Vermont ; its length is about 180 miles, its average breadth 65. But its variety of climate, productions, and geographical features have no parallel in any section of equally limited area on the American continent. By its physical features it is divided into three long and narrow parallel sections—the valley of the Jordan, the hill country of Central Palestine, and the rich and fertile lowlands which border on the Mediterranean. On the north the hills rise into mountains, reaching, in the Lebanon and Anti-Lebanon, a height of from 6000 to 8000 feet above the level of the ocean. In the south they drop down into the level plains of the desert, while the waters of the Dead Sea are 1316 feet below the Mediterranean. Politically, at the time of Christ Palestine was divided into four sections — Judea, Samaria, Galilee, and Perea. See Luke 3 : 1, note and map.

Perea (*beyond*). The region east of the river Jordan, including Bashan and Gilead, because lying *beyond* the river Jordan, so called ; in modern literature it is often entitled the trans-Jordanic region. In the time of Christ it was fertile and populous, and inhabited by a mixed population, partly Roman, partly Jewish. It is said that the Jordan valley alone contains the ruins of 127 villages. Most of the events and incidents in Luke, chaps. 10-18, occurred in this district.

Salim. Site unknown.

Samaria. The province of Samaria once included all of Palestine north of Judea. That portion east of the Jordan which originally belonged to it was taken away by the kings of Assyria ; then the northern portion, Galilee, shared the same fate ; and Samaria was reduced to the dimensions which it possessed in the time of Christ. 1 Chron. 5 : 26 ; 2 Kings 15 : 29 ; Luke 9 : 51-56 ; 10 : 25-37 ; John 4 : 39-42.

Sidon, or **Zidon.** An ancient city of Phœnicia, about 20 miles north of Tyre, and nearly 40 miles south of *Beirut*. See Matt. 11 : 21, note.

Sychar. A celebrated city of Palestine ; called also Sichem, Shechem, and Sychem. The modern town is called Nablous, and contains about 8000 inhabitants. It is beautifully located in a fertile valley between Mt. Ebal and Gerizim, about seven miles south of Samaria. Gen. 23 : 18-20 ; Josh. 24 : 1-23, 32 ; Judges 9 ; 1 Kings 12 : 1-25 ; 2 Chron. 10 ; Jer. 41 : 5 ; John 4 : 5.

Tyre. A commercial city of Phœnicia, on the eastern shore of the Mediterranean. Its present population numbers between 3000 and 4000, the half being Christians. See Matt. 11 : 21, note.

THE GOSPEL ACCORDING TO
MATTHEW.

CHAPTER I.

THE book of the generation[a] of Jesus Christ, the son of David,[b] the son[c] of Abraham.

2 Abraham[d] begat Isaac; and Isaac[e] begat Jacob; and Jacob[f] begat Judas and his brethren;

3 And Judas begat Phares[g] and Zara of Thamar; and Phares begat Esrom;[h] and Esrom begat Aram;[i]

a Luke 3 : 23, &c.....b ch. 22 : 45 ; Ps. 132 : 11 ; Acts 2 : 30.....c Gen. 22 : 18 ; Gal. 3 : 16.....d Gen. 21 : 2–5.....e Gen. 25 : 26.....f Gen. 29 : 35, &c.....g Gen. 38 : 27, 30, &c.....h Gen. 46 : 12.....i Ruth 4 : 19.

1 : 1–17. THE GENEALOGY OF JESUS CHRIST.—THE OLD TESTAMENT PREPARES FOR THE NEW.—CHRIST IS THE CONSUMMATION OF JEWISH HISTORY.—HARLOTS (RAHAB, THAMAR, BATHSHEBA) SHARE IN THE PREPARATION FOR HIS COMING.—JEW AND GENTILE, SAINT AND SINNER (ABRAHAM, RUTH, AND RAHAB) ARE AMONG HIS ANCESTORS; THUS THE LOWLIEST ANCESTRY PREPARES FOR THE NOBLEST BIRTH.—THE SON OF A PEASANT, THE SON OF DAVID, THE SON OF GOD ARE ALL ONE.—GOD PRESERVES FOR HIS PURPOSE THE PIOUS FAMILY. "IT MAY GO DOWN, BUT NOT GO OUT; IT STANDS BECAUSE IT WITHSTANDS."

1. The book of the generation, *i. e.*, the genealogical register of Jesus Christ. This is the title of the first seventeen verses of this chapter, not of the whole Gospel as has sometimes been supposed. It was customary for the Jewish families to keep with care records of their pedigree. Among the Jews the land was divided among the tribes, and according to families, the monarchy and the priesthood were both hereditary; and these facts gave to such genealogical registers of the Jewish families a peculiar value. Instances of such records are afforded by Gen. 5 : 1 ; 3–32; 35 : 22–26. First Chronicles is full of such genealogies. These records were revived at the time of the restoration, and the re-settlement of the land of Israel under Ezra and Nehemiah, and the allotment of priestly and other offices was apparently determined according to them (Ezra, chaps. 2, 8 ; Neh., chaps. 7, 10, 12). **Son of,** *i. e.*, descendant of. The term *son* is frequently used in Scripture in this enlarged sense. The Messiah promised by the prophets was to be a son of David (Jer. 23 : 5 ; Ps. 132 ; 10, 11), and the chief object of this genealogical register of Jesus Christ appears to have been to show the Jews that he was a descendant of David, and a child of Abraham, and so fulfilled the prophecies respecting the Messiah.

Another genealogical register is given in Luke 3 : 23–28. The wide differences between them have occasioned biblical students some difficulty. Luke gives the whole record from Adam ; Matthew begins at Abraham, and omits many names which appear in the O. T. history. Such omissions of unimportant names in the genealogical register are, however, common. But between David and Joseph the two lists are almost entirely different. This is a more serious difficulty. Without entering here into a full explanation of the difficulty and its solution, for which the reader must be referred to the treatises which have been written on the subject, it must suffice to say : 1st. That both genealogies were undoubtedly taken from the public registers, that of Luke probably from the record made out for the purpose of the census ordered by Augustus, and referred to in Luke 2 : 1, 3. 2d. That both are unquestionably the genealogy of Joseph : genealogies of women were unknown to the Jews, and a careful comparison of the two refutes the old hypothesis that one is the genealogy of Joseph, and the other of Mary. 3d. That David had four sons by Bathsheba, and that Luke traces the genealogy from Nathan, one of these four sons (Luke 3 : 31), while Matthew traces it from Solomon, another son, and the inheritor of his father's throne. Thus Matthew's register shows the regal descent of Jesus Christ from David through Solomon, and his consequent right, so to speak, to sit on the throne of his father David—while Luke gives his natural and actual descent through Nathan, and the two come together at Salathiel. 4th. That it is probable that Mary was the cousin of Joseph, her husband ; so that in point of fact, though not in form, both genealogies are hers as well as his. 5th. That the fact that Jesus was a descendant of David does not rest alone upon the testimony of these genealogies. Psalm 132 : 11 ; Luke 1 : 32 ; Rom. 1 : 3 show very clearly that Mary also was of the family of David. The reason why Jesus is shown to be of the family of David, by tracing his descent through Joseph, his putative father, and not through Mary, his real mother, is to be found in the fact that the Jews would not have recognized any fulfillment of the ancient prophecy in a genealogy through the mother, which that age never recognized.

2–6. Judas, Greek form of patriarch Judah, eldest son of Jacob, and progenitor of the tribe of Judah, to which Jesus Christ belonged. From his name come the words Judea and Jews. **Phares and Zara,** same as Pharez and Zarah (Genesis 38 : 27, 30). The rest of the genealogy to

4 And Aram begat Aminadab; and Aminadab begat Naasson;^j and Naasson begat Salmon;^k
5 And Salmon begat Booz of Rachab;^l and Booz begat Obed^m of Ruth; and Obed begat Jesse;
6 And Jesse begat Davidⁿ the king; and David the king begat Solomon^o of her *that had been the wife* of Urias;
7 And Solomon begat Roboam;^p and Roboam begat Abia; and Abia begat Asa;
8 And Asa begat Josaphat; and Josaphat begat Joram; and Joram begat Ozias;
9 And Ozias begat Joatham; and Joatham begat Achaz; and Achaz begat Ezekias;
10 And Ezekias^q begat Manasses; and Manasses begat Amon; and Amon begat Josias;
11 And Josias begat Jechonias and his brethren, about the time they were carried away to Babylon;
12 And after they were brought to Babylon, Jechonias begat Salathiel;^r and Salathiel begat Zorobabel;^s
13 And Zorobabel begat Abiud; and Abiud begat Eliakim; and Eliakim begat Azor;
14 And Azor begat Sadoc; and Sadoc begat Achim; and Achim begat Eliud;
15 And Eliud begat Eleazar; and Eleazar begat Matthan; and Matthan begat Jacob;
16 And Jacob begat Joseph the husband of Mary, of whom was born Jesus, who is called Christ.
17 So all the generations from Abraham to David *are* fourteen generations; and from David until the carrying away into Babylon *are* fourteen generations; and from the carrying away into Babylon unto Christ *are* fourteen generations.
18 Now the birth^t of Jesus Christ was on this wise: When as his mother Mary was espoused to Joseph,

---

j 1 Chron. 2 : 10; Num. 1 : 7,.....k Ruth 4 : 20.....l Jos. 6 : 25; Ruth 4 : 21.....m Ruth 4 : 13.....n 1 Sam. 17 : 12.....o 2 Sam. 12 : 24.....
p 1 Chron. 3 : 10, &c.....q 2 Kings 20 : 21; 1 Chron. 3 : 13.....r 1 Chron. 3 : 17, &c.....s Neh. 12 : 1.....t Luke 1 : 27, &c.

David is the same as that in Ruth 4 : 18-22, except that the Greek and Hebrew forms are different, as Aram for Oram, and Booz for Boaz, &c. It is worthy of note that Ruth was a Moabite, and that thus, in the very genealogy of Christ, there is implied a rebuke of the Jewish pride of birth and disdain of the Gentile world. Boaz, too, is declared to be the son of Rachab, *i. e.*, probably Rahab the harlot (Josh. ch. 2), who was also a Gentile, and whose name, as well as that of Bathsheba, and Thamar, appears to be inserted here for the purpose of rebuking that form of Phariseeism which visits the sins of the mother on the children. Four women are mentioned in this genealogy; of whom three are described in the sacred history as unchaste at one time in their lives, though apparently subsequently repentant.

7-11. These verses give the regal succession from the accession of Solomon to the captivity of the Jews in Babylon. Some confusion is produced by the fact that the form of the names is changed from the Hebrew to the Greek. If we change them back to their Hebrew, *i. e.*, to their O. T. forms, they will read thus : Solomon, Rehoboam, Abijah, Asa, Jehosaphat, Jehoram (there were two kings of this name, one the son of Ahab, and king of Israel, the other the son of Jehosaphat and king of Judah), Uzziah, Jotham, Ahaz, Hezekiah, Manasseh, Amon, Josiah (1 Chron. 3 : 15, 16).

12. Jechonias begat Salathiel. Jeremiah (22 : 30) prophesied that Jechonias should be "childless, a man that shall not prosper in his days; for no man of his seed shall prosper, sitting upon the throne of David, and ruling any more in Judah." This prophecy may be understood to mean, however, not that he should have no offspring, but that he should have none to succeed him on the throne, as Alford interprets it ; or it may be that Salathiel, though not his son, but the son of Neir, and so a descendant of David through Nathan (Luke 3 : 27), was adopted as the heir of Jechonias, as Lord Hervey supposes (see art. on Salathiel in Smith's Bib. Dict.). Zorobabel, probably the natural son of Pedaiah, Salathiel's brother (1 Chron. 3 : 19), but adopted by his uncle Salathiel and succeeding him as head of the house of Judah.

12-17. These verses give the genealogy from the time of the Babylonian captivity to the birth of Christ. A similar register is given in 1 Chron. 3 : 19-24, and some of the persons here mentioned are also mentioned in Luke. The difference in the statements appears at first to be considerable ; but they are all due, probably, to the omission from one or the other of the genealogies of names deemed unimportant, or to a difference in the form of word employed for the same name, or to the employment of different names for the same person ; thus Hannaniah (Chron.) and Joanna (Luke) are the same name, as also probably are Abiud (Matt.), Juda (Luke), and Hadaiah (Chron.).

16. Jacob begat Joseph. Luke says that Joseph was the son of Heli; while both Luke and Matthew agree in representing Joseph's grandfather as Matthan or Matthat. Jacob and Heli were accordingly brothers. By Jewish law even if a man died without issue, his brother was required to marry his widow, and the first-born succeeded to the rights of the childless husband (Deut. 25 : 5-10); Jacob and Heli probably married in succession the same wife according to this law, and Joseph, who was the true son of one, was also legally the son and heir of the other.

17. So all the generations . . . . . are fourteen. In counting these tables the first person is twice counted ; once as the beginning of a table, and once as the end of the preceding table. Thus Abraham is the first, and David the last in the first fourteen, David is the first and Josiah the last in the second fourteen, and Josiah is the first and Joseph the last in the third.

1 : 18-25. **THE BIRTH OF JESUS.**—See Note

before they came together, she was found with child of the Holy Ghost.

19 Then Joseph her husband, being a just *man*, and not willing to make her a public example, was minded" to put her away privily.

20 But while he thought on these things, the angel of the Lord appeared unto him in a dream,^{v} saying, Joseph, thou son of David, fear not to take unto thee Mary thy wife; for that which is conceived in her is of the Holy Ghost.

21 And she shall bring forth a son, and thou shalt call his name JESUS: for he shall save^w his people from their sins.

22 Now all this was done, that it might be fulfilled which was spoken of the Lord by the prophet,^{x} saying,

u Deut. 24 : 1......v Job 33 : 15, 17......w Acts 5 : 31 ; 13 : 23, 38......x Isa. 7 : 14.

BELOW ON NAMES OF JESUS; AND ON THE INCARNATION SEE NOTES ON JOHN 1.

18. Now the birth of Jesus Christ. According to the chronology, which regulates our present system of dates, Jesus was born in the year of Rome 754, and in the first year of the present system of reckoning, *i. e.*, A.D. 1. But it is now generally agreed that this places his birth some years too late. Herod died in the year of Rome 750, *i. e.*, B.C. 4. Jesus was born during the lifetime of Herod, and certainly within less than two years previous to his death (Matt. 2 : 16), *i. e.*, between the years of Rome 748 and 750, or between 6 and 4 B.C. The time of year of his birth is entirely unknown. There is no reason for supposing it to have occurred on the 25th of December; that month was fixed upon for the commemoration of his birth (in the sixth century) for the purpose of drawing off heathen converts from the heathen festivities. (See *Abbott's Popular Religious Dictionary*, article *Christmas*.) **In this wise,** *i. e.*, the circumstances attending his birth were as follows. **Espoused.** Among the ancient Jews the espousal or betrothal, answering to our modern marriage engagement, was a formal and solemn contract, almost as much so as the subsequent wedding itself. It was ratified on both sides with oaths by the parties or their representatives. After betrothal the woman was considered to a certain extent a wife; the contract could only be set aside by a solemn renunciation of it, answering to a divorce; and if, after the betrothal, the woman was guilty of infidelity, she was considered guilty of adultery, exactly as if the marriage had taken place (Ezek. 16 : 8 ; Deut. 22 : 23, 24). **Came together.** The woman continued to live at her father's house prior to the marriage, which was completed by a public bringing of the woman to the home of her husband. Before this was accomplished, and Joseph and Mary had begun to live together as man and wife, she was found to be with child.

19. Joseph, her husband, so called, and so in some sense regarded, though they were as yet unmarried (comp. Gen. 29 : 21 ; Deut. 22 : 24). **Being just,** *i. e.*, having a character such as rendered him unwilling to pass by what he deemed a flagitious offence against good morals and the law of God; **And yet not willing to make her a public example,** being also kind and merciful, and probably greatly attached to her despite what he supposes to be her sin. **Intended to put her away privately.** According to the original he not merely thought of doing so, but had resolved to do so. By Jewish law the husband was final judge in all cases in which his wife was suspected of infidelity, so far at least that he might himself annul the marriage, provided, however, he gave her a bill of divorcement, setting forth the reasons for his course. This must be in writing, and by the rabbinical law was required to be given to her in the presence of at least two witnesses—(*Lightfoot*). This, however, apparently involved her in no condemnation, since she might in that case marry again (Deut. 24 : 1-4). But she could not be proceeded against criminally without a trial; in such case, if found guilty of adultery, she was put to death by stoning (Deut. 22 : 22-24). Joseph proposed not to bring any criminal complaint against Mary, but simply to give her a writing of divorcement under the provision of the former of these two laws, and so separate from her. On these provisions of divorce, and their bearing on the questions of marriage and divorce, we comment elsewhere (Matt. 19 : 3-9).

20. Take unto thee Mary, thy wife, *i. e.*, Take Mary to be thy wife; do not fear to complete the marriage relation begun by the betrothal. **For that which,** etc. See on Luke 1 : 30, etc. **Jesus,** same as Joshua. The name of Joshua is rendered Jesus once in Acts 7 : 45, and once in Hebrews 4 : 8. See below on the names of Jesus.

22, 23. Now all this was done, etc., The prophecy referred to is to be found in Isaiah 7 : 14-16. About 740 B.C., Ahaz being king of Judah, an invasion was threatened by the combined armies of Syria and Israel. Ahaz was alarmed, and determined to call in aid from Assyria for his defence. God promised deliverance to Judah, and invited Ahaz to ask a sign in confirmation. This Ahaz declined to do. Isaiah then, under divine inspiration, uttered a prophecy, which is confessedly somewhat enigmatical, and which Henderson renders as follows. The reader will do well to compare this translation with that of our English Bible.

Behold, the virgin shall conceive and bear a son;
And shall call his name Immanuel.

23 Behold, a virgin shall be with child, and shall bring forth a son, and they shall call his name Emmanuel; which being interpreted is, God? with us.
24 Then Joseph, being raised from sleep, did as the angel of the Lord had bidden him, and took unto him his wife;
25 And knew her not till she had brought forth her first-born* son: and he called his name JESUS.ª

y John 1 : 14.....z Ex. 13 : 2.....a Luke 2 : 1.

Butter and honey shall he eat,
When he shall know to reject what is evil,
And to choose what is good.
But before the youth shall have knowledge
To reject what is evil and to choose what is good,
The land, which thou destroyest [Eng. vers. abhorrest], shall be forsaken by both its kings.

Shortly after uttering this prophecy Isaiah had a child by one who was, *at the time of the prophecy,* a virgin, and the declaration was then made by God (Isaiah 8 : 1-4) that before this son should be able to cry, "My father and my mother," the riches of Damascus and the spoil of Samaria should be taken away before the king of Assyria (Isaiah 8 : 1-4). Ahaz carried out his contemplated plan, secured the aid of the king of Assyria, and by doing so repelled the invaders. Damascus, the capital of Syria, was taken, and Rezin was slain. Shortly after Samaria was besieged by the same Assyrian king, and Israel was carried away captive. Thus, some years before the maturity of Isaiah's son, both the allied nations, leagued against Judah, were effectually destroyed (2 Kings 16-17 ; 6).

There are two explanations of Isaiah's prophecy. One is that he referred to the birth of his own son, Mahershalalhashbaz; that his declaration should be translated as in our Bible, "the land that thou *abhorrest* shall be forsaken of both her kings;" and that this prophecy was literally fulfilled by the destruction of Damascus and the death of Rezin, and by the destruction of Samaria and the captivity of Israel, as recorded in 2 Kings 16 and 17. According to this view Isaiah did not himself have in mind the future birth of the Messiah, though the birth of his own son, and the consequent deliverance of Israel, was itself a prophecy of a greater deliverance to come, just as the raising of the brazen serpent in the wilderness was prophetic of the crucifixion of Christ. The other view is that the prophecy of Isaiah was not intended as a sign of deliverance but was a rebuke to Ahaz for persisting in his appeal to the king of Assyria; that the prophecy should be translated as Henderson translates it in the passage quoted above; that by it God declared to Ahaz that though temporary relief should come, yet the end of the Jewish nation was not far off, and that before the Messiah, long-promised and long-expected, should come to years of maturity, the land which Ahaz by his wickedness corrupted and destroyed, *i. e.,* the land of Canaan, Jehovah's land, should be forsaken of both her kings, discrowned and subjected to a foreign power. This in fact occurred: for, at the time of the birth of Jesus, Herod was nominally king of the Jews, and after Herod's death, Archelaus, his son, reigned in his stead; but in the 12th year of our Lord, the very year in which he evinced his wonderful discrimination by disputing with the elders in the temple (Luke 2 : 49-46), Archelaus was banished, and Judea was reduced to a Roman province. The former of these two interpretations is the more common one; the latter appears to me to consort best with the original prophecy, and its divine fulfillment by the birth of Jesus Christ. It seems not reasonable, on the one hand, to imagine, as some have done, that the birth of Jesus Christ was foretold by Isaiah as a sign for the purpose of assuring Ahaz of national deliverance, when, in fact, the deliverance preceded the sign over seven centuries; nor consonant with the direct declaration of Matthew that the birth of Jesus fulfilled this prophecy, if, in fact, the prophecy had only an indirect reference to it; nor does the birth of a child, who does not appear to have been called Immanuel, by a woman who was not at the time a virgin, appear to be a real fulfillment of the prophecy; nor does it seem reasonable to suppose that God would encourage Ahaz in going on with his appeal to Assyria, a heathen ally, to whom he gave "the silver and gold that was found in the house of the Lord" (2 Kings 16 : 8); while it entirely accords with the circumstances of the case to understand that the prophecies of Isaiah 7 : 14-16 and 8 : 1-4 are distinct prophecies, the latter a declaration that Judah shall be delivered speedily from Syria and Israel; the former that immediately subsequent to the birth of the long-anticipated Messiah the entire land, Israel and Judah, should be deprived of its national glory, its kings discrowned, and itself reduced to a subject province. Actual history fulfils both prophecies, if thus understood, and thus gives to this interpretation an additional confirmation.

24. Then Joseph took unto him his wife; perhaps so as to preclude suspicion attaching to her; perhaps to convince her that no suspicion lingered in his own mind. It was, at all events, a strong attestation of his belief in the divine message. **Knew her not till she had brought forth her first-born son.** Certainly there is nothing in this verse to imply the perpetual virginity of Mary. There is some doubt whether the word **first-born** belongs here. Alford thinks not, and suggests that it was bor-

CHAPTER II.

NOW when Jesus was born in Bethlehem of Judæa in the days of Herod the king, behold, there came wise men from the east to Jerusalem,

2 Saying, Where is he that is born[b] King of the Jews? for we have seen his star[c] in the east, and are come to worship[d] him.
3 When Herod the king had heard *these things*, he was troubled, and all Jerusalem with him.

b Zech. 9:9.....c Num. 24:17; Isa. 60:3.....d John 5:23.

rowed from Luke 2:7. The phrase seems to imply that she had other children, a question elsewhere considered (Matt. 13:55).

THE NAMES OF JESUS.—It was the Hebrew custom to give names possessing a special signification (Gen. 27:36; Exod. 2:10); and sometimes to change the name as an indication of a change of character. Thus Abram (*high father*) was changed to Abraham (*father of a multitude*), and Jacob (*supplanter*), to Israel (*a prince of God*). Names given by parents might of course be meaningless, or might prove inappropriate, as Absalom (*father of peace*), and Rehoboam (*liberator*). The names of Jesus were given by God with the distinct recognition of their significance, and are therefore important indications of his character and work. Each of his three names, Christ, Emanuel, Jesus, are symbols of truths respecting him and his relations to us.

Christ, is a Greek word corresponding to Messiah, which is Hebrew. Both mean the "Anointed One," and both are titles rather than names. The original in the O. T. is sometimes translated Messiah, sometimes the Anointed; and is applied to the high priests and to kings (Lev. 4:3, 5, 16; 1 Sam. 12:3, 5; 16:6; 2 Sam. 1:14; Ps. 18:50; 28:8; Is. 45:1). Kings were not always anointed, but the essential element in the inauguration ceremonies of the high priest was anointing, and he was emphatically the "Anointed" to the Jews, as to the Romanist the pope (*i. e.* papa) is emphatically the Holy Father. The reiterated declaration of the prophets that redemption should come through the Messiah (Anointed One), was equivalent to a declaration that it should come through a Great High Priest; and the high priest himself was a perpetual and living prophecy of the coming of such a deliverer. To us Jesus is the Christ, the Messiah, the Anointed One, *i. e.* the one whom God has anointed to be our Great High Priest, through whom we have access "with boldness to the throne of grace" (Heb. 1:9; 4:14-16; ch. 5).

Emanuel or Immanuel is a Hebrew term signifying "God with us." The heathen religions generally represent God as afar off or unknown (Acts 17:23). Natural religion also represents him as the "Unknown" and "Unknowable." "The soul can never find the soft bosom of the mother in whose heart it can nestle."—(*O. B. Frothingham.*) "It is alike our highest wisdom and our highest duty to regard that through which all things exist as the 'Unknowable.'"—

(*Herbert Spencer.*) Christianity represents him as our Shepherd, our Guardian, our Guide, our constant Companion, our supreme Comforter in sorrow, our strength in temptation, Immanuel, God with us. It represents him in the O. T. a Guide and a Deliverer (Ps. 18:23; Ps. 104, 105, 107); in the N. T. a "God manifest in the flesh" (John 1:14; 1 Tim. 3:16; Heb. 1:3. Compare Phil. 2:5-11); and in the daily experience of the Christian he is disclosed as a God with us here and now, because he dwells with us and in us, unknown to the intellect but known to the heart (Matt. 5:8; John 14; 16-20; and see John 14 and 15 throughout; and compare Gal. 2:20, and similar passages).

Jesus is a Hebrew term, signifying help, deliverance, salvation. It is a modification of the name Joshua, which is itself an abbreviation of Jehosua, *i. e.*, Jehovah his help (Numb. 13:16; 1 Chron. 7:27). Its meaning is interpreted by the angel in verse 21, "For he shall save his people from their sins;" observe, not from the consequences of their sins, but *from their sins*, *i. e.*, from the power and dominion of sin itself (Phil. 4:13; Rom. 7:23; 8:27; Eph. 6:11, &c., &c.). This he does because as our Messiah, *i. e.* our high priest, he takes away the burden of the past, and as our Immanuel, *i. e.* God with us, he gives strength in the present, and assurance of victory in the future. Thus the three names of our Saviour—Christ, "the anointed high priest;" Immanuel, "God with us;" and Jesus, "he that saves"—embody the great doctrines of the Gospel, that he makes atonement for the past, is our companion in the present, and so delivers us from the power of sin now, and its penalty hereafter.

2:1-12. VISIT OF THE MAGI. THE LIGHT OF NATURE IS BUT STARLIGHT.—IT LEADS HONEST INQUIRERS TO CHRIST BY FIRST LEADING THEM TO THE SCRIPTURE.—HE WHO FOLLOWS WHAT LIGHT HE HAS WILL BE GIVEN MORE LIGHT.—THE HEATHEN ENTER THE KINGDOM OF CHRIST BEFORE THE SCRIBES (Matt. 8:11, 12).—GOD ADAPTS HIS TEACHING TO THE LEARNER; HE TEACHES THE MAGI BY THE STARS, THE SCRIBES BY THE SCRIPTURES.—IT IS BETTER TO BELIEVE THE TEACHING OF NATURE AND OBEY IT, THAN TO BELIEVE THE TEACHING OF THE SCRIPTURE AND DISOBEY IT.—HEROD IS AN EXAMPLE OF AN UNBELIEVING BELIEVER; HE BELIEVES THE SCRIPTURE, BUT "HOLDS IT IN UNRIGHTEOUSNESS," AND WRESTS IT TO HIS OWN HURT (Rom. 1:18 and note; 2 Pet. 3:16).—THE SCRIBES POINT TO CHRIST AND YET ARE CAST-AWAY (1 Cor. 9:27).—THE NEAR ARE SOMETIMES AFAR OFF; AND THE AFAR OFF NEAR.—THE MAGI SAW THE STAR, AND REJOICED; HEROD HEARD OF CHRIST, AND WAS

BETHLEHEM.
Looking west from the Convent of the Nativity.

TROUBLED (1 Kings 18:17; Matt. 10:34). DOES THE COMING OF CHRIST GIVE YOU JOY OR TROUBLE?

1. Now when Jesus was born. The evangelist passes over the intervening results and the account of Christ's birth, and the reasons which had led his parents to Bethlehem, all of which are given in Luke 2:1-20. **Bethlehem of Judea.** A village five miles south of Jerusalem. Its name Beth-lehem (*house of bread*) was due to the fertility of the adjacent cornfields. The modern village contains about five hundred houses, a famous convent, within which is a large rock-hewn cave which the monks point out as the manger where Christ was born. Over this cave stands the Basilica built by St. Helena A.D. 325-327, in honor of Christ, the oldest monument of Christ existing in the world. Bethlehem is one of the oldest towns in Palestine, and has a sacred history. Near it is the tomb where Jacob buried Rachel. The supposed site is still shown to travelers. In the adjoining fields Ruth gleaned for grain and gained a husband. Here David was born and anointed king (Gen. 35:16, 19; Ruth 1:19; 1 Sam. 16:1-13; 2 Sam. 23:15-17). And here, in the fourth century after Christ, Jerome, fleeing from persecution, accomplished the great work of his life, the "Vulgate," the translation of the Scriptures into Latin, the accepted version of the Roman Catholic Church. It is called Bethlehem in Judah or Bethlehem-Judah (Judg. 17:7,8,9; 1 Sam. 17:12), to distinguish it from another Bethlehem in the tribe of Zebulun near the sea of Galilee (Josh. 19:15). It was also called Ephrath, *the fruitful* (Gen. 35:19; 48:7), or **Ephratah** (Micah 5:2).

Herod the king. Herod is the name of a family which plays an important part in the history of Palestine. Seven of that name are mentioned in the N. T., as follows:

I. Herod the Great.

II. Herod Archelaus. He was a son of Herod the Great, was made by his father's will one of his heirs; the will was confirmed by Augustus Cæsar, and Herod Archelaus, with the title of monarch, received the one-half of his father's dominions, viz., Judea, Samaria, and Idumea, with the cities of Joppa and Cæsarea. He is the Herod referred to below in ver. 22.

III. Herod Antipas, another son of Herod the Great, and by his father appointed tetrarch of Galilee and Perea. His illicit marriage to Herodias, wife of his half-brother Philip, was rebuked by John the Baptist; the rebuke led to the latter's execution. He was the Herod before whom our Lord was sent by Pilate during the Passion week (Luke 23 : 7). For some account of his life and character see Matt. 14 : 1, note.

IV. Herod Philip I, known in the N. T. as Philip, a third son of Herod the Great, the first and lawful husband of Herodias, and the father of Salome (Matt. 14 : 3, 6). He must not be confounded with the tetrarch Philip. Owing to his mother's treachery he was excluded from all share in his father's possessions and lived in a private station.

V. Herod Philip II, a fourth son of Herod the Great and made tetrarch of Batanea, Trachonitis, Auranitis and some parts about Jamnia. His territory lay east of Galilee and north of Perea. He was the founder of Cæsarea Philippi, and made a new city, which he called Julius, out of Bethsaida, on the northern shore of the Sea of Galilee. He married Salome, the daughter of Herod Philip I and Herodias. He was by far the best of the ruling sons of Herod the Great; is referred to in the N. T. only in Luke 3 : 1.

VI. Herod Agrippa I, a grandson of Herod the Great. He is the Herod mentioned in Acts 12 : 1–3, 23. See notes there.

VII. Herod Agrippa II, a son of Herod Agrippa I. In A.D. 52, he was made ruler, with the title of king, of northern Palestine, the previous dominions of Philip and Lysanias. He is the Agrippa before whom Paul was tried (Acts 25 : 13, 22, 23 ; 26 : 27, 28). See notes there for life and character. There were other members of the Herodian family, but these are the only ones mentioned in the N. T.

The Herod here referred to is the father, Herod misnamed the Great, the second son of Antipater, an Idumean, appointed procurator of Judea by Julius Cæsar, B.C. 47, and subsequently receiving the title of "King of Judea" from the Roman Senate. He possessed energy of character, but an unscrupulous ambition, and was remorselessly cruel. He was made governor of Galilee at the early age of fifteen, and distinguished himself by his campaign against the brigands who infested the mountains. He transferred his allegiance without scruple from Cassius to Antony, and from Antony to Cæsar, as in succession they secured the possession of the political power of Rome. By Antony's influence he was made king of Judea, and on Antony's fall was confirmed in his position by Cæsar. He rebuilt the temple in great magnificence in Jerusalem, which is consequently known in history as Herod's Temple, to distinguish it from Solomon's Temple; he also constructed another on Mt. Gerizim for the Samaritans and established heathen worship in Cæsarea for the Romans. By nature jealous and suspicious, a terrible distemper, which finally brought his wretched life to a more wretched end, aggravated the asperities of his temper. In succession, his wife's grandfather, his wife herself, and three of his own sons were slain by his command. His course on hearing that another "king of the Jews" was born, was quite in keeping with all that secular history records of his character. He died miserably in the 70th year of his age, and the 38th year of his reign, issuing on his death-bed a characteristic order for the massacre of the courtiers whom he had called about him in his last illness. Thus he said he should secure universal mourning at his death. The events recorded in this chapter took place near the close of his reign, probably during the last year.

There came wise men from the east. Concerning these "wise men" three questions naturally call for some answer: (1) Who were they? (2) From what country did they come? (3) How should they know that the star foretold the coming of Christ?

(1.) The original expression is "*Magi from the East.*" The term *magi* is that from which comes our modern word "magician." Its etymology is uncertain. It is probably derived from a word (*mogh*, priest) found in the Zend, the ancient language in which the sacred books of the Persians were written, and is connected with a similar word (*mahat*, great) in the Sanscrit, from which the Latin *magnus* and our words major, magnify, magnificent, etc., are derived. This derivation corresponds with what is known of the magi, who were the priests and the great men, first of Media, afterwards of the Medo-Persian empire. The earliest notice, in Scripture, of this class is in Jer. 39 : 3, 13, where mention is made of Rab-mag, which is probably not a proper name, but a compound word signifying chief magi, after the analogy of such words as chief eunuch and chief butler. The same class is referred to in Jeremiah 50 : 35, where our English version entitles them "wise men." But the most frequent references to them are in the book of Daniel. To this class Nebuchadnezzar appealed in vain for the exposition of his dream (Dan. 2 : 1–13), and Belshazzar for the interpretation of the handwriting on the wall (Dan. 5 : 1–9). Daniel himself seems to have been in some measure identified with them, intercedes to save them from death (Dan. 2 : 24), and accepts the office of the "master of the magicians" (Dan. 5 : 11), which was probably that of Rab-Mag or Chief-Magi. The origin of this class is involved in obscurity. It is believed, however, to have originally existed in the Chaldean empire, to have

4 And when he had gathered ᵉ all the chief priests and scribes of the people together, he demanded of them where Christ should be born.

5 And they said unto him, In Bethlehem of Judæa; for thus it is written ᶠ by the prophet;

6 And thou Bethlehem, *in* the land of Juda, art not

ᵉ Ps. 2:2....ᶠ Micah 5:2; John 7:42.

---

been preserved in the successive changes which wars of conquest produced in the political organization and national complexion of the eastern world, and to have remained intact, though modified, in the successive Assyrian, Median, and Persian kingdoms. This hypothesis of the origin of this priestly class is confirmed by the fact that in the O. T. it is not unfrequently designated by the title Chaldeans (Dan. 2:4, 5, 10, etc.). It certainly was not of Persian origin, and it is equally certain that it was reorganized and reformed by contact with the Persian religion. Under the Persian empire the magi existed in three orders; they wore a peculiar dress; they had direction of the education of the monarch, who, as the special privilege of his rank, was permitted to become acquainted with their learning; next to the king's wives and eunuchs, they stood nearest to his person, and constituted his chief counsellors (Esther 1:13). These peculiar prerogatives were due to the religious veneration which was paid to them (see Dan. 2:46). They performed all public religious rites, were the teachers of all religious truths, and were regarded as the sole medium of communication between the Deity and his creatures. They practised divination, and by various means—auguries, dreams, and especially a study of the stars—assumed to read the destiny of mankind, and to interpret the problems of the future. It was Daniel's pre-eminent success in interpreting the dream which the magi could not interpret that placed him at their head (Dan. 2:47, 48). The fact that he accepted this office, and still more the fact that Nebuchadnezzar introduced as a novelty a golden image to be worshipped, and Darius, by special edict, forbade all petitions to god or man for thirty days (Dan., chaps. 3 and 6), indicate that the magi were not image-worshippers, and that their superstitions were mainly, or at least largely, those of honest seekers after truth, having, however, no other manifestation of God than was afforded them by nature. In later days they degenerated into mere soothsayers and fortune-tellers. In the N. T., except in this one passage in Matt., they appear only as impostors. To this class belonged, or pretended to belong, Simon the Sorcerer (Acts 8:9-11) and Bar-jesus (Acts 13:8). In classic history they are treated as a despicable class. But the itinerant magi, seeking personal aggrandizement among the ignorant, by the use of an honored name, may have been impostors, and yet the true magi in their own country, studying nature as the sole revelation given to them of an unknown God, may have been honest, honorable, and learned men, and sincere seekers after the truth; and this appears to have been the case with those magi who followed the star in the East in their search for the Messiah. Of the later legends respecting them it must suffice to say that there is nothing historical in any of them; the legend that they were kings possibly grew out of such passages as Psalms 68:29; 72:10, 11, 15, and Isaiah 60:3, which it is hardly necessary to say do not refer to the worship and gifts proffered by the magi to the infant Jesus; the legend that they were three in number, preserved in song and in art, is said to have grown out of a desire to find in their visit a confirmation of the doctrine of the Trinity, or to see in them representatives of the three great divisions of the human family, descended from Noah. During the middle ages the bodies of these magi were, it was pretended, discovered; they were brought to Constantinople, thence to Milan, and finally to Cologne, in whose cathedral the shrine of the three kings is still shown as the greatest of its many treasures.

(2.) "*The East*" was then, as it now is with us, a very general term. Probably the country indicated to the mind of any Palestinian Jew would be the region stretching forward from the Jordan to the Euphrates. Somewhere in this general district we must look for the home of the magi who visited the infant Jesus; but whether in Arabia, Persia, Chaldea, or Parthia cannot with certainty be known.

(3.) Secular history affords some answer to the third question—How should they know that the star foretold the coming of Christ? An opinion, derived possibly through the Scriptures, prevailed throughout the ancient world that a Messiah would come at about this time. Confucius, in China, had prophesied the appearance of such a deliverer, and a deputation of his followers, going forth in search of him, were the means of introducing Buddhism into China. This belief is also recognized by Roman writers, as Tacitus and Justinius. But the clearest of all these prophecies was one by Zoroaster, the founder of the reformed religion of Persia, who had foretold the coming of a prophet, supernaturally begotten, who should found a kingdom of righteousness and peace; and later traditions, borrowed perhaps from the faith of the Jews and the prophecies of Daniel, during the captivity, led the Zoroastians to expect that this Messiah would be of the seed of Abraham. Thus prepared to expect the coming of a Messiah in Judea, the appearance of a remarkable star traveling westward would naturally lead the magi to recognize in it an augury of the Messiah's coming, and to follow it to his birth-place. The coming of these magi affords a singularly literal fulfillment of the prophecy of Isaiah 60:1-3; comp. that of Numb. 24:17.

2. We have seen his star in the East. The ancients regarded any peculiarly bright star as a portent of the advent of some great personage, and they also believed that at death their heroes migrated into some star. Thus Julius Cæsar was deified at his death, it is said, because of a star which appeared at that time, and into which it was believed he had gone. Respecting the star in the East an extensive literature has been written. The opinions respecting it are given below. The *facts*, as reported by Matthew, our sole authority, are these. The magi, coming from the East to Jerusalem, reported that they had seen a star in the East, which portended the advent of an anticipated "king of the Jews," and they came to Jerusalem to worship him; they learned from the Council where he should be born, viz., Bethlehem; when they left Jerusalem the star again preceded them, and guided them to "where the young child was," an expression which may indicate either the town of Bethlehem or the house in the town. Concerning it the principal hypotheses may be classified as follows: (1.) That it was not a *star*, but a miraculous light, created for the special purpose of guiding the magi to Christ. This is perhaps the most common opinion, but it does not accord with the language of the Evangelist, who describes it as a *star* (ἀστήρ), not as a light (λύχνος). (2.) That it was a meteor, or a comet. The second hypothesis is conceivable, the first scarcely so. For though the Greek word rendered star is used for a meteor (Jude 13), no meteor, according to any known laws of its existence, could have guided the magi so far, and its extinction would have been an omen full of evil to them. (3.) That it was one of the stars of heaven, then first created, or then first seen, and that the guiding was due, not to the real motion of the body itself, but to a miraculous diversion of its rays, in a manner analogous to that which is by many believed to have produced the apparent standing still of the sun and moon (Josh. 10:13), and the going back of the sun-dial (2 Kings 20:11). This view is maintained, with no inconsiderable power, by F. W. Upham, in a monograph on The Star of our Lord. (4.) That it was a conjunction of planets, not in a true sense a miraculous phenomenon, and that God thus employed nature to guide to Christ those who were seeking in nature for a clearer revelation of God and divine truth. It is now certain that in the year 747 of Rome, on the 20th of May, a conjunction of Jupiter and Saturn occurred in that part of the heavens in which, according to astrology, signs denoted the most notable events. It was repeated on the 27th of October, and again on the 12th of November. The first of these conjunctions would rise, to the Assyrian, in the East, three and a half hours before sunrise. The journey to Bethlehem would occupy about five months, and the November conjunction would be before them, in the direction of Bethlehem, when they were at Jerusalem. It was a tradition with the Jews that a similar conjunction of Jupiter and Saturn preceded the birth of Moses, and there are indications that not only the Jews but also the Chaldeans regarded such a conjunction as an indication of the near approach of the Messiah. The chief objection proposed to this hypothesis is that such a conjunction could not indicate "where the young child was," and the notion that another body of a meteoric nature did this guiding does not agree with the narrative, which identifies it as the same star. Each of these opinions is purely hypothetical; each has difficulties. I incline to regard the latter as most consonant with the narrative, and to interpret the language of verse 9 to indicate simply that the town wherein the magi were to find the Messiah was indicated to them by the star. Not more than two years (verse 16) nor less than five or six months intervened between the birth of Jesus and the appearance of the magicians at Jerusalem. The visit of the shepherds (Luke 2:8-16) having preceded, the babe was no longer dwelling in the stable, but in a house (verse 11).

We have come to worship him. Do homage in the eastern fashion of prostration. Civil honors due to a king, not divine honors to a God, are here indicated. Yet it must be remembered that the ancient heathen drew no clear distinction between the two, and used the same word and the same sign of homage in both cases (see Matt. 8:2, note).

3. Troubled—agitated, thrown into tumult. The same word is used in John 5:4, to indicate a stirring up of water. This is the original meaning of the word. The idea of uneasiness or discomfort is secondary. Josephus represents the commotion as stirred up by the Pharisees, who prophesied a revolution.

4. Chief priests. The priesthood were divided into twenty-four courses, each having its own chief or president (1 Chron. 24:6). The term here used probably includes the high priest and any who had held that office, together with the chiefs of the priestly courses. **Scribes**—Jewish doctors or rabbis learned in the law and the commentaries thereon, the theologians of the first century. What Herod probably summoned was the Sanhedrim. It was the chief legislative

the least among the princes of Juda: for out of thee shall come a Governor, that shall rule my people Israel.

7 Then Herod, when he had privily called the wise men, inquired of them diligently what time the star appeared.

8 And he sent them to Bethlehem, and said, Go and search diligently for the young child; and when ye have found *him*, bring me word again, that I may come^b and worship him also.

9 When they had heard the king, they departed; and, lo, the star, which they saw^i in the east, went before them, till it came and stood over where the young child was.

10 When they saw the star, they^j rejoiced with exceeding great joy.

11 And when they were come into the house, they saw the young child with Mary his mother, and fell down, and worshipped him; and when th had opened their treasures, they presented unto him gifts; gold, and frankincense, and myrrh.

12 And being warned of God in a dream that they should not return to Herod, they departed into their own country another way.

13 And when they were departed, behold, the angel of the Lord appeareth to Joseph in a dream, saying, Arise, and take the young child and his mother, and flee into Egypt, and be thou there until I bring thee word: for Herod^m will seek the young child, to destroy him.

14 When he arose, he took the young child and his mother by night, and departed into Egypt:

15 And was there until the death of Herod, that it might be fulfilled which was spoken of the Lord by the prophet, saying, Out^o of Egypt have I called my son.

---

and judicial body of the Jews, consisted of seventy-one members, comprised the chiefs of the priestly courses, rabbis learned in the literature of the church, and elders chosen from the laity. It was the body before which Jesus was arraigned, and subsequently the apostles, as recorded in the Acts (Matt. 26:57,59; Acts 4:5; 5:27; 6:15).

5. Prophet—Micah 5:2. The quotation is not exact, but the substantial thought is the same. The very body which subsequently crucified Jesus as an impostor, officially testifies that his birth in Bethlehem fulfills the prophecy uttered seven hundred years before respecting the Messiah.

6. Princes. The Jewish nation was divided into twelve tribes, each tribe into families. The heads or chiefs of these families are here indicated. In Micah the language is "*thousands of Judah.*" Here the term *princes* stands for the family and its city which the prince represented. Thus Bethlehem itself was the city of David.

7. Then Herod when he had secretly called the magicians, without the knowledge of the council, lest his object should be suspected and defeated. **Inquired the exact time when the star appeared,** that he might know what was the exact age of the infant whom he wished to slay.

8. Sent them to Bethlehem. They had evidently lost sight of the star (verse 10), and depended on Herod for information where the child should be found. **I may come,** etc. His purpose was to make sure of the child that he might slay him.

11. House. The throng brought together by the requirement of the census had dispersed, and Joseph and Mary were no longer in the stable (Luke 2:7). **With Mary.** Possibly Joseph was not present at the time; possibly he is not mentioned because the Evangelist recognized the fact that he was not in reality but only in securing the father of the child. **Treasures**—chests or boxes. It was customary in visits to a sovereign to offer him gifts (1 Kings 10:2, &c.). **Frankincense**—a vegetable resin, obtained by incisions in the bark of a tree called the *arbor thuris*, bitter to the taste, used for its odor in sacrifices (Exod. 30:34-36), and imported by the Hebrews generally from Arabia (Isaiah 60:6; Jeremiah 6:20), though the best is said to come from Persia. **Myrrh**—an aromatic gum highly prized by the ancients, and used in incense and perfumes. It distils from incisions from a small thorny tree, which grows chiefly in Arabia. It is mentioned in Exod. 30:23 as one of the ingredients of the holy oil; in Esther 2:12, Psalm 45:8, Prov. 7:17, Sol. Song 1:13, 3:6, etc., as a perfume. It was used also as an anodyne (Mark 15:23), and for embalming (John 19:39).

12. Their own country another way. They could easily go direct from Bethlehem to the Jordan river, leaving Jerusalem to the north and west. See map of Palestine.

2:13-23. FLIGHT INTO EGYPT.—CHRIST COMES TO HIS OWN, AND HIS OWN RECEIVE HIM NOT (John 1:11); HE IS CAST OUT OF JUDEA, AND GOES TO THE HEATHEN. THUS THE CHRIST-CHILD PROPHESIES THE FUTURE OF HIS OWN GOSPEL.—HEROD EXEMPLIFIES THE FOLLY AND WRETCHEDNESS OF FIGHTING AGAINST GOD (Ps. 2:2-4).—LITTLE CHILDREN ARE THE FIRST MARTYRS. EVEN THEY ENTER THE KINGDOM OF HEAVEN THROUGH SUFFERING.—THEY ARE THE FIRST TO SUFFER, ARE KEPT CLOSEST IN THEIR FATHER'S CARE (Matt 18:10), ARE GREATEST IN THE KINGDOM OF HEAVEN (Matt. 18:4).—JOSEPH'S IMPLICIT OBEDIENCE IS AN EXAMPLE TO US. "DUTIES ARE OURS; EVENTS ARE GOD'S."—CHRIST'S HUMILIATION AS A NAZARENE PREPARES FOR HIS EXALTATION AS KING OF KINGS (Phil. 2:5-11).

13. Arise—at once; there was no time for delay. **Into Egypt.** It was not more than three hundred miles distant, was a Roman province, was much inhabited by Jews, and was independent of Herod. It therefore afforded a convenient and safe refuge. Jesus was probably between one and two years old at this time; certainly not over the latter age (verse 16).

14. By night. That is, that same night.

16 Then Herod, when he saw that he was mocked of the wise men, was exceeding wroth, and sent forth, and slew all the children that were in Bethlehem, and in all the coasts thereof, from two years old and under, according to the time which he had diligently inquired of the wise men.

17 Then was fulfilled that which was spoken by Jeremy the prophet, saying,

18 In Rama was there a voice heard, lamentation, and weeping, and great mourning, Rachel weeping *for* her children, and would not be comforted, because they are not.

19 But when Herod was dead, behold, an angel of the Lord appeareth in a dream to Joseph in Egypt,

20 Saying, Arise, and take the young child and his mother, and go into the land of Israel: for they are dead which sought the young child's life.

21 And he arose, and took the young child and his mother, and came into the land of Israel.

22 But when he heard that Archelaus did reign in

o verse 7....p Jer. 31 : 15....q Ex. 4 : 19.

15. Out of Egypt. This prophecy is in Hosea 11 : 1. It primarily refers to the nation of Israel, and describes what God had done for it, ages before the prophet wrote, in the emancipation of the Jews from slavery. How then is it a prophecy of Christ's return from Egypt? Because the historical events in the O. T. are many of them prophetic, and point to a fulfillment in the New: the raising of the brazen serpent to the cross of Christ, the riven rock to the piercing of the side of Christ, the emancipation of Israel to the greater emancipation of humanity from sin by Christ. So the calling of Israel 1500 years before out of Egypt was itself a prophecy of the fact that Jesus should be called out of Egypt to dwell in the land of promise. "The subject of all allusions, the represented in all parables and dark sayings was HE who was to come, or the circumstances attendant on his advent and reign."—(*Alford*.)

16. When Herod saw that he was mocked. The Evangelist describes his feelings; it was one of rage against them as having deceived him and so disappointed him in his purpose. **Slew all the children**—i. e., male children; the number would not have been great in a town of the size of Bethlehem. **The coasts thereof**—the borders, i. e., the country in the immediate vicinity. There is no authentic reference to this slaughter in secular history; but it accords exactly with what we know of Herod's character. (See on verse 1, above.)

17, 18. Jeremy. Jeremiah. The passage is chap. 31 : ver. 15. **Rama**—A small town in the tribe of Benjamin, and six miles north of Jerusalem. It was the birth-place and burial-place of Samuel, and the spot where Saul was anointed king (1 Sam. 1 : 19, 20 ; 2 : 11 ; 8 : 4 ; 10 : 18 ; 25 : 1). Not far distant from Ramah, yet south of Jerusalem and in the more immediate vicinity of Bethlehem, was the tomb of Rachel and the supposed place of her burial (Gen. 35 : 19—20 ; 48 : 7). The passage in Jeremiah refers originally to an event which occurred very soon after the prophecy was delivered. Jerusalem was captured by Nebuchadnezzar the king of Babylon; Zedekiah, the king of Judea, was taken captive, all his sons were put to death before his face, his eyes were then put out, and he was carried in chains to Babylon; the walls of Jerusalem were broken down, and the chiefs of the city were carried away into captivity; and Jeremiah himself was taken in chains as far north as Ramah, the first station where the captives with their guards would rendezvous, where he was released (Jer. ch. 39 ; 40 : 1—6 ; 2 Kings ch. 5). It was in reference to this event that the prophecy in Jer. 31 : 15 was uttered. "It is," says Michaelis, "an exquisite figure. Rachel, during all her life ardently desirous of children, dying in childbirth, and buried on the border of Benjamin, lifts her maternal head from her tomb, looks around on the wide waste of ruin, and sees not one of her children in all the land! She pours out her heart in most bitter tears; then God appears for her consolation." But while this prophecy receives its immediate fulfillment in the capture of Jerusalem and the terrible events which accompanied it, it received a second and further fulfillment in the event recorded in this chapter. The one was a type and prophecy of the other. "Divine prophecies," says Lord Bacon, "being of the nature of their author, with whom a thousand years are as one day, are not punctually fulfilled at once, but have springing and germinant accomplishment throughout many ages;" and Dr. Wordsworth adds, "have, at length, their summer blossom and autumnal ripeness in Christ."

19. When Herod was dead. He died soon after at about seventy years of age, of a dreadful disease, at Jericho. The stay in Egypt is variously estimated. Ellicott thinks that not over a fortnight elapsed between the flight into Egypt and the death of Herod. Greswell allows seven months; other writers make it still longer. **They are dead.** The plural form is often used in speaking of kings. It is possible there is a reference to those who were concerned in the massacre; perhaps to Antipater, a son of Herod, who was put to death by his father just previous to Herod's own death.

21. Land of Israel. Not the northern portion of Palestine; it is here used as a general term for the Holy Land.

22. Archelaus. On the death of Herod the Great his kingdom was divided between his three sons, Archelaus, Antipas, and Philip. Philip's domains lay all east of the Jordan, and outside of that portion of Palestine in which Christ conducted his chief ministry. He is referred to in Luke 3 : 1. Antipas was made tetrarch of Galilee and Perea,

Judæa in the room of his father Herod, he was afraid to go thither: notwithstanding, being warned of God in a dream, he turned aside into the parts of Galilee:*

23 And he came and dwelt in a city called Nazareth:* that it might be fulfilled which was spoken by the prophets, He shall be called a Nazarene.¹

r ch. 3:13; Luke 2:39....*s* John 1:45..*t* Num. 6:13; Jud. 13:5; 1 Sam. 1:11; Amos 2:10-12; Acts 24:5.

i. e., the region east of the Jordan. He is called in the N. T., Herod the tetrarch (Matt. 14:1; Luke 3: 19; 9:7; Acts 13:1). To Archelaus fell Idumea, Judea, and Samaria. His proper title was ethnarch, the kingly title perishing with his father, Herod the Great; but in the beginning of his reign he assumed the title of king. This division of the kingdom is represented in a map inserted at Luke 3:1. Archelaus was dethroned in the ninth year of his reign, and banished to Vienne, in Gaul, where he is thought to have died. The fear of Joseph was very natural. The Jewish deputies in their complaints to Rome of the tyranny of Archelaus said, "he seemed to be so afraid lest he should not be deemed Herod's own son that he took especial care to make his acts prove it." See Josephus, Antiq. 17:11, 2. **Notwithstanding, being warned, etc.** This is ambiguous. It does not mean that he went to Galilee *despite* the fact that he was warned of God, but that *in consequence* of the divine direction he did so. **He turned aside into the parts of Galilee.** Matthew writes in seeming oblivion of the fact that Joseph and Mary came from Galilee in the first instance (Luke 2:4). He may not have known the fact; or, writing chiefly for the Jews, he may have wished only to emphasize the fact that the birth of Jesus took place at Bethlehem in accordance with prophecy. It is observable that throughout his account he points out the fulfillment of prophecy. There are in these first two chapters five references to the Hebrew prophets (1:22; 2:5, 6, 15, 17, 18, 23). **Galilee.** The northernmost of three provinces or districts into which Palestine, west of the Jordan, was divided at the time of Christ. (See map.) Its scenery was more rugged than that of Judea, its inhabitants a simple, humble peasantry; industrious, unpretending, without wealth or culture, but also without those religious prejudices which excluded the Gospel from the hearts of the Judeans. Twenty of their chief cities had been given by Solomon to Hiram, king of Tyre (1 Kings 9:11), but had been restored to Solomon again (2 Chron. 8:2). The people had intermixed with other and heathen races, and thus had lost both Jewish purity and Jewish pride. Their very speech was provincial (Matt. 26:73). Galilee was the scene of Christ's most abundant labors; and all his apostles, except Judas Iscariot, were Galileans.

23. Nazareth. Here first mentioned in the Bible. It reposes in the bosom of a beautiful valley on the northern edge of the plain of Esdraelon and about five miles west of Tabor. The modern Nazareth is one of the better class of Eastern villages and has a population of three or four thousand. All the inhabitants of Galilee were looked on with contempt by their wealthier and more cultured neighbors of Judea; but Nazareth suffered under special opprobrium, and this among the Galileans as well as among the Jews (John 1:46). The origin of this disrepute is not known. **Called a Nazarene.** No specific prophecy is referred to; but probably (this at least we think to be the better interpretation) those declarations in the prophets which declare of the Messiah that he should be despised and rejected of men. In fulfillment of this prophecy, he was, from the very beginning, known as a citizen of despised Nazareth (Isaiah 53 and Ps. 22).

THE BIRTH OF JESUS.—The incidents connected with the birth of Jesus are narrated *only* by Matthew and Luke. Mark and John begin his life with his baptism. Matthew and Luke do not relate the same incidents; it is only by comparing them that we get the entire story. To Matthew we are indebted for the account of the betrothal, the divine warnings to Joseph, the visit of the magi, the flight into Egypt, the return to Nazareth. None of these incidents are mentioned by Luke. To Luke we are indebted for the account of the annunciation, Mary's psalm of thanksgiving, the cause of the visit of Joseph and Mary to Bethlehem, the birth of Christ in a stable, the visit of the shepherds, the presentation of the child at the Temple, and the prophecy of Simeon. The probable order is as follows: Mary is espoused to Joseph (Matt. 1:18); the birth of Jesus is announced to her, possibly before her betrothal (Luke 1:26-38); and she visits her cousin Elizabeth and utters her psalm of thanksgiving (39-56); Joseph discovers that she is with child, and is told by God to take her, notwithstanding, as his wife (Matt. 1:18-25). They go up to Bethlehem together, where Jesus is born, and the same night the shepherds visit the child, having been told of his advent by the angels (Luke 2:8-20); the child is presented in the Temple and the prophecy of Simeon is uttered (21-38). Meanwhile the star in the east has appeared to the magi, and they have commenced their journey toward Palestine. After a journey which occupies several months, they find the child, now removed to a house, and offer their gifts (Matt. 2:1-12). The flight into Egypt and the massacre of the infants follow (13-23); and the accounts of the two Evangelists come to-

CHAPTER III.

IN those days came John^u the Baptist, preaching in the wilderness of Judæa,

2 And saying, Repent ye: for the kingdom of heaven is at hand.
3 For this is he that was spoken of*v by the prophet Esaias, saying, The voice of one crying in the wilder-

u Luke 3:2; John 1:6....v Isa. 40:3.

gether again with the return of Joseph and Mary and the child to Nazareth (Matt. 2:23; Luke 2:39, 40). There is no inconsistency in the accounts; but each narrates incidents which the other passes by in silence.

3:1-12. PREACHING AND BAPTISM OF JOHN.—SEE ON LUKE 3:1-18.

1. In those days. A general term, indicating possibly the days when Jesus was living with his parents at Nazareth, but more probably simply synonymous with "in that age or era." The phrase is used in this way by the Old Testament writers, e.g. Exod. 2:11, where a long interval is evidently to be supplied between the 10th and 11th verse, Moses having grown to manhood meanwhile, and similarly by us at the present time, e. g. in such phrases as "in these days of steam and electricity." An interval of about thirty years (Luke 3:23) occurred between the birth of Jesus and the first public preaching of John the Baptist. Concerning the life of Jesus meanwhile, only one incident is recorded by the sacred writers (Luke 2:41-52). Concerning Christ's education meanwhile, nothing is positively known. He certainly did not receive an education in the Rabbinical schools (John 7:15, and note there). Jewish law required every man to teach his son a trade, even though he were destined to a learned profession as a theologian, and it is therefore probable that Christ worked at his father's bench learning the art of the carpenter (Mark 6:3). It is probable, too, that he attended the synagogue school; for there was one connected with every Jewish synagogue, in which the children of the village were taught to read and to cipher, and were instructed in their own national history and in the Jewish Scriptures, and to some extent in the commentaries of the scribes thereon. It is certain, from the incident recorded in Luke 2:41-52, that Jesus early showed a great aptitude for religious studies, and particularly for the deeper truths of religion. Meanwhile, great political changes had taken place in Palestine. Archelaus had been banished, the semblance of kingly authority possessed by Herod the Great had been taken away, and Judea was ruled directly by the Romans, through a governor or procurator, Pontius Pilate. Galilee continued under the rule of Herod Antipas, and all of Christ's life and ministry continued under the civil administration of these two men, Antipas in Galilee and Pontius Pilate in Judea (Luke 3:1).

John the Baptist. He was the son of Elizabeth, a cousin of Mary, and was, therefore, a second cousin of Jesus. The circumstances of his birth are recorded in Luke 1. He was a Nazarite (Luke 1:15, and note there; for an account of the vows of a Nazarite, see Numb. ch. 6); had shut himself up to a solitary life of prayer and meditation (Luke 1:80), from which he emerged to preach the doctrine of repentance as a preparation for the coming of the kingdom of God. His character was that of an ascetic; he dressed in a rough garment woven of camel's hair, and lived on locusts and wild honey, food furnished him by the wilderness (see below, ver. 4). A fuller account of his preaching is given in Luke 3:4-18; it, however, changed in its nature after the baptism of Christ, from which time he preached not only repentance and good works as a fruit of repentance, but also faith in the Lamb of God that taketh away sin (John 1:29-36; 3:25-36). **Preaching**, literally, *proclaiming as a herald*. As one runs before a king announcing his coming, so John the Baptist came before Christ proclaiming the coming of the kingdom of God. **Wilderness of Judea.** The region between Jerusalem and the river Jordan and the Dead Sea. "This tract was not strictly a *desert*, but thinly peopled, and abounding in pasture for flocks."—(*Alford.*) The idea embodied is simply that he was ministering, not in the city and under the influence of the hierarchy, but in the country, and had rural habits and a rural education. The region is more definitely fixed by Luke 3:3, and by his baptism of the people, as being in the immediate vicinity of the river Jordan. He was at this time about thirty years of age, the age when, if he had intended to enter the priesthood inherited from his father, he should have come up to Jerusalem to be examined by the Sanhedrim.

2. Repent. This word in the Greek is composed of two words—(μετά), *after*, and (νοέω), *to perceive, i. e.*, to perceive afterwards; hence, to change one's view, mind, or purpose. It has been even translated *change your minds.* But this, in the sense in which those words are ordinarily used, appears to be clearly inadequate. No idea of sorrow for sin is involved in the *word;* and though certainly genuine repentance does necessarily involve sorrow for the past, the radical and fundamental idea is, not so much sorrow as a change; a change, however, be it observed, not merely of conduct, but of the thinking and immortal part—a change of one's view of life and truth, and a consequent change of one's pur-

ness, Prepare ye the way of the Lord, make his paths straight.

4 And the same John had his raiment* of camel's hair, and a leathern girdle about his loins; and his meat was locusts* and wild honey.

5 Then went out to him Jerusalem, and all Judæa, and all the region round about Jordan,

6 And were baptized of him in Jordan, confessing their sins.

7 But when he saw many of the Pharisees and Sad-

---

* ch. 11:8; 2 Kings 1:8.... x Lev. 11:22.... y Acts 1:5; 2:38; 19:4, 5, 16.

---

pose regarding life. It is interpreted by John himself in his directions to the people when they asked him what they should do (Luke 3:10-14), and by Jesus in the parable of the Prodigal Son, who gave evidence of his repentance not by tears, but by leaving the far country and his old companions, and his sins and consequent wretchedness, and returning to his father with confession and a humble prayer for pardon. "In the N. T., especially in St. Luke and in the Revelations, it denotes a change of moral thought and reflection;" hence, "to repent of anything is not only to forsake it, but to change one's mind and apprehensions regarding it."—(*Cremer's Biblical Theol. Dict. of N. T. Greek.*) Another Greek word is used in four passages in the N. T., which is unfortunately translated repent (Matt. 21:29, 32; 27:3; 2 Cor. 7:8; Heb. 7:21). This word involves more distinctly the idea of sorrow, and it is evident from its use in Matt. 27:3, that the idea which it embodies—sorrow in consequence of sin—is not the *fundamental or principal* element in a true repentance.

Kingdom of Heaven. This phrase is used only by Matthew. The synonymous phrase, Kingdom of God, is used by Mark and Luke, "writing more especially for the Gentiles, who were to be disabused of their notion of local Deities, and taught the unity of God."—(*Wordsworth.*) Sometimes the phrase Kingdom alone is used, without any explanatory word (Matt. 8:12; 9:35, etc.). The phrase appears, at first sight, to be used in different senses, but the meanings are really essentially the same. It always indicates a state of cheerful submission to the will of God as the Supreme King. When applied to the individual, it denotes that state of heart in which God's will is recognized as the Supreme authority (Matt. 3:2). Applied to the community, it indicates the advent of the Messiah as the Supreme Lord (in which sense it is used here by John the Baptist), or his final advent, when all will recognize his supreme authority (Matt. 16:28). Applied to the future life, it indicates that state in which there shall be perfect submission by every heart to the Divine will (Matt. 25:34). The expressions "Kingdom of Heaven" and "Kingdom of God" are common in the rabbinical writers, who generally mean the theocracy, and who expected in the establishment of the Kingdom of Heaven the restoration of political power to the Jews and Jewish rulers, and hence to themselves, just as to the Romanist the supremacy of the church

indicates, not the triumph of the principles of Christ in all organizations, but the political supremacy of the pope and the priesthood. The peculiarity of the preaching of John the Baptist was that he taught that all the people, Jews as well as Gentiles, priests as well as people, must change their views of truth, their moral conceptions of God and his kingdom, and their moral purposes respecting their own life, in order to enter into this kingdom. Thus it approached the preaching of Jesus to Nicodemus in his declaration, "except a man be born again he cannot see the kingdom of God."

3. Esaias—Greek form of Isaiah. The passage is chap. 40:3. The prophet, contemplating the restoration of the Jews from their captivity in Babylon, announces the mission of John the Baptist as a herald of the Messiah. Some commentators regarded this passage as primarily a prophecy of the restoration of the Jews from Babylon, and so fulfilled long before the birth of John the Baptist, to whom they regard it as only applicable by a sort of accommodation (see Mr. Barnes on Isaiah 40:3). The better opinion (so Alford, Henderson and Cowles) regards it as more probably referring wholly to John; "first, because the words are expressly quoted by three of the inspired Evangelists as receiving their fulfillment in John (Matt. 3:3; Mark 1:3; Luke 3:4-6); and secondly, because the way was to be prepared not for the Jews but for Jehovah himself." The language here is not that of John the Baptist but that of Matthew respecting him. It is not "I am," but "this is." But John himself refers to the same prophecy, and to himself as its fulfillment (John 1:23). Isaiah's symbol is borrowed from a common practice among Eastern monarchs, whose kingdoms possessed no such broad highways as modern civilization has formed for all the people, and who therefore, on setting out on any great journey, were accustomed to send out pioneers to open roads through the wilderness for them, cutting through the hills and the forests, and filling up the hollows. Such a preparation for Christ's coming was the preaching of John the Baptist; it was his mission to awaken the expectations of an inert and sluggish people; and he succeeded wonderfully in this work (Luke 3:15).

4. Camel's hair. Not the camel's skin with the hair on, but a garment made of the shaggier camel's hair, woven into a coarse fabric like our drugget. It was recognized as a garb of the prophets (Zech. 13:4), and is still worn in the East by the poor or those who affect austerity. His dress resembled that of Elijah, and in this respect also he fulfilled the prophecy of Malachi 4:5, being in other respects than his attire and ascetic habits an antitype of Elijah (Matt. 11:14). **Locusts and wild honey.** "*Locusts*" have been thought to designate, not the insect of that name, but the long sweet pods of the locust tree, which are still called St. John's bread by the monks of Palestine. This is a mistake. The locust proper was permitted as an article of food by Moses (Lev. 11:22). Different species of the family are referred to in the Bible, generally in connection with their great numbers, or the devastations which they commit (Exod. 10:12-15; Deut. 28:38; Joel 1:4-7). They are, however, eaten in all parts of the world which they frequent, and in some places form an important article of food, especially among the peasantry and lower classes. In Palestine they are eaten either roasted or boiled in salt and water; but when preserved for future use they are dried in the sun, their heads, wings and legs picked off, and the bodies ground into dust. This dust has naturally a rather bitter flavor, which is corrected by mixing it with camel's milk or honey, the latter being the favorite substance; hence we may suppose that the food of John the Baptist was, like his dress, that of those of the people who lived at a distance from towns, and that there was no more hardship in the one than in the other. **Wild honey.** This existed in such abundance in the trunks of trees and the crevices of the rocks that to the ancient Israelites the land was described as "flowing with milk and honey" (Exod. 3:8). There is a "honey," so called, which exudes from the trees, and which has been supposed to be referred to here and in 1 Sam. 14:25; but the supposition is unnecessary and improbable. In some parts of northern Arabia the bees are said to be so abundant that no sooner is a hive deposited than it is filled. Compare Samson's experience in Judg. 14:5-9.

5. **Then went out to him Jerusalem,** etc. Not merely persons from these localities, but such multitudes that it might be said that all Judea was there; so we say now on the occasion of a great procession, all New York turned out to see it (Compare 11:7-15). **About Jordan—** *i. e.*, the regions in the vicinity of Jordan besides Judea and Jerusalem. It would include parts of Perea, Samaria, Galilee, and Gaulonitis. (See map.) Among those that came were a delegation from the Sanhedrim at Jerusalem, and several Galileans who subsequently became Christ's disciples (John 1:19, 35-45). It should be added that the best chronologists are of the opinion that John commenced his preaching in the Sabbatical year (see Andrews' Life of our Lord, p. 139), when the laws of Moses forbade all agricultural labor, and the people, relieved from their ordinary toil, were at leisure for the hearing of the truth (Exod. 23:10, 11; Lev. 25: 2-7; Deut. ch. 15).

The Jordan—the principal river of Palestine. It rises among the Lebanon mountains in the north of Palestine, and flows almost exactly due south, first through a marshy plain to the Lake Huleh or Merom (Josh. 11:5), then about nine miles to the Lake of Gennesaret or Sea of Galilee, descending in this distance 600 feet, and reaching, at the surface of the lake, a point 653 feet below the surface of the Mediterranean, and thence issuing a headlong torrent, crooked and precipitous, through a narrow and desolate valley, occupying 200 miles in its course, though traversing but 60 in a straight line, falling rapidly meanwhile, and finally issuing in the Dead or Salt Sea, whose surface is over 1300 feet below the level of the Mediterranean. Its average width between the two seas is from 70 to 80 yards, though at its mouth it is 180 yards. (Mr. Barnes says ninety feet, but this is evidently an error. See Lieut. Lynch's report.) The Jordan thus divides the Holy Land into two sections very clearly separated, partly by its waters, yet more by the valley or gorge through which it flows. This separation exerted an important influence on the history of the Jewish people, a part of the tribes, Reuben, Gad, and half of Manasseh remaining, in the distribution of the land, east of the Jordan, and never fully assimilating with their brethren. In O. T. times this region is described sometimes as the land "on this side Jordan" (Numb. 32:19), and sometimes as the land "beyond Jordan" (Josh. 13:8), or "the other side Jordan" (Josh. 2:1), according as the location of the writer is east or west of the river. But the phrase "beyond Jordan," in the N. T. (John 1:28; 3:26), signifies the district east of the river. It is known in secular history by the name Perea, signifying "beyond."

6. **And was baptized.** See note below on baptism of Jesus. **Confessing their sins.** The idea of a public and united confession appears to be involved in the original Greek word, which is composed of three words (εκ ομος λεγω) and signifies to speak out together. It is clear, both from this word and from Luke 3:10-15, that it is not a private confession to John which is indicated, and that the passage affords no foundation for the doctrine of auricular confession, in support of which it has been quoted. The same word is used in Acts 19:18, where the confession evidently was open and public, and in James 5:16, where the original shows that a mutual and common confession of faults, not a private confession to the ear of the priest alone, is intended.

7. **Pharisees and Sadducees.** Phari-

sees. This term meets us here for the first time in the Bible. The Pharisees are generally defined as a Jewish sect, but in fact they constituted the orthodox party in Judaism, and embraced the great body of the people. Historically the Pharisees were the reformers of the second century before Christ. The sect arose as a protest against heathen corruptions during the period subsequent to the captivity. The two characteristic features of their creed were faith in immortality and faith in the absolute decrees of God. They believed that all things were ordered by his will, that nothing therefore went wrong. They borrowed their hope from the future, and believed that whatever appeared to go wrong here God would set right hereafter. But the laws of Moses contain no clear revelation of any future state. In the main they represent God's government as administered by temporal rewards and punishments. The Pharisees, accordingly, invented a singular fiction to give authority to their belief. They asserted that during the forty days which Moses spent in the Mount, Jehovah gave him an additional revelation, in which he promulgated the doctrine of a future life and the duty of prayer, and afforded an authoritative interpretation of all the written law. This additional revelation, it was said, had been handed down orally from generation to generation, and it was regarded by the rabbis as of equal binding force with the Scriptures. Such a doctrine opened wide the door to corruption. These oral traditions soon outgrew the written word, and became to the Pharisees what, in the middle ages, the decrees of the Church were to the Romanist. The Scriptures took a subordinate place; to read them, except in the light of the authoritative interpretation, was denounced as equivalent to atheism. This doctrine led in the first century, as in the middle ages, to a rigorous but fruitless ceremonialism. All outward forms of the law were observed by the Pharisaic leaders; but to personal morals they were for the most part profoundly indifferent (see Matt. 15: 2-6, and note there). It is true that some of the rabbis inculcated a pure and high-toned morality, but more frequently the spirit of even their purest ethics was mercenary. The basis of their morality was the maxim, "Consider for whom thou dost work, and what is thy master who will pay thee thy wages." There were among the Pharisees some pure spirits, who desired if they did not fully appreciate a more spiritual religion, and who thus were in some measure prepared for at least the ethical teachings of Jesus (Luke 10: 25-28; Mark 12: 33; 15: 43; John 7: 50; Acts 15: 5). But this party was neither strong in numbers nor in courage. Thus despite some pure precepts in their inculcations, the characteristic feature of their religion was a pious formalism thinly covering an intensely selfish spirit. They fasted and prayed with great regularity and precision, but generally in public and for applause. They paid tithes of all they possessed, but their almsgiving was without genuine love. They ignored the precepts of religion in their lives, but were careful to inscribe them on pieces of parchment bound on their foreheads, and to engrave them upon the lintels of their doors. Religion became a trade. "Three things," so ran their proverb, "will make thee prosper—prayer, alms, and penitence." They were not all hypocrites; there were many honest but mistaken souls among them. Such was Saul of Tarsus, a Pharisee of the Pharisees. Their hypocrisy, too, was for the most part unconscious, and they hid from themselves more effectually than from others the selfishness of their hearts by the rigor of their lives. This was the school which constituted Christ's bitterest foe while he lived, which compassed his death, and which endeavored in vain to destroy the effect of his teachings. And it is hardly too much to say that the spirit of Pharisaism has continued to be in all ages the most dangerous and deadly enemy of Christianity, even when it has assumed the name and pretended to revere the memory of Jesus Christ.

Sadducees. The infidels and materialists of the first century. They probably derive their name from one Zadok, who is supposed to have been their founder. They maintained that justice is administered in this life, denied the existence of the soul beyond the grave, repudiated not only the oral tradition of the Pharisees, but also the books of the Bible, except the Pentateuch; insisted, theoretically, that virtue should be practiced for its own sake, not for the sake of any hoped-for reward; denied, not the existence of a God, but his control over and interest in the affairs of men; were naturally led by this theology into a loose and easy morality, the motto of which was, "Let us eat and drink, for to-morrow we die;" and were quite ready to affiliate with the Gentiles if place, power, or wealth could be obtained by so doing. The Pharisees were popular with the common people, who revered them for the real austerity of their doctrine and the seeming austerity of their lives. The Sadducees consisted wholly of men of a cold and heartless culture, but embraced a considerable portion of the priestly class, who performed with unconcern ceremonies in which they no longer had any faith. Their philosophy was a purely negative philosophy, though the same principles reappear in new forms from age to age, in the same or a similar class of minds. Sadduceeism, as a distinct school of philosophy, has long since perished from Judea, and not even a trace of its influence or a remnant of its literature has survived, except that which is incidentally found in the

ducees come to his baptism, he said unto them, O generation of vipers, who hath warned you to flee* from the wrath to come?

8 Bring forth therefore fruits meet for repentance:
9 And think not to say within yourselves, We have Abraham to our father: for I say unto you, that God

a ch. 12 : 34; 23 : 33 ; Isa. 59 : 5 ; Luke 3 : 7....a Jer. 51 : 6 ; Rom. 1 : 18.

four Gospels and in the writings of the theological opponents of the Sadducees, the Pharisees.

To this mention of the two principal Jewish sects or schools of philosophy should be added, perhaps here, a paragraph concerning a third, which is not, however, directly referred to in the N. T.—the *Essenes*, who may be briefly described as the Shakers of their age. "They lived in communities by themselves. They discouraged marriage. The higher orders forbade it. They maintained an absolute community of goods. They abhorred alike war, slavery, and commerce. Their wages were regulated by an inflexible system, administered by an absolute ecclesiastical superior. The hours of prayer, meals, labor, were all fixed by rigorous rules. Their doctrine was simple, but mystical. Their morals were pure, but austere. Their religious forms were observed with a rigor which even surpassed that of the Pharisees, but were accompanied with a life of practical virtue which rarely found a parallel in the Pharisaic life. They were initiated into the order by a secret service and a novitiate of three years, and were, at its close, bound by the most solemn oaths 'to observe piety, justice, obedience, honesty, and secrecy.' For violation of his oath, the offender was excommunicated. Having sworn that he would receive no food save from his own sect, and driven by excommunication from their table, he perished miserably of starvation. Four thousand of these ascetics lived in settlements of their own, chiefly in the wild region which borders the Dead Sea. They did not intermingle with their own countrymen. They exerted no influence upon the religious opinions and practices of their neighbors. They never seem to have come in contact with Christ." —(*Abbott's Jesus of Nazareth*.) It has been soberly maintained by De Quincy that this latter sect were disciples of Christ, who were misrepresented by Josephus, from whom most of our knowledge of them is derived, while other and skeptical critics have endeavored to maintain that Christianity was itself an outgrowth of Essenism. Neither view, however, has any warrant in history. The strongest antagonism exists between the life of bondage of the one and the spirit of freedom of the other. Doubtless the monastic habits of early and mediæval Christianity were analogous to those of the Essenes, but they were not in accordance with the precepts of Jesus Christ.

Come to his baptism. Why? Some think to oppose it. This is not probable, and there is nothing in the account to indicate it. It is clear,

on the other hand, from Matt. 21 : 32, and Luke 7 : 30, 33, that the Pharisees were not in any considerable number baptized by John. Apparently, his preaching had produced a very great agitation, and they came as onlookers, and to some extent as inquirers. The latter fact is indicated by the statement of John (1 : 19), that a delegation were sent out from Jerusalem to inquire respecting him. **Offspring of vipers**, in contrast with their proud belief that they were the favorites of God because the children of Abraham (verse 9; and compare analogous contrast in Christ's teaching, John 8 : 39, 44). The viper was a species of serpent; but the term is here used as a general term, and equivalent to serpent, which was among the Jews a symbol of cunning (Gen. 3 : 1), and malice (Ps. 58 : 4), and an emblem of the devil (Gen. 3, Rev. 12 : 9, 14, 15); so that this phrase, offspring of vipers, was analogous to the subsequent declaration of Christ, that the Pharisees were of their "father the devil." Vehemence of invective may be rarely right; but it cannot be always condemned. There are times when nothing else will awaken the conscience and start the sluggish soul. **The wrath to come.** The prophet Malachi, who had foretold the coming of John the Baptist, also foretold that his advent would be followed by "the great and dreadful day of the Lord" (Mal. 3 : 1-3; 4 : 5), as it was by the destruction of Jerusalem and the dispersion of the Jews among all lands, witnessed by some of that generation and probably by some of John the Baptist's auditors. For among his audience is believed to have been John the Evangelist (John 1 : 35; 41, and note there), who was still living at the destruction of Jerusalem. The primary reference here undoubtedly is to this wrath so soon to come upon the nation, though it as undoubtedly refers secondarily to that greater and more dreadful day of the Lord, the day of final judgment, of which we have, in Matt. ch. 24, Christ's own warrant for asserting the destruction of Jerusalem to be a symbol.

8. Bring forth therefore fruits worthy of a change of heart. Compare Matt. 7 : 16, 19. For a catalogue of the fruits of the new life, see Gal. 5 : 22, 23; and 2 Peter 1 : 5-7. Observe, first, that John and Christ, as well as the apostles, call for something *more than fruits*, viz. ; a change of character (compare John 3 : 3 ; 2 Cor. 5 : 17); and second, that they recognize as an evidence of a change of heart, not a creed, a ceremony, or a profession, but *fruits worthy of repentance*. Compare Matt. 7 : 21-23; John 14 : 21; Romans, ch. 12; James 2 : 14-17. See the whole

is able of these stones to raise up children unto Abraham.
10 And now also the axe is laid unto the root of the trees: therefore every tree which bringeth not forth good fruit, is hewn^b down, and cast into the fire.

11 I indeed baptize you with water^c unto repentance: but he that cometh after me is mightier than I, whose shoes I am not worthy to bear; he shall baptize you^d with the Holy Ghost, and *with* fire:
12 Whose fan *is* in his hand, and he will throughly

b John 15 : 6....c Luke 3 : 16; Acts 19 : 4,...d Acts 1 : 5.

---

truth embodied in Ephes. 2 : 10. We are God's workmanship, but we are created *unto* good works.

9. And do not fancy that you may say in yourselves. He interprets their own plea, not uttered, but secretly nourished in their own hearts. **We have Abraham to our father.** Contrast with verse 7 above. The common Jewish idea, especially the Pharisaic idea, was that the children of Abraham were favored of God. Says the Talmud: "A single Israelite is worth more before God than all the people who have been or shall be." A similar feeling underlies the pride of birth, wherever it exists. The ideas set in contrast are that which regard moral character as an inheritance, and so the exclusive prerogative of a few, and that which declared it to be the gift of God, and available to all. Compare John 1 : 13, and note there. **Of these stones.** The pebbles or shingle on the beach of the Jordan. Out of the unlearned and despised fishermen of Galilee he raised up his apostles (John 7 : 48). Out of the hated and outcast Gentiles he built up his church, the "new Jerusalem." The head of the corner was itself a "stone which the builders despised" (Matt. 21 : 42). So God daily raiseth up children to himself from the stones of the desert; the church is not made up from the rich and wise (1 Cor. 1 : 26-29); stony hearts he converts to hearts of flesh (Ezek. 36 : 26).

10. Is laid at the root, ready for use. The cutting down of the unfaithful nation has not yet commenced, but everything has been made ready for it (compare Luke 13 : 6-9). **Every tree, etc.** The only measure of character is its fruit-bearing character (compare John 15 : 2). **Is cut down.** The present form of the verb indicates that John speaks of a law always operating in God's kingdom. He always destroys what has ceased to serve a useful purpose; the nation that no longer serves humanity, as Persia, Babylon, Egypt, Greece, Rome, is dissolved; the tree that no longer bears fruit for food, or leaves for shade, perishes; the soul that ceases to bear any fruit for God and humanity is destroyed. The destruction may be, and often is, delayed to give space for repentance; but it is inevitable, except by repentance and faith the character is changed and made fruitful (Luke 13 : 6-9; Rom. 2 : 4-10). **Cast into the fire.** The destruction is final. There is no restoration (compare Matt. 13 : 30; Luke 3 : 17; John 14 : 6; Heb. 6 : 8). In these and similar passages fire is used as a symbol of utter destruction, not of purification.

11. In water. Not *with water*. The Greek preposition (*εν*), here translated *with*, properly signifies *in*, and certainly should be so translated here. It implies that John's baptism involved a going into the water, though not necessarily complete immersion in it. See note below. **Unto repentance.** It was not Christian baptism, *i. e.*, in the name of the Father, the Son, and the Holy Ghost, which was not established until after Christ's resurrection. See below. **Is mightier than I.** "I call to repentance, he remits sin; I preach the kingdom of heaven, he bestows it. I baptize with water, he with the Spirit also."—(*Wordsworth*.) **Whose shoes I am not worthy to bear.** In the other Gospels it is "to unloose" (Mark 1 : 7; Luke 3 : 16; John 1 : 27). It was the office of the slave to loose the shoe, to tie the same, or to carry it with other necessary articles of apparel before his master to the bath. Shoes proper were worn by the Greeks and Romans, but it appears to be the better opinion of biblical scholars that the Jews wore only, or at least chiefly, sandals which consisted simply of a sole fastened to the foot, and protecting its lower but not its upper surface. It was fastened to the foot by thongs or straps. It was sometimes beautifully ornamented, inwrought with lines of gold, silver, or silk, and occasionally embroidered with jewels. The materials were either leather, felt, cloth, or wood. It was occasionally shod with iron. Palm-leaves and papyrus-stalks were also sometimes used. Shoes or sandals do not appear to have been worn at all periods as with ourselves: they were laid aside when in-doors, and only put on by persons about to leave home. **In the Holy Spirit and fire.** A prophecy literally fulfilled at the Pentecost (Acts 2 : 1-4). Observe that the same language is used here as before respecting water, *in* not *with*. Yet the apostles were not *immersed* in fire. There is, says Jerome, a threefold baptism with fire: the fire of the Holy Spirit as at Pentecost (so termed because it makes the recipient fervent, that is, burning in spirit, Rom. 12 : 11), the fire of earthly trials (which are compared to a fire because of their purifying power, 1 Pet. 1 : 7; 4 : 12, 13), and the fire which at the last shall try every man's work, the great trial which is to test all life and character (1 Cor. 3 : 13). While John simply offers a symbolical test of character, the willingness of his hearers

Ch. III.] MATTHEW. 71

purge his floor, and gather his wheat into the garner; but he will burn up the chaff with unquenchable fire.

13 Then cometh Jesus from Galilee to Jordan, unto John, to be baptized of him.

14 But John forbad him, saying, I have need to be baptized of thee, and comest thou to me?

15 And Jesus answering, said unto him, Suffer *it to* be so now; for thus it becometh us to fulfill all righteousness. Then he suffered him.

16 And Jesus, when he was baptized, went up straightway out of the water: and, lo, the heavens were opened unto him, and he saw the Spirit of God descending like a dove, and lighting upon him;

17 And, lo, a voice from heaven, saying, This is my beloved Son, in whom I am well pleased.

_{a Mal. 3:7,8....f Ps. 2:14; Mal. 4:1; Mark 9:44....g Mark 1:9; Luke 3:21....h Isa. 11:2; 42:1; 61:1; John 3:34....i Ps. 2:7; Luke 9:35; Eph. 1:6; 2 Pet. 1:17.}

to acknowledge publicly their sins, and profess their change of purpose by a water baptism, Christ would test them by earthly trials and by his final judgment. While John could only bid them repent, and symbolize their purification by the washing of water, Jesus would really purify them, and give them a new heart by the Holy Spirit, and the fire of divine life and love.

12. Whose fan, etc. A metaphor drawn from the method of threshing and winnowing pursued in the Holy Land. A level spot was selected for the threshing-floor, in a situation where advantage might be taken of the wind for winnowing or separating the grain from the chaff; the sheaves, being thickly spread on the floor, were trodden down by oxen driven over them, or by a threshing instrument or sledge made of thick planks, the bottom being studded with sharp stones or pieces of iron, or sometimes made with rollers of wood, iron or stone. Sometimes for lighter grains flails or rods were used. By these processes the straw was broken up, and the grain separated from it. A shovel or "fan" was also used for winnowing. This was done by throwing the grain against the wind, and thus separating it from the chaff. **Chaff.** All that is not wheat, including the straw, which was commonly used in the East for fuel. **Unquenchable fire.** "Lest after the winnowing the chaff should be blown back and mingled with the wheat, the Jews were accustomed to put fire to it at the windward side, which was only extinguished when it had utterly consumed the chaff." "—(*Burders' Oriental Customs.* See Isaiah 5:24.) For the spiritual significance of this passage compare Matt. 13:24-30, 36-43, 47-50. It is not only in the future that Christ will sift out the straw from the wheat. His fan is in his hand; the sifting process is going on now; his Gospel is measuring men; every day is a day of judgment.

For a consideration of John the Baptist's character and preaching see Luke 3:18, and note there.

Ch. 3:13-17. BAPTISM OF JESUS.—SEE NOTE BELOW.

13. Then. The time is uncertain. Jesus was about thirty years of age (Luke 3:23). **To Jordan.** Beyond Jordan (John 1:28; see note there); the exact site is unknown.

14. John forbad him. Rather sought to hinder him. "The word implies the active and earnest preventing with the gesture, or hand, or voice."—(*Alford.*) (Compare John 1:33, and note there.) **I have need to be baptized of thee.** With the Holy Spirit and fire (verse 11).

15. Now. Compare John 13:7, 8. **Us.** Not merely me, but *you and me.* **To fulfill all righteousness.** You by yielding to the will of your Lord, even in a matter the propriety of which you do not understand (John 13:7); me by taking my place under the law, and acting as one made in the image of sin, though I know no sin (Matt. 17:27). See note below.

16. From the water, not *out of the water.* The Greek preposition here is not (ἐκ) *out of,* but (ἀπό) *from.* The same preposition is used in Matt. 8:1, *from* the mountain, which clearly does not mean *out of* the mountain. In Mark 1:10 the preposition is (ἐκ), *out of,* in the best manuscripts. But nothing is very clearly indicated as to the mode of baptism by the phraseology employed in either place. (See note below.) **And, lo, the heavens.** The Greek word here employed sometimes signifies the starry firmament, the blue canopy (Mark 13:25; Rev. 6:13, 14); sometimes the clouds and the cloud region (Matt. 6:26; *air,* 26:64). **Opened.** Compare the experience of Stephen (Acts 7:56) and of Peter (Acts 10:11). **He saw.** Christ, and also John the Baptist (John 1:32-34). There is nothing to indicate that the opening of the heavens or the descending of the dove were seen by any others. The vision in Stephen's case appears to have been confined to him; and at the time of Saul's conversion, while a sound was heard by the men who accompanied him, they saw no man and understood not the meaning of the words addressed to Saul (compare Acts 9:7, with 22:9). Moreover, it was not the divine way to manifest the character of Jesus by such manifestations to the multitude. These were afforded only to those who already believed on him because of the supreme excellence of his character and teachings, as in the transfiguration, which was seen only by Peter, James, and John, and in the ascension, which was witnessed only by the disciples (Matt. 17:1; Acts 1:9; compare Matt. 12:39). **Descending like a dove.** In Mark, 1:10, the language is, "like a dove descending." The plain meaning is, not merely that the Spirit descended as a dove descends, but that John and Jesus saw the Spirit taking on the form and appearance of a dove, and so descending. The dove was a sacrificial animal which the poorest could afford, and which, in the case of the poor, was permitted as a substitute for a more costly sacrifice (Lev. 5:7). If the worshipper could buy none, he could catch one of the wild pigeons which dwell among the hills of Palestine (Jer. 48:28; Sol. Song 2:14). Its coming was one of the prophecies of spring (Sol. Song 2:12, where "turtle" signifies a turtle-dove). It was historically connected in the Jewish mind with the abatement of the waters after the flood, and has become, as well as the olive-branch, a symbol of peace among all Christian people (Gen. 8:8-11), and it is referred to by Christ as a symbol of harmlessness and gentleness. It was thus a fitting emblematic form for the Holy Spirit to take on in giving a divine endorsement to him who is a sacrifice for all, whose coming brings life to the world, and the assurance of the peace of God to the soul which accepts him, and who was holy, harmless, undefiled, separate from sinners (Heb. 7:26). There is not a shadow of basis for the old gnostic notion, which some have since attempted to revive, that Christ received at this time the gift of the Holy Spirit, and though before a mere man, now first became in a true sense the Son of God. **Lighting upon him.** He was praying at the time (Luke 3:21). "The ordinances of religion will commonly be ineffectual without prayer."—(*Barnes.*) John (1:32) tells us that "it abode upon him." That is, it was not a mere transient vision.

17. A voice from heaven. Compare Matt. 17:5; John 12:28; 2 Pet. 1:17. **My beloved Son.** Christians are called "sons of God" (1 John 3:2); but nowhere is the term beloved Son applied by God to any one but Jesus Christ, to whom it is given both here and in the hour of his transfiguration (Matt. 17:5).

NOTE ON THE BAPTISM OF JESUS BY JOHN.

The ceremony of baptism performed by John, which has given him his title, the Baptist or Baptizer (Matt. 3:1; 11:11, 12, etc.), is intimately connected with the rite of Baptism maintained in the Christian Church ever since the resurrection of Jesus Christ, if not during his lifetime. John 4:1, 2, is the only reference to baptism by Jesus or his disciples during his life. This connection gives it an importance which it would not otherwise possess, and leads me to group here such scanty information as the Bible and other authentic sources give concerning it.

History. The origin of baptism as a religious rite is unknown. It is certainly very ancient; Grotius even imagines that it is as old as the Deluge, and was established in commemoration of that event. Ceremonial ablutions of some sort were certainly common in the time of Christ, not only in Palestine, but also in adjoining lands. The Egyptian priests bathed twice a day and twice in the night, and inaugurated their feasts with a grand ceremony of purification.—(*Wilkinson*, 1:324.) The Greeks and Romans prepared for sacrifice and other religious rites by lustration; and not only the priests performed this ceremony—it was also performed by private individuals when they had polluted themselves by any real or supposed criminal action, from the stain of which they desired purification. A similar rite was performed at times by the shepherd on his sheep, and even on the army or the fleet before entering on a campaign. It was in such cases performed by sprinkling the water on the person or persons, usually from a branch of olive or laurel. (See Smith's Dictionary of Antiq., Art. *Lustratio*, and authors there cited.) The O. T. abounds with examples of lustrations of various descriptions, of the person, the clothing, and objects offered for sacrifice. It was performed on both priests and people (Exod. 19:10; 29:4; 30:20; 40:12-15; Lev. ch. 8; 16:26, 28; 17:15; 22:4, 6; Deut. 23:10, 11; 2 Chron. 4:2, 6). The spiritual significance of these lustrations is rendered evident by other passages which refer to washings as a symbol of moral purification, in a way to leave no doubt that it was recognized by pious and intelligent Jews that a mere washing of the person in water was not enough, but that the soul must be cleansed through repentance by the power of God (Ps. 26:6; 51:2, 7; 73:13; Isaiah 1:16; 4:4; Jer. 4:14; Zech. 13:1). The act of Pilate in washing his hands before the people, and declaring himself innocent of the blood of Jesus (Matt. 27:24), would have possessed no significance if both Jew and Roman had not recognized the moral meaning of washing as a sign of purification from sin. The N. T. also contains frequent reference to ceremonial washings which had been instituted by the Pharisees, and through their traditions engrafted on the laws of Moses (Mark 7:4, 8, 14; Luke 11:38; Heb. 9:10).

Baptism of Proselytes.—Of these washings none was more significant or more universally recognized, if we may judge from the rabbinical writings, than the baptism of Jewish proselytes. Heathen converts on entering the Jewish church ratified their change of faith by two ceremonies, baptism and sacrifice; in the case of males circumcision was added. The baptism was administered in the daytime by the immersion of the whole person; and while standing in the water the proselyte was instructed in certain portions of the law. The whole families of proselytes, including infants, were baptized. (See Lightfoot on Matt. 3:6.) By this act of baptism the proselyte signified that he was washed of his past sins and errors and entered his new life, cleansed and purified, a new man.

John's Baptism.—When, therefore, John commenced his public ministry by preaching the necessity of repentance, and added to it baptism as a symbol, its meaning would be readily understood. It was interpreted by his declaration that it was not enough to be a child of Abraham, but that Israelite and Gentile alike needed to repent of sin, a doctrine subsequently more emphatically repeated by Paul (Matt. 3:9, 10; Rom. 2:12, 17-24; 3:9, etc.). By baptizing the people, John emphasized this declaration and said to them, by a formal and solemn ceremonial, You need, no less than the despised Gentile, to wash away the past, to be cleansed, morally and personally, as a preparation for the Kingdom of God. Every one who submitted to baptism at his hands publicly recognized the truth that personal repentance of sin was as necessary to the Jew as to the Gentile. And it is a noteworthy fact that the delegation from the Sanhedrim who inquired by what authority he baptized (John 1:25), did not inquire the meaning of the rite, showing evidently that they understood its significance.

Baptism of Jesus.—Why Jesus should have been baptized is a question which has given rise to much discussion. The same perplexity which John felt then, the Christian Church has felt since; for Jesus had no sins that needed to be washed away, and could not, therefore, become strictly a disciple of the doctrine of repentance, as by submitting to baptism he appeared to do. Various answers have been given, some of them certainly fanciful, others mystical, needing explanation more than the fact itself. Thus it has been said that the object of the baptism was to point out Jesus Christ as the sacrificial Lamb of the World, and to prefigure his death for sin, as baptism symbolizes death to sin; that he was baptized as a priest, and because the priests received a like lustration before entering on their priestly duties, that by his baptism he pledged himself to the whole righteousness of the law, promising to fulfill all; that he brought the baptism of John to its consummation and inaugurated Christian baptism in its place, as by partaking of the Last Passover he converted it into a Christian ordinance; that he sanctified by this act the water to the mystical washing away of sin; and that in him the whole Christian Church were baptized into a new life, he acting as the type and representative of humanity. But here, as everywhere throughout Scripture, the rational and simple meaning is the best. The significance of John's baptism, as interpreted above, explains the significance of the baptism of Jesus. It was not merely like his submitting to circumcision and the purification (Luke 2:21, 22), because they were rites required by the law, while baptism was not. It was *a public renunciation of sin and a public profession of religion*. It is true that Christ himself knew no sin and needed no repentance (John 8:46; 14:30), but he was numbered with the transgressors, was made sin for us, and bore our infirmities and carried our transgressions (Isaiah 53:12; 2 Cor. 5:21). In taking upon him human nature he took *all* its humiliation and *all* its duties, though none of its real degradation, and fittingly commenced his public life by a public renunciation of sin for himself and his followers. Observe, too, that the religion which by this act he professed, was that of the *spirit* as opposed to the religion of *form and ceremonies*. His baptism was a public and solemn enunciation of his position as a teacher of personal righteousness, and his endorsement of the fundamental doctrine of which John the Baptist was a herald, but which received its fullest exposition in the teachings of Jesus and the Apostles, that they only are the true children of God who, whatever their birth or place in humanity, repent of their personal sins and bring forth fruits meet for repentance. The true follower of Christ must follow him in this public renunciation of sin and profession of religion. It is not true, as sometimes said, that Christ professed religion only by his life.

Form of Baptism.—There is no clear and certain information in the Scripture as to the mode in which John the Baptist administered baptism. The question is important only in its bearing upon another, viz., what is the proper mode of Christian baptism. Without considering the latter question here, it is enough to say that the indications are that the baptism of John was performed by a partial or total immersion. These indications are the following: 1. The Greek word ($\beta \alpha \pi \tau \iota \zeta \omega$), generally translated "baptize" in our version, and the corresponding Hebrew word sometimes rendered "baptize" and sometimes rendered "dip," imply primarily a partial or complete immersion. At the same time it appears clear that in biblical usage neither word necessarily involves the idea of complete submersion. Thus, in Mark 7:4, we have a reference to the washing (Gr. $\beta \alpha \pi \tau \iota \sigma \mu \acute{o} \varsigma$) of tables (perhaps couches or beds, see note there), which certainly does not indicate a submersion of the table or bed in water as a means of purification. The only passages in the O. T. in which the original Hebrew word is used, are the following: Lev. 4:6; 14:6-51; Num. 19:18; Ruth 2:14; Ex. 12:22; Deut. 33:24; Ezek. 23:15; Job 9:31; Lev. 9:9; 1 Sam. 14:27 (*twice*); 2 Kings 5:14; 8:15; Gen. 37:31; Josh. 3:15. In the N. T. the only passages where the word occurs in which it is not translated baptize or baptism, which is in fact no translation but only an English form of the original Greek word, are Mark 7:4, 8, and Hebrews

9:10. The word translated dip, in Luke 16:24; John 13:26; and Rev. 19:13, is etymologically the same, however, though slightly different in form. The English reader who is desirous to investigate more fully the biblical use of the word can do so by an examination of these passages. The result of a fair and impartial examination will be that which the best scholarship has reached, viz., that the word does generally involve the idea of dipping into water, though not necessarily a complete immersion, still less a complete submersion in it. 2. Although ceremonial washings were performed both by Greek and Romans, and by Jews by means of sprinkling (see above, and Numb. 7:7; 19:19; Ezek. 36:25), yet the baptism of proselytes, from which probably the baptism of John was borrowed, was by immersion. It was regarded as indispensable that this should be complete. "If," said the rabbinical writers, "any wash himself all over except the very top of his little finger, he is still in his uncleanness." 3. The language of the passage descriptive of his baptism, "I baptize you *in* water" (see note on verse 11, above), tends to confirm this impression, as does the fact that John baptized in the Jordan. The catacombs contain rude pictures of the baptism of Jesus by John. They never represent it as done by sprinkling, or by immersion, but by pouring; Jesus stands in the water and John pours water upon his head from a vessel, in a manner analogous to that pursued in the anointing of a priest according to the O. T. ritual (Exod. 29:7). There are some other considerations which throw light on the method pursued in the N. T. times in later Christian baptism, but they will be considered hereafter. It should be added that nothing is known as to the formula, if any, used by John; he certainly did not baptize in the name of the Father, the Son, and the Holy Ghost (Matt. 28:19; Acts 19:1-5; compare also Rom. 6:3, 4). Evidently baptism into "Christ's death" could not precede his death. See an able essay on the essential difference between Christ's baptism and the baptism of John, by Robert Hall.

Ch. 4:1-11. TEMPTATION OF JESUS CHRIST.—
SEE THOUGHTS ON THE TEMPTATION, BELOW.

PRELIMINARY NOTE. This incident is recorded also fully in Luke 4:1-13, and briefly in Mark 1:12, 13; it is not mentioned in John. It is confessedly one of the most difficult passages in the Gospels to understand. The various interpretations may be conveniently classed under six different heads.

1. That no such event really occurred, but that Christ, in the form of a parable, of which he made himself a central figure, taught his disciples how it is that temptations assail us all, and how we are to resist them. This interpretation is rejected by nearly all Christian commentators; for while this lesson is taught by Christ's example, the language is that of historical narration, not of a parable.

2. That it is an historical narrative, but of a natural event; that the devil was a human tempter, or animated a human tempter, and offered the temptation through him; for example, that the tempter was one of the delegation which came up from Jerusalem to attend the preaching of John the Baptist (John 1:19), and that the temptation really consisted of propositions which they made to him to join their party. "Probably," says Lange, "he was transported in a figurative sense to the summit of the temple pinnacle by the ostentatious offers of the deputies of the Sanhedrim." "The mountain on which they placed him was Mount Zion, according to its spiritual significance, in the last age of the world. The tempter displayed to him the prospect of the theocratic government of the world. Probably into this disclosure plots against the Romans were introduced. And Christ was urged to approve of their hierarchical plan for the conquest of the world." This view, though defended by Lange and Bengel, is unmistakably an afterthought. There is nothing in the narrative itself to suggest or to warrant it. It has, so far as I know, no other respectable endorsers.

3. That it is a vision or a dream, having its parallel in Ezekiel's vision of the valley of bones (Ezek. 37:1-14), and of Paul's experience of being caught up into the third heaven (2 Cor. 12:1-4). But there is nothing whatever in the narrative to imply a vision or a dream, and the true spiritual significance of the hour, as one of real temptation, is taken away by such an interpretation.

4. That it is a personal and internal experience, in which certain circumstances suggest temptations which Jesus overcomes only after a bitter struggle. "A stone by its shape or color suggests to an imagination affected by bodily cravings the appearance of a loaf of bread, and gives rise to the first temptation. His foot strikes against a stone and he stumbles; perhaps is in danger of a serious fall. Instantly there occurs to him another passage of Scripture, 'He will give his angels charge over thee, lest at any time thou dash thy foot against a stone.' Since he has angels attending him, why may he not go to the city, ascend one of the pinnacles of the Temple, cast himself off and display to the astonished crowd his miraculous power? Once more he finds himself upon an eminence which commands an extensive view; he feels the stirring of personal ambition, and bethinks him how, if he would only fall down and worship the evil thought, he might possess himself of universal dominion. The tempter and the temptation were within his own soul." (Condensed from Furness's Notes on Schenkel's Character of

CHAPTER IV.

THEN was Jesus led up of] the Spirit into the wilderness, to be tempted⁾ of the devil. 2 And when he had fasted forty days and forty nights, he was afterward an hungred.

3 And when the tempter came to him, he said, If thou be the Son of God, command that these stones be made bread.
4 But he answered and said, It is written, Man shall not live by bread alone, but by every word that proceedeth out of the mouth of God.

j 1 Kings 18 : 12; Eze. 11 : 1, 24; Acts 8 : 39....k Mark 1 : 12; Luke 4 : 1; Heb. 2 : 18....l Deut. 8 : 3.

Jesus.) This view will at once be rejected by all those who hold that Jesus Christ was the sinless Son of God, in whose pure heart no solicitations of evil could arise of themselves to lure him to sin. If we accept the narrative at all, we must accept, *as the very essence of it*, that the suggestion of recreancy did not spring spontaneous in his heart from evil desires which lurked unrecognized there, but that they were suggested to him by the tempter only to be instantly and indignantly rejected.

5. That it is a literal narrative; that Satan really appeared in tangible form to Jesus, and proposed to him to convert the stones into bread, carried him bodily to the pinnacle of the temple, and showed him from some high eminence a view which at least suggested all the kingdoms of the world. This is a common view among evangelical interpreters; to it there are serious objections, objections which seem to me to be conclusive. *a.* We must either impute to the devil a degree of supernatural power, which the Bible nowhere else attributes to him, or must suppose that Jesus exercised it in his flight to the pinnacle of the temple, and this for the very purpose of entering into temptation. *b.* There is no mountain from which all the kingdoms of the known world could be seen; in part, then, the narrative cannot be a literal one. *c.* The Bible nowhere else represents the devil appearing undisguised to man; on the contrary, his power lies in his disguises and concealments (Gen. ch. 3; 2 Cor. 11 : 3). *d.* In this particular case the temptation, especially the last, would be robbed of all its power if the devil had been recognized before his proposition. It seems impossible that the suggestion of literal worship to a bodily fiend could offer any temptation—we will not say to Jesus—to any one of ordinary purity of heart and strength of conscience.

6. That it describes in dramatic language a real but internal experience, that Satan was really present, whispering the suggestions of evil to the soul of Jesus, as he still does to us (see note on verse below), but unrecognized until the last, the subtlest and worst of the three temptations; that the narrative describes a succession of pictures which passed before Christ's imagination, by which Satan endeavored to seduce him; that it was in imagination that Jesus was carried to the pinnacle of the temple, and in imagination was shown the kingdoms of the world, and that he was invited to gain control of them, not by a literal worshiping of the bodily fiend, but by yielding to the arts of the evil one, and serving him as the previous conquerors of the world, Cyrus and Alexander, for example, had done. This opinion is also beset with difficulties. Our temptations possess their strength and their bitterness in large measure because we possess a fallen nature which Christ did not. To us Satan is often undisclosed, and our sluggish consciences do not recognize *quickly* the evil when covertly disguised as good. But we cannot attribute to Christ a blunted and insensitive moral nature. These and kindred difficulties, however, *are inherent in any conception of Christ's temptation here, and in any attempt to understand his experiences of conflict elsewhere recorded*. We can only reverently accept the declaration that he was tempted in all points like as we are, yet without sin, and interpret his experiences by our own, fully recognizing the truth that our souls cannot gauge and measure his, and that the utmost study and thought will yet leave in this passage, as in all of Christ's mysterious life, an utterly inexplicable element, a mystery that is insoluble. Fully recognizing this, I adopt the last of the interpretations given above as on the whole the one most consonant with other Scripture, the narrative itself, and with reason. The grounds on which I accept this interpretation, have been in part indirectly stated in disposing of the other views; they will appear more fully in interpreting the passage itself. It is to be remembered that, though Satan is more distinctly embodied in this narrative than in any other, yet he is repeatedly referred to in Scripture as bringing trouble or temptation in cases in which no other than a purely spiritual and unrecognized presence is indicated (1 Chron. 21 : 1; Job 2 : 7; Matt. 18 : 19, 39; Luke 13 : 16; John 13 : 2).

1. **Then.** Immediately after the baptism and the descent of the Spirit. "Thou didst take up arms, not to be idle, but to fight."—(*Chrysostom.*) After the baptism of grace comes the battle. It is the wilderness, not Jordan and the dove, which tries us and shows our true character. Compare 2 Cor. 12 : 7-10. **Was Jesus led.** Rather brought or carried. The word is used to signify something more than a mere leading, and is the same translated *brought* in Luke 2 : 22; Acts 9 : 39; 12 : 4. It is used also in describing the bringing of sacrifice to the altar. In Acts 7 : 41, it is translated *offered*. Under an irresistible impulse Christ was carried away into the wilderness (compare Acts 7 : 39). **By the Spirit,** *i. e.*,

the Holy Spirit. God tempteth no man, but he sometimes brings us into temptation (compare Matt. 6:13; 26:41; Job 1:12; 2:6; 2 Cor. 12:7). **Into the wilderness** (see note on Matt. 3:1). Between Jericho and the Mount of Olives is a wild region, where is a mountain called Quarantana, which Robinson describes as "an almost perpendicular wall of rock, twelve or fifteen hundred feet above the plain." This is fixed on by tradition as the site of the temptation, and particularly as the mountain to which Christ was carried in the last one. But the tradition is entirely untrustworthy. The site is wholly a matter of conjecture. **To be tempted.** This was the purpose for which he was led into the wilderness. "As he had been subject to his earthly parents at Nazareth, so now he is subject, in the outset of his official course, to his Heavenly Parent, and is by his will thus carried up to be tempted."— (*Alford.*) **By the devil.** Not by his own heart, nor by a human tempter. The term, "the devil," is always used in the Bible to signify an evil spirit, *never to personify the evil in man or in the world*. On the contrary, the work of evil spirits is contrasted with the evil influence of the world (Eph. 6:12). Judas Iscariot is called *a* devil but not *the* devil (John 6:70); and in Rev. 2:10, the devil working in the hearts of malignant persecutors is intended; the word is not put for the persecutors themselves. The word devil (Gr. διάβολος) signifies accuser (Rev. 12:9, 10). He is also called Abaddon (Hebrew) or Apollyon (Greek), *i. e.*, destroyer (Rev. 9:11); Belial, *i. e.*, a good-for-nothing (2 Cor. 6:15); Satan, *i. e.*, an adversary (Job 2:1). See also for descriptive titles: John 8:44; 12:31; 2 Cor. 4:4; Ephes. 6:12; 1 Pet. 5:8; 1 John 3:8; Rev. 12:7; 20:10. Less is disclosed concerning him in Scripture than many suppose; much of the popular impression concerning him is derived from mediæval theology, and yet more from Milton's Paradise Lost. It certainly is not true that the idea of a personal devil was derived by the Jews from Persian philosophy during their captivity, for he appears by implication, though not expressly named, in the history of the fall (Gen. ch. 3), and more distinctly, probably, in Job, one of the oldest books of the Bible, if not the very oldest, than anywhere else (Job 1:6; 2:3-7; compare also 1 Chron. 21:1). He is represented in the N. T. as an adversary of human souls, endeavoring by various snares to take us captive, suggesting evil thoughts to our minds, or erasing good impressions which have been produced there, or putting hindrances in the way of Christian work, or inspiring persecutors of the faithful, and as certain at last to be bound in chains, and finally cast into torment (Matt. 13:19; Luke 22:31; John 13:2; 2 Cor. 2:11; 11:3, 14; Ephes. 6:11; 1 Thess. 2:18; 2 Tim. 2:26; 1 Pet. 5:8, 9; Rev. 2:10; 12:9; 20:1-3 and 7-10).

2. Fasted. This does not necessarily imply that he ate nothing (Dan. 10:2, 3). Some commentators think that his fasting may have consisted simply of abstaining from all ordinary food and subsisting only on the scanty supplies of the desert (compare with Matt. 3:4; 11:18). But the language of Luke 4:2, taken with Exod. 34:28, and 1 Kings 19:8, implies that he literally ate nothing, being miraculously sustained during the period of fasting. Observe that the duration of Christ's fast was the same as that of Moses and that of Elijah, who were transfigured with him (Matt. 17:3). According to Luke 4:2, and apparently Mark 1:13, he was subjected to temptations during this whole period of forty days; those here recorded would seem to be the culmination of these temptations.

3, 4. THE FIRST TEMPTATION. It appeals to a natural and sinless appetite—hunger. It suggests an act seemingly innocent. Why should not Christ make bread of the stones, and so supply his wants? Because he had taken upon himself the nature of man and the condition and sufferings of mankind (Psa. 9:6-8). To have availed himself of his divine power to escape the bodily discomforts of humanity, would have been to fail in his mission of becoming our pattern and our sympathizing high priest at the very outset. Accordingly, there is no case in the N. T. in which Christ exercises miraculous power for his own benefit. The escapes recorded in Luke 4:30, John 8:59, and 10:39, are sometimes regarded as miraculous, but there is no Scripture authority for so regarding them; and the taking of the tax-money from the fish's mouth (Matt. 17:27) was for a moral purpose. (See note there.) I doubt whether there is *any* case in Scripture in which a genuine miracle is recorded as being wrought for the benefit of him at whose bidding it is performed.

3. If thou be. Rather, Since thou art. The "if," says Alford, "implies no doubt."

4. It is written, in Deut. 8:3. The reference there is to the feeding of Israel with manna in the wilderness, and may be literally rendered, "by every outgoing of the mouth of the Lord;" *i. e.*, by the whole course of God's providential care over those who obey his word. The meaning is the same as that involved in Matt. 6:24-34, viz.: that he who seeks first the kingdom of God and his righteousness may leave all questions of food and raiment to God. If man obeys the divine will, he may trust himself to the divine providence. The divine will respecting Christ was that he should be found in condition as a man. He obeys that will, and leaves to God to provide for his physical wants (compare Deut. 29:5, 6). "They that taunted him on the cross, 'He saved others, himself he cannot save,' bore an unconscious testimony to the unselfishness of

5 Then the devil taketh him up into the holy city,ᵐ and setteth him on a pinnacle of the temple.
6 And saith unto him, If thou be the Son of God, cast thyself down, for it is written, Heⁿ shall give his angels charge concerning thee: and in *their* hands they shall bear thee up, lest at any time thou dash thy foot against a stone.

7 Jesus said unto him, It is written again, Thouᵒ shalt not tempt the Lord thy God.
8 Again, the devil taketh him up into an exceeding high mountain, and sheweth him all the kingdoms of the world, and the glory of them;
9 And saith unto him, All these things will I give thee, if thou wilt fall down and worship me.

m ch. 27 : 53; Neh. 11 : 1....n Ps. 91 : 11, 12....o Deut. 6 : 16.

his spirit and the thoroughness with which he took upon himself the life of common humanity. He that fed five thousand in the wilderness, from two small loaves and five little fishes, would not supply himself, except by ordinary means, with one."

5-7. THE SECOND TEMPTATION. The devil appeals to love of fame, and proposes to Christ to found his kingdom upon fame. A single miracle wrought before all the people shall secure their reverence and allegiance. A single trial of the divine power which belongs to the Son of God will put an end to all doubts, in Christ's own mind and in the mind of the people. "If he would have a prosperous following and an easy victory over the world, let him become the master of marvels. Let him show men that a Divinity was among them, not by the inspiration of a higher life in their souls, but by such a use of divine power as should captivate the fancy of all who saw the wonders of skill, of beauty, of daring, which he should show."—(*Beecher's Life of Christ.*) This, I think, is the true interpretation of the second temptation, which is one of ambition, or rather vain glory, not one of *mere* presumption, as supposed by Alford. The same demand for a wonder-working evidence of his divine authority is frequently repeated throughout Christ's life (Matt. 12 : 38, 39), and always refused. It reappears in demands of modern skeptics for modern miracles, and in the language of Renan, who treats Christ as a thaumaturgist, *i. e.*, a mere wonder-worker.

5. The holy city. Jerusalem. **Pinnacle of the temple.** The temple was built on Mount Moriah, on a foundation built up of solid masonry, so as to present a nearly perpendicular wall of over 200 feet from the floor of the temple to the valley below, "almost equal in height to the tallest of our church spires." On this wall, overhanging the valley of the Kedron, was Herod's royal portico. From the roof of that portico to the valley below was not less than 300 feet. "The valley was very deep, insomuch that if any one looked down from the top of the battlements, he would be giddy, while his sight could not reach to such an immense depth."—(*Josephus.*) According to Alford, it was the roof of this porch which is intended by the description here. According to others, it was the apex of the temple proper from which he was called upon to cast himself down into the court below among the people who were always assembled there. If we suppose the whole event to have taken place in thought only, the location could not have been very definitely described, because it would not necessarily have been very definitely conceived. The essence of the temptation appears to me to be its publicity, and, therefore, whatever point of the temple was brought to Christ's mind, it must have been one from which the miracle proposed could have been generally observed.

6. It is written, in Psalm 91 : 11; not, however, as a prophecy of the Messiah, but as applicable to all the children of God. Christ has replied to the devil's first suggestion as a man, and the devil cites a promise of God applicable to all men in his second temptation. Observe that the devil misapplies Scripture, using it to lead into error. "If," says Jerome, "the text which he quotes refers to Christ, he ought to have added what there follows against himself—the dragon shalt thou tread under thy feet" (verse 13).

7. It is written, in Deut. 6 : 16; **thou shalt not tempt,** *i. e.*, try him, put him on trial, presume on his aid, and therefore attempt exploits which he does not command, or neglect precautions which reason dictates.

8-10. THE THIRD TEMPTATION. An appeal to ambition. The Pharisees expected a literal establishment of a universal Jewish domain. As Alexander had conquered all the world, so they expected Judaism would conquer all the world, and Jerusalem would be its capital. This was unmistakably the expectation of Christ's own disciples, even to the close of his life (Matt. 20 : 20, 21; Luke 19 : 11; 24 : 21). The third temptation of the devil was an appeal to Christ to realize this dream of the nation. "There was a tremendous temptation to exhibit before men his real place and authority; to appear as great as he really was; to use his energies that men should admit him to be greater than generals, higher than kings, more glorious than temple or palace."—(*Beecher's Life of Christ.*) "It was a proposition to use physical force for the accomplishment of moral results—to turn from the path of suffering and labor and martyrdom for the truth."—(*Deems' "Jesus."*) "'All this power and glory will I give thee, if thou wilt fall down and worship me.' In other words, the glory and power shall be the Messiah's, if he consents to act in the spirit of the prince of this world."—(*Pressense's*

10 Then saith Jesus unto him, Get thee hence, Satan: for it is written, Thoup shalt worship the Lord thy God, and him only shalt thou serve.

11 Then the devil leaveth him, and behold, **angels** came and ministered unto him.

p Deut. 6 : 13; 1 Sam. 7 : 3....q Heb. 1 : 6, 14.

Life of Christ.) "The seductive promise was whispered in the ear of Jesus, 'This victory shall be thine. Only yield something of your religious zeal; only consent to join hands with the priestly aristocracy of Judea; only consent to look in silence on their sins; only compromise a little with conscience; only employ the arts of policy and the methods of state diplomacy, by which, always and everywhere, men mount to power. Be not righteous overmuch, for why shouldst thou destroy thyself."—(*Abbott's Jesus of Nazareth.*) This temptation was repeated in different forms several times in Christ's life, especially in the effort of the people to make him king (John 6 : 15), and in the endeavors of the disciples to dissuade him from his voluntary sacrifice of himself (Matt. 16 : 22, 23). Compare his language to Peter in the last-quoted passage with verse 10 here.

8. Of course there is no such mountain, and on a round globe can be none. The language "all the glory of them" indicates a picture seen in imagination rather than a literal view from any height. We must at all events dismiss at once all such puerile explanations as that the devil showed him the entire Holy Land, *i. e.*, the Jewish domain, or the Roman Empire, which could not all be seen from any elevation, or pointed out the direction of all kingdoms. Either the sight was one afforded in imagination only, or there was a miraculous extension of Christ's vision for the purpose. But the whole theory of a series of miracles *wrought for the express purpose of affording a temptation*, is inconsistent with the general tenor of Scripture, and directly contradictory of James 1 : 13; and the difficulty of understanding how Christ's imagination could be made a means of temptation is only part of the greater and insoluble difficulty of understanding how he could be truly subject to any temptation. Of the location of this mountain, if we suppose the scene to be real, not in imagination only, nothing is known. (See note on ver. 1.)

9. **All these things will I give thee.** There would seem to be little or no temptation in this promise if we suppose that the proposition was made by a fiend in bodily form, and involved a demand of divine homage paid to him. Christ, who knew that the devil was a liar from the beginning (John 8 : 44,) would not be deceived by so self-evident a lie as this would be if it were made in this form. Nor is the supposition that he did not till the last recognize the devil in these suggestions of evil, inconsistent with the degree of supernatural knowledge attributed to him by the N. T. (See notes on Matt. 6 : 10; Mark 13 : 39; and Heb. 5 : 8.)

10. **Satan.** Christ now first calls him by name, as though he now for the first time recognized the source whence these suggestions came to his mind. **It is written.** A quotation, but a free one, and somewhat modified, of Deut. 6 : 13.

11. **Then the devil leaveth him.** For a season, but only to return with various temptations in the subsequent life of Christ (Luke 4 : 13). From this time the devils recognize the Lord, acknowledge his power, and are cast out by his word (Mark 1 : 24, 34; 3 : 11; 5 : 7). **Angels came and ministered unto him.** The primary meaning is with food or other supplies, as in the case of Elijah, 1 Kings 19 : 6, 7.

THOUGHTS ON THE TEMPTATION OF JESUS CHRIST.

I. The nature of temptation is here indicated. It does not necessarily involve sin or even moral imperfection. We are tempted whenever desires, such as *may be right in themselves*, conflict with principles which are morally superior and should be their masters, as when appetite conflicts with trust in God; love of approbation with humble obedience to and waiting on God; love of influence and power, with a supreme love for and allegiance to God. We sin only when the higher principle yields to the lower propensity. In us temptation is strengthened by the fact that we have yielded to it; yet before we have yielded we learn obedience by experience of conflict.

II. Christ was "in all points tempted like as we are, yet without sin;" *i. e.*, he possessed the same propensities and was subject to the same conflicts, but never yielded (Hebrews 4 : 15). That he really felt the power of temptation and conquered only after a struggle analogous to our own heart struggles, is abundantly indicated not only in this passage and in the account of the struggle in Gethsemane and on the cross (Matt. 26 : 36-56; 27 : 46, and parallel passages), but also in such incidents as those recorded in Luke 12 : 50; John 12 : 27; and 16 : 32, and in such direct declarations as those of Hebrews 2 : 10, and 5 : 8.

III. In this threefold temptation there is noticeable a regular progression. The first appealed to the body; the second to love of admiration; the third to love of power. The first to a mere bodily appetite; the second to a more honorable desire of fame, founded on human sympathy; the third to a noble ambition which

CH. IV.] MATTHEW. 79

12 Now when Jesus had heard that John was cast into prison, he departed into Galilee:
13 And leaving Nazareth, he came and dwelt in Capernaum, which is upon the sea coast, in the borders of Zabulon and Nephthalim:
14 That it might be fulfilled which was spoken by Esaias the prophet,' saying,
15 The land of Zabulon, and the land of Nephthalim, *by* the way of the sea, beyond Jordan, Galilee of the Gentiles

r Isa. 9 : 1, 2.

Satan tried to pervert. The first called for an act seemingly miraculous; the second for one ostentatious and presumptuous, the third for one blasphemously wicked. The first disguised itself under an appeal to reason; the second sustained itself by an appeal to Scripture; and in the third all disguise was cast off, and Satan revealed himself. The first was the most deceptive; the second the most plausible; the third the most audacious. In the first, Satan tried to mislead by hiding the sin; in the second, by sanctioning the sin because of a greater good to be accomplished by it; in the third, to compensate for the sin by a promised reward.

IV. Christ receives the temptation as a man and resists it as a man. As he is tempted in all points like as we are, so his resistance is an example to us how to resist. He conquers the temptation through bodily hunger by trust in God, the temptation to presumption and ostentation by humble obedience to and patient waiting on God, the temptation to worldly ambition by supreme love and reverence for God; thus in every onset it is *faith in God* which is the shield that quenches the darts of the adversary (Ephes. 6 : 16).

V. We share Christ's first experience when poverty tempts us to violate God's law that we may provide for our daily wants; we share the second experience when we are tempted to neglect duties which God's providence lays upon us or to run into needless dangers or difficulties, or to assume uncalled-for hazards, and trust the result to God, or to make an ostentatious display of our faith in God; we share the third experience when we are tempted, for the sake of power, wealth, or influence, to conform to the world and to employ Satan's instruments in even seeming to do God's service. We yield to the first temptation when we distrust God's providential care; we yield to the second when we presume unwarrantably on his grace, or make a show of our reliance on his word; we yield to the third when we are conformed to this world and adopt its policies and methods and imbibe its spirit for the sake of its rewards. The first sin is forbidden by Matt. 6 : 25, the second by 6 : 1-7, the third by 6 : 24. We resist the first temptation when we seek first the kingdom of God and his righteousness, and trust food, raiment, and shelter to Him; we resist the second when, in humble trust in Him, we do all that God has given us power to do, looking to Him only to protect us from ills against which we cannot, by

reasonable precaution, guard ourselves, and patiently waiting for Him to bring about his own results in his own time and way; we resist the third when we make a supreme love to God the sole inspiration of our hearts, and a supreme allegiance to Him the sole rule of our lives.

Ch. 4 : 12-25. CHRIST'S FIRST MINISTRY IN GALILEE.—THE MISSION OF CHRIST: TO GIVE LIGHT TO THOSE IN DARKNESS, LIFE TO THOSE IN DEATH. THE MESSAGE OF CHRIST: REPENT, FOR THE KINGDOM OF HEAVEN IS AT HAND. THE CALL OF CHRIST: TO CHRISTIAN LABOR: I WILL MAKE YOU FISHERS OF MEN.—HOW TO ACCEPT CHRIST'S CALL: IMMEDIATELY, THOUGH IT REQUIRE US TO LEAVE PROPERTY, BUSINESS, FRIENDS.—CHRIST, THE MODEL FOR THE PREACHER; CHRIST, THE MODEL FOR THE PHYSICIAN.

12. Now. An interval of about a year, perhaps more, elapses between verses 11 and 12. During this time Christ goes from the wilderness to Cana of Galilee, where he performs the miracle at the wedding feast (John 2 : 1-11), goes up to Jerusalem to inaugurate his ministry there (John 2 : 13-25; 3 : 1-21); after the Passover, joins the Baptist in Enon (John 3 : 22-36); leaves Judea to avoid threatened controversy, going through Samaria on his way, and arriving at the residence either of his mother or some friends in Cana, where he heals the sick child by a word (John, ch. 4), and where he hears of the imprisonment of John the Baptist, which takes place about this time. There is some uncertainty as to the chronology, but this I think to be the most probable order of events. See *Abbott's Jesus of Nazareth*, p. 139, note. **Jesus had heard.** John (the Evangelist) says the reason why he departed into Galilee was that "the Lord knew how the Pharisees had heard that Jesus made and baptized more disciples than John," *i. e.* the Baptist (John 4 : 1, 2). The true explanation seems to be that this was the reason of his leaving the vicinity of the Jordan, viz.: to avoid the collision of his disciples with those of the Baptist, but that he did not commence public preaching in Galilee until after John's imprisonment. **John was cast into prison.** For account of this imprisonment and its result, John's death, see Matt. 14 : 3-12; Mark 6 : 14-29.

13. And leaving Nazareth. He was driven out of it by a mob, in consequence of a sermon in which he disclosed the opening of the door of salvation to the Gentiles (Luke 4 : 16-31). Alford places this sermon later; but his reasons for differing from the opinions of most other scholars

16 The people which sat in darkness saw great light: and to them which sat in the region and shadow of death, light is sprung up.
17 From that time Jesus began to preach, and to say, Repent: for the kingdom of heaven is at hand.
18 And Jesus, walking by the sea of Galilee, saw two brethren, Simon called Peter, and Andrew his brother, casting a net into the sea: for they were fishers.
19 And he saith unto them, Follow me, and I will make you fishers of men.
20 And they straightway left *their* nets, and followed him.
21 And going on from thence, he saw other two

are not satisfactory. Indeed, his views in general on chronology are not more satisfactory than might be expected of one who in express terms asserts the "impracticability of constructing a formal harmony of the three synoptic Gospels." **Capernaum.** One of the chief cities of Galilee. It had a synagogue, in which Jesus often taught, a Roman garrison, and a customs station, and was the residence of Andrew, Peter, James, and John, and probably also of Matthew (Matt. 9:1-9; Mark 1:21; Luke 7:1, 8; 5:27; John 6:59). It was denounced by our Lord for its rejection of him (Matt. 11:23), and its destruction has been so complete that its very site is a matter of uncertainty. The better opinion fixes it at Tel Hum, on the northern shore of the Sea of Galilee. The new name corresponds with the old, Cafar or Kefer, signifying *village*, and Tel *a deserted site*. The ruins of an ancient synagogue have been recently discovered at Tel Hum, not impossibly the very one in which Christ preached.

14-16. That it might be fulfilled. As the life of the individual is ordered by God in such a way as to fulfill the divine but undisclosed purpose, so the life of Christ was ordered in such a way as to fulfill the divine will concerning him disclosed in the prophets, and for the purpose of so doing. **Esaias.** Isaiah 9:1, 2. The quotation does not follow the original literally, nor indeed are the quotations in the New Testament from the Old Testament generally verbally exact. **Zabulon and Nephthalim.** The territories allotted to the tribes of Zebulon and Naphthali are referred to. They embrace the territory west of the Sea of Galilee, and constituted one of the most important, if not the most important, field of Christ's ministry. **The way of the sea, beyond Jordan.** Our version is unfortunate, if not inaccurate. These words are not descriptive of Zabulon and Nephthalim, but descriptive of other regions, the whole being embraced in the last term of the sentence, Galilee of the Gentiles. (See paraphrase below.) **Galilee of the Gentiles.** So called because of the intermixture of heathen with the Jewish population in Galilee. **Which sat in darkness.** A symbol of hopeless gloom. It signifies more than "walked in darkness;" they do not even attempt to escape from it. Zabulon and Nephthalim occupied the most northerly portion of the Holy Land, and were the tribes most distant from Jerusalem. The history and character of Galilee (see note on Matt. 2, 22) had brought it into contempt among the Judeans, and its people, intermixed with Gentiles, were certainly in ignorance of the ecclesiastical rules and the traditions and ceremonies which prevailed in Judea, and constituted in all respects a more common and simple population. The prophet declares that this region of darkness and ignorance should be the scene of the Messiah's illustrious appearance. **Shadow of death.** A common metaphor in the Old Testament (Job 10:21; Ps. 23:4; Jer. 2:6; and many other similar passages). Death is represented like a cloud that intervenes between the sun and the landscape; it thus casts a gloom on the face of the nation. **Light is sprung up.** "The light of itself sprung up and shone forth; it was not that they first ran to the light."—(*Chrysostom.*) Compare Ephes. 2:4, 5; John 4:10. The whole passage then may be paraphrased thus: "The territories of Zabulon and Nephthalim, the region about the Sea of Gennesaret, the country beyond the Jordan, yea, the whole of Galilee, which you contemptuously designate Galilee of the Gentiles, whose inhabitants sit in the darkness of ignorance and under the gloom of impending death, from which there is no one to deliver, shall be the first to see the light which the Messiah brings."

17. From that time. Though he had commenced his ministry at Jerusalem by casting out the traders, and by his conversation with Nicodemus (John 2:13; ch. 3), and some public instruction in Samaria is implied by John 4:40-42, his sermon at Nazareth appears to have inaugurated his entry upon his life-work as a preacher of righteousness. There is no cessation of that work from this time until his death. Even during his retirement, after his rejection by the Galileans (John 6:66 and Matt. 15:21), he occupied himself with instructing his disciples in the principles of Christianity, and the nature and work of the Christian Church. His preaching is, however, at first only a preaching of repentance, like that of John the Baptist. It grows more explicit in its disclosures of the true nature of the kingdom of heaven afterwards.

18-22. THE CALL OF FOUR DISCIPLES. The account in Luke 5:1-11, is much more full. See notes there. **Sea of Galilee.** Also called Lake of Gennesaret (Luke 5:1), Sea of Chinnereth (Numb. 34:11), of Cinnereth (Josh. 11:2), of Cinneroth (1 Kings 15:20), and of Tiberias (John 6:1). See map, Mark, ch. 1.

brethren,ˣ James, *the son* of Zebedee, and John his brother, in a ship with Zebedee their father, mending their nets; and he called them.

22 And they immediately left the ship and their father, and followed him.

23 And Jesus went about all Galilee, teachingʸ in their synagogues, and preaching the gospelᶻ of the kingdom, and healing all manner of sickness, and all manner of diseaseᵃ among the people.

24 And his fame went throughout all Syria: and they brought unto him all sick people that were taken with divers diseases and torments, and those which

---

x Mark 1 : 19, 20....y ch. 9 : 35; Luke 4 : 15, 44....a ch. 24 : 14; Mark 1 : 14....a ch. 8 : 16, 17; Ps. 103 : 3.

FISHERMAN CASTING HIS NET.

Simon called Peter. The name Peter had been previously given to him by our Lord at or about the time of his own baptism by John the Baptist (John 1 : 42). The reason of the new name is given in Matt. 16 : 18. See note there. **And Andrew his brother.** Simon Peter, Andrew, and John had already met Jesus at the ford of the Jordan, where they had partially attached themselves to him under the influence of John the Baptist's preaching (John 1 : 35-42, *note*). The fact of their acquaintance with him, coupled with the miraculous draft of fishes recorded in Luke, accounts for the readiness with which they responded to his call. It was not the call of a stranger, but of one whom they had already recognized as a prophet if not as the Messiah.

20. And they straightway left their nets, etc. "Mark both their faith and their obedience. For though they were in the midst of their work (and ye know how greedy a thing fishing is), when they heard his command they delayed not, they procrastinated not, they said not, 'let us return home and converse with our kinsfolk,' but they forsook all and followed, even as Elisha did to Elijah."—(*Chrysostom*.) Compare Matt. 7 : 21, 22, and ch. 19 : 27-30.

21. Zebedee. The husband of Salome. The latter became a follower of Christ, and watched him on the cross, and ministered to him even in the grave (Matt. 27 : 55, 56; Mark 15 : 40; 16 : 1). It is in-

ferred from the mention of Zebedee's hired servants (Mark 1 : 20), and from the acquaintance of John with the high priest (John 18 : 15), that the family were in easy circumstances; and that the father and sons were actively engaged in manual labor does not militate against this opinion. Zebedee is never mentioned after this incident, and there is no reason to believe that he ever became a disciple of Jesus. Compare Matt. 24 : 40, 41. One is taken and the other left in the call of Christ, as in his final coming.

22. Left the ship and their father. Not only their property and their business, but their home and their father—for Christ's sake. Compare Matt. 10 : 37, and contrast Luke 14 : 18-20.

23. Jesus went about. John preached in one locality to the people who came to him. Jesus went about seeking the people (Mark 1 : 37, 38). **Teaching in their synagogues.** Places of religious assembly among the Jews. Synagogues were first constituted during the captivity in Babylon, when access to the Temple was denied, and received their full development on the return of the Jews from captivity. They were built generally on elevated ground; worshippers, as they entered and as they prayed, looked toward Jerusalem. When finished, they were set apart, as the Temple had been, by a special prayer of dedication. The common acts of life, such as eating, drinking, reckoning up accounts, etc., were forbidden in them. Even if the building ceased to be used for worship, it was not to be applied to any base purpose. At the Christian era there were synagogues in every town, and in Jerusalem, according to the rabbinical writings, there were upwards of 450. The people assembled in them on Sabbath and other sacred days, for public prayer and the hearing of portions of Scripture (Luke 4 : 16; Acts 13 : 15). In the interior arrangements of the synagogue may be traced an obvious analogy to those of the Tabernacle. At the upper end stood the ark or chest which contained the Book of the Law. Here were the "chief seats" (Matt. 23 : 6; James 2 : 2, 3). In front of the ark was a lamp kept constantly burning, and an eight-branched lamp, lighted only on great

were possessed with devils, and those which were lunatic, and those that had the palsy; and he healed them.

25 And there followed him great multitudes[b] of people from Galilee, and *from* Decapolis, and *from* Jerusalem, and *from* Judæa, and *from* beyond Jordan.

b Luke 6 : 17, 19.

festivals. A little farther toward the middle of the building was a raised platform; and in the middle of this rose a pulpit, in which the Scripture was publicly read and the sermon or address was delivered. The officers of the congregation were composed of a college of elders (Luke 7 : 3; Mark 5 : 22; Acts 13 : 15), presided over by one who was the ruler of the synagogue (Luke 8 : 41, 49; Acts 18 : 8, 17). These managed the affairs of the synagogue and possessed the power of excommunicating. There were also an officer who was the chief reader of prayers, a minister of the synagogue (Luke 4 : 20), who had duties of a lower kind, resembling in part those of the modern sexton, in part those of the Christian deacon or sub-deacon, and who also often acted during the week as schoolmaster of the town or village, and ten men whose functions are not well ascertained. The latter were to be men of leisure, able to attend the week-day as well as the Sabbath services, and were probably simply a body of men permanently on duty making up a congregation (ten being the minimum number), so that there might be no delay in beginning the service at the proper time. The service was a ritual, probably borrowed and modified from the established service of the Temple. The first five books of the Old Testament were read through in a course of lessons, one lesson being read every Sabbath; the prophets were read as second lessons. There was also a sermon or exposition of the passage of Scripture which had been read, on which, however, any rabbi present might speak, by invitation of the ruler of the synagogue (Luke 4 : 16, 17; Acts 9 : 20; 13 : 15). The liberty of preaching was not ordinarily granted to any who were not versed in the lore of the rabbinical schools; but it was accorded to prophets and others who were recognized as leaders of new sects or representatives of new opinions, in order that they might not be condemned unheard. Hence the permission granted to Christ, and subsequently to his apostles, to speak in the synagogues. The synagogue was a place of trial, and even, strange as it may seem, of the infliction of punishment (Matt. 10 : 17; 23 : 34; Acts 22 : 19).

And heralding the glad tidings of the kingdom. The word translated *preaching*, signifies literally proclaiming as a herald or public crier; the word gospel is composed of two words, god—spell, good tidings, and answers almost exactly to the Greek, which is a compound word, signifying good news. An illustration of Christ's preaching is afforded by Luke 4 : 16-32. The characteristics of Jesus as a preacher are indicated by references in the various Evangelists. He possessed in a remarkable degree that mysterious personal magnetism which is the secret of all true oratory. No sooner did he rise to speak than all eyes were fastened on him (Luke 4 : 20). He spoke with ease and grace (Ib., verse 22), but with peculiar power (Mark 1 : 22; Luke 4 : 32). For illustration of this power, see Luke 4 : 30; John 10 : 39; 7 : 32, 45, 46; 18 : 6. He showed no respect for rabbinical lore (Matt. 15 : 3-9; Mark 7 : 5-13); but was familiar with and referred constantly to the Old Testament Scriptures (Matt. 19 : 5-7; 22 : 21, 32, 42-45; Mark 7 : 25, 26; John 5 : 39). He loved nature and interpreted her lessons (Matt. 6 : 26-29; 7 : 24-27, etc.), and drew innumerable illustrations from the common events of life (Matt. 13 : 3-9, 24-30, 33, 45-50; Luke 5 : 10; 14 : 16-24), and from public and political events of importance (Matt. 10 : 7-15; Luke 13 : 1-5; 19 : 12-28, and note). His discourses were generally brief, and abounded in apothegms, proverbs, and even startling paradoxes (see, for example, Matt. 5 : 10-12, 14, 29, 30, 44; 6 : 3, 21, 24, 34; 7 : 1, 7, 19, 20).

And healing. For a graphic description of a day's work, see Mark 1 : 21-35. To this period of his ministry are thought to belong the casting out the devil in the synagogue (Mark 1 : 21-28; Luke 4 : 31-37), the healing of Peter's mother-in-law and others (Mark 5 : 14-17), the healing of the leper (Matt. 8 : 2-4), and of the paralytic (9 : 2-8). The fuller accounts of these cures thus given show plainly that they were miraculous. Though Jesus sometimes used some of the simple remedies of his day (Matt. 9 : 29; Mark 6 : 13; Luke 4 : 10; John 9 : 6, 7), and though some of the diseases, such as lunacy in its milder forms, hysteria, and some cases of paralysis, can be relieved, if not cured, by a strong influence acting upon the system through the mind and brain, yet this is not true of the diseases which Christ for the most part treated, such as malarious fever (Matt. 8 : 14-17), chronic paralysis (Luke 13 : 11-17), congenital epilepsy (Matt. 17 : 14-21), long-continued ophthalmia (Matt. 9 : 27-30), or leprosy (Mark 3 : 2-5; 9 : 25; see also Matt. 8 : 5-13; 9 : 18, 19, 23-26; Luke 7 : 1-16; John 4 : 46-54; 17 : 12-19). No natural causes can possibly explain these manifestations of Christ's power. His miracles, too, were characteristically unlike the acts of a necromancer. He never shrouded them in mystery; he cured in his own name (Matt. 8 : 3), in open day, and before all the people (Mark 3 : 2-5; 9 : 25), by a word (Mark 3 : 5), a touch (Matt. 9 : 29), a command (John 5 : 8). For a full consideration of Jesus Christ as a preacher and healer, see Jesus of Nazareth, by Lyman Abbott, chapters 11, 12, and 13, from which this note is condensed.

21, 25. Comp. Mark 1 : 28. The Sea of Galilee was the centre of a busy traffic, and on the highway between Damascus and the Mediterranean. The caravans would carry his fame in both directions. **Possessed with devils.** See note on Matt. 8 : 28-34. **Lunatic.** Literally, *moonstruck;* probably subject to epilepsy. The same word is employed in describing a specific case in Matt. 17 : 15 ; see note on Mark 9 : 7, 8. **Palsy.** See, for cure of a specific case of palsy, Matt. 9 : 1-8 ; Mark 2 : 1-12 ; Luke 5 : 17-26 ; and for description of disease, notes on the passage in Mark. **Decapolis** (*ten cities*), a region in the northeastern part of Palestine, near the lake of Gennesaret, and so called because it contained ten cities, which seem to have been endowed by the Romans with some peculiar privileges. Their population was mostly heathen. **Jerusalem :** including the territory round about Jerusalem. **Beyond Jordan.** East of the Jordan. In secular history and in modern books of travel it is known as Perea (*beyond*). It is even to this day a comparatively unknown land. See as to its character, note on Matt. 19 : 1.

Ch. 5, 6, 7. SERMON ON THE MOUNT.—THE RELIGION OF JESUS CHRIST IS A RELIGION OF SPIRITUAL BLESSEDNESS (1-16), OF SPIRITUAL OBEDIENCE (17-48), OF HUMBLE PIETY (6 : 1-18), OF SINGLENESS OF SERVICE (19-24), OF CHILDLIKE TRUST IN GOD (24-34), OF CHARITY AND PURITY (7 : 1-6). IT IS A DIVINE GIFT, IS TO BE ATTAINED BY PRAYER (7-12), BY SELF-DENIAL (13, 14), BY PRACTICAL OBEDIENCE (15-27). THE KINGDOM OF CHRIST CONTRASTED WITH EARTHLY KINGDOMS (1-16), WITH THE MOSAIC COMMONWEALTH, *i. e.*, THE LAW (17-48), AND WITH THE RELIGION OF FORMALISM (6 : 1 to 7 : 6). THE CONDITIONS OF CITIZENSHIP IN CHRIST'S KINGDOM (7 : 7-27).—SEE NOTE ON OBJECT OF DISCOURSE, AND ANALYSIS BELOW.

PRELIMINARY NOTE.—Of this sermon there are two reports having some points in common and some marked differences, one and the fullest here, the other in Luke 6 : 20-49. The sermon is not reported by Mark or John. In reconciling these two accounts there are several hypotheses proposed, of which the principal are the following : I. That Luke has given a report of the sermon, and that Matthew has grouped around it a collection of the sayings of our Lord, uttered at different times during this period of his ministry. But this is inconsistent with ch. 5 : 1, 2, which represents the discourse as given at one time, and no less so with the structure of the discourse, which is as remarkable for its unity of thought as for the richness and the power of isolated passages (see analysis below). II. That Matthew has given a full report and that Luke has condensed from it. But Luke adds matter which Matthew does not give (Luke 6 : 24-26), nor is there anything in his account to indicate that it is borrowed or condensed from the previous report of another. III. That there were two distinct discourses, one preached by Christ to the disciples alone and recorded by Matthew, the other and briefer preached to the multitude, and reported by Luke. This opinion is maintained by Dr. Eddy (*Life of Christ,* pages 312, 313), Lange (*Life of Christ,* ii. 380-383), H. W. Beecher (*Jesus the Christ,* chap. xiv), following Tholuck, "Sermon on the Mount," and apparently Augustine. This hypothesis is pronounced "clumsy and artificial" by Jamieson, Faussett, and Brown, and "unlikely and unnatural" by Alford, and is rejected by Ellicott (*Life of Christ,* page 171, note), because it "has so much the appearance of having been formed simply to reconcile the differences as to locality and audiences, which appear in the two Evangelists, and involves so much that is unlikely and indeed unnatural." It can at best be said to be but a possibly true explanation. IV. That there was but one discourse, that it was delivered to the disciples in the presence of the multitude, and with reference to the wants of both the infant church and the great body of the people, and that of it we have different reports, with such variations as would naturally occur in the subsequent record by different writers. This is the view of Pressense (*Life of Christ,* page 361), Ebrard (*Gospel History,* pages 270-272), Neander (*Life of Christ,* page 224), Bengel (Gnomon on Matthew 5 : 1 ; Luke 6 : 17), Olshausen (*Commentary,* Matt. 5 : 1), Wordsworth (*Commentary,* Luke 6 : 20), Robinson (*Harmony of the Gospels,* § 41), and Townsend (*New Testament,* page 75, Pl. III, note 42). Those who believe in the verbal inspiration of the Scripture will reject this view. Those who believe that the Evangelists were left to use their natural faculties in recalling and recording the events and discourses they reported, being guarded by the Spirit of God from all material error, such as could affect the truth they were appointed to teach, will generally regard it, as I do, as the most rational and probable opinion. "It is," says Alford, "the view taken by ordinary readers of Scripture," and is "also taken by most of the modern German commentators."

OBJECT OF THE DISCOURSE. Luke has given the time of the discourse ; Matthew has not. Jesus had carried on his ministry for some time in Galilee ; his fame had extended throughout the Holy Land ; he had wrought the cures which Matthew subsequently records. While his popularity was constantly increasing among the common people (Mark 1 : 45 ; Luke 5 : 15, 16), his declaration that the Gospel was for the Gentiles (Luke 4 : 24-28), his disregard of the Pharisaic ceremonials, and his controversies with the Pharisees respecting Sabbath observance, as recorded in Matt. 12 : 1-9 ; Mark 2 : 23-28 ; 3 : 1-6 ; John, ch. 5, which had taken place previous to this time though re-

CHAPTER V.

AND seeing the multitudes, he went up into a mountain: and when he was set, his disciples came unto him:

2 And he opened his mouth, and taught them, saying,[c]

3 Blessed *are* the poor in[d] spirit;[e] for their's is the kingdom of heaven.

c Luke 6 : 20, etc....d Isa. 57 : 15; 66 : 2....e Jas. 2 : 5.

---

corded by Matthew subsequently, indicated the collision which was inevitable between his teachings and those of the Scribes and Pharisees. He summoned from the many that followed him, twelve to be his apostles (Luke 6 : 13-16) and the founders under him of the church which was to carry on the preaching of the Gospel after his death, and having consecrated them to their work he preached this sermon, primarily to them, but also to the great multitude who crowded to hear (Luke 6 : 17). It was thus in a proper sense an inaugural discourse. It sets forth to his disciples and to the people the character of that kingdom of heaven which he had declared to be at hand, but it does this by contrasting it, firstly, with the old theocracy which it was to fulfill, and secondly, with the righteousness of which the scribes were the expositors, and which it was to overthrow.

ANALYSIS.—The sermon may be briefly analyzed as follows. The kingdom of God is one of blessedness, a blessedness which does not consist, however, in wealth and honor, but in character, in a lowly spirit, a merciful disposition, a pure heart. It brings earthly persecution but eternal reward (vers. 1-12), and no one is worthy of it who has not the spirit to endure suffering for its sake (13-16). To make clear the nature of this kingdom, Christ points out its contrast with, first, the Mosaic law, and second, the traditional and ceremonial religion of the Scribes and Pharisees. He has been accused of disregarding the laws of Moses (Mark 2 : 24; John 5 : 10, 16). It is not true. The Messiah comes to fulfill, not to repeal, the Old Testament law. He has been charged with irreligion; he replies that the religion of his disciples must exceed that of their accusers or they can never enter the kingdom of God (17-20). He explains his first declaration by showing how the laws of the kingdom of heaven require all that the Mosaic law required, and much more, and illustrates this truth by pointing out that while the Mosaic law forbade murder, adultery, and perjury, and restrained revenge within certain definite bounds, Christ's law forbids anger and unhallowed thoughts, and requires simplicity in all speech, and love toward all men (21-48). He next illustrates the second declaration by depicting the vices which nullify all that is seemingly good in Pharisaism, the ostentation of the three good works of all formal religions—alms-giving, prayer, and fasting; the greed which accompanies their pretended piety; and the censoriousness which is the result of their self-righteous spirit (ch. 6 ; ch. 7 : 1-6). He finally, in a few brief aphorisms, points out the way by which the soul may enter the kingdom of God (ch. 7 : 7-14); cautions his hearers against preachers of false doctrine; gives a simple test of truth which every man, however unlearned, can easily apply for himself (15-23); and he closes by the declaration that discipleship consists not in hearing the truth, nor in professing the truth, but in living the truth (24-27).

The fact that this discourse possesses a unity as characteristic as that of any address of equal length in the Bible, if not in any literature, is a sufficient refutation of the idea that it is a mosaic of Christ's sayings, put together by Matthew; the fact that it was preached for a specific purpose, viz., to exhibit the contrast of the religion of the Spirit with that of external observance, sufficiently indicates the reason why it contains no distinct enunciation of those doctrines of an atoning sacrifice, and a new and spiritual birth, which Jesus had already enunciated in private conversation with Nicodemus (John 3 : 1-8), and which he at a later period emphasized, not only in addresses delivered to his own disciples, but in those delivered to the people (Matt. 27 : 11-13; 28 : 1-13, John ch. 6; ch. 10, etc.). At the same time the fundamental truth that the kingdom of heaven is the gift of God, is indicated clearly in chapter 7 : 7-11. See notes there.

1. And seeing the multitudes. To escape from them and to secure a private interview with his disciples (compare Mark 3 : 9, 13). **Mountain.** Not necessarily a particular mountain; rather into the "hill-country." Luke says (ch. 6 : 17) that he came down and stood in the plain (literally, *level place*). Nothing more is indicated by this than that he descended from one of the higher peaks to the plateau to give this discourse, where it might be heard by the people as well as by the twelve. A tradition points out a hill, known as Mount Hattin, as the place where the sermon was delivered. The tradition is of no weight, but the hill itself contains a platform "evidently suitable for the collection of a multitude, and corresponding precisely to the 'level place' to which he would 'come down,' as from one of its higher horns, to address the people."—(*Stanley's Sinai and Palestine*, page 360.) **And when he was set.** The Jewish rabbis gave their instruction sitting, both in the schools and in the public preaching in the synagogues (Luke 4 : 20). **His disciples.** It is evident from Luke

4 Blessed *are* they that mourn;*f* for they shall be comforted.*g*
5 Blessed *are* the meek: for they*h* shall inherit the earth.
6 Blessed *are* they which do hunger and thirst after righteousness: for*i* they shall be filled.
7 Blessed *are* the merciful: for*j* they shall obtain mercy.

f Isa. 61 : 3; Ezc. 7 : 16.....*g* John 16 : 20; 2 Cor. 1 : 7.....*h* Ps. 37 : 11.....*i* Ps. 145 : 19; Isa. 65 : 13...*j* Ps. 41 : 1, 2.

6 : 13–16, that the twelve had been chosen and set apart to the apostleship immediately preceding this sermon. The account of their selection is given later by Matt. (10 : 1–5) in connection with the command given to them to preach the gospel. This commission must, however, have been preceded by some preparatory special instruction. Comparing Luke and Matthew, the whole narrative will read as follows: "And it came to pass in those days that he went up into a mountain (rather, *the hill country*) to pray, and continued all night in prayer to God. And when it was day he called unto him his disciples, and of them he chose twelve, whom also he named apostles (Matt. 5 : 1; Luke 6 : 12, 13); and he came down with them, and stood in the plain (rather, *a level place*) with the company of his disciples, and a great multitude of people out of all Judea, etc., which came to hear him (Luke 6 : 17); and he opened his mouth and taught them saying" (Matt. 5 : 2).

2. And he opened his mouth. A not infrequent introduction to a solemn and weighty discourse (Job 3 : 1; Psalm 78 : 2, referred to in Matt. 13 : 35; Dan. 10 : 16; Acts 8 : 35; Ephes. 6 : 19). In the light of these references such deductions as those of the fathers, "He who before had opened the mouth of Moses and the prophets opens now his own mouth" (*Gregory*), "in his very silence he gave instructions, and not when he spoke only" (*Chrysostom*), though true, must be regarded as fanciful and far-fetched.

Ch. 5 : 3–16. FIRST GENERAL DIVISION.—THE CHARACTERISTICS OF CHRIST'S TRUE DISCIPLES.

3–12. THE BEATITUDES. These, which are eight in number (Luke adds four woes, 6 : 24–26), are not promises of blessings to be fulfilled in another life; they are enunciations of certain general principles, according to which each grace of disposition receives its own peculiar experience of blessedness. The Jewish people were looking for political supremacy, a kingdom like that of Greece and Rome, when the long promised and now more lately heralded kingdom of God should come. In these beatitudes Christ teaches, first, what are the characteristics of the kingdom of God, and second, what is its true pomp and glory. It is in some sense a contrast with the earthly rewards promised by the Old Testament (Deut. 30 : 20; Isaiah 1 : 19, 20). Yet a hint of the beatitudes is to be found even in the Old Testament (see references below). "Prosperity is the blessing of the Old Testament; adversity is the blessing of the New; which carrieth the greater benediction

and the clearer revelation of God's favor. Yet even in the Old Testament, if you listen to David's harp you shall hear as many hearse-like airs as carols; and the pencil of the Holy Ghost hath labored more in describing the afflictions of Job than the felicities of Solomon."—(*Lord Bacon*.)

3. Poor in spirit. Those who possess a disposition the reverse of proud in spirit and haughty. The world still honors the high and haughty spirit; it is the lowly in spirit whom Christ declares blessed. **Theirs is the kingdom of heaven.** *Is now*, not shall be hereafter. The kingdom of heaven represents not a future state, but the condition of obedience to God here. (See note on chapter 3 : 2, and compare Rom. 14 : 17.) To the lowly in spirit repentance and confession are not difficult, and, therefore, to them the door of entrance into the kingdom of heaven swings open readily. A parallel teaching is that of Psalm 51 : 17, and Isaiah 66 : 2. "By spirit he hath here designated the soul, and the faculty of choice. Since many are humble not willingly, but compelled by stress of circumstances, letting these pass (for this were no matter of praise), he blesses them first who by choice humble and contract themselves."—(*Chrysostom*.) This beatitude comes first because it is the foundation of all that follow, as repentance and confession are the entrance door into all the blessings which are attributed to the other graces—graces that belong alone to the kingdom of God.

4. Blessed are they that mourn; not merely for their sins. It is an absolute promise to all those who *in the kingdom of heaven* are brought into the experience of mourning, and is to be interpreted by such passages as Romans 5 : 3–5, Hebrews 12 : 11, and Rev. 7 : 14. "Tears like rain-drops have a thousand times fallen to the ground and come up in flowers."—(*H. W. Beecher*.) "Every praying Christian will find that there is no Gethsemane without its angel." —(*Binney*.) Compare with this promise Eccles. 7 : 2, 3; Isaiah 61 : 2, 3; 66 : 13.

5. Blessed are the meek. The Greek word here rendered meek (πραΰς) occurs also in Matt. 21 : 5 and 1 Pet. 3 : 4, and in a slightly different form in James 1 : 21; 3 : 13, and 1 Pet. 3 : 15. A comparison of these passages, together with those where the English word is the same, but the Greek is different in form, though from the same root, indicates its significance in the Scripture. Meekness is a spirit the opposite of the ambitious and self-seeking one which is charac-

8 Blessed *are* the pure in heart: for they shall see God.
9 Blessed *are* the peacemakers: for they shall be called the children of God.
10 Blessed *are* they which are persecuted for righteousness' sake: for their's is the kingdom of heaven.
11 Blessed are ye, when men shall revile you, and persecute you, and shall say all manner of evil against you falsely, for my sake.
12 Rejoice, and be exceeding glad; for great *is* your reward in heaven; for so persecuted they the prophets which were before you.

k Ps. 24 : 3, 4; Heb. 12 : 14; 1 John 3 : 2, 3....l Ps. 34 : 14....m 1 Pet. 3 : 13, 14....n 2 Cor. 4 : 17.

teristic of kings (Matt. 21 : 5), the opposite of the ambitious and self-assertive one which is characteristic of controversialists (1 Pet. 2 : 15). The root of meekness is the dominance of spiritual over earthly desires. It is the characteristic of one who seeks first the kingdom of God and his righteousness, and leaves all other things to God's care (Matt. 6 : 33). **Inherit the earth.** Not the new heavens and the new earth, nor the land of promise, *i. e.*, the heavenly kingdom hereafter, nor great spiritual blessings here, but literally *the earth.* Christ declares that the enjoyment of earthly blessings belongs not to those who grasp for them, and assert and maintain with vehemence and care their right to them, but to those who hold them lightly, and who, ranking them inferior to spiritual blessings, are not burdened by them while they possess them, nor harassed lest they lose them. "Selfish men may possess the earth; it is the meek alone who inherit it from the heavenly Father, free from all defilements and perplexities of unrighteousness."—(*John Woodrow's Journal*, page 35.) This beatitude is found almost in the same form in Psalm 37 : 11; and the substance of the same truth is contained in Isaiah 57 : 13; 60 : 21. See also Matt. 19 : 29.

6. Hunger and thirst. Not merely desire, but so desire that we cannot be denied. Though it is Satan who said, "All that a man hath will he give for his life" (Job 2 : 4), it is, nevertheless, substantially true; and he who has a similar desire for righteousness will count no sacrifice too great to secure it (Matt. 10 : 37-39, and parallel passages). **Righteousness.** Perfect conformity to the will of God respecting us, as represented to us in the life and character of Christ, our example. **Shall be filled.** All other desires are liable to be disappointed; the desire for righteousness, if it be supreme—not merely the wish, but the *choice* of the soul, can never be disappointed. Even success fails to satisfy other desires; the desire for righteousness shall be *filled.* Compare Psalm 17 : 15; 65 : 4; 107 : 9.

7. Merciful. Mercy as a feeling is that habit of mind which leads one to feel pity and compassion rather than resentment toward a wrong-doer; and as an act, it is the exercise of forgiveness in the largest sense, *i. e.*, of good-will and helpfulness toward those who have wronged us and who are deserving of punishment. It is the highest exercise of love, because it is love toward not only the undeserving, but the ill-deserving, and involves sympathy not only for the unfortunate, but for the wrong-doer. **Shall obtain mercy.** Not only from men, because the tender consideration of the merciful from others reacts in tender regard of others for ourselves, but also from God (Ps. 18 : 26; Prov. 3 : 34; compare Matt. 18 : 23-35). "Mercy turns her back to the unmerciful."—(*Quarles.*)

8. Pure in heart. They who are not merely clean ceremonially or morally, *i. e.*, in external conduct, but in motive and purpose. Compare Psalm 51 : 6; Prov. 4 : 23. **Shall see God.** Not merely hereafter, but now. True knowledge of God comes not through an intellectual study of his attributes, but through a spiritual conformity to his character (John 14 : 15, 17, 21, 23; 2 Cor. 3 : 18; Heb. 12 : 14; 2 Pet. 1 : 8). As we grow in grace we grow in the knowledge of God (2 Pet. 3 : 18). The converse is also true; when we see him as he is, we shall be by the sight made like him (1 John 3 : 2). For parallel to this promise, see Psalm 24 : 4, 5. "We must be in some way like God in order that we may see God as he is."

9. Peace-makers. Not merely they who reconcile differences between man and man, though such peace-making is included, but they who, by their presence and disposition, as well as by their conscious acts, carry with them the spirit of peace and quietness, and bring peace to others who are perturbed and troubled. See for a wondrous illustration of such peace-making John 14 : 27. One condition of such peace-making is the maintenance of a quiet and peaceful heart amidst all experiences of turmoil. As Solomon contrasts him who maintains peace in himself with the conqueror (Prov. 16 : 32), so Christ contrasts him who produces peace with the war-makers whose victories were the envy of the Jews, and by whose prowess they expected to see the kingdom of God ushered in. **Shall be called.** Shall not only be the children of God, but shall also be recognized as such. It is this peace-giving quality which above all others is counted among men as saintliness. Observe that, as in James 3 : 17, so here, purity precedes peace, and that there is no true peace-making which is not also in so far pure-making. "No peace was ever won from fate by subterfuge or agreement; no peace is ever in store for any of us, but that which we shall win by victory over shame or sin—victory over the sin that oppresses

CH. V.] MATTHEW. 87

13 Ye are the salt° of the earth; but if the salt have lost its savour, wherewith shall it be salted? it is thenceforth good for nothing, but to be cast out, and to be trodden under foot of men.
14 Ye are the light° of the world. A city that is set on an hill cannot be hid.

15 Neither do men light a candle, and put it under a bushel, but on a candlestick; and it giveth light unto all that are in the house.
16 Let your light so shine before men, that they may see your good works, and glorify⁹ your father which is in heaven.

o Mark 9 : 50....p Phil. 2 : 15....q 1 Pet. 2 : 12.

---

as well as over that which corrupts."—(*Ruskin*.) In this truth is found the reconciliation of such passages as this with Matt. 10 : 34.

10. Compare 1 Peter 3 : 14. Not merely because a heavenly reward compensates the persecuted for their sufferings, though this is true (see Luke 16 : 25; and Rev. 7 : 14), but more because the persecution itself intensifies the martyr's abhorrence of evil, and drives him to a closer refuge in God. The truth is illustrated in many a Christian experience, is embodied in the hymns of the Christian Church, as in the lines,

> Man may trouble and distress me,
> 'T will but drive me to thy breast,

and is exemplified in the fact that the greatest purity of the Christian Church has been in times of persecution, its greatest corruption in the time of its wealth, its honor, and its worldly prosperity. "So long as the waters of persecution are upon the earth, so long we dwell in the ark; but where the land is dry, the dove itself will be tempted to a wandering course of life, and never to return to the house of her safety."—(*Jeremy Taylor*.)

11, 12. The preceding verse is the last of the beatitudes, each of which is seen to be the enunciation of a law which connects with each seeming lowliness of character, or bitterness of sorrow, a real experience of grace and glory. The 11th and 12th verses are addressed more directly and immediately to Christ's own disciples, as an encouragement in view of approaching contumely and persecution. In the other promises Christ says not, blessed are ye, but blessed are the poor, they that mourn, the meek, etc. Observe the qualifications of this blessing: "Lest thou shouldest think that the mere fact of being evil spoken of makes men blessed, he hath set two limitations; when it is for his sake, and when the things that are said are false; for without these he who is evil spoken of, so far from being blessed, is miserable."—(*Chrysostom*.) **Reward.** Of grace, not of debt. See Romans, ch. 4, and parable of the laborers, Matt. ch. 20, and note there. **For so persecuted they,** etc. Compare Matt. 23 : 29-31. Every age persecutes its own prophets, and reveres the prophets whom the preceding age has persecuted.

13. **Ye are the salt of the earth.** The significance of the metaphor consists not merely in the fact that salt is the great antiseptic, but also in its peculiar quality of imparting a flavor to everything with which it is mixed. Livy calls Greece "the salt of the nations." Observe that salt must be mingled with whatever it is to flavor; and Christians are to mingle with men, not to live in monkish solitude apart from them; they are to carry religion into daily life, not to keep it for the closet and the church. **Lost its savour.** "It is a well-known fact that the salt of *this country* (Palestine), when in contact with the ground, or exposed to rain and sun, does become insipid and useless. From the manner in which it is gathered much earth and other impurities are necessarily collected with it. Not a little of it is so impure that it cannot be used at all, and such salt soon effloresces and turns to dust—not to fruitful soil, however. It is not only good for nothing itself, but it actually destroys all fertility wherever it is thrown; and this is the reason why it is cast into the street. So troublesome is this corrupted salt that no man will allow it to be thrown on to his field, and the only place for it is the street, and there it is cast to be trodden under foot of men."—(*Thompson's Land and Book*, vol. ii, p. 44.) **Good for nothing.** Salt is a great antiseptic. Its function in ordinary culinary purposes is to prevent decay and corruption. This is the function of the Christian Church. It does this by its spirit of self-sacrifice; by showing itself willing to suffer for truths and principles which the world but dimly recognizes, or not at all. If the church loses this spirit of self-sacrifice, it becomes itself corrupt, ceases to be a purifier and preserver, and is "*good for nothing*." Observe, that the salt cannot restore that which is decayed, but only preserve from decay. "That men should be set free from the rottenness of their sins was the good work of Christ; but their not returning to it again any more was the object of these men's diligence and travail."—(*Chrysostom*.)

14. **Light of the world.** Because Christ is in the midst of his church, which otherwise possesses no light (John 1 : 9; 8 : 12; Ephes. 5 : 8; Rev. 1 : 13). It is not truth in abstract forms, but truth embodied in living men, and chiefly incarnate in the man Christ Jesus, which is the light of the world; *i. e.*, example is more than precept, life is more than philosophy. **A city set on a hill.** Possibly an allusion to Jerusalem. There is no authority for the notion that some city was in sight

17 Think not that I am come to destroy the law, or the prophets: I am not come to destroy, but to fulfill.

18 For verily I say unto you, Till heaven and earth pass, one jot or one tittle shall in no wise pass from the law, till all be fulfilled.

r ch. 3 : 15....s Isa. 42 : 21,....t Ps. 40 : 7, 8,...u Luke 16 : 17.

at the time of the delivery of this sermon, though that may have been the case.

15. Candle. This word often occurs in our version of the Scripture, where a lamp is more probably meant (Job 18 : 6 ; Ps. 18 : 28). But candles made of wax or tallow, with the pith of a kind of rush for the wick, were used at this time among the Romans and probably among the Jews.

16. Good works. Does this conflict with what Paul says about good works? No! for though we are saved by faith, it is *unto* good works (Ephes. 2 : 10). Let your light so shine . . . that they may glorify your Father. The Pharisee displays his light (see ch. 6) ; the true Christian simply *lets his shine.* The Pharisee glorifies himself by his works ; the true disciple of Christ glorifies only his heavenly Father. Observe that in these verses (13–16) Christ teaches that the pre-eminence which Christian character and conduct gives to the true disciple is a part of the divine intention ; and hence rebukes the fear of being odd, and the tendency to conform to the world in its habits and usages ; also that he puts example above precept, and thus impliedly teaches, what Paul declares most clearly, that the greatest heresies are not in doctrine, but in life (1 Tim. 1 : 9-10).

Ch. 5 : 17–48. SECOND GENERAL DIVISION.—THE LAWS OF THE KINGDOM OF CHRIST CONTRASTED WITH THOSE OF MOSES.

17. Think not that I am come to destroy. This charge had already been made against Jesus (John 5 : 16, 18); was substantially made against Paul (Acts 21 : 20, 21 ; Rom. 3 : 8, 21 ; 6 : 1); in the sixteenth century was made against Luther; and is still made against every one who preaches the liberty of the Gospel. **I am not come to destroy, but to fulfill,** *i. e.,* to fill to the full the ancient laws with their own true and spiritual meaning. But see further below. In these words Christ declares the relations of the law and the Gospel, a theme to which we must constantly recur, especially in Paul's writings. Without essaying a full interpretation, a work which belongs to the preacher rather than to the commentator, it must suffice to say here :

I. That by the term *law* the whole Mosaic system is meant. The Bible *nowhere makes a distinction between the moral and the ceremonial law.* The whole is treated as one system, and the relation of the Gospel to the one is its relation to the other. Observe that it is a portion of the ceremonial law which is apparently retained by the council of Jerusalem (Acts 15 : 28, 29) ; and the moral law, written in the hearts of the Gentiles as well as in the books of the Jews, which is treated of in Romans, chaps. 2 and 3. It is tampering with the plain meaning of Scripture to suppose that Christ destroyed the ceremonial but retains and enforces the moral law. See particularly verse 18, and James 2 : 10.

II. The N. T. nowhere treats any part of the law as abolished or repealed. The popular idea that it repeals the Jewish Sabbath and re-enacts a new one has no warrant in Scripture. *There is no repealing clause in the New Testament;* and nothing in it to set aside the O. T., or any part of it, as obsolete, common, old-fashioned, and useless. Paul may seem to treat a part of the law as repealed, in such passages as Ephes. 2 : 15 and Col. 2 : 14 ; but he carefully and indignantly repudiates this inference in Rom. 3 : 31, and impliedly so in 1 Timothy 1 : 8.

III. The proximate object of law is the protection and welfare of the community ; its ultimate object is the development of character ; but this it essays to accomplish only by forming right habits of conduct. Law, therefore, *regulates only the external conduct.* In the nature of the case, civil laws, enforced by civil penalties, cannot deal directly with the heart. While, therefore, the ultimate object of law (1 Tim. 1 : 5) and its indirect effect (Ps. 19 : 7, 8,) is the improvement of character, it is composed necessarily of specific precepts commanding or forbidding *actions*. It prohibits adultery, not lust ; murder, not anger; because this is all mere *law* can do.

IV. The Gospel operates directly on the heart. It not only requires purity in thought and love, and forgiveness in feeling (see below) ; it bestows moral and spiritual power (John 1 : 12) ; and so, by making the *character divine,* removes all occasion for laws regulating the *conduct.* When the character is conformed to the divine image, the end of the law is fulfilled, and the law itself becomes useless and is forgotten. "As the shell breaks when the bird is hatched ; as the sheath withers when the bud bursts into leaf ; as the rough sketch is done with when the picture is finished ; as the toys of boyhood are laid by in adolescence ;" so the system of law, which is preparatory only, is superseded, not repealed or destroyed, and this just in the proportion in which the individual, the community, or the race comes into a moral state in which it no longer needs to be commanded and forbidden (Gal. 3 : 24, 25; 4 : 1–6).

V. The mere external law regulating conduct was all that was recognized by the Pharisees or by the great majority of the Jews; just as even now the precepts of Christ constitute in the thought of many the chief part of Christianity. Yet in the O. T. are hints that the law looked towards something higher than a well-regulated *conduct*. See, for example, such commands as Exod. 20:17; Lev. 19:18; Deut. 6:5; 10:12; and such passages as Isaiah 1:16, 17; 66:2; and Micah 6:8. Indeed, the prophets are full of a constant protest against a mere obedience to the letter of the law, and insist on a spiritual life. Thus Christ does not destroy even that conception of the law which the ancient Jews—that is, the best among them—entertained, but fulfils the meaning of the ancient statutes by the disclosure of a life more deeply spiritual than any of which the prophets had ever conceived. It is to the contrast between the mere legal obedience rendered by the Pharisees and the spiritual life to which the law, rightly interpreted, should conduct, that Christ refers in verse 20.

In three ways, then, does Christ fulfill the law; *first*, by giving it in his exposition a fuller and more spiritual meaning than the Pharisees imputed to it or than we now ordinarily impute to it, or even to his precepts; *second*, by illustrating its end and object, the development of a perfect character, by his own life, free from reproach, even by the Pharisees (John 8:46), because perfect in spirit; and *third*, by giving to his disciples the *power*, which the law never gave, of obedience, by changing the desires and aspirations of the heart, and so making the character to act out, naturally and free from restraint, the life which the *law* alone required from unwilling subjects through fear, but was unable to secure (Rom. 8:3, 4; Heb. 2:15). These principles will be recurred to hereafter in this work, and are embodied here in a brief statement partly for that purpose. They explain and are explained by the illustrations which follow. What becomes of the law against murder to one who is never under the dominion of anger, or of the law against adultery to one who is perfectly pure in thought, or of the law against forswearing to one who has been cured of the evil, from which all exaggerations and undue expletives come (see verse 37), or of the law against excessive punishment and revenge to one who *loves* his enemies?

Observe in this connection how Christ set himself before the people as the one that was to come, and as the fulfiller of the whole imperfect and prophetic system of Moses. "When you know what it means and how long mankind had been kept waiting for it, there is sublimity in the composure with which this simple preacher of God sets himself forth as the fulfiller."—(*Dykes.*) Observe, also, that he declares it his mission to fulfill the prophets as well as the law; that is, in him and the kingdom he has come to establish, the whole system of O. T. prophecy, type, and symbolism, is fulfilled.

18. Verily. A common precursor of a solemn and weighty declaration; but so used only by Christ. See, for examples, 6:2, 5; John 3:3, 5, 11; and Concordance, word *verily*. It is the Greek word Amen, and is used in the N. T. as an appellation of Christ (Rev. 3:14), and also as a solemn close of prayer, being repeated by the people as their ratification or endorsement of it (1 Cor. 14:16; Rev. 5:14; 19:4), in which case it is rendered in our version by the word Amen. **I say unto you.** Christ appeals to himself as authority, here and elsewhere, in his most solemn and weighty disclosures of truth; his "I say unto you" is equivalent to the prophetic formula, "thus saith the Lord." **Jot or tittle.** Jot is the Hebrew *Jod*, the smallest letter in the Hebrew alphabet; *tittles*, literally horns, are the little turns of the strokes by which one Hebrew letter differs from another similar to it. At the time of Christ the O. T. scripture existed of course only in manuscript. In the Hebrew Bible are over 66,000 jots. The Hebrew copyists were scrupulous to the last degree, and regarded the slightest error in their copy fatal. For the purpose of illustration, Christ takes this well-known veneration of the copyists for the most minute details in their copying. **Till all be fulfilled.** Just in the proportion in which, by the baptism of the spirit and the regeneration and sanctification of the character, the law is fulfilled, it ceases to bind, *but no farther*. If lust and anger are still in the heart, the law against adultery and murder are not superseded. It is in the failure to recognize this truth that the Antinomians fell into capital error.

The note of Dean Alford on this verse appears to me so important that I transcribe the most essential portion of it in full: "It is important to observe in these days how the Lord here *includes the Old Testament and all its unfolding of the divine purposes regarding himself, in his teaching* of the citizens of the kingdom of heaven. I say this, because it is always in *contempt and setting aside of the Old Testament* that rationalism has begun. First, *its historical truth*, then its *theocratic dispensation* and the *types* and *prophecies* connected with it are swept away; so that Christ came to fulfill nothing, and becomes only a teacher or a martyr; and thus the way is paved for a similar rejection of the New Testament, beginning with the narratives of the birth and infancy, as theocratic myths, advancing to the denial of his miracles, then attacking the truthfulness of his own sayings, which are grounded on the Old Testament as a revelation from God, and so finally leaving us nothing in the Scriptures

19 Whosoever therefore shall break one of these least commandments, and shall teach men so, he shall be called the least in the kingdom of heaven: but whosoever shall do and teach *them*, the same shall be called great" in the kingdom of heaven.

20 For I say unto you, That except your righteousness shall exceed" *the righteousness* of the scribes and Pharisees, ye shall in no case enter the kingdom of heaven.

21 Ye have heard that it was said by them of old

v 1 Sam. 2 : 30.....w ch. 23 : 23–28; Phil. 3 : 9.

but, as a German writer of this school has expressed it, 'a mythology not so attractive as that of Greece.' That this is the course which unbelief *has run* in Germany should be a pregnant warning to the decriers of the Old Testament among ourselves. It should be a maxim for every expositor and every student, that Scripture is a *whole*, and stands or falls together."

19. Break. Rather *relax*. The Greek word here used (λύω) is generally translated *loose*, and when not used metaphorically embodies the idea of freeing from restraints, as in Mark 1 : 7; Luke 13 : 15; 19 : 30, 31; John 11 : 44. The same idea appears to be generally involved in its metaphorical use, as in Matt. 16 : 19; Acts 2 : 24. And even when it embodies the idea of destruction, a general dissolution is ordinarily involved, as in 2 Pet. 3 : 11, 12. **Least in the kingdom of heaven.** See note on next clause; and on meaning of phrase, kingdom of heaven, see note on Matt. 3 : 2. **Whosoever shall do**—in the spirit and fulness with which Christ fulfilled all righteousness—**and teach**—expounding the law as Christ in this chapter expounds it, so as to bring out its spiritual meaning, and accomplish its spiritual purposes—**shall be called great in the kingdom of heaven.** Chrysostom, and following him Owen, interpret the phrase "kingdom of heaven" here as equivalent to the "time of the resurrection and that awful coming," and "least in the kingdom" as equivalent to cast out from it. But our Lord does not say that he who loosens the obligations of the law shall be excluded from the kingdom, but shall be *least in it*, and our duty is to find out what he says, not to substitute for it something which we regard as equivalent. The question of admission to or exclusion from the kingdom is not raised here at all, and to regard "least in the kingdom" as equivalent to excluded from it, and great "in the kingdom" as not denoting grade or rank, but a full and free entrance into it, is not only to miss the meaning of this passage, but to make admission into the kingdom to rest upon obedience to law, *which is never recognized in the N. T. as the condition of admission*. The natural and plain meaning of Christ's words affords the true interpretation. To relax the obligation of law either by precept or example is not the way to attain eminence in piety ourselves, or to promote it in others. The true way to overcome the spirit of externalism and legalism in the church is not by *relaxing* the obligations of obedience, but by teaching men the doctrine of a *higher obedience*. The true way, for example, to correct a formal technical and servile observance of the Sabbath, is not by relaxing the Sabbath-law, but by leading up to a higher appreciation of Sabbath rest and Sabbath worship; and so of all law. Of such true teaching Paul's Epistle to the Romans affords, when studied as a whole, a wondrous illustration.

20. Scribes. This term, which is sometimes used in the N. T. to designate certain officers whose duty it was to keep the official records of the Jewish nation, or to act as private secretaries of distinguished individuals, is ordinarily applied in the N. T. to persons devoted to reading and expounding the law. They generally appear in connection with the Pharisees; but it would appear from Acts 23 : 9, that there were Scribes attached to the other sects also. The Scribes customarily opposed themselves to our Lord; watching him to find matter of accusation (Luke 6 : 7, 11); perverting his sayings and his actions (Matt. 9 : 3; Luke 5 : 30; 15 : 2); and seeking to entangle and embarrass him by questions (Matt. 12 : 38; 21 : 23; Luke 10 : 21, 22). They took the place, though they did not fulfill the functions, of the ancient prophets; and their authority as expounders of the law is recognized by our Lord himself (Matt. 23 : 1, 2). They kept schools for the teaching of the law and the commentaries thereon (Luke 2 : 46; Acts 5 : 34; compare with 22 : 3, and see Jos. Antiq. 17 : 6, 2); they also copied the law, and at a later date wrote commentaries upon it, and engaged with each other in fruitless and often heated discussions, respecting questions in rabbinical theology and casuistry. **Pharisees.** See note on Matt. 3 : 7. Their righteousness was one of external obedience to law merely; that of Christ's disciples must be higher—the obedience of the heart and the spirit. Observe, that Christ does not denounce the obedience of the Pharisees, here or anywhere in the N. T (compare 23 : 23); he denounces their hypocrisies; but he overturns formalism and legalism, not by denouncing it, but by propounding a higher standard. The true way to overcome evil is always by pointing out and inciting to a better way. **Ye shall in no case enter, etc.** Compare 7 : 21; 25 : 31–46; John 3 : 5; Phil. 3 : 4–10.

21–48. These verses embody in five examples illustrations of the general principles laid down in verses 17–20. They show how it is that Christ fulfills the law, and in what sense the Christian

time,ˣ Thou shalt not kill; and whosoever shall kill shall be in danger of the judgment:
22 But I say unto you, That whosoever is angry with his brother without a cause, shall be in danger of the judgment; and whosoever shall say to his brother, Raca, shall be in danger of the council; but whosoever shall say, Thou fool, shall be in danger of hell fire.

x Ex. 20:13; Deut. 5:17.

righteousness must exceed that of the Scribes and Pharisees.

21–26. FIRST EXAMPLE. *Law against murder.*

21. Ye have heard—viz., in the synagogues where the O. T. Scriptures were read in a course of lessons, on the Sabbath (compare Luke 16:29; Acts 13:27) —**that it was said by them of old time** —rather, probably, **to them of old time.** Either rendering is grammatically correct, but the weight of authority appears to sanction the latter, and the contrast throughout this chapter is not between Christ and Moses as law-givers, but between the laws addressed to the world in its childhood, and those addressed to the disciples of Christ as the children of God; between the law of servitude of the old time, and the law of liberty which Christ ushers in (Gal. 4:1–3, 7; James 1:25). **Thou shalt not kill.** Murder was prohibited (Exod. 20:13); the penalty was death (ch. 21:14); but provision was made for the escape of one accidentally killing another, from the revenge of the next of kin, and for determining whether the killing was or was not intentional (Numb., ch. 35). **Judgment.** Not the final judgment; the laws of Moses, like any other code of civil laws, depended for their enforcement on temporal rewards and punishments. Judges were appointed in every city (Deut. 16:18), according to Josephus, seven to each city. It was by this tribunal the case of the manslayer was determined (compare Numb. 35:13, 24, 25 with Josh. 20:4). It is to this judgment Christ here refers. The tribunal might, if they could not determine the case, certify it for decision to the Sanhedrim, the chief court of the Jews at Jerusalem.—(*Josephus' Ant.* 4:8, 14.)

22. Without a cause. There is some doubt whether this word has not been inserted by the copyists to soften the apparent rigor of the precept. However that may be, the Bible recognizes elsewhere a righteous anger (Ephes. 4:26; James 1:19; Ps. 7:11; Rev. 6:16). **Judgment,** *i. e.*, in Christ's kingdom, not as in verse 21, judgment in the Jewish commonwealth. There is between verses 21 and 22 a transition from the ancient law, which was enforced by temporal punishments, to the spiritual law, which is enforced by the judgments of God. But the Jewish terms "judgment," "council," and "hell-fire" are used metaphorically to indicate degrees in the divine penalties of the future world. **Raca**— *empty.* A general term of contempt. **Council.** The Sanhedrim, the highest court of judicature, answering as a judicial body to our Supreme Court, or rather to the English House of Lords, since it exercised both judicial and legislative functions. **Fool.** Rather, probably, *rebel.* *Raca* is a Hebrew word; probably the word used here was also, in the original, Hebrew; but in attempting to preserve the Hebrew sound in Greek characters, a Greek word was used. The Greek word means *fool,* the Hebrew *rebel.* If we preserve the Hebrew significance here the climax is preserved. Fool and Raca would, on the contrary, be nearly synonymous. If I am right in this the obnoxious word embodies a bitter judgment of one's spiritual state, decrees him to certain destruction, and answers to the most common form of modern profanity. **Hell-fire.** There are two words in the N. T. translated hell. One is *Hades* ($\mathring{q}\delta\eta\varsigma$), and always signifies simply the place of departed spirits; the other is *Gehenna* ($\gamma\epsilon\epsilon\nu\nu\alpha$), and is the word used here. It indicates, by a significant metaphor, the place of future punishment. To the southeast of Jerusalem was a deep and fertile valley called the vale of Hinnom, or, in Greek, Gehenna. In a particular portion of this valley, known as Tophet (Isa. 30:33; Jer. 7:31, 32; 19:6, 11), the idolatrous Jews burned their children in sacrifice to Moloch. In the reformation instituted by Josiah (2 Kings 23:10) this valley was polluted, and thereafter became the place for casting out and burning offal and the corpses of criminals. Hence the phrase, "fire of Gehenna," translated "hell-fire," was employed to indicate the place of future punishment. Here and in Matt. 10:28; 18:9; 23:15, 33; Mark 9:43, 45, 47; Luke 12:5; Jas. 3:6, the word translated by hell is *Gehenna;* and the idea conveyed is, undoubtedly, a place of punishment. In all other passages in the Bible where the word hell occurs, the meaning of the original would be more appropriately expressed by the word Hades.

Observe: 1. That the comparison of *judgment, council,* and *hell-fire* indicates that future punishment is adjusted according to the sin of the condemned; 2. That adjustment of punishment is graded exactly according to the sin, "to unjust anger the just anger and judgment of God, to public reproach a public trial, and hell-fire to that censure that adjudgeth another thither."— (*Lightfoot*); 3. That the outward expression of anger in words enhances the sin; the highest duty is not to be angry; nevertheless, if one is angry, it is a secondary duty to restrain all expression of it. Observe, also, how these two verses illustrate the meaning of the general prin-

23 Therefore, if thou bring thy gift° to the altar, and there rememberest that thy brother hath aught against thee,

24 Leave there thy gift before the altar, and go thy way; first be reconciled to thy brother, and then come and offer thy gift.

25 Agree with thine adversary quickly, whiles thou art in the way with him; lest at any time the adversary deliver thee° to the judge, and the judge deliver thee to the officer, and thou be cast into prison.

26 Verily I say unto thee, Thou shalt by no means come out thence, till thou hast paid the uttermost farthing.

27 Ye have heard that it was said by them of old time, Thou shalt not commit adultery:

28 But I say unto you, That whosoever looketh° on

y Deut. 16:16, 17....z Prov. 25:8; Luke 12:58, 59....a Job 31:1; Prov. 6:25.

ciple laid down in verse 17. "Is 'Be not angry' contrary to 'Do no murder?' or is not the one commandment the completion and the development of the other? Clearly, the one is the fulfilling of the other, and that is greater on this very account. Since he who is not stirred up to anger will much more refrain from murder, and he who bridles wrath will much more keep his hands to himself. For wrath is the root of murder, and you see that he who cuts up the root will much more remove the branches, or, rather, will not permit them so much as to shoot out at all."—(*Chrysostom.*)

23, 24. Gift. Sacrifice. Compare Matt. 8:4; 23:18, 19. **Altar**—in the Temple. To bring a sacrifice to the altar was the Jewish method of public worship. The modern equivalent would be, "If thou goest to church." **Hath aught,** *Justly or unjustly.* The question whether you are in the right or wrong does not arise. If there is a variance, it is to be reconciled. As God in Christ sought to reconcile the world unto himself (2 Cor. 5:19), so are we to seek to reconcile those that are in enmity to us. He that is sure he is right is the one to seek reconciliation. **Against thee.** If others have any complaints against us, and *we have not done all we can to remove them*, our worship is unacceptable; on the other hand, if we have aught against others, we are to forgive before we bring our offering (Mark 11:25, 26). **Leave there thy gift, . . . then come and offer thy gift.** The whole language implies the urgency of the case. It is better to let even the worship of God be interrupted than that brotherly love should not continue; and indeed there is no true worship where the heart fails in brotherly love. Compare with this teaching John 14:21, 23, with 15:12, 17; and 1 John 4:7, 8, 20. It gives a hint why prayer is often unavailing and worship unsatisfying. Compare John 9:31 and Isaiah 1:10-15.

Is Christ's direction here to be literally interpreted? Must the Christian, for example, stay away from the communion table if there is an unreconciled variance between himself and another? No! not if either, first, he has done all he can to remove it, or, second, he is ready to do all that he can and will put his resolution in execution at the first opportunity. If, however, he is unwilling to obey Christ's law of love, his worship is worse than useless. "The important thing is to go to thy brother, not with the feet, but with the heart."—(*Augustine.*) Provided, however, that the feet go as soon as possible. It is the love, not of sentiment, but of action, which is commanded. Compare James 2:15, 16.

25, 26. Officer. An official among the Jews whose position and duties were substantially those of a modern constable or police-officer. There is some difficulty in the interpretation of these verses, and an effort has been made to give them a symbolical meaning. But such a meaning is certainly secondary, not primary. **Adversary.** Not the devil, for we are not to agree with him; nor God, who is never represented in the N. T. as our adversary. The Roman law directed the plaintiff and defendant to make up the matter on their way to the judge; after the case came before the judge, the law must take its course. The primary reference is perhaps to this provision. It is, at all events, counsel on the side of earthly prudence. Worldly wisdom, as well as duty toward God, advises to speedy reconciliation; and the more imperious your opponent and the farther the quarrel has gone, the wiser is it to seek reconciliation. This is substantially the view of Chrysostom, of Lightfoot, and of Barnes. Alford adds a spiritual deduction, which is legitimate and may have been intended, but is not necessarily involved in the words. "As in worldly affairs it is prudent to make up a matter with an adversary before judgment is passed, which may deliver a man to a hard and rigorous imprisonment, so reconciliation with an offended brother in this life is absolutely necessary before his wrong cry against us to the Great Judge, and we be cast into eternal condemnation." **Farthing.** A small coin equal to two mites and equivalent to about seven mills of our money. "These words, as in the earthly example they imply future liberation, because an earthly debt can be paid in most cases, so in the spiritual counterpart they amount to a negation of it, because the debt can never be discharged."—(*Alford.*) Matt. 18:30; Luke 7:42.

27-32. SECOND EXAMPLE. *Law against adultery.*

27. Thou shalt not commit adultery. (Exod. 20:14.) By the Mosaic law the punishment of this crime was the death of both parties by stoning, Lev. 20:10; Deut. 22:22-27; but if the woman were a slave she was to be whipped, not put to death, and the man was to bring a tres-

a woman to lust after her, **hath committed adultery** with her already in his heart.

29 And if thy right eye offend thee, pluck it out, and cast *it* from thee; for it is profitable for thee that one of thy members should perish, and not *that* thy whole body should be cast into hell.[b]

30 And if thy right hand offend thee, cut it off, and cast *it* from thee: for it is profitable for thee that one of thy members should perish, and not *that* thy whole body should be cast into hell.

31 It hath been said, Whosoever shall put away his wife, let him give her a writing of divorcement:[c]

32 But I say unto you, That whosoever shall put away his wife,[d] saving for the cause of fornication, causeth her to commit adultery: and whosoever shall marry her that is divorced, committeth adultery.

33 Again, ye have heard that it hath been said by them of old time, Thou shalt not forswear thyself,[e] but shalt perform unto the Lord thine oaths;

34 But I say unto you, Swear not at all;[f] neither by heaven; for it is God's throne;

35 Nor by the earth; for it is his footstool; neither by Jerusalem; for it is the city of the great King.

36 Neither shalt thou swear by thy head, because thou canst not make one hair white or black.

37 But let your communication be, Yea, yea; Nay,

b Rom. 8:13; 1 Cor. 9:27....c Deut. 24:1; Jer. 3:1; Mark 10:2-9....d ch. 19:9; 1 Cor. 7:10, 11....e Lev. 19:12; Num. 30:2; Deut. 23:23...f ch. 23:16-22; Jas. 5:12....g Rev. 21:2, 10.

---

pass offering (Lev. 19:20-22). In case a wife were suspected of adultery by her husband, a singular ordeal was provided for her trial, the only case of trial by ordeal known to the Jewish law (Numb. 5:11-31).

28. Looketh .... to lust. Not every rising of evil inclination is classed with adultery; not every lust, nor every looking, but the *looking to lust*, *i. e.,* the *indulgence* in an evil imagination. Whether the evil act be outwardly committed, or be committed in imagination only, the outward act being restrained by fear or shame, does not determine the question of guilt. Neither does our Lord say that there is no difference between the act of imagination and the actual overt sin; but that God sees, recognizes, and condemns the former as a real violation of the law against adultery: as a civil statute it affects only the conduct; as interpreted by Christ, it applies to the inward man also. (Compare Job 31:1; Prov. 6:25.) For illustration of the violation of this law, thus interpreted, and the crimes to which it led, see the story of David and Bathsheba, 2 Sam., ch. 11.

29. If thy right eye—the more important of the two—**offend thee**—*i. e.*, tempts thee to sin. The original means primarily to cause one to stumble, or to fall. It is used in the N. T. generally, if not exclusively, in the sense of leading one into sin, or at least into moral perplexity. The following passages will suffice to indicate its various uses: Matt. 15:12; 17:27; 18:6; John 6:61; 1 Cor. 8:13. **Pluck it out.** A symbol of the thoroughness of the work. If self-denial is required, it is best to do it quickly and completely. **For it is better.** The greatest self-sacrifice is really for our self-interest. "The eye to be plucked out is the eye of concupiscence, and the hand to be cut off is the hand of violence and vengeance; *i. e.*, those passions are to be checked and subdued, let the conflict cost us what it may."—(*Porteus.*) But much more than that is meant; these verses make short work of all defenses of habits and recreations confessed to be injurious in their effects, but defended on the ground that they are not wrong *per se*. The hand and eye are not only in themselves *innocent*, they are, in their right use, *highly important*. To deprive one's self of them is both to maim the person and to lessen one's means of usefulness. Whatever, then, tempts the individual, or his neighbor, or the community, into sinful courses, *even though it be not only in itself innocent, but in its right employment important*, is to be put away until it ceases to be a source of temptation. Asceticism—that is, the denial of a real good for the sake of a higher good—has its root in a right principle, though its common manifestations have many of them been egregiously wrong. Compare for other illustrations of this general principle, in its wider application, Matt. 18:6-10; Rom. 14:19-21.

31, 32. The law referred to is to be found in Deut. 24:1. **Fornication.** This is not cited as another example of the contrast between the external law of Moses and the spiritual law of Christ, but as a further illustration of the subject of adultery. To put away one's wife, save for the one cause, or to marry one that has been put away, Christ declares to be embraced among the sins which the law against adultery, spiritually interpreted, prohibits. The general subject of divorce is more fully considered by Christ in Matt. 19:3-9. See notes there.

33-37. THIRD EXAMPLE. *Law against swearing.*

33-35. Thou shalt not forswear thyself—swear falsely. False swearing and profane and idle use of the name of God are both prohibited by the third commandment (Exod. 20:7). The Hebrew word which answers to *in vain* may certainly be rendered either way, and probably includes both. Compare Lev. 19:12. False swearing is yet more distinctly forbidden by Numb. 30:2 and Deut. 23:21-23. The false witness received the same punishment which was due for the crime to which he testified. (Deut. 19:16-18.) **Neither by heaven . . . nor by the earth.** "The Jews held all those oaths not to be binding in which the sacred name of God did not directly occur."—(*Alford* quoting Philo.) So *Lightfoot* quoting from the rabbinical books, "If any one swear by the heavens, by the earth, by the sun, it is not an oath." See, however, Matt. 23:16-22. Swearing, in ordinary conversation, is much

nay; for whatsoever is more than these, cometh of evil.[b]

38 Ye have heard that it hath been said, An eye for an eye, and a tooth for a tooth

[b] Jas. 5:12...J Ex. 21:24.

more common in the East than here. "The people now use the very same sort of oaths that are mentioned and condemned by our Lord. They swear by the head, by their life, by heaven, and by the Temple, or what is in its place, the church. The forms of cursing and swearing, however, are almost infinite, and fall on the pained ear all day long."—(*Thompson's Land and Book*, 2 : p. 284.) **God's throne .... God's footstool ... the city of the great King.** The significance of an oath consists in its calling God to witness the truth of the assertion. All such *quasi* oaths do this indirectly.

36. Neither ..... by thy head, because thou canst not make one hair white or black. Protestations of friendship were frequently confirmed by touching the forehead and swearing by it; and this custom is still maintained in the East. Christ says: Even your head is not your own; to swear by it is to swear by him who made it.

Christ here condemns all those "half-veiled" blasphemies which, common in our times as in his, are nearly all traceable, historically, to an appeal, more or less direct, to the name of God. They are either, (*a*,) like I *swan*, I *swore*, I *vum*, corruptions of I swear, I vow; or, (*b*,) like *gosh, god, golly*, corruptions of the name of God; or, (*c*,) like *gracious, goodness, mercy, glory*, etc., appeals to God by some one of his prominent attributes; or, (*d*,) like *mercy on me*, or *laws-a-massey*, an abbreviation of the solemn oath, "If this be not true, may the Lord have mercy on me;" or, (*e*,) like *darn it, dang it, darnation*, palpable abbreviations of damn and damnation, the most solemn possible of all forms of imprecation, generally on an enemy, real or imaginary, living or inanimate, a travestie on the Christian appeal to the God of Justice to do justice to wrong-doers (Rom. 12:19); or, (*f*,) like the *deuce*, the *dickens*, the *old nick*, all terms for the devil, and abbreviations of "to the devil," or "the devil take it," a less solemn form of the same imprecation; or, (*g*,) like *confound it, plague take it*, etc., an unconscious prayer to God to bring real or supposed enemies into confusion and failure (compare Psalm 40:14; 70:2); or, (*h*,) like *upon my soul, by my life*, a pledging of one's life, or one's eternal destiny, in support of his assertion, as in Josh. 2:12-14, in which case there is an implied call on God to execute the penalty. Thus nearly all the expletives used in common and even fashionable life to strengthen or confirm our assertions are degenerate oaths, a direct violation of the third commandment as Christ here interprets it. And it is no answer to this to say that those who use such phrases do not intend blasphemy by them; frequently those who use more directly the name of God in vain, mean nothing by their imprecation. *The meaningless use of such language is itself a violation of the simplicity of Christian discourse*, even when it does not indicate a bitter, angry, or irreverent mood.

37. Cometh of the evil. The word here translated "evil," when coupled with the article as it is here, in the Greek though not in our version (ὁ πονηρός, the evil), sometimes stands for the evil-one, *i. e.* Satan (Matt. 13:19; 1 John 2:13, 14), and is rendered *the wicked one*. This signification here would be in accordance with James 3:6. In the other and more general sense, it is true that all swearing, genteel or otherwise, *comes of evil*, *i. e.*, of an underlying consciousness that simple assertion is not enough, that our word is not to be trusted, that some witness must be called in to attest it; and as God, who knows all things, is the only witness, we call on him. If truth were perfect there would be no occasion to emphasize our assertions by such appeals; and in point of fact, falsehood and profanity generally are close companions. Throughout this chapter Christ is giving directions for the individual character, not for the community. This passage does not, therefore, necessarily forbid oaths in courts of justice, any more than verses 38 and 39 forbid punishment from being inflicted by the State. Yet it is true that even judicial oaths *come of evil*; *i. e.*, if truth were never violated in the community, there would be no need of solemn asseverations to give weight to testimony in the administration of justice. And, in fact, in Christian courts the oath, as an appeal to God, has been in a considerable measure superseded by a mere affirmation.

38-42. Fourth example. *Law of retaliation.*
38. An eye for an eye, etc. Exod. 21:24; Lev. 24:20; Deut. 19:21. Natural revenge does not stop at mere retaliation. For an insult is given a blow: for a blow with the fist one with the knife. The laws of Moses were a check on personal revenge and undue severity of punishment, for they forbade the injury inflicted to exceed the injury received. The same principle, viz., that the punishment should be *as* the offence, and determined by it, is found in the laws of Solon of Greece, in the laws of the twelve tables of Rome, and others. On the other hand, the laws of Draco (7th century B.C.) punished every crime, even petty theft and idleness, with death; and those of England, A.D. 1600,

CH. V.] MATTHEW. 95

39 But I say unto you, That ye resist not evil: but whosoever shall smite thee on thy right cheek, turn to him the other also.
40 And if any man will sue thee at the law, and take away thy coat, let him have *thy* cloak also.

41 And whosoever shall compel thee to go a mile, go with him twain.
42 Give to him that asketh thee, and from him that would borrow of thee turn not thou away.

j Prov. 20 : 22 ; 24 : 29 ; Rom. 12 : 17–19... k Isa. 50 : 6... l Deut. 15 : 7, 11.

263 crimes in the same manner, while those of Moses provided capital punishment but for twelve crimes. The Mosaic law of retaliation was permissive, not compulsory. The injured party might require retaliation in kind at the hands of the magistrate; but except in the case of murder (Numb. 35 : 31) he might take satisfaction in money, in which case the damages were adjusted according to the injury done (see Exod. 21 : 30). Such money redemption was ordinarily substituted for the infliction of the penalty. This law was for the regulation of the administration of justice by the government. Christ does not condemn it as a law of *justice*, but he declares in this and the next section (43–48) that his followers are to be governed in their personal relations by the law of *love*.

39. Resist not the evil—literally *the evil*, i. e., *the evil one*. Christ implies here what the Scripture elsewhere abundantly asserts, that the malice and wrong-doing of the world to the disciples of Christ is the work of the devil (compare 1 John 2 : 13, 14; Rev. 2 : 10). So he transfers our anger from the instrument to the real cause of the wrong-doing. "What then, it is said ; ought we not to resist the evil-one ? Indeed we ought, but not in this way, but as he hath commanded, by giving one's-self up to suffer wrongfully ; for thus shalt thou prevail over him."—(*Chrysostom*.) So Christ conquered Satan by yielding himself an unresisting victim to his malice.

40. Coat . . . cloak. The coat was a tunic made commonly of linen, and extending to the knees. The cloak or mantle was larger and more expensive, was commonly made nearly square, and was wrapped round the body like a cloak, but was thrown off for the purposes of labor. It was also used as a wrapper at night, hence *might not be taken by a creditor* (Exod. 22 : 26, 27). Christ's precept, then, is in principle, Submit to even a palpable injustice, without color of law, rather than resist even by an appeal to the law. This is not merely a precept of worldly wisdom, though worldly wisdom justifies it, nor an obsolete requirement applicable only to the heathen tribunals of Christ's day, nor an absolute law, so that a follower of Christ cannot ever apply to the courts for redress without violating Christ's prohibition. *These aphorisms are expressions of a Christian spirit, not enactments of a new law.* See below. It is, nevertheless, noticeable that the tendency of Christianity has been, first, to lessen personal resistance to evil, and second, to discourage lawsuits ; and that while the commentators have difficulty with this passage, Christian lawyers constantly advise their clients, *as matter of worldly wisdom*, to submit to almost any injustice rather than to involve themselves in a lawsuit. "To seek the redress of grievances by going to law is like sheep running for shelter to a bramble-bush."—(*Selwyn*.) "To go to law is for two persons to kindle a fire at their own cost to warm others, and singe themselves to cinders."—(*Bentham*.) A lawyer "is a learned gentleman who rescues your estate from your enemies, and keeps it himself."—(*Brougham*.) So far has this conviction gone that the abolition of all laws for the collection of debt, except in cases of fraud, is seriously considered by able jurists in this country. And yet English and American justice is immeasurably superior to that administered by Oriental or Roman courts in the time of Christ. Compare with this precept 1 Cor. 6 : 7.

41. Whosoever shall compel thee to go, etc. The word translated *compel* is of Persian origin. Footmen were employed from a very early period of history in carrying despatches (1 Sam. 22 : 17 ; 2 Chron. 30 : 6, 10). At a later period this service was performed with mules and camels (Esther 8 : 13, with 15 ; 8 : 10, 14). It was continued under the Roman government, and these heralds were authorized to compel any person to accompany them as guides or assistants, or to lend them a horse, boat, or other means of transportation. A similar law is in force in Persia to this day. The Jews particularly objected to the duty thus imposed on them. Christ's disciples were to yield to the demand, though oppressive and injurious.

42. Give to him that asketh of thee. Compare for a proper understanding of this verse Christ's promise to his disciples (John 14 : 14), and his own practical interpretation of it. He does not always give what we ask, but often far different (2 Cor. 12 : 8, 9). Sometimes, too, we do not receive because we ask amiss (James 4 : 3). In this, as in all else, Christ is his own interpreter, and his example explains his precept. "To give every thing to every one—the sword to the madman, the alms to the impostor, the criminal request to the temptress—would be to act as the enemy of others and ourselves."—(*Alford*.) It must never be forgotten that Christ throughout this sermon is speaking of the *spirit* which should animate his followers ; and the spirit of Christianity is one which leads the followers of Jesus

43 Ye have heard that it hath been said,ᵐ Thou shalt love thy neighbour, and hate thine enemy:

44 But I say unto you, Loveⁿ your enemies, bless them that curse you, do good to them that hate you,

m Deut. 23 : 6....n Rom. 12 : 14, 20.

Christ to give to every true want; judgment keeps it from becoming indiscriminating, and so injurious. Borrow. Contrast with this verse the spirit of the heathen world, as exemplified in the saying of Cicero, that alms should be given to a stranger only when it involves no privation to ourselves. Compare with it, as an evidence and illustration that Christ does but fulfill the spirit of the ancient law, the provision in Deut. 15 : 8-10.

CHRIST'S PRINCIPLES RESPECTING RETALIATION. In considering the significance of this entire passage respecting retaliation (vs. 38-42), it is to be remembered, (a,) that Christ throughout this sermon inculcates principles for the government of the individual, not of the community; and that, therefore, it does not affect, except indirectly, the right or duty of the community to use force in protecting itself or its members from evil; (b,) that it does not affect the question of the right of the community to overturn a tyrannical government, and substitute another and more just and equitable one in its stead; (c,) that it does not necessarily deny the right or duty of one to use force, if need be, in defending others intrusted to his protection, as the husband his wife, or the father his child; (d,) that it inculcates the *spirit* in which the disciple of Christ is to receive injuries personal to himself, and that to interpret it as a series of mere *rules* for the regulation of conduct is to fall into the very error of Phariseeism, which the Sermon on the Mount is aimed to correct. With these qualifications (if they are to be regarded as qualifications) the precepts are not difficult to be understood; the only serious difficulty is in complying with them. To set them aside, by treating them as Oriental forms of speech, as exaggerations which we are to qualify, as impracticable rules proposed only to stimulate us to greater gentleness, as an ideal which we are not to expect to realize in the present state of society, but only to strive toward, appears to me to be subversive of all right reading of the Bible. Let us either frankly say that Jesus was mistaken, and laid down principles which cannot be applied in the common intercourse of life, or let us accept those principles as coming with divine authority from a divine master, and measure our common intercourse of life by them. So accepted they will be seen to cover the whole ground of *personal resistance and retaliation* to wrong. They include injustice inflicted by personal violence (v. 39), that attempted to be inflicted by an appeal to the law (v. 40), and that inflicted by an oppressive and tyranical government (v. 41). In each case Christ counsels submission to wrong, rather than resistance to it; and he has abundantly interpreted these precepts by his own illustrious example; the first precept by his patient suffering of personal indignity (Matt. 26 : 67, 68; and compare Isa. 50 : 7); the second by his payment of a tax unjustly exacted (Matt. 17 : 24-27, and note there); the third by his yielding to the infliction of scourging and crucifixion after a trial which violated the forms of law as palpably as it contravened justice, and his refusal to permit the use of violence as a means of rescue. See report of his trial, and notes there, and compare Matt. 26 : 51-53; Luke 22 : 50, 51. Observe that, yielding himself, he protested against the injustice to which he nevertheless submitted (Matt. 26 : 55; John 18 : 19, 23), and, *seemingly* by a miracle, provided for the escape of his disciples (John 18 : 6-8).

On the other hand observe that, *even regarded merely as laws*, these aphorisms do not require *unlimited* yielding to wrong. Turning the other cheek does not require continued submission if experiment proves it unavailing; giving the cloak does not forbid the Christian from having recourse to the law; going two miles is not going indefinitely. Paul's precept, "If it be possible, as much as lieth in you, live peaceably with all men" (Rom. 12 : 18), evidently implies limits to non-resistance. He recognizes a right use of the sword (Rom. 13 : 4); and he himself appealed to Roman law for protection (Acts 16 : 37; 22 : 25), and directly to Cæsar from an unjust judge and a malignant prosecutor (Acts 25 : 11).

43–48. FIFTH EXAMPLE. *The law regulating our relations with enemies.*

43. No law is to be found in the O. T. answering the description here given. But the O. T. does inculcate in many passages an abhorrence of heathen character and heathen habits (Deut. 7 : 1, 2, 16, 23-26; 12 : 27, 32; Josh. 23 : 12, 13; Ps. 139 : 21, 22); while the law of love has an appearance of being confined in its application to the Israelites (Lev. 19 : 17, 18; compare Deut. 23 : 3-6). As we teach our children to abhor that which is evil in character and conduct, and to avoid all evil companions, but afterward build up on that a love for those who are evil and a spirit that seeks them out to redeem them, so God, in the childhood of the race, taught it only to abhor the evil practices and character of the heathen; but on this Christ built up the higher law of personal love to the wrong-doer, a love which is practically perfectly consonant with an abhorrence of their sinful practices, and of the sinful character of which those practices are the fruit. The Pharisee had con-

and pray for them which despitefully use you, and persecute you;
45 That ye may be the children of your Father which is in heaven: for he maketh his sun to rise on the evil and on the good, and sendeth rain on the just and on the unjust.

46 For if ye love them which love you, what reward have ye? do not even the publicans the same?
47 And if ye salute your brethren only, what do ye more *than others?* do not even the publicans so?
48 Be ye therefore perfect, even as your Father which is in heaven is perfect.

o Luke 23:34; Acts 7:60....p Job 25:3,...q Gen. 17:1; Deut. 18:13; Luke 6:36, 40; Col. 1:28.

founded the moral abhorrence of the sin with *personal* hate of the man; and the exact parallel to the precept here condemned is to be found in the rabbinical writings; *e. g.*, "An Israelite who sees another Israelite transgressing and admonishes him, if he repents not, is bound to hate him."

44. Love your enemies. This is in a measure interpreted by what follows. Yet it is a law of the heart, not of conduct merely; it means more than bless, do good, pray for; it is interpreted by God's love for us when we were yet enemies (Rom. 5:8; Ephes. 2:4, 5), and it is quite consistent with the utmost abhorrence of their wrong-doing, from which by love we seek to redeem them. **Bless them that curse.** Seek God's blessing on those who call down upon you God's curses (compare Rom. 12:14, 19–21). The Greek word (εὐλογέω), which in our version is here translated "*bless,*" never means in the N. T. to speak well of, nor does the word (καταράομαι), translated curse, ever mean to slander. The one signifies to invoke the divine blessing, the other to imprecate a curse. The latter is composed of two Greek words, signifying *prayer against.* For parallel to the direction of this verse, see Ephes. 4:32; for illustration of the precept Joseph's treatment of his brethren, Gen. ch. 45, especially verses 5, 10, 11, 15, and ch. 50:15–21. It should, perhaps, be added that the clauses in this verse, "Bless them that curse you and do good to them that hate you," are omitted from some of the best manuscripts. But as they appear in Luke 6:27, 28, where there is no question of their genuineness, there is no reason to doubt that they were uttered by Christ as we have them in our present report, though Matthew may have omitted them and they have been transferred from Luke to Matthew by some of the copyists of the latter. The 44th verse is the climax to which the sermon from verse 21 has conducted. "Seest thou how many steps He hath ascended, and how He hath set us on the very summit of virtue? Nay, mark it, numbering from the beginning. A first step is, not to begin with injustice; a second, after he hath begun, not to vindicate one's self by equal retaliation; a third, not to do unto him that is vexing us the same that one hath suffered, but to be quiet; a fourth, even to give one's self up to suffer wrongfully; a fifth, to give up yet more than the other wishes, who did the wrong; a sixth, not to hate him who hath done so; a seventh, even to love him; an eighth, to do him good also; a ninth, to entreat God himself on his behalf."—(*Chrysostom.*)

45. In this way ye shall become the children of your Father. Both a reason for and the reward of so loving and doing good to our enemies. As the climax of Christian duty is loving one's enemies, so the climax of Christian reward is the becoming like God (compare Ephes. 5:1.

46. The publicans. The Roman tax-gatherers. See note on Matt. 9:10, 11. They are here a type of purely worldly men. If the Christian acts on the same principles as the man of the world, what right has he to expect any different regard or treatment from God?

47. Salute. The Oriental salutation was generally in form a prayer for divine blessing (Gen. 43:29; Ruth 2:4; 1 Sam. 15:13; Ps. 129:8). The Pharisees only saluted members of the same religious faith; the modern Mohammedan confines his salutation to Mohammedans. Hence, Christ's inculcation was a direct innovation on the almost universal usage of his day. Its application to professing Christians who refuse to speak to those who have offended them is so plain as to need no enforcement. **More than others.** The Christian may not compare himself with others and be satisfied because he is *as* others. Both God and men expect *more* of him than of others, and this in the common intercourse of daily life.

48. Perfect. Rather *complete.* The word never signifies in N. T. usage sinlessness, but completion in Christian character in contrast with a half-finished and partial character, a character that is Christian in some parts and worldly and selfish in others. This verse sums up that portion of the Sermon on the Mount in which Christ has developed the Christian ideal of character. It is the complement of verses 17 and 20. In it Christ explains in what consists the fulfillment of the law and the prophets. "The ancient statutes," says Christ in effect, "forbade murder, adultery, false-swearing, cruelty in revenge. A complete obedience embraces the whole man, and brings the spirit as well as the members under allegiance to these laws. The ancient statute commanded love to your neighbor; the spirit of that statute requires love to all mankind. You are to aim not at an external

CHAPTER VI.

TAKE heed that ye do not your alms before men, to be seen of them: otherwise ye have no reward of your Father which is in heaven.

2 Therefore when thou doest *thine* alms, do not sound a trumpet before thee, as the hypocrites do in the synagogues and in the streets, that they may have glory of men. Verily I say unto you, They have their reward.

obedience to laws and regulations, but at the attainment of a character which in all its conduct shall conform to the law, and in all its faculties to the image of Him whose sons you are called to be." In brief, one may be an imperfect, but one cannot be a partial Christian. He may obey Christ imperfectly, but he cannot obey in part and disobey in part (6:24; compare Ephes. 4:13; Col. 1:28; 4:12). The lesser interpretation, as Alford, "Complete in your love of others, not one-sided or exclusive," has grown out of a fear of giving countenance to the doctrine of human perfectibility. But the passages which require perfection, *i. e.*, completion of character, are numerous and cannot be explained away. God requires perfection of his disciples as the wise teacher continually holds perfection before his pupils; not condemning those who fall short (see Rom. 8:1), but not allowing them to rest satisfied with incomplete attainment. "The goal is not brought to the racers, but the racers must strive to reach the goal."—(*Conder.*)

Ch. 6:1-34; 7:1-6. THIRD GENERAL DIVISION.—THE PRINCIPLES OF LIFE IN CHRIST'S KINGDOM CONTRASTED WITH THE PRACTICES OF THE PHARISEES.

1-18. The first eighteen verses of this chapter constitute a warning against the dangers of ostentation in religion, applied to *almsgiving*, 2-4; *prayer*, 6-15; and *fasting*, 16-18. The word *almsgiving* in the first verse should be rendered righteousness (see below), and the verse itself constitutes a general precept of which the verses following are particular applications, and constitutes, as it were, the text of this portion of the discourse, as do verses 17-20 of chapter 5 of the rest of that chapter. It may be paraphrased thus: I have set before you the nature of that righteousness of the spirit which the laws of God, as spiritually interpreted, require of you; I now warn you to be on your guard lest you fall into the snare of doing the deeds of your righteousness before men for the sake of securing their approval, instead of seeking only the approval of your heavenly Father.

1-4. FIRST EXAMPLE. *Almsgiving.*

1. Take heed. For the danger of ostentation in religion is one that must be watched against, one that easily ensnares the unwary disciple (compare Exod. 23:13; Deut. 11:16; Deut. 26:41; 1 Cor. 10:12). **Not to do your righteousness.** The best manuscripts have here *righteousness* (δικαιοσύνη), not *alms* (ἐλεημοσύνη), as in the received text and in our English version. There is some uncertainty about the reading; that which I have adopted is sustained by Lange, Schaff, Wordsworth, Alford, Tregelles, Tischendorf, Lachmann, Griesbach. **To be seen.** This qualifies the preceding clause. Not all doing of righteousness before men is condemned, not all public almsgiving, prayer, and fasting, but that *the object of which is human applause.* "We are to be seen to do good, but not to do good to be seen (Gal. 1:10)."—(*Wordsworth.*) **Otherwise,** *i. e.*, as explained below, if your object is human applause. **No reward of your Father.** Not no reward, but no reward from God. They who do righteousness for public applause receive public applause, *i. e.*, the very reward for which they strive.

2. Therefore. A specific deduction from the general principle. **When thou doest alms.** There is no question here as to whether almsgiving is or is not a wise form of charity, nor how far it is to be carried; nor in the sections below are the general questions of prayer and fasting considered. Christ simply takes the three chief "good works" of Pharisaism to illustrate the principle that in our religious life we are to avoid ostentation. Almsgiving, however, is abundantly enforced as a religious duty both in the Old and the New Testaments. The laws of Moses required provision to be made for the poor (Lev. 19:9, 10; 23:22; Deut. 14:28, 29; 15:11; 24:19; 26:9-13); and the importance of obedience to these precepts is recognized elsewhere in the Scriptures (Job 29:13; Ps. 41:1; 112:9; Prov. 14:31). The N. T. abounds not less in precepts whose spirit requires charity toward the poor (Luke 14:13; Acts 11:27-30; 20:35; Rom. 15:25, 27; 1 Cor. 16:1-4; Gal. 2:10; 1 Tim. 5:10); while at the same time the systematic begging carried on by the mendicant monks finds no sanction in its pages, and we are impliedly guarded against encouraging idleness by indiscriminate giving (2 Thess. 3:10). **Do not sound a trumpet.** "Not that they had trumpets, but he means to display the greatness of their frenzy by the use of this figure of speech, deriding and making a show of them thereby."—(*Chrysostom.*) It was customary to call the people together by a trumpet to see a great spectacle (Numb. 10:3; 2 Kings 9:13; Ps. 81:3); and even up to as late a period as the fifth century, when bells were first introduced in the churches, the people were summoned to public worship by the blowing of a trumpet. It is probable the reference is to this custom. It is possible that Mr. Barnes' conjecture may be correct, and that the Pharisees really did summon the beggars by the use of a trumpet, blown ostensibly to call them together,

3 But when thou doest alms, let not thy left hand know what thy right hand doeth.
4 That thine alms may be in secret: and thy Father, which seeth in secret, himself shall reward' thee openly.

5 And when thou prayest, thou shalt not be as the hypocrites *are:* for they love to pray standing in the synagogues and in the corners of the streets, that they may be seen of men. Verily I say unto you, They have their reward.*

r Luke 6 : 17 ; 14 : 14....s Prov. 16 : 5 ; Jas. 4 : 6.

really to make public proclamation of the charity about to be bestowed. It is said that the Mussulmen to this day are accustomed to call the poor together by a trumpet to receive gifts of rice and other kinds of food. **Hypocrites.** Literally, stage-player or actor; *i. e.,* one who puts on his religion as an actor puts on his character for the evening's performance. The virtues which he assumes as Hamlet and the vices which he represents as Macbeth are not his own. The word is said to be found in a religious sense only in the N. T. Our translation and our habitual usage of the word hypocrite deprives the sentence of its keen but delicate satire. **They have.** Gr. (ἀπέχω), *receive in full.* In Phil. 4 : 18, "I have all," the verb is the same. **Their reward.** The reward they seek.

3. Let not thy left hand know. Simply a pithy enforcement of the doctrine. Compare with it the Eastern proverb, "If thou doest any good, cast it into the sea ; if the fish shall not know it, the Lord knows it ;" or the rabbinical maxim, "He who gives in secret is greater than Moses himself ;" or the saying of Dryden, "The secret pleasure of a generous act is the great man's great bribe." For illustration of this precept, see Ruth 2 : 15-17.

4. Openly. Not only in the judgment at the last day (Matt. 25 : 40 ; Luke 12 : 8), but also in the bestowal of the divine favor, in the recognition of the invisible world now (Heb. 12 : 1), and sometimes in providential disclosures in this life. See for example the case of Cornelius, Acts 10 : 4, whose secret almsgiving has been published to the whole world. Observe that Christ does not condemn the desire for the approval of others ; but he lifts it up into a higher sphere. Strive, he says, not for the approval of *men,* whose standard of moral judgment is low, but for the approval of God and his holy angels. "It were not meet for him who desires glory to let go this our theatre, and take in exchange that of men. For who is there so wretched as that when the king was hastening to come and see his achievements, he would let him go, and make up his assembly of spectators of poor men and beggars ?"—(*Chrysostom.*)

In this passage Christ does not forbid public giving which he elsewhere commends (Mark 12 : 44), which the apostles by their example approved and by their words commanded in connection with the services of the early church (Acts 4 : 34, 35 ; 11 : 30 ; Romans 15 : 26, 27 ; 1 Cor. 16 : 1, 2), but giving for the sake of publicity *to be seen of men.* It is the *spirit* of ostentation which our Lord here condemns, as it is the *spirit* of purity and love which he has before commended. Neither does he directly condemn all appeals to men to give for the sake of what is expected of them by us ; and Paul based appeals to the Corinthians on this ground (2 Cor. 8 : 24 ; and see that chapter throughout). But all exhibiting charities, whether given with public announcement in great congregations or with a blazoning forth in the newspapers, are, *when bestowed thus publicly in order to be seen and applauded of men,* contrary to the spirit of these precepts ; of such givers we may say, as our Lord did, They receive here their full reward.

5-15. SECOND EXAMPLE. *Prayer.*

The significance of this passage is interpreted by an acquaintance with the prayer customs of the East formerly in existence among the Jews and still among the Mohammedans. The former had eighteen stated prayers which the pious were expected to repeat every day ; a summary of these was composed for those who had not the time or the memory to repeat the fuller forms. Special prayer was given by individual rabbis to their disciples for special occasions. Ejaculations, prayers, and blessings were added, to be repeated on various occasions. Certain set times for prayer were established, which the pious observed, leaving their work and repeating their prayer wherever they chanced to be. Long pauses were added before and after these prayers, so that it was not unfrequent to see a Jewish Rabbi in a praying position for three hours together. In their liturgies they repeated over and over again the same petition in slightly different phraseology ; and it was a proverb with them, "Every one that multiplies prayer is heard." The same practices still exist among the Mohammedans. The rules for daily and especial prayer are prescribed with a most minute detail. Five daily canonical prayers are prescribed ; they must be uttered at the appointed time, wherever the Mussulman may chance to be, whether in the mosque, the market-place, or the house ; each prayer must be repeated a prescribed number of times and in a prescribed posture ; any failure in the slightest particular ruins the whole, and the prayer must be repeated again from the beginning. Notwithstanding Christ's precepts, the same ritualism was introduced into the Christian church. In the fourth century seven times of devotion were required to be ob-

6 But thou, when thou prayest, enter into thy closet, and, when thou hast shut thy door, pray to thy Father which is in secret; and thy Father, which seeth in secret,⁴ shall reward thee openly.
7 But when ye pray, use not vain repetitions,ʷ as the heathen *do:* for they think that they shall be heard for⁵ their much speaking.
8 Be not ye therefore like unto them; for your Father knoweth⁶ what things ye have need of, before ye ask him.

⁴ Ps. 34 : 15 ; Isa. 65 : 24. . . . ⁵ Ecc. 5 : 2. . . . ⁶ 1 Kings 18 : 26, etc. . . . ʷ Luke 12 : 30 ; John 16 : 23-27.

served at least by all the clergy and members of religious bodies; prayers were appointed to be said and Psalms to be repeated for each hour; and to such an extent was the ritualism carried, that if the entire service were observed, it would have required nearly the whole twenty-four hours. These canonical hours of prayer are still maintained by the religious devotees of the Roman Catholic church.

5. Standing. This was not in itself a sign of ostentation; it was a common attitude of prayer (1 Sam. 1 : 26 ; 1 Kings 8 : 22). It is not the standing, but standing *in public places*, which Christ condemns; and this not as an act, but as an indication of an ostentatious spirit. **Synagogues.** As with the Roman Catholic the cathedral, and with the Moslem the mosque, so with the Jews the synagogue stood open for purposes of prayer.

6. Closet. Sometimes in the women's apartments, sometimes over the porch or on a part of the roof, is a room in most Oriental houses, from which all are excluded except the women, their domestics, and the master of the house. This was, perhaps, the inner chamber referred to in 1 Kings 20 : 30 and 22 : 25, and the closet referred to here and in Matt. 24 : 26 ; Luke 12 : 3.

The true significance of these verses is lost if they are made a rule for the regulation of times or places of prayer. The whole gist of the caution is in the words, "*that they may be seen of men.*" If one makes an ostentation of his secret prayer, he violates the spirit of this law; if he prays in public places, but in secrecy of heart and feeling, he obeys its spirit. Certainly Christ does not condemn public prayer, nor even all private prayer in public places; at least his own disciples did not so understand him, for they went to the Temple to pray (Acts 3:1). The habit of employing the church as a place of private prayer, universal in the Roman Catholic church, and borrowed by that church from the East, probably grew out of the fact that the worshippers had not, and many of them still have not, any privacy at home. To such the church is the closet. Compare Luke 18 : 10 for an instance in which it was a closet to the publican and a public place to the Pharisee. There may even be cases in which it becomes a duty to pray publicly to be seen of men; in Daniel's case retirement would have been cowardice (Dan. 6 : 10). On the other hand, there is no virtue in a closet. "Isaac's closet was a field (Gen. 24 : 63); David's closet was his bed-chamber (Ps. 4 : 4 ; 77 : 6); our Lord's closet was a mountain (Matt. 14 : 23); Peter's closet was a housetop" (Acts 10 : 9). It is as possible to be ostentatious of private prayer as it is to be humble and indifferent to men in prayer in public places. The commentators, especially the ancient ones, have given to this deduction its true significance. "If thou shouldest enter into thy closet, and having shut the door, shouldest do it for display, the doors will do thee no good."—(*Chrysostom.*) "Enter into the secret chamber of thine own mind, wherever thou art, shut the door thereof against the world, and commune with God."—(*Ambrose.*) "We may enter the chamber of our hearts even in a crowd."—(*Wordsworth.*) "Every man can build a chapel in his heart."—(*Jeremy Taylor.*) Christ condemns not the place, the attitude, or the act, but the spirit which chooses the place, determines the attitude, and inspires the act.

7, 8. Use not vain repetitions, etc. The meaning of this prohibition is interpreted to us by the Eastern custom of repetition in prayer, on which see note above. Not much praying is condemned (see Luke 11 : 5-8 ; 18 : 1-7 ; 21 : 36 ; Rom. 12 : 12 ; Ephes. 6 : 18 ; 1 Thess. 5 : 17); nor even every kind of repetition (Matt. 26 : 44); but repeating *for the sake of repetition*, of which the devotions of the prophets of Baal afford an illustration (1 Kings 18 : 26). This warning does not affect the use of a liturgy in public prayers, nor even in private devotion, but the repeating of prayers, *whether written and learned, or fallen into as a mere routine*, without real consideration of its meaning, which latter habits many parents, with the best intentions, unconsciously form in their children. It condemns all mere *saying of prayers*. The practice in the Roman Catholic church of repeating *pater nosters, i. e.,* the Lord's prayer, and measuring the merit of the observance by the number of times the prayer is repeated, is in direct contravention of the precept here given. Thus the very prayer which our Lord gave, not as a form, but as a prohibition to all formalism in prayer, has been made a means of perpetuating the very evil which he required his disciples to shun, a striking illustration of the truth of the precept, "the letter killeth." Contrast with Christ's prohibition the direction of Liguori, a Roman Catholic writer of acknowledged standing in that church: "We must always act like beggars with God, always saying, Lord, assist me ; Lord, assist me ; keep your hand upon me ;

9 After this manner therefore pray ye: Our Father which art in heaven, Hallowed be thy name. 10 Thy kingdom come. Thy will be done in earth, as *it is* in heaven.

give me perseverance; give me your love." **Your Father knoweth what things ye have need of before ye ask him.** And better than we know, and answers more fully than we ask or even think (Ephes. 3:20), and teaches us both how to pray and what to pray for (Rom. 8:26). *Why then pray?* Because God wills it (Ezek. 36:37); it forms in us the wish, though it does not inform Him of the need; it prepares us to receive what he is willing to grant; it strengthens us, because it brings us into communion with Him who is our strength; it is due to Him as well as needed by ourselves. "Not to inform Him, but to exercise ourselves in communion with Him."—(*Chrysostom.*) "It is one thing to inform the ignorant and another thing to beseech the omniscient."—(*Jerome.*) Nor is this all. Though he knows what things we have need of, he has made our preferring of requests the condition of his promise to supply our need (Ezek. 36:37; Matt. 18:19; 21:22; Luke 11:13; John 14:13, 14; Heb. 4:16, etc.); and he vouchsafes blessings in answer to persistent prayer which are not given to the prayerless, nor even to the lukewarm petitioner (Matt. 17:21; Luke 18:1–8). If we ask why, the sufficient answer is, Even so, Father, for so it seemed good in thy sight. But the recognition of this truth that our Father knoweth what things *we have need* of, and not merely what things we desire, should always underlie our praying: if it does, it will make "Thy will, not mine, be done," to be the accompaniment of every prayer.

9–13. THE LORD'S PRAYER. This prayer is given in a slightly different form by Luke 11:1–4, who says that Christ gave it to his disciples in answer to their request, "Teach us to pray." The improbability that Christ should have twice taught the same form of prayer to his disciples, or that they, having once received from him a form of prayer, should have requested one again, has led some to the opinion that the prayer was really given at that time, but was inserted by Matthew here because cognate to the subject of the sermon. But this opinion is, at best, only a *surmise*, and the question is not very important. We have the prayer; when it was given, and whether once or twice, is a matter of secondary moment. The opinion that it is composed largely of forms then already existing in Jewish formulæ is said by Alford to rest on "very slender proof." That there are parallels to some petitions in the rabbinical writings is certain; but it is also certain that no one can be sure how much of the seemingly Christian precepts of the Talmud, no part of which was reduced to writing until the 2d century after Christ, was in fact taken from the instructions of Christ. The literature upon this prayer would of itself make a library. For eighteen centuries the Christian church has been studying it. To attempt to condense into a few paragraphs the fruits of this study would be idle; the result would be unsatisfactory. I shall simply attempt to give the meaning of the petitions of which the prayer is composed, leaving the reader to deduce his own spiritual conclusions, or to look for them in some of the sermons and homilies that have been written on this prayer of prayers.

9. After this manner. Does Christ prescribe this as a set form of prayer for public or private use, or both, to take the place of the forms of prayer in vogue then among the Jews, and now among the Mohammedans, or does he merely indicate the spirit and manner in which we should approach God? In favor of the first opinion are—first, The language of this verse, which is literally *Thus therefore pray ye*, and that of Luke, which is yet more definite, "*When ye pray say;*" second, The fact that the early fathers all treated it as not only a pattern or model of prayer, but also as a form to be used in the words in which Christ prescribed it; their opinions are collated in Bingham's Antiquities, book 13, chap. 7. In favor of the latter opinion are—first, That it is reported in different forms by Matthew and Luke, and if the Holy Spirit had intended to give a form, that form would have been preserved unimpaired by the Evangelists in both reports; second, That there is no indication that it was ever used as a form by Christ himself, or by his Apostles subsequent to his ascension; it first appears as part of a ritual in the third century, (see Tholuck on the Lord's Prayer); third, Christ here offers this prayer in illustration and enforcement of the doctrine that our prayers are not to be vain repetitions; and the doctrine that substituted one form for another, and *made its use obligatory on his followers*, violates the spirit of his teaching here and elsewhere, which is, not indeed against all religious forms, but strongly against all formalism in religion (compare John 4:23, 24). I need not say that I hold to the latter view; though in that view there is nothing opposed to the practice of employing the Lord's Prayer in formal service either in the family, the Sabbath school, or the church, *provided it is not imposed on the worshipper as a law*, but is simply employed as a vehicle for the expression of his real desires.

Our Father. Observe the significance of the word *our*. "How can we look round upon the people whom we habitually feel to be separated from us, those of an opposite faction, or whom we have reason to despise, or who have made themselves vile and are helping to make others vile, and then teach ourselves to think that in the very highest exercise of our lives they are associated with us, that when we pray we are praying for them and with them, that if we do not carry their sins to the throne of God's grace we cannot carry our own?"—(*Condensed from Maurice on the Lord's Prayer*.) So Chrysostom, referring to the use of the plural number throughout (see verses 11, 12 and 13), deduces the doctrine that, whether we pray alone or in common with others, we are always to pray for our brethren. To the same effect Augustine: "The Prayer is fraternal; he does not say 'My Father,' but 'Our Father.'" The Fatherhood of God does not here appear for the first time. Some traces of it are to be found in the O. T. (Isa. 1:2; 63:16; Mal. 1:6). The simile was not unknown in heathen religions. Among the North American Indians the Great Spirit was sometimes known as the "Father and Mother of Life." In the hymns of the Vedas, of the Hindoos, he is addressed sometimes as "Father." In the Zend-Avesta, the Persian sacred writings, is an appeal to him "who was from the beginning the Father of the pure creatures." In Plato's Timæus is a reference to "the supreme God, Father and Maker of all things." And Plutarch both embodies and interprets the symbol in the declaration, "Since, therefore, the world is neither like a piece of potter's work nor joiner's work, but there is a great share of life and divinity in it, which God himself communicated to and mixed with matter, God may properly be called Father of the world." But in all *heathen* use of this symbol, so far as I have been able to discover, the idea involved is *not parental love, or parental care*, but simply *production and begetting*. God is represented as the Father, not particularly of humanity but of all life, because all comes forth from him. The same belief underlaid even the worship of Baal and Ashtoreth, who personified the producing powers of nature, one in the person of a male, the other in the person of a female. But nowhere in literature, outside of the Bible, and that which has been inspired by the Bible, is to be found a recognition of the truth that the relation of a father to his child, and the government of a father over his child, that is, the government of a personal, providing, sympathizing love, is the best symbol for the interpretation of the relations between God and man. Even the early fathers would not allow any but communicants to use this passage, because "no one that was not baptized could presume to say 'Our Father which art in heaven.'" —(*Theodoret, quoted in Bingham's Antiquities*, 10:5.) And some relic of this idea lingers in modern theology. Yet that there is a peculiar sense in which those are the children of God who have been adopted into the household of faith through Jesus Christ, is implied in such passages as Rom. 8:14; Gal. 3:26; 1 John 3:1. For practical deductions from this truth see Gal. 4:6; Ephes. 5:1; 2 Pet. 1:4; 1 John 3:10; 5:1.

Which art in heaven. The abode of the blessed, which is generally represented in the Bible as in the heavens. The Bible, while it recognizes and teaches the omnipresence of God, teaches also, and nowhere more clearly than here, his proper personality. We are not, however, to conclude from this or other parallel passages (e. g., Ps. 115:3; Isa. 57:15; 66:1) that God has, in any proper sense of the term, a local habitation; on the contrary, while it sometimes pictures him to our thought as in the heavens, in order to give definiteness to our conception, it also declares that he dwells in the hearts of the contrite and humble (Isa. 57:15; compare John 14:20, 23), and that no place is without his presence (Psalm 139:7-10). Contrast with the spirit of this opening address of our Lord's Prayer the modern philosophy which declares that "God is the highest dream of which the human soul is capable," of that he is "an Inscrutable Power," whose "nature transcends intuition and is beyond imagination," and whose mode of being may "transcend Intelligence and Will." Let any one who wishes to contrast modern philosophy and the religion of Jesus essay a prayer to "The Inscrutable Power," or "The Infinite," or "The Ultimate Cause," or the "Unconditional," the common appellations which rationalism employs.

Hallowed be thy name. At first it might seem this should be a commandment addressed to us rather than a prayer addressed by us. In truth, however, the whole prayer is an amplification of this. God's name is hallowed, honored, lifted up for worship and adoration, just in the measure in which his kingdom comes, his will is done, his providential care and his forgiving kindness is manifested among men. The highest appeal we can make to him is for his own name's sake, for his great mercy's sake, or for Jesus' sake, which is, in fact, the same thing (Psalm 6:4; 25:11; 31:3, 16; 44:26). To suppose that we are required to begin every prayer with an ascription of praise to God is entirely to miss the meaning. But underlying every true prayer is the deep wish, born of a supreme and filial love for God, that in all that he does for us, and enables us to do, his name may be hallowed. We come into the true spirit of prayer only as, in all our praying, his name is in our thought

11 Give us this day our^d daily bread:
12 And forgive us our debts,^e as we forgive our debtors.

13 And lead us not into^f temptation, but deliver us^g from evil: For thine^h is the kingdom, and the power, and the glory, forever. Amen.

d Prov. 30 : 8; Isa. 33 : 16. ...e ch. 18 : 21-35; Luke 7 : 40-48....f ch. 26 : 41; Luke 22 : 40, 46....g John 17 : 15....h Rev. 5 : 12, 13.

above every name, and we have the desire to see it everywhere so recognized.

10. Thy kingdom come. (See on Matt. 3 : 2.) Here the kingdom of God means all that the words in all their applications involve; the perfect obedience and allegiance of all created beings to the will and word of God. **Thy will be done**—*respecting* us, in God's providential dealings (Luke 22:42; Acts 21:14); *by* us, in our daily life (John 6:38; 17:18; Ephes. 6:6.); *in* us, by the conformity of our character to the divine image (John 17:23; Rom. 12:2; Col. 4:19; 1 Thess. 4:3). Observe that this is much more than a mere *submission* to the will of God. It is not "Give us such and such things, nevertheless thy will be done." This petition stands first in the prayer as it should stand first in our hearts; the expression of the pre-eminent desire of our souls that God's will, not our own, may be accomplished, and that ours may be made subject to it. **In heaven.** Not among the heavenly bodies, though the perfect conformity of the stars to the divine law may serve as an illustration of that perfect obedience for which we are to look and pray, but in the spiritual heavens. "Not by blind agents, but by intelligent, spiritual creatures; by wills which might have fallen but which stood in holy, cheerful obedience."—(*Maurice.*)

11. Our daily bread. There is some difficulty in translating the Greek word rendered in our version *daily*. The better opinion appears to be that it signifies not daily but *necessary for our sustenance*. It is, then, a prayer simply for sufficient bread to satisfy our real wants, and receives an interpretation from Paul's exhortation, "having food and raiment, let us be therewith content" (1 Tim. 6:8). The word translated bread (ἄρτος) is said to stand generally for food, and by Mr. Barnes to denote everything necessary to sustain life. Yet literally it signifies only bread, and the fact that this word is used, and not one of the more general ones (ἰχθύα or τροφή) translated respectively *meat* and *food*, is an indication of the simplicity which should characterize our earthly desires, and our petitions for their satisfaction. The ancient commentators considered that the term bread, as here used, signifies food for the soul as well as food for the body, and some of them even referred it directly to the body of Christ, and from it framed an argument for the daily celebration of the Lord's Supper. But the word bread (ἄρτος) is never used in the N. T. to signify anything but mate-

rial food, except in cases where the context clearly indicates a purely metaphorical use, as in John, ch. 6, where Christ employs it emblematically, but distinguishes spiritual from material food by such phrases as "bread from heaven," or "true bread," or "bread of life." We are to take the words of Scripture in the sense in which the speaker or writer would have expected his audience or readers to have taken them, except where he himself gives a different interpretation, or peculiar circumstances compel the belief that he was willing to be misunderstood for the time; and it is very clear from John 6 : 34 (compare John 4 : 15, and Mark 8 : 15, 16), that the disciples would not have understood this passage in a spiritual sense. This petition is not, then, a prayer for a supply of *all* our wants; so to interpret it is to lose its significance. It is our warrant for carrying to God our *physical* wants. The lowest and most animal of them all, hunger, is taken because that includes by necessary implication all the rest; and the limits on our right of petition, so to speak, are given in the fact that we are taught to pray for just so much bread as is necessary day by day for our sustenance, leaving all the future in God's hands. He who can be content with to-day's loaf, and trust the morrow wholly to God, has learned the spirit of this prayer as interpreted by verses 25-34 below.

12. And forgive us. The Greek word translated *forgive* is the same translated *left* in Matt. 4 : 20, 22; *sent away* in ch. 13 : 36; Mark 4 : 36; *put away* in 1 Cor. 7 : 11, 12. I refer to these passages to give the English reader an idea of the primary meaning of the word, which is to *send away, dismiss, set free*. The Bible idea of forgiveness is not merely a remission of penalty or an absence of vengeance, *but an absolute putting away of the sins*, so that he who is wronged remembers them no more against the wrongdoer, and he who has done the wrong carries them no more in his memory as a burden. It is interpreted by such passages as Isa. 1 : 18; 43 : 25; Micah 7 : 19; John 1 : 29; and by the annual ceremony among the ancient Jews of binding the sins of the nation upon the scape-goat, and sending them away into the wilderness (Lev. 16 : 21, 22). But these symbols are not satisfied by a mere literal forgetting of the transgression; on the contrary, it is clear from Matt. 5 : 44 that we are often to remember the wrong we have suffered that we may repay it by love, and from Paul's experience (1 Tim. 1 : 12-17), the wrong we have done that we may augment our love to Him who has forgiven us. **As.** Not merely *inasmuch as*, or *because*, but literally *as, i. e., in the manner in which* we forgive. As elsewhere the Bible makes the divine forgiveness a type and model for us in the forgiveness of personal wrong, so here we are required to make our forgiveness interpret to God the forgiveness which we ask from him (compare Ephes. 4:32; Col. 3:13). If any Christian is perplexed by the question—How does Christ's law of forgiveness require that I should feel toward him who has wronged me? he may answer it by another question—How do I wish Christ to feel toward me? **Debts—debtors.** Sins are compared to debts because they represent all that duty and love which we owe to him but have never by our past lives paid, all that in which we have come short of the glory of God. Not merely our positive sins need forgiveness, but our failures as children and servants of God to fulfill the mission in life he lays upon us. So the phrase "our debtors" includes not only those who owe us confession and reparation for positive wrong-doing, but also all those who are in a more literal sense our debtors, all who in the common walks of life have come short of their duty to us. As we treat, not merely our enemies, but our children, our servants, our employees, all who are under obligations of service to us, so we may expect God to treat us; as we are willing he should exact of us, we may exact of them. Observe, the prayer assumes that we have forgiven and do habitually forgive or release. If we understand this as a mere rule of prayer we miss its meaning; the whole relates to the spirit rather than to the form of prayer, and this petition is interpreted by ch. 5:23, 24.

13. Lead us not into temptation. More strictly and properly, trial; *i. e.*, experiences that try the character. The term is general, but it includes those experiences that involve temptation to sin. Though God never tempts any man, that is, never solicits him to evil (James 1:13), yet he orders our life and decides what shall be the measure of its trials and temptations (1 Cor. 10:13; compare Job 1:12; 2:6). Directly contrary to the spirit of this prayer is the temper which courts trial for the sake of displaying to others or to one's self the strength of resistance; the temper which twice led Peter into presumption and consequent danger (Matt. 14:28-30; 26:69-75). In entire accordance with it is the spirit which, when God's providence does bring us into temptation, boldly faces it, and, by faith in him, vanquishes it, and even rejoices in the conflict and the victory (compare James 1:2; 4:7). Observe the spirit with which Christ met the tempter in the wilderness, and observe that it is after that experience of temptation that he instructs his disciples to include this petition in their prayer. *To lead into* temptation is not equivalent to *bringing under the power* of temptation; God never does that. **Deliver us from the evil one.** Not merely evil, either in the moral or the physical sense; but the devil, the author of all temptation. Compare with this petition Christ's prayer for us (John 17:15). **For thine is the kingdom, etc.** There is considerable doubt whether this doxology was not added subsequently, when the prayer came into use as a liturgy. This appears to be the opinion of the best scholars, among whom may be mentioned Tischendorf, Wordsworth, Alford, Bloomfield, Lange. On the other hand, Chrysostom comments on it without any apparent doubt of its authenticity. For a statement of the arguments for and against it, see note by Dr. Schaff in Lange on Matthew, Addenda, 567. It grounds the entire petition on the *royalty* of God, being an appeal of a subject to his Lord and King; on the *power* of God, being an appeal of weakness to One mighty and able to help (compare 8:2); and on the honor and good name of God (compare Exod. 32:11, 12), our victory over the evil one being not to our glory, but to God's (compare 5:16; 1 Pet. 2:12; Ephes. 2:8-10).

The commentators have undertaken to analyze the Lord's Prayer, to divide it into sections, to trace in it a parallel to the Ten Commandments on the one hand, and to the beatitudes on the other, and even to find in its arrangement an evidence of the doctrine of the Trinity, all of which the reader will find at some length in Lange's Commentary. To me this all seems quite foreign to a prayer whose beauty is its perfect simplicity. The best analysis is the quaint one which Matthew Henry affords: "This prayer, as indeed every prayer, is a letter from earth to heaven. Here is the inscription, *Our Father*; the place, *in heaven*; the contents, in the several errands; the close, *for thine is the kingdom*; the seal, *Amen*; and, if you will, the date too, *this day*." More important to study than any analysis of this prayer is the spirit which breathes through it all, and which it is its chief object to inculcate. It approaches God not with fear and awe, but with childlike confidence; it finds him not hard to be entreated; its petitions are framed in the simplest possible forms; it is humble, without being groveling; submissive, without being abject; earnest, without being clamorous. We have in Christ's history two records of prayer offered by him (Matt. 26:39, 42, 44 and John, ch. 17). The same spirit breathes in his example as in his precept. The true significance of both is interpreted by the contrast which is afforded in the prayers of the prophets of Baal (1 Kings 18:26). Alas! that so much of public prayer should conform more to the example of the heathen prophets than to that of Jesus of Nazareth.

14 For if ye forgive men their **trespasses**, your heavenly Father will also forgive you.
15 But if ye forgive not men their trespasses, neither will your Father forgive your trespasses.¹
16 Moreover, when ye fast, be not, as the hypocrites, of a sad countenance: for they disfigure their faces, that they may appear unto men³ to fast. Verily I say unto you, They have their reward.
17 But thou, when thou fastest, anoint **thine head**, and wash thy face;
18 That thou appear not unto men to fast, but unto thy Father which is in secret: and thy Father, which seeth in secret, shall reward thee openly.
19 Lay not up for yourselves treasures upon⁴ earth, where moth and rust doth corrupt, and where thieves break through and steal:
20 But lay up for yourselves treasures in¹ heaven, where neither moth nor rust doth corrupt, and where thieves do not break through nor steal;
21 For where your treasure is, there will your heart be also.
22 The light of the body is the eye:ᵐ if therefore thine eye be single, thy whole body shall be full of light:
23 But if thine eye be evil, thy whole body shall be full of darkness. If therefore the light that is in thee be darkness, how great is that darkness!
24 No man can serve two masters:ⁿ for either he

1 Eph. 4 : 31; Jas. 2 : 13....j Isa. 58 : 3, 5....k Prov. 23 : 4; Luke 18 : 24, 25; Heb. 13 : 5....l Isa. 33 : 6; Luke 12 : 33, 34; 1 Tim. 6 : 19....
m Luke 11 : 34, 36....n Luke 16 : 13.

14, 15. Compare 18 : 23-35, and 5 : 7, and references there. "He that cannot forgive others breaks the bridge over which he must pass himself; for every man has need to be forgiven."—(*Lord Herbert.*)

16-18. THIRD EXAMPLE. *Fasting.* For a general discussion of the question whether fasting is appropriate under the Christian dispensation, and for some information respecting Jewish fasts, see Matt. 9 : 14, 15, and notes.

16. Disfigure their faces. By leaving them unwashed and by covering them with ashes (Esther 4 : 3; Job 2 : 8; Lam. 3 : 16; Dan. 9 : 3; Jonah 3 : 6). This use of ashes, which, with sackcloth, had been at first a symbol of mourning, and was its natural expression in an age and among a people who gave expression to feeling by symbolic acts rather than by words, had been perverted by the Pharisees, and they employed the symbols of mourning without the real sorrow which alone gave the symbol significance. They forbade all washing or anointing of the body during fasting; and it was a 'rabbinical proverb, "Whoever makes his face black in this world, God shall make his face to shine in the world to come." The spirit of Christ's precept forbids not merely disfiguring of the person, but all simulating of feeling of sorrow, and, impliedly of any feeling, for the purpose of appearing unto men to possess it. Compare, on the spirit of true fasting, Isaiah 58 : 3-7.

19-34. FURTHER CONTRAST OF PHARISAISM AND THE CHRISTIAN RELIGION.

From a rebuke of the ostentation of Pharisaism Christ passes to a rebuke of its spirit of greed. The two vices generally accompany each other (Matt. 23 : 14; compare Luke 16 : 14). Through this discourse Christ does not merely nor chiefly rebuke the wrong, but points out a more excellent way; so here, from a mere condemnation of greed (19-23), he proceeds to set forth the principle upon which and the spirit in which his disciples are to solve the problem presented by the twofold demands which this life makes on the body and the higher life makes on the soul (24-34). For a paraphrase of the passage and a consideration of its general significance, see note below.

19. Treasure not for yourselves treasures. All laying in store is not forbidden; but hoarding; *i. e.*, the accumulation of wealth *as our treasure in which our heart is*. Compare, for an illustration of the spirit forbidden, Luke 12 : 16-21. **Where moth and rust.** *The first reason for not laying up our treasures upon earth.* All such treasures are transient; they are *liable* to be taken from us, and we are *certain* to be taken from them (Prov. 23 : 5; 1 Tim. 6 : 7, 8; compare also Eccles. 5 : 10; 6 : 2). One of the most common forms of riches in the East was garments, which were liable to moth (Josh. 7 : 21; 2 Kings 5 : 22; compare James 5 : 2, 3). **Rust.** The Greek word would be more literally rendered "*eating*," and it is so translated in 1 Cor. 8 : 4. It signifies here the whole corrosive influence of time, "which eats into and consumes the fairest and the best-protected possessions."

20. But treasure up for yourselves treasures in heaven. Compare Luke 12 : 33. How? By charity administered as unto Christ (Matt. 25 : 40; 1 Tim. 6 : 18, 19); by spiritual labors for others (James 5 : 19, 20); by personal growth in grace (2 Peter 1 : 5-11).

21-23. *The second reason for not hoarding; its corrupting influence on the soul.* **Where your treasure is, there will your heart be also.** The *heart* is, in Scripture, used for the seat and centre of man's life, especially the desires and aspirations, out of which are the issues of life (Prov. 4 : 23). If we amass our treasures on earth, our desires and aspirations, and so our life, will be of the earth earthy.

22, 23. The light of the body is the eye. If thine eye be clear, thy whole body shall be full of light; but if thine eye be diseased, thy whole body shall be full of darkness. What the eye is to the body, the *heart*, not the intellect, is to the soul. If the heart be pure, we see God and heavenly things, and take hold on the truth, and are made righteous (Matt. 5 : 8; Rom. 10 : 10); if it be corrupt, all is corrupt (Matt. 12 : 33, 35; 15 : 19), and the very power

MATTHEW. [CH. VI.

will hate the one, and love the other; or else he will hold to the one, and despise the other. Ye cannot° serve God and mammon.

25 Therefore I say unto you, Take no thought*p for your life, what ye shall eat, or what ye shall drink; nor yet for your body, what ye shall put on. Is not the life more than meat, and the body than raiment?

26 Behold the fowls of the air: for they sow not, neither do they reap, nor gather into barns; yet your heavenly Father^q feedeth them. Are ye not much better than they?

27 Which of you by taking thought can add one cubit unto his stature?

28 And why take ye thought for raiment? Consider

o Gal. 1 : 10 ; 2 Tim. 4 : 10 ; Jas. 4 : 4....p 1 Cor. 7 : 32 ; Phil. 4 : 6....q Job 38 : 41 ; Luke 12 : 24, etc.

---

of moral and spiritual discernment is abated and finally destroyed; for the soul which begins by practically disregarding spiritual truths, ends by losing the power of perceiving them (1 Cor. 2 : 14). **If the light be darkness, etc.** If that which is intended to be the light of the soul be darkened, in what total darkness will the whole soul be plunged? "When the pilot is drowned and the candle is put out, and the general is taken prisoner, what sort of hope will there be after that for those that are under command."—(*Chrysostom*.) See Luke 11 : 34-36, note.

24. The connection appears to be this: Not only you must not make it your object to accumulate your treasures on earth; you cannot have two objects and two treasures, one on the earth and one in heaven. **Serve.** Literally, be the slave of, belong to. Evidently one may serve two masters if *one is subordinate to the other*, as the slave serves both the overseer and the owner, or the soldier both the captain and the colonel. He who keeps the world always in subordination to the Lord obeys this precept; he who attempts to *belong to both* contravenes it. **Mammon.** A word of Syriac origin, meaning riches. It has been said to be the name of an idol worshipped as the god of riches. But this assertion rests on slender authority and is probably incorrect. Observe that in this passage Christ does not condemn the *possession* of riches, but the *serving* of them; and the poor and successful man may serve, while the rich man may master wealth. He that serves riches labors for them; he who is the master of riches knows how to make them labor for him, and through him for others. "Job was rich, but he served not mammon, but possessed it and ruled over it, and was master, not slave."—(*Chrysostom*.) (See Job 29 : 11-17).

25. Therefore. The whole of the following verses to the end of the chapter are a deduction from verse 24, and are to be interpreted accordingly. **I say unto you.** See on 5 : 18. Here this expression is the seal of a divine promise which underlies all that follows. **Take no thought.** The original Greek word signifies a division or distraction of mind. The command is literally, "be not divided in mind respecting your life." It thus follows logically from the prohibition of the preceding verse, against serving God and mammon, and leads naturally to the conclusion of the whole, "Seek first the king-

dom of God and his righteousness" (v. 33). See note at close of chapter. The word thought has the significance of anxiety in old English. Lord Bacon speaks of one who "died with thought and anguish." Compare, for similar use, 1 Sam. 9 : 5. **Is not the life, etc.** *First reason for not being anxious.* Our anxiety is about matters of trivial importance. As the life is more than meat which serves it, and the body than raiment which clothes it, so the soul is more than either; for both life and body exist only for the development of the soul. But our anxieties are not for the soul, but only about the outer things, the mere food and raiment. This appears to me to be the meaning, not, as most of the commentators interpret it, God, who has given you life, will much more give you food. Compare Matt. 10 : 28.

26. Behold the fowls of the air. *Second reason for not being anxious*, viz.: our Father's care for us, as illustrated in his care of the birds. Compare with this Psalm 104, especially 10-12, 21, 27, 28. It is very evident from our Lord's illustration that he does not forbid foresight and provision for the future. For though the birds neither sow nor reap, nor gather into barns, yet while winter storms linger afar off they foresee the evil, and by their flight into southern climes guard themselves against it; and when spring comes, they provide beforehand for the little ones yet to come, the father foraging in the fields and the mother plucking from her own bosom the down to furnish for them a resting-place. Rightly considered, therefore, there is nothing in this verse inconsistent with wise forethought, nothing to conflict with the lesson from the ant drawn in Prov. 6 : 6-8. Chrysostom, and, following him, Alford, notice that Christ does not say we must not sow, nor reap, but that we must not be distracted and anxious. The illustration is an argument from the less to the greater, analogous to the argument in Luke 18 : 1-7, from the unjust judge to the just God. If the birds, incapable of sowing, reaping, storing, are cared for in the way God appoints to them, how much more will you be cared for in the way of your duty, to whom God gives the capacity of forethought and the means of providing for future necessities. **Much better.** Rather of more value (ch. 10 : 31). It is not that we are better, morally, than the birds, and so more deserving of a Father's

the lilies of the field, **how they grow**; they toil not, neither do they spin:

29 And yet I say unto you, That even Solomon in all his glory was not arrayed like one of these.

30 Wherefore, if God so clothe the grass of the field, which to day is, and to morrow is cast into the oven, *shall he* not much more *clothe* you, O ye of little faith?

31 Therefore take no thought,*r* saying, What shall we eat? or, What shall we drink? or, Wherewithal shall we be clothed?

32 (For after all these things do the Gentiles seek:) for your heavenly Father knoweth that ye have need of all these things.

---

r Ps. 37:3; 55:22; 1 Pet. 5:7.

---

care, but of a higher order, to whom suffering is sharper and life larger and grander, and to whom, therefore, the divine care is more important, and for and in whom it will produce more important results.

27. Which of you by thought can add to his age one cubit. *A third reason for not being anxious;* viz., the uselessness of anxiety. A cubit is equivalent to about a foot and a half in length. It would be not a small but a very considerable addition to a man's height. The word here translated *stature* is rendered *age* in John 9:21, 23. This would better convey the meaning here. Measures of space are sometimes employed by a metaphor in estimates of life (see for example Psalm 39:5). The idea, then, here is that anxiety and care do nothing to lengthen out the duration of life; and this is in truth the object of all our solicitude.

28, 29. Consider the lilies of the field. This whole series of illustrations is an incidental enforcement of the truth that nature is full of unobserved lessons for us, an incidental appeal to us to study nature for the ascertainment of her moral and spiritual meaning (compare Job 12:7, 8). **The lilies of the field.** Several flowers have been suggested as answering to the lily of the field. Dr. Thompson's *Land and Book* describes one of these, the Huleh lily. "It is very large, and the three inner petals meet above and form a gorgeous canopy, such as art never approached and king never sat under, even in his utmost glory. And when I met this incomparable flower, in all its loveliness, among the oak woods around the northern base of Tabor and on the hills of Nazareth, where our Lord spent his youth, I felt assured that it was this to which he referred." It seems quite as likely that no special flower was intended, but that the language is general for wild flowers. These of the most brilliant hue—lilies, daisies, anemones, wild tulips and poppies—abound in the Holy Land. **Solomon in all his glory, etc.** Solomon represented to the Jewish mind the ideal of regal magnificence (see 1 Kings, ch. 10). In two respects this declaration is literally true; first, because his glory was external, a glory put on, while that of the flower is its own, being developed from within; second, because the beauty of the most perfect fabric is imperfect and shows itself rough and coarse under the microscope, while the beauty of the flower has no imperfection, but, on the contrary, discloses under the microscope glories unseen by the naked eye. These verses indicate a *fourth reason for not being anxious* and troubled about earthly needs. Our worry and anxiety are for the most part not for the food and clothing which is necessary for our life and usefulness, but for the means to equal or surpass our neighbors in display; and yet, with all our striving, the wild flowers of the field surpass us.

30. The grass of the field * * * cast into the oven. Weeds and grass were and still are used in the East as fuel. Ovens were constructed in various ways: sometimes of earth; sometimes a pit, lined with cement, served the purpose; sometimes baking was done simply on stones heated by fire previously kindled on them. The oven here mentioned was a large round pot of earthen or other materials, two or three feet high, narrow towards the top. This being first heated by a fire made within, the dough or paste was spread upon the sides to bake, thus forming their cakes. In all these cases the fuel was, cast *into* the oven, and when the oven was sufficiently heated, was raked out again to make room for the bread, after the manner in vogue in the use of the old brick oven. The verse recurs to the underlying reason for not being anxious; God who cares for birds and flowers much more cares for us his children. **Oh ye of little faith.** He cares even for the untrusting (2 Tim. 2:13).

31-34. These verses sum up the conclusion of Christ's warning against greed and its concomitant care.

32. For after all these things do the Gentiles seek. An additional argument, interpolated by Christ in his summing up. If you are as anxious and concerned about food and raiment as the heathen, how are you any better off than they (compare chap 5:46, 47)?

33. Seek ye first. Not in order of time merely, but in order of importance. Interpret this command by verse 24. **The kingdom of God** (see on Matt. 3:2). **Righteousness** (see on Matt. 5:6). **And all these things.** All what things? Not an accumulation of food and raiment; piety is not a short road to wealth; but *all of those things of which your heavenly Father knows you have need;* i. e., enough day by day to supply daily need. The promise is interpreted by David's testimony (Psalm 37:25), and by Paul's experience and assurance (Phil. 4:11, 19). So in-

33 But seek ye first* the kingdom of God, and his righteousness, and all these things shall be added¹ unto you.

34 Take therefore no thought for the morrow: for the morrow shall take thought for the things of itself.ᵃ Sufficient unto the day is the evil thereof.

* 1 Tim. 4 : 8....1 Lev. 25 : 20, 21 ; 1 Kings 3 : 13 ; Ps. 37 : 25 ; Mark 10 : 30.... a Deut. 33 : 25 ; Heb. 13 : 5, 6.

terpreted, life proves it true; those that give themselves wholly to God's service often live in poverty, but they rarely or never suffer for want of necessary food and raiment.

34. Take therefore no thought for the morrow; for the morrow shall take thought for the things of itself. That is, the future will bring not only its own trouble, but also with it the grace that is needed to bear it, or the guidance that is needed to escape it (Deut. 33 . 25 ; 1 Cor. 10 : 13 ; Heb. 13 : 6). **Sufficient unto the day is the evil thereof.** "Every day brings its own troubles, and to anticipate is but to double them."—(*David Brown.*) This verse indicates the line between the forethought that is a duty and the care that is a sin. Forethought considers a future possible ill only in so far as it is necessary to determine present duty. Care brings, by imagination, the possible evil from the future, and inflicts it on us here and now.

NOTE ON CHRIST'S TEACHING RESPECTING CARE (vs. 19–34).

The general significance of this passage may be indicated perhaps by a

Paraphrase.—Do not make it your object to accumulate treasures on the earth, because all such treasures are transitory, and the life which is devoted to accumulating them darkens and destroys the soul. Nor think to divide your energies, and to devote a part to God's service and a part to the accumulation of wealth. This you cannot do. You must choose your master, and serve him with single devotion. Having chosen God, do not allow your life to be distracted by the ambition for wealth, or by fears respecting the future. This is folly; for your soul alone is worthy of your care. It is needless; for your heavenly Father, who feeds the birds, will care for you. It is useless; for with all your worry you cannot prolong your life. It is wasted energy; for it is spent, in truth, not on satisfying the real necessities of the body, but on vieing in display with others, and the highest success leaves you at last inferior to the wild flowers of the field. It is unchristian; for he who is guilty of it is in so far no better off than the heathen who know of no heavenly Father on whom they can cast their cares. God, your heavenly Father, knows what is necessary for you and will provide it. You have only to do day by day your daily duty, making the sole object of your life to promote in your own heart and in the hearts of others, allegiance to him, and attending faithfully to each day's cares and duties, sure that the *present* duty is all that God means you to perform, and that with to-morrow's problems will come grace and wisdom for their solution.

A fair and reasonable interpretation of Christ's words does not forbid forethought or provision for the future, as is evident from, first, the general significance of the whole passage if read as it should be together, not dissected into separate and independent precepts; second, from the very illustrations employed, particularly that of the birds (v. 26), who do exercise forethought, and from the express declaration that we have needs which God recognizes (v. 32), and for which as they arise we are to provide (v. 34); third, from the example of Christ himself, who appointed a treasurer of his little band of disciples, provided a bag with money to meet their simple wants, and carried provisions on their journeys (Matt. 14 : 17 ; John 12 : 6 ; 13 : 29); fourth, from other precepts and examples in the Bible (Gen. 41 : 33-36; Ephes. 4 : 28 ; 1 Tim. 5 : 8; and also compare Prov. 6 : 6 with ch. 22 : 3). It is clear, on the other hand, that it does forbid, as essentially unchristian, all making of acquisition and accumulation of wealth the object of life, and all attempt to divide the mind between two objects, one the promotion of the divine life in ourselves and others, the other the accumulation of wealth, or the vieing with others in external signs of earthly prosperity. This is alike forbidden by the general tenor of this passage, by the example of Christ, and by other biblical precepts (compare especially Luke 12 : 16-21 ; Col. 3 : 2 ; Heb. 13 : 5, where conversation means "course of life"; 1 John 2 : 15). In brief, this passage offers a cure of care by forbidding its real cause, a divided heart and life, and by pointing to the true remedy, moderate desires and trust in God for their gratification. That the original verb translated "take no thought" bears the significance I have given it throughout these notes, is agreed to by all the commentators. "No thought," says Mr. Barnes, "means no anxiety." "Take no thought," says Alford, "does not express the sense, but gives rather an exaggeration of the command, and this makes it unreal and nugatory. * * * It is, Be not anxious, as at sea tossed about between hope and fear." "Our Lord," says Wordsworth, "does not forbid provident forethought, but he forbids anxious, restless, distrustful solicitude about earthly things."

CHAPTER VII.

JUDGE[v] not, that ye be not judged.
2 For with what judgment ye judge, ye shall be judged; and with what measure ye mete,[w] it shall be measured to you again.
3 And why beholdest thou the mote that is in thy brother's eye, but considerest not the beam that is in thine own eye?
4 Or how wilt thou say to thy brother, Let me pull out the mote out of thine eye; and, behold, a beam is in thine own eye?
5 Thou hypocrite, first cast out the beam[x] out of thine own eye; and then shalt thou see clearly to cast out the mote out of thy brother's eye.
6 Give not that which is holy unto the dogs, neither cast ye your pearls before swine, lest they trample them under their feet, and turn again and rend you.

---

v Luke 6 : 37; Rom. 2 : 1; 1 Cor. 4 : 5....w Judges 1 : 7....x Gal. 6 : 1....y Prov. 9 : 7, 8; 23 : 9.

1-6. THE CENSORIOUSNESS OF PHARISAISM REBUKED. These verses continue the contrast between the principles which must actuate Christ's disciples and those which do actuate the Pharisees. Censoriousness is the common accompaniment of a self-righteous spirit (Luke 7 : 39; 18 : 11), and against that spirit these verses are directed, except the last, which is a qualification of the general precept of the first verse.

1. Judge not. See, on the meaning of this verse, note below.

2. For with what judgment ye judge, ye shall be judged. Firstly, by *ourselves*, because by judging others we condemn ourselves, being guilty of the same sins, not necessarily in form, but in spirit (Rom. 2 : 1); secondly, by *our fellow-men*, for men habitually judge leniently those that exercise lenient judgments, and severely those that judge severely (Luke 6 : 37, 38); and rightly, because he who customarily suspects the motives of others thereby testifies to the ground of his suspicion, which is the consciousness of evil motives in himself; and thirdly, by *God*, who will at the last judge us severely if we have so judged our fellow-men (James 2 : 13). **And with what measure, etc.** In Mark 4 : 24 the same aphorism is employed and the same principle is applied to those that impart truth to others; and in Luke 6 : 38 to all beneficence. It may here be equivalent to "the standard by which you measure others, they will use in measuring you;" but it is more probable that it is the amplification of a general principle, that Luke's report is fuller, and that it is as if Christ had said, As you judge you shall be judged, in accordance with the general and universal principle that as you give to others they will give to you, charity for charity, severity for severity; generosity for generosity, niggardliness for niggardliness.

3. And why beholdest thou, seeing it from without,—**the mote,**—the lesser fault,—**in thy brother's eye, and considerest not,**—by weighing well from within,—**the beam,**—the larger fault, in thyself? Our own faults ought to be to us beams; our neighbor's faults should be but motes. In our common estimates the reverse is the case; we magnify the faults of others and palliate our own. So runs the old proverb: Men carry their own sins on their back and those of their neighbors before. But besides this, the spirit which rejoiceth in iniquity is always a beam, generally a more flagrant violation of the spirit of love (1 Cor. 13 : 5) than the sin over which it rejoices and which it condemns.

4. Or how wilt thou say. The preceding verse asserts that the Christian spirit will lead us to consider more carefully our own faults than those of our neighbor; this and the next asserts that we cannot cure our neighbor's faults except in a spirit of humility, because of our own. It is interpreted by Gal. 6 : 1. In the rabbinical books is this saying: "If any one says to another, 'Take out the mote from thine eye,' he will be answered, 'Take out the beam from thine own.'" If this was really a proverb in the time of Christ, he gives it a new significance and direction. From a mere expression of the spirit which resents reproof, it becomes a direction to him who would administer reproof. Victory over evil in ourselves can alone give the clearness of moral vision necessary to perceive, and the sympathy necessary to eradicate, evils from our neighbors.

5. Hypocrite. Every man who pretends to zeal in reform, but is zealous only to reform his neighbor, but indifferent respecting himself, is but a pretender—a hypocrite, though sometimes a self-deceived hypocrite. **Shalt thou see clearly.** He that rids himself of the spirit of censoriousness and seeks to discern the good and not the evil in his neighbor, is prepared to help him to get rid of the evil. It is not the spirit of criticism, but the spirit of charity, which is curative. Before he had only *beheld* the mote; now he *sees to cast it out*. "The beholding was vain and idle; the seeing clearly is for a blessed end, viz.: (18 : 15) to gain thy brother."—(*Alford*.)

OF JUDGING OUR FELLOW-MEN.—This passage has given rise to much difficulty from failing to note the proper meaning of the word *judge*. The Greek word (κρίνω) here translated *judge* signifies primarily to separate; then to form a judicial sentence, because that involves a separation of the good from the evil, as illustrated by the parables in Matt. 13 : 30, 49; 25 : 32. It is frequently used in the N. T. in this strict sense to express a judicial and official decree, as in 1 Cor. 6 : 2, and in Acts 15 : 19, in which latter passage it is rendered by *my sentence is*. It is also frequently used metaphorically for a *quasi* judicial decision (see illustrations below), and in one or two cases it is employed to express a personal conclusion, *but always one that is irrevocably fixed.* Of this use an illustration is afforded by 2 Cor. 5:14: "We thus *judge* that if one died for all, then were all dead," where not an opinion or probable conclusion, but a deliberate and settled conviction is expressed; and another in Acts 20:16: "Paul had *determined* to sail by Ephesus," where not a mere purpose, but a settled determination is indicated, one so unalterable that the subsequent entreaties of his friends could not swerve him from it (Acts 21:14). Our translators have then almost exactly preserved the meaning of the original word in this passage. It is not equivalent to condemn nor to condemnatory judgment on the one hand, nor does it, on the other, signify every mental opinion concerning others; *but such opinions as are judgments, i. e., in their nature judicial.* Christ certainly does not prohibit all formations of opinions respecting our fellow-men; this is not only necessary to be done, but directly commanded both by Christ and his apostles (Matt. 18:15-17; 1 Tim. 5:20; 2 Tim. 4:2), and it is impliedly required in this very passage in verse 6. Nor is his prohibition of judging satisfied by interpreting it as a mere warning against harsh, unkind, and censorious condemnation of others. It includes this, but both here and in the parallel passages (Luke 6:37, where condemnation of others is also rebuked; Rom. 2:1; 14:4, 10, 13; 1 Cor. 4:3, 5; James 4:12) much more is indicated than this. We get to the gist of the command here, as I am persuaded we shall do generally in Christ's sayings, not by departing from, but by adhering to his exact words. *All assuming of God's judgment-seat,* all undertaking to reach any final and conclusive judgment concerning our fellow-men, is prohibited by the spirit and the words of this passage and its parallels in the New Testament. It prohibits absolutely all attempts by man to fix the eternal state of any soul, or to declare what it is or will be, and so all excommunication which involves an imprecation of an everlasting curse; all imprecation of men in the mass, as by the anathemas of the Roman Catholic church and the damnatory clauses of the Athanasian creed; all such discussions respecting the character and eternal destiny of individuals as often occur after the death especially of public men—and this whether conducted in public or private; all formation of ineradicable prejudices or final and settled judgments against any, such as cannot be readily set aside by clearer evidence or by their repentance and reformation (compare 1 Cor. 5:4, 5, with 2 Cor. 2:5-8); and all judging of men's moral character and status before God and their final condition by reason of their divergence from us in points of doctrine or of practice (Rom., ch. 14, throughout). But it does not forbid such tentative and partial judgments both of conduct and character as are formed in the spirit of love and meekness, as are accompanied in our own minds with the recognition of the truth that they are imperfect, and that all the data for a perfect judgment are not and cannot be before us, as are held subject to revision or reversal on adequate evidence or in case of repentance and reform, and as are necessary for our own guidance in determining what shall be our conduct toward or in respect to the persons in question. Such passages as 1 Cor. 16:22; 2 Pet., ch. 2; and Jude, v. 4, do not militate against this precept, which does not forbid our judging of principles and practices, but of assuming to judge individuals; nor does Christ's example in Matt., ch. 23, contradict his precept, because he knew what was in man, and could judge then as he will judge finally (John 5:22, 27).

6. This verse can scarcely be regarded as a qualification, but rather as an interpretation, of what precedes. If one is evidently past our influence, whether violent as the dog or given over to sensuality as the swine, we may adjudge him to be so, and need not go on casting pearls before him (compare Prov. 9:7, 8). But observe that it was never the practice of the apostles to account any unworthy to receive the Gospel till by their own act they had rejected it, and so counted themselves unworthy (Acts 13:46; Titus 3:10). **Holy.** The meat offered for sacrifice, a part of which was reserved for the priests (Lev. 2:3, etc.), was regarded among the Jews as peculiarly sacred, as much as the bread and wine, when consecrated for the Eucharist, were regarded in the early church and still are in many of the modern churches. To give such meat to the dogs would be, to the Jewish mind, the extreme of profanation. No unclean person was permitted to eat of it (Lev. 22:4, 10, 14, etc.; compare Exod. 22:31). **Dogs—swine.** The dog was never a pet or a favorite among the Jews. They lived and still live in Oriental cities in packs, half wild, generally without masters or owners, and barely tolerated as scavengers. Both dogs and swine are common symbols in the Bible of vileness and uncleanness (Lev. 11:7; 14:10, 11; Prov. 11:22; Matt. 15:27; Phil. 3:2; Rev. 22:15). **Turn again and rend you.** Proclaiming the truth to those that are determined against it only provokes their anger. See, for interpretation, Matt. 10:23.

Ch. 7:7-27. FOURTH GENERAL DIVISION.—HOW TO ENTER THE KINGDOM OF HEAVEN.

The connection in this part of Christ's discourse is not as close as in the preceding portion. Neither must it be forgotten that Eastern teaching was more aphoristic than ours. Nevertheless, there is a connection which would be recognized more readily were it not for our division of the sermon into chapters and

7 Ask, and it shall be given you;ᵃ seek, and ye shall find; knock, and it shall be opened unto you;
8 For every one that asketh receiveth; and he that seeketh findeth; and to him that knocketh it shall be opened.
9 Or what man is there of you, whom if his son ask bread, will he give him a stone?
10 Or if he ask a fish, will he give him a serpent?
11 If ye then, being evil, know how to give good gifts unto your children, how much more shall your Father which is in heaven give good things to them that ask him?
12 Therefore all things whatsoever ye would that men should do to you, do ye even so to them: for this is the law and the prophets.
13 Enter ye in at the strait gate: for wide is the gate,

z Isa. 55:6; Prov. 2:4, 5. a Ps. 81:10, 16; John 14:13, 14; 16:23, 24; 1 John 3:22; 5:14:15....b Prov. 8:17; Jer. 29:12, 13.... c Luke 11:11, etc....d Lev. 19:18; Rom. 12:8-10; Gal. 5:14.....e Luke 13:24.

verses. The two conditions of entering into the kingdom are faith (7-11) and obedience (13-27). Character is the gift of God and is to be sought by prayer from him (7-11). Nevertheless, not every praying receives, but that which accompanies a life of non-conformity to the world (13-14) and of practical righteousness, from which many false prophets will seek to turn men away. They are to be known by their fruits, for the product of moral teaching is its best test (15-23). And though the false religion will find many to applaud it now, he whose religion consists in practical obedience to Christ's precepts, and he alone, has built upon a rock (24-27). It is noticeable that in this portion of the sermon, which gives the condition of entering into his kingdom, neither any public ceremony nor any formal creed is prescribed.

7-11. First condition. *The prayer of faith.*

7. The connection is thus given by Chrysostom: "For inasmuch as he had enjoined things great and marvelous, and had commanded men to be superior to all their passions, and had led them up to Heaven itself, and had enjoined them to strive after the resemblance, not of angels and archangels, but of the very Lord of all (ch. 5:48), * * * * that they might not say these things are grievous and intolerable * * * * he adds also the pinnacle of all facility, devising us no ordinary relief to our toils, the assistance derived from persevering prayers." This is not all, however. He puts prayer first, the striving afterwards, so signifying that the first step toward the kingdom of God is seeking of God. Compare with this command John 4:10; Rom. 6: 23; and in the O. T. Isa. 55:1. Observe that even here where character is represented as bestowed on the soul by the Spirit of God, we are represented not as mere passive receivers of an irresistible grace, but as agents asking, seeking, knocking. For the kind of seeking, see Prov. 2:3, 4; 18:17; Jer. 29:13; Luke 13: 24, and note there. Contrast with this teaching, where man is represented as seeking and knocking, other passages where the Lord is represented as the one seeking and we as the found (Luke 15: 3, 10; Rev. 3:20). And compare ch. 5:6, where the mental state is described as hunger and thirst after righteousness, of which asking, seeking, knocking, is the expression or utterance, the activity to which it leads.

8. For every one that asketh. The argument here is from the greater to the less and from the general to the specific. In the whole realm of life energetic faithful endeavor is generally crowned with success. Even the Pharisee who seeks the praise of men by his public alms, prayers and fasting, has his reward. How much more shall he that asks, seeks, knocks, receive in the kingdom of God's grace.

9-10. Or what man is there of you. Second reason for faith in prayer; analogy from the earthly to the heavenly parent. Observe that the N. T. almost never, and the O. T. but rarely, employs nature as a symbol to represent God. He is represented to us by images drawn from the higher and better experiences of human nature; or, in theological language, the N. T. symbolism is anthropomorphic. Modern philosophy argues from the apparent inflexibility of nature that God does not hear prayer; Christ answers from the mobility of the soul, as illustrated by the common parental experience, that God does hear and answer. The root of modern unbelief lies just here, in an assumption that God is like nature. But the Bible does not say, As mountains stand immovable, as the thunderbolts strike irresistible, as the sea, as the river, as the earth, but "As a father pitieth his children," "as one whom his mother comforteth," "as a shepherd feedeth his sheep." Observe, too, that there is here implied, not merely a promise to give some answer to the prayer, but to give *the thing asked for or something better.* God may do more for us than we ask or think; but never less. The argument here, as in the preceding verse, is from the less to the greater. This is brought out clearly in the verse following. Compare with this passage Luke 11:12, where is added, "If he shall ask an egg, will he offer him a scorpion?"

11. Being evil. "He said this not to condemn our race as bad; but in contrast to his own goodness he calls parental tenderness evil, so great is the excess of his love to man."—*Chrysostom.* Yet Stier well observes that the remark is a strong indirect support of the doctrine of original sin. Even in our highest holiest relations there is evil; selfishness is mingled with

and broad *is* the way, that leadeth to destruction, and many there be which go in thereat:
14 Because strait *is* the gate: and narrow *is* the way, which leadeth unto life; and few' there be that find it.

15 Beware of false prophets,ᶠ which come to you in sheep's clothing, but inwardly they are raveningʰ wolves.
16 Ye shall know them by theirⁱ fruits. Do men gather grapes of thorns, or figs of thistles?

f ch. 20 : 16 ; 25 : 1-12 ; Rom. 9 : 27, 29, ...g Deut. 13 : 1-3 ; Jer. 23 : 13-16 ; 1 John 4 : 1....h Acts 20 : 29-31....i ch. 12 : 33.

our most unselfish love. **Good things.** Luke (11 : 13) says Holy Spirit. But the greater includes the less. "He that spared not his own Son, how shall he not with him also freely give us all things." (Rom. 8 : 32.)

12. Therefore all things whatsoever ye would that men, etc. From the general theme of his discourse, which is here a statement of the conditions of entering the kingdom of heaven, Christ turns aside to enforce a high standard of human duty by his consideration of the goodness of God to us. Therefore connects the golden rule directly with the preceding teaching, respecting divine compassion. The connection is the same in substance in ch. 5 : 48; and ch. 6 : 14, 15. Because God is so ready to answer our prayers, we ought to show like sympathy and love to our fellow-men. This precept is found not alone in the teaching of Christ. In a negative form the same rule of conduct is found in the rabbinical writings: "Thou shalt not do to thy neighbor what is hateful to thyself." **Do ye even so to them.** Observe that it is not said do *that* to them, but so to them, *i. e.* in like manner. The rule does not require us to do *the things* which they ask, but to act toward them in the manner and spirit in which we should wish them to act toward us. Observe, too, that this rule works in two ways; while directly it requires us to act toward others as we should wish them to act toward us, in spirit and by implication it requires us to wish from others no more than we should be willing to render to them if our positions were reversed. **This is the law and the prophets** (Lev. 19 : 18 ; Isaiah 1 : 17 ; Rom. 13 : 10). That is, the object of the law and the prophets is to produce that state of heart and life of which the golden rule is the natural expression in daily conduct.

13-20. THE SECOND CONDITION. *Obedience.* Verses 13, 14, state simply that obedience involves a non-conformity to and a separation from the world; 15-20 warns the disciples against false teachers who will attempt to substitute some other conditions than faith and obedience, and so, under one pretence or another, attempt to widen the gate (Ephes. 6 : 6, and reference below); and verses 21-27 emphasize the doctrine that there is no true religion which does not show its spirit by its actual obedience to the precepts of the Master (John 14 : 21 ; 15 : 14; and reference below).

13, 14. The strait gate, *i. e.,* a narrow and difficult gate. The word is not the same as *straight*. The idea of narrowness is preserved in our use of the word *straits* to indicate a passage either in the mountains or from one sea to another, as "Straits of Gibraltar"; the idea of difficulty is illustrated by its use in the verse, "I am in a strait betwixt two." Observe, the gate is put *before the way*. It is not, therefore, the gate out of life at the end of the pilgrimage, but the gate into Christian life, as Bunyan represents it in Pilgrim's Progress (compare Psalm 118 : 19, 20). The entrance into Christian life is narrow, *i. e.* requires a true spiritual separation from the world (Ephes. 5 : 11), and the life is beset with difficulties which must be counted on before entering (Luke 9 : 57, 58, and notes). As used here, the gate is not equivalent to the door in John 10 : 2. The strait gate is the spirit of real and hearty allegiance to Jesus Christ, by which we enter in to him. It is the patient continuance in well-doing described in Romans 2 : 7 as the condition of entrance into eternal life; it was too strait for the rich young man described in Matt. 19 : 16-22; through it the apostles entered into the way (ch. 19 : 27, and see ch. 4 : 20, 22 ; ch. 9 : 9); Christ has entered into glory by the same door and way (Phil. 2 : 9, 10; Heb. 12 : 2). It is not because the gate is difficult to find, but because we are unwilling to find and to enter in *through this gate*, that there are few who enter. It is wide enough to admit any soul, but too narrow to admit any sin. Observe, too, that not only the gate is strait, but the subsequent way narrow. Like a mountain path cut in the rock, a little deviation is attended with dangerous consequences—deviation not from circumscribed rules but from the spirit of Christ's precepts. There is possible significance in the fact that the word here translated *narrow*, is the participle of the verb elsewhere translated *troubled* (*e. g.,* 2 Cor. 4 : 8 ; 7 : 5). The way is narrow because it is a way hemmed in by persecution, especially to the early Christians, from which persecution they were constantly tempted to escape by going out of the narrow path. The temptation was the strait gate to Christ; the trial-hour of Gethsemane and Calvary a part of the narrow way. Contrast with this teaching Ps. 119 : 45; Isa. 35 : 8. Though the way is narrow, it is a highway in which mere ignorance cannot go astray; though compressed, it is to him whose heart is fully set to walk in it the way of *life* and of *liberty*.

15-20. WARNINGS AGAINST FALSE TEACHERS. The Hebrew word translated prophet is derived from a root signifying to boil over, and embodies

Ch. VII.] MATTHEW. 113

17 Even so every tree bringeth forth good fruit: but a corrupt tree bringeth forth evil fruit.
18 A good tree cannot bring forth evil fruit, neither can a corrupt tree bring forth good fruit.
19 Every tree that bringeth not forth good fruit is hewn down, and cast into the fire.
20 Wherefore by their fruits ye shall know them.
21 Not every one that saith unto me, Lord, Lord, shall enter into the kingdom of heaven: but he that doeth the will of my Father which is in heaven.
22 Many will say to me in that day, Lord, Lord, have we not prophesied in thy name? and in thy name have cast out devils? and in thy name done many wonderful works?

23 And then will I profess unto them, I never knew you: depart from me, ye that work iniquity.
24 Therefore whosoever heareth these sayings of mine, and doeth them, I will liken him unto a wise man, which built his house upon a rock:
25 And the rain descended, and the floods came, and the winds blew, and beat upon that house; and it fell not: for it was founded upon a rock.
26 And every one that heareth these sayings of mine, and doeth them not, shall be likened unto a foolish man, which built his house upon the sand:
27 And the rain descended, and the floods came, and the winds blew, and beat upon that house; and it fell: and great was the fall of it.

---

j Luke 6 : 43, 45....k ch. 3 : 10; John 15 : 2, 6....l ch. 25 : 11, 12; Isa. 48 : 1, 2; Luke 6 : 46; 13 : 25; Rom. 2 : 13....m Num. 24 : 4; 1 Kings 22 : 11, etc.; Jer. 23 : 13, etc.; Acts 19 : 13-15; 1 Cor. 13 : 2....n ch. 25 : 41; Ps. 5 : 5; Rev. 22 : 15....o Luke 6 : 47, etc....p Ps. 111 : 10; 119 : 99, 130....q Ps. 92 : 13-15....r 1 Sam. 2 : 30; Jer. 8 : 9....s 1 Cor. 3 : 13....t Heb. 10 : 26, 27.

---

the idea of a fountain bursting forth from the heart of man into which God has poured it. It thus signifies not merely a foreteller, nor, on the other hand, every religious teacher, but such as teach under divine inspiration. A false prophet is not merely an erroneous teacher, but a lying teacher, strictly speaking one pretending to an inspiration which he does not possess; secondarily, any teacher deliberately deceiving others; it does not properly signify one deceiving himself, and so unconsciously deceiving others (see ch. 24 : 24; 2 Tim. 2 : 17, 18; 2 Pet. 2 : 1; 1 John 4 : 1-3). The caution applies directly to such in our time as claim to possess communication with the spirit-world, or to be invested with direct and infallible authority to speak for God; indirectly to all who put on a semblance of piety for selfish purposes, and so get a position of honor as teacher in the church; or who, without even that pretence, maintain the position for worldly purposes. Its application, as is made clear in the next verse, is not so much to open and avowed teachers of error, men who deny the fundamental principles of the Gospel, as to those who pretend to maintain but really undermine and destroy them. So Chrysostom: "By false prophets I think he shadows out not the heretics, but them that are of a corrupt life yet wear a mask of virtue, whom the majority are wont to call by the name of impostors." **Sheep's clothing.** The metaphor is of a wolf putting on the sheep's skin; the thing signified is a selfish and designing man putting on the garb of meekness, gentleness and piety (2 Cor. 11 : 13, 15; 2 Tim. 3 : 5). **Ye shall know them.** Literally *fully, perfectly know them*. The infallible test of all religious teaching is its practical result in the lives of those that receive it. The answer to modern eulogists of Buddhism and Confucianism is India and China; the answer to the papal claim of infallibility is Spain and Italy; the answer to the eulogists of "pure reason" and a Bible overthrown is Paris during the Revolution and Paris during the Commune. New England is the best refutation of those that sneer at Puritanism; and Christendom, contrasted with the heathen world, is a short but conclusive reply to all advocates of a universal and eclectic religion. Here the test is applied only to religious teaching; but elsewhere the same test is applied to the estimate of individual character (John 15 : 6, 8).

21-23. THE FRUITS OF TRUE RELIGION. *Practical obedience in daily life.* **He that doeth the will.** That will embraces trust in Christ as our strength (John 6 : 29), love to our fellow-men (John 15 : 12), personal purity of character (1 Thess. 4 : 3), and the cultivation of the graces that are the fruit of the Spirit (1 Thess. 5 : 18; 1 Pet. 2 : 15; 4 : 2, etc.). It is by God's Spirit alone that we are enabled to do his will (Heb. 13 : 21; Rev. 2 : 17). **Devils.** See note on demoniacal possession (ch. 8 : 28-34). **Then will I profess.** Greek, *publicly profess*. The disclosure of the false character of the fruitless professor of religion will be before men and angels (Matt. 25 : 32). **Depart from me.** God now abides even with the ungodly, that he may lead them to repentance (Rom. 2 : 4). He will then separate them from him for ever (2 Thess. 2 : 9).

Compare with this entire passage 1 Cor. 13 : 1-3, and observe that in the only passage where Christ pictorially describes the judgment-scene, the judgment is portrayed as dependent upon the course of daily life (Matt. 25 : 31-46); and that the sentence, as recorded in Rev. 22 : 11, is a simple fixing, eternally and irreversibly, of the character formed here.

24-27. CONCLUSION OF THE DISCOURSE. *The test of true religion.* The symbol which Christ employs here, would possess a significance for his hearers which it has not for us. In the East the peasants' huts are often unsubstantial structures, built of mud or sun-burnt brick, and sometimes washed away by a single furious rain-storm. Their mountain streams, too, are of a peculiar character. These water-courses, called *wadies*, are in the summer perfectly dry, in the rainy season they are swollen streams. The shepherd builds his hut by one of these water-courses, which often in the summer weather affords the only herbage which is not burnt up by the sun. If the house is built high up on the rock it is safe; if down on the sandy soil, though there is no water at the time, the treacherous

28 And it came to pass, when Jesus had ended these sayings, the people were astonished*a* at his doctrine:
29 For he taught them as *one* having authority, and not as the scribes.

CHAPTER VIII.

WHEN he was come down from the mountain, great multitudes followed him.

2 And, behold, there came a leper*c* and worshipped him, saying, Lord, if thou wilt, thou canst make me clean.
3 And Jesus put forth *his* hand, and touched him, saying, I will; be thou clean. And immediately his leprosy was cleansed.
4 And Jesus saith unto him, See thou tell*w* no man; but go thy way, shew thyself to the priest, and offer

a Jer. 23 : 29 ; Mark 6 : 2....*v* Mark 1 : 40, etc. ; Luke 5 : 12, etc....*w* ch. 9 : 30; Mark 5 : 43.

---

foundation gives away with the first freshet; and these often come with almost no note of warning, and as a result of rains further up the stream. A friend of the writer, journeying through Palestine, pitched his tent, one fair night, in one of these *wadies*, and was before morning awakened by the sound of water, from which he and his party had barely time to escape with the loss of clothing, books and instruments. So the trial of the last great day will come, without warning (Matt. 24 : 36-39, 42-44), and overwhelming those whose exterior was fair, but the foundation of whose life was insecure. As the builder would know, or easily might know, the danger of building on the sand, and yet build there for the sake of ease and transient convenience, so many, who confess that it is not safe to build on any other foundation than a practical obedience to Jesus Christ, yet do build otherwise, and trust to a vague hope to escape the day of trial when it comes.

The building on the rock is building on Christ Jesus. "The Rock, as signifying him who spoke this, is of too frequent reference in Scripture for us to overlook it here (2 Sam. 22 : 2, 47 ; 23 : 3; Ps. 29 : 1; 31 : 2; Isa. 26 : 4; 32 : 2 ; 44 : 8 ; 1 Cor. 10 : 4, etc.)."—(*Alford.*) Yet the contrast is not between those who build on him and those who lay other foundations, but between those who build on him by mere intellectual belief and external profession, and those who build by practical obedience to his precepts. Compare ch. 21 : 28-32. See for a similar metaphor of the judgment-day, Isaiah 28 : 15-18.

This close gives a solemn significance to the whole discourse, which indicates the superstructure of character to be reared, while this metaphor indicates the foundation on which alone it can be built (1 Cor. 3 : 11). No building of kindness and good-will towards others, and of purity, and of seeming simplicity, complies with the Sermon on the Mount, unless the foundation is laid in faith in Christ, and the building is that of a real and hearty obedience to him.

28, 29. Ch. 8 : 1. EFFECT OF CHRIST'S PREACHING. **Doctrine,** *i. e.,* teaching. Not only what he taught, but the method and spirit of his teaching. **As, one having authority.** Not only because, as Chrysostom, "He did not say what he said on the authority of others, quoting Moses or the prophets, but everywhere alleging himself to be the One who had the power;" but also because his appeal was not to any external authority but to the moral consciousness of his hearers, to the law of God written in their own hearts, and because he spoke out of a perfect and personal assurance of the truth of every utterance; for *he was the truth.* In this sense every religious teacher should imitate the example of him who is the great preacher. He will speak with authority just in so far as the truth is *a part of his own being,* not merely an external dogma intellectually apprehended, and as he appeals to the dormant consciousness of moral truth, which is in the heart and conscience of every man.

Ch. 8 : 1. Great multitudes followed him. His preaching not only singularly and powerfully affected his hearers, but it attracted hearers to him. During this early period of his ministry he was thronged by multitudes, not only curious to see or desirous to receive the benefit of his miracles, but also fascinated by the moral and spiritual power of his teaching.

Ch. 8 : 2-4.—CURE OF THE LEPER.—LEPROSY A TYPE OF SIN, INSIDIOUS, DEADLY, HEREDITARY, OFTEN CONTAGIOUS.—THE SPIRIT OF TRUE PRAYER: IF THOU WILT THOU CANST.—CHRIST TOUCHES THE LEPER; CHRIST IS THE TOUCH OF GOD'S HAND ON A SINFUL WORLD.—CHRIST'S CLEANSING; PERFECT, IMMEDIATE, CLEANSES FROM THE FOULEST AND THE MOST INERADICABLE DISEASES (1 John 1 : 9).—THE DUTY OF THE CLEANSED; A PUBLIC ACKNOWLEDGMENT OF HIS PURIFICATION, AND A PUBLIC RETURN TO THE CHURCH.

2-4. This incident—the healing of the leper—also recorded in Mark 1 : 40-45; Luke 5 : 12-15, occurred during Christ's first missionary tour through Galilee, as described in Mark 1 : 21-45. Its apparent connection with the Sermon on the Mount is due to the modern division of the N. T. into chapters. Verse 1 of this chapter properly belongs with the preceding chapter, and the words "and behold" mark a transition from the preceding narrative. If Christ were on a tour of healing, and the leper had heard of the cures Christ had wrought, his appeal for help would not be extraordinary; but it is incredible that such faith as he manifested should have been awakened by a sermon which he could not possibly have heard. Nor is it probable that he would have been found in the midst of the multitude mentioned in verse 1; nor, if the cure had been performed in their hearing, would the caution of verse 4 be likely to have been given. These considerations lead most harmonists to prefer the order indicated in Mark to that which seems to be implied by Matthew. The cure took place in a city (Luke 5:12), apparently not Capernaum (Mark 1:38-40).

2. **There came a leper.** Luke says "full of leprosy;" an indication that it was an aggravated form of the disease from which he suffered. In coming to Christ, in the city, for cure, the leper violated the letter of the ancient law (Lev. 13:46), but not its spirit. See on verse 3, below.

In the absence of accurate medical knowledge the term leprosy was used in ancient times to designate diseases whose natures were radically different, but whose symptoms were somewhat analogous. In its worst forms, leprosy (*elephantiasis Græcorum*) is the most terrible of all diseases. From a commencement slight in appearance, with but little pain or inconvenience, it goes on in its strong but sluggish course, generally in defiance of medical skill, till it reduces the patient to a mutilated cripple, with dulled or obliterated senses. This disease assumes several forms, the most common of which is known as the *tuberculated elephantiasis*. It generally first shows itself by inflamed patches in the skin, on the face, ears, or hands, of a dull red or purplish hue, from half an inch to two inches in diameter. These soon change to a brownish or bronze color, with a metallic or oily lustre, and a clearly defined edge; and in this state they very often remain for weeks or months. By degrees the discolored surface becomes hard, and rises here and there into tubercles, at first reddish, but afterward either bronzed or white. The scarf-skin often scales off. After another period of weeks, months, or even years, many of the tubercles subside, and leave a kind of cicatrix thinner than the surrounding skin. The tubercles which do not subside, or which break out again, may vary from the size of a pea to that of a pigeon's egg, and, after continuing, it may be, for years, they ulcerate, discharging a whitish matter. The ulcers often eat into the muscle till they expose the bones; should there be any hair on the tubercles it either falls off or turns white, and the hair of the head and eyebrows mostly disappears. When the disease is fully formed, the distorted face, and the livid, encrusted, and ulcerated tubercles, the deformed, sightless and uncovered eyes, the hoarse whispering voice, the fœtid breath and cutaneous excretion, the contorted joints, which are often buried in or absolutely dislocated by tubercles, the livid patches on those parts of the body not yet tuberculous, all form a picture which is not exceeded in the horror of its features by any other malady. The disease for the most part creeps on with irresistible progress until it attacks some vital organ and occasions death.

Whether leprosy is contagious or not has greatly perplexed both the divines and physicians. The cases of Naaman and Gehazi (2 Kings 5:1, and 27, with ch. 8:4) indicate very clearly that some forms of the disorder were not so regarded. It is also asserted by Trench that the leper was allowed a place, though apart from the rest of the worshippers, in the synagogue, and in later times in Christian churches. On the other hand leprosy is universally regarded as a contagious disease in the East, where it is chiefly prevalent. "No healthy person would touch them, eat with them, or use any of their clothes or utensils, and with good reason." (*Thompson's Land and Book*, 2:517.) And it is only upon the theory of contagion that it is possible to account for the Mosaic precepts and provisions referred to below. The fact appears to be, that of the several diseases designated in the Bible as leprosy, the worst form (tubercular leprosy) is contagious, but the milder (squamous leprosy) is not; and that the provisions contained in Lev. ch. 13 were for the purpose of determining officially whether the person suspected of having the leprosy really had the contagious or only the milder form of the disease.

In its worst form leprosy was universally regarded by the Jews as a divine punishment; and the disease was several times inflicted by God in judgment for flagrant transgressions (Numb. 12:10; 2 Kings 5:27; 15:5; 2 Chron. 26:19). The leper was exiled from the haunts of men, bore about with him the emblems of death, and wherever he went cried, as a warning of his coming, "Unclean, unclean" (Lev. 13:45; compare Numb. 12:12; Ezek. 24:17); his disease was regarded by universal consent as hopeless of cure; and this opinion, so far as regards its worse forms, is confirmed by modern science. The same opinions and sentiments respecting it reappear at a later date, as in Europe during the middle ages, when the leper was clothed in a shroud, and had mass for the dead read over him; and at the present day, not only in Palestine but also in Persia, China, Japan, and indeed throughout the East where the disease is well known. Lepers associated together in communities of their own as they still do (2 Kings 7:3; Luke 17:12), and the leper-houses which now exist in the vicinity of Jerusalem, Damascus, Nablus, and Ramleh probably originated at a very early period. The Mosaic law provided for the official determination of the question whether a person suspected of being afflicted by leprosy was really subject to it or not, and whether the leprosy was of the more dangerous forms or no. These provisions are recorded in Lev. ch. 13. If the leprosy were the milder form, affecting the skin only, or if it covered the whole body with a white eruption (verses 12, 13), a sign that it was not the contagious form of the disease, but what is known as the *lepra vulgaris*, the patient was to be pronounced clean and discharged.

The whole character of this disease made it a type of sin; it was a *"living death," appeared insidiously, was incurable except by divine grace, and separated its victim from the people of God.* "The Jews called it 'the finger of God,' and emphatically 'the stroke.' It attacked, they said, first a man's house, and then, if he refused to turn, his clothing; and lastly, should he persist in sin, himself."—(*Trench*.) "The same emblems were used in his misery as those of mourning for the dead; the same means of cleansing as for uncleanness through connection with the dead, and which were never used except on these two occasions. Compare Numb. 19:6, 13, 18, with Lev. 14: 4-7. All this exclusion and mournful separation imported the perpetual exclusion of the abominable and polluted from the true city of God, as declared in Rev. 21:27."—(*Alford*.)

Worshipped. No great stress can be laid upon this word, or the word "Lord," as indicating the divinity of Jesus Christ. The Greek word (προσκυνεω), translated *worshipped*, is a general one, expressive of the homage paid by an inferior to a superior. "According to Herodotus, the ancient Oriental, and especially Persian mode of salutation was, between persons of equal rank, to kiss each other on the lips; when the difference of rank was slight, they kissed each other on the cheek; when one was much inferior, he fell upon his knees and touched his forehead to the ground, or prostrated himself, kissing his hand at the same time towards his superior. This latter mode Greek writers express by (προσκυνεω) *proskuneo*."—(*Robinson's Lexicon*.) This word is uniformly translated, in the N. T., *worship*. The act of the leper is more fully described by Mark 1:40, as "beseeching him and kneeling down to him." Similar homage was paid by Lot to the angels (Gen. 19:1); Joseph's brethren to Joseph (ch. 42:6); and by Joseph to his father (ch. 48:12). And in the Septuagint, the Greek version of the O. T., the same Greek word (προσκυνεω) is used. Compare Matt. 20:20, and Rev. 3:9. On the other hand, the same word is used in the N. T. to express the highest worship of God, as in John 4:20-24, and Rev. 7:11; 19:10, etc. It should also be noted that the term Lord (κυριος) is not used exclusively as an appellation of the Deity. It is employed as a common form of address to a superior, answers to our "sir," and is so occasionally translated (Matt. 13:27; 21:30; 27:63); it is addressed to the apostles in one important instance, and received by them without rebuke (Acts 16:30); and it is rendered "master" and "owner" (Matt. 6:24; Luke 19:33); and if translated *lord* is spelt with a small *l* in those passages where the translators regard it as not involving any idea of divine homage (Matt. 24:45-50; 25:18, 19). The same English word "lord" is employed in England to this day as a title of nobility. But though the fact that the leper paid this homage to Christ does not indicate that he conceived him to be possessed of a divine character, the fact that Christ in this and other instances received the homage without question, indicates that he assumed at least a super-human character. Compare his instructions to his disciples in Matt. 25:8-10, and Peter's reception of similar homage when offered to him in Acts 10:25, 26.

If thou wilt. Contrast Mark 9:22. The leper does not doubt Christ's power, he does not dictate to his will. "He did not say, 'If thou request it of God,' nor 'If thou pray,' nor 'Lord, cleanse me,' but leaves all to him, and makes his recovery depend on him, and testifies that all the authority is his."—(*Chrysostom*.) Observe that the prayer is not for a spiritual benefit, but for a temporal blessing, which Christ may refuse to impart (2 Cor. 12:8, 9), and which must always be asked for subject to the higher will of God. In this the leper's prayer is a model in spirit for us. Observe, too, that if the leper were mistaken in attributing to Christ the power to cleanse from leprosy, it was Christ's place to correct the error, and to attribute the power to God, as the apostles did in a somewhat similar case (Acts 3:12). On the contrary, he confirms it with his "*I will*." Contrast with this assumption of power to heal, Moses' prayer for the healing of Miriam (Numb. 12:13). It was a general belief among the Jews, taught by their rabbinical books, that one of the signs of the Messiah would be his power to cure leprosy.

Clean. The curse of leprosy was not merely in the suffering it caused, but yet more in the odium it entailed, and in the fact that it made the Jew "unclean," *i. e.*, an outcast, and classed with swine and dogs and all odious and abhorrent creatures. The leper's prayer is not therefore, Make me well, but, Make me CLEAN, take away the shame and the moral pollution of this disease.

3. Be thou clean. The diseases, as the devils, obey Christ. **Touched him.** Mark gives the reason, "moved with compassion;" the touch was a touch of pity, the more wonderful because not only a universal prejudice, but also the Levitical law forbade touching any unclean thing (Lev. 5:3). Yet even in this act Christ exemplifies the truth that he had come to fulfill the law, though he seemed to violate it, and did violate its letter. For the object of the law was the preservation of purity; but Christ did better than preserve himself from impurity; by his

the gift that Moses commanded,ˣ for a testimony unto them.

5 And when Jesus was entered into Capernaum, there came unto him a centurion,ʸ beseeching him,

x Lev. 14 : 3, etc....y Luke 7 : 2, etc.

touch he communicated purity to the impure. *It is never wrong to come in contact with evil for the purpose of curing it, if we are strong in God to accomplish our beneficent purpose.* To touch the dead was forbidden, yet both Elijah and Elisha did so (1 Kings 17 : 21 ; 2 Kings 4 : 34), for the law of love is always superior to any mere ceremonial regulation. **Immediately.** Mark says, "As soon as he had spoken." Observe that, assuming that we have a true account, there was no room for mistake or for the operation of natural causes. The leper was "full of leprosy," and was cured "immediately."

4. Shew thyself to the priest. The Levitical law provided that when a leper claimed to be healed, he should present himself to the priest, his healing should be officially passed upon by the priest, and certain sacrificial ceremonies performed, among which was the giving by the man of three lambs, with fine flour and oil; if he were poor a less costly gift might be substituted. The directions are contained in Lev. ch. 14. The birds and cedar-wood, and scarlet and hyssop, there referred to (verse 4) were no part of the gift, but were provided by the priest. The object of this ceremonial was both sanitary and ceremonial. It secured the community against the contagion of lepers who had not been really healed, by requiring the official sanction of the priest, and it also kept alive the symbolism which represented leprosy as a type of sin which, for its cleansing, requires divine pardon as well as physical cure. It must be remembered that the priests were the learned class of the early ages, and that the practice of medicine was chiefly confined, in ancient lands, to the priesthood and the temples. Jesus directed the leper to comply with this law, and thus *reunite himself with the church from which his leprosy had separated him.*

See thou tell no man. Because, (*a*,) Jesus would not have the leper make a boast of his miraculous cure, glory in it and in himself as a special object of divine favor; (*b*,) if the reputation of his marvellous cure preceded him to Jerusalem, the priests might deny that the man had ever been a leper, or was now truly cleansed, otherwise they would condemn themselves and their opposition to Jesus out of their own mouth; (*c*,) Christ customarily imposed silence on the subjects of his cures, because he would not that the faith of the people should rest upon the external evidence afforded by miracles, but upon their spiritual apprehension of the truth itself. (See Matt. 12 : 15-21, 38, 39.) The evidence from miracles he always treated as less valuable than the evidence which the truth carried in itself (John 14 : 11). *Christ and Christian truth are always the best evidence of Christianity.* **Testimony unto them.** These words are to be connected with Christ's command, not with that of Moses. The original may be translated as in our version, or "*for* a testimony *against* them." Both ideas are involved. Their official recognition that the leper was truly cleansed would render the miracle a conclusive testimony *to* them of Christ's healing power; it would be no less a testimony *against* them, because by accepting the gift and recognizing the cure the priests would testify against their own incredulity and rejection of Jesus as the Messiah.

Ch. 8 : 5-13. THE CURE OF THE CENTURION'S SERVANT.—EXEMPLIFICATION OF FAITH (10) ; IT IS HUMBLE (8), CONFIDENT (8, 9), ACCOMPANIES PRACTICAL BENEVOLENCE (6, Luke 7 : 1), HAS ITS REWARD (13).—CHRIST'S KINGDOM IS COMPREHENSIVE, INCLUDES THE OUTCASTS OF EARTH (11) ; IS EXCLUSIVE, CASTS OUT THE NATURAL BUT UNWORTHY HEIR (12).—IN THE KINGDOM OF HEAVEN ARE LIGHT, JOY, CHRISTIAN SOCIETY (11) ; IN THE KINGDOM OF SATAN DARKNESS, DESPAIR, OUTCASTS (12).

This incident is recorded by Luke (7 : 1-10) more fully than by Matthew; for that the two accounts are of the same incident is beyond reasonable doubt. It is not to be confounded with the cure of the nobleman's son (John 4 : 46-54 ; see notes there). It appears from Luke that the miracle was wrought immediately after Christ's Sermon on the Mount, and on his descent from the mountain; that the sick person, who is here called boy or child (see on verse 6, below), was a servant who was dear to the centurion; that the centurion was a favorite with the Jews, having built a synagogue for them; that he did not go in person, but sent the elders of the Jews to intercede for him; and that when he heard that Jesus was coming he sent a second delegation with the message, "I am not worthy," etc. The careful study of these two accounts is itself a lesson in biblical interpretation. They show that the Evangelists give only the essential facts, those that are necessary to an understanding of the moral significance of the teaching or the miracle.

5. Capernaum. See Matt. 4 : 13. **Centurion.** A Roman military officer. All Palestine was under Roman military government; this centurion was probably connected with the garrison at Capernaum. The Roman army was divided into legions, answering to our army corps, varying in size from three thousand to six thousand men; each legion was divided into ten cohorts, usually called in the N. T. the "band;"

6 And saying, Lord, my servant lieth at home sick of the palsy, grievously tormented.
7 And Jesus saith unto him, I will come and heal him.
8 The centurion answered and said, Lord, I am not worthy[a] that thou shouldest come under my roof: but speak the word only,[a] and my servant shall be healed.
9 For I am a man under authority, having soldiers under me: and I say to this *man*, Go, and he goeth; and to another, Come, and he cometh; and to my servant, Do this, and he doeth *it*.
10 When Jesus heard *it*, he marvelled, and said to them that followed, Verily I say unto you, I have not found so great faith,[b] no, not in Israel.
11 And I say unto you, That[c] many shall come from

---

a Ps. 10:17; Luke 15:19, 21....a verse 3; Ps. 33:9; 107:20....b ch. 15:28....c Isa. 9:2,3; Luke 13:29; Acts 11:18; Eph. 3:6; Rev. 7:9.

---

the cohort was divided into three maniples, and each maniple was divided into two centuries. These last contained from fifty to one hundred men, answering to our company, and each one was commanded by a centurion, answering to our captain. There were thus in each legion sixty centuries, each under the command of a centurion.

6. My servant. The Greek word (παῖς), translated *servant*, answers very nearly to the French term *garçon*, and to our term *boy;* but it indicates that the relation between this centurion and his servant or boy was one unusually tender (see Luke 7:2). Such instances of affection are more common in military than in domestic service. The regard which the master should have for his servant, especially in case of sickness, has been noted by the commentators as one of the morals indicated by this incident. "This centurion did not act as many masters do when their servants are afflicted—have them immediately removed to an infirmary or a work-house."—(*Adam Clarke.*) **Lieth at home sick of the palsy.** The disease indicated is not certain, for the ancients grouped many diseases together because of a certain similarity in symptoms which modern science discriminates, on account of their different causes and their intrinsic nature. It may have been a form of paralysis, which is sometimes accompanied with severe pain; or it may have been tetanus, or lock-jaw, which in the East is not infrequently connected with paralysis. He was in great pain, "grievously tormented," and was "ready to die" (Luke 7:2).

8. Answered. By a second delegation which the centurion sent when he heard that Christ was coming (Luke 7:6). What is done through another is often spoken of in Scripture, as in other books, as done by the person who directs it. See Gen. 40:22; 41:56; and compare Mark 10:35 with Matt. 20:20. **I am not worthy.** Observe three estimates of the centurion's character; first, his own, *not worthy*, because a Gentile, and because a sinner; second, the Jewish estimate, *worthy*, because he had built a Jewish synagogue, the highest encomium of character which a Jewish elder could pass on a Gentile outcast (Luke 7:4, 5); third, Jesus' estimate, *worthy, because of his faith*, and needing no commendation from Jewish elders, but himself an example and a rebuke to them. **Come under my roof.** "Counting himself unworthy that Jesus should enter into his doors, he was counted worthy that Jesus should enter into his heart."—(*Augustine.*) **Speak the word.** Contrast the centurion's faith, who trusts all to the word of Christ, with Martha's, who trusts only to his prayer to God. John 11:21, 22.

9. Under authority. The military authority of the East is even greater than in our own country. "No one ever inquires into the reason of an order of the rajah."—(*Burder's Oriental Literature.*) The idea appears to be, I am *under* authority; yet my servants do my bidding without questioning; you are no subordinate, how much more will disease obey you without questioning or requiring your presence to confirm your command. But it is in no way probable that the centurion had any clear comprehension of an Almighty power in Christ, or regarded him in any other light than as a prophet and a worker of miracles. To deduce from this an argument for the divine power and character of Jesus is to attribute to the uninstructed centurion not only a *faith* but a *knowledge* which the apostles did not acquire until after the resurrection of Jesus from the dead.

10. When Jesus heard it he marvelled. The significance of such declarations as this is not to be impaired by such interpretations as that of Augustine, "for our good that we may imitate the centurion's faith." It is difficult to understand how Christ, endowed with perfect knowledge of what was in man, could marvel at any disclosure; but not more difficult than to understand how he could rejoice, weep, be tempted, have spiritual struggles. It is a part of that inexplicable mystery which belongs to a nature too deep for our comprehension. It is not to be explained away in the vain endeavor to make a clear and easily comprehensible analysis of his character. What David said of the knowledge of God (Psalm 139:6) we may say of the character of Christ; It is too wonderful for us, we cannot attain unto it. **So great faith.** "To have high imaginations concerning him, this especially is of faith and tends to procure the kingdom and his other blessings."—(*Chrysostom.*) But this surely is not all. It was not merely belief, or hope, or expectation, which was exemplified, but *faith*, as a moral power impelling to action against moral obstacles. It was not merely an *intellectual perception*, but also a *moral resolution*, which made the naturally skeptical Roman

Сн. VIII.] MATTHEW. 119

the east and west, and shall sit down with Abraham, and Isaac, and Jacob, in the kingdom of heaven.
12 But the children of the kingdom⁴ shall be cast out into outer darkness: there shall be weeping⁵ and gnashing of teeth.

13 And Jesus said unto the centurion, Go thy way; and as thou hast believed, so be it done unto thee. And his servant was healed in the selfsame hour.
14 And when Jesus was come into Peter's house, he saw his wife's mother laid,ᶠ and sick of a fever.

d ch. 7 : 22, 23....e ch. 13 : 42, 50....f Mark 1 : 30, 31; Luke 4 : 38, 39.

apply to a messenger of the God of the Jews, which made the naturally proud Roman apply to a prophet of a people whom the Romans despised and classed with slaves, which made a naturally haughty military officer recognize the superior authority of one who was under his military control, but whose power was from above, which made the naturally callous Roman appeal for help, not on his own behalf, but on that of a mere chattel servant.

11. Many shall come. The question is sometimes still asked whether any of the heathen, who have never known of and received Christ, will be admitted to heaven. Christ answers the question, at least by implication, here and in Luke 13 : 29. Compare Romans 2 : 8-11, and observe that the Gentiles referred to in the latter passage, and to whom Paul declares there is at least a possibility of salvation, are those that never have received a written law, i. e., the Bible (verses 12-15), and that in the case of the centurion the *spirit* of faith preceded any knowledge of Christ, and that there is nothing to show that this Roman had any clear and correct intellectual apprehension of Christ's character, or of his kingdom. **Sit down.** To sit at table with other immortals is a common metaphor among ancient writers to express future felicity.

12. Cast out into outer darkness. "An emblem of such as are rejected and cast out of the door at the marriage-feast to which they had come. In despair they weep and gnash their teeth. The Jews generally had their great feasts in the evening; those cast out are therefore in darkness."—(*Burder's Oriental Literature.*) See for fuller interpretation notes on Matt. 25 : 1-13. Observe that, (*a*,) the kingdom of heaven is represented as one of light and joy; (*b*,) that punishment consists in exclusion from God and the companionship of the holy. There is no suggestion here of positive *torments*, and although there are such intimations elsewhere (Matt. 11 : 50; 18 : 34, 35; Mark 9 : 43-48; Luke 16 : 24), yet the contrast is very marked throughout Christ's teachings between his representations of future punishment and those found in heathen literature. See, for example, the following quotation from the (Hindoo) Institutes of Manu: "Multifarious tortures await the wicked. They shall be mangled by ravens and owls, and shall swallow cakes boiling hot, and shall walk over inflamed sands, and shall feel the pangs of being baked like the vessels of the potter; they shall assume the form of beasts continually miserable, and suffer alternate afflictions from extremes of cold and heat, surrounded with terrors of various kinds. They shall have old age without resource, diseases attended with anguish, pangs of innumerable sort, and lastly unconquerable death." For the most part the Bible representations of future punishment are of a fixity in a state of sin (Rev. 22 : 11), and of banishment from the presence of God (2 Thess. 1 : 9).

13. Was healed. Evidently this cure is not one which can be attributed to any known natural causes; not merely because severe paralysis is extremely difficult of cure, if not incurable (on this much stress cannot be laid since we are not sure of the disease), but because Jesus did not even see his patient, so that no remedy could have been employed, and there could have been no opportunity even for the operation of mental causes in relieving the sufferer.

Ch. 8 : 14-17. HEALING OF PETER'S MOTHER-IN-LAW AND OTHERS.—CHRIST CURES IN THE HOUSEHOLD AS WELL AS IN THE CHURCH.—HE CURES INSTANTLY, WHOLLY.—HE THAT CASTS OUT DISEASE ALSO IMPARTS STRENGTH (2 Peter 1 : 3).—HE THAT IS HEALED BY CHRIST SHOULD IMMEDIATELY BEGIN TO SERVE CHRIST —HE HEALS NOT ONLY HIS FRIENDS BUT THE MULTITUDE. —HE SUFFERS THAT HE MAY HEAL, AND THUS EXEMPLIFIES THE LAW OF BURDEN-BEARING FOR OTHERS (Gal. 6 : 2).—WE MAY BRING TO HIM NOT ONLY OUR PAST SINS, BUT ALSO OUR PRESENT INFIRMITIES OF TEMPER AND SICKNESSES OF SOUL.

These incidents are reported in Mark 1 : 29-34, and Luke 4 : 38-41, more fully than here. They occurred before the Sermon on the Mount, during Christ's first missionary tour of Galilee, on Sabbath evening, and immediately after his healing of the demoniac in the synagogue (Mark 1 : 23-28, 29, etc.; Luke 4 : 33-35, 38, etc.). The house was in Capernaum where Peter lived, and near which town he had been called to follow Christ (Matt. 4 : 18-20). The healing followed almost immediately after this call. Thus Peter, who left all to follow Christ, gained by it a mother (Mark 19 : 29). Peter, Andrew, James, and John were all with Christ at the time. The three had followed Peter with Christ from their fishing just previously (Matt. 4 : 18-22; Mark 1 : 19).

14. Fever. Malarious fevers, of a malignant type, are common in the vicinity of Capernaum; they are due, probably, to marshes near by. In the very imperfect medical language of that day fevers were simply divided into little and great fevers. Luke, who was a physician, character

15 And he touched her hand, and the fever left her: and she arose, and ministered unto them.
16 When the even was come, they brought unto him many^g that were possessed with devils: and he cast out the spirits with *his* word, and healed all that were sick:
17 That it might be fulfilled which was spoken by Esaias^h the prophet, saying, Himself took our infirmities, and bare *our* sicknesses.
18 Now when Jesus saw great multitudes about him, he gave commandment to depart unto the other side.

19 And a certain scribe came, and said unto him, Master, Iⁱ will follow thee whithersoever thou goest.
20 And Jesus saith unto him, The foxes have holes, and the birds of the air *have* nests; but the Son of man hath not where to lay *his* head.
21 And another of his disciples said unto him, Lord,^j suffer me first to go and bury my father.
22 But Jesus saith unto him, Follow me; and let the dead bury their dead.
23 And when he was entered into a ship, his disciples followed him.

g Mark 1 : 32, etc.....h Isa. 53 : 4; 1 Pet. 2 : 24.....i Luke 9 : 57, 58.....j 1 Kings 19 : 20.

izes this as a "great fever." That she was entirely prostrated by it is evident from the language here, "laid and sick of a fever."

15. And he touched her hand. According to both Mark and Luke he was asked to cure her. He not only touched her hand but lifted her up (Mark 1 : 31). **The fever left her.** Mark says *immediately*, which is implied here. **She ministered unto them.** Such a fever invariably leaves the patient weak. The period of convalescence is always long and trying, often full of danger. The fact that she ministered to them, *i. e.*, served in the ordinary duties of the household, shows that Christ in healing the disease also imparted health and strength, and it demonstrates the miraculous character of the cure.

16. When the even was come. It was on the Sabbath day (Mark, ch. 1), on which the Pharisaic law allowed no works of healing. The Sabbath ended at sunset. The Talmud says, "If in the going out of the Sabbath one do any work after one star is seen, he is bound to a sacrifice for sin; if after two, to a sacrifice for transgression; if after three, he is clear." It was during this twilight hour that the people brought their sick to Christ. Observe, that he heals Peter's mother-in-law without waiting for sunset, and thus privately teaches his disciples that it is lawful to heal on the Sabbath-day, a lesson which he subsequently repeated publicly (Matt. 12 : 12; John 5 : 16, 17). **They brought unto him.** *i. e.*, the people generally. Mark gives an idea of the throng by his expression, "All the city was gathered together at the door." **Many.** "In one word the Evangelist traverses an unspeakable sea of miracles."—(*Chrysostom.*) Compare John 20 : 30. **Devils.** See note at end of this chapter. Mark and Luke both add that he suffered them not to speak.

17. That it might be fulfilled. The passage referred to is Isaiah 53 : 4, 5. There the reference is clearly to sins and heart-sorrows; here to physical disease. Matthew interprets the one by the other, and leaves us to draw the conclusion that *as Christ bore the sicknesses of those he healed, in like manner he bears the sins of those he redeems*; *i. e.*, his character as a physician is the symbol of his character as a savior. How, then,

did he bare the infirmities of the sick? Not literally. He removed them from others, but did not become diseased himself. Neither in removing sins from others does he become stricken with sin himself. (Compare John 1 : 29 with Hebrews 4 : 15.) But he did not merely heal the sick, he truly bore their sicknesses, not in his body, but in his heart. The metaphor both here and in Isaiah is of one who removes a burden by putting his own shoulder under it, and bearing it away *upon himself*. This Christ did, because he entered through compassion into the sorrows and sicknesses he healed (Mark 7 : 34; John 11 : 33, 35). So, *not by any literal transfer of sins from others to himself*, but by a spiritual and sympathetic bearing of the burden of the world's sins in his own heart, he bore them away from all those who cast their burden on him. (Compare Gal. 6 : 2; 1 Pet. v : vi.)

18-22. CONDITIONS OF FOLLOWING CHRIST. There is some uncertainty when this incident occurred. Mark does not record it, but he narrates the miracle of the stilling of the tempest, which he places immediately after the parables recorded in Matt. ch. 13 (Mark 4 : 35), and with that miracle Matthew connects this incident (verse 18); Luke places it at a later period in Christ's life (Luke 9 : 57). The hypothesis that the same incidents occurred twice is utterly indefensible. On the whole, the probability appears to be that it occurred on Christ's taking ship to depart to the other side of the lake, after preaching the parables on the kingdom of God, as recorded in Matthew, ch. 13. But as Luke's account is the fullest, I reserve comments on the practical and spiritual significance of the incident for the passage in Luke.

18. The other side, *i. e.*, of the Sea of Galilee. His object was to escape the throng, and secure quiet with his disciples. The offer of the scribe was therefore, if not an impertinence, certainly an intrusion.

21. Another of his disciples. According to an ancient tradition this was Philip. It seems more probable that the phrase disciple is here used only in the more general sense of one who had loosely attached himself to Jesus as a learner. It appears from Luke that his request was in response to Christ's command, "Follow me."

24 And behold,[b] there arose a great tempest in the sea, insomuch that the ship was covered with the waves: but he was asleep.
25 And his disciples came to *him*, and awoke him, saying, Lord, save us: we perish.
26 And he saith unto them, Why are ye fearful, O ye of little faith? Then he arose, and rebuked[c] the winds and the sea; and there was a great calm.

27 But the men marvelled, saying, What manner of man is this, that even the winds and the sea obey him!
28 And[m] when he was come to the other side, into the country of the Gergesenes, there met him two possessed with devils, coming out of the tombs, exceeding fierce, so that no man might pass by that way.
29 And, behold, they cried out, saying, What have

b Mark 4 : 37, etc.; Luke 8 : 23, etc....l Job 38 : 11; Ps. 89 : 9; 107 : 29....m Mark 5 : 1; Luke 8 : 26, etc.

23–27. STILLING THE TEMPEST. Recorded also in Mark 4 : 35–41 and Luke 8 : 22–25. The account is fullest in Mark. It there appears that Christ departed *as he was*, i. e., without making any preparations; that there were other ships or boats accompanying him; that the waves filled the boat so that it seemed to be in danger of foundering; that Christ was asleep in the hinder part of the boat on a pillow or cushion; and that the disciples not only aroused him, but did so with words which implied fault-finding, because of his supposed indifference to their danger. The incident occurred immediately after the preaching of the parables concerning the kingdom of God, recorded in Matt. ch. 13. See notes on Mark 4 : 35–41.

Ch. 8 : 28–34. HEALING OF THE DEMONIACS. THE DEVILS CANNOT KEEP THE SOUL FROM CHRIST.—THEY HAVE NOTHING TO DO WITH JESUS THE SAVIOUR; BUT MUCH TO DO WITH THE SON OF GOD, THE JUDGE.—THE CREED OF THE DEVILS IS THE SAME AS PETER'S CREED (Matt. 16 : 16); THE BELIEF IS THE SAME BUT NOT THE FAITH (James 2 : 19).—THE HOLY ARE A TORMENT TO THE WICKED.—SIN PROTESTS AGAINST INTERFERENCE. ITS CRY IS ALWAYS LET US ALONE; WHAT HAVE WE TO DO WITH THEE (1 Kings 18 : 17; Acts 16 : 20; 17 : 6). —THE DEVIL'S POSSESSION IS ALWAYS FOR DESTRUCTION.—THE DEVIL PROMISED ALL THE KINGDOMS OF THE EARTH TO JESUS (ch. 4 : 8); HIS AGENTS CANNOT EVEN TAKE POSSESSION OF A HERD OF SWINE WITHOUT CHRIST'S PERMISSION.—THE POWER AND THE POWERLESSNESS OF THE DEVIL BOTH EXEMPLIFIED.—TO THE COVETOUS SWINE ARE WORTH MORE THAN THE SAVIOUR.—THE SENTENCE OF THE JUDGMENT-DAY, "DEPART" (ch. 25 : 41), WILL ONLY ECHO THE PRAYER OF THE SINNER.

This miracle is recorded also in Mark 5 : 1–21 and Luke 8 : 26–40, which, with the notes on the latter passage, see for some details omitted here.

28. The other side. The eastern shore of the Sea of Galilee. **Gergesenes.** Mark and Luke have Gadarenes, and some manuscripts substitute that word here. For a time the seeming conflict between the sacred writers in this respect caused great perplexity to biblical students, and in the minds of rationalistic critics threw doubt over the whole narrative. The city of Gadara is three hours to the south of the southern shore of the lake, and the miracle could not have been performed in its vicinity; and it is hardly probable that the citizens of so distant a city would have turned out *en masse* for a journey of three hours to see the one who had wrought this miracle. But recently Dr. William Thompson has discovered a Gergesa, now called Chersa or Gersa, on the eastern shore of the lake, and on the borders of the district or province which took its name from Gadara, one of the chief cities of Decapolis. This Gersa or Gergesa, so insignificant that it has escaped the attention of most travelers, was unknown to the Roman world. Mark and Luke therefore, who wrote for the Gentiles, described the miracle as occurring in the country of the Gadarenes, a description which would have been readily comprehended, since Gadara was one of the chief Roman cities of Palestine, and widely known. Matthew, who had been a tax-gatherer on this very shore, was familiar with every village and hamlet, and wrote for Jewish readers, described it as occurring in the country of the Gergesenes, thus fixing its locality more definitely. Chersa or Gersa answers to all the conditions of the narrative: it is within a few rods of the shore; a mountain rises immediately above it, so near the shore that the swine, rushing madly down, could not stop, but would be inevitably driven on into the water and drowned; the ruins of ancient tombs are still found in this mountainside, and Capernaum is in full view on the other side, "over against it" (Luke 8 : 26). See *Thompson's Land and Book*, vol. ii., pp. 34, 35.

Two possessed with devils. Mark and Luke mention but *one*; probably the fiercer of the two. He was naked (Luke 8 : 27), had been chained but had broken his chains, and had cut himself with stones until he was doubtless covered with blood. He ran to Jesus and worshipped him; i. e., as the devils worship, not by paying him a true reverence, but by a compulsory acknowledgment of his power. See Mark for a graphic picture of his condition. On the nature of demoniac possession, see below.

Out of the tombs. These were caves formed by nature or cut in the rocks, with cells at the sides for the reception of the dead. They were ceremonially unclean (Numb. 19 : 11, 16; Matt. 23 : 27; Luke 11 : 44), and dwelling in them was of itself a sign of degradation. Trench (*Notes on the Miracles*) quotes from *Warburton's Crescent and the Cross* a striking illustration of this account: "I found myself in a cemetery, whose sculptured turbans showed me that the neighboring

we to do with thee, Jesus, thou Son of God? art thou come hither to torment us before the time?
30 And there was a good way off from them, an herd of many swine, feeding.
31 So the devils besought him, saying, If thou cast us out, suffer⁰ us to go away into the herd of swine.°

32 And he said unto them, Go. And when they were come out, they went into the herd of swine and, behold, the whole herd of swine ran violently down a steep place into the sea, and perished in the waters.
33 And they that kept them fled, and went their

a Job 1 : 10–12; 2 : 3–6.... o Deut. 14 : 8; Isa. 65 : 3, 4.

village was Moslem. The silence of the night was now broken by fierce yells and howlings, which I discovered proceeded from a naked maniac, who was fighting with some wild dogs for a bone. The moment he perceived me he left his canine comrades, and bounding along with rapid strides, seized my horse's bridle, and almost forced him backward over the cliff by the grip he held of the powerful Marmeluke bit." **Exceeding fierce.** Mark adds that he could neither be tamed nor bound, and Luke that the evil spirit drove him into the wilderness.

29. Comparing this account with Mark and Luke, the facts appear to be that the maniac made a rush towards Jesus and the twelve, perhaps purposing to destroy them; that Christ stopped him by word of command, requiring the evil spirits to leave the man, and that the expostulation given in this verse was the devil's response to that command. Christ then asks his name, and is told it is "Legion." The devils beseech that they may not be sent "out into the deep" (Luke 8 : 31, and note), literally into the *abyss*, i. e., back into their prison-house, but instead may be suffered to enter into the herd of swine. **What have we to do with thee?** A common Jewish phrase, signifying a wish not to be troubled by the importunity or the interference of another (Judges 11 : 12; 2 Sam. 16 : 10; 2 Kings 9 : 18; Ezra 4 : 3; John 2 : 4). **To torment us.** Compare Mark 1 : 24. "Herein the true devilish spirit speaks, one which counts it a torment not to be suffered to torment others, and an injury done to itself when it is no more permitted to be injurious to others."—(*Trench*.) **Before the time.** When the devil and his angels shall be shut up in the fire prepared for them (Matt. 25 : 41; Jude 6; Rev. 20 : 10).

30. And there was * * * an herd of many swine. Mark gives the number, about 2000. The flesh of swine was forbidden as food by the Levitical law (Lev. 11 : 7; Deut. 14 : 8). It is generally believed that its use in hot countries tends to induce cutaneous disorders, and would render the eater more liable to leprosy and kindred diseases. It is to the present day held in great abhorrence among the Jews (see Isaiah 65 : 4; 66 : 3, 17). The rabbinical law forbade the keeping of swine. Whether this herd was kept by Jews or by heathen is a matter of uncertainty. The cities of Decapolis were largely filled with Romans, with whom swine's flesh was deemed a luxury.

31. So the devils besought him, etc. This, as appears in both Mark and Luke, was in response to Christ's command to the evil spirit to come out of the man. Adam Clark remarks on this passage that since the evil spirit cannot enter the body of even a swine without divine permission, those need not fear the devil whose trust is in God.

32. It is impossible for an honest interpreter to understand this narrative in any other than its plain and natural sense, viz., that there were evil spirits in the man controlling his personality, that they left him and entered into the herd of swine, and that in consequence, either driven by fright or acting under the impulses of the evil spirits, the entire herd rushed headlong into the sea. Any such *pseudo* interpretation as that offered by Lange, in his *Life of Jesus*, but apparently abandoned in his *Commentary*, that the cries of the demoniac man, when the evil spirit came out of him, frightened the herd and threw them into a panic, are not interpretations at all, but the substitution of a new narrative for those which the Evangelists have given us; the supposition of Mr. Livermore that "Jesus miraculously transferred the insanity from the men to the swine" (*Livermore's Commentary*, Matt. 8 : 32) needs only to be stated; it bears its own refutation on its face. The general question of demoniac possession I consider below; but some special questions, raised by this part of the narrative, may be briefly answered here. *Why should Christ have permitted the evil spirits to enter the swine?* A difficult question; but less so than the question why God should have permitted them to enter into the man, or indeed sin to enter into the world at all. *Why should they have destroyed the herd of swine, and so deprived themselves, so to speak, of a terrestrial abode?* Perhaps the act of the swine was the result of panic, and in spite of the evil spirits. But Trench well remarks that it is the very nature of evil thus to outwit itself; "stupid, blind, self-contradictory, and suicidal, it can only destroy, and will involve itself in the common ruin rather than not destroy." *What right had Christ to allow the destruction of the property of another?* He had the same right which he constantly exercises through the destructive agencies of nature to do what he will with his own. His destroying cattle by murrain, cities by earthquakes, ships with their living freight by storm, is all a part of the same in-

ways into the city, and told every thing, and what was befallen to the possessed of the devils.

34 And, behold, the whole city came out to meet Jesus: and when they saw him, they besought *him* that he would depart⁰ out of their coasts.

CHAPTER IX.

AND he entered into a ship, and passed over, and came into his own city.

2 And,ᵃ behold, they brought to him a man sick of

p Job 21 : 14; Luke 5 : 8; Acts 16 : 39. ...q Mark 2 : 3, etc.; Luke 5 : 18, etc.

scrutable mystery. Here we can at least see that the destruction of the herd of swine, standing in contrast with the salvation of the man, has given the cure a significance it could not have possessed otherwise, and their panic-stricken flight affords a sort of testimony, coming from the lowest animals, against the consent which alone allows the devil ever to gain possession of us. If the herdsmen were Jews, they deserved the loss of their herd. *How are we to understand the devils entering into the swine, i. e., "the working of the spiritual life in the bestial?"* We know so little of the means by which even through physical organs of speech, sight, and hearing, one spirit acts upon the other, that we may well admit the mystery of this possession of the swine by an evil spirit. But we daily see the horse and the dog catching the spirit of their master, emboldened by his courage or panic-stricken by his fear; facts which may illustrate, if they cannot fully explain, how a herd of swine might be possessed by evil spirits. "The very fierceness and grossness of these animals may have been exactly that which best fitted them for receiving such impulses from the lower world as those under which they perished."—(*Trench.*)

33. **Went * * * into the city.** Not Gadara, which was three hours distant, but Chersa or Gergesa, which was close at hand. See on verse 28. **Told everything, and what had befallen to the possessed.** Evidently first what had befallen the swine entrusted to their keeping, next what salvation had come to the man.

34. **The whole city.** See note on Matt. 3 : 5. **Besought him that he would depart.** It appears from Mark and Luke that the sight of the well-known maniac clothed and in his right mind filled the people with fear. Awe at the miracle, mingled with dread because of the destruction of their property, led them to beseech Christ to depart. The loss of 2000 swine was more to them than the saving of a soul.

Ch. 9 : 1. And he took ship. This verse belongs with the preceding chapter, and narrates Christ's response to the people's request. It does not connect the embarkation for the western shore of Galilee with the miracle following—the healing of the paralytic. See on verse 2. Twice in this narrative Christ hears the prayer whose petition is for evil—the prayer of the evil spirit, which ends in the destruction of the swine and in the exile of the evil spirits and their being driven back from earth into their own place again, and now the prayer of the people that he would depart from their coasts. "God sometimes hears his enemies in anger (Numb. 22 : 19, 20), even as he [sometimes] refuses to hear his friends in love (2 Cor. 12 : 8, 9)."—(*Trench.*) Christ appears never to have visited the country of the Gadarenes again. He does not abide where he is not wanted (compare Exod. 10 : 28, 29; Acts 24 : 25). Mark and Luke add to this account that the demoniac "published throughout the whole city how great things Jesus had done unto him;" an incidental evidence of the completeness of his cure. **And came into his own city,** *i. e.,* Capernaum (Matt. 4 : 13).

OF DEMONIACAL POSSESSION.

Of all the cases of demoniacal possession recorded in the N. T. this is the most striking. The difficulties peculiar to it have been considered above. It remains to speak briefly of the general subject.

The N. T., and especially the Evangelists, repeatedly mention individuals whom they describe as possessed by devils. For the most part these persons seem to have been harmless; sometimes, however, of a violent and dangerous character. The possession was often accompanied by physical disease—blindness, dumbness, epilepsy. In one case it accompanied a disorder which was congenital, if not hereditary. The victim seems usually to have been possessed of a double consciousness. His acts were unwitting. And when, by the word of Jesus, the devil was cast out,

and he appeared clothed and in his right mind, he was with peculiar significance a new creature in Christ Jesus (Matt. 12 : 22; Mark 9 : 18, 20, 21; Luke 8 : 29; and see references below). In respect to the narratives of these cases two important questions arise: 1st. *What are we to suppose the writers meant by their narratives; i. e.,* how did they understand these cases. 2d. *Is their understanding to be accepted? i. e.,* did they correctly interpret the phenomena which they recorded, or are we to give to those phenomena, in the light of modern science, a different interpretation?

In respect to the first question there is really no difficulty. It was the universal belief of their age, both among the Jews and among the heathen, that evil spirits operated upon and sometimes controlled both nature and the human soul. Disease was often, and lunacy was generally, attributed to the influence of evil spirits. The Evangelists unquestionably believed and intended to be understood as asserting that the persons described as possessed with evil or unclean spirits were really and literally under the control of disembodied spirits, agents of Satan. They are frequently distinguished from those afflicted with mere physical disorders (Mark 1:32; 16:17,18; Luke 6:17, 18); the demons are distinguished, nowhere, perhaps, more clearly than in this narrative, from the persons whom they control, and are represented as recognizing in Jesus the Son of God, a title not given to him even by his disciples until toward the close of his ministry (see verse 29; Mark 1:24; 5:7; Luke 4:41; compare Matt. 16:16). No honest interpreter can doubt that the Evangelists shared the common opinion of their day, and intended to be understood as asserting that these individuals were under the control of evil spirits, and that Christ literally emancipated them from this diabolical servitude, and cast the evil spirits out.

The second question is really the only one in the case, viz.: Did they correctly interpret the phenomena which they recorded, or are we to give to those phenomena, in the light of modern science, a different interpretation?

It is certain that they bear a curiously striking resemblance to cases of what is in modern scientific language called "moral insanity." In both there is a clear recognition of the difference between right and wrong; in both there is the testimony of the patient that he is impelled by a power beside himself; both are accompanied sometimes by acts of violence, sometimes by attempts at suicide; both are, in their worst forms, attended with epileptic convulsions; both are frequently manifested in periodic returns of disorder, with intervals of sanity; both are sometimes traceable to willful self-indulgence in some form of sin as their provoking cause; and in both there is at times, in a remarkable degree, an appreciation of the character of persons with whom the insane are thrown in contact, who are sometimes peculiarly affected by the presence of persons of a pure and holy character (Mark 1:24; 5:6,9; 9:17, 18-22; Luke 4:33). The reader who is curious to investigate this parallelism will find the material in Abbott's *Jesus of Nazareth*, chap. 13, and still more full reports of modern cases analogous to the demoniacal possession of the N. T., in Ray's *Medical Jurisprudence*, chap. 7, § 5, pp. 202-260; Henry Maudsley's *Physiology and Pathology of the Mind*, chap. 3, pp. 306-316, and Forbes Winslow's *Obscure Diseases of the Brain and Mind*, pp. 175-211. These parallels have led a certain class of critics to the conclusion that the persons described in the N. T. as possessed of evil spirits were in fact only lunatics, and that the narrative of their disease and their cure is to be interpreted accordingly. The great majority of Evangelical scholars agree, however, in the opinion that the individuals described as possessed by evil spirits, were really under their control, and that the cures described consisted in fact, as well as in appearance, in the casting out of the evil spirit. This opinion, which I think is the only one consistent with belief in the historical trustworthiness of the Scriptures, or confidence in the truthfulness of Christ, rests on the following grounds:—1st. *It best accords with the facts testified to by modern science, if not best with its hypotheses.* In certain of the cases of so-called "moral insanity," the patient not only recognizes the difference between right and wrong, and abhors the crime to the commission of which he is impelled, seemingly by a will stronger than his own, but subsequently, in his sane moments, or previously, in anticipation of the paroxysm, declares himself conscious of the indwelling of another spirit too strong for his resistance, and asserts that he is "prompted by Satan," while on the other hand medical examination, in many cases, fails to find any physical cause for the phenomena. These circumstances have led some of the highest authorities in mental disease to acknowledge the cause of those forms of "moral insanity" to be inscrutable (see both Henry Maudsley and Forbes Winslow), and others to recognize demoniacal possession, as a modern phenomenon, to be the most probable and rational explanation of them. This is the view of Esquirol, who stands at the head of the French school, if not of all schools, as a student of mental disorders. 2d. *It best accords with other teachings of Scripture.* This represents that there is a world of disembodied spirits, both good and bad; that they are not wholly separated from man, but exert a powerful influence upon him; that their influence is not a thing of the past, but that the Christian has still need to watch and pray against it (Judges 9:23; 1 Sam. 16:14-23; 18:10,11; 19:8,10; 1 Kings 22:22; Luke 22:31; John 13:27; Acts 5:3; 2 Cor. 4:4; Ephes. 6:11,12; 1 Tim. 3:7; 1 Pet. 5:8). 3d. *It accords with the teaching and conduct of Jesus Christ.* He distinctly recognized the personality and presence of demons, distinct from the man in whom they were, and from whom they were cast out (Mark 1:25; 5:19; 9:25; Luke 10:17-20; 11:17-26). Either his words are falsely reported, *i. e.*, demoniacal possession is a mythical addition of a later date, or he was himself under a delusion respecting these cases, *i. e.*, he shared the ignorance and superstition of his age, or he ratified and confirmed that superstition for the purpose of adding to his prestige by seeming to cast out spirits that had no existence; *i. e.*, he lent himself to imposture, or *evil spirits really exercised a control over the impulses and the will of those whom they were sent to*

the palsy, lying on a bed: And Jesus seeing their faith, said unto the sick of the palsy, Son,¹ be of good cheer; thy sins be forgiven thee.

3 And, behold, certain of the scribes said within themselves, This man blasphemeth.

4 And Jesus knowing their thoughts,⁸ said, Wherefore think ye evil in your hearts?

5 For whether is easier, to say, *Thy* sins be forgiven thee; or to say, Arise, and walk?

6 But that ye may know that the Son of man hath power on earth to forgive¹ sins, (then saith he to the sick of the palsy,) Arise, take up thy bed, and go unto thine house.

7 And he arose, and departed to his house.

8 But when the multitudes saw *it*, they marvelled, and glorified⁶ God, which had given such power unto men.

9 And⁷ as Jesus passed forth from thence, he saw a

---

r Mark 5 : 34....s Ps. 139 : 2 ; John 2 : 24, 25 ; Heb. 4 : 12, 13 ; Rev. 2 : 23....t Micah 7 : 19....u Acts 4 : 21 ; Gal. 1 : 24....v Mark 2 : 14 ; Luke 5 : 27, etc.

---

possess, and *Christ really drove them out from their possession, and emancipated the soul from their control.* If the question is asked why this demoniac possession is unknown now, the answer is, that it is not unknown ; that, on the contrary, demoniacal possession is the most natural explanation of certain forms of so-called " moral insanity ; " that it should exist in less degree and extent is just what we should expect from the declarations of Scripture (Zech. 13 : 2 ; 1 John 3 : 8). How far the victim of demoniacal possession was responsible for his condition, how far he is to be regarded as guilty, and how far as simply unfortunate, is a difficult if not an insoluble question. " The common characteristic of all was cowardice, a cowardly surrender of a weak and lowered consciousness to wicked influences."—(*Lange*.) Every such surrender by the soul is one step toward a complete enthrallment of the soul by evil, though that enthrallment rarely becomes complete in this life.

Ch. 9 : 2–8. HEALING OF THE PARALYTIC. The accounts of this miracle in Mark 2 : 1–12, and Luke 5 : 17–26, are fuller than that given here. From these accounts it appears that the crowd was so great that the friends of the paralytic could not reach the house in which Christ was teaching, and that they uncovered the roof and let the patient down with the bed or mattress on which he was lying. This constituted the evidence of their faith, commended by the Lord. The miracle took place, not, as might be supposed, on Christ's return from the country of the Gadarenes, but more probably at about the time of the healing of the leper, recorded in Matt. 8 : 2–4. For notes on the miracle see Mark 2 : 1–12.

Ch. 9 : 9–13. THE CALL OF MATTHEW.—A BAD BUSINESS IS A POOR EXCUSE FOR NOT FOLLOWING CHRIST; FOLLOW HIM OUT OF IT.—THE POWER OF CHRIST'S CALLING: IT SUMMONS FROM ALL RANKS AND ALL AVOCATIONS.—CHRIST'S SOCIABILITY THE TRUE MODEL OF CHRISTIAN SOCIABILITY.—A RIGHT AND A WRONG WAY TO ASSOCIATE WITH SINNERS ; A RIGHT AND A WRONG WAY TO BE SEPARATE FROM THEM. CHRIST ATE WITH SINNERS BUT WAS SEPARATE FROM THEM ; THE PHARISEES SCORNED THEM BUT WERE ONE WITH THEM.—MATTHEW AN EXAMPLE OF A FISHER OF MEN ; CALLED HIMSELF, HE CALLS OTHERS.—SIN IS BOTH A WEAKNESS AND A DISEASE ; PERSONAL SYMPATHY AFFORDS SPIRITUAL STRENGTH AND IS A SPIRITUAL MEDICINE.—THERE IS LESS RELIGION IN SACRIFICE WITHOUT MERCY THAN IN MERCY WITHOUT SACRIFICE ; TRUE RELIGION CONSISTS IN SACRIFICE AND MERCY.—THE EXCLUDED AND THE INCLUDED IN CHRIST'S CALLING: THE EXCLUDED ALL THE SELF-RIGHTEOUS ; THE INCLUDED ALL CONSCIOUS OF SIN.

The call of a publican, and a subsequent feast given by him in honor of the Lord, are recorded by Mark 2 : 13–17, and Luke 5 : 27–32 ; but in Mark and Luke the publican is called Levi. Matthew never speaks of himself as Levi in his own gospel, and is never spoken of as Levi by the other Evangelists in any other passage. This has led some commentators to suppose that there were two persons and two feasts, a supposition which is quite improbable, and is now universally rejected. Changes of name in commemoration of any great event were not uncommon among the Jews, of which the cases of Abram or Abraham, Jacob or Israel, and Saul of Tarsus or Paul (Gen. 17 : 5 ; 32 : 28 ; Acts 13 : 9) are striking illustrations ; that of Simon changed to Peter (John 1 : 42, and note there) is still more in point. If, as is probable, the name Matthew means the same as the modern name Theodore, Gift of God or Given to God, its very significance would help to account for the change. Chrysostom and Jerome note the "self-denial of the Evangelist who disguises not his former life, but adds even his name, when the others had concealed him under another appellation." Observe that in ch. 10 : 3 Matthew calls himself "Matthew the publican," while neither Mark nor Luke so characterize him in the lists of the apostles. There can be no doubt that the call of Matthew preceded the Sermon on the Mount, which was an ordination sermon following the solemn consecration of the twelve to their apostolic office (Luke 6 : 13–20) ; nor that it immediately succeeded the cure of the paralytic, with which Matthew directly connects it by his phrase "as Jesus passed forth from thence." At what time the feast was given by Matthew to Christ is not so certain. All the Evangelists connect it with the call of Matthew ; it is a rational supposition that Matthew gave it at this time ; in that case he would naturally invite his old associates to the feast ; whereas, after entering on his apostolate, and breaking off his old

man, named Matthew, sitting at the receipt of custom: and he saith unto him, Follow me. And he arose, and followed him.

10 And it came to pass, as Jesus sat at meat in the house, behold, many publicans and sinners came and sat down with him and his disciples.

life with them, he would be less likely to invite them; and it seems almost certain that this feast preceded the charges brought against Jesus, and recorded in Matthew 11:19. On the other hand, Matthew connects this feast directly with the healing of Jairus' daughter (see verse 18, below), which Mark and Luke place immediately after the cure of the Gadarene demoniac, but without any definite note of time. The better opinion is that the feast was given at the time of Matthew's call, though this is by no means certain.

Accepting this opinion, and combining the accounts of the three Evangelists, the fact and its significance may be concisely stated thus: Christ calls a tax-gatherer to leave his office and join the band of itinerant disciples; the call is accepted with alacrity; and as a means of knowing his new master, and at the same time bringing him to a knowledge of his old associates, Levi gives a feast to which both Christ and his disciples, and his own former companions, are invited. At the same time he takes on the new name of Matthew, which he henceforth bears. By accepting the invitation Christ enters into familiar intercourse with a class of men whose moral character was bad, whose reputation was worse, and whose iniquitous avocation was justly odious to all men. The Pharisees ask the disciples, tauntingly, for an explanation, and Christ replies by declaring his object to be the elevation and redemption of sinners, and by referring them to the Scriptures which they pretended to teach, but whose spirit they totally misapprehended (see ch. 3: 12, 16), as the authority for his course.

9. As Jesus passed forth from thence. This indisputably connects the call of Matthew with the preceding miracle, and places both in the period of Christ's earlier ministry in Galilee, where it is placed by Mark. Chrysostom observes that Christ calls Matthew immediately after having asserted and demonstrated in the preceding miracle his power to forgive sins. **Matthew.** Luke says that he was the son of Alphæus. This was a not uncommon name among the Jews. It is not probable it was the same Alphæus who is described in Matthew 10:3 (see note there) as the father of James. This is the first mention of Matthew in the Gospels. On his life and character, see note at end of chapter 10. **Sitting at the receipt of custom.** The taxes levied by the Roman government on the inhabitants of Palestine may be roughly divided into two classes—internal taxes and tolls. The former included all taxes levied on persons and property directly; the latter, all customs levied on goods in transit; and answered to our modern custom dues. They are distinguished in Rom. 13:7 as tribute and custom. The customs were levied on all goods imported for trade, though not, ordinarily, on such as were imported for the purchaser's personal use; they were levied at harbors, piers, and gates of cities; they amounted to a sum varying at different times from one-eighth to one-fortieth of the value of the goods; any attempt at concealment was punished by the confiscation of the articles. Matthew probably sat in the custom-house of Capernaum to gather some rate or toll of those that crossed the sea. Luke adds that he was a publican (see also Matt. 10:3); and some knowledge of the character of the publicans is necessary to understand the significance of his call and the attending circumstances, as well as to explain the frequent references to them in the N. T.

OF THE PUBLICANS. These were inferior officers employed as collectors of the Roman taxes, which were of a character to make any collector sufficiently odious. Every article exported or imported paid a customs-tax; every article sold paid a tax on each sale; every house, every door, every column, had its special tax; all property, real and personal, was taxed; and the citizens of subordinate provinces, including therefore the Jews, paid in addition a poll-tax. The method of collecting these taxes made them the more burdensome, and those employed in their collection more odious. The provinces were farmed out by the Roman government to wealthy individuals, or joint-stock companies, who paid large sums for the privilege of collecting the taxes. They in turn let these provinces in smaller districts to sub-contractors, who employed in the collection of the taxes the lowest and worst class of the native population, since no others would assume a task so hateful. They were required to pay over to their superiors the exorbitant sum fixed by the law, and depended for their profit on what they could make by fraud and extortion. They overcharged, brought false charges of smuggling to extort hush-money, seized upon property in case of dispute and held it until their levy was paid, forbade the farmer to reap his standing crops until they had wrung from him all that his penury could produce. They were universally feared, hated, and despised throughout the empire; but nowhere more than in Palestine. The Jews not only accounted all payment of tribute to a foreign and heathen government as a national degradation, but also the servitude which compelled such payment as a condition dishonoring to God;

11 And when the Pharisees saw *it*, they said unto his disciples, Why eateth your Master with publicans and sinners?"
12 But when Jesus heard *that*, he said unto them, They that be whole need not a physician, but they that are sick.

13 But go ye and learn what *that* meaneth, I* will have mercy, and not sacrifice: for I am not come to call the righteous, but sinners to repentance.⁷
14 Then came to him the disciples of John, saying, Why do we and the Pharisees fast oft, but thy disciples fast not?

---

w ch. 11 : 19; Luke 15 : 2; Heb. 5 : 2....x ch. 12 : 7; Prov. 21 : 3; Hosea 6 : 6; Micah 6 : 8....y Luke 24 : 47; Acts 5 : 31; 2 Pet. 3 : 9.

---

hence the publicans were in their eyes not only odious as tax-collectors, but yet more hateful as traitors to their nation and apostates from their religious faith. The Talmud classes them with thieves and assassins, and regards their repentance as impossible. No money known to have come from them was received for religious uses. They were classed with sinners, with harlots, with heathen in public estimation, and probably in their actual and customary companionships (Matt. 9 : 11 ; 11 : 19 ; 18 : 17 ; 21 : 31, 32). Nor was their ill-repute confined to the Holy Land. Cicero declares theirs to be the basest of all livelihoods. It was a current Latin proverb throughout the empire, "All the publicans are altogether robbers." Even Nero made an attempt to abolish both the nefarious system and the order of publicans which sprang from it, but their moneyed influence was too great, and he abandoned the endeavor. It was out of the lower class of these publicans that Matthew was called; and from them and their natural associates the guests were composed who attended the feast which Matthew gave.

10. In the house, *i. e.*, in Matthew's house. He gave the feast (Luke 5 : 29), using it, as a fisher of men, to catch his old associates. **Reclined with him.** The posture at meal was that of reclining, as indicated in the cut. Thus, *to recline*

at table with publicans and sinners was to come into the most intimate social relations with them. That culture which is so refined that it cannot bear *contact* with the sinful is not Christian culture.

11. Unto his disciples. Not to Christ, of whom they habitually stood in awe (compare Matt. 22 : 46). Perhaps there was in this question an endeavor to estrange the disciples from their Lord. Luke says they murmured, *i. e.*, talked over in a low voice privately, not intending that Jesus should hear. Their complaint was probably made subsequent to the feast; for the Pharisees could not have been present at it without stulti-

fying themselves. **Why eateth.** Observe the tenor of the complaint; it is not that he taught sinners, but that he *associated with them*. The same complaint would be made now against any clergyman who should associate with the same outlawed class in the community. It is not always true that the man is known by the company he keeps; nor always true that we are to avoid bad company. There is no instance in the Gospels in which Christ refused an invitation to a social gathering; and none in which he refused to associate with any on account of their social or moral character, though both he and Paul recognize the necessity of casting some out from all fellowship with us (Matt. 18 : 17; 1 Cor. 5 : 9). But the significance of Christ's social life is interpreted by the two verses which follow, and by his uniform practice of availing himself of these social opportunities to teach some truth to or to inspire a higher life in the guests of the occasion (Luke 11 : 38, etc.; 14 : 1, etc.; 19 : 5-10).

12, 13. Jesus * * * said unto them. The disciples made no answer. It is possible that they were as much perplexed as the Pharisees (see Acts 10 : 14, 15). It is not improbable that they were overawed by the assumed religious superiority and purity of the religious teachers of Judaism. **They that be whole;** rather, *strong*. Sin is a disease needing cure; it is a moral weakness; the victim needs moral strength rather than instruction; and it is through social fellowship that the way is opened to impart the needed strength to the moral nature and enable it to conquer its temptations.

13. Go ye and learn. This is said to have been a common form of speech among the Jewish rabbis when they referred their hearers to the Scriptures; Jesus thus treats the religious teachers as themselves pupils, and sends them to their own sacred writings to study their meaning. "He signifies that not he was transgressing the law, but they; as if he had said, Whereof accuse me? Because I bring sinners to amendment? Why then ye must accuse the Father also for this."—(*Chrysostom*.) **I will have mercy and not sacrifice.** The quotation appears to be from Hosea 6 : 6, but its spirit is embodied in many passages in the O. T. (1 Sam. 15 : 22; Ps. 50 : 8-15); especially in the prophets (Isaiah 1 : 11-17; Amos 5 : 21-24; Mic. 6 : 7, 8). It would appear utterly incomprehensible that the Bible students of the first century could have failed to apprehend the meaning of

15 And Jesus said unto them, Can the children of the bridechamber mourn, as long as the bridegroom^a is with them? but the days will come, when the bridegroom shall be taken from them, and then shall^a they fast.

16 No man putteth a piece of new cloth unto an old

a ch. 25 : 1, 10 ; John 3 : 29 ; Rev. 21 : 2....a Isa. 22 : 12.

these passages, and have discovered only a religion of fruitless formalism in the O. T., were there not so many similar misinterpreters at the present day. Sacrifice was the chief part of the ceremonial law, and represents here the religion of formal obedience to ceremonial rules ; mercy expresses that spirit of love to the fallen which seeks their restoration. The very essence of the Jewish sacrificial system was that it expressed the infinite mercy of God, in providing a way of pardon for sin. To be without the spirit of mercy was really to lose the meaning and heart of the sacrifices ; as now, to hold to the doctrine of Christ's atoning sacrifice, but to be without the spirit which leads to personal self-sacrifice for the salvation of others, is to be without the spirit of Christ (Phil 2 : 5, etc. ; 1 John 3 : 16).

Not * * * the righteous but sinners. This is not exactly equivalent to "those who think themselves righteous" and "those who confess themselves sinners," as Wordsworth explains it. Christ takes the Pharisees at their own estimation of themselves, and the publicans at the Pharisees' estimation of them, and says : " I have come to preach the doctrine of repentance as the condition of entering the kingdom of heaven (Matt. 4 : 17). Evidently the doctrine of repentance is for sinners such as these publicans are, not for the righteous such as you are !" It is in so far a keen irony of their self-righteousness. Chrysostom refers to Gen. 3 : 22 and Psalm 50 : 12, as similarly ironical. Compare for significance of the entire passage John 9 : 39–41 ; 1 Tim. 1 : 15 ; Rev. 3 : 17. **To repentance.** These words are not found here or in Mark in the best manuscripts ; but there is no doubt of their authenticity in Luke, and therefore no doubt that they are a part of Christ's response, and qualify and interpret his declaration. He comes to sinners that he may bring sinners to himself ; he does not conform to them, but conforms them to him by the renewing of their minds. His example is authority for social mingling with sinners, but not for acquiescing in or giving even tacit sanction to their sinful practices. These words, "to repentance," are the answer to the charge of Celsus (second century). "Jesus Christ came into the world to make the most terrible and dreadful society, for he calls sinners and not the righteous ; so that the body he came to assemble is a body of profligates, separate from good people, among whom they were before mixed. He has rejected all the good and collected all the bad."

Ch. 9 : 14–17. OF FASTING.—THE CAUSE OF CHRISTIAN JOY IS THE PRESENCE OF CHRIST; THE CAUSE OF CHRISTIAN MOURNING IS HIS WITHDRAWAL.—THE JOYOUSNESS OF THE RELIGION OF JESUS; IT IS A WEDDING FEAST.—TRUE AND FALSE FASTING.—THE LAW OF CHRISTIAN REFORMATION: ENTIRE, INTERNAL.—THE NEW LIFE CANNOT BE PATCHED UPON THE OLD; THE NEW SPIRIT CANNOT BE CONTAINED IN OLD FORMS.—THE FERMENTING POWER OF THE GOSPEL.

This incident is recorded also in Mark 2 : 18–22 and Luke 5 : 33–38, and in the same connection. No doubt it occurred on the occasion of Matthew's feast.

14. The disciples of John, i. e., the Baptist. Luke adds "and the Pharisees." John the Baptist was in prison ; he was himself perplexed by the course of Christ's mission (Matt. 11 : 2, 3) ; it is not strange that his disciples felt aggrieved that Jesus, instead of sorrowing and fasting over the national degeneracy that suffered the imprisonment of their master, should be feasting with publicans and sinners. Observe how, customarily, Christ left his sometimes enigmatical example to work out its own effect without explaining it, unless called on for an explanation. **We and the Pharisees fast oft.** Mark says they "used to fast ;" literally, "*were fasting,*" which may mean that at this time they were observing a fast, with which the joyousness of Matthew's feast seemed incongruous. In addition to the fast of the Day of Atonement, prescribed by Moses (Lev. 23 : 26–32), the Jews had instituted several national fasts, chiefly to commemorate respectively the several captures of Jerusalem by alien armies ; special fasts were also common (Esther 4 : 15–17 ; Jer. 36 : 9 ; Joel 1 : 14) ; and the stricter of the Pharisees observed the fifth and the second day of every week (Luke 18 : 12) as a fast day, because on the fifth Moses was believed to have gone up into Sinai, and on the second to have come down. Fasts were connected with their superstitions as well as with their religion ; they fasted to obtain auspicious dreams, or to secure the fulfillment of a dream, or to escape the fulfillment of an inauspicious dream, or to secure any desired object, or avert any threatened ill. This fasting was sometimes an absolute deprivation of all food, sometimes only an exclusion of all viands but those of the simplest and plainest description (Dan. 10 : 2, 3).

15. Children of the bridechamber. The companions of the bridegroom, answering to our modern groomsmen. The wedding ceremonies of the Jews lasted often for days ; the bride-

garment; for that which is put in to fill it up taketh from the garment, and the rent is made worse.

17 Neither do men put new wine into old bottles, else^b the bottles break, and the wine runneth out, and the bottles perish: but they put new wine into new bottles, and both are preserved.

b Job 32 : 19.

groom, with the children of the bridechamber, went to the house of the bride, and brought her to the bridegroom's house, where a great feast was given; the nuptials were always celebrated with great festivities and mirth; and the Talmud, which forbade to eat, to drink or to wash the face on the Day of Atonement, made an exception in favor of the bride. The simile used by Christ could not fail to recall to the disciples of John their master's use of the same simile (John 3 : 29), whom Christ thus cites, though indirectly, in answer to their question. The significance of the metaphor is unmistakable. *Christ is the bridegroom; the church is the bride; the ordained teachers in the church are the children of the bridechamber, who are instrumental in bringing together bride and groom; the whole period of time intermediate Christ's first public ministry and his second coming is the wedding-feast, during which the children of the bridechamber are bringing their Lord to the bride; the marriage-supper of the Lamb in the heavenly kingdom is the final consummation of the wedding ceremony.* There is significance in the fact that this metaphor employed in the O. T. to designate the relation between God and his chosen people is used in the N. T. to symbolize the relation between Christ and his Church (Isa. 54 : 5 ; Jer. 3 : 14 ; Hosea 2 : 19, 20 ; Matt. 22 : 1-14; 25 : 1-13; Eph. 5 : 30-32; Rev. 19 : 7). **Mourn.** Observe that, while John's disciples ask why Christ's disciples do not fast, he replies that they cannot *mourn*. Fasting is only the external symbol of mourning, or its natural expression and effect; where there is no mourning, there is no virtue in fasting. Luke's report is: "Can ye *make* the child of the bridechamber fast while the bridegroom is with them?" i. e., Can you by laws and regulations make them while in the period of their joy, fast in truth? **Shall be taken from them.** The first distinct intimation afforded by Christ of his own crucifixion. Its meaning can have been but imperfectly understood by either the disciples of John or by his own disciples; but its pathos could not but have been felt. **Shall they fast.** Rather, will they fast; it is not imperative, but simply prophetic; it indicates a fact, it does not embody a command. In fact, the disciples suffered no persecution while Christ lived, and neither knew any especial experience of mourning, prior to his passion, nor observed any seasons of fasting. Luther remarks on the two kinds of self-denial and suffering, the one which we inflict on ourselves (1 Kings 19 : 28), the other that which God lays upon us, and to which we cheerfully submit (John 18 : 11). There is no virtue in the first; there is benefit in the second.

What does Christ here teach respecting the obligation of fasting? The laws of Moses prescribed many feast days and but one fast day. Christ himself prescribed no set fasts, and none were observed by the apostolic church. But occasional fasts were observed throughout the O. T. history by the Jews (1 Sam. 7 : 6 ; Neh. 1 : 4 ; Joel 2 : 12. Compare Isaiah 58 : 3-6), and in the N. T. history both by Christ and his apostles (Matt. 4 : 2 ; Acts 13 : 2, 3 ; 14 ; 23). Reading Christ's declaration in the light of this history, the plain inference from it appears to be this: Fasting is the expression of mourning; while Christ was with his disciples in the body, there was no occasion for mourning or fasting; so when the soul is conscious of his spiritual presence, when the bridegroom is with the children of the bridechamber, they cannot be made to fast in reality and truth; but whenever Christ has withdrawn from the soul, whenever times of darkness hide, or experiences of sin banish him from the soul, or the strong need of a clearer sense of his presence overcomes the desire for food, or a failure in his work indicates a lack of his presence and power (Matt. 17 ; 21), then there will be fasting. In other words, fasting is Christian only when it is the natural expression of a Christian experience. "Fasting should be the genuine offspring of inward and spiritual sorrow, of the sense of the absence of the Bridegroom in the soul—not the forced and stated fasts of the old covenant, now passed away. It is an instructive circumstance, that in the Reformed Churches, while those stated fasts which were retained at their first emergence from popery are universally disregarded even by their best and holiest sons, nothing can be more affecting and genuine than the universal and solemn observance of any real occasion of fasting placed before them by God's providence."—(*Alford.*)

16. **No man puts a patch of unfinished** (*unfulled*) **material upon an old garment; for the patch tears away from the garment and a worse rent takes place.** The student will get the significance of the original in several particulars which may escape him otherwise, if he will compare this transaction with that of our English version. Garments in the East were made sometimes of leather, sometimes of cloth. The leather which had not been dressed, and the cloth which had not been fulled, i. e., **soaked and cleansed with water,**

130 MATTHEW. [CH. IX.

18 While he spake these things unto them, behold, there came a certain ruler, and worshipped him, saying, My daughter is even now dead : but come and lay thy hand upon her, and she shall live.
19 And Jesus arose, and followed him, and *so did* his disciples.

20 And, behold, a woman, which was diseased with an issue of blood twelve years, came behind *him*, and touched the hem of his garment ;
21 For she said within herself, If I may but touch his garment, I shall be whole.
22 But Jesus turned him about ; and when he saw

<small>e Mark 5 : 22 ; Luke 8 : 41, etc....d John 11 : 25.....e Mark 5 : 25 ; Luke 8 : 43....f Acts 19 : 12.</small>

was sure to shrink, and if such undressed or unfulled (not merely *new*) material was used in repairing a garment it would soon tear out the old cloth ; the consequence would be, *not that the old rent would be made worse*, but that *a new and worse rent would be produced*. Luke (ch. 5 : 36) puts it a little differently, see note there ; and he gives the reason of the new rent, "the piece that was taken out of the new, agreeth not with the old." The disciples of John the Baptist looked not for a new religion, but for a re-formation, a patching up of the old Jewish religion. To them Christ responds that he has come to give the world new garments, not to patch the old ones ; any attempt to attach his religion of the spirit of love to the old religion of forms would be sure to make a worse state of things than that which he attempted to cure ; both because *the old is old*, worn out, and can bear no strain, and because *the new is new*, and has as yet, as it exists in the minds of the disciples, none of that flexibility which would enable it to adapt itself to the prejudices and prepossessions of others. The spirit in the apostolic church which was offended and stumbled at eating meat offered to idols, represents the old garment ; the spirit which could not yield, and for the sake of others abstain, represents the unfulled piece of cloth (Romans 14 : 14, 15). It is true that the apostle sought to fuse these two factions, but by instructions which destroyed the factions and drove out the spirit of intolerance from the one, and of headiness or impatience from the other. In every religious reformation some have attempted to put on new patches on old garments ; *e. g.*, John the Baptist, Erasmus, the Old Catholics of to-day. Let us beware lest, in our own souls, we attempt patchwork reformation.

ANCIENT BOTTLE.
(From a painting at Pompeii.)

17. New wine into old bottles. The bottles of the East were and still are made of the skins of animals, the entrails being taken out, the form of the animal preserved, and the hair left on the outside. Hence the reference to wine bottles of the Gibeonites "old and rent and bound up" (Joshua 9 : 4). "New wine" is wine not yet fully fermented. In its fermenting it expands and would thus burst the bottle. *Establishing new truths in the hearts of men is always by a process of fermentation ; of excitement and agitation. To confine new truths in old forms only results in shattering the old.* Note as examples the effect of Old Catholicism in Germany, and the ecclesiastical reformation of Henry VIII in England. "The new wine is something too living and strong for so weak a moral frame ; it shatters the fair outside of ceremonial seeming ; and the wine runneth out, the spirit is lost, the man is neither a blameless Jew nor a faithful Christian ; both are spoiled."—(*Alford.*)

The connection of these two verses with the preceding question about fasting is unmistakable. Fasting was prescribed by the old dispensation and still more by the Pharisees as a law, as it still is by the Roman Catholics. Christ's system recognizes no other law than that of love ; and it cannot be patched on to one which makes a virtue of a fast. But here, as often, Christ takes occasion of a question which relates only to an external service to enunciate a principle of much broader application. *In so far as the soul receives the spirit of Christ as a new inspiration, it will work out for itself a new expression ;* it may use but it cannot be confined within old forms, whether of devotional expression or of doctrinal statement.

18-26. RAISING OF JAIRUS' DAUGHTER. HEALING OF WOMAN WITH ISSUE OF BLOOD. It is clear from the account here that these two miracles were wrought immediately after Matthew's feast. They are recorded in Mark 5 : 22-43 and Luke 8 : 41-56 as immediately succeeding Christ's return from the land of the Gergesenes, and his casting out of the devil there. It appears from their accounts that Jairus was a ruler of the synagogue, probably at Capernaum, that his daughter was twelve years old, that the first message to Jesus was that she was dying, and that afterwards a second message was sent him, while he was on his way to the ruler's house, to the effect that she was already dead ; the two being embodied in one message in Matthew's account, and that the father and mother of the girl, with Peter, James and John, went with him into the room, and were witnesses of her resurrection from the dead. The accounts in Mark and Luke also give details respecting the healing of the woman with

her, he said, Daughter, be of good comfort; thy faith hath made thee whole. And the woman was made whole from that hour.

23 And when Jesus came into the ruler's house, and saw the minstrels and the people making a noise,

24 He said unto them, Give place; for the maid is not dead, but sleepeth. And they laughed him to scorn.

25 But when the people were put forth, he went in, and took her by the hand, and the maid arose.

26 And the fame hereof went abroad into all that land.

27 And when Jesus departed thence, two blind men followed him, crying, and saying, Thou son of David, have mercy on us.

28 And when he was come into the house, the blind men came to him: and Jesus saith unto them, Believe ye that I am able to do this? They said unto him, Yea, Lord.

29 Then touched he their eyes, saying, According to your faith be it unto you.

30 And their eyes were opened: and Jesus straitly charged them, saying, See that no man know it.

g Luke 7:50; 17:19; 18:42; Acts 14:9....h John 4:53....i Mark 5:38; Luke 8:51....j 2 Chron. 25:25....k Acts 10:10....l 2 Kings 4:33, etc.....m ch. 15:22; 20:30, 31....n ch. 12:16; Isa. 42:2.

an issue of blood, omitted by Matthew. See for notes on the two miracles, Mark 5: 22–43.

Ch. 9: 27–34. HEALING OF THE BLIND AND THE DUMB.—CHRIST THE LIGHT OF THE WORLD (John 8: 12). HE MAKES THE BLIND TO SEE (John 9: 39).—PERSISTENT FAITH FOLLOWS CHRIST DESPITE HIS SEEMING REFUSAL TO HEAR (Matthew 15: 21–28).—THE GIFT OF GOD IS TO US ACCORDING TO OUR FAITH (Hebrews 11: 6).—TRUE FAITH ILLUSTRATED; PERSONAL TRUST IN A PERSONAL SAVIOUR.—SILENCE FOR CHRIST IS SOMETIMES AS SACRED A DUTY AS SPEECH.—HE MAKETH THE DUMB TO SPEAK (Psalm 51: 15).

These incidents are peculiar to Matthew. Other cases of healing of the blind are recorded in Matt. 12: 22; 20: 29–34; 21: 14; Mark 8: 22–26; Luke 7: 21; and John, ch. 9. Blindness is very common in the East; the dust, the hot sun, the sleeping in the open air, are among the causes said to produce it. Trench quotes a "modern traveler" as reporting that there are four thousand blind in Cairo alone; Volney says that out of one hundred persons he met in that city twenty were quite blind, ten wanted each one eye, and twenty others suffered from ophthalmia. Blindness is not as common in Syria as in Egypt, but the references in the Scripture indicate that it was not infrequent (Lev. 19: 14; Deut. 27: 18). This is also indicated by the fact that it was prophesied respecting the Messiah as one of the signs of his character and mission that he should open the eyes of the blind (Isaiah 29: 18; 35: 5; 42: 7). There is nothing in the original to indicate the nature or cause of the blindness in this case. It is worthy of note that the cure was instantaneous and complete, so that the blind men apparently straightway went out from his presence to proclaim their cure; whereas in all cases of natural cure the eyes must go through a long process of protection from extreme light which in their weakened state they cannot bear.

27. **And when Jesus departed thence.** Possibly from the house, perhaps from Capernaum, perhaps from that general region of country; the phrase is very vague and does not identify the time or place of the cure. **Crying:** Rather, calling aloud, as Bartimeus did (Mark 10: 46, 47). **Son of David.** A common appellation among the Jews for the Messiah (Mal. 21:9; 22:42; Ezek. 34:23, 24). Thus their appeal was a confession of their faith not only in his power to heal as a physician, or a prophet, but a distinct recognition of his Messianic character. **Have mercy on us.** Physiological ailments were accounted among the Jews as an indication of and a punishment for special sin (John 9:2). The spiritual significance of this cry is not to be pressed here; nothing more is necessarily signified by the original than Have pity on us. Yet as disease is a fruit and a type of sin, so healing is a fruit and a type of divine mercy in the strictest sense of that term. The cry of suffering to God is always a cry for mercy as well as for pity.

28. **And when he was come into the house.** Possibly, as Dr. Adam Clark, "the house of Peter at Capernaum where he ordinarily lodged." But the phrase does not necessarily indicate any particular house; "merely as we sometimes use the phrase 'the house' as opposed to 'the open air.'"—(Alford.) Why should our Lord wait until he comes into the house before he answers their prayer? Chrysostom replies: "To repel the glory that cometh from the multitude. Because the house was near he leads them thither to heal them in private. And this is evident from the fact that he charged them to tell no man." Calvin, and so most of the commentators, that he may try the pertinacity of their faith, not only by his subsequent inquiry, but also by his seeming to withdraw from them without heeding their request. He thus also illustrates the virtue of that importunity of prayer which he subsequently enforces by his direct teaching (Luke 11: 5–8; 18: 1–8). He further sounds the depths of their faith by a question: **Believe ye that I am able to do this?** In the light of the prophecies above referred to (note on ver. 26) this was again a question as to their faith in him, not as a mere prophet, but as the Messiah. "He did not say, Believe ye that I am able to entreat my Father, that I am able to pray, but that I am able to do this?"—(Chrysostom.)

29. **He touched their eyes.** He is never

31 But they, when they were departed, spread abroad his fame in all that country.

32 As they went out, behold, they brought to him a dumb man° possessed with a devil.

33 And when the devil was cast out, the dumb spake:ᵖ and the multitudes marvelled, saying, It was never so seen in Israel.

34 But the Pharisees said, Heᵍ casteth out devils through the prince of the devils.

35 Andʳ Jesus went about all the cities and villages, teaching in their synagogues, and preaching the gospel of the kingdom, and healing every sickness and every disease among the people.

36 But when he saw the multitudes, he was moved with compassion on them, because they fainted, and were scattered abroad, as sheepᵗ having no shepherd.

37 Then saith he unto his disciples, The harvestᵘ truly *is* plenteous, but the labourers *are* few ;

38 Pray ye therefore the Lord of the harvest, that he will send forthᵛ labourers into his harvest.

o ch. 12 : 22 ; Luke 11 : 14....p Isa. 35 : 6....q ch. 12 : 24 ; Mark 3 : 22 ; Luke 11 : 15....r ch. 4 : 23.....s Numb. 27 : 17 ; 1 Kings 22 : 17 ; Ezek. 34 : 5 ; Zech. 10 : 2....t Luke 10 : 2 ; John 4 : 35....u Ps. 68 : 11.

said to have healed the blind by a mere word, but always, where any details are given, used some instrumentality (Matt. 20 : 34; Mark 8 : 23; John 9 : 6, 7). **According to your faith be it unto you.** The universal answer of God to all our prayers for spiritual blessings. He is ready to grant more than we can ask or even think ; but we can receive only in proportion as our faith is prepared to receive. "Faith which in itself is nothing is yet the organ for receiving everything."—(*Trench*.)

30-31. Straitly charged. The original word occurs in Mark 14 : 5, where it is rendered *murmured*, and in John 11 : 33, 38, where it is rendered *groan*. He so charged them as to imply indignation if they disobeyed. Why should he have given this caution which was often repeated (Matt. 8 : 4 ; 12 : 16 ; Mark 1 : 34, 43, 44 ; 3 : 12 ; 5 : 43 ; Luke 4 : 41 ; 8 : 56)? Was it because he himself in the spirit of his own precepts shrank from having his benefactions blazoned abroad (Matt. 6 : 3, 4 ; Isaiah 42 : 2)? or was it that the faith of the people might not rest upon his miracles but upon the truth itself (Matt. 12 : 39 ; John 14 : 11)? since the faith that rested on the miracles wholly misapprehended his mission (John 2 : 12 ; 6 : 11, 15). See note on ch. 8 : 4. If this last be the true explanation, is it not a mistake for us to rest the evidence of Christianity so largely on miracles of which Christ made so little, instead of resting it on the truth itself, of which Christ made so much? As to the course of the blind men in spreading abroad their cure, one may admire, as the Roman Catholic writers do, their spirit of gratitude, without justifying their disobedience of Christ's command. The effect of this and other similar acts of others was to bring to him a crowd, not of appreciative hearers, anxious to hear the truth, but of mere wonder-gazers, curious to witness his miracles. Their popularity only impeded his work (Mark 3 : 20; 6 : 31 ; Luke 12 : 1, etc.).

32-34. An instance of a miraculous cure, very similar, is recorded in Matthew 12 : 22-24 ; Luke 11 : 14, 15, etc. The report of the accusation of the Pharisees, and of Christ's reply, is fuller there than here. Whether the incident is really the same or not is uncertain ; most harmonists regard it as different. For notes on the Pharisaic accusation, see on Matt. 12 : 22, etc.

Ch. 9 : 35-38. PREPARATION FOR THE COMMISSION OF THE APOSTLES.—CHRIST'S TRAINING OF HIS DISCIPLES IS THEORETICAL AND PRACTICAL; FIRST THE SERMON ON THE MOUNT, THEN A MISSIONARY CIRCUIT. HE EXEMPLIFIES THE WORK OF THE MINISTRY BEFORE HE COMMISSIONS THE APOSTLES TO IT.—IN THE FIRST MISSIONARY WORK HEALING OF THE BODY AND OF THE SOUL GOES TOGETHER.—THE CONDITION OF SUCCESS IN CHRISTIAN WORK: "MOVED WITH COMPASSION."—THERE WERE MANY RABBIS, BUT NO SHEPHERDS; THERE MAY BE MANY RELIGIOUS TEACHERS, BUT NO TRUE PASTORS.—WORK FOR ALL IN CHRIST'S VINEYARD ; NO ONE CAN SAY, "NO MAN HATH HIRED US."— THE REAL IMPEDIMENT TO THE SPREAD OF THE GOSPEL; LACK OF CHRISTIAN LABORERS.

35. Cities and villages. A distinction similar to that which prevails in modern times between incorporated and unincorporated towns existed in the time of Christ. The city proper was environed by walls ; a council of elders, and a government answering to the modern common council and mayor, administered the government ; there were night-watchmen ; lights were unknown, except torches carried in the hand ; there was usually no sewerage ; the houses were crowded close together ; the streets were narrow and unpaved. The villages were unwalled collections of huts of stone or mud. Nearly the entire population of Palestine was gathered in cities and villages as a protection against robbers, etc. After commissioning his disciples Jesus continued his ministry among the *cities* (Matt. 11 : 1), while his apostles preached the gospels in the unwalled *towns or villages* (Luke 9 : 6), where the word "town" (κώμας) is the same here translated "village." **Healing every sickness.** (νόσος), *positive ailment ;* **and every disease** (μαλακία), *weakness, want of health and vigor.* Christ not only takes away our disease, he gives us health and strength. In the moral life weakness is sometimes the worst form of disease. **Among the people.** This is an addition not found in the best manuscripts. The language descriptive of this tour is almost identical with that employed in Matt. 4 : 23. See note there for description of the synagogue, and for references indicating the general character of Christ's preaching and miracles of healing. Observe that the commission of the twelve is preceded by a tour in which Christ exemplifies to the commissioned apostles the nature of the work they are to do. This particular journey is generally characterized by the harmonists as Christ's third missionary circuit; but there is no evidence that his ministry was divided in fact, or in the thought of the sacred writers, into any such definite circuits.

36. He was moved with compassion. This fact concerning our Lord is repeatedly stated by the Evangelists (ch. 14:14; Mark 1:41; 6:34); and it affords, humanly speaking, the secret of his power. We get influence over the debased and ignorant only as they awaken a feeling of true compassion and yearning, rather than of resentment, distaste, and aversion. Observe, that his compassion was for publicans and sinners. "Christ pities those most that pity themselves least: so should we."—(*Matthew Henry.*) **Fainted.** This is the correct translation of the received text (ἐκλελυμένοι), but the best authorities give another word (ἐσκυλμένοι), the proper translation of which is *harassed*. What moved his compassion was not their physical weariness, but their harassment and perplexity under the burdensome ritualism imposed on them by the Pharisees (Matt. 23:4–13, etc.). **Scattered abroad as sheep having no shepherd.** There were many scribes and doctors of the law, but no shepherd, no one who watched over and tended and cared for their spiritual welfare (1 Kings 22:17; Ezek. 34:1–6).

37. The harvest truly is plenteous. "Mark how he points out the facility and necessity of the thing. For what saith he? The harvest truly is plenteous, but the laborers are few. That is: Not to the sowing, saith he, but to the reaping do I send you (John 4:38). And these things he said, at once repressing their pride and preparing them to be of good courage, and signifying that the greater part of the labor had already come."—(*Chrysostom.*) Observe, too, here, and yet more in John 4:35, the plain intimation that the impediment to the spread of the gospel is not the hardness of heart and unpreparedness of the world for it, but the lack of activity in the church. The harvest of souls is ready; but there are either no laborers, or they lack the true spirit of Christ—are rabbis, not shepherds. The harvest is a frequent symbol in the Bible of Christian work. God is the husbandman (John 15:1); the world is the field (Matt. 13:38); Christians are workmen whom the Lord employs (Matt. 20:1); souls are God's husbandry (1 Cor. 3:9, and note); the true children of God are separated from sinners by a process of threshing and winnowing (Isaiah 21:10; Matt. 3:12); the end of the world witnesses the gathering of the grain into barns, and the destruction of the tares (Matt. 13:30). Compare Psalm 126:5; Isaiah 9:3; 1 Cor. 3:6; and especially Matt. 13:24–30, 34–73.

38. Pray ye therefore, etc. "Though they were but twelve he made them many from that time forward, not by adding to their number, but by *giving them power*."—(*Chrysostom.*) Observe that he who bids to pray sends forth the laborers, teaching us that we are to help to the answer of our own prayers. Observe, too, that he bids those that were to go forth pray for laborers; pray, that is, that God would send them forth. *Those only can labor successfully for God whom God sends forth.* Compare for such a prayer Isaiah 6:8. **Send forth.** The original word (ἐκβάλλω) certainly generally carries with it the idea of force. It is rendered *drive* in Mark 1:12; John 2:15; *thrust*, in Luke 4:29; *put forth*, in John 10:4; *expel*, in Acts 13:50. As the Holy Spirit uses a certain compulsion to bring sinners to Christ (Luke 14:23), so he impels Christian workers, against their first inclinations, into Christian work. So God impelled Moses (Exod. 4:1, 10–17); so by a goading of the conscience and a divine vision he impelled Saul; so by early persecutions he sent the early Christians out of Jerusalem, and scattered them everywhere, preaching the Gospel (Acts 8:4). Compare chap. 10:23, and note. So in a sense we may say that no one is competent to preach, either publicly or privately, the gospel to others, who is not impelled thereto by the strong power of the Holy Spirit. Compare Ezek. 3:14; Acts 9:26; 1 Cor. 9:16.

Ch. 10:1–42. THE MISSION OF THE TWELVE.

Ch. 10:1–15. THEIR COMMISSION.—THE WEAKNESS AND THE POWER OF THE APOSTLES (2 Cor. 4:7).—CHRISTIAN WORK, LIKE CHARITY, BEGINS AT HOME (vs. 5, 6).—THE FOUNDATION OF THE GOSPEL: THE KINGDOM OF HEAVEN IS AT HAND (V. 7).—THE WORK OF THE GOSPEL: HEALING, CLEANSING, LIFE-GIVING, DEVIL-CONQUERING (V. 8).—THE TRUST OF THE GOSPEL MINISTRY: GOD AND THE PEOPLE. THEIR SUPPORT: THE VOLUNTARY CONTRIBUTIONS OF THEIR HEARERS (vs. 9–13).—THE SIN OF REJECTING THE GOSPEL IS THE MOST HEINOUS OF ALL SINS (vs. 14, 15).

The conflict between Christ and the Pharisees had already commenced. They had attacked him for breaking the Sabbath (Matt. 12:2, 10, 14; John 5:16), and for associating with publicans and sinners (Matt. 9:11), and accused him of casting out devils by the Prince of devils (Matt. 12:24). He had made several missionary tours through Galilee, preaching the Gospel and healing the sick. Prior to this commission are undoubtedly to be placed, not only the miracles previously recorded by Matthew, but also those of the raising of the son of the widow of Nain (Luke 7:11–17), and the healing of the impotent man at the pool of Bethesda (John 5). He had also been mobbed at Nazareth (Luke 4:29, 30), and had already not only vigorously exposed the errors of the Pharisees in the

CHAPTER X.

AND when he had called unto *him* his twelve disciples, he[v] gave them power *against* unclean spirits, to cast them out, and to heal all manner of sickness and all manner of disease.

2 Now the names[w] of the twelve apostles are these: The first, Simon, who is called Peter, and Andrew his

[v] Mark 3:13, 14; 6:7, etc.; Luke 9:1, etc.....[w] Luke 6:13.

Sermon on the Mount, but had denounced them and their hypocrisy before all the people (Matt. 14: 33-39; Luke 11:37-54), and had preached the parables concerning the Kingdom of God recorded in Matt. XIII. Meanwhile his popularity among the people had only been increased by the opposition of the Pharisees. Wherever he went crowds gathered about him thronging the streets through which he passed (Mark 2:15; 5:24; Luke 7:11; 8:45), crowding the houses he entered (Mark 2:2), treading each other under foot in their eagerness (Luke 12:1), breaking in on his sleep and meals (Mark 3:20), and following him on foot when he endeavored to escape them by boat (Matt. 14:13). Without entering here into the reasons for placing this commission at a later date than appears to be assigned to it by Matthew, it may suffice to say that it appears clear from Mark 6:7-14 that the commission was given, if not after the death of John the Baptist, certainly about the same time. Two reasons appear to have led to this commissioning of the twelve: first, the growing eagerness of the people to hear the news of the kingdom could not be satisfied by one preacher; second, the growing opposition of the Pharisees made apparent the necessity of not only appointing but training men to preach Christ's Gospel when he should be slain. *This commission* was, however, for a purely temporary service, and the instructions which accompanied it apply directly only to this single preparatory mission (see notes below). There is nothing *in this chapter* to indicate that the twelve understood that they were appointed to any permanent office in the church, or that there was any permanent apostolic office created, or even that they comprehended that a church of Christ would be organized to promote the kingdom of heaven after Jesus' death, much less that a succession was established for all future time. Other passages of Scripture (e. g. Matt. 28: 19, 20; Acts 1:15-26), taken in conjunction with the previous calling and present appointment of the twelve, seem to indicate that our Lord intended to confer upon them a *quasi* leadership in the infant church. Yet there are other indications that this leadership was not authoritative, such as the position of James, the Lord's brother (Acts 15:13; 21:18; Gal. 2:12; comp. Gal. 1:19), and that of Paul, both of whom are called apostles in the N. T. (1 Cor. 15:9; 2 Cor. 11:5). The significance of these passages will be considered in due course; it must suffice now to say that this chapter throws little or no light on the nature of the office and functions of the twelve in the church, as is evident from the fact that almost the same powers were conferred and almost the same directions given to the seventy (Luke 10:1-16).

1. When he had called unto him his twelve disciples. The call and ordination of the twelve to be *apostles* had taken place some time previously; in connection with it the Sermon on the Mount was delivered (Luke 6:13). The language here "his twelve disciples" indicates very clearly that they had already been chosen and set apart to the ministry. He gave them power. See on verse 8.

2. The names of the twelve apostles are these. Of the twelve apostles there are four lists, the other three being found in Mark 3:16; Luke 6:14; and Acts 1:13. They differ in the following particulars. Luke in the book of Acts does not insert the name of Judas Iscariot, who was then dead; both in his Gospel and in Acts he entitles the Simon who is here and in Mark called the Canaanite, Simon Zelotes; Matthew gives as the tenth disciple Lebbeus; Mark calls him Thaddeus; Luke and Acts *Judas of James; i. e.* either son or brother of James; and Mark says that James and John were surnamed by Christ Boanerges, *i. e.,* The sons of thunder. In other respects the four lists are identical, except that the names are given in a slightly different order by the different writers. They all agree, however, in putting Simon Peter first and Judas Iscariot last, and all agree in arranging them in groups of four, Simon Peter being first of the first group, Philip of the second, James the son of Alphæus of the third. There are three pairs of brothers among them, Andrew and Peter, James and John, James the less, and Judas or Thaddeus. James and John I believe to have been own cousins of our Lord. See note below. With the exception of Judas Iscariot all were Galileans; several of them were by trade fishermen, a laborious and profitable calling; they were all laymen, that is, there was neither priest nor scribe among them. They have generally been regarded as illiterate men (Acts 4:13); but by this must be understood, not that they were specially ignorant, but that they were not versed in the rabbinical literature, the scholastic theology of their age. Philip and Peter both appear to have been acquainted with the Greek. This is indicated by the application of the Greeks to Philip (John 12:20, 21) and by the fact that the epistles of Peter were written in Greek. Matthew

CH. X.] MATTHEW. 135

brother; James *the son* of Zebedee, and John his brother;
3 Philip, and Bartholomew; Thomas, and Matthew the publican; James *the son* of Alphæus, and Lebbæus, whose surname was Thaddæus;

4 Simon the Canaanite, and Judas Iscariot, who also betrayed him.
5 These twelve Jesus sent forth, and commanded them, saying, Go not into the way of the Gentiles, and into *any* city of the Samaritans* enter ye not;

x 2 Kings 17 : 24; John 4 : 5, 9, 20.

was a ready and methodical writer; John evidently was a man of culture, as his writings show, and his social position was such as gave him ready access to the high priest's palace during the trial of Jesus (John 18:16); and there are unmistakable indications that several of the twelve possessed wealth or wealthy connections, for the father of James and John had hired servants, Peter apparently lived in his own house, and Matthew (Sen.) had the means to give a large party to many friends (Mark 1:29; Luke 4:38; 5:29). Several of them, Andrew, John, Philip, probably Peter and perhaps Nathanael or Bartholomew, were disciples of John the Baptist, and in attendance on his ministry first became acquainted with our Lord (John 1:36, 37, 42, 44, 45, 49). I have grouped together, in a note at the end of this chapter, a brief account of the information which the Scripture affords us of their individual lives.

The first, Simon who is called Peter. In the lists of the apostles Peter is always named first in order; yet it is certain that he was not the first to come to Christ, for Andrew his brother brought Peter to him (John 1:40, 41), nor is there any other indication that he was the oldest than such as may be thought to be afforded by the fact that he was married (Mark 1:30), and that he was generally foremost as spokesman of the twelve. (See below.) The precedence given to him, not only in the lists of the apostles but in the mention of him elsewhere in the Gospels, (Matt 17:1; Mark 5:37; 9:2; 14:33; 16:7; Luke 8:51; 9:28, and see references below), is one of the grounds on which the Roman Catholic church bases its belief that Christ made him and his successors the visible head of the church. Here and elsewhere the Scripture indicates that he possessed a certain pre-eminence among the twelve, but it affords no hint of an ecclesiastical or official supremacy. On the contrary, though foremost in the early history of the church as a preacher of great power (Acts 2:14, 41), he was less an ecclesiastical leader than James the Lord's brother (Acts 12:17; 15:13; 21:18; Gal. 1:19), who is not to be confounded with either of the twelve of that name (see note below), and less a founder and builder of the church than Paul. (See note on Matt. 16:13-20.) On the place which the N. T. assigns to Peter, Alford's note is so admirable that I quote it entire.

"We find Simon Peter, not only in the lists of the apostles, but also in their history, prominent on various occasions before the rest. Sometimes he speaks in their name (Matt. 19:27; Luke 12:41); sometimes answers when all are addressed (Matt. 16:16); sometimes 'our Lord addresses him as principal even among the three favored ones (Matt. 26:40; Luke 22:3); sometimes he is addressed by others as representing the whole (Matt. 17:24; Acts 9:33). He appears as the organ of the apostles after our Lord's ascension (Acts 1:15; 2:14;4:8; 5:29); the first speech, and apparently that which decided the Council, is spoken by him (Acts 15:1). All this accords well with the bold and energetic character of Peter, and originated in the unerring discernment and appointment of our Lord himself, who saw in him a person adapted to take precedence of the rest in the founding of his Church (Acts 5:3, 9) and shutting (Acts 5:3, 9) and opening (Acts 2:14, 41; 10:5, 46) the doors of the kingdom of heaven. That, however, no such idea was current among the apostles as that he was destined to be the primate of the future Church is as clear as the facts above mentioned. For (1) no trace of such a pre-eminence is found in all the Epistles of the other apostles; but when he is mentioned it is either, as in 1 Cor. 9:5, as one of the apostles, one example among many, but in no wise the chief; or, as in Gal. 2:7, 8, with a distinct account of a peculiar province of duty and preaching being allotted to him, viz. the apostleship of the circumcision (see Pet. 1:1), as distinguished from Paul, to whom was given the apostleship of the uncircumcision; or, as in Gal. 2:9, as one of the principal pillars, together with James and John; or, as in Gal. 2:11, as subject to rebuke from Paul as from an equal. And (2) wherever by our Lord himself the future constitution of his Church is alluded to, or by the apostles its actual constitution, no hint of any such primacy is given, but the whole college of apostles are spoken of as absolutely equal. Matt. 19:27, 28; 20:26, 28; Eph. 2:20. Again (3) in the two Epistles which we have from his own hand, there is nothing for, but everything against, such a supposition. He exhorts the presbyters as being their co-presbyter (1 Pet. 5:1); describes himself as a partaker of the glory that shall be revealed; addresses his second Epistle to them that have obtained the like precious faith with ourselves (2 Pet. 1:1), and makes not the slightest allusion to any pre-eminence over the other apostles."

5. These twelve Jesus sent forth. On the names, character and lives of the twelve, see note at the end of this chapter. **And commanded them saying.** John gives no ac-

6 But go rather to the lost sheep² of the house of Israel.

7 And, as ye go, preach, saying,ᵃ The kingdom of heaven is at hand.

y Acts 13 : 46....z Ps. 119 : 176; Isa. 53 : 6; Jer. 50 : 6, 17; Eze. 34 : 5, 6, 8; 1 Pet. 2 : 25....a ch. 3 : 2; 4 : 17; Luke 9 : 2; 10 : 9.

count of this discourse; Mark (6 : 7–13) and Luke (9 : 1–6) present fragmentary reports of it. They were not apostles and were not present; Matthew was, and his report is much the fullest. It is clear, both from the structure of the discourse and from Matthew 11 : 1, that it is no collection of our Lord's sayings uttered at different times, but a report of a single discourse delivered at one time and for a specific purpose. But similar precepts were given by Christ at the ordination of the seventy (Luke 10 : 1–6) which should be compared carefully with this discourse, and some of the aphorisms found here and there are found elsewhere in the Gospels. Apparently Christ frequently repeated certain proverbial expressions in his itinerant preaching. Compare with verse 14, Luke 10 : 11; verse 17, Mark 13 : 9; verse 24, Luke 6 : 40, John 13 : 16; 15 : 20; verses 29–31, Luke 12 : 6, 7, etc. Much of Luke 12 : 1–11 appears to duplicate portions of this address. Comparing the reports of the three Evangelists, the following features are found characteristic of the mission of the twelve. The apostles were to go in pairs (Mark 6 : 7), "for they were to be accustomed to work in brotherly fellowship, and when difficulties arose one was to have the counsel and aid of the other" (*Schenckel's Character of Jesus*); (verses 7 and 8); were to preach in the towns and villages while Christ continued his ministry in the cities (compare Luke 9 : 6 with Matt. 11 : 1); were to preach only to the Jews (verses 5, 6); and in their ministry were to follow the example and adopt the habits of the ancient prophets (See note below). The discourses to them may be divided into three parts: *first*, their commission proper (verses 5–15); *second*, warnings of obstacles and persecution (verses 16–23); *third*, promises and encouragements (verses 24–42). The *first* comprises specific directions directly applicable only to this temporary mission, and part of them were subsequently declared by Christ inoperative in their later and wider ministry (see notes below); the *second* is more general, and applies to the Christian ministry in all times of religious persecution; the *third* appears to be universally applicable to all followers of Christ, whether engaged directly in the work of preaching the Gospel or not. The first part contains (*a*) the limitation of the apostles' missionary commission (verses 5–6); (*b*) their commission itself (verses 7, 8); (*c*) their provision (verses 9, 10); (*d*) directions as to their methods (verses 11–15).

Go not into the way of the Gentiles, i. e., into the Gentile territory. **And into a city of the Samaritans enter ye not.** The Samaritans were a mongrel race produced by an intermixture of Jews and heathen. Their religion was a composition of the worship of the true God and of idolatry (2 Kings 17 : 24–41). The enmity of the Jews against them was intense (John 4 : 9), and their character and conduct were characteristic of an apostate race. (See note on parable of Good Samaritan, Luke 10 : 25–37, and on John 4 : 9).

6. But go rather. The very form of this prohibition affords an intimation that it was not intended to be permanent. **To the lost sheep of the house of Israel.** Not to any particular class of Israelites, but to the Jews, who were as sheep without a shepherd (chapter 9 : 36; 15 : 24; John 10 : 16).

What was the cause and what is the significance of this prohibition? It certainly was not because Christ shared the prejudices of the age which caused the Jewish rabbis to forbid teaching the law to a Gentile (see to the contrary, Matt. 8 : 10–12; 28 : 19; Acts 1 : 8); nor because any inherent necessity required that the Gospel should be preached exclusively to God's chosen people before it was offered to the Gentiles, for Jesus had already preached it to the Samaritans (John 4 : 40); nor because he must by his death break down the middle wall of partition between Jew and Gentile before they could be made inheritors of the promise (Ephes. 2 : 14), for Christ before his death declared them to be sharers in the New Covenant (Luke 4 : 24–27). Two reasons are apparent, though none are declared by Christ himself; *first*, because if the twelve had begun by preaching the Gospel to the Gentiles they would have intensified the Jewish prejudices against it, and so closed the door to Jewish hearts; *second*, because they did not themselves understand the universality of the Gospel until long after, and if they had attempted to preach it to the Gentiles they would have inevitably became preachers of the Jewish law, and made at best only converts to a reformed Judaism. The practical significance of the command is that our work for Christ should begin with those nearest to us; that we are to preach the Gospel to our neighbors and friends, and so test our capacity before reaching out with religious ambition for a larger field of personal work among the heathen at home or abroad. But it affords no justification for refusing aid to those who have proved their capacity and have entered on the larger work.

7. And as ye go. The ministry was to be an itinerant one. **Preach, saying the King-**

8 Heal the sick, cleanse the lepers, raise the dead, cast out devils: freely⁵ ye have received, freely give.
9 Provide° neither gold, nor silver, nor brass, in your purses;
10 Nor scrip for *your* journey, neither two coats, neither shoes, nor yet staves; for⁴ the workman is worthy of his meat.
11 And into whatsoever city or town ye shall enter,

b Acts 8 : 18, 20....c Luke 22 : 35; 1 Cor. 9 : 7, etc....d Luke 10 : 7, etc.

dom of Heaven is at hand, *i. e., draws nigh*. Compare the following passages, where the Greek word (ἐγγίζω), here translated at hand, is rendered *draw nigh* or *come nigh* (Matt. 21 : 1, 34; Mark 11 : 1; Luke 15 : 25). The phrase Kingdom of Heaven first appears in the N. T., but this metaphor is employed in the prophecies of Daniel (Dan. 4 : 8, 34 ; 7 : 13, 14), whence it passed into the rabbinical books, where it is used sometimes in a general and almost a scriptural sense to signify a state of complete and perfect submission to the divine will, sometimes in a more restricted sense to signify that political reformation and national exaltation which the Jews expected would follow the coming of the Messiah (see Luke 17 : 20; 19 : 11). The disciples were not directed to explain in what the Kingdom of Heaven consisted; they were simply to proclaim that it was near. In this respect their preaching was to be patterned after that of John the Baptist (Matt. 3 : 2). It was their office *in this mission* not to instruct the nation, but simply to raise an expectancy, and so prepare the way for instruction which Christ afterward afforded in his sermon at Capernaum (John 6), and which the apostles themselves were afterward directed to give to the Gentiles (Matt. 28 : 19; compare 1 Cor. 2 : 2 ; Col. 1 : 26-28). It is not a law nor even a precedent for us; but is it not always the first work of the preacher, whether lay or clerical, to awaken a spiritual appetite, even if it be not very intelligent at the beginning? And is it not always to be done by proclaiming the kingdom of God as at hand, by making vivid the presence and power of God in nature and life, or awakening an expectation of his early coming in death and the judgment, or otherwise producing a sense of personal responsibility to God? The immediate effect of this mission was to extend the fame of Jesus (Matt. 14 : 1 ; Mark 6 : 31).

8. Heal the sick, etc. This command was accompanied with the conferring of power (verse 1), the first bestowal of miraculous power on the disciples. In the call of the Seventy it led to a mistaken exultation which Christ corrected (Luke 10 : 17-20). To those who see in the external acts of Christ's ministry a parable of his spiritual work, and especially in his ministry to the body a type of his ministry to the soul, it will not seem fanciful to trace that parallel here. The wise apostle of Christ will sometimes treat sin as a sickness to be cured (compare Gal. 6 : 1, 2), sometimes as a leprous pollution to be cleansed away (Acts 8 : 22, 23), sometimes as a spiritual death, the remedy for which is a spiritual resurrection (Eph. 2 : 4, 5), sometimes as a possession of the soul by an evil spirit that must be cast out (Acts 13 : 10-12; 19 : 15, 19). He needs to exercise sometimes gentleness and long-suffering, sometimes the purifying power of loving-kindness, sometimes spiritual vehemence, sometimes courage in combat with opposing evil. Christ healed his disciples of unworthy ambition (Mark 9 : 34-37), cleansed the woman that was a sinner (Luke 7 : 47, 48), raised Matthew from the dead (Matt. 9 : 9), and cast the devil out of Peter (Matt. 16 : 23). It should be added that the phrase "raise the dead" is omitted from some MSS., and placed in others before "cleanse the lepers."

Freely ye have received, freely give. This clause properly belongs with the two verses following, and enunciates the general principle which they illustrate. Freely is here equivalent to gratuitously (see Isaiah 51 : 1; Acts 8 : 18-23). It is only as the minister, lay or clerical, *receives* from the Lord that he can *impart* in his name. As to the bearing of this verse on the question of free churches, see below.

9. Provide neither gold. The articles referred to in this and the succeeding verses were the ordinary provision of travelers. They are of three kinds, money, food and clothing. **Gold, silver, brass;** rather *copper*. Mark and Luke have in our translation the general term *money;* but in the Greek, Mark has *brass* or *copper*, and Luke *silver*. All money in the East, in the time of Christ, was coined, and these three words embrace all coins; the apostles were not to provide themselves with money. **Purses;** literally *belt* or *girdle*. One end of the girdle was folded back so as to form a pocket: and it was used to carry money or an inkstand (Ezek. 9 : 2), a use to which it is still put in the East.

10. Nor scrip. "A bag used for carrying food or other necessaries; it was generally made of leather, and slung over the shoulder (1 Sam. 17 : 40); a similar article is still used by Syrian shepherds."—(*Kitto.*) Mark and Luke interpret this direction by their phraseology, "*no scrip, no bread.*" The apostles were to carry no food, and not even the traveler's bag or wallet in which to put such as might be provided for them. **Neither two coats,** literally tunics. The tunic (Greek χιτών) was the inner garment, worn next the skin, usually with sleeves and reaching to the knees. It answered rather to our *shirt* than to our *coat*. Apparently two tunics were sometimes worn, probably of different stuffs, by per-

12 And when ye come into an house, salute it.
13 And if the house be worthy, let your peace come

inquire who in it is worthy, and there abide till ye go thence.

sons of rank, wealth, or official station. To this fact John the Baptist refers probably in Luke 3 : 11. In Mark 14 : 63, the high priest is said to have "rent his clothes," literally, "*his tunics*," indicating that he had on more than one ; and Mark, in his account of this commission, says, "*and not put on two coats*" or *tunics*. **Neither shoes.** Mark (ch. 6 : 9) gives the converse direction "*be shod with sandals.*" "Shoes were of more delicate use ; sandals were more ordinary and more for service. A shoe was of softer leather ; a sandal of harder."—(*Lightfoot.*) The whole prohibition is aimed at luxury and delicacy of attire. **Nor yet staves.** The proper reading is *neither a staff*. According to Mark (ch. 6 : 8) the apostles were allowed each to take a staff ; probably the reading here has been changed to harmonize the two accounts. But no traveler would think of taking an extra staff. According to Mark they are permitted to take a staff, *i. e.*, the one which they already possessed ; according to Matthew they were not to *provide staves for this journey*; they were to go as they were, without any additional provision. **For the workman is worthy of his meat.** This assigns the reason for the prohibition of special provision; they are to be supported by those whom they serve. In the accompanying cut, from an Italian marble, a Roman peasant is shown, with his *staff*, and with his *scrip* or wallet slung over his shoulder.

From these provisions in verses 9 and 10 regarding the support of the twelve in this their first missionary tour, too much has sometimes been deduced respecting the support of the Christian ministry and their true method of operation. The commission was for a temporary service; the requirements were adapted to the customs of society ; the apostles were cast upon the hospitality of the people partly to try their own faith, partly to try that of the people, and measure their readiness to receive the Gospel, partly because they thus conformed to the habits of the ancient prophets (1 Kings 17 : 9 ; 2 Kings 4 : 8), and so assumed an office and position with which the people were measurably familiar. It is no more just to assume that the ministry must always be itinerant and without a settled support, than to conclude that they must not preach to the Gentiles, and must confine their preaching to a mere heralding of the coming of the kingdom of heaven (verses 5-7). In subsequent directions for their later ministry, Christ gave the apostles commands directly opposite to certain precepts here (*compare verse 5 with Acts 1 : 8*), and his own practice did not ordinarily conform to the precepts here given, forbidding provision. The band had a treasurer, and usually carried both money (John 12 : 6 ; 13 : 29) and provisions (Matt. 14 : 17 ; 15 : 34 ; 16 : 5, 7) ; and Christ himself expressly declared later that these directions were not applicable in their subsequent ministry (Luke 22 : 35, 36) ; observe that the disciples were abundantly provided for by the hospitality of the people (Luke 22 : 35). But while we shall miss the meaning of these precepts if we regard them as *rules* for the permanent government of the church, we shall also miss their meaning if we do not gather from them for our guidance the *spirit and principles* which underlie them. They certainly involve this much, viz., that (*a*), the ministry are to seek, as well as to save the lost, and therefore are to go after them ; (*b*), they are to give freely, and not make a merchandise of the Gospel ; (*c*), they are to avoid all ostentation in attire and luxury in food ; (*d*), they are to depend on the voluntary contributions of the people for their sustenance, as did the O. T. priesthood to a large extent, and the O. T. prophets altogether (Numb. 18 : 20, 21 ; Deut. 10 : 8, 9 ; 18 : 1, 2) ; and not on the acquisition of property by the church so as to render its ministry independent of the people, as the Roman Catholic hierarchy do, nor on the support of the state, as do the ministry of all established churches ; (*e*), their dependence is that of a laborer who *earns* his bread, not that of a beggar who receives it as a gratuity. But whether the wages are paid in chance and occasional contributions, or in a permanent and regular stipend is a matter not determined here, nor, so far as I can now see, anywhere in the Scripture.

11-15. These verses give further directions as to the method in which the apostles are to prosecute their mission now given to them. With these directions compare those given to the seventy reported in Luke 10 : 5-12.

11. Who in it is worthy. For an interpretation of the kind of worth signified, see Acts 13 : 46, 48 ; 17 : 11. It is not moral excellence, but a readiness to receive the Gospel message. In this sense Zaccheus, though a publican, was worthy to be a host of Christ (Luke 19 : 5, 9). Chrysostom notes that Christ requires his apostles to exercise circumspection. They are not to trust to the hospitality of every one, but to enquire where they will be likely to find a welcome. **There abide.** They are not to go from house to house (compare Luke 10 : 7), lest the time that should be devoted to the preaching of the Gospel be frittered away in receiving hospitality and entertainment. A comparison of this direction

upon it: but if it be not worthy, let your peace return° to you.

14 And whosoever shall not receive you, nor hear your words, when ye depart out of that house or city, shake¹ off the dust of your feet.

15 Verily I say unto you, It ͬ shall be more tolerable for the land of Sodom and Gomorrha in the day of judgment, than for that city.

16 Behold, I send you forth as sheep in the midst of wolves: be ye therefore wise ͪ as serpents, and harmless¹ as doves.

17 But beware ʲ of men: for they ᵏ will deliver you

● Ps. 35 : 13....f Neh. 5 : 13; Acts 13 : 51; 18 : 6....g ch. 11 : 22, 24....h Rom. 16 : 19; Eph. 5 : 15....i Phil. 2 : 15....j Phil. 3 : 2....
k ch. 24 : 9 ; Mark 13 : 9.

---

with the apostolic practice subsequent to Christ's resurrection (Acts 2 : 46, but see note there), affords a hint of the right and the wrong kind of pastoral visiting; the right kind goes for the preaching of the Gospel, the wrong kind for mere social entertainment.

12. And when ye come into the house salute it. Not the house that is worthy, but any house which they enter. They are not to stand on ceremony and the dignity of their office and await a welcome; they are at once to offer the customary salutation. The ancient Jews, like the modern Mohammedans, did not salute one of a different religious faith; but the apostles were not to wait until they had ascertained how they would be received before proffering their blessing. For form of salutation see Luke 10 : 5 ; and compare Numb. 6 : 23-26.

13. Let your peace return to you. The prayer for blessing will receive no answer if the heart refuses to receive the blessing. Nor are the apostles to be disturbed in mind because of such refusal, still less to follow their rejected benediction with an anathema. Their peace is *to return to them.* "If your peace finds a shut instead of an open door in any household, take it back to yourselves who know how to value it, and it will taste the sweeter to you for having been offered, even though rejected."—(*Dr. Brown.*) There is no peace like that which comes from bearing insult and wrong with sweetness and serenity.

14. And whosoever shall not receive you * * * shake off the dust of your feet. Mark and Luke add by way of explanation "*for a testimony against them.*" Compare Luke 10 : 11. The Scribes taught that the dust of heathen lands defiled those who came in contact with it; accordingly it was a custom of the Pharisees, when they entered Judea from a heathen country, to shake off the dust of the land as a testimony that they had no part or lot with heathenism. The apostles, if rejected, were to turn from the city or house that rejected them and hold no further intercourse with it. It was to be to them as a Gentile city to a Jew. Compare Matt. 18 : 17; and see for illustration of this precept Acts 13 : 51 ; 18 : 6. Is the Christian minister, then, to refuse all intercourse with and all second attempts to win those who reject Christ in the first presentation? No! because these are not rules for the permanent ministry, but for a specific and necessarily rapid mission, whose object was not so much to win souls as to awaken attention and prepare for a future ministry. On this point Chrysostom's homily is admirable ; I quote a single paragraph : "For I indeed oftentimes pronounce peace to you, and will not cease from continually speaking it ; and if, besides your insults, you receive me not, even then I shake not off the dust ; not that I am disobedient to our Lord, but that I vehemently burn for you. And besides I have suffered nothing at all for you ; I have neither come a long journey, nor with that garb and that voluntary poverty am I come, nor without shoes and a second coat ; and perhaps this is why ye also fail of your part."

15. It shall be more tolerable for the land of Sodom and Gomorrha in the day of judgment than for that city. Compare chap. 11 : 21-23, and Luke 10 : 13-15. Observe, *first,* that as there are degrees of guilt, so there will be degrees of punishment in the future world (Luke 12 : 47, 48) ; and *second,* that the guilt of rejecting the Gospel is marked by Christ as greater than that of moral impurity of life. Neither secular nor sacred history contains a record of immorality and vice more loathsome and flagrant than that of the cities of the plain (Gen. 18 : 20 ; 19 : 4-15) ; but Christ pronounces a heavier woe against those that refuse the proffer of the Gospel, because *the refusal to accept help out of sin* is more fatal than any form of immorality, however grievous.

Ch. 10 : 16-23. WORDS OF WARNING. THE CHRISTIAN, LIKE CHRIST, IS A SHEEP AMONG WOLVES (Isaiah 53 : 7).—THE CHRISTIAN IS IN AN ENEMY'S COUNTRY (vs. 17, 18). THE DANGER IN THE FIRST CENTURY WAS FROM OPEN ATTACK, IN THE NINETEENTH IT IS FROM TREACHEROUS AMBUSCADE.—THE CHRISTIAN'S BEST PREPARATION FOR THREATENED DIFFICULTY AND DANGER: THE BAPTISM OF THE HOLY SPIRIT (vs. 19, 20). —A TRUE INSPIRATION IS THE PERPETUAL HERITAGE OF GOD'S PEOPLE.—TRIBULATION IN THE WORLD; GLORY BEYOND THE WORLD (vs. 21, 22; John 16 : 33). —PERSECUTION IS A WIND THAT CARRIES THE SEEDS OF TRUTH ON ITS WINGS (v. 23).

16-23. In these verses Christ passes from the immediate and temporary mission to the future work of the apostles, and warns them of the danger which their consecration to his service will involve. It is certain that these warnings are not exclusively, and it is doubtful whether they are even primarily, applicable to the immediate and

up to the councils, and they will scourge¹ you in their synagogues ;

18 And ye ᵐ shall be brought before governors and kings for my sake, for a testimony against them and the Gentiles.

19 But ⁿ when they deliver you up, take no thought

---

l Acts 5 : 40 ; 2 Cor. 11 : 24....m Acts, chs. 24 and 25....n Mark 13 : 11 ; Luke 12 : 11 ; 21 : 14, 15.

---

temporary mission laid upon them in this discourse. It is observable that these warnings and the subsequent encouragements are not found in the discourse to the seventy (Luke 10 : 1-15). Observe that Christ always sets before the disciples the hazards and dangers of discipleship, and bids them count the cost before entering on their work. Compare Luke 14 : 25-36.

16. Behold I send you forth. *I*, who give all power, both send and direct in what spirit and by what methods you are to execute your mission. "In saying 'Behold, I send you forth as sheep,' he intimates this, 'Do not therefore despond, for I know certainly that in this way more than any other, ye will be invincible to all.'"—(*Chrysostom*.) Observe Christ's tacit claim of power in this declaration, which is quite incompatible with the humility which would belong to Jesus if he were mere man. Compare Isaiah 6 : 8. **As sheep in the midst of wolves.** "Not *to the wolves*, but *in the midst of* wolves, in order to seek out those who would receive the kingdom."—(*Lange*.) Yet the symbol is intended to teach, not merely their apparent helplessness, but their real power, "the unresistable might of weakness." "For thus shall I best show forth my might when sheep do get the better of wolves, and receiving a thousand bites, so far from being consumed, do even work a change on them ; a thing far greater and more marvellous than killing them, to alter their spirit and to reform their mind ; and this being only twelve, while the whole world is filled with wolves."—(*Chrysostom*.) Christ himself was as a sheep among wolves. See Isaiah 53 : 7 ; and compare Psalm 44 : 22 ; Rom. 8 : 36. There is possibly here a reference to the passage in Psalms. Has the church always been a sheep among wolves ? Was not the inquisition rather a wolf among sheep ? **Be ye therefore shrewd as serpents and simple as doves.** The Greek word (ἀκέραιος) translated *harmless*, occurs also in Romans 16 : 19 and Phil. 2 : 15, and probably signifies *unmixed*, *simple*. *i. e.* the opposite of a character in which many motives mingle and every act is complex, and the aims covered up and concealed. There is in this aphorism of Christ's a contrast in terms which the translators have endeavored to soften, and which the above translation but imperfectly renders. The serpent was among the Jews a common symbol of diabolical craft, while the dove was proverbial for its stupidity ; it was an Arab proverb, There is nothing more simple than the dove ; both conceptions are embodied in the O. T. Scripture (Gen. 3 : 1 ; Hosea 7 : 11) ; and a proverb very analogous in words, but very different in application to that of our Lord's, is found in the rabbinical books : "Ye shall be toward me as upright as the doves, but toward the Israelites as cunning as serpents." The Christian worker is to combine these two contradictory qualities in his conduct toward all men. He is to be guileful like the serpent (2 Cor. 2 : 16) and guileless like the dove (1 Pet. 2 : 1, 21, 22). Of the wisdom of the serpent, Christ's replies to the Pharisees in the last days of his mission afford an example (Matt. 22 : 15-46); the simplicity of the dove he exemplified during his trial (Matt. 26 : 63, 64). "These qualities are opposed to each other ; they never occur combined in nature, or in the natural disposition of man. But the spirit of Christ combines in higher unity these natural antagonisms. The serpent slips innumerable times from the hand of the pursuer [and catches its prey by guile, see reference above]; the dove does not settle in any unclean place, it approaches him who is gentle, and will never do harm to the persecutor ; its safety lies in flying upward." It may be added that Christian virtue often consists in holding in even balance opposing qualities, either of which alone or in excess becomes a vice.

17. But beware of men, *i. e.*, of all men (verse 22), not merely of particular persecutors, but of the enmity of mankind. See below. **Councils.** The local tribunals established in every town. Their origin is indicated in Deut. 16 : 18. They consisted, according to Josephus, of seven judges ; according to the rabbinical books, of twenty-three. See on chap. 5 : 21. **Scourge you in their synagogues.** In every synagogue there was a bench of three magistrates, who had authority to inflict certain punishments, of which scourging was one. "The number of stripes could not exceed forty (Deut. 25 : 3); whence the Jews took care not to exceed thirty-nine (2 Cor. 11 : 24). The convict was stripped to the waist and tied in a bent position to a low pillar, and the stripes, with a whip of three thongs, were inflicted on the back between the shoulders."—(*Smith's Bib. Dict., Am. Ed., Art. Punishments.*) This punishment is not to be confounded with the Roman scourging to which our Lord was subjected under Pilate (Matt. 27 : 26), which was a still more dreadful infliction. For general account of synagogues, see note on Matt. 4 : 23 ; for evidence of direct fulfillment of this prophecy, see Acts 5 : 40 ; 22 : 19 ; 26 : 11.

18. And ye shall be brought before gov-

CH. X.] MATTHEW. 141

how or what ye shall speak? for it shall be given you in that same hour what ye shall speak.
20 For it is not ye that speak, but the Spirit of your Father which speaketh in you.
21 And the brother shall deliver up the brother to death, and the father the child: and the children shall rise up against *their* parents, and cause them to be put to death.
22 And ye shall be hated of all *men* for my name's sake; but he° that endureth to the end shall be saved.

o Dan. 12 : 12, 13; Rev. 2 : 11.

ernors, i. e., Roman officials, e. g., Felix (Acts, ch. 24), Festus (Acts, ch. 25), Gallio (Acts 18 : 12), Paulus (Acts 13 : 7). **And kings,** e. g., Herod Agrippa (Acts, ch. 26), and Cæsar, i. e., Nero (Acts 25 : 12). **For my sake.** Compare Matt. 5 : 11, 12, and Acts 5 : 41. **For a testimony against them.** Neither *against* them, as in our version, nor *to* them, as in some commentaries, but *both against and to them* (2 Cor. 2 : 15, 16). "It was a testimony in the best sense *to* Sergius Paulus (Acts 13 : 7), but *against* Felix (Acts 25 : 25) ; and this double power ever belongs to the word of God as preached—it is a two-edged sword" (Rev. 1 : 16 ; 2 : 12).—(*Alford.*) **And the Gentiles,** rather the nations. Compare Matt. 24 : 14, and for an illustration of the effect of the bringing of an apostle before the kings, see Phil. 1 : 12–18.

19. Take no thought. Literally, be not divided in mind, i. e., between desire to be faithful to the truth and a desire to act prudently and to escape threatened evil. The Greek word here (μεριμνάω) is the same as that used in Matt. 6 : 25 ; see note there. Alford renders it, *Take no anxious thought. Be not distracted,* still more closely reflects the meaning of the original. Observe the qualification, "*When they deliver you up,*" and the contrary direction, contrary in words though not in spirit, given to those disciples, the grounds of whose faith were inquired into, "Be always ready to give an answer to every man that asketh you a reason of the hope that is in you, in meekness and fear" (1 Pet. 3 : 15). "As long as the contest is among friends, he commends us to take thought; but when there is a terrible tribunal, and frantic assemblies, and terrors on all sides, he bestows the influence from himself, that they may take courage and speak out, and not be discouraged nor betray the righteous cause."—(*Chrysostom.*) This verse is best interpreted by such practical illustrations as are afforded by Acts 4 : 19, 20 ; 5 : 20–32 ; and see especially Dan. 3 : 16–18. **How or what ye shall speak,** i. e., they are neither to be anxious concerning the *matter* nor the *manner* of their reply. Compare Romans 8 : 26 ; "for we know not *what* we should pray for *as* we ought." **For it shall be given you in that same hour what ye shall speak.** Even irrespective of the more distinct promise of the succeeding verse, it is generally safer in time of threatened danger to trust to the intuition of the hour and speak boldly and simply the truth than to study an answer which by much thinking is apt to become an evasion. *Mental distraction never inspires moral courage.* That this verse should ever have been quoted as an authority for giving instruction in the principles of the Gospel without previous study and thought affords one of the most amazing examples of the capacity of the mind to misinterpret and misapply the truth.

20. For it is not you that speak, etc. Compare Exod. 4 : 12; Jer. 1 : 7; Acts 4 : 8. And observe in the latter case how obedience to Christ's precept rendered the reply of the apostles a witness for Jesus to the Sanhedrim. (See verse 13.) **The Spirit of your Father.** The Holy Spirit, more explicitly promised in John 15 : 26, 27. This promise here given does not imply the inspiration of the Scriptures, but it does necessarily involve the strongest possible assurance of *a divine inspiration, i. e.,* of a divine influence acting upon and giving peculiar power to the heart and mind of the disciple. The careful student should combine here the note of Alford and that of Chrysostom. The first observes that "in the great work of God in the world, human individuality sinks down and vanishes, and God alone, his Christ, his Spirit is the great worker;" the latter notes that "from first to last part is God's work, part his disciples'. Thus, to do miracles is his, but to provide nothing is theirs. Again, to open all men's houses, was of the grace from above ; but to require no more than was needful, was of their own self-denial. Their bestowing peace was of the gift of God ; their inquiring for the worthy and not entering in without distinction unto all, was of their own self-command. Again, to punish such as received them not, was his ; but retiring with gentleness from them without reviling or insulting them, was of the apostles' meekness. To give the Spirit and cause them not to take thought, was of him that sent them ; but to become like sheep and doves, and to bear all things nobly [and to abstain from distracting thoughts], was of their own calmness and prudence. To be hated and not to despond, and to endure, was their own ; to save them that endured, was of him who sent them." Observe, too, how the promised inspiration is characterized by the very form of the promise, "speaketh *in* you." It is not a divine dictation of words to the speaker, but a divine inspiring of *his own natural faculties,* so that the Spirit speaks not *to* the disciple, nor *through* the disciple, but *in* the disciple. Compare 1 Pet. 1 : 21.

23 But when they persecute you in this city, flee[p] ye into another: for verily I say unto you, Ye shall not have gone over the cities of Israel, till the Son of man be come.

[p] Acts 8 : 1.

21. And the brother shall deliver up the brother, etc. Natural affection is not adequate to counteract the power of religious bigotry. No power for evil is greater than that of a corrupted and misdirected religious zeal; none is more unscrupulous and cruel.

22. Hated of all. For the reason why, see John 15 : 18, 19. For the Christian's answer to the world's hate, see Matt. 5 : 44. This verse, compared with such injunctions as Matt. 5 : 16, affords a striking illustration of the seeming contradictions of which the Bible is full; but not fuller than life itself. Christian character commends itself to the consciences of men, but is hated because it crosses their self-interest, and rebukes, by its very purity, their sin. See for illustrations of good works that led men both to glorify God and to hate his disciples Acts 4 : 13, 18; 5 : 28, 40. Chrysostom remarks on the combination of dangers of which Christ warned his disciples; the courts of justice, kings, governors, synagogues of Jews, nations of Gentiles, rulers, ruled, their own kinsfolk, and finally the whole combined enmity of mankind. The spiritual power of Christ is exemplified in the fact that he could describe such dangers, and yet inspire the twelve with courage to go forth undaunted to meet them. Chrysostom's practical application to our own times is also worth quoting and worth pondering, "What then must we deserve, having such high patterns, and in peace giving way to effeminacy and remissness? With none to make war we are slain; we faint when no man pursues: in peace we are required to be saved, and even for this we are not sufficient."

But he that endureth to the end shall be saved. Some of the commentators, among others Alford, Schaff and Owen, see in this promise a primary reference to the destruction of Jerusalem, the end being, in their view, the overthrow of the holy city, and the being saved the deliverance referred to in Matt. 24 : 15–18. There appears to me to be nothing either in the context or in the parallel passages where this aphorism occurs, to warrant this view. The promise is simply the general one; he who endures persecution until its completion, and so by implication until it has completed in the soul its work of purification (Rom. 5 : 3–5; James 1 : 3, 4), shall be saved, i. e. ransomed and presented perfect before the throne of grace. So Dr. Alexander interprets it. See for parallels Matt. 24 : 13; 13 : 21; Ephes. 6 : 13; Hebrews 3 : 6; 10 : 23, 38, 39; Rev. 2 : 10, 17, 26.

23. But when they persecute you in this city, flee you into another. It has been noticed that this implies a promise that they should find another provided, that they should not be without a refuge. In seeming contrast to this direction is John 10 : 11, 13; "the hireling fleeth because he is an hireling and careth not for the sheep." Wordsworth suggests the true reconciliation: "If a person has a flock committed to his care which will be scattered or torn by wolves if he flies, then he must not fly." Christ himself exemplified on more than one occasion the meaning of the direction *flee* (Luke 4 : 29-30; John 8 : 59; 10 : 39). Through obedience to it persecution became in the apostolic era an instrument for the spread of the Gospel (Acts 8 : 1; 11 : 19). The same principle in the later history of the church has wrought in the same way; e. g., the flight of the Puritans from the persecutions of the Stuarts, and of the Huguenots from persecutions in France, led to the religious foundation which was imparted to the American colonies. Directly contrary to the spirit of this precept was the spirit of Christians in the early church. The passion for martyrdom became so great that men accused themselves to receive the martyr's crown, or openly disturbed heathen worship for the same purpose; and this singular fanaticism had finally to be repressed by the admonitions of the clergy, and even by a canon which refused the title of martyrdom to those who sought it by publicly destroying idols. True Christian principle is quite compatible with true Christian prudence.

For verily I say unto you. A common introduction to a peculiarly solemn affirmation. See note on Matt. 5 : 13. **Ye shall not have gone over.** Literally, Ye shall not complete. But it is hardly possible to give to this the sense which Alford gives: ye shall not have preached the Gospel *effectually*. The meaning afforded by our English version is much the more natural. Dr. Owen paraphrases it, Shall not have finished passing through the cities to preach the Gospel. **Till the Son of man be come.** The phrase, *Son of man*, is used in the O. T. sometimes to designate the descendants of Adam (Job 25 : 6; Psalm 144 : 3; 146 : 3; Isaiah 51 : 12; 56 : 2) and in Ezekiel that prophet is addressed by this appellation about eighty times. In Daniel (7 : 13) it is applied prophetically to the Messiah, and in this sense alone is it used in the N. T. In the Evangelists the writers themselves never use it of Christ, but *he* uses it in describing himself, especially when speaking of himself as the Messiah (Matt. 9 : 6; 11 : 19; 12 : 8; 13 : 41; 17 : 9, 22; 24 : 27–30, etc.). It is also used elsewhere by third persons, but always

24 The disciple is not above *his* master, nor the servant above his lord.

25 It is enough for the disciple that he be as his master, and the servant as his lord. If they have called

q Luke 6 : 40 ; John 13 : 16 ; 15 : 20. . . . r John 8 : 48.

in speaking of him in his exaltation and manifested glory (Acts 7 : 56 ; Rev. 1 : 13 ; 14 : 14). And the *coming of the Son of man*, wherever used in the N. T., prophetically signifies the disclosure of Jesus as the Messiah (Matt. 24 : 27, 37, 39 ; 25 : 31 ; Mark 8 : 38 ; Luke 17 : 24), but not always his final coming to judge the world (Matt. 16 : 28). It is evident that in this promise Christ cannot refer directly to his final coming in judgment, because he did not know when that event would take place (Mark 13 : 32). This much is clear; but in the light of these facts the interpretation of this prophecy, Ye shall not have gone over the cities of Israel till the Son of man be come, must be confessed to be difficult. The principal explanations are the following: 1. Before they had fulfilled their task Christ himself, following them, would overtake them and be ready to give them future directions. So Chrysostom, Lange, and apparently Alexander. But this does not agree with the universal usage by Matthew of the phrase "coming of the Son of man," nor with the facts in the case, for Christ did not overtake the apostles, but they returned to him (Mark 6 : 30 ; Luke 9 : 10). 2. Before the work of *effectually* preaching the Gospel to the Jews, *i. e.* before the Jews were all converted, Christ would come in power and glory to judge the world. But he does not say before all missionary work is done, but before *their work is done*. The plain meaning of the promise is that it is to be fulfilled *during their life-time.*, 3. Before their mission was ended the destruction of Jerusalem should take place, *i. e.* Christ should in his power by his providence come to judge the Jewish nation. This is the common view of most commentators, *e. g.* Alford, Brown, Bloomfield, Barnes, Owen, &c. It appears to me to be untenable. In no proper sense did the Son of man come in the destruction of Jerusalem. It may be conceded that this national judgment was itself a prophetic symbol of the final judgment when the Son of man shall come in power and glory; but the promise here made to the apostles of his personal coming to aid them in their mission, is not fulfilled by an event *which is not the coming of the Son of man at all, but only a prophecy and symbol of that coming*. 4. Before their preaching to the Jewish nation should be completed, Jesus should be revealed as the Son of man, *i. e.* as the Messiah, a promise which was fulfilled by his crucifixion, resurrection, and second spiritual coming to dwell in the hearts of his disciples. This is apparently the view of Lightfoot and Calvin. It appears to me to be the true one for the following reasons : (*a*) The Son of man did not fully come until his crucifixion and his resurrection, which not only disclosed his Messianic character (Matt. 27 : 54 ; Rom. 1 : 4), but also completed his Messianic mission (Luke 24 : 26 ; John 19 : 31, 34 ; Acts 17 : 3). (*b*) Not until then did or could he fulfill the promise of his second and spiritual coming to *abide* in the hearts of his disciples (John 14 : 18, 19, 21-23). That promise was fulfilled at the day of Pentecost by the descent of the Holy Spirit; for the clearly marked distinction between the three persons of the Godhead belongs to a later epoch in theology, and Christ himself speaks of the coming of the Spirit and his own coming as all one (compare John 14 : 16, 17 with verses 18-23), and the apostles speak of the indwelling of the Spirit and of Christ as one (compare Acts 4 : 8 with verse 13, and Gal. 5 : 6, 24 with verses 16 and 25, and see Rom. 8 : 1). (*c*) It is after the disclosure of Christ as the Messiah by his resurrection and his second and spiritual coming, that the apostles begin to preach that Jesus is the Christ, that is, to declare that the Son of man, a Messiah, has come ; this forms the burden of their first preaching subsequent to the ascension (Acts 2 : 36 ; 3 : 18 ; 4 : 10-12 ; 8 : 5, and note 9 : 20 ; 10 : 42), and the revelation made to them by the Holy Spirit of Jesus as the Messiah is recognized by them as a fulfillment of the prophecies of the O. T., respecting the Messiah's coming (Acts 2 : 16-21 ; 3 : 19). (*d*) Finally it was not until after this spiritual coming of Christ, subsequent to his resurrection and ascension, that the disciples made an end of preaching the Gospel to the cities of Judea and began to preach to the Gentiles. This promise, then, may be paraphrased thus : Go on ; fear not ; before your mission to the Jews (vers. 5) is completed, the Messiah will be revealed and the Messiah's kingdom established : and this promise was fulfilled by Christ's passion, resurrection, ascension and subsequent spiritual coming on the day of Pentecost, though in a manner very different from that which the disciples had anticipated.

Ch. 10 : 24–42. CHRISTIAN ENCOURAGEMENTS. CHRIST'S EXAMPLE THE CHRISTIAN'S INSPIRATION IN SUFFERING AS IN ACTION (VS. 24, 25).—INJUSTICE SUFFERED HERE WILL BE SET RIGHT BY GOD'S JUSTICE HEREAFTER (V. 26).— FEAR OF GOD CASTS OUT FEAR OF MAN (V. 28).—GOD CARES FOR HIS LEAST DISCIPLES. GOD'S GREATNESS IN LITTLE THINGS (VS. 29-31). EARTHLY DISREPUTE THE ROAD TO HEAVENLY HONOR (VS. 32, 33).— FOREWARNED IS FOREARMED (VS. 34, 35).— LOVE EASILY CARRIES ALL CROSSES (VS. 37, 38).—SELF-SACRIFICE IS THE HIGHEST SELF-SERVICE (V. 39) —THE CHRISTIAN'S MISSION IS CHRIST'S MISSION (John 17 : 18), AND THE CHRISTIAN STANDS IN CHRIST'S STEAD (V. 40).

the master of the house Beelzebub, how much more *shall they call* them of his household?

26 Fear them not therefore: for* there is nothing covered, that shall not be revealed; and hid, that shall not be known.

27 What I tell you in darkness, *that* speak ye in light: and what ye hear in the ear, *that* preach ye upon the housetops.

28 And fear' not them which kill the body, but are not able to kill the soul: but rather fear him which is able to destroy both soul and body in hell.

29 Are not two sparrows sold for a farthing? and

Mark 4 : 22; Luke 12 : 2, 3; 1 Cor. 4 : 5....Δ Isa. 8 : 10, 13; 51 : 7, 12; 1 Pet. 3 : 14.

THE ALL-SEEING SEES, AND THE ALL-LOVING REWARDS THE LEAST SERVICE (VS. 41, 42).

Verses 24–42 consist of aphorisms whose general purpose appears to be to encourage the disciples in view of the warnings already given. They are more general than those warnings, and are applicable to all Christians and in all ages of the world. Several of them are repeated elsewhere; and there is a close parallelism between this portion of the discourse and one reported in Luke 12 : 1-12. It is possible that Matthew may have collected here utterances really delivered at other times in Christ's ministry; it is more probable that Christ repeated the same proverbs on different occasions. The connection in this part of the discourse is not so marked as in the preceding portions. It is indicated in the notes below.

24, 25. The scholar is not above his teacher, nor the slave above his lord. * * * If the head of the house they have called Beelzebul, how much more the members of his household. The three relations in which Christ stands to his people here mentioned, are elsewhere brought out in Scripture. He is teacher, and they learners (Matt. 5 : 1; 7 : 27, 8; Luke 6 : 20); he is lord or owner, they servants (Luke 12 : 35-48; John 13 : 13; Rom. 1 : 1; 2 Pet. 1 : 1; Jude 1); he is head of the household, they its members (Matt. 24 : 45; 26 : 26-29; Luke 24 : 30). Compare for the significance of the last metaphor, Hebrews 3 : 6 with Ephes. 3 : 14, 15, in one of which Christ, in the other the Father, is described as head of the family. Observe how each of these metaphors interprets the other; as teacher, Christ is lord, and speaks with authority (Matt. 7 : 29); as lord, he is over friends, not slaves, and rules by love, not law (John 15 : 15); observe, too, how Christ's claim of supremacy depends, not on isolated passages, but is woven into the texture of all his teachings. **Beelzebul,** not *Beelzebub.* There is no account of Christ being called Beelzebub, but the Pharisees referred his miracles to the power of Beelzebul. *i. e.,* of Satan (Matt. 9 : 34; 12 : 22; John 8 : 48). See notes on Matt. 12 : 24.

26. Fear them not therefore; for there is nothing covered—with slander, **that shall not be uncovered**—at the judgment day (Eccles. 12 : 14), **and hid,** of the true glory of Christian truth and Christian character (Col. 3 : 3; 1 John 3 : 2), **that shall not be known.** "When Christ shall be manifested who is our life, then shall we also with him be manifested in glory" (Col. 3 : 4; see note there). For the effect which this truth should have on those suffering from slander, see 1 Pet. 2 : 23; 4 : 19. The connection with the preceding verse Chrysostom thus gives: "For why do ye grieve at their calling you sorcerers and deceivers? But wait a little, and all men will address you as saviours and benefactors of the world—yea, for time [still more the disclosures of the last judgment] discovers all things that are concealed; it will both refute their false accusations and make manifest your virtue."

27. What ye hear in the ear. According to Lightfoot, the Jewish rabbis who explained the law in the schools in Hebrew, whispered their explanations to the ear of the interpreters, who then repeated them aloud to the scholars. There is, perhaps, a reference to this custom here. **Preach ye upon the housetops.** The Jewish housetop was flat. The ministers of the ancient synagogue on Sabbath eve sounded six times a trumpet to announce the coming in of the Sabbath. The Turkish crier calls to prayers from the housetop. Local governors in country districts cause their proclamations to be announced in the same way, generally in the evening on the return of the people from their labors. The metaphor here is borrowed from, and illustrated by, these uses of the housetop. Of Christ's whispering in the ear, see illustrations in Matt. 13 : 11, 18, 36; 16 : 20; of the disciples preaching on the housetop, see illustrations in Acts 2 : 6-11, etc. Christ speaks in darkness parables which the people do not understand, but which are subsequently interpreted to his disciples and thus to all mankind (Matt. 13 : 11, 18, 36). He spoke in the ear, chapters 14, 15, 16 and 17 of John, which the evangelist has repeated by his Gospel in the light. He still, by the inspiration of his Spirit, speaks in the ear experience which his followers are to interpret publicly by life and words (1 Cor. 2 : 7-13).

28. And fear not them which kill the body * * * rather fear him who is able to destroy both soul and body. Observe the double contrast, (1) between men whose power extends only to the *body,* and God, whose power endangers *both soul and body ;* (2) between man, who can only *kill* the body, beyond which comes the resurrection and the new life, and God, who can *utterly destroy* (Gr. ἀπόλλυμι) both

one of them shall not fall on the ground without your Father.
30 But ᵃ the very hairs of your head are all numbered.
31 Fear ye not therefore; ye are of more value than many sparrows.
32 Whosoever therefore shall confess me before men, him ᵛ will I confess also before my Father which is in heaven.
33 But whosoever ʷ shall deny me before men, him will I also deny before my Father which is in heaven.
34 Think not that I am come to send peace on earth: I ˣ came not to send peace, but a sword.

a Acts 27 : 34....v Rev. 3 : 5....w 2 Tim. 2 : 12....x Luke 12 : 49, 53.

soul and body. As in several other passages of Scripture, there is an implication here that the punishment of the wicked is *a true destruction*, not a living in suffering. But it is only an implication, and there are other passages which certainly appear to teach otherwise. For a consideration of the whole question, see note on Matt. 13 : 50. I assume that *Him* whom we are to fear is God, as do most commentators, not Satan, as do Stier and some others; for (a) It is not true that Satan can destroy either body or soul; he has no power except such as God permits him to exercise (Job 1 : 12; compare James 4 : 12); he is himself shut up in hell (Matt. 25 : 41; Rev. 20 : 10), "does not destroy soul and body in hell, but *before* that time, and for the purpose of having them consigned *to* hell."—(*Lange*.) (b) The fear of Satan is but a sorry protection against the fear of man, but "The fear of the Lord is the beginning of wisdom" (Prov. 9 : 10). (c) The context of the discourse calls for this interpretation. We are both to fear and to trust the All-powerful. See next verses.

In hell. *Gehenna.* See note on Matt. 5 : 22. Dr. Owen concludes that Christ does not here speak of annihilation, "for the destruction spoken of takes place in Gehenna." But since the fires of Gehenna did in fact utterly consume the corpses of the criminals cast upon them, his deduction is hardly warranted. On the other hand, the metaphor does not necessarily imply annihilation. That question of the true punishment of the lost must be determined by the teachings of other passages, or at least by a comparison of this with other passages.

29. Are not two sparrows sold for a farthing? The *farthing* (Gr. ἀσσάριον) is a Roman coin which was equal to about a cent and a half in value. The word occurs in the N. T. only here and in the analogous passage in Luke 12 : 6. The **sparrow** is a general term for a large variety of birds, of which there are known to be above one hundred different species. The corresponding Hebrew term is generally rendered bird or fowl. It is in the O. T. a symbol of weakness (Psalm 11 : 1). The various species of sparrow are very numerous in Palestine. They are snared in great numbers and sold for food. The markets of Jerusalem and Joppa are said to be saturated at the present day by many fowlers who offer for sale long strings of little birds of various species, chiefly sparrows, wag-tails and larks. It is to this snaring and sale of the sparrow our Lord alludes here. **Without your Father.** Observe he does not say *their* Father nor *our* Father, but *your* Father, *i. e.*, without his knowledge and his permission (Luke 12 : 6). This verse certainly forbids the construction put by Stier upon the preceding one, that it is the devil who can destroy both soul and body. Not even the sparrow can fall to the ground by the power of the devil without permission of God. Observe that nature as strikingly illustrates God's greatness in little as in great things, a truth of which the microscope affords abundant illustration.

30. But the very hairs of your head. A metaphorical expression to signify the minuteness of God's care. Compare 1 Sam. 14 : 45; Luke 21 : 13; Acts 27 : 34. The lesson inculcated is not only that God cares for us despite our insignificance, but also that he cares for us in respects that seem the most insignificant.

31. Of more value. Compare Matt. 6 : 26, and note. This is God's answer to David's question: "What is man that thou art mindful of him, and the son of man that thou visitest him?" (Psalm 8 : 4). Observe, that nature inspires both question and answer: the stars the question, the birds the answer.

32, 33. Every one therefore who shall confess in me. Observe the phraseology of the original of which the above is a literal translation. The promise is to *every one* (πᾶς) who confessed *in Christ* (ἐν ἐμοί). It is not a mere public profession before the church which is meant, for it must be "*before men*," *i. e.*, as interpreted by verses 17 and 18, councils, synagogues, governors, kings, in time of peril, when confession costs something; nor is it even every public profession before men which is meant, but a confession in Christ, *i. e.*, such a confession as has its root in Christ, and shows a living union with him. Such a confession in Christ the apostles witnessed before the Sanhedrim (Acts 4 : 13), and such Christ himself witnessed in God before Pontius Pilate (1 Tim. 6 : 13; compare John 18 : 37; 19 : 6, 11, 12). Christ also confesses *in us*; that is, not only acknowledges us his disciples, but shows himself *in* us and us to be *in* him (John 17 : 21, 26). "The context shows plainly that it is a practical, consistent confession which is meant, and also a practical and enduring denial." The Lord will not confess the confessing Judas, nor deny the denying Peter."—(*Alford.*)

35 For I am come to set a man at variance? against his father, and the daughter against her mother, and the daughter in law against her mother in law.
36 And* a man's foes *shall be* they of his own household.
37 He* that loveth father or mother more than me, is not worthy of me: and he that loveth son or daughter more than me, is not worthy of me.

38 And he that taketh not his cross, and followeth after me, is not worthy of me.
39 He* that findeth his life, shall lose it: and he that loseth his life for my sake, shall find it.
40 He* that receiveth you, receiveth me; and he that receiveth me, receiveth him that sent me.
41 He* that receiveth a prophet in the name of a prophet, shall receive a prophet's reward; and he that

y Micah 7 : 5, 6....z Ps. 41 : 9....a Luke 14 : 26....b ch. 16 : 25.....c ch. 18 : 5 ; 25 : 40, 45; John 12 : 44.....d 1 Kings 17 : 10 ; Heb. 6 : 10.

Observe how Christ here ranks himself with God in judging not with man in being the object of judgment.

34. Think not I am come to sow peace on the earth. The metaphor is that of a husbandman sowing seed ; Christ's seed is a sword. Yet in the O. T. Christ is called a prince of peace (Isaiah 9 : 6) ; his birth is announced by the angels as a precursor of peace (Luke 2 : 14; compare 1 : 19) ; he bestows peace upon his disciples in his parting benediction (John 14 : 27) ; he declares that the peace-makers shall bear his own title and be called the sons of God (Matt. 5 : 9) ; and the peace of God is declared by the apostle to be among the fruits of the spirit (Gal. 5 : 22). We are not to reconcile these passages by saying, with De Wette, that divisions were not the purpose, but only the inevitable result of Christ's coming, for " with God *results* are all *purposes.*"—(*Alford.*) Christ comes to declare war against the devil and all his works (Ephes. 6 : 11, 12 ; 1 Tim. 6 : 12), and to bring peace only with victory. The first coming of Christ always brings war, whether to the individual soul or to the community. War is the stalk, peace the ripened grain. Romans 7 : 23 depicts the sword, 7 : 25 and ch. 8, the peace. Compare Matt. 13 : 33, and note.

35. For I am come, etc. This verse is substantially quoted from Micah 7 : 6 ; it is illustrated by John 7 : 1–5.

36. A man's foes shall be they of his own household. This declaration finds abundant illustration in the history of religious persecutions ; not less in daily life. Husbands, wives, parents, children are helps, but also often hindrances ; the same one is sometimes a spiritual friend, sometimes a spiritual foe. Christ found foes in his warmest friends, Matt. 16 : 22, 23.

37. He that loveth father, etc. * * * **more than me.** Compare with this the parallel passage, Luke 14 : 26. Observe that the test of love according to Christ is not emotional experience, but obedience (John 14 : 21) ; hence this declaration is substantially embodied in Matt. 5 : 24. No man can *serve* two masters. For illustration of loving Christ more than father or mother, see Matt. 4 : 21, 22. For parallel and illustrative teachings, John 21 : 15 ; 2 Cor. 5 : 14, 15 ; Phil. 3 : 7–9. **Is not worthy of me,** *i. e.* to be called my disciples. Compare Ephes. 4 : 1 ; Col. 1 : 10 ; 1 Thes. 2 : 12. For he only is Christ's disciple who learns like Christ to sacrifice *all* for God. "Stier well remarks, that under the words 'worthy of me,' there lies an exceeding great reward which counterbalances all the *seeming asperity* of this saying."—(*Alford.*)

38. He that taketh not his cross. The Roman custom obliged the crucified to carry their own cross to the place of punishment. To this custom reference is here made. The meaning of the symbol is, whoever is not willing freely to deny himself, even unto death, and that the most painful and shameful, is not worthy of me. It is, of course, a prophetic reference to Christ's own death, a prophecy which, at the time, the disciples could have only imperfectly understood (John 12 : 16). Observe that it is not only *cross-bearing* but *cross-taking* that is required of the disciple ; not merely submission to burdens which God's providence lays upon them, but a voluntary assuming of burdens, even the burden of death, for the sake of Christ and humanity. In slightly different forms this aphorism repeatedly appears in Christ's teaching (Matt. 16 : 24 ; Mark 10 : 21 ; Luke 9 : 23). Paul, by his use of the metaphor in Galatians (2 : 20 ; 5 : 24 ; 6 : 14), gives a partial interpretation to it. We take up our cross when we mortify the deeds of the flesh for the sake of the Spirit (Col. 3 : 5), or when we gladly suffer the loss of all things that we may be found in Christ (Phil. 3 : 8-10), or share his sufferings and self-sacrifices that we may minister to his suffering ones (Matt. 25 : 35, 36).

39. He that findeth his life shall lose it. Repeated in Matt. 16 : 25 ; Luke 17 : 33 ; John 12 : 25. Not merely, he that finds the life of this world shall lose eternal life in the world to come, though this is implied in John, nor he that finds the lower earthly life shall lose the higher and spiritual life. The significance of the saying does not depend upon any such play on the word life. The aphorism goes deeper. *All self-seeking is self-losing.* Even in spiritual things, he who is perpetually studying how to secure joy and peace *for himself* loses it. A certain measure of self-forgetfulness is the condition of the highest success even in Christian grace. Observe that *finding* implies *seeking ;* so that this proverb is not at all, He that gains this life loses the next, but, He that makes his own life the chief object of his endeavor and seems to succeed, really fails.

40. He that receiveth you receiveth me.

receiveth a righteous man in the name of a righteous man, shall receive a righteous man's reward.

42 And whosoever shall give to drink unto one of these little ones a cup of cold *water* only in the name of a disciple, verily I say unto you, he shall in no wise lose his reward.

The primary reference is to the twelve apostles in their commission ; the receiving is that referred to in verses 13, 14, receiving to the house with hospitality (compare Hebrews 13:2). Underneath this is a deeper meaning of wider application. He who receives the servant of Christ and his message in his heart, receives Christ ; he who opens his heart to Christlike influence from men, opens it, even though unconsciously, to Christ. Compare 2 Cor. 5 : 20.

41. In the name of a prophet, *i. e.*, as a **prophet, because he is a prophet.** The word prophet in N. T. usage signifies not necessarily a foreteller of events, but an inspired teacher of God. See illustrations of this truth in 2 Kings, ch. 4. The joys of Christ's kingdom are awarded according to the spiritual aspirations, not according to the intellectual abilities and actual achievements in work. If one, however humble his station, shows himself in his spiritual sympathy one with the prophets, he shall receive the prophet's place ; if, however imperfect his character, he approves himself the friend of righteousness, he shall receive the reward of righteousness. Observe that that reward is a perfect character (Col. 1:22); so that the promise is involved in Matt. 5 : 6.

42. Whosoever shall give * * * a cup of cold water. "This he saith lest any one should allege poverty."—(*Chrysostom*.) It is never, even in our intercourse with each other, the largeness of the gift, but always the spirit which inspires the giver, which determines its value. It is not the service we render to Christ's cause or church, but the will to render it which Christ looks at. Compare Luke 21 : 1-4. **In the name of a disciple,** *i. e.*, "because ye belong to Christ " (Mark 9:41). **To one of these little ones ;** not, as De Wette, to the despised and meanly esteemed for Christ's sake ; nor necessarily, as Alford, to children that *may* have been present ; but to one insignificant and unknown in Christ's kingdom in contrast with the inspired teacher and the well-known righteous man. It is explained by Matt. 25 : 40. Dr. Brown notices here "a descending climax—' the prophet,' 'a righteous man,' 'a little one,' signifying that however low we come down in our service to those that are Christ's, all that is done for his sake, and that bears the stamp of love to his blessed name, shall be divinely appreciated and owned and rewarded." Chrysostom, on the other hand, notices the climax in the entire passage, the connection of which he thus indicates : "Seest thou what mighty persuasions he used, and how he opened to them the houses of the whole world ? Yea, he signified that men are their debtors, first by saying, The workman is worthy of his hire ; secondly, by sending them forth bearing nothing ; thirdly, by giving them up to wars and fightings in behalf of them that receive them ; fourthly, by committing to them miracles also ; fifthly, in that he did by their lips introduce peace, the cause of all blessings, into the houses of such as receive them ; sixthly, by threatening things more grievous than Sodom to such as receive them not ; seventhly, by signifying that as many as welcome them are receiving both himself and the Father ; eighthly, by promising both a prophet's and a righteous man's reward ; ninthly, by undertaking that the recompense shall be great even for a cup of cold water."

CHAPTER XI.

AND it came to pass, when Jesus had made an end of commanding his twelve disciples, he departed thence, to teach and to preach in their cities.

Ch. 11 : 1. When Jesus had made an end, *i. e.*, for the time, had finished this special discourse. **He departed thence.** The locality is not fixed. The address was delivered during a journey in Galilee (Matt. 9:35). **To preach in their cities.** They preached in the towns or villages (Luke 9:6), that men should repent (Mark 6:12), basing their preaching on the announcement that the kingdom of Heaven was at hand (Matt. 10:7). Their preaching thus corresponded to that of John the Baptist and the earlier ministry of Jesus (Matt. 3:2; 4:17).

THE TWELVE APOSTLES: THEIR LIVES AND CHARACTERS.

For the convenience of the student, I embody here very brief references to the Scriptural information concerning the twelve apostles, and shall refer to this note in other parts of the commentary when their names occur.

SIMON PETER (*rock*). His original name was Simon or Simeon (Acts 15:14) ; he was born at Bethsaida on the Sea of Galilee (John 1:44) ; with his father Jonas and his brother Andrew carried on the trade of a fisherman on the Sea of Galilee (Luke 5:3; John 21:3) ; was married, and his mother-in-law lived with him (Mark 1:29, 30) ; was originally, with his brother Andrew, a disciple of John the Baptist ; joined Jesus temporarily at the ford of Bethabara (John 1:40, 41), where he received his new name of Peter (verse 42) ; he resumed his fishing, and was a second time called to follow Christ, which he did, with Andrew his brother, and with James and John (Luke 5:6-11). The healing of his mother-in-law followed almost immediately (Mark 1:29-31; Luke 4:38, 39). The subsequent incidents in his life indicate a warm, affectionate, impulsive but unstable character. He starts to walk to Jesus on the wave, but loses courage almost as soon as his feet touch the water (Matt. 14:28-30); impetuously refuses to let Christ wash his feet, and as impetuously offers his head and his hands (John 13:6, 8, 9); draws his sword to fight single-handed the Roman soldiers, yet turns and flees with the others when Christ surrenders to the band (John 18:10; Matt. 26:56); follows Christ into the palace, but there denies with vehemence and oaths that he is a disciple (Matt. 26:69-75; John 18:15, 17, 25-27); is one of the first to baptize the Gentiles, then refuses to fraternize with them from fear of opposition in the church (Acts 10:47, 48; Gal. 2:11-13; but compare Acts 15:7, etc.) After the resurrection and ascension of our Lord, Peter appears to have taken a leading position in the church, but as an orator rather than as an organizer or ecclesiastical leader (Acts 1:15; 2:14-41; 4:8). He traveled about in missionary work, taking his wife with him (1 Cor. 9:5), ministering to the Gentiles, and probably traveling as far east as Babylon (1 Pet. 5:13). If he ever visited Rome, which is uncertain, it was not until the later years of his life, and after the founding of the Christian church. According to tradition, he was crucified under Nero, with his head downward, and to this event our Lord is thought to refer in John 21:18. The personal friendship between himself and John, illustrated by many incidents (Luke 5:1-11; John 13:23, 24; 18:15, 16; 21:7; Acts 3:1; 4:13), is one of the most touching and tender of the minor episodes in Gospel history, all the more so from the incidental indication of the contrasts in their characters (John 20:3-9; 21:7).

ANDREW (*manly*). A son of Jonas and brother of Peter. He brought the latter to Christ (John 1:40-42), and with him was subsequently called by Christ to become a disciple, and later an apostle (Matt. 4:21; Luke 6:14). The only other incidents respecting him recorded in the Gospels are those narrated in Mark 13:3, John 6:8, and 12:22, and these give little or no information respecting his character. After the resurrection of our Lord, he appears only in the list of apostles in Acts 1:13. Tradition reports him to have preached the Gospel in Scythia, Greece, and Asia Minor, and to have been crucified upon a cross in the form of a X, which is called, accordingly, St. Andrew's cross.

JAMES (same as Jacob, *i. e.*, *Supplanter*). He was a son of Zebedee; his mother's name was Salome (compare Matt. 27:56 with Mark 15:40). He probably resided at Bethsaida; joined Jesus with his brother John at the Sea of Galilee (Matt. 4:21); is never mentioned in the Gospels except in connection with his brother John; was martyred under Herod Agrippa, A. D. 44 (Acts 12:2). There is reason to believe that he and his brother John were own cousins of our Lord. This opinion rests on the account given by Matthew, Mark, and John, of the women at the crucifixion. They describe these women as follows:

				Mary, mother of James and Joses.	Mother of Zebedee's children.
Matt. 27:56.	....	Mary Magdalene.			
Mark 15:40.	....	"	"	Mary, mother of James the less.	Salome.
John 19:25.	Mary, mother of Jesus.	"	"	Mary, wife of Cleophas.	Sister of Jesus' mother.

It is evident, from a comparison of these accounts, that Salome and the mother of Zebedee's children are the same; that is, that Salome was the mother of James and John. It is a question whether the sister of Jesus' mother mentioned by John is to be identified with Salome or with Mary, wife of Cleophas; whether, that is, John mentions two or three persons in addition to Mary, the mother of Jesus. If Mary, wife of Cleophas, were the sister of Jesus' mother, there would have been two sisters of the same name, Mary, which is not impossible, as Jewish records show, but is improbable. On the whole, I think the better opinion to be that which identifies the sister of Jesus' mother with Salome, the mother of Zebedee's children, in which case Jesus was own cousin to James and John. See note on Matthew 13:55.

JOHN (*grace of the Lord*). He was a brother of James, and of course is not to be confounded with John the Baptist. Several references in the N. T. indicate that his family was one of some wealth and social position (Mark 1:20; Luke 8:3; 23:55, comp. with Mark 16:1; John 19:27). He appears to have accompanied our Lord in his first ministry in Judea, and he is the only one of the Evangelists who gives any account of that ministry. He is mentioned frequently in connection with Peter and James as especially intimate with Jesus (Matt. 17:1, Mark 5:37; John 13:23); and of those three, he appears to have been the one most beloved of our Lord (John 13:23; 19:26; 20:2; 21:7, 20, 24). Of his personal history subsequent to the crucifixion little is known. He went into Asia, exercised a pastoral supervision over the Asiatic churches, was banished to Patmos, and probably died in extreme old age a natural death. Of his personal character much has been written, yet it is certain he has been greatly misunderstood. He was naturally impetuous and ambitious (Matt. 20 : 20, 21 ; Mark 3 : 17 ; 10 : 35-37 ; Luke 9 : 54), and of all the apostles, he appears to have been the most courageous ; he alone of the Evangelists, apparently, accompanied Jesus in his earlier Judean ministry, since he is the only one who gives any account of it; and he alone clung to him and followed him during the trial in the court of Caiaphas and before Pilate's judgment-seat ; this is evidenced by his narrative, which is unmistakably that of an eye-witness. His gentleness, patience, love, and spiritual apprehension of Christ's interior teaching, seem to have been the effect of Christ's personal influence upon him. He was the beloved disciple, because of all the disciples he was the most docile and most ready to yield to and receive Christ's teaching and influence. See further on his character, Introduction to Gospel of John. We have, in the N. T., four books from his pen : one Gospel and three Epistles.

PHILIP (*warlike*). He was a native of Bethsaida ; brought Nathanael, who was probably the same as Bartholomew, to Jesus ; and is generally mentioned in connection with Bartholomew. The only direct reference to him in the Gospels, except the mere mention of his name here and in other lists of the twelve, are in John 1 : 43-45 ; 12 : 21, 22 ; 14 : 8, 9. Of his life and labors nothing else is known ; and the traditions respecting him are conflicting. He is not to be confounded with Philip, the deacon, mentioned in Acts 6 : 5 ; 8 : 5-12, 26-40 ; 21 : 8, 9.

BARTHOLOMEW (*son of Tholmai*). It is generally thought by Biblical scholars that this apostle is identical with Nathanael. John alone mentions Nathanael (John 1 : 45-49 ; 21 : 2), whom Philip brought to Jesus ; Matthew, Mark, and Luke do not mention him, but give the name of Bartholomew in connection with Philip. This fact, coupled with their otherwise singular omission of the name of Nathanael, and with the fact that Bartholomew is not properly a name at all, but a descriptive title, meaning son of Tholmai, have led to the hypothesis which identifies the two. It is, however, but an hypothesis, though certainly a reasonable one. Nothing is known of his life or character, except what may be gathered from the above reference.

THOMAS (*twin*). This word is of Hebrew origin ; its Greek equivalent is Didymus, and his name occurs in this form (John 11 : 16 ; 20 : 24 ; 21 : 2). He was doubtless a Galilean, but neither his parentage, birth-place, nor call are mentioned.

There are but four incidents in his life recorded in the N. T. (John 11 : 16 ; 14 : 5 ; 20 : 24-29 ; 21 : 2). These indicate that he possessed an affectionate spirit but a skeptical mind. The earnestness and fidelity of his love was unaccompanied by a faith and hope at all comparable to it (John 11 : 16) ; he could not understand the "mansions" which Christ, after his death, would prepare for his followers (John 14 : 5) ; he refused to believe in his Lord's resurrection without tangible evidence (John 20 : 24-29). Of his history subsequent to the ascension of Christ, nothing is known with any certainty ; the Syrian Christians, however, claim him as the founder of their church.

MATTHEW (probably, *gift*). He is also called Levi (Luke 5 : 27-29 ; and see note on Matt. 9 : 9). He was a publican, i. e. tax-gatherer and the son of Alphæus (Mark 2 : 14) ; but whether of the same Alphæus mentioned in this history as the father of James the less is uncertain ; most scholars think not. The name Alphæus is a common one in Jewish records, and if Matthew were a brother of James, the two would probably have been mentioned together, as are Simon Peter and his brother Andrew and James and his brother John. Of his life, subsequent to his call, the N. T. gives no information, except that his Gospel indicates that he accompanied Christ to the last. No reliance can be placed on the traditions respecting his later history.

JAMES, THE SON OF ALPHÆUS. His father's name is given by John as Cleophas or Cleopas, a different form of the same word ; his mother's name was Mary (Mark 15 : 40), assuming, as I do from reasons which will appear elsewhere (see note on Brethren of our Lord on Matt. 13 : 55), that there are three persons of the name of James mentioned in the N. T., James the brother of John, James the son of Alphæus, and James the Lord's brother, and that the latter was the author of the Epistle General of James, nothing more is known concerning this James, who is generally in Biblical literature distinguished from James the brother of John by being entitled James the less.

LEBBÆUS (the meaning is uncertain). In Mark 3 : 18 he is called Thaddæus, and it is probable that the addition here of the words, "whose surname was Thaddæus," has been added by some copyist to harmonize the two accounts. In the lists given in Luke 6 : 14, etc., and Acts 1 : 13, neither Lebbæus nor Thaddæus appears, but in their place the name of Judas of James, which our translators interpret Judas the brother of James. This is, however, merely their interpretation, the word *brother* being added by them ; the better opinion appears to be that the proper interpretation would be *son* of James. This Jude or Judas, also called Lebbæus and Thaddæus, is by many critics regarded as identical with the Judas mentioned in Matthew 13 : 55, and as the

2 Now° when John had heard in the prison the works of Christ, he sent two of his disciples,

3 And said unto him, Art thou he that should come, or do we look for another?

c Luke 7 : 19, etc.

writer of the epistle of Jude. While the question, like that of the possible identity of James the less with James the Lord's brother is beset with difficulties, I think the better opinion is that which considers that there were two persons of the name of Jude or Judas, one the apostle who is mentioned only in the lists of the twelve and is identical with Lebbæus or Thaddæus, the other Jude the brother of James the Lord's brother, and so the brother of our Lord (Matt. 13 : 55 ; Jude, verse 1), and the author of the Epistle which bears his name. See Introduction and notes to that epistle.

SIMON (*that obeys*) THE CANAANITE. In Luke and Acts he is called Simon Zelotes, *i. e.* Simon the Zealot. He is not to be confounded with Simeon the brother of Jesus (Matt. 13 : 55, and note there). The Zealots were a faction of the Jews who were conspicuous for their fierce advocacy of the Mosaic ritual ; their fanatical violence was one of the principal causes which led to the destruction of Jerusalem. Nothing is known of his life and character.

JUDAS ISCARIOT. The derivation of this name is uncertain ; it is probably (*Of Kerioth*, a town of Judea (Josh. 15 : 25). In that case Judas Iscariot was the only Judean among the twelve, and this fact would afford a key to his enigmatical character and career. His father's name was Simon (John 6 : 71). He followed Christ with the other disciples, received from him a commission to preach the Gospel, and apparently preached it endowed with the same power to "heal all manner of sickness and all manner of disease," was entrusted with the funds of the little band, and adhered to Christ and his cause until the unmistakable declaration of Jesus respecting his death, when he deserted and betrayed him. For a consideration of his enigmatical character and career see Abbott's *Jesus of Nazareth*, chap. 29, and notes hereafter, especially on chap. 27 : 3-10.

Ch. 11 : 2-19. JOHN'S EMBASSY AND JESUS' DISCOURSE ON JOHN. QUIET BRINGS TEMPTATION TO UNQUIET SOULS.—THE PERPLEXITY OF THE DISCIPLE TO WHOM CHRIST IS NOT CLEARLY REVEALED: "DO WE LOOK FOR ANOTHER?"—THE EVIDENCE OF CHRISTIANITY, BOTH IN THE SOUL AND IN THE WORLD : A WORK OF DIVINE POWER, OF DIVINE HEALING, OF DIVINE LOVE.—THE BEST EVIDENCE IS A PRESENT EVIDENCE; WHAT WE DO NOW HEAR AND SEE.—CHRIST IS BOTH A STUMBLING-STONE AND THE STONE OF THE CORNER (verse 6; Matt. 21 : 42, 44).—JOHN THE BAPTIST A TRUE PREACHER; NEITHER SHAKEN BY ADVERSITY, NOR SEDUCED BY PROSPERITY.—THE GLORY OF JOHN THE BAPTIST, THE GLORY OF THE TRUE PREACHER: A HERALD OF THE LORD.—THE GREATEST IN THE O. T. DISPENSATION IS LESS PRIVILEGED THAN THE LEAST IN THE NEW.—THE KINGDOM OF HEAVEN IS WORTHY OF OUR ENTHUSIASM. —THE FULFILMENT OF PROPHECY IS IN UNEXPECTED WAYS; THE JEWS LOOKED FOR ELIJAH AND BEHOLD JOHN THE BAPTIST.—THE UNWILLING CAN ALWAYS FIND AN EXCUSE FOR REJECTING BOTH THE WARNINGS AND THE INVITATIONS OF THE GOSPEL.—THERE ARE MANY MESSENGERS, YET BUT ONE MESSAGE; MANY INVITATIONS, YET BUT ONE DIVINE LORD.

Of this embassy of John the Baptist to Jesus (vs. 2-6), and the subsequent discourse concerning him (vs. 7-19), there is also an account in Luke (7 : 18-35). It occurred apparently immediately after the resurrection of the son of the widow of Nain (Luke 7 : 11-17) ; and probably prior to the commission of the twelve ; for Herod beheaded John while the disciples of Christ were absent on their mission (Mark 6 : 30; Matt. 14 : 13).

2. When John (Baptist) **had heard in the prison.** For an account of his imprisonment, see Mark 6 : 17-30. For brief history of his life, see notes on Matt. 14 : 1-12. The prison was the castle of Machærus, east of the Dead Sea. Next to Jerusalem it was the strongest fortress of the Jews. "It is, as it were, ditched about with such valleys on all sides, and to such a depth that the eye cannot reach their bottoms." —(*Josephus' Wars of Jews*, 7, §§ 1, 2.) Its ruins still exist. The citadel, an isolated and almost impregnable work, small, circular, and exactly one hundred yards in diameter, was placed on a summit overlooking the city. The wall can be clearly traced. There are also remains of two dungeons ; the holes where staples of wood and iron had once been fixed are clearly visible. See description of the ruins in Tristram's *Land of Moab*. John, in this prison, heard of the works of Jesus through his own disciples (Luke 7 : 18). Tristram supposes that John was confined in one of the above dungeons. But it is not probable that at this time his imprisonment was very close, for his disciples had access to him ; and Herod, who was educated in the Jewish religion, stood in awe of John as a prophet whom the people revered (Matt. 14 : 5).

The works of Christ. Primarily of course, and chiefly, the miracles which Christ had wrought ; but the phrase may also here include those features in Christ's ministry which perplexed the disciples of John the Baptist, such as Christ's not keeping any fasts (Mark 2 : 18). It is observable that it is said John had heard of the works of *Christ*, *i. e.* the Messiah, not the works of *Jesus*. It is the only place in Matthew where

4 Jesus answered and said unto them, Go and shew John again those things which ye do hear and see :
5 The blind receive their sight, and the lame walk, the lepers are cleansed, and the deaf hear, the dead are raised up, and the poor have the gospel preached to them.
6 And blessed is *he*, whosoever shall not be offended⁴ in me.

4 Isa. 6 : 14, 15 ; 1 Cor. 1 : 22, 23 ; 1 Pet. 2 : 6.

the name Christ stands by itself in lieu of Jesus or Jesus Christ, and it indicates that John recognized in those works an evidence of the Messiahship of our Lord, even though he shared with the disciples their perplexity at Christ's course. See note below. **Two of his disciples.** Some manuscripts have here *by his disciples.* The difference is important only in its bearing on the question whether John sent to satisfy his own doubts or theirs. Luke says that he sent two, so that there is no question as to the fact.

3. And said unto him. Observe that both here and in Luke (7 : 20), the message is represented as that of John the Baptist, not as that of his disciples. **Art thou he that should come?** Literally, *The coming one* (Greek ὁ ἐρχόμενος). The phrase is an unmistakable reference to the Messiah, as to the one whom the prophets had foretold, and for whom the Jews looked. The same Greek word is used in the Septuagint in Psalm 118 : 26, and a different form of the same verb in Zech. 9 : 9. Compare Matt. 10 : 23 and note. The question then is this : Art thou the Messiah long prophesied, for whom we have looked, or are we still to look for the fulfilling of those prophecies in the coming of another? This is the common question of all dispirited and discouraged Christians. Has the Lord Jesus really come to me, or am I to look for some other experience of his coming? And the answer is always that which the Lord makes here (*verse 4*). If your eyes see the truth more clearly, your limbs are stronger to run the Christian race, your disease of sin is even partly purged away, and you have begun to walk in newness of life, do not be disheartened because the kingdom of God comes without observation, nor look for another and more marvelous coming. In the soul, as in the world, God's work of love is best demonstrated by the fruits of love.

4. Jesus answered and said. Luke says (7 : 21), "In the same hour he cured many of their infirmities and plagues, and of evil spirits ; and unto many that were blind he gave sight." **Go and shew John again.** The word *again* is not in the original. It is one of the illustrations of the need of a new translation of the Bible that the Greek here and in Luke is precisely the same (πορευθέντες ἀπαγγείλατε), but the English is quite different. In Luke the rendering is "*Go your way and tell.*" Observe, they were to shew *John*, an indication that the doubt, which led to the question, was truly his. **"Those things which ye do hear and see."** Observe that the *truths heard*, as well as the *miracles seen*, are included among the evidences of Christ's divine character and mission. For by this phrase *what ye do hear*, we are not to understand that they were to report rumors of miracles heard of by them ; such rumors John had already heard. They were to carry the testimony of their own observation.

5. The blind receive their sight. "As the article is wanting in each of these clauses, the sense would be better perceived by the English reader thus, though scarcely tuneful enough : 'Blind persons are seeing, lame people are walking, leprous persons are getting cleansed, deaf people are hearing, dead persons are being raised.'"—(*Dr. Brown.*) The reference to the O. T. prophecies respecting the Messiah is unmistakable ; see in particular Isaiah 35 : 5 ; 61 : 1-3, and the application of the latter passage by Christ to himself in Luke 4 : 16-21. This is the principal, if not the only place in the N. T., in which Jesus Christ employs the argument from miracles directly in support of his mission ; and it is to be noticed that he refers to them, not to convince an opponent, but to strengthen the faltering faith of a friend. In John 5 : 36 and 10 : 38 the appeal is not merely to his miracles (σημεῖοι) but to *works* (ἔργα), which includes much more. The argument is as potent now as it was in the time of Christ ; viz., the healing and evangelizing power of the Gospel of Christ, not as it is reported to us from the past, but as *we do hear and see its beneficent effects now.*

The poor receive good news. (Greek εὐαγγελίζομαι). Our English version gives the true sense, but not as John would have apprehended it ; for the Gospel, in the modern sense, dates from the death of Christ. Observe that it is characteristic of every revival of the Christian religion that it proclaims the Gospel without money and without price, and therefore makes the poor full participants in its privileges. But the language here also embraces the poor in heart-life, all who suffer heart-hunger, the meek, the broken-hearted, the captives, the bound of Isaiah 61 : 1.

6. Shall not be offended in me. Shall not be caused to *stumble* in me. Compare Mark 14 : 27. See note on Matt. 5 : 29. Christ is a stumbling-stone, a rock of offence, to many, as he was to John the Baptist (Rom. 9 : 33 ; 1 Cor. 1 : 23), because his character and mission are lowly, and because he does not immediately accomplish the redemption of the world, or of the individual soul. That he should be such a stumbling-block was prophesied by Jeremiah (6; 21). John (see note below) shared the general expectation of an immediate and temporal reformation to be wrought by the Messiah. Christ's reply is well paraphrased by Andrews: "Blessed is he who shall understand the work I now do, and not stumble at it."

JOHN'S EMBASSY TO JESUS. This embassy has given rise to some perplexity, and there are two principal interpretations of it. One supposes that John himself was in no doubt respecting Christ's Messianic character, but that his disciples were, and that he sent them to Jesus for the purpose of solving their doubts, selecting for that purpose two whose testimony would be conclusive to the others. In support of this opinion, it is argued that John the Baptist had repeatedly borne testimony to Christ's character as the divine Son and Lamb of God (Matt. 3:11, 14; John 1:27, 29, 32, 34; 3:20); that Christ, in his subsequent discourse, expressly repudiated the idea that John was one easily shaken by stress of trial (verse 7); that he utters no word of rebuke, but much strong commendation; and that while there are no other indications of a faltering faith in John, there are many that the disciples of John were skeptical respecting Jesus, and jealous of his growing fame and influence (Matt. 9:14; John 3:25, 26). This view was generally entertained by the early fathers, who seem to have adopted it to exculpate the Baptist. Wordsworth, who reflects their opinions throughout his commentary, even declares of this embassy that "it was the crowning act of St. John's ministry." "He thus guarded against a schism between his own disciples and those of Jesus; he bequeathed his disciples to Christ; he had prepared the way for Christ in the desert, he now prepared it in the prison." But this opinion rests wholly upon conjecture. The other opinion is that John was himself in perplexity, and sent his disciples to solve both his own and their doubts. This opinion accords best with the natural meaning of the narrative. The message came from John; the answer is sent to him, not to them, "Go and show John;" the message closes with a benediction, which indicates that John was in danger of stumbling at the course of Jesus; and the discourse which follows is on the character of John, and gives no indication that the question was not truly his own. This view is entertained by nearly all modern commentators, and requires no conjectural addition to the narrative to support it. Various attempts have been made to explain the cause and nature of John's doubts; e. g., DeWette, Lange, and Dr. Schaff think the doubt was not respecting our Lord's mission, but his way of manifesting it; Olshausen attributes it to the discouraging effects produced by imprisonment on John's mind; Lightfoot, and, apparently, Dr. Brown, to his dissatisfaction at not being liberated from prison; Matthew Henry, to the neglect of Jesus to visit him there; Alford, and similarly Neander, to impatience at the slow and unostentatious course of our Lord's self-manifestation, and a desire to impel Jesus to a public acknowledgment of his own character and mission; still others, referred to by Alford, to a doubt whether the one of whose miracles rumors reached him in prison was really the Jesus whom he baptized, and to whom he testified. All this is but matter of conjecture; the sacred narrative is silent as to the Baptist's motives, and leaves us only in possession of the fact. Observe, however, that his doubt is not distrust, for he sends to Jesus for its solution; that Jesus carefully guards the people against the supposition that the temporary doubt really shakes his religious faith and character (verse 7); that similar experiences of perplexity at the course of God's providential dealings are recorded of Moses (Exod. 17:4), Elijah (1 Kings 19:10), David (Ps. 10:1), Jeremiah (Jer. 12:1, 2; Lam., ch. 3), and the unknown author of Psalm 77, written during the Babylonian captivity; that it is not unnatural to suppose that John the Baptist shared the universal expectation among the Jews and Christ's own disciples of the temporal reign of the Messiah, and may, therefore, have been perplexed by the fact that there was no sign of the establishment of the kingdom of God in the nation; that experience of doubts are a peculiar temptation of active natures in times of enforced inactivity; and finally that the result of this embassy was probably to solve his doubts, certainly to put an end to the doubts and jealousies of his disciples. "The happy result of this mission is intimated in those touching words, 'His disciples took up the body of John and buried it, and came and told Jesus,' Matt. 14:12."—(*Wordsworth.*) Observe, too, that Christ makes no direct answer, affords to John the Baptist no peculiar assurance or evidence, but leaves his faith to rest on the common evidence on which the faith of all the disciples is built. The moral of the incident thus interpreted is plain, viz.: that the strongest disciple is liable to incursions of unbelief; that the true solver of doubts, in such times, is Jesus himself; that he solves them by pointing us to those evidences of Christianity which are open to all—the beneficent works of this Gospel; and that the argument from miracles is valid rather to sustain the faltering faith of the disciple than to compel the reluctant assent of a willing skeptic. Compare effect of miracles on Pharisees, Matt. 12:14, 24.

7-19. DISCOURSE ON JOHN THE BAPTIST. This discourse evidently followed directly the departure of the disciples of John. Whether

7 And, as they departed, Jesus began to say unto the multitudes concerning John, What went ye out into the wilderness to see? A reed shaken with the wind?
8 But what went ye out for to see? A man clothed in soft raiment? behold, they that wear soft *clothing* are in kings' houses.

9 But what went ye out for to see? A prophet? yea, I say unto you, and more than a prophet.
10 For this is *he* of whom it is written, Behold, I send my messenger before thy face, which shall prepare thy way before thee.
11 Verily I say unto you, Among them that are born of women there hath not risen a greater than

e Luke 7:24, 30....f Eph. 4:14; James 1:6....g Isa. 40:3; Mal. 3:1; Luke 1:76....h John 5:35.

---

the subsequent portion of this chapter is a part of the same discourse is uncertain. See preliminary note verses 20-24, below. Luke (7:29, 30) adds an account of the effect this discourse produced.

7. As they departed. Christ utters no word of commendation of John while the disciples are present. "He would not flatter John, nor have his praises reported to him. * * * Pride is a corrupt humor, which we must not feed either in others or in ourselves."—(*Matthew Henry.*) What he has before said is in reply to the question of John, and is addressed to John's disciples; what he now says is in reply to the *thoughts* of the people, lest they shall misinterpret and misjudge the Baptist. But, as often in his sayings, the occasion becomes a text for spiritual instruction respecting his kingdom. He begins with John the Baptist; he ends with the privileges of the least in the kingdom of heaven. **What went ye out into the wilderness to see?** The reference is to the earlier ministry of John the Baptist, when it is said of him that Jerusalem and all Judea, and all the region round about Jordan, went out to him (Matt. 3:5). **To see.** Rather, *to gaze upon*. The original verb here is not the same as in the succeeding verse. **A reed shaken with the wind?** The word reed is a general one, standing, as with us, for a variety of plants of a similar character. The Jordan abounded with these reed-like plants. In Scripture, the reed is an emblem of weakness (2 Kings 18:21; Isaiah 42:3). The contrast surely is not, as Alford interprets it, between a reed, or the banks of the Jordan with its reeds, and a man; the former is employed as a symbol of a weak and wavering character, easily bending before the storm of adversity. Because John has sent this message, the people are not to imagine that he is yielding to fear and persecution. John is "not a reed planted in the morass of a weak and watery faith, and quivering in the wind of doubt. Not a reed—but a rock."—(*Wordsworth.*) The question requires no answer; Christ gives it none.

8. A man clothed in soft raiment? Contrast his real raiment (Matt. 3:4). Chrysostom gives the connection: "He was not himself a waverer. * * * Much less can any one say this, that he was indeed firm, but having made himself a slave to luxury, he afterwards became languid." **Behold they that wear soft**

clothing. Luke interprets and at the same time adds to this declaration: "*Behold they which are gorgeously apparelled and live delicately.*" "Had he been minded to wear soft raiment he would not have lived in the wilderness, nor in prison, but in the king's courts; it being in his power, merely by keeping silence, to have enjoyed honor without limit."—(*Chrysostom.*)

9. A prophet? All the people regarded John as a prophet (Matt. 21:26). Jesus thus appealed to their public recognition of his character. Observe how our Lord begins by strengthening and clarifying their appreciation of John as a prophet, and so establishing sympathy between himself and them, as a preliminary to leading them on to higher matters. The underlying thought is this: Ye were attracted, not by an ardent, impulsive orator, easily swayed from his purpose by adversity, nor by any glitter of external show, but by the moral qualities of a religious and inspired teacher. **More than a prophet.** *More*—because himself the object of prophecy; because the last in the succession of the prophets and the clearest in his prophecies of the coming King; because he pointed out the Messiah whom others only foretold, and saw Him whom kings and prophets desired to see, but died without the sight (Matt. 13:17); and chiefest of all because he was a forerunner as well as a prophet, and, as a herald, went before the Lord, preparing his way. For it was characteristically his office, not merely to foretell the coming of the Lord, but to bring about among the people a state of heart and mind which should make them ready to receive the Lord (Luke 3:4; 7:27). See next verse, which gives the reason for the declaration in this.

10. For. Equivalent here to *because*, and introduces the ground of the preceding assertion. **This is he of whom it is written.** The reference is to Malachi 3:1. Alford notes the change from the first to the second person; in Malachi it is "*the* way before *me;*" here "*thy* way before *thee;*" and this change is preserved by all the Evangelists in their citations (Mark 1:2; Luke 7:27). That Christ thus changes the language, "making that which is said by Jehovah of himself to be addressed to the Messiah, is, if such were needed (compare also Luke 1:16, 17, and 76), no mean indication of his own eternal and coequal Godhead." Alford's deduction is also note-

John the Baptist: notwithstanding, he¹ that is least in the kingdom of heaven is greater than he.

12 And from the days of John the Baptist until now the kingdom of heaven suffereth violence, and the violent take¹ it by force.

13 For all the prophets and the law prophesied until John.

14 And if ye will receive it, this is Elias, which* was for to come.

15 He¹ that hath ears to hear, let him hear.

i John 1 : 15, 27 ; 3 : 30. ... j Luke 16 : 16 ; Eph. 6 : 11-13. ... k ch. 17 : 12 ; Mal. 4 : 5. ... l Rev. 2 : 7, etc.

worthy: "If John was thus great above all others, because he was the forerunner of Christ, how above all prophets and holy men of old must Christ himself be." **Behold I send my messenger.** Observe that John attributes to himself the humbler prophecy which designates him as "the voice of one crying in the wilderness" (John 1 : 23), while Christ designates him as "my messenger." The contrast illustrates Luke 14 : 11. **Prepare thy way before thee.** See note on Matt. 3 : 3.

11. There hath not risen a greater than John the Baptist; notwithstanding, he that is least in the kingdom of heaven is greater than he. This is the climax in the ascending scale, for which the preceding verses have been a preparation. John the Baptist is more than a mere impetuous orator, fickle-minded and easily swayed by storm, more than a king gorgeously apparelled, more than a prophet, yea, greatest of men, yet the least in my kingdom is greater than he. The object of the whole discourse is to lead up the mind to an appreciation of the greatness of this kingdom and those who are in it. On the meaning of the phrase **kingdom of heaven**, see Matt. 3 : 2. Observe, that there John is represented as preaching, not in the kingdom, but as a herald who *precedes* it. Here, as there, the phrase points to the advent of the Messiah as King and Lord, and the inauguration of Christ's kingdom by his crucifixion.

What is meant by "least in the kingdom of heaven?" Chrysostom and many of the fathers understand Christ himself. "Less in age and according to the opinion of the multitude," says Chrysostom, referring to verse 19, and to chapter 13 : 55. Wordsworth revives this opinion, which is now generally abandoned, which certainly the plain reader would never attach to the words, and which is indefensible, because, (a,) Christ is never spoken of in the N. T. as *in* the kingdom of heaven, but rather as its Lord and King; (b,) the words "little" and "least" (Gr. μικρός, μικρότερος) applied to the kingdom of heaven have a well-defined meaning in N. T. usage = to humble in position, authority and influence (Matt. 10 : 42; 18 : 6, 10, 14; Mark 9 : 42; Luke 9 : 48; 17 : 2 ; compare Matt. 13 : 32, and Acts 8 : 10); it is only in Mark 15 : 40, "James the Less," that the word bears the meaning of *younger*. The key to the interpretation is given by Maldonatus, quoted by Wordsworth and Alford: "The least of the greatest is greater than the greatest of the least."

It is here not greater in personal character, nor in eternal condition, but in *present* privilege, prerogative, station, as the least child is greater than the highest servant. John was a servant, we are sons of God (Gal. 4 : 7; compare John 15 : 15). There is a significance, too, in the language used here, "*born of women*." Whoever enters the kingdom of heaven is born of the Holy Ghost (John 3 : 5). Alford embodies the contrast well. "John not inferior to any that are born of women ; but these, even the least of them, are born of another birth. John, the nearest to the King and kingdom, but never having himself entered; these in the kingdom, subjects and citizens and indwellers of the realm ; He the friend of the Bridegroom ; they, however weak and unworthy, his Body and his Spouse." Observe, that Paul calls himself "least of the apostles" (1 Cor. 15 : 9).

12. And from the days of John the Baptist until now the kingdom of heaven suffereth violence, etc. The metaphor is that of a city to which long siege has been laid, and into which at last the victorious troops pour joyfully, seizing on it as their prey. The preaching of John the Baptist inaugurated the new dispensation, in which the poor had the Gospel preached unto them. Crowds thronged to hear him, as now they were thronging to hear Christ, eager to seize hold of the kingdom which both John and Jesus declared to be at hand. There was no such eagerness to lay hold on the preaching of the Scribes ; this very contrast was an evidence that the kingdom of heaven was at hand, and it dated from the advent of John, who was thus pointed out as the messenger sent before the Lord (verse 10), the Elias that was for to come (verse 14). Other interpretations have been proposed, as, (a,) that the kingdom of heaven forces itself on others, breaks in upon them with violence, an interpretation explained by Joel 2 : 28-32, and Acts 2 : 16-21 ; (b,) it is forcibly resisted, and thus suffers violence ; e. g., at the hand of the Pharisees; (c,) it yields only to a *quasi* violence, a spiritual resoluteness and importunity, as implied in Luke 14 : 25-33. Either of these interpretations is grammatically defensible ; the one I have given alone agrees with the context, and is now generally adopted. Observe in this metaphor thus interpreted, a justification of intense enthusiasm in the religious life. Compare for spiritual interpretation 2 Cor. 7 : 11.

13. For all the prophets and the law

16 But[m] whereunto shall I liken this generation? It is like unto children sitting in the markets, and calling unto their fellows,

17 And saying, We have piped unto you, and ye have not danced; we have mourned unto you, and ye have not lamented.

[m] Luke 7:31.

prophesied until John. That is, until John the whole dispensation was typical and prophetic; he introduced the new dispensation, that of fulfillment; for,

14. **This is Elijah which was for to come,** i. e. he fulfilled the prophecy of Malachi 4:5: "Behold I will send you Elijah the prophet before the coming of the great and dreadful day of the Lord." How he fulfilled it is explained in Luke 1:17; he came "in the spirit and power of Elijah." That John the Baptist fulfilled this prophecy is again, if possible, more distinctly stated by our Lord in answer to the arguments of the scribes (Matt. 17:10-13), "Elijah is come *already*." The rabbis held that as Elijah ascended bodily into heaven, so he is destined to reappear bodily upon the earth before the advent of the Messiah; and some Christian scholars, Alford for example, seem to hold the same view, believing that the literal resurrection and reappearance of Elijah will precede the second coming of Christ. But our Lord neither here nor in Matt. 17:10-13 gives any hint of this. *There is no more reason to regard John the Baptist as a typical fulfillment of the prophecy of the coming of Elijah than there is to regard Jesus of Nazareth as a typical fulfillment of the prophecies regarding the Messiah.* Christ thus gives the sanction of his authority to the spiritual interpretation of the O. T. prophecies; these are largely books of inspired poetry, and are to be read and interpreted accordingly. The advent of Christ was to the Jewish nation the "great and dreadful day of the Lord," because it ushered in the destruction of Jerusalem and the dispersion of the Jews. Observe that the closing words of the O. T. canon prophesy the advent of John the Baptist, and that in the opening chapter of the N. T. canon the fulfillment of that prophecy is recorded. John the Baptist, when asked, said that he was not Elijah (John 1:21). It is not probable that he fully understood his own mission, or the extent to which he fulfilled the O. T. prophecy, and ushered in the N. T. dispensation. The greatest and best men rarely understand their own mission fully, or are understood by others, till after their death. **If ye will receive.** Not receive *it*, as in our English version, *i. e.* the statement of Christ, nor *him*, *i. e.* John the Baptist, as a prophet, but *receive* simply, *i. e.* accept the divine teaching and influence *whencesoever it comes.* The function of Elijah, as described by Malachi (4:6), was to produce domestic peace and concord by the preaching of repentance as a preparation for the coming of the Prince of Peace (compare Malachi 3:1). How far John would fulfill this prophecy depended on how far the people would receive and yield to instructions, which he gave in the spirit of the prophet Elijah.

15. **He that hath ears to hear, let him hear.** A phrase frequently used to point out the fact that there is a deep significance in the instruction afforded, which requires thoughtful hearing. (Mark 7:16; Luke 14:35; Rev. 2:7, etc.) Its meaning is indicated by the reference in Matt. 13:13, 14 to those who, having ears, hear not.

16. 17. **This generation * * * like unto children sitting in the market.** The markets were always held in an open street or square, as in many of our cities; and these market-places were used, not only for business, but, like the streets and open squares of to-day, by children in their sports. **Piped unto you * * * mourned unto you.** The metaphor is drawn from the sports of children, imitating the serious business of life, here weddings and funerals. "Among the Jews, the Greeks, and the Romans it was customary to play the flute, especially at marriage dances. Similarly, solemn wailing was customary at burials."—(*Lange.*) Dancing in that age was radically different from the modern dance; it is, however, worthy of note that Christ implies its common use as a recreation, and incidentally compares his gospel to a call to the dance, as it is elsewhere compared to an invitation to a feast (Luke 14:16-24). Observe, too, in this metaphor, one of the many indications in the N. T., not only of Christ's love for children, but also of his sympathy for them in their childish sports and games. Of this parable, for such it is, in fact, three interpretations have been proposed: (*a*,) that the children represent the Jews, who called to John and to Jesus, but were dissatisfied with the mourning of the one, and the joyousness of the other; (*b*,) that the children and their fellows represent different classes of the Jews, one part desiring one thing, and another another, so that they could agree in nothing; (*c*,) that the children represent Jesus and John, the one of whom called to joyousness and the other to mourning, and both of whom were rejected. The latter is the older interpretation, it accords best with the context, and it is that which the ordinary reader would at once gather from the passage. The objection that Christ says "*this generation* is like unto children

18 For John came neither eating nor drinking, and they say, He^a hath a devil.
19 The Son of man came eating^o and drinking, and they say, Behold a man gluttonous, and a winebibber, a friend of publicans^p and sinners. But wisdom^q is justified of her children.

_{a ch. 10 : 25; John 7 : 20....o ch. 9 : 10; John 2 : 2....p Luke 15 : 2; 19 : 7....q Ps. 92 : 5, 6; Prov. 17 : 94.}

sitting and calling," is not conclusive, for he similarly says (Matt. 13:24), "The kingdom of heaven is likened unto a man who sowed good seed," while he afterwards (ver. 37) explains that the sower is the Son of man; compare similar use of language in Matt. 13 : 45. The objection that it is undignified or harsh to understand of the children John the Baptist and Jesus is even less forcible, for Christ elsewhere compares himself to objects lowlier and less dignified than children playing, *e. g.* to a road-way, to bread, to a gate, etc. See also for Biblical use of very lowly imagery, Ezekiel 4 : 1–3; 5 : 1, etc. I accept, therefore, the interpretation which is the most common and natural, though many of the ablest commentators, Lange, Schaff, Olshausen, and Alford among others, reject it. John comes mourning and warning, but the nation mourns not; Jesus comes rejoicing and calling to joy, but the nation rejoices not.

18. For. This connects the following verses with the preceding metaphor, and shows them to be an interpretation of it. **John came neither eating nor drinking;** *i. e.*, sociably. He lived the life of an ascetic, almost of an hermit (Matt. 3:4). **He hath a devil.** This charge is nowhere else reported against John, though it is reported as brought against Jesus (Matt. 9 : 34; 12:24; John 7:20; 8:48, 52; 10:20). But the Pharisees, who rejected Jesus, and charged him with laxity of morals in mixing with sinners, also rejected John, whose spirit was the reverse of that of Jesus in this respect (Matt. 21:25; Luke 7:30). Dr. Brown remarks: "When men want an excuse for rejecting or disregarding the grace of the Gospel, they easily find it. * * * One preacher is too austere; another too free; one is too long; another too short; one is too sentimental; another is too hard."

19. The Son of man came eating and drinking; *i. e.*, he mingled in the social festivities of his age. There is no record in the N. T. of his ever having declined an invitation. His habit in this respect is illustrated by his presence at the marriage at Cana of Galilee (John 2:1-11), the feast at Matthew's house (Matt. 9:9, 10), the house of Simon (Luke 7:36), the dinner given him by the Pharisees (Luke 11:37; 14:1), and the supper given by Mary and Martha (John 12:1, 2). Christ's example justifies a right enjoyment of social festivity, and affords no ground for asceticism. **They say.** Note the value of a "*they say;*" *i. e.*, the weight that belongs to mere common report. **Behold a man gluttonous and a wine-bibber.** Observe that Christ did not permit the fear that his example would be misunderstood and misinterpreted to prevent his participation in social festivities, in which there was then, as there is now, sometimes excess. It is not true that we are to avoid all appearance of evil, as that language is ordinarily understood (see note on 1 Thess. 5 : 22); and the apostle's principle, "If meat make my brother to offend, I will eat no flesh while the world standeth," is to be qualified by Christ's example. An example that is a stumbling-block to others *sometimes becomes a duty*. **A friend of publicans and sinners.** A sublime truth, though uttered as a slanderous lie.

But wisdom is justified by her children, *i. e.*, the divine Spirit is recognized by the children of God. *Wisdom* is not here equivalent to Christ; it is the spirit of divine Wisdom which was manifested both in John the Baptist and in Jesus (see Prov. ch. 8). *Justified* is equivalent to *recognized as right* (compare, for use, Matt. 12 : 37; Luke 7 : 29; 10 : 29; 16 : 15; 18 : 14). In the Gospels, as in its theological use in Romans, it signifies, not *a making* right, but *regarding* as right, *treating* as right. *Her children* are the children that are begotten of the divine Wisdom, *i. e.*, the sons of God (John 1 : 12, 13). The true meaning of the passage is indicated by Luke's declaration (Luke 7 : 29); "All the people that heard him and the publicans *justified God*, being baptized with the baptism of John." For contrast between the effect produced by the Gospel on the children of foolishness and the children of wisdom, see 1 Cor. 1 : 23, 24. Observe that the Pharisees, the wise and mighty and rich of Judea, were stumbled, while the publicans and sinners, the foolish and weak and base, justified God (1 Cor. 1 : 26-29; compare John 7 : 48, 49).

Ch. 11 : 20-24. WOES PRONOUNCED AGAINST GALILEAN CITIES. THE OBJECT OF CHRIST'S MIGHTY WORKS: THE PRODUCTION OF REPENTANCE—THE GROUND OF ETERNAL CONDEMNATION; THE REFUSAL TO REPENT.—THE HEATHEN CONDEMN CHRISTENDOM.— THE PROSPERITY OF GREAT CITIES OFTEN FALLACIOUS. —THE HISTORY OF DIVINE JUDGMENTS IN THE PAST AN EXEMPLIFICATION OF DIVINE JUDGMENTS IN THE FUTURE.—DIFFERENCES IN SIN AND IN PUNISHMENT.— THE GREATER THE GRACE, THE GREATER THE SIN, AND THE GREATER THE JUDGMENT.

This discourse and that contained in the following part of the same chapter (ver. 25-30), appear only in Matthew. But thoughts almost identical with those down to verse 27, appear in Luke 10 : 13-16, 21, 22, in connection with the commis-

20 Then[f] began he to upbraid the cities wherein most of his mighty works were done, because they repented not:
21 Woe unto thee, Chorazin! woe unto thee, Bethsaida! for if the mighty works which were done in you had been done in Tyre and Sidon, they would have repented long ago in sackcloth and ashes.
22 But I say unto you, It[s] shall be more tolerable for Tyre and Sidon at the day of judgment, than for you.
23 And thou, Capernaum, which art[u] exalted unto heaven, shalt be brought down to hell: for if the mighty works which have been done in thee had been done in Sodom, it would have remained until this day.

f Luke 10 : 13, etc....s John 12 : 21....t ch. 10 : 15....u Isa. 14 : 13-15; Lam. 2 : 1.

sion and the return of the Seventy. Most commentators regard the connecting words, "then he began to upbraid," as an indication that this entire chapter is one discourse. So Alford: "I would regard the 'then he began,' as the token of the report of an ear witness, and as pointing to a pause or change of manner on the part of our Lord." The original is, however, certainly susceptible of a more general signification. This occasion marked a change in Christ's ministry, from a mere proclamation that the kingdom is at hand to a warning of divine judgments against the people for rejecting it. Observe that from this time onward, these warnings grow more and more terrible to the close of his ministry. See Luke 11 : 39-54; 13 : 1-5; 16 : 15, and their strongest and most terrible expression in Matt. ch. 23. Whether the same woes were twice pronounced in the cities of Galilee, once at the time indicated here by Matthew, and again at the time indicated by Luke, or whether the two evangelists give in different connections reports of the same address, is a question which cannot be answered with any certainty.

20. The cities (of Galilee), **wherein most of his mighty works were done.** The Greek word (δύναμις) here translated "mighty works," is elsewhere translated miracles (Mark 9 : 39; Acts 2 : 22). It unquestionably here means works of a miraculous nature. That there were many such miracles unrecorded is testified to in Luke 4 : 23 and John 21 : 25. Compare Matt. 9 : 35; Mark 1 : 34; Luke 7 : 21. **Because they repented not.** The object of his miracles, as his preaching, was to produce repentance. Compare Matt. 4 : 17. "He does not say because they *believed* not; for some kind of faith [belief?] many of them had, as that Christ was a teacher come from God; but because they *repented not*; their faith [belief?] did not prevail to the transforming of their hearts and the reformation of their lives."—(*Matthew Henry.*)

21. Woe unto thee, Chorazin. Chorazin is mentioned only here and in Luke 10 : 13. Its situation is not with certainty known; the latest researches identify it with modern Kerazeh, two miles north of Capernaum, modern Tel Hum, and this agrees with the testimony of Jerome. Nothing is known of its history. **Bethsaida.** There is no adequate ground for the hypothesis that there were two cities of this name in Galilee, one on the northern and one on the western shore of the lake, an hypothesis invented to reconcile Luke 9 : 10 with Mark 6 : 45. There are some passages in later writers, referred to in Smith's Bib. Dict., which seem to substantiate this hypothesis, but there is no relic of a Bethsaida on the western shore, and no adequate evidence of such a town to overcome the inherent improbability of two towns of the same name in such close proximity. There was a well-known town of this name, a fisherman's village (the name signifies *house of fish*), on the north shore, where the Jordan enters the Sea of Galilee. See note on Mark 6 : 45.

Tyre and Sidon. Phœnician cities on the Mediterranean coast (see map). **Sidon,** named from the son of Canaan (Gen. 10 : 15), was one of the oldest cities in the Holy Land. **Tyre,** an offspring of Sidon, became the chief commercial city of Palestine, if not of all the East. Joshua did not drive out the aborigines from the neighboring plains (Josh. 11 : 8, with Judg. 1 : 19); and David and Solomon made treaties with the kings of Tyre (2 Sam. 5 : 11; 1 Kings 5 : 1-12). The Tyrian manufactures and commerce are graphically described in Ezekiel, ch. 27. Carthage, long the rival of Rome, was a Tyrian colony. Both Tyre and Sidon fell into the hands of Alexander the Great, and Phœnicia became a province of Syria. Still, in the time of Christ, Tyre was the chief commercial city of Palestine, and the largest city, probably, except perhaps Jerusalem. Both cities are now comparatively in ruins. The harbor of Tyre is filled up, the fishermen dry their nets on its rocks, and even if Palestine should become a prosperous nation again, Tyre never could be rebuilt as a commercial city, for want of a harbor, a striking illustration of the truth of Ezekiel's prophecy, "Thou shalt be built no more" (Ezek. 26 : 14). The warnings denounced against Tyre and Sidon in Ezekiel, chaps. 26, 27, and 28, rendered these cities notably a type of warning to the Jews.

In sackcloth and ashes. Sackcloth is a coarse texture of a dark color made of goats' hair. It was worn by mourners in a garment resembling a sack in shape, with holes for the arms. For illustration of use, see 2 Kings 6 : 30; Job 16 : 15; Isaiah 32 : 11; Joel 1 : 8; Jonah 3 : 5. Ashes were also put upon the head and face as a symbol of mourning. See 2 Sam. 13 : 19; Esther 4 : 1; Job 2 : 8; Isaiah 58 : 5, etc.

24. But I say unto you, That' it shall be more tolerable for the land of Sodom in the day of judgment, than for thee.
25. At" that time Jesus answered and said, I thank thee, O Father, Lord of heaven and earth, because thou hast hid these things from the wise and prudent, and hast revealed them unto babes.
26 Even so, Father: for so it seemed good in thy sight.
27 All things are delivered unto me of my Father:

22. More tolerable. See note on Matthew 10 : 15.

23. And thou, Capernaum, shalt thou be exalted unto heaven? Thou shalt be brought down unto death. There is some uncertainty as to the reading ; that which I have adopted in this rendering is that of the Sinaitic manuscript, and is adopted by Lachmann, Tregelles, Conant, and Alford in his last edition. The word translated "hell" is not Gehenna (γέεννα), the place of punishment, but Hades (ᾅδης), the place of the dead. See note on Matt. 5 : 22. The declaration is not that the inhabitants of Capernaum shall be eternally punished, but that Capernaum itself, which was the chief commercial city of the Sea of Galilee, should not have its expectation of future greatness realized, but should be obliterated. This prophecy has been so literally fulfilled that the very site of Capernaum is a matter of uncertainty. See note on Matt. 4 : 13. Of course, the spiritual lesson is involved in the symbol, the judgment that has fallen on the *place* is typical of the judgment that will fall on the people, as on all those that refuse to repent at the preaching and mighty works of Jesus. **Had been done in Sodom.** Christ elsewhere compares the suddenness of the judgment which overtook Sodom to that which will overtake the world (Luke 17 : 29, 30). The O. T. prophets compared the sins of Israel to those of Sodom (Isaiah 1 : 10 ; Lam. 4 : 6 ; Ezek. 16 : 46-57).

It would have remained. It is then clear (*a*) that the destruction of Sodom and Gomorrah was not brought about by the mere operation of natural law or an inevitable decree, but by divine Providence as a punishment for iniquity, a fact clearly stated in the O. T. narrative (Gen. 18 : 20, 21 ; 19 : 13), but here directly confirmed by Christ ; (*b*) that the decrees of God are not irrevocable, but are held by him subjected to change on the repentance and reformation of those warned of impending punishment, a truth illustrated in the history of Nineveh (Jonah 3 : 10) ; (*c*) that there is no sin and no sinner that cannot obtain pardon and absolution through repentance, since even Sodom might have escaped if it had repented.

24. More tolerable in the day of judgment. History affords an illustration of this declaration ; for "the name and perhaps even the remains of Sodom are still to be found on the shore of the Dead Sea, while that of Capernaum, on the Lake of Gennesareth, has been utterly lost."—(*Stanley*).

The moral meaning of these woes and their practical application is plain. "Unto whomsoever much is given, of him shall much be required" (Luke 12 : 48). In the divine judgment the flagrant vices of ignorance are less culpable than the rejection of pardon and spiritual life by those educated in the Gospel. The historical fulfillment of these warnings, in the destruction of the cities, points forward to a further spiritual fulfillment ; for the declaration is that it *shall be* more tolerable for the land of Sodom *in that day*, which evidently looks to a judgment of Sodom, *i. e.,* of its people, yet to come ; but the judgment on the place, *as a place*, had long since been fulfilled. If Tyre and Sidon, and Sodom and Gomorrah would have repented if further opportunity and greater manifestations had been awarded them, the question naturally occurs, why were these not given ? The answer is, that sufficient opportunity and sufficient warnings were given, and as no laborer in the vineyard has a right to call God to an account for giving a penny to all alike (Matt. 20 : 10-14), so no outcast has a right to call God to account for not giving all the same opportunity. If still the disciple, perplexed, asks why such seeming inequalities in the administration of divine grace, why the gift of Christ to the cities of Galilee and the withholding of Christ from the cities of the plain, the gift of Christianity to Europe and the withholding it from India, there is no other answer than, Even so, Father ; for so it seemed good in thy sight.

Ch. 11 : 25-30. CHRIST'S INVITATION. THE WARNING OF DANGER AND DOOM IS FOLLOWED BY THE INVITATION TO REFUGE AND REST.—SPIRITUAL TRUTH IS DISCERNED, NOT BY INTELLECTUAL POWER, BUT BY CHILD-LIKE DOCILITY. THE HUMBLE CHILD IS WISER THAN THE CONCEITED PHILOSOPHER.—ALL THINGS ON EARTH ARE IN THE HANDS OF INFINITE MERCY.—THE MYSTERY OF CHRIST'S NATURE ; NO THEOLOGY CAN FULLY INTERPRET HIM.—CHRIST THE GREAT REVEALER.—WITHOUT CHRIST GOD IS THE UNKNOWN AND UNKNOWABLE.—WHO ARE INVITED ? ALL IN NEED ; TO WHOM INVITED ? TO JESUS, WHO SAVES FROM SIN (Matt. 1 : 21) ; FOR WHAT INVITED ? FOR REST IN TROUBLE HERE, FROM TROUBLE HEREAFTER.—CHRIST'S YOKE, SELF-DENIAL FOR THE SAKE OF OTHERS ; LIGHT, BECAUSE BORNE FOR CHRIST AND BORNE WITH CHRIST. CHRIST'S YOKE, BECAUSE BORNE BY HIM FOR US, BY US FOR HIM, AND BY IT WE ARE YOKED TO CHRIST.—THE TRUE CHRISTIAN TEACHER MUST BE MEEK AND LOWLY IN HEART.—CHRIST'S GIFT, A YOKE, YET PERFECT REST ; A SERVICE WHICH IS JOY AND PEACE.

25. At that time. Not necessarily in the same discourse. It may mean at this period in his ministry, though the discourse from verse 7 may be all one. Compare for signification of phrase, Matt. 12:1; 14:1; Mark 10:30, etc. This much is certain; at the same period in which Jesus began to pronounce woes against the cities of Galilee, he commenced to give to his ministry a tenderer aspect toward the weary and heavy-laden. Luke records the same acknowledgment of God's mystery of grace with a more definite note of time, "in that hour" (Luke 10:21), *i. e.*, in the same hour with the return of the Seventy. Robinson supposes it to have been twice uttered, and this is quite possible. See above, note on 20-24. **I thank thee.** The Greek verb (ἐξομολογέω) so rendered here is nowhere else in the N. T. so translated, except in the parallel passage in Luke. The general idea is "*confess,*" but with the idea of publicity. It is here "*I publicly acknowledge to thee * * * that thou hast hid,*" etc. **Father, Lord of heaven and earth.** It is to be observed that he does not address the Father as his Lord, but as Lord of heaven and earth. But see John 20:17, where he says "My Father and your Father, and my God and your God. **These things.** That is, the mysterious operation of that divine power which destroys the cities of Galilee and raises up other nations to become light-bearers, as set forth in Matt. 21:43. Compare Rom. 11:33, and observe that Paul's expression there is in view of the casting out of Israel and the admission of the Gentiles. Both the warnings (Luke 19:42) and the invitations (2 Cor. 4:3) of the Gospel are hid from the eyes of such as are wise in their own conceit. Compare 1 Cor. 2:6-8. **From the wise and prudent.** The wise in philosophy, the prudent in worldly affairs (Acts 13:7). Observe, that the contrast is not with the unwise and imprudent, but with *babes*. The words (σοφός and συνετός), here rendered "wise and prudent," are never used alone in the N. T. in a bad sense, unless 1 Cor. 3:19 be an exception. The word wise (Gr. σοφός) is employed to designate an attribute both of God and good men (1 Cor. 3:10; Rom. 16:27), and the negative *foolish* (Gr. ἄσοφος, Ephes. 5:15 only) and *without understanding* (ἀσύνετος, Matt. 15:16; Rom. 1:31, etc.), are used only in a bad sense. The doctrine conveyed, then, is that religious truth is *not acquired by any mere intellectual process, however good in itself;* it is revealed not to philosophical wisdom, or intellectual culture, or practical sagacity in affairs, but to childlike humility and docility. Compare Job 11:7; Luke 18:17; 1 Cor. 1:12-21. The babes here are the disciples, contrasted with the wise and prudent (1 Cor. 1:26), unfamiliar with the wisdom of the Scribes (Acts 4:13), and disregarding worldly prudence in leaving all to follow Christ. The language here indicates that Luke has given this part of the discourse in the right connection, viz., immediately after the return of the Seventy from their mission. "When the Seventy came telling him about the devils, then he rejoiced and spake these things; which, besides increasing their diligence, would also dispose them to be modest."—(*Chrysostom.*)

27. All things are delivered unto me of my Father. Not *revealed* to me, but *delivered* to me; *i. e.*, the whole administration of human life is handed over to me. Compare Col. 1:16-19, and Hebrews 1:8. But observe that the power of Christ is represented as derived from the Father (delivered unto me by my Father), and that all will at the last be delivered to the Father again (1 Cor. 15:28). Compare, as to both truths, Matt. 28:18; John 5:26, 36; 14:10. **No man knoweth the Son.** The designation of Jesus as "*the Son*" occurs frequently in the Gospel of John, but only here, in Luke 10:22, and in Mark 13:32, in the synoptic Gospels. This verse finds, both in the spirit and the truth enunciated, a parallel in many passages in John; *e. g.*, John 1:18; 6:46; 14:6, 9, 10. The commentators note in it "a connecting link between the synoptists and John, and an incidental testimony by Matthew to the originality and credibility of the weighty discourse of Christ concerning his relation to the Father, which are only recorded in the fourth Gospel."—(*Schaff.*)

No one knoweth the Son but the Father. *Knows perfectly, fully* (Gr. ἐπιγινώσκω). Compare Matt. 7:20, and note. Observe that it is not, as in our version, no *man* knoweth, but no *one* knoweth—man, angel, archangel. That is, Christ claims a character which only the Infinite can fathom, because only the Infinite can fully understand the Infinite. Compare 1 Cor. 2:11. Observe, too, how the declaration of this mystery of Christ's nature is coupled with the declaration that the mysteries of the King and the kingdom are revealed to the childlike and hid from the wise and prudent; and that any system of theology is unscriptural which undertakes fully to interpret the nature of either the Father or the Son. **Neither knoweth any one the Father but the Son, and he to whom the Son wills to reveal him.** No man knows the Father except he add to the knowledge gained from other sources—history, science, nature, and his own thoughts—that special knowledge of God's grace and love which the Son affords; nor unless his study of nature, etc., is under the direction of and in submission to the Son. Philosophy is in so far right that to the Christless God is the Unknowable. Compare, for the way in which the Son reveals the Father, and to whom he will reveal him, John 14:15-24.

and no man knoweth the Son, but the Father; neither knoweth[a] any man the Father, save the Son, and *he* to whomsoever the Son will reveal *him*.

28 Come unto me, all *ye* that labour[a] and are heavy laden, and I will give you rest.

29 Take my yoke upon you, and learn[b] of me; for I am meek and lowly[c] in heart: and ye[d] shall find rest unto your souls.

30 For my yoke *is* easy,[e] and my burden is light.

a John 1 ; 18 ; 1 John 5 : 20. ...a Isa. 55 : 1–4....b Phil. 2 : 5–8 ; 1 Pet. 2 : 21....c Zech. 9 : 9....d Jer. 6 : 16....e 1 John 5 : 3.

28. Come unto me. Observe the utter incongruity of such an invitation as that here given, and its accompanying promise, in the mouth of a merely inspired prophet, or even an angel or archangel. Compare with it John 1 : 29, and Isaiah 53 : 4; and observe that Christ carries not only our sins, but also our griefs and our sorrows.

All that labor and are heavy laden. This is not to be limited or qualified, as an invitation to the Jews, "who groaned under the weight of their ceremonial laws and the tradition of their elders" (*Barnes*), or to "those, and those only, that are sensible of sin as a burden, and groan under it, that are not only convinced of the evil of sin, of their own sin, but are contrite in soul for it."—(*Matthew Henry*.) Of course, the invitation includes those burdened by a consciousness of sin, and the laborer serving under the law, as the greater includes the less. Observe, too, that the burden and weariness of labor is a fruit of sin (Gen. 3 : 17–19), and is thus a symbol of the bitterer spiritual labor and weariness of the soul under a sense of sin. But this invitation is not merely to the penitent and the remorseful, but *to all who, for any reason whatever, feel the want of a rest which the world cannot give* (compare Ps. 46 : 1 and Heb. 4 : 16). Thus, *the travail of life echoes Christ's invitation to spiritual rest* (Rom. 8 : 22, 23). The burden and labor of the leper was his leprosy; of the centurion, was his sick child; of the palsied, was his palsy; of the woman that was a sinner, was her sin and shame; of the prodigal, was at first only his hunger and his degradation (Matt. 8 : 2–4, 5, 6 ; 9 : 2 ; Luke 7 : 38 ; 15 : 16, 17). The coming to Christ is interpreted by his name, Jesus, Saviour from sin (Matt. 1 : 21), and by the coming of the apostles (*e. g.*, Luke 5 : 11), of Paul (Acts 9 : 5, 6), and of the rich young man who did not truly and finally come (Matt. 19 : 16–22); not less so by the coming of the many burdened by disease who came to him for cure. Whoever comes must take up his cross and follow Jesus (Luke 14 : 25–35). Chrysostom's interpretation is as broad as the original invitation itself. "Not this or that person, but all that are in anxiety, in sorrows, in sins, come—not that I may call you to account, but that I may do away your sins; come—not that I want your honor, but that I want your salvation."

I will give you rest. Not necessarily *from* your burden; if not, that then rest *in* your burden. The rest is described in the next verse, "*rest unto your souls.*" Compare John 14 : 27; 16 : 33; and observe that Christ's promise of peace there recorded was followed immediately after by external experiences of dire tribulation both to him and to his disciples. Compare, for fulfillment of this promise, 2 Cor. 12 : 9, 10; and for parallel to it, Heb. 12 : 11–13.

29. Take my yoke upon you. The yoke is used symbolically in the Bible to denote a condition of servitude (Lev. 26 : 13 ; 1 Kings 12 : 4, 9–11 ; Isaiah 9 : 4, etc.); and hence, in the N. T., of bondage under the law as opposed to the freedom of the Gospel (Acts 15 : 10 ; Gal. 5 : 1 ; 1 Tim. 6 : 1). Only here is it used in the N. T. of allegiance to Christ. The metaphor was well understood in his time. To express the subjugation of the conquered nations, the Romans were accustomed to make their captives pass under a yoke, made by placing two spears upright a short distance apart, and a third across the top. To pass under it, they were compelled to stoop. To take Christ's yoke, then, is to become captive to him in love. *But the yoke is never borne by one alone.* And Christ also became subject to a yoke for love's sake (see Phil. 2 : 7, 8), and sends us into the world as he was sent into the world (John 17 : 18). Hence, to take Christ's yoke is not only to yield ourselves servants to him in righteousness; *it is also to be yoked to Christ, i. e., become yoke-fellow and co-laborer with him* (see 1 Cor. 3 : 7). All burdens become easy when we are yoked with Christ, and he bears them with us.

And learn of me. By my teaching, my example, my indwelling. **For I am meek.** See note on Matt. 5 : 5. **And lowly in heart;** *i. e.*, of a heart to condescend to men of low estate. It is explained by Rom. 12 : 16, and Phil. 2 : 5–8, etc. The qualification, even of the Lord Jesus Christ, to be our divine teacher is not so much his infinite wisdom as his infinite meekness and condescension. And we attain his peace by becoming like him in character. **Ye shall find rest unto your souls.** Compare Jeremiah 6 : 16. Observe that there the condition of the promise is, "Ask for the old paths." Christ himself fulfilled the law and the prophets, so that they who came to him for rest came unto old paths, those through which the patriarchs and prophets entered into their rest.

30. For my yoke is easy. Rather, *kindly serviceable*. This is the proper meaning of the original ($\chi\rho\eta\sigma\tau\delta\varsigma$). That a yoke is *easy* is not an argument for it, for none at all is still easier.

CHAPTER XII.

AT that timeᶠ Jesus went on the sabbath day through the corn; and his disciples were an hungred, and began to pluckᵉ the ears of corn, and to eat.

2 But when the Pharisees saw *it*, they said unto him, Behold, thy disciples do that which is not lawful to doʰ upon the sabbath day.

3 But he said unto them, Have ye not read what David didⁱ when he was an hungred, and they that were with him;

f Mark 2 : 23, etc.; Luke 6 : 1, etc. ...g Deut. 23 : 25....h Exod. 31 : 15....i 1 Sam. 21 : 6.

But Christ's yoke is *useful;* it is by his yoke that we ourselves are brought into the image of God; by sharing his death we are made participants in his life here (2 Cor. 4 : 10) and hereafter (2 Tim. 2 : 11), and are also enabled to do service to him as represented in our fellow-men. "The yoke of Christ is like the plumage of a bird, which adds to its weight, but enables it to soar to the sky."—(*Wordsworth*, quoting from the Fathers.) **My burden is light.** Compare Matt. 23 : 4. For a contrast between the yoke which Christ breaks and the rest he gives, see Romans chaps. 7 and 8; 7 : 21-24 interprets the burden; 8 : 1, 38, 39 indicates the rest. If, as is thought by many of the harmonists, the incident of the woman who was a sinner, recorded in Luke 7 : 36-50, occurred immediately after this discourse, her acceptance of the invitation here offered affords the best possible interpretation of its true spiritual significance. Compare with Christ's invitation and his absolute promise of *rest* to all who come to him, the dying discourse of Socrates : "Cebes answered with a smile, 'Then, Socrates, you must argue us out of our fears; and yet, strictly speaking, they are not our fears; but there is a child within us to whom death is a sort of hobgoblin; him, too, we must persuade not to be afraid when he is alone with him in the dark.' Socrates said, 'Let the voice of the charmer be applied daily until you have charmed him away.' 'And where shall we find a good charmer of our fears, Socrates, when you are gone?' 'Greece,' he replied, 'is a large place, Cebes, and has many good men, and there are barbarous races not a few; seek for him among them all far and wide, sparing neither pains nor money; for there is no better way of using your money. And you must not forget to seek for him among yourselves too; for he is nowhere more likely to be found.'"—(*Phædo*, Jowett's translation.)

Ch. 12 : 1-14. THE LAW OF THE CHRISTIAN SABBATH ILLUSTRATED. IT IS ALWAYS EASY TO CRITICISE CHRISTIANS.—THE SERVICE OF CHRIST IS MORE THAN THE SERVICE OF THE TEMPLE.—THE LIBERTY OF THE O. T. ILLUSTRATED BY DAVID, BY THE TEMPLE SERVICE; HOW MUCH GREATER THE LIBERTY OF THE N. T. —THE SERVICE OF MERCY, MORE THAN THE SERVICE OF SACRIFICE; THE SERVICE OF CHRIST, MORE THAN THAT OF THE TEMPLE.—THE SABBATH PERMANENT: CHRIST IS ITS LORD; UNIVERSAL: MADE FOR MAN.—TWO FUNDAMENTAL PRINCIPLES OF SABBATH OBSERVANCE: IT IS MADE FOR MAN'S USE, SO ITS BEST USE IS ALWAYS ITS RIGHT USE; IT IS LAWFUL TO DO GOOD ON THE SABBATH DAY.—THE SABBATH OF EARTH LIKE THE SABBATH OF HEAVEN, A REST FROM THE HARASSMENT OF EVIL, BUT NOT FROM WORKS OF LOVE.—WITH EVERY COMMAND OF CHRIST COMES POWER FROM CHRIST.—THE EFFECT OF MIRACLES ON UNCANDID MINDS IS ONLY TO ANGER, NOT TO CONVINCE.

The incidents here recorded are found also in Mark 2 : 23-28; 3 : 1-6, and Luke 6 : 1-11. The time is uncertain. The most definite indications are the references in Luke 6 : 1, to "the second Sabbath after the first" (see note there), and the fact that the grain was ripe for plucking. The barley harvest was in April, the wheat harvest was in May, sometimes as late as June. Most harmonists place both incidents immediately succeeding that recorded in John, ch. 5. They probably occurred prior to the Sermon on the Mount, certainly prior to the commission of the twelve. The place is also uncertain. The connection in all three of the Evangelists, neither of whom gives an account of Christ's early Judean ministry in detail, indicates Galilee. But see note below, on verse 9.

1. At that time. See note on chap. 11 : 25. **On the Sabbath day.** The Jewish Sabbath, the seventh day of the week, answering to our Saturday. There was no observance of the first day of the week till after the resurrection of Christ. **Corn.** Rather grain, probably barley or wheat. The principal grains known to the Hebrews were wheat, barley, millet and spelt, the latter rendered sometimes rye (Exod. 9 : 32; Isaiah 28 : 25), and sometimes fitches (Ezek. 4 : 9). Recent discoveries indicate that maize or Indian corn was known to the Egyptians, but whether it was cultivated by the Hebrews or not is matter only of conjecture. **Were an hungered.** The rabbinical law allowed no eating on the Sabbath, except in case of sickness, prior to the morning prayers of the synagogue. A similar canon in the ritualistic churches of to-day forbids breaking the fast before partaking of the communion. **Began to pluck the ears of corn.** Luke adds, "rubbing them in their hands," in order to separate the kernel from the chaff.

2. That which is not lawful to do upon the Sabbath day. The Jewish law expressly permitted plucking the standing grain with the hand in passing through a field (Deut. 23 : 25); so that the objection was not that there was any dishonesty or theft; and the spirit of the law allowed

4 How he entered into the house of God, and did eat the showbread, which was not lawful for him to eat, neither for them which were with him, but only* for the priests?
5 Or have ye not read in the law, how that on the sabbath days the priests in the temple™ profane the sabbath, and are blameless?

6 But I say unto you, That in this place is *one* greater° than the temple.
7 But if ye had known what *this* meaneth, I° will have mercy, and not sacrifice, ye would not have condemned the guiltless.
8 For the Son of man is Lord even of the sabbath day.

j Ex. 25 : 30....k Ex. 29 : 32, 33...J Num. 28 : 9....m John 7 : 22, 23,...n ch. 23 : 17-21 ; 2 Chron. 6 : 18 ; Mal. 3 : 1,...o Hos. 6 : 6.

doing on holy days what was necessary to supply needful food (Exod. 12 : 16). But the rabbinical rules forbade any approximation to labor on the Sabbath. "One might not walk upon the grass because it would be bruised, which would be a kind of threshing ; nor catch a flea, which would be a kind of hunting; nor wear nailed shoes, which would be a sort of burden; nor, if he fed his chickens, suffer any corn to lie upon the ground, lest a kernel should germinate, which would be a kind of sowing."—(*Abbott's Jesus of Nazareth*.) And a special rule forbade to pluck the ears of corn, because that would be a kind of reaping. The punishment awarded by the rabbis for a presumptuous violation of this law was stoning. (See *Lightfoot*.)

3. **Have ye not read?** Compare chapter 9 : 13, and note there. Observe the delicate irony of the question. **What David did.** The account is in 1 Sam. 21 : 1-9. **They that were with him.** In Samuel, Ahimelech is represented as asking, "Why art thou alone, and no man with thee?" but verse 4 of 1 Sam. ch. 21, shows clearly that he was not absolutely alone, only, for a king's son, comparatively unattended.

4. **And did eat the showbread.** This consisted of twelve loaves placed fresh every Sabbath day on the table in the sanctuary (Exod. 25 : 25-30 ; 29 : 36). It could be eaten only in the sanctuary and by the priests (Lev. 24 : 5-9). To get this bread, David told a lie ; and the consequence was disastrous in the extreme (see 1 Sam. ch. 22 : 17-19). Christ does not commend his course *in this respect ;* the only question before him relates to Sabbath observance, and the right of man to modify or set aside a ceremonial regulation in case of necessity. Observe, that fresh bread had just been put upon the table when David arrived (1 Sam. 21 : 6), he taking that which was carried away ; the day, therefore, was the Sabbath (Lev. 24 : 8).

5. **The priests in the temple profane the Sabbath.** By kindling fires for the burnt offerings and bearing the sacrifices and utensils through the temple. The Sabbath was the priests' busiest day of labor. Work was required of the priests (Numb. 28 : 9, 10); though in general forbidden (Exod. 20 : 10 ; Neh. 13 : 19 ; Jer. 17 : 21, 22, 27) **Blameless.** Because the greater duty of temple service set aside the law of Sabbath rest. Compare John 7 : 22, 23.

6. **A greater than the temple is here.** Not merely mercy is greater than the temple, but, as Dean Alford interprets it, "If the priest in the temple, and for the temple's sake, profane the Sabbath, as ye account profanation, and are blameless, how much more these disciples who have gone hungry in their appointed following of Him who is greater than the temple, the true Temple of God on earth, the Son of man."

7. **I will have mercy and not sacrifice.** Quoted from Hosea 6 : 6. See note on Matt. 9 : 13. If, in the service of sacrifice, the Sabbath law may be seemingly set aside, how much more in my service, which is the service of mercy.

8. **For the Son of man.** Mark inserts here before this verse the important addition, *The Sabbath was made for man, not man for the Sabbath. Therefore the Son of man is Lord also of the Sabbath.* The Son of man is never, in N. T. usage, equivalent to man, but always signifies the Messiah. Christ's declaration is not, as Grotius, Because the Sabbath was made for man, man is Lord of the Sabbath, which would be a singular *non sequitur ;* but, Because the Sabbath is made for humanity, the Lord of humanity is Lord of the Sabbath. Observe, *is* Lord of the Sabbath. He does not, then, abolish it, but retains and rules over it. While the direct bearing of this incident and teaching respects the Sabbath observance, it goes deeper. It strikes at the root of all ceremonialism. The Christian must be willing to die for a principle (Luke 14 : 26); he is not required even to suffer a pang of hunger merely to preserve intact a ceremonial. If the Sabbath, the oldest and the most sacred of all religious observances, was made for man, much more all lesser observances.

9-13. HEALING OF THE MAN WITH THE WITHERED HAND. Mark 3 : 1-6, and Luke 6 : 6-11, add some features not given here. Combining these accounts, it appears that Christ entered the synagogue on the Sabbath to teach (Luke); that the Scribes and Pharisees, observing the man with the withered hand, watched to see whether Christ would heal, that they might find a ground of accusation against him (Luke); that they first put the question to him, Is it lawful to heal on the Sabbath days? (Matt.) that he, knowing their purpose, replied with a question which disclosed their hypocrisy, Is it lawful to do good on the Sabbath day, or to do evil ? to save life, or to kill ? to which they could make no reply (Mark, Luke); that he looked about upon them with

CH. XII.]   MATTHEW.   163

9 And when he was departed thence, he went into their synagogue:
10 And, behold, there was a man which had *his* hand withered. And they asked him, saying, Is it lawful to heal on the sabbath days? that they might accuse him.
11 And he said unto them, What man shall there be among you, that shall have one sheep, and if it fall into a pit on the sabbath day, will he not lay hold on it, and lift *it* out?
12 How much then is a man better than a sheep? Wherefore it is lawful to do well on the sabbath days.
13 Then saith he to the man, Stretch forth thine hand. And he stretched *it* forth; and it was restored whole, like as the other.
14 Then the Pharisees went out, and held a council against him, how they might destroy him.
15 But when Jesus knew *it*, he withdrew himself from thence: and great multitudes followed him, and he healed them all;

p Mark 3 : 1, etc.; Luke 6 : 6, etc. ...q Luke 14 : 3. ...r Deut. 22 : 4.

anger, being grieved at the hardness of their hearts, then answered their question and his own by the illustration of the sheep (Matt.), which he seems to have subsequently repeated in a slightly different form on another occasion (Luke 14 : 5); he then performed the cure, but with a word, *doing nothing*, and so giving no ground on which they could base an accusation.

9. Departed thence. Nothing more is necessarily indicated by this than that the two incidents did not occur in the same place. Luke says the healing was wrought "on another Sabbath." **Their synagogue.** That is, a synagogue of the Pharisees, one in which their influence predominated.

10. Had his hand withered; *i. e.*, dried up from a deficient absorption of the nutriment. Luke says his "right hand." The disease here indicated results in a loss both in size and in power of the arm; for it there is no remedy known to man. **They asked him, saying, Is it lawful to heal on the Sabbath day?** Their object was to provoke him to some act on which they could base an accusation of Sabbath-breaking, the punishment for which was death. The Mosaic law did not forbid works of healing; but the rabbinical tradition and interpretations did. "Let not those that are in health use physic on the Sabbath day." "He that hath the toothache, let him not swallow vinegar to spit it out again; but he may swallow it, so he swallow it down." Lightfoot gives a number of these minute and absurd Sabbath regulations. See Luke 13 : 14.

11. And he said unto them. He first asked them a question which they could not answer: "Is it lawful to do good on the Sabbath days? to save life or to kill?" (Mark 3 : 4, and note.); *i. e.*, to save life, as I am seeking to do, or to kill, as you are seeking to do, in endeavoring to find a ground of accusation against me.

What man shall there be among you, etc. Later rabbinical law forbade the owner of a beast that fell into a pit to lift it out; he might, however, bring food, or even lay planks for the beast to come out on. That this regulation was of a later date is evident from Christ's language here, which indicates that the saving of the beast in such case was a thing allowed (compare Luke 14 : 15). It is not improbable that the subsequent regulation was added by some of the rabbis to meet the very point of Christ's argument in this case.

12. How much better then is a man than a sheep. Compare Matt. 6 : 26, and note there. **It is lawful to do well on the Sabbath days,** *i. e.*, to do good to others. The language (καλῶς ποιεῖν) is the same as that employed in Matt. 5 : 44, "Do good to them that hate you." Work, *the sole object of which is true benefit to others*, is legitimate Sabbath labor.

13. Then saith he to the man. As the cure is wrought only by a word, the Pharisees have no ground of accusation; there has been no infraction of the letter of even their own regulations. Observe that with the word of command here, as in others of Christ's miracles (Matt. 9 : 6; John 5 : 8, etc.), comes power to obey it. So he requires what are impossibilities of withered souls, but with the command imparts power to fulfill (John 1 : 12).

14. Took counsel. Not the gathering of an official body, but an informal consultation is indicated. The Herodians joined in these deliberations (Mark 3 : 6). This is the first mention of any deliberate plan formed to put our Lord to death. The attempt at his destruction in Nazareth (Luke 4 : 29) was the sudden impulse of a mob. Observe, in the effect of this miracle, how utterly inefficacious are miracles to persuade uncandid souls. See an illustration of the same principle in Luke 16 : 31. Modern miracles would not convince modern skepticism.

The LESSON OF THESE INCIDENTS. In considering the general significance of Christ's example and words in these two incidents, it is to be observed, 1st. That Christ chose the Sabbath as an occasion for many cures. Seven such are recorded in the Gospels (Mark 1 : 21, 29; Luke 13 : 14; 14 : 1; John 5 : 9; 9 : 14). 2d. That in these incidents there is nothing to indicate that the Lord intended to do away with the Sabbath day. 3d. That, on the contrary, his assertions, The Sabbath was made for *man*, and, The Son of man *is* Lord of the Sabbath day, indicate its perpetuity as a Christian institution. 4th. That he does vigorously sweep away the traditions and interpretations of the rabbis, who had converted this

16 And charged them that they should not make him known:

17 That it might be fulfilled which was spoken by Esaias the prophet, saying,

a Isa. 42 : 1.

day of rest into a day of irksome bondage. 5th. That by implication he repudiates all inflexible rules which trammel the Sabbath day, and settles it on a new basis of principle, enunciated in the two declarations, The Sabbath was made for man, and he is, therefore, to use it in the way best calculated for his highest good, and It is lawful to do good on the Sabbath days, *i. e.*, work, the *sole object* of which is the true welfare of others, is not prohibited by the requirements of a true Sabbatical rest.

Ch. 12 : 15-21. THE GENTLENESS OF JESUS. JESUS ILLUSTRATES HIS OWN TEACHINGS: DOES NO RIGHTEOUSNESS TO BE SEEN OF MEN (Matt. 6 : 1).—HIS HONOR: THE BELOVED OF GOD; HIS POWER: THE SPIRIT OF GOD; HIS OFFICE; THE DIVINE REVEALER TO ALL NATIONS; HIS METHODS: QUIET, GENTLE; HIS TENDERNESS: HE DESPISES NOT THE POOR AND FEEBLE; HIS GLORY: THE SAVIOUR OF ALL NATIONS.

Parallel with verses 15 and 16 is Mark 3 : 7-12, which is fuller. He departed to the sea, and procured a small boat to escape from the multitude. The rest of this passage (vers. 17-21) is peculiar to Matthew.

15. But Jesus knowing this. The implication of the original, unlike that of our translation, is that he knew it at once. Compare Matt. 9 : 4. **Withdrew himself.** By his example he enforces his directions to his disciples (Matt. 10 : 23). **Great multitudes followed him.** His enemies were the ecclesiastical leaders; he was still popular with the common people. Healed them all, *i. e.*, all that were in need of healing. Compare chap. 8 : 16, and note there.

16. And charged them, etc. See note on Matt. 8 : 4.

17. That it might be fulfilled. The original is nearly equivalent to *so was fulfilled* (Gr. ἵνα πληρωθῇ). It, however, embodies the idea that both the prophecy and the fulfillment were in accordance with God's purpose. For it is true that it was the purpose of Christ in life, character, and death, to fulfil God's will concerning him.

I may take this occasion to say to the Greek student, that I dissent from Alford's conclusion that "it is impossible to translate ἵνα (*hina*) in any other sense than 'in order that.'" Sophocles (*Greek Lex.*, art. ἵνα) has given a number of illustrations, some from the Septuagint, showing that it is used in the later Greek otherwise than in a telic sense; and there are passages in the N. T. where it cannot be rendered "*in order that*," without forcing an unnatural meaning upon the sacred text. John 13 : 34 affords a striking illustration: "A new commandment I give unto you, That (ἵνα) ye love one another; as I have loved you, that (ἵνα) ye also love one another." It is certainly unnatural though not impossible to render the first ἵνα (*hina*) "in order that," *i. e.* to suppose Christ's declaration to be, I have given you a new commandment *in order that* ye love one another; but it neither accords with common sense nor with other teachings of Scripture to give that meaning to the second ἵνα, so as to read, I have loved you *in order that* ye love one another; for the springs of Christ's love are in himself. So here, while ἵνα has a qualified telic sense, yet "in order that" would not fairly represent its true significance, for it is impossible to believe that the reason why Christ was gentle, did not strive nor cry, bore patiently and long with the bruised reed and smoking flax, was that he might fulfill a prophecy. This would make Christ for the prophecy, whereas the prophecy is for Christ. The mistake—for in spite of Dean Alford's very positive assertion, I cannot regard it but as a mistake—arises from forgetting that the language of the N. T. is popular, not abstruse, and conforms in many respects rather to the later than to the classical Greek. I may add that while Winer (§ 53, ¶ 10, sec. 6) in the main appears to sustain Alford's view, though he is less positive and seems to allow of some exceptions, the other view is maintained by Olshausen, Note on Matt. 1 : 21; Owen, Note on same; Ellicott, Note on Ephes. 1 : 17; Sophocles, Gr. Lex., Art. ἵνα; Robinson, Gr. Lex. of N. T., Art. ἵνα, and other scholars quoted in those authorities. Olshausen's argument appears to me to be quite conclusive on this subject. "This Evangelist (John) has used ὥστε once only (John 3 : 16) in all his writings; and in that instance it is after a preceding οὕτως; ὥστε, too, occurs only in John 11 : 57. But it is inconceivable that John should not sometimes have wished to express the notion of mere consequence without intention. Such passages as John 4 : 34; 9 : 2; 15 : 13; 16 : 7; 17 : 3, show that he employed ἵνα for this purpose."

17. Which was spoken by Esaias, *i. e.* **Isaiah.** The quotation is from Isaiah 42 : 1-4. It is apparently a quotation from memory, for it follows neither the original Hebrew nor the Greek version (the Septuagint) with verbal accuracy. The N. T. quotations from the O. T. afford a striking illustration of the biblical disregard of the letter, and a conclusive argument against the doctrine of verbal inspiration, *i. e.* the doctrine that the Holy Spirit dictated the words, and that the writers were mere amanuenses. That the English

18 Behold my servant, whom I have chosen; my beloved, in whom my soul is well pleased; I will put my spirit upon him, and he shall shew judgment to the Gentiles.
19 He shall not strive, nor cry; neither shall any man hear his voice in the streets.
20 A bruised reed shall he not break, and smoking flax shall he not quench, till he send forth judgment unto victory.
21 And in his name shall the Gentiles trust.
22 Then¹ was brought unto him one possessed with a devil, blind and dumb: and he healed him, insomuch that the blind and dumb both spake and saw.

1 Mark 3 : 11 ; Luke 11 : 14.

---

reader may note the contrast in phraseology, I transfer Henderson's translation of the original passage:

"Behold my servant whom I uphold;
Mine Elect in whom my soul delighteth;
I have put my spirit upon him;
He shall cause judgment to go forth to the nations;
He shall not cry nor raise his voice,
Nor cause it to be heard in the streets.
A bruised reed shall he not crush;
And a glimmering wick shall he not quench;
For permanence he shall cause judgment to go forth.
He shall not glimmer [be dim], neither shall he be bruised,
Till he have established judgment on the earth,
And the maritime lands have waited for his law."

18. My servant. The same word ($παῖς$) is translated child in Acts 4 : 27. It is the one employed in Matt. 8 : 6 ; see note there. The phrase is used by Isaiah in various senses. It is applied to himself (Isaiah 20 : 3), to Eliakim (22 : 20), to the Jewish people (41 : 8, 9 ; 44 : 1, 2, 21 ; 45 : 4), and to the Messiah (42 : 1 ; 50 : 5-10 ; 52 : 13). Its application to the Messiah, in the passage from which this quotation is made, is recognized by most Jewish rabbis, and in the Chaldee paraphrase the interpretation is incorporated in the text, which reads, Behold my servant, the Messiah. **Whom I have chosen.** The Greek word ($αἱρετίζω$) here rendered *chosen* occurs no where else in the N. T. It is a different word from that employed in such passages as John 15 : 16, and does not involve the idea of selection from many, but of preferment and love. **In whom my soul is well pleased.** Compare Matt. 3 : 17; 17 : 5. And for the reason why God the Father is well pleased with the Son, see Phil. 2 : 9 ; Hebrews 1 : 9. **I will put my Spirit upon him.** Compare Matt. 3 : 16, 17; John 1 : 32-34 ; 3 : 34 ; 10 : 38 ; 14 : 10. Observe that in some passages the Spirit of God is represented as taking on human nature (Phil. 2 : 6, 7 ; Heb. ch. 2 : 16) ; and elsewhere, as here, the man Christ Jesus is represented as clothed with and inspired by the indwelling Spirit of God. Thus the Bible uses both forms of expressing the incomprehensible character of Jesus Christ (see ver. 27) which in the church have been employed separately by antagonistic schools of theology. To the devout Arian Jesus Christ is a man in whom the Spirit of God peculiarly dwells; to the devout Athanasian, he is the Spirit of God dwelling in and with a perfect man. **And he shall announce judgment to the Gentiles ;** rather to the nations, *i. e.* to all nations, including the Jews, but also including pagans. Compare Matt. 3 : 12, and note ; 25 : 31, 32 ; John 5 : 22, 27.

19. He shall not strive. Compare 2 Tim. 2 : 24. Observe that though error was common in Christ's day, as in ours, he rarely if ever entered into a theological discussion. His preaching was not controversial, though sometimes doctrinal. He denounced sin (Matt. ch. 23), corrected error by instructing in the truth (chaps. 5 and 6), but avoided debate (ch. 21 : 23-27). **Nor vociferate.** Christ's preaching was not vociferous; his power was gentle. Compare Psalm 18 : 35. **Neither shall any man hear his voice in the streets.** Of course to be understood as an elaboration of the preceding clause. Christ was characteristically a street and field preacher.

20. A bruised reed. The reed was itself an emblem of weakness (see note on ch. 11 : 8). A bruised reed is one broken, but not entirely in two. The flax floating in oil was a common form of lamp; the smoking flax is one almost extinguished. The half-formed purpose he will not discourage; the disheartened aspiration he will not extinguish; the least glimmer of faith and love he will accept as a beginning; he will not, by coldness or rebuke, destroy. Read this metaphor in the light of chap. 11 : 28. "He who holds not a hand to the sinner, nor carries the burden for his brother, breaks the bruised reed ; he who despises the spark of faith in a little one extinguishes the smoking flax."—(*Jerome.*) Simon would have broken the bruised reed in the woman that was a sinner; Christ forbade and strengthened the faltering purpose (Luke 7 : 37-48). The Pharisees would have extinguished the smoking flax in Zaccheus ; Christ fanned it into a flame of true penitence (Luke 19 : 1-10). Peter was a bruised reed whom Christ broke not (Luke 22 : 55-62). **Till he send forth judgment unto victory,** *i. e.,* until he brings long conflict with evil to an end by taking the judgment-seat and becoming conqueror as judge over all (1 Cor. 15 : 25 ; Rev., ch. 20). The implication is, that the work of redemption will cease with the final judgment.

21. And in his name shall the Gentiles trust. For parallel declarations of the univer-

23 And all the people were amazed, and said, Is not this the son of David?
24 But when the Pharisees heard *it*, they said, This *fellow* doth not cast out devils, but by Beelzebub the prince of the devils.
25 And Jesus knew their thoughts,* and said unto them, Every kingdom divided against itself is brought to desolation; and every city or house divided against itself shall not stand:
26 And if Satan cast out Satan, he is divided against himself; how shall then his kingdom stand?
27 And if I by Beelzebub* cast out devils, by whom

u Ps. 139 : 2; John 2 : 24, 25.... v verse 34.

sality of Christ's kingdom of grace, see Isaiah 49 : 6, 12; 51 : 4, 5; Matt. 28 : 19; Mark 16 : 15.

12 : 22-42. HEALING OF DUMB AND BLIND, AND DISCOURSE THEREON. NO EVIDENCE CAN CONVINCE A DETERMINED SKEPTIC.—THE ARGUMENT FROM MIRACLES, OF HEALING IN THE PAST, OF GRACE IN THE PRESENT; NONE BUT GOD IS STRONGER THAN SATAN.—IN THE CONFLICT BETWEEN GOOD AND EVIL THERE CAN BE NO NEUTRALITY. EVERY MAN IS A SUBJECT OF GOD OR OF SATAN.—WITH CHRIST IS ALWAYS FOR CHRIST; TO BE SEPARATE FROM CHRIST IS ALWAYS TO BE AGAINST HIM.—ALL WORK THAT IS NOT WITH CHRIST, WASTES.—THERE ARE BOUNDS TO GOD'S PARDONING GRACE.—THE UNPARDONABLE SIN: TREASON AGAINST THE HOLY GHOST.—THE TREE IS MORE THAN ITS FRUIT; THE CHARACTER THAN CONDUCT.—WORDS ARE THE INCARNATION OF THOUGHTS. THE INTERPRETERS OF THE SOUL.—OUR WORDS ARE WRITTEN IN THE RECORD OF OUR LIFE.—THE RESURRECTION OF CHRIST THE EVIDENCE OF CHRISTIANITY.

The time when this miracle was wrought, and the accompanying charges of the Pharisees and Christ's reply were uttered, is uncertain. There is no reasonable doubt that the three accounts given by Matthew here, by Mark (ch. 3 : 19-30), and by Luke (ch. 9 : 14-20), are all of the same incident and discourse, though some scholars have supposed its occurrence twice. Robinson places it almost immediately after the Sermon on the Mount. Townsend does the same. The internal evidence—the facts that so serious a charge was definitely brought against Jesus as that of cooperation with Beelzebul, and that the people designated him the Son of David, i. e., the Messiah, the first time this designation was given to him by the multitude—appears to me to point to a later period. It was probably subsequent to the charges made of eating with publicans and sinners (ch. 9 : 11) of blasphemy (ch. 9 : 3), and of Sabbath breaking (ch. 12 : 2, 10, etc.). The place appears from Mark 3 : 22 to have been Galilee, and from same chapter, verses 20, 21, to have been in a house

22. One possessed with a devil, or *demon*. See note on Demoniacal Possession, ch. 8, p. 85.

23. Son of David. A common Jewish appellation of the Messiah. See references in note on ch. 8 : 27.

24. But when the Pharisees heard it. That is, when they heard what the people said. That they were present is indicated by Luke's phraseology "Some of them said." Mark gives a more definite description of these critics; they were "scribes who came down from Jerusalem." There is nothing inconsistent in these different descriptions. They were, in office scribes, in sentiment Pharisees, at the time present with and part of the multitude. **They said.** Not openly, but to one another. This is evident from the language of the next verse. **But by Beelzebul the prince of devils.** All the authorities agree that the reading here should be Beelzebul. Beelzebub, or Baal-zebub (*lord of flesh*), was a god of the Ekronites (2 Kings 1 : 2). By the change of a single letter the Jews converted it into Baal or Beelzebul (*lord of filth*), and applied it to the prince of devils. In their demonology, the demons were divided into ranks or classes, Satan, or Beelzebul, or the devil, being the prince or chief of all. See on his character note on ch. 4 : 1.

Observe that during Christ's life it was never denied by his bitterest foes that he wrought miracles. Compare John 11 : 47. Even the Pharisees were compelled to admit the miracles which they attributed either, as here, to demoniacal agency, or, as in their later books, to magical powers. A blasphemous Life of Jesus, compiled from the rabbinical authorities, asserts that he wrought them by possessing himself secretly of the incommunicable name of God kept in the Holy of Holies, and carefully guarded there; and that the cause of his death was his deprivation, through the treachery of Judas, of the manuscript on which he had written this name and other mysteries there acquired. The first open denial of the reality of the miracles appears as late as the second century in the works of Celsus.

25. And Jesus knew their thoughts. Compare ch. 9 : 4; Heb. 4 : 13. **Every kingdom divided against itself.** The German version expresses the idea happily: Every kingdom not at one with itself (*uneins*). History affords abundant illustration of this principle in human affairs. The principle itself constitutes an incidental but strong argument against sectarianism. See 1 Cor. 1 : 13. Observe that Christ recognized and set the seal of his approval on the Jewish conception of two kingdoms, of good and evil, with their angels and archangels. The kingdom of Satan is as definitely recognized by Jesus as the kingdom of God. **And every * * house** (οἰκία), here equivalent to household.

26. If Satan cast out Satan. Satan is

CH. XII.] MATTHEW. 167

do your children cast *them* out? therefore they shall be your judges.
28 But if I cast out devils by the Spirit of God, then the kingdom* of God is come unto you.
29 Or else how can one enter into a strong man's house, and spoil* his goods, except he first bind the strong man? and then he will spoil his house.
30 He that is not with me, is against me:* and he that gathereth not with me, scattereth abroad.
31 Wherefore I say unto you, All* manner of sin and

* ch. 6 : 33; Dan. 2 : 44; Luke 11 : 20; 17 : 21; Rom. 14 : 17 . . . x Isa. 49 : 24; 53 : 12; Rev. 12 : 7-10; 20 : 2, 3. . . . y 1 John 2 : 19. . . .
z Mark 3 : 28; Luke 12 : 10.

here evidently synonymous on the one hand with Beelzebul, on the other with the demon which Christ has cast out, who is treated as one of Satan's emissaries. The passage shows conclusively that in New Testament usage demon is nearly equivalent to devil with us, not merely to spirit, as in classical usage. **He is divided against himself: how shall then his kingdom stand?** It is true that the kingdom of Satan is in perpetual discord and anarchy, for to this the spirit of selfishness inevitably leads; but in relation to the kingdom of heaven, it is at one. "Just as a nation or kingdom may embrace within itself infinite parties, divisions, discords, jealousies, and heart-burnings; yet if it is to subsist as a nation at all, it must not, *as regards other nations*, have lost its sense of unity; when it does so, of necessity it falls to pieces and perishes."—(*Trench.*) There is, however, a real as well as seeming unity in the kingdom of evil; every evil influence co-operates with others, and tends to render the soul more subject to sin and Satan; and in all conflicts the hosts of evil naturally and instinctively ally themselves together; while the truth tends to the development of the individual conscience and to liberty of judgment and action in the individual, and so leads at first to divisions which only time and a riper development can cure. Contrast, for example, the unity of the Papal Church with the divisions among Protestants.

28. By whom do your children cast them out? There are two interpretations of this verse. Chrysostom and the fathers generally understand by "your children" the apostles. "He saith not 'my disciples,' nor 'the apostles,' but 'your sons,' to the end that if, indeed, they were minded to return to the same nobleness with them, they might derive hence a powerful spring that way."—(*Chrysostom.*) And he interprets the argument thus: "If I so cast them out, much more those who have received their authority from me. Nevertheless, no such thing have ye said to them. * * * Therefore, also he added, 'they shall be your judges.' For when persons from among you, and having been practised in those things, both believe me and obey, it is most clear that they will also condemn those who are against me both in deed and word." But this interpretation is unnatural, and has probably been invented to avoid the difficulty felt in supposing that Christ imputes miraculous powers to the followers of the Pharisees. The later and better interpretation understands by "your children," the disciples of the Pharisees (see 2 Kings 2 : 3), and the argument to be, Your own disciples assume to cast out devils; how do they accomplish it? If in them it is an evidence of divine authority, what is it in me? They, therefore, shall judge. *Did, then, the disciples of the Pharisees cast out devils?* That they pretended to do so is certain. There is no other evidence in Scripture of such a practice than that contained here; for the persons mentioned in Luke 9 : 49, and in Acts 19 : 13, 14, assumed to cast out devils only in Christ's name; the latter incident, however, implies a not uncommon practice of exorcism. But there is abundant evidence of this practice in the rabbinical books. Josephus refers to it: "He (*i. e.* Solomon) left behind him the manner of using exorcism, by which they drive away demons, so that they never return, and this manner of cure is of great force unto this day" (Antiq. viii., ch. 2, § 5). And he proceeds to give an account of the method pursued—a species of incantation. In one passage (Wars of Jews, viii., ch. 6, § 2) he gives an account of a root called barras, which can only be plucked in a particular manner, but which "quickly drives away those called demons, which are no other than the spirits of the wicked, that enter into men that are alive, and kill them, unless they can obtain some help against them." That the Pharisees claimed power to cast out devils is then clear; but, notwithstanding Alford's argument, there appears to me to be nothing in the words of Jesus here to warrant the belief that they really possessed any such power. The argument is simply one *ad hominem*, and it is equally strong whether the exorcism of evil spirits was real or pretended.

28. But if I cast out devils by the Spirit of God. Literally *in the Spirit of God, i. e.* in the power of his Spirit; Luke says "with the finger of God." **Then the kingdom of God is come unto** you; rather, as rendered in Luke, *upon you.* It comes upon the Pharisees and the devils, *unto* the disciples and the victims possessed of devils.

29. Or else, *i. e.*, if the kingdom of God has not come, if one *stronger* than Satan is not here. **How can one.** Luke says "*a stronger than he,*" *i. e.,* than Satan. The same Greek word (ἰσχυρότερός) here translated "stronger," is used by John the Baptist to designate Jesus (Matt. 3 : 11; Luke 3 : 16, there translated "mightier"). **Enter**

blasphemy shall be forgiven unto men: but the blasphemy *against* the *Holy* Ghost^a shall not be forgiven unto men.

32 And whosoever speaketh a word against the Son of man,^b it shall be forgiven him; but whosoever speaketh against the Holy Ghost, it shall not be forgiven him, neither in this world, neither in the *world to come.*

a Heb. 10 : 29 ; 1 John 5 : 16....b Luke 7 : 34 ; John 7 : 12 ; 1 Tim. 1 : 13.

into a strong man's house, except, etc. The strong man is Satan, his house is the whole domain of evil. It is only by binding Satan that his power over the souls of men can be broken. Compare for interpretation of metaphor Isaiah 40:10 ; 49:24, 25 ; 53:12 ; Col. 2:15, and note on Luke 11 : 21, 22, where the metaphor is given more fully than here.

30. He that is not with me is against me, etc. The converse of the proposition is also true, He that is not against us is on our part (Mark 9:40 ; Luke 9:50). This is the consummation of the first part of the discourse, and leads to the second part. See on next verse. It sets forth the division of all moral beings into two kingdoms of good and evil, God and Satan, *in one or other of which every person is of necessity ; for there is no third kingdom.* **He that is not gathering with me,**—for the final harvest,—**is scattering abroad,** does not gather for any harvest, but scatters, wastes. This is not a mere repetition of the first clause of the verse. The first asserts that he who is not Christ's follower is his foe, and it classes the multitude, who were listening but not obeying, with the Pharisees, and both with Satan and the devils ; the second asserts *that every act and influence in life, of the disciple as well as of him who is not,* if it gather nothing for Christ and with him, scatters and wastes that which has been or is being gathered. Every *act* as well as every *individual* is with and for Christ or against him. For meaning of the word "gathering" see Matthew 3:12 ; 13:30 ; of the word "scattering" see John 10:12. Observe that throughout this verse the contrast is not between him who is *for* Christ or who gathers *for* Christ and him who is against Christ or scattereth, but between him who is *with* Christ (Gr. μετά) or gathereth *with* Christ (συνάγω) and him who is against Christ or scattereth. One can be *for* Christ only as he is *with* Christ. We are *against* him when we are not *with* him, i. e., in his fellowship. When we are in his fellowship we cannot be against him. Unwisdom may make our work apparently scattering, wasteful, useless ; but he gathers it if we have worked with him. Mary doing no work, only sitting at Jesus' feet, was *for* him ; Martha, cumbered about much serving, though *for* him, scattered, wasted her energies, because she was not *with* him in sympathy (Luke 10 : 38-42).

30. Wherefore. This conjunction connects the discourse following respecting blasphemy against the Holy Spirit closely with what precedes concerning the kingdoms of good and evil, God and Satan. Mark (3:30) gives the connection still more definitely : "Because they said, He hath an unclean spirit." **I say unto you.** A common introduction of a solemn assertion. See note on Matt. 5: 18. **Every sin and blasphemy shall be forgiven.** Our English version doubtless gives the sense : not every sin shall be forgiven, but every kind of sin ; that is, there is forgiveness through repentance for all sins except the one about to be mentioned. **But the blasphemy of the Spirit.** The word Holy is inserted by the translators in this verse to make it conform to the verse following. On the meaning of word blasphemy see below.

32. Against the Son of man, *i. e.,* the Messiah. See note on Matt. 10:23. It is not true, as some commentators have supposed, that the contrast is between speaking against the Messiah in his veiled condition and unfinished work, and slandering the same Person after the change of glory which the Holy Ghost was soon to throw around his claims, and in the full knowledge of that, for the phrase "Son of Man" is used by Christ in describing himself both as coming in spiritual glory and power on the day of Pentecost (Matt. 10 : 23, and note), and subsequently to judge the world (Matt. 26 : 64), and is quoted from Daniel and the rabbinical books, where it is an appellation of the Messiah. **Neither in this world, neither in the world to come.** All such attempts as that of Dr. Adam Clark to break the force of this language by such interpretations as "Neither in this dispensation, viz., the Jewish, nor in that which is to come, viz., the Christian," or that of Wordsworth, following certain of the fathers, "Is very unlikely to obtain pardon," are utterly inadmissible. The contrast here recognized between this world and the world to come is a common one among the Jewish rabbis, and no phrases could have been better adapted to cover, to the Jewish mind, the whole period of the soul's existence. There is certainly in this verse no necessary implication that there is forgiveness of any sin in the life to come, though that deduction has been drawn, even by Augustine ; on the other hand, there is positive assertion that there is a sin for which there can never be pardon. It would be impossible to employ language more definitely inconsistent with the idea that all men will be finally pardoned and restored to divine favor.

OF BLASPHEMY AGAINST THE HOLY GHOST. Volumes have been written respecting this utter-

33 Either make the tree good, and his fruit good; or else make the tree corrupt, and his fruit corrupt: for[c] the tree is known by *his* fruit.

34 O generation[d] of vipers! how can ye, being evil, speak good things? for out[e] of the abundance of the heart the mouth speaketh.

c ch. 7 : 16, 17....d ch. 3 : 7....e Luke 6 : 45.

ance of Christ. In the early church conflicting sects charged each other with this sin. The fathers attributed it to the Arians because they denied the divinity of Christ, to the Macedonians because they denied the Godhead of the Holy Spirit, and, in brief, to all heretics because they spoke evil of the Holy Spirit's work. In later times multitudes have yielded themselves to despair, supposing themselves guilty of it. It has been variously defined as, Persistent resistance to the influence of the Third Person of the Trinity; Impious speaking against the Holy Ghost; Attributing the works of God to Satan; A wanton and blasphemous attack on the divine nature and power of Christ; A contemptuous treatment of Christ, not as he then appeared in his humiliation, but as he was ere long to appear, when his mission and character should be attested by the Holy Ghost; Not a particular act of sin but a state of sin, a wilful, determined opposition to the blessed power of the Holy Spirit; Not a sinful state of mind, but one great and deadly sin, which, when committed, renders forgiveness absolutely impossible. It has been supposed that the Pharisees had committed it, and Christ denounced this woe upon them; that they had not committed it, but approached its commission, and Christ warned them of their danger. To a certain extent the sin appears to be left purposely undefined, the note of warning to be indefinite, that it may caution all against transgressing the bounds beyond which forgiveness never reclaims. In seeking to understand Christ's meaning, and governing ourselves by the canon, we are to understand him as he would expect to be understood by his auditors, the following facts are to be considered. (*a*) There is an unpardonable sin; a sin, be it act or state, for which there is no space for forgiveness. It is possible to go beyond the reach of God's mercy. (*b*) There are hints of such a sin elsewhere in the N. T. In the study of this subject these should be carefully examined. The principal passages are the following: Heb. 6 : 4–6; 10 : 26–31; 12 : 15–17; 1 John 5 : 16. (*c*) The connection in this discourse is close between Christ's previous reference to the oppugnance of the two kingdoms of good and evil, and his allusion here to blasphemy against the Holy Ghost. "Wherefore," *i. e.*, because he that is not with me is of necessity against me, "I say unto you, All manner of sin and blasphemy shall be forgiven except the blasphemy against the Holy Ghost." (*d*) It is also closely connected with the accusation brought against Christ by the Pharisees, This fellow doth not cast out devils but by Beelzebul the prince of devils. (See Mark 3 : 30.) If they were not guilty of this sin they were approaching it. (*e*) The language used by Christ in describing the sin had a more definite meaning with the Jews than it has with us. The Spirit of God was not first revealed at Pentecost. The phrase is of constant occurrence in the O. T. (Exod. 31 : 3; Numb. 11 : 26; 1 Sam. 10 : 10; 19 : 20; Psalm 137 : 7; 143 : 10; Isaiah 48 : 16; Ezek. 11 : 24, etc.). As used here by Jesus, it would be understood by his auditors in the O. T. sense, viz., neither as the Third Person of the Trinity, for the doctrine of three Persons in one God was unknown to the Jews, nor as the divine power in Jesus Christ, for his divinity was not recognized fully, even by the disciples, till a later period, but as *God manifest in personal presence and power in and upon the hearts of men*. (*f*) The word *blasphemy* had a well defined meaning to the Jews. It was the designation of a crime defined by statutes, and punishable by death. Under the theocracy Jehovah was king of the Jews. He at first appointed directly all subordinate officers, and held, in his own name, all the land; later the kings were his own anointed, and ruled in his name. To do aught to diminish reverence and allegiance to him was the blasphemy of the O. T., a crime answering to treason in our own times, and was carefully defined and rigorously punished by the Mosaic laws. (For laws, see Exod. 20 : 1–7; 22 : 20; Deut. 13 : 1–5; 18 : 19, 20; Numb. ch. 16; 20 : 7–12; 1 Kings 18. See also Abbott's Jesus of Nazareth, ch. xxiv.) It was of this crime that Jesus was accused, and for it condemned by the Sanhedrim, because he assumed a divine character, and claimed divine honors (Matt. 26 : 63–66). (*g*) The warning here was uttered by Christ, not to infidels and open opposers of the kingdom of God, nor to hardened, flagrant, and undisguised sinners; but to the Pharisees, who claimed to be leaders in the Jewish theocracy, citizens in the kingdom which the Messiah was to inaugurate.

I conclude, then, that by blasphemy against the Holy Ghost Christ's auditors would understand, not a hardness of heart, a state of wilful, determined, obdurate sin, though only out of this could it spring, nor every kind of evil speaking against either the Third Person in the Trinity or the divine nature and office of Christ, but *treason by professed members of the kingdom of God against the Spirit of God*, manifested in this instance by wilfully confounding the two kingdoms of good and evil, God and Satan, and attributing to the

35 A good man out of the good treasure of the heart bringeth forth good things; and an evil man, out of the evil treasure, bringeth forth evil things.
36 But I say unto you, That every idle word that men shall speak, they shall give account^f thereof in the day of judgment:
37 For by thy words^g thou shalt be justified, and by thy words thou shalt be condemned.

38 Then certain of the scribes and of the Pharisees answered, saying, Master, we would see a sign^h from thee.
39 But he answered and said unto them, An evil and adulterous^i generation seeketh after a sign; and there shall no sign be given to it, but the sign of the prophet Jonas:
40 For^j as Jonas was three days and three nights in

f Ecc. 12 : 14; Eph. 5 : 4, 6; Jude 15... g Prov. 13 : 3... h ch. 16 : 1; 1 Cor. 1 : 22... i Isa. 57 : 3... j Jonas 1 : 17.

diabolical agency of the latter the blessed operations in merciful healing wrought by the former. But all wilful, wanton, determined opposition to the work of the Holy Spirit, either in others' hearts or our own, especially when engaged in by those who profess allegiance to the Holy Ghost, approximates this sin.

33. **Either make the tree good and his fruit good, or else make the tree corrupt and his fruit corrupt.** The direct connection with the preceding verses appears to be this: Be consistent; either represent the casting out of the devil from the possessed as bad, or else acknowledge the power that has done it to be good. But the lesson is of wider application; for it is not without significance that Christ uses the word *make* (Gr. ποιεω), which never appears to be used in the N. T. as merely equivalent to *represent*. The parable has a bearing on all work of reformation, public or individual, as well as on all judgments of real or *pseudo* reformation. We must always work at the tree if we wish to affect the fruit. See John 3 : 6. **For the tree is known by his fruit.** Nevertheless, the tree is more than the fruit, just as the treasure of the heart (ver. 35) is more than the speaking. Compare with this verse Matt. 7 : 15-20, and note.

34. **O offspring of vipers.** See Matt. 3 : 7, and note. **How can ye, being evil, speak good things.** Observe how even here, where Christ gives prominence to *conduct* (of the tongue), he still recognizes *character* (the *being evil*) as the source and root of conduct, and as that which must be changed. It is not merely the speaking against the Holy Ghost which is the unpardonable sin, but that kind of *being evil* which leads to such speaking. **For out of the abundance.** Literally *overplus* (Gr. περισσευμα, *what is over and above*). The speaking not only indicates the state of the heart, but indicates much more than appears in the words. And observe the implication, that the words are evil because they are indicators of the evil state within.

35. **The good man out of the good treasure,** *i. e.*, out of the *character*, which is a treasure or accumulation of all previous education, training, and habits. The words "*of the heart*" are not in the best manuscript; they were probably inserted there from the preceding verse. Luke (6 : 45) gives almost the same aphorism in his report of the Sermon on the Mount.

36. **Every idle word.** This is not merely equivalent to *evil* word, though it includes such. The original (ἀργός) is used in the N. T. to designate unemployed persons (Matt. 20 : 3, 6, etc.; 1 Tim. 5 : 13, etc.), and in the classics, money lying without interest, and land untilled, and a fallacious argument, *i. e.*, one that comes to no true result. Here the meaning is every non-productive word; every word that adds nothing, either to the present happiness or the permanent usefulness of others, all talking for the mere sake of talking, and of course all words of falsehood, malice, and injury. "That is idle which is not according to the fact, which hath in it unjust accusation; and some say that which is vain also, for instance, provoking inordinate laughter, or what is filthy, and immodest, and coarse."—(*Chrysostom.*) Compare Ephes. 4 : 29; 5 : 3, 4.

37. **For by thy words, etc.** Literally *out of thy words*. Compare Rev. 20 : 12, where the same Greek preposition (ἐκ) is rendered *out of*. The dead were judged *out of* those things which were written in the books. Here the declaration is that words form a basis for the last judgment. But the reason must not be forgotten; because the words are indicators of the heart which is to be judged. By our words we are writing the history of our lives and preparing the record for the judgment day. Compare with this portion of Christ's discourse, James, ch. 3.

38. **Then certain * * * answered, saying, Master.** Observe the language of respect. A portion had tried open reproach; others tried flattery. Compare Matt. 22 : 16-24; Luke 20 : 21-28; and observe how Christ receives the hypocritical advances of pretended respect. **We would see a sign from thee.** The same Greek word (σημειον) is often rendered miracle. A miracle had just been wrought in the casting out of the evil spirit. Luke explains the demand more definitely: "A sign from heaven" (compare Matt. 16 : 1), *i. e.*, a sign in which the interference from above should be more evident and palpable, a miracle not wrought by him but from above. The same demand is made by modern scepticism, which calls for a repetition now of the N. T. miracles. See, for example, Renan's *Life of Jesus*, p. 44, intro. Am. Ed.

39. **An evil and adulterous generation.** It was literally an adulterous generation. See Matt. 19 : 3-9, and notes. But the O. T. symbol-

the whale's belly; so shall the Son of man be three days and three nights in the heart of the earth.
41 The men of Nineveh shall rise in judgment with this generation, and shall condemn^k it; because they repented at the preaching of Jonas; and, behold, a greater than Jonas *is* here.

42 The^m queen of the south shall rise up in the judgment with this generation, and shall condemn it: for she^n came from the uttermost parts of the earth to hear the wisdom of Solomon; and, behold, a greater than Solomon *is* here.
43 When^o the unclean spirit is gone out of a man, he^p

^k Rom. 9:27...J Jonas 3:5...m Luke 11:31, etc...n 2 Chron. 9:1...o Luke 11:24...p Job 1:7; 1 Pet. 5:8.

ism gives to the phrase here a spiritual significance. Israel was married to God (Isaiah 54:5; Jer. 3:14), and because faithless to him was compared to an adulteress (Jer. 3:8-13; Ezek. 16:38; ch. 29, etc.). It is the godless that demand a sensuous manifestation of the Deity; the true children of God know him by his spiritual presence (John 14:17. Compare 1 Cor. 1:22, 23). **But the sign of the prophet Jonas,** *i. e.,* of *Jonah.* This declaration is interpreted by the following verse.

40. For as Jonah * * * was in the belly of the great fish. The account is given in Jonah, chaps. 1 and 2. The word *whale* is a mistranslation. There is nothing in the original Greek here to indicate the species of fish, and nothing in the O. T. account. Observe that Christ gives his personal sanction to the account of this miracle, which, more than any other in the O T., has been subjected to criticism and even ridicule. We must either accept the O. T. history of this miracle or believe that Jesus was a deceiver or was himself deceived. **So shall the Son of man be three days and three nights in the heart of the earth.** He, in fact, died Friday afternoon at three o'clock, and rose again on Sabbath morning, so that he was in the heart of the earth only two nights and one day and a part of two others. But Jewish reckoning accounted part of a year as a whole one in estimating royal reigns, and a part of a day as a whole one in statements of time; so that Christ's statement accords exactly with the facts as the Jews would have stated them. See for illustration Gen. 40: 13, 20; 1 Sam. 30; 12, 13; 2 Chron. 10: 5, 12. The birth of Christ is typified by the birth of Isaac and Mahershalalhashbaz, his death by that of Abel and the substitute for Isaac and the appointed sacrifices in the Temple, his resurrection by the deliverance of Isaac from death, Daniel's deliverance, and most of all by Jonah's. Observe that Jonah (2:2) speaks of his prayer as being heard "out of the belly of hell," *i. e.,* Hades (see note on Matt. 5:22). Christ unmistakably recognizes in the miraculous deliverance of Jonah a parable of his own resurrection. Luke gives it, if possible, even more clearly (chap. 11:30): *As Jonah,* not his preaching, but Jonah himself by his deliverance, *was a sign unto the Ninevites, so shall also the Son of man be,* by his resurrection from the dead, *to this generation.* Observe that the first preaching of the apostles, on and after Pentecost, consisted largely of a personal testimony to the resurrection of Jesus Christ (Acts 2: 24-36; 3:15; 4:33; 7:56, 56; 10:39, 40; 1 Cor. 15:3-8, etc.).

41. The men of Nineveh shall rise in judgment. Observe the incidental confirmation of the doctrine of a general resurrection of *both good and evil,* and of a general judgment. **A greater than Jonah is here,** *i. e.,* there is more in the presence and power of Christ and his word to produce repentance than in the preaching of Jonah. The practical application is that at the present day the argument for the truth of Christianity is stronger, and the influence to produce repentance for sin and faith in a Saviour are greater, than they ever were before; wherefore, the condemnation of those that resist is heavier. Compare with this and the succeeding verse, Matt. 10:15, and note.

42. The queen of the south. The incident referred to is related in 1 Kings 10:1-13, where she is called the Queen of Sheba, *i. e.,* probably the Sabeans, descendants of Seba. There were two, a son of Cush, whose descendants settled in Ethiopia, and a son of Joktan, whose descendants settled in Arabia. Both these countries have traditions respecting the visit of a queen to Solomon. Josephus and the rabbinical writers place the kingdom of Sheba in Ethiopia; but it appears to be the better opinion that the queen referred to came from Arabia. This accords best with her gifts (1 Kings 10:2), and is maintained by Alford, Rawlinson, Poole, and others. **From the uttermost parts of the earth.** It is estimated that she must have taken a journey of no little hazard, and of over 1,000 miles. To the ancient Jews her kingdom was on the extreme borders of the known world. **To hear the wisdom of Solomon.** Observe, not attracted by the fame of his external grandeur, but by that of his wisdom. Compare 1 Kings 10:1: "she came to prove him with hard questions." **A greater than Solomon is here.** Not merely because moral greatness is greater than temporal, but because spiritual wisdom is greater than political. Observe, too, that Jesus assumes pre-eminence above Jonah the prophet, Solomon the king, and Abraham the patriarch (comp. John 8:58).

Ch. 12:43-45. PARABLE OF THE UNCLEAN SPIRIT. TRUE AND FALSE REFORMATION. THE TRUE: GOD CASTS THE EVIL SPIRIT OUT; THE FALSE: THE EVIL SPIRIT GOES OUT; THE TRUE: GOD OCCUPIES THE SOUL;

walketh through dry places, seeking rest, and findeth none. 44 Then he saith, I will return into my house from whence I came out; and when he is come, he findeth it empty, swept, and garnished. 45 Then goeth he, and taketh with himself seven other spirits more wicked than himself, and they enter in and dwell there: and the last *state* of that man is worse than the first. Even so shall it be also unto this wicked generation. 46 While he yet talked to the people, behold, *his*

mother and his brethren[s] stood without, desiring to speak to him. 47 Then one said unto him, Behold, thy mother and thy brethren stand without, desiring to speak with thee. 48 But he answered and said unto him that told him, Who is my mother? and who are my brethren? 49 And he stretched forth his hand toward his disciples, and said, Behold my mother, and my brethren! 50 For whosoever shall do the will[t] of my Father which is in heaven, the same is my brother, and sister, and mother.

q Heb. 6 : 4 ; 10 ; 26 ; 2 Pet. 2 : 20, 22.....r rk 3 : 31, etc. ; Luke 8 : 19, etc.....s ch. 13 : 55.....t ch. 7 : 20 ; John 15 : 14 ; Gal. 5 : 6 ; Heb. 9 : 11 ; 1 John 2 : 17.

THE FALSE: IT REMAINS EMPTY.—MERELY NEGATIVE REFORMATION IS NEVER PERMANENT.

43-45. This is a parable; nothing, therefore, is to be deduced from it concerning demoniacal possessions, except perhaps the reality of such possessions. **Unclean spirit.** See note on Demoniacal Possession at close of chapter 8, p. 85. **Dry places.** Rather desert places, which the Jews believed to be the abode of evil spirits. See Isaiah 13 : 21, and 34 : 14, where satyr probably represents an imaginary demon, half man half goat. **My house.** Still his, for he has *gone*, not *been cast* out by divine power. **Empty.** Literally at leisure, idle, and so vacant. The same Greek word (σχολάζων) appears in the Septuagint in Exod. 5 : 8, 17. Idleness is always a preparation for the devil. **Generation.** (Gr. γενεά.) This word here, as often in the N. T., would be better rendered *nation*.

The lesson of this parable is twofold. Every reformation is transient unless: (*a*) The evil is cast out by the power of God (compare John 3 : 5); (*b*) is supplanted by the indwelling of God (compare John 15 : 4). The direct application is to the Jewish nation. The evil spirit of idolatry had gone out, but no spirit of true allegiance to God had taken its place; and the nation, without any true religious life, was prepared for the worse spirit which showed itself in the rejection of our Lord, the fearful excesses which accompanied the death of Jesus, and their subsequent history. The indirect application is to all reformation, which is permanent only when we overcome evil with good (Rom. 12 : 21), in church, state, or individuals. It is illustrated historically by France, out of which went the spirit of Jesuitism, only to make room for that of atheism and socialism, and individually by thousands who cast out an evil habit, but receive not the Spirit of God. Compare Heb. 6 : 4-6; 2 Pet. 2 : 20-22.

Ch. 12 : 46-50. ATTEMPT BY CHRIST'S MOTHER TO INTERRUPT HIS PREACHING. CHRIST OBEYS HIS LAW; FORSAKES MOTHER AND BRETHREN TO PREACH THE GOSPEL.—THE TRUE DISCIPLES OF CHRIST ARE THE NEAREST TO HIM IN LOVE.—CHRIST'S LOVE FOR HIS DISCIPLES IS PERSONAL, THE LOVE OF A BROTHER.—THE CONDITION OF NEARNESS TO CHRIST: DOING THE WILL OF HIS FATHER.

This incident is recorded also in Mark 3 : 31-35, and Luke 8 : 19-21. Luke places it after the parable of the sower; Mark agrees in order with Matthew. The circumstances—the crowd, the discourse delivered in the house, the enmity of the Pharisees, confirm Matthew's chronology.

46. His brethren. Presumptively his real brethren as his real mother. See note on chapter 13 : 55. **Stood without,** *i. e.*, without the house in which he was teaching (Mark 3 : 19, 20). **Desiring to speak with him.** Mark explains why: "They went out to lay hold on him; for they said, He is beside himself" (Mark 3 : 21). Their endeavor was to interrupt his preaching, and so to rescue him from the danger of a conflict with the Pharisees, which he was provoking. To the worldly-wise, spiritual enthusiasm always seems craziness. Compare Acts 26 : 24; 2 Cor. 5 : 13. **47. And one said to him, Behold,** etc. Mark says that his mother and brethren sent unto him. **48. Toward his disciples,** *i. e.*, toward the twelve. **49. For whosoever shall do the will of my Father.** Compare Matt. 7 : 21 and note, and John 14 : 23. **The same is my brother, and sister, and mother.** The personality of our relationship to Christ is elsewhere illustrated (John 10 : 3, 14; 15 : 15; Ephes. 5 : 25, 32), but nowhere more clearly. "To be the brother of Christ and the Son of God—have we ever measured the full meaning of those words?" Observe that Christ places every true disciple on an equality with his mother. For the bearing of this passage on Mariolatry, see Chrysostom, whose comments show what the early fathers would have thought of that practice and the doctrines with which it is connected. "That which she wanted to do was of superfluous vanity.; in that she wanted to show the people that she hath power and authority over her son." "How many women have prayed that they might become such mothers? What, then, is there to hinder? It is granted not to women only, but to men also, to be of this rank, or rather of one yet far higher."

His practical deduction is also worth noting: "There is only one nobleness, to do the will of God. This kind of noble birth is better than the other, and more real." Compare with Christ's example here his teaching to his disciples in such passages as Matt. 10:35-37; Luke 9:59-62; and 14:26.

Ch. 13 : 1-53. PARABLES BY THE SEA-SHORE. CHRIST A POPULAR PREACHER.—HIS AUTHORITY SANCTIONS FIELD PREACHING (V. 2).—HIS USE OF ILLUSTRATIONS: NOT TO ENTERTAIN, NOT MERELY TO INSTRUCT, BUT TO GIVE TRUTH ENTRANCE TO RELUCTANT HEARTS (V. 13).—HIS MAGAZINE OF ILLUSTRATIONS: NATURE AND COMMON LIFE.—THE SEVEN SYMBOLS OF THE KINGDOM OF GOD.—IT GROWS GRADUALLY (Mark 4 : 26-29).—ITS OBSTACLES IN THE HUMAN HEART: INDIFFERENCE, IRRESOLUTION, WORLDLINESS (VS. 18-23).—THEIR SECRET CAUSE: EVIL SEED SOWN BY SATAN (VS. 37-43).—ITS PROGRESS: FROM THE LEAST SEED TO THE LARGEST HERB (VS. 31, 32).—THE METHOD OF ITS GROWTH: BY PERMEATION, BY AGITATION, SECRETLY, SILENTLY, SURELY (V. 33).—ITS VALUE AND ITS COST: ALL THAT A MAN HATH (VS. 44-46).—ITS FINAL PERFECTION: COMPLETE PURIFICATION, AFTER DEATH, IN THE DAY OF JUDGMENT (VS. 47-50).—SEE, FURTHER, THOUGHTS ON EACH PARABLE.

PRELIMINARY NOTE.—Of these parables we have three reports. See Mark 4:1-34 and Luke 8:4-15. Matthew's report is the fullest; several of the parables are given only by him, but Mark gives one omitted by the others (Mark 4:26-29). Luke gives only the parable of the Sower.

1. *Were these seven parables uttered at one time?* It is tolerably evident that they did not constitute one discourse, for it is incredible that Christ should have interrupted such a discourse to interpret the parables to the twelve, and then resumed it again (ver. 10, 36). It is clear that they were delivered at one period in his ministry, probably on the same day (ver. 53). They are all upon the same theme—the kingdom of God; they are therefore to be studied together, however they may have been uttered.

2. *What is a parable?* The original Greek word (παραβολή) signifies, literally, *placing side by side*—hence a comparison. The parable always teaches by comparing a spiritual truth with some type or symbol, in nature or human experience. It differs from a *fable*, which teaches only maxims of a prudential morality, and which, in its teaching, violates the truth of nature—representing the brute and inanimate world as reasoning, reflecting, speaking. This the parable never does, for it always compares *truth* with *truth* or with *realistic fiction*—never with an impossible and unnatural narrative. Judges 9:7-16 is, I believe, the only instance of a fable in the Scriptures. It differs from a *myth*, which represents fiction as fact, and in such guise that it is assumed to be a fact by the auditor, who often sees no moral meaning underneath it. Thus the myth of William Tell shooting the apple from his son's head was long received as history, and its original signification is now entirely lost. This can never be true of a parable. It differs from an *allegory*, which upon its face declares itself to be a symbol of spiritual truth, and conveys the truth in the story, not by an application or interpretation of it; whereas the office of a parable is to veil the truth until it has been admitted into the mind reluctant to receive it. John 15:1-8, "I am the Vine," is an allegory; Luke 13:6-9, "A certain man had a fig-tree," is a parable. It differs from a *proverb* in that it elaborates dramatically what proverbs, or rather certain kinds of proverbs, state concisely. Thus, "If the blind lead the blind, both shall fall into the ditch," could be readily converted into a proverb. So, again, Psalm 103:13, "Like as a father pitieth his children, so the Lord pitieth them that fear him," is a proverbial utterance which the Parable of the Prodigal Son embodies in a dramatic form. A parable, then, is *a fictitious narrative, true to nature, yet undeceptive, veiling a spiritual truth, under a symbol, for the purpose of conveying it to minds reluctant or indifferent*. It differs from the proverb in being a *narrative*, from the fable in being *true to nature*, from the myth in being *undeceptive*, from the allegory in that it *veils the spiritual truth*.

3. *Why did Christ speak in parables?* He answers the question in this chapter (ver. 11-15); and his language in Mark is still more definite: "That (Greek ἵνα) seeing they may see and not perceive; and hearing they may hear and not understand" (Mark 4:12). This answer is interpreted by the nature of the parable and its general object, viz., to veil the truth for the purpose of inculcating it. Christ did not use the parable because (a) he would have hazarded his life if he had openly taught the truth (*Barnes*); for when did he refuse to hazard his life for the sake of teaching the truth? and was it not the plainness of his final teaching which led to his crucifixion? Nor (b) to compel his auditors to give closer attention if they would get the benefit of his teaching (*Kuinoel, Bloomfield, Andrews*); for God's avowed and unmistakable design is to afford in Christ a revelation of truth for the plain and the simple (Isa. 35:8; compare Psalm 19:7; 119:130). Nor (c) did he veil the truth as a punishment for the sins of the people in rejecting him (*Scott, Doddridge*); for as yet they had not rejected him, but had received him with enthusiasm, even now crowded him into a boat for his pulpit, later sought by force to make him king (John 6:15). Nor is it rational to suppose that he would teach the truth blindly as a punishment for their rejection of him; rather he would cease to teach; and after their rejection of him at Capernaum this was in fact his course (compare John 6:65 with Matt. 15:21). Nor (d) to make his meaning clear to

174　　　　　　　　　　　　　MATTHEW.　　　　　　　　　[Ch. XIII.

CHAPTER XIII.

1 THE same day went Jesus out of the house, and sat by the sea-side.
2 And great multitudes were gathered together unto him, so that he went into a ship,ᵃ and sat; and the whole multitude stood on the shore.
3 And he spake many things unto them in parables, saying, Behold,ᵇ a sower went forth to sow:
4 And when he sowed, some *seeds* fell by the way-side, and the fowls came and devoured them up:
5 Some fell upon stony places, where they had not much earth; and forthwith they sprung up, because they had no deepness of earth:

a Luke 5:3....b Mark 4:2; Luke 8:5, etc.

---

common understandings, as an orator commonly uses tropes and figures, for this is directly inconsistent with Christ's own declaration, "That seeing they may see and not perceive," and equally so with the fact that even his own disciples had to come to him for an interpretation of his parables (ver. 10, 36). His object was so to veil the truth that it might be received by those who, *if they saw*, would not perceive, and, *if they heard*, would not understand, lest they should be converted; *i. e.*, who were *determined* not to receive the truth, since its acceptance would have required repentance and a change of life. His object is illustrated strikingly in other passages where by veiling he compelled the Pharisees to condemn themselves. See Matt. 21:28-45; Luke 10:29-37. It is further illustrated by a consideration of—

4. *The object of the parables in this chapter.* Up to this time Christ's preaching had been chiefly confined to a simple proclamation, The kingdom of heaven is at hand (Matt. 4:17; 10:7). The Sermon on the Mount afforded some interpretation of the principles of that kingdom, but primarily to his own disciples, and chiefly in contrast with the Mosaic law and the Pharisaic system. See Preliminary Note and Analysis there, pp. 45, 46. In these parables Christ discloses those features respecting his kingdom which were surest to encounter prejudice and opposition; its growth depends on its acceptance by its subjects (verses 19-23); it grows up with the kingdom of evil, not separated from it by natural or geographical boundaries (verses 27-29); it is a gradual growth, does not immediately appear (Mark 4: 26-29); it is obtained only through a process of conflict (verse 33), and by self-sacrifice (vers. 44-46). These truths were in this exposition received without opposition because but half understood; later, when distinctly declared, they were vehemently rejected. Compare for illustration the declaration here (verse 33), "The field is the world" (Gr. ὁ κόσμος) with the reception of the same truth when more plainly declared by Christ (Matt. 21: 45-46), and by Paul (Acts 22:21, 22).

5. *Time, place, and circumstances of the utterance of these parables.* The time is uncertain. It was toward the latter part of Christ's Galilean ministry. This is evident from the order of the three evangelists, and from the facts that the throng had now so increased that Christ sought refuge from it in a boat, and that now first he began to interpret the nature of his kingdom, and to do so in parables. It was certainly subsequent to the developed hostility of the Pharisees (chap. 12), and prior to the feeding of the 5,000 (chap. 14), which was followed by the sermon in the synagogue at Capernaum (John, ch. 6), and Christ's withdrawal from Galilee (Matt. 15:21), and the close of his ministry there. The place is also uncertain. It was by the sea (ver. 1), *i. e.*, of Galilee, on the western shore (see Mark 4:35, and note). The common life of the place affords the imagery of these parables. The fertile plain of Gennesaret (see note on Matt. 14:34), with its thorn bushes and its underlying and occasionally out-cropping basaltic rocks in the midst of the fields of grain, suggests the stories of the Sower and the Tares. The commerce from the East to the Mediterranean, the remains of which in an occasional caravan are still seen in the vicinity of the lake, the parable of the Merchantman; the fishermen at work along the sea-shore, as on the day when Christ called four of his disciples here (Luke 5:1-11), the parable of the Drag net. It is worthy of note that the location of many of Christ's parables can be measurably determined by their adaptation to special localities or local customs. Thus the parable of the Good Samaritan (Luke 10:29-37); of the Vineyard (Luke 13:1-9), of the Good Shepherd (John 10:1-14), and probably of the Pharisee and the Publican (Luke 18:9-14), all belong to Judea, as that of the Sheep lost in the Wilderness (Luke 15:4-7) to Perea, that of the Ten pounds (Luke 19:12) to Jericho, where Archelaus, whose history suggested it, had a palace, and those here given to the region about the Sea of Galilee. See notes on above parables, and on John 7:37 and 8:12.

1. **The same day.** The Greek word (ἡμέρα), here translated *day*, is sometimes used loosely as equal to time or nearly so, and is so translated in Acts 8:1 (compare John 8:56; Acts 2:20). Here it may indicate nothing more than, At this period in Christ's ministry. Nearly all the chronological notes in the Evangelists are indefinite. The **house**, apparently where the previous discourse had been delivered (ch. 12:46, and note). The house could no longer hold his audience. **Sea-side.** The Sea of Galilee. See notes on Matt. 4:18.

2. **Ship,** *i. e.*, fisherman's boat; perhaps his own. See Mark 3:9. **Sat.** The usual attitude of the Jewish doctors in teaching. Compare Matt.

CH. XIII.] MATTHEW. 175

6 And when the sun was up, they were scorched; and because they had no root, they withered away;
7 And some fell among thorns; and the thorns sprung up, and choked them:
8 But other fell into good ground, and brought forth fruit, some an hundredfold, some sixtyfold, some thirtyfold.
9 Who* hath ears to hear, let him hear.

10 And the disciples came, and said unto him, Why speakest thou unto them in parables?
11 He answered and said unto them, Because it is given unto you to* know the mysteries of the kingdom of heaven, but to them it is not given.
12 For⁷ whosoever hath, to him shall be given, and he shall have more abundance; but whosoever hath not, from him shall be taken away, even that he hath.

w ch. 11 : 15. ...x ch. 11 : 25; Mark 4 : 11; 1 Cor. 2 : 10, 14; Eph. 1 : 9, 18; 3 : 9; Col. 1 : 26, 27; 1 John 2 : 27.... y ch. 25 : 29; Luke 19 : 26.

5 : 1, and Luke 4 : 20. Observe that we have the highest authority for street and field preaching. Observe, too, how utterly incongruous such an informal service with the idea that any kind of ritualism is an essential accompaniment of religious instruction.

3. Many things. At least one parable not recorded by Matthew. See Mark 4 : 26–29. In parables. See above, Preliminary Note, § 2.

3-9. PARABLE OF THE SOWER. See interpretation below. (Mark 4 : 2–9; Luke 8 : 4–8.) The seed-time in Palestine is from 1st October to 1st November. But Thomson's *Land and Book*, i., 113, implies that sowing is done in spring. It is always done by hand; the ground is first scratched with a plough, which runs about four inches deep; the seed is sometimes covered with a harrow, sometimes trodden in by the feet of animals; the fields are not fenced or hedged; the pathways run directly through them; clumps of thorns are interspersed with the grain; the farmers, who live in villages to guard against robbers, *go forth* to do their sowing. Stanley (*Sinai and Palestine*, ch. xiii., p. 418) gives a graphic description of Gennesaret as he saw it, the probable scene of this parable. "There was the undulating cornfield descending to the water's edge. There was the trodden pathway running through the midst of it, with no fence or hedge to prevent the seed from falling here and there on either side of it, or upon it; itself hard with constant tramp of horse, mule, and human feet. There was the 'good' rich soil, which distinguishes the whole of that plain and its neighborhood from the bare hills, elsewhere descending into the lake, and which, where there is no interruption, produces one vast mass of corn. There was the rocky ground of the hillside protruding here and there through the corn-fields, as elsewhere through the grassy slopes. There were the large bushes of thorn—the 'Nabk,' that kind of which tradition says that the Crown of Thorns was woven—springing up, like the fruit-trees of the more inland parts, in the very midst of the waving wheat."

Way-side. Road or pathway. **Stony places** (Gr. πετρώδης). Rather, *rock-like, i. e.* places where the underlying rock came close to the surface, having only a thin covering of soil. **Thorns.** There are a variety of thorny weeds common to Palestine. Smith's *Biblical Dictionary* describes five varieties. There is nothing in the original word here (ἄκανθα) to determine whether any particular species was intended. **A hundredfold * * * thirtyfold.** Dr. Thomson (*Land and Book*, i., 117) says that thirty-three per cent. is now regarded a good crop; but both land and laborers have deteriorated.

10-17. CHRIST'S REASON FOR TEACHING IN PARABLES.

For general interpretation of this and the parallel passage in Mark 4 : 10–12 and Luke 8 : 9, 10, see Preliminary Note above, § 3.

10. And the disciples. Not merely the twelve, but others with them (Mark 4 : 10). **Came unto him.** "When he was alone" (Mark), and therefore not, as Alford, during a pause in the discourse, but subsequent to it. Perhaps Matthew has interpolated the account of the interview here in order to combine the interpretation with the parable. **Unto them.** "To them that are without" (Mark), *i. e.*, to the multitude. **In parables.** Parables were a common method of instruction in vogue among the scribes. The rabbinical books abound with them. There is no sufficient reason for supposing that the rabbis borrowed this method from Christ; it is more probable that he adopted the popular mode of his day, but gave new character to it. *Trench on the Parables* (Introd., § 4) gives some illustration of these Jewish parables. What surprised the disciples was not parabolic teaching, but its adoption, now for the first time, by our Lord.

11. Because it is given. Observe that the language here and in the following verse is of grace as a *gift*. Compare Rom. 6 : 23; Ephes. 2 : 8. **Unto you.** To whom? To those that were "about him with the twelve," who came to him "and asked him of the parable" (Mark 4 : 10), *i. e.*, to those who sought to know the truth. There is no selection by Christ of a few for special instruction. He gives it *to all those that seek it*. Compare Isa. 55 : 1; Rev. 22 : 17. **To know the mysteries.** Scripture truth is always a mystery to the unspiritual (1 Cor. 2 : 7–14). It can only be hinted at by parallels drawn from nature or common experience, *e. g.*, the Saviour's care by the Shepherd's care, God's love by the love of an earthly father.

12. For whosoever hath, etc. See same aphorism with a different application in ch. 25 : 29. Here it is: If one possess some spiritual knowl-

13 Therefore speak I to them in parables: because they seeing, see not; and hearing, they hear not, neither do they understand.
14 And in them is fulfilled the prophecy of Esaias, which saith, By hearing ye shall hear, and shall not understand; and seeing ye shall see, and shall not perceive:
15 For this people's heart is waxed gross, and their ears are dull of hearing, and their eyes they have closed; lest at any time they should see with their eyes, and hear with their ears, and should understand with their heart, and should be converted, and I should heal them.
16 But blessed are your eyes, for they see: and your ears, for they hear.
17 For verily I say unto you, That many prophets and righteous men have desired to see those things which ye see, and have not seen them; and to hear those things which ye hear, and have not heard them.
18 Hear ye therefore the parable of the sower.
19 When any one heareth the word of the kingdom, and understandeth it not, then cometh the wicked one,

---

edge and desire, these lead to more; if he has no appreciation of such spiritual truths as he can discern, he will lose even that power of spiritual discernment. The first part of this declaration is illustrated by Prov. 4:18; the second part by Rom. 1:28.

13. Therefore speak I unto them in parables. See above Preliminary Note, § 3.

14. Esaias. Isaiah 6:9, 10. Compare Isa. 44:18. Observe that in the former passage the command is, Make the heart of this people fat, etc.; here they are represented as making themselves stupid. When God leaves man to himself he makes himself gross, dull, spiritually dead. **Hearing * * * shall not understand,** i. e., with the heart (ver. 15). **Seeing * * * shall not perceive,** i. e., though they see the truth intellectually they shall not appreciate it spiritually; they see it as the horse sees the same prospect with his rider, without appreciation.

15. Waxed gross; literally, fat. The growth of a fatty tissue about the heart is a common result of self-indulgence and luxurious living, and dulls and deadens the whole system. Here the physical disease is a type of the spiritual. **Their ears are dull of hearing.** Literally, with their ears they hear heavily, i. e., they are not sensitive to the truth. **Their eyes they have closed.** The spiritual ignorance and obtuseness which Christ condemns is willful, deliberate, resolute. Compare Rom. 1:22-32, and the account in Matt. 12:24 of the Pharisees, who, seeing the miracle, would not perceive in Christ the power of God. Compare Matt. 11:16-19. This is made yet clearer by the clause which follows: **Lest at any time they should perceive**—not see; the Greek word here is (ἴδω) the same translated perceive in ver. 14. It differs from (εἶδον) see; that conveys the idea of a mere external sight, but this of an interior perception, here a spiritual perception. For its signification see John 1:18, "No man hath seen God at any time," i. e., understood his nature; John 8:38, "I speak that which I have seen with my Father, and ye do that which ye have seen of your father," i. e., we each speak out of the treasure of our own personal experience; Acts 8:23, "I perceive that thou art in the gall of bitterness," i. e., I see through the fair seeming, and recognize your spiritual death. **And should be converted, and I should heal them.** Mark (4:12) indicates the kind of healing: "Lest their sins should be forgiven them" (Mark 4:12). The reason why men shut their eyes to the truth is lest they should be led to repentance and reformation. Compare 2 Cor. 4:3, 4. Observe, too, that the fault of remaining unforgiven is never because forgiveness is wanting, but always because repentance and reformation are refused. Even the Pharisees might have been converted by receiving the truth which Christ inculcated and following it.

16, 17. Observe the connection between the O. T. and N. T., that the latter is not the abrogation, but the fulfillment of the former (Matt. 5:17, and note), and that the O. T. saints lived in faith of Christ, represented more or less distinctly in the promises and types of the old dispensation. Compare Heb. 11:39, and see for illustration of the longing here referred to, 2 Sam. 23:5; Job 19:23, 27; Luke 2:29, 32. For the reason why the eyes of the true disciples see and their hearts understand, see Psalm 119:110; Prov 24:35.

18-23. Interpretation of the Parable of the Sower.

18. Hear ye, i. e., with spiritual discernment (compare verses 15 and 16 above). Luke commences the explanation by the statement, The seed is the word of God (Luke 8:11). The "word of God" sometimes stands for the written or spoken word (Mark 7:13; Luke 5:1), and sometimes for Christ himself (John 1:1, and notes there). But these are not incongruous representations; the written word has life only because Christ is in it; Christ makes it a seed. "Christ is the live seed, and the Bible the husk that holds it."—(Arnot.) Christ is also the Sower in this parable as in the following one (verse 37), and the only sower; all good seed is sown by him; apostles, prophets, ministers, teachers, and parents sow only as Christ is in them sowing the seed, as the Father was in Him (John 14:10; 2 Cor. 5:20; compare Matt. 19:40). There is nothing inconsistent in the double character thus attributed to him, for he sows himself (Luke 4:16-22).

19. Every one hearing the word of the kingdom, i. e., the word or message concern-

Ch. XIII.]   MATTHEW.   177

and catcheth away that which was sown in his heart. This is he which received seed by the way side.
20 But he that received the seed into stony places, the same is he that heareth the word, and anon with joy^k receiveth it;
21 Yet hath he not root in himself, but dureth for a while; for when tribulation or persecution ariseth because of the word, by and by he is offended.¹
22 He also that received seed among the thorns, is he that heareth the word; and the careⁱ of this world and the deceitfulness of riches* choke the word, and he becometh unfruitful.

k Is. 53 : 2 ; Eze. 33 : 31, 32 ; John 5 : 35 ; Gal. 4 : 15 . . . l John 6 : 66 . . . j Luke 14 : 16-24 . . . k Mark 10 : 22 ; 1 Tim. 6 : 9 ; 2 Tim. 4 : 10.

ing the kingdom of God, whether spoken, as by Christ and his apostles, or written, as in the N. T and in books of interpretation and of spiritual application. **And understanding it not.** The original (συνίημι) signifies literally to put together, and so affords the true idea of spiritual understanding, which consists in putting the truth with the life, *i. e.*, applying it to the life. This the teacher cannot do; every hearer must do it for himself. Christ signifies not a failure to comprehend the truth intellectually, but to receive and apply it spiritually. For illustration of non-understanding of the truth see James 1: 23, 24. Compare 1 Cor. 2 : 6-8, 14 ; 2 Cor. 3 : 14, 15 ; how to come to an understanding is told in verse 16 of same chapter. The reason why it is not understood is indicated here in verse 4. The heart is a road made hard by the traffic of the world. The seed cannot penetrate. **Then cometh the wicked one.** Luke says (8:12) the devil. Observe that in the parable it is the fowls of the air which carry away the seed, and that in the application Christ imputes those wandering thoughts, which do the work of truth-robbers, to the evil one whose agents and instruments they are. **And catcheth away.** The same verb (ἁρπάζω) is rendered in John 10 : 12 *catcheth*, in same chapter, ver. 28, 29, *pluck*, in Acts 23 : 10, *take by force.* The devil is a robber, and is to be resisted as a robber. **That sown in his heart.** A transient impression on the affections appears to be recognized even in this class of hearers. **This is he sown by the wayside.** Not, as in our English version, *He that received seed by the way-side.* It is implied here that the seed and the product are identical, and this is more clearly stated in Luke (8:14), *That which fell among thorns are they who * * * are choked with cares, etc.* The "word" is not a mere intellectual proposition; it includes faith and love in the teacher, who thus becomes the germ of faith and love in the taught. As the seed reproduces itself in the grain, so the living truth, the truth that springs from the heart, reproduces itself in the heart; and thus as Christ is *the Word* of God, so every Christian is to be *a* word of God, an embodiment of the truth which he has received (see 2 Cor. 3 : 2).

20. But that which is sown upon the rock; not *upon stony places*, but in a soil which forms a thin covering of a ledge. The hardness of the second hearer is greater but less apparent than that of the first. **Is he that heareth the word, and straitway with joy receiveth it.** The joy that is one of the fruits of the spirit (Gal. 5 : 22) rejoices alway (Phil. 4 : 4). The transient glow of quick emotion is often the sign of a shallow nature, not of deep feeling.

21. Yet he hath no root in himself. The root gives the plant both life and stability. The hearer now described depends for both on others, not on sources within himself. Compare for analogous use of this metaphor Jer. 17 : 8 ; Hosea 9 : 16 ; Eph. 3 : 17 ; Col. 2 : 7. **But is for the time** (πρόσκαιρός ἐστιν). Not merely "*dureth for a while*," but *is*, by the nature of his hold upon the truth, *only for the occasion which begot his interest.* **When tribulation or persecution ariseth through the word.** This answers to the *when the sun was up* of the parable (verse 6). Observe that, as the sun which sustains the healthy plant withers the weak and ill-rooted, so tribulation strengthens real grace, and destroys the counterfeit. Observe, too, that the withering is not because of the sun, but "*because they had no root.*" The professed disciple never fails because of his circumstances, but always because *the root is not in him.* **Straitway he is offended,** *i. e.*, caused to fall into sin. See note on Matt. 5 : 29. Luke says "fall away." Compare 1 Tim. 4 : 1, and Heb. 3 : 12. where the Greek verb (ἀφίστημι) rendered *depart*, is the same as that in Luke 8 : 13 rendered "*fall away.*" In *Pilgrim's Progress*, Obstinate received the seed by the way-side, Pliable on stony ground.

22. He that received * * * is he that heareth, etc. See above on verse 19. **The care of the world and the deceitfulness of riches.** Observe the double aspect in which life presents its temptations—cares, anxieties, pressures to the poor, the deceitfulness of riches to the rich. It alternately threatens and cajoles. Compare Prov. 30 : 8, 9. Mark affords a hint of the secret cause of the temptation in both : *The lusts of other things.* Observe, too, Luke's language: Are choked with cares and riches and pleasures of this life. "Marvel not at his calling luxury *thorns.* For it pricks sharper than any thorn, and wastes the soul worse than care, and causes more grievous pain both to body and soul."—(*Chrysostom.*) **Choke the word.** Doubly—both by drawing from the root its moisture, the thoughts and attention from spiri-

23 But he that received seed into the good ground, is he that heareth the word, and understandeth *it;* which also beareth fruit,¹ and bringeth forth, some an hundredfold, some sixty, some thirty.

1 John 15 : 5.

tual things to worldly cares, and by excluding from the stalk the sun—shutting out from the soul the rays of divine grace. The church at Laodicea was thus choked with thorns (Rev. 3 : 17). **Becometh unfruitful.** Luke says, *Bring no fruit to perfection.* In the care-filled heart, as in the weedy soil, there may be some fruit, but it is both small in quantity and immature. Observe, the difficulty here is not merely with the soil, but with subsequent lack of cultivation. In spiritual as in earthly husbandry the reception of the seed must be followed by persistent and careful labor to make it fruitful. In both Nicodemus and Judas Iscariot there were weeds; one rooted them out, the other suffered them to grow. Observe, too, that the cares which choke, like the seeds of thorns, are unrecognized, till they have grown; and note Dr. Arnot's remark: "The thorns are at home, the wheat is an exotic; the thorns are robust and can hold their own, the wheat is delicate and needs a protector."

23. But that which is sown upon good ground is he that heareth the word and understandeth it. Rather, *Personally applies it* (Gr. συνιων). See above on verse 19. The interpretation is fuller in Luke : *which in an honest and good heart having heard the word.* Observe that Christ recognizes a measure of goodness in the heart before the word is received; and observe, also, that the goodness recognized consists not in any moral and spiritual life, but in a readiness to receive moral and spiritual life. "No heart can be said to be absolutely a good soil ; yet comparatively it may be affirmed of some that their hearts are a soil fitter for receiving the seed of everlasting life than those of others." (*Trench.*) For illustration of good heart-soil, see Acts 17 : 11. **Which also beareth fruit.** The three conditions of useful hearing are indicated in this verse ; *he that heareth the word*, with attention ; *and understandeth it*, by personal application ; *who also beareth fruit*, by actual obedience. Compare Matt. 7 : 17 ; James 1 : 23, 24. **Some an hundredfold, some sixty, some thirty.** The usefulness of all Christians is not alike ; but all are alike dependent on the Sower for the seed of truth and life, which can alone bear fruit.

LESSONS OF THE PARABLE OF THE SOWER. Luke indicates Christ's object in this parable in the conclusion, *Take heed, therefore, how ye hear* (Luke 8 : 18). Its general lessons are as follows : All spiritual life depends on a divine seed sown in the heart by the Divine Sower (1 Pet. 1 : 23). He sows on all hearts alike ; the life of the seed depends on, *first*, receiving it ; *second*, rooting it ; *third*, cultivating it. The unfruitful hearers described are of three classes : The first hear, but heed nothing ; the second heed, but resolve nothing ; the third resolve, but persist not. The first hear, but without really apprehending the truth ; the second apprehend, but only for a transient emotional enjoyment—the truth gets no hold, and produces no real moral convictions or changed life ; the third hear, apprehend, and begin a new life, but suffer it to be choked by the world. The first receive a hindrance at the outset ; the second after the seed has germinated ; the third after it is well grown. In the first case the seed does not spring at all ; in the second it springs, but dies before it grows up ; in the third it grows up, but does not ripen. The first have no life ; the second have life, but only on the surface ; the third have life, but it is hindered and made unfruitful by the world. The first hearers are illustrated by the Pharisees, who refused to receive the word ; the second by the Galileans, who heard with joy, but departed from Christ when he told them of his cross (John 6 : 66) ; the third by the heathen, who suffered Christianity to be corrupted and choked by their heathen habits and lives. Gallio (Acts 18 : 17) exemplifies the first, the rich young ruler (Matt. 19 : 22) the second, Judas Iscariot the third. The first danger described is that of careless hearing ; its cause is a heart made hard by worldliness, and inattentive by wandering thoughts ; to guard against it, keep the heart tender and the attention fixed. The second danger is that of mistaking emotion for principle—glad reception of the truth for resolute practice of it ; its cause is an underlying selfishness of life ; to guard against it, count the cost of following Christ (Luke 14 : 25–33 ; 2 Tim. 2 : 3, 4). The third danger is worldliness, whether cares and anxieties, or pleasures and luxuries ; its cause is a divided heart and a divided service (Matt. 6 : 24) ; to guard against it, seek first the kingdom of God and his righteousness, and watch and pray against the first appearance of worldly-mindedness. The first danger is passed when the truth is really received in the heart ; the second, when the good resolution has been tried by actual tribulation ; the third, never this side heaven. The first belongs peculiarly to childhood, the second to youth, the third to maturity. Most Christians in their experience illustrate each class. They are all at first utterly unreceptive of the word of God, because the heart is hardened by the world ;

24 Another^m parable put he forth unto them, saying, The kingdom of heaven is likened unto a man which sowed good^o seed in his field:

25 But while men slept, his enemy came and sowed tares among the wheat, and went his way.

26 But when the blade was sprung up, and brought forth fruit, then appeared the tares also.

27 So the servants of the householder came and said unto him, Sir, didst not thou sow good seed in thy field? from whence then hath it tares?

28 He said unto them, An enemy hath done this. The servants said unto him, Wilt thou then that we go and gather them up?

29 But he said, Nay; lest while ye gather up the tares, ye root up also the wheat with them.

30 Let both grow together until the harvest; and in the time of harvest^o I will say to the reapers, Gather ye together first the tares, and bind them in bundles to^p burn them: but gather the wheat^q into my barn.

31 Another parable put he forth unto them, saying, The kingdom of heaven is like to a^r grain of mustard seed, which a man took, and sowed in his field:

32 Which indeed is the least of all seeds, but when it is grown, it is the greatest among herbs, and becometh a tree,^s so that the birds of the air come and lodge in the branches thereof.

m Isa. 28:10, 13....o 1 Pet. 1:23....o 1 Tim. 5:24....p Mal. 4:1....q Luke 3:17....r Mark 4:30....s Eze. 17:23.

next they are awakened and rejoice in the truth, but do not take hold of it with practical resolution to realize it in their life; then they begin the work of carrying it into life, and find it continually choked with cares and ambitions, which must be weeded out; finally it brings forth fruit. Thus the progress of the truth is from the first to the second, from the second to the third, from the third to the last; there is more hope for the second than for the first, more hope for the third than the second; but if the second gets no root, the condemnation is greater than if he had never received the seed, and if the third goes at last to thorns, his condemnation is greater than if the seed had never taken root.

24-30. PARABLE OF THE TARES.—Peculiar to Matthew. For interpretation see verses 37-43, and notes.

24. **The kingdom of heaven is likened unto a man which sowed.** Not merely to the man, which represents Christ (verse 37), nor merely to the sowing; but the progress of the kingdom and the obstacles which it encounters are illustrated by the experience of a farmer beset by an enemy who sows tares in his field. Neither one of these parables illustrate Christ's kingdom in its entirety; each illustrates a certain phase or aspect of it.

25. **While men slept.** Not while *the man* slept, there is no intimation of any withdrawal of Christ, or any cessation of his personal activity; nor while *the men* slept, there is no intimation of negligence on the part of his servants; but simply while *men slept*, i. e., at night. For similar use of this phraseology see Mark 4:27. It is nevertheless true that, in the moral realm, the devil sows evil seed while good men are spiritually asleep, and at night, i. e., secretly, and under cover; for all his works are works of darkness.

Tares. A weed probably identical with the English darnel, and in character resembling the American chess or cheat. It grows frequently with the wheat, so nearly resembles it as to be practically indistinguishable until the grain is headed out, is hence called bastard wheat, is believed by the Eastern farmers to be merely a degenerate wheat or barley, produced from the seed of wheat or barley by an inauspicious season, especially by rain, and this opinion is sanctioned by some ancient writers and even by some biblical scholars. It is a mistake, but one not unnatural. For sometimes the wheat will be drowned out with the rain, and the field will grow up to tares; its seeds are light, they are carried by insects and birds and on the winds; and the rain which destroys the wheat, is favorable to the tares. So the very air is full of the seeds of evil, always ready to spring up in hearts whose culture has seemingly all been Christian. The taste of the tares is bitter, its effect to nauseate; when mixed with wheat in bread it produces sickness, and sometimes, if eaten in considerable quantities, death. It is said to be the only poisonous grass, a fitting symbol of the fruit of the devil's sowing. When intermixed with wheat the farmer makes no attempt to weed it out, both from the difficulty of distinguishing it, and from the practical impossibility of separating it from the wheat with which its roots are often intermixed. They are therefore left to grow together till the harvest. Cases of malicious sowing of the tares or darnel by an enemy are not infrequent. Roberts (*Oriental Illustrations*) describes this as common in India; Trench narrates a similar injury practised on an incoming tenant by an outgoing tenant in Ireland; and Dean Alford narrates in his commentary an instance of the same act of malice practised on himself by the sowing of charlock on a field belonging to him in England.

Went his way. It was enough to sow the evil seed. He did not need to remain and cultivate it. "He knew the soil; he knew how the seed would take root and grow. He had only to sow the seed and let it alone. So Satan knows the soil in which he sows his doctrine. He knows that in the human heart it will take deep and rapid root. It needs but little culture."—(*Barnes*.)

31, 32. PARABLE OF THE MUSTARD SEED. Mark 4:30-32; Luke 13:18-21. Dr. Robinson supposes that Christ uttered this and the next parable twice—once at this time, once at the time

33 Another parable spake he unto them: The kingdom of heaven is like unto leaven, which a woman took, and hid in three measures of meal, till the whole was leavened.

seemingly indicated by Luke. The mustard seed, of which four to six come in the pod, was used by the rabbis as a symbol to express the most diminutive quantity, and in one other instance was so used by our Lord (Luke 17 : 6); it was, in fact, the smallest of the various kinds of seed in common use in Jewish husbandry. The product is a bush which grows sometimes as tall as a horse and his rider, though its common height is less. The birds, attracted by its seeds, often settle on it in great numbers. I cannot find that they ever built their nests in it, though this is indicated by the phrase here employed, "lodge in the branches thereof" (Gr. κατασκηνοῦν), literally *pitch tent*). It is, however, a bush rather than a tree, and the phraseology in Luke, where it is called "a great tree," must be regarded as qualified by the expression here, "greatest among herbs," *i. e., garden plants.* Some writers have indeed supposed that our Lord here refers to a tree which is found in Palestine (*Salvadora persica*), the seeds of which are said to be used in Syria as a substitute for mustard, but the identification of the plant of the parable with garden plants renders that opinion improbable. See this question fully discussed in Smith's *Bible Dictionary*, art. Mustard.

INTERPRETATION.—In the preceding parables Christ has presented certain obstacles to the growth of his kingdom; in this and the following parable of the leaven he reassures his hearers of the certainty of its growth, despite small and secret beginnings, and great obstacles. O. T. symbols throw light on this parable. Daniel uses the growth of the tree to typify that of an earthly kingdom (Dan. 4 : 10-12), Ezekiel to symbolize that of the kingdom of God (Ezek. 17 : 22-24; compare Psalm 80 : 8-11). The parable is illustrated and fulfilled historically by (*a*) the *external* growth of the church from the smallest beginnings—the despised Nazarene, the unlearned Galilean fishermen, the church to which not many wise, mighty, or noble were called (1 Cor. 1 : 26)—to a great tree overspreading the whole earth; (*b*) the *internal* growth of the Church, as a system of truth and ethics, from the seed of the four Gospels, out of which all that is true Christianity, in doctrine or life, has grown; (*c*) the *spiritual* life of the *individual*, which is always a gradual growth from a small seed, the repentance bred of hunger in the prodigal becoming the tree whose fruits are the robe, the ring, the shoes, the fatted calf, the father's home and love. The law of Christian growth here set forth is exemplified in the Lutheran reformation, the Wesleyan reformation, in the rise of Puritanism, in every revival of religion. It gives hope to every Christian worker who plants but small seeds, and must leave time to develop the tree; to every Christian soul, who must expect his religious life to be *in its beginning* an instantaneous planting of the seed of grace, but *in its development* a gradual growth. Incidentally it is worthy of notice that the mustard seed is *pungent, penetrating, searching,* and must be *bruised* before it will give out its virtues, and when it is grown gives *shelter and house-room* to the birds. So the seed of truth must be pungent, penetrating, searching; so Christ, who is the seed, because he is the living and life-giving truth, must needs be bruised before he could save; so the church of Christ, as an organization, and the Christian, in his individual life, gives shade and shelter to the oppressed and the tempted (compare Zech. 3 : 6).

33. PARABLE OF THE LEAVEN. Found also in Luke 13 : 20, 21. **Leaven** among the Jews generally consisted of a lump of old dough, in a high state of fermentation, inserted in the bread preparatory to baking. Like our yeast, its object was to ferment the bread, and the process and the result was analogous to that of yeast. The **three measures of meal**, equal to one ephah, was equivalent to a little over a bushel, more nearly four pecks and a half. Some of the commentators have seen a spiritual significance in the *three* measures; *e. g.,* Olshausen, who supposes it to refer to the body, soul, and spirit, and Stier to the three sons of Noah by whom the whole earth was overspread. But neither appears to me to be natural. Three measures or an ephah was a usual quantity for baking (Gen. 18 : 6; Judges 6 : 19; 1 Sam. 1 : 24).

INTERPRETATION. Leaven, being itself corrupt, and leavening by a process of corruption, is usually in the Bible a symbol of evil (Matt. 16 : 6; 1 Cor. 5 : 6-8; Gal. 5 : 9), and, perhaps for this reason, was generally excluded from the offerings under the O. T. (Exod. 13 : 3; Lev. 2 : 11; Amos 4 : 5). Woman, too, is often employed as a symbol of an apostate church and its ministry (Prov. 9 : 13; Zech. 5 : 7-11; Rev. 17 : 3, etc). Hence, some commentators have regarded leaven here as a symbol of corruption, and the parable as illustrative rather of the opposition which the kingdom of God must encounter than of its process and progress. But this view is *unnecessary*, because (*a*) the Scripture uses the same thing to symbolize sometimes good, sometimes evil, *e. g.,* the lion as an emblem both of the devil and of Christ (1 Pet. 5 : 8; Rev. 5 : 5), the tree as an emblem of both pious and wicked men (Psalm 1 : 3; 37 : 35), the dove as an emblem of both an evil and a right simplicity (Hosea 7 : 11; Matt. 10 : 16); (*b*) leaven itself was in one instance required in a

34 All these things spake Jesus unto the multitude in parables ;* and without a parable spake he not unto them ;
35 That it might be fulfilled which was spoken by the prophet,* saying, I will open my mouth in parables ; I will utter things which have been kept* secret from the foundation of the world.

36 Then Jesus sent the multitude away, and went into the house : and his disciples came unto him, saying, Declare unto us the parable of the tares of the field.
37 He answered and said unto them, He that soweth the good seed is the Son of man :
38 The field is the world :* the good seed are the

---

t Mark 4 : 33....u Ps. 78 : 2....v Luke 10 : 24 ; Rom. 16 : 25, 26 ; Col. 1 : 26....w Rom. 10 : 18 ; Col. 1 : 6.

---

sacred offering (Lev. 23 : 18), and could not, therefore, have been always regarded as an emblem of evil ; (c) it is a natural emblem of a good, warming, pervasive influence, imparting its own savor and virtue to the lifeless lump. This view is also *indefensible*, because (a) Christ directly compares the kingdom of heaven to the operation of leaven, and it flatly contradicts his language to regard the parable as a symbol of the operation of the kingdom of Satan ; (b) he distinctly asserts that the leaven abides in the meal till *all is leavened*, which, if leaven be a symbol of corruption, would involve the idea that the Gospel is to be conquered and the influence of Satan become victorious ; (c) its connection with the preceding parables point to a further and fuller illustration of the progress of the kingdom of God. I conclude, then, that the natural and plain meaning of the parable is the true one, and that Christ means exactly what his words mean, viz., that the operations of the influence of God in the community and in the individual heart are analogous to those of leaven in the dough. Why ? Because the latter is a foreign power, not merely an awakening of life dormant in the dough ; it brings new life with it ; it is hidden in the dough ; it does its work secretly, silently, by a process of fermentation and agitation ; it is itself that which the dough is to become. The parable is historically illustrated by the progress of Christianity in the world, which proceeds from the Bread which came down from heaven and was mingled with our common humanity ; came not with observation, being unrecognized as a divine life-giving force by Jew or Gentile ; it permeates all society ; has won its way by a process of agitation, bringing first the sword, then peace (Matt. 10 : 34) ; and has proceeded from the interior outward ; and, by a process of infection or contagion of beneficent influence, is leavening all society — governments, commerce, social customs, as well as church organizations and the professed disciples of Christ. It is illustrated in the history of every Christian soul ; for Christ is hidden in the soul, and becomes the secret source of its life ; to him it gradually becomes conformed ; he is unrecognized by the world, though the sweetness and life produced by his presence is perceived ; and he gradually and silently pervades the whole being, until the whole is leavened.

Observe, too, that as each part of the dough becoming leavened acts as leaven, stimulating life in that which adjoins, so each true Christian, leavened by Christianity, operates as leaven upon his neighbor.

34, 35. Use of Parables. Without a parable spake he not to them, *i. e.*, in this discourse his entire explanation to the multitude of the kingdom of God was by parables only ; the interpretation was reserved for his own disciples.

35. That it might be fulfilled. The Greek participle here is ὅπως, not ἵνα (*hopōs* not *hina*) ; but what I have said concerning the latter in note on Matt. 13 : 17 is substantially applicable to the former. The reference here is to Psalm 78 : 2. That Psalm was written, according to the Hebrew inscription, by Asaph ; it contains no reference directly or indirectly to Christ, and it consists of an account, in poetical form, of the history of God's dealings with Israel, which are, however, a parable in this sense, that they are an ensample of his spiritual dealings with his people in all times (1 Cor. 10 : 6, 11). Only in this very general sense, in which the whole of the O. T. is prophetic of the New, can these words, and Asaph in uttering them, be regarded as prophetic of Christ and his method of instruction. **Things kept secret.** In these parables Christ was interpreting the spiritual nature of his kingdom, which was an enigma to the Jewish nation.

36-43. Interpretation of the Parable of Tares.

37. Then Jesus sent the multitude away and went into the house. The parable of the leaven appears to have ended the public discourse concerning the kingdom of God ; the subsequent parables appear to have been uttered to the disciples alone. **His disciples.** Not necessarily the twelve alone, but those who accepted him as their teacher, and wished to learn of him. Compare the language of Mark 4 : 10, which interprets that of Matt. 13 : 10, the same as that employed here. **Declare unto us,** *i. e.*, interpret to us.

37. He that soweth the good seed is the Son of man, *i. e.*, Jesus Christ. See note on Matt. 10 : 23. Observe that all sowing, whether done by prophet, apostle, preacher, teacher, or parent, is done by *Christ in him*. See note on verse 18, above.

children of the kingdom ;* but the tares are the children of the wicked one:
39 The enemy that sowed them is the devil: the harvest is the end of the world ;* and the reapers are the angels.*

40 As therefore the tares are gathered and burned in the fire ;* so shall it be in the end of this world.
41 The Son of man shall send forth his angels, and they shall gather out of his kingdom all things that offend, and* them which do iniquity ;

x 1 Pet. 1 : 23. ...y John 8 : 44 ; Acts 13 : 10 ; 1 John 3 : 8. ...a Joel 3 : 13 ; Rev. 14 : 15. ...a Rev. 14 : 15–19. ...b verse 30. ...c Luke 13 : 27.

38. The field is the world. Not the church; the word *world* (κόσμος) never represents the church in the N. T., but the whole world of humanity. See 1 John 2 : 2, where the contrast between the church and the world is drawn. Observe that the world is *his* field (verse 24, above); the whole world of humanity is the kingdom of Christ, though only a part recognizes its duty of allegiance to him; much of it is a kingdom in rebellion. Observe, too, that it is for the whole world Christ has died (John 3 : 16; 1 John 2 : 2), and that throughout the whole world the seed is to be sown (Matt. 28 : 19, 20). In the Donatist controversy, famous in ecclesiastical history, the Catholic commentators read, The field is the church, an interpretation which they endeavor to sustain by ingenious arguments, and which is, singularly, sustained by the great body of commentators since. It is, however, only an instance of the power of dogmatic prejudice to modify Scripture. The object was to prove from Scripture that the church was not to purge out by discipline all its evil, heretical, and hypocritical members. This may be indirectly implied; it is not directly asserted. At all events, the direct and unambiguous words of Christ, The field is the world, are not to be departed from either (*a*) by confounding the world and the church, for (see above,) the word *world* (κόσμος) never stands in the N. T. for the church; nor (*b*) by supposing that it is used parabolically for the church, for Christ is explaining the parable, not giving another, still less interpreting it by one more difficult to be understood; nor (*c*) by supposing that the church is commensurate with the world, for it is not, the greater part of it still lying in heathenism, like portions of a field given over to tares. The application of the parable is not, except indirectly, to discipline in the church. See this matter well discussed in *Arnot on the Parables*. And see, for general teaching of parable, note below. **The good seed are the children of the kingdom.** In the parable of the sower the seed is the word of God; but the two interpretations are not incongruous; one includes the other. See note on verse 19, above. **The tares are the children of the wicked one.** Observe here, as throughout the Scriptures, the broad line is drawn between the two classes of men; they do not, in fact as in appearance, resemble one another. One is produced from good seed, the other from evil seed; one class are the children of God, the other are the children of the devil; one belong to the kingdom of light, the other to the kingdom of darkness. Compare Matt. 12 : 30, and note; John 8 : 44; 1 Thess. 5 : 5. But the difference is not ineradicable here; the great gulf which begins on earth becomes impassable only at death (Luke 16 : 26). "We are not to suppose that the wheat can never become tares, or the tares wheat; this would be to contradict the purpose of Him who willeth not the death of a sinner, but rather that he should be converted and live; and this gracious purpose shines through the command, Let both grow together till the harvest."—(*Alford*.)

39. The enemy; who sowed the tares. Is the devil. See note on Matt. 4 : 1. Observe that here, as elsewhere, the personality of the devil is recognized by our Lord in unmistakable terms. This is no parable, but the interpretation of a parable; it is no concession to popular prejudice, for it is uttered to his own disciples alone; the devil cannot stand for the evil in the human heart, for it is contrasted therewith, the natural evil of the heart being symbolized in the parable of the sower, the direct agency of Satan in this parable of the tares. Evil and false teaching is attributed directly to his influence; of him are wicked and evil-producing men, who are the children of the wicked one, as good men are the children of the kingdom of God and seed sown by God. Observe, too, the nature of his work, fair in seeming, deadly in reality. "He at once mimics and counter-works the work of Christ."—(*Trench*.) **The harvest is the end of time.** The Greek word rendered here *world* (αἰών) signifies not the physical world, but rather the present era or cycle; the reference is not to the destruction of the world, though elsewhere it is implied that such a destruction takes place at the judgment, but to the completion of the present cycle. Observe the implication that the judgment takes place *at the end of the world*, not as Swedenborg teaches, simultaneously with the world's existence, and for each man at the end of his life. **The reapers are the angels.** These are frequently represented as accompanying the Lord in his coming at the day of judgment (Matt. 16 : 27 ; 24 : 31 ; 2 Thess. 1 : 7 ; Rev. 19 : 14).

41. Gather out of his kingdom. Observe that as the tares are represented as sown in Christ's field, so here the whole world of good and evil is represented as *his* kingdom, from which the evil is to be gathered out. See note

42 And⁴ shall cast them into a furnace of fire: there shall be wailing and gnashing of teeth. 43 Then shall the righteous shine' forth as the sun in the kingdom of their Father. Who hath ears to hear, let him hear. 44 Again, the kingdom of heaven is like unto treas-

d ch. 3 : 12 ; Rev. 19 : 20 ; 20 : 10. ... e verse 50 ; ch. 8 : 12. ... f Dan. 12 : 3 ; 1 Cor. 15 : 49.

on verse 38, above. **All things that offend,** *i. e.*, tempt to sin. Compare note on Matt. 5 : 29. **And them which do iniquity.** Compare Matt. 7 : 23, and Rev. 21 : 8 ; 22 : 15. Observe that not merely those who deliberately *do iniquity*, but also those who so carry themselves as to lead others into sin, are outcast.

40-42. Fire was employed as a punishment by the Chaldeans (Jer. 29 : 22 ; Dan. 3 : 6), and has been similarly used in later times by the Persians. By fire Antiochus persecuted the Jews (Dan. 11 : 33 ; 1 Cor. 13 : 3), as in medieval times the Romanists persecuted the Reformers. Herod the Great burned to death certain who had opposed his authority in his last days (*Wars of Jews*, i., 33, § 4). Weeds also were used among the Jews as a fuel, especially for heating their ovens; a fire was kindled inside, and subsequently removed to make room for the bread (Matt. 6 : 30). From this double use comes the employment of fire in the Bible as a metaphor of the punishment of the ungodly. It is thus employed frequently in the O. T. (2 Sam. 23 : 6, 7 ; Isaiah 5 : 24 ; 10 : 16, 17 ; Mal. 4 : 1). Here and elsewhere it is adopted by Christ for the same purpose, and assuredly with a full sense of the terrible significance which the Jewish mind would attach to the metaphor (Matt. 7 : 19 ; John 15 : 6). And it is used elsewhere in the N. T. in a similar manner (Matt. 3 : 10, 12, and note ; Heb. 6 : 8 ; 10 : 27). This fire is represented not as something external to the sinner, but as consisting of his sins, and as proceeding from himself (Isaiah 9 : 18, 19 ; 31 : 11, 12). An examination of these passages will make it clear that (*a*) fire is used in them as a symbol not of purification but of punishment; (*b*) that it represents a punishment which is a finality, and from which there is and can be no deliverance or restoration ; (*c*) that being borrowed from the most painful form of death in use among men, it stands for a terrible penalty, such as could be interpreted only by a physical symbol ; (*d*) that it is symbolical merely, and to give it a literal interpretation, and found on it a doctrine of physical torture, is wholly to miss the meaning and ignore the usage of Biblical symbolism ; (*e*) that it does not necessarily imply the literal destruction of the sinner, though the chaff, stubble, tares are utterly consumed, for in no other way could a physical symbol interpret spiritual penalty. The fire is represented as everlasting and unquenchable (Isaiah 66 : 24; Matt. 25 : 41), and it is represented as an instrument, not merely or mainly of destruction, but as one of true penalty, involving suffering, as here in the words, There shall be weeping and gnashing of teeth. The question whether immortality is denied to the impenitent, or whether they possess an immortal but suffering life, must be determined by a consideration of other passages of Scripture. The symbolism of fire throws little or no light upon that problem.

Wailing and gnashing of teeth. A symbol not only of suffering, but even more, of rage (Acts 7 : 54). Compare Matt. 8 : 12, and note.

43. Then. When the tares are removed, the obstructions to growth in holiness and godliness are removed. **Shall the righteous shine forth.** Light is a symbol of joy, of clear apprehension of truth, of a light and joy-giving example. Now, hindered and darkened by admixture with evil men, the light is not clear; then it will shine out with unobstructed glory, both *in* and *from* the saints (Rom. 8 : 18 ; Col. 3 : 3, 4. Compare Dan. 12 : 3).

LESSONS OF THE PARABLE OF THE TARES. The key-note of this parable is afforded by verse 30, "Let both grow together till the harvest." Its direct lesson is that man may not use force to purify the kingdom of God of evil elements that mingle in it ; the reason assigned is, Lest ye root up also the wheat with the tares, both (*a*) by mistaking wheat for tares, as in the middle-ages the honest but perverted zeal of the hierarchy mistook truth and piety for heresy and sin, and (*b*) by uprooting tares which patience and instruction might turn into wheat. Its direct application is to civil governments, which never have the right to punish sin for the purpose of avenging it, or of representing and carrying into effect divine justice, or of perfecting the purification of society, but only so far as is needful for the protection of society and the offender's reformation ; its indirect application is to the church, which is not to use discipline for the purpose of excluding all from its communion whom it deems unworthy, nor even all who offend and do iniquity, but only such as, by their presence and influence, are destructive of the vitality of the church. It incidentally applies to all Christian work and Christian organizations, the duty of the Christian, in church, Sabbath school, and social life, being a duty of patience and long-suffering with the children of the wicked one, not of Pharisaic withdrawal from them, or indignant excision of them from social and Christian fellowship. It interprets the ground of God's being long-suffering, who bears with the tares that he may change them to wheat

ure hid in a field; the which when a man hath found, he hideth, and for joy thereof goeth and selleth all that he hath, and buyeth that field.

45 Again, the kingdom of heaven is like unto a merchant man, seeking goodly pearls;

46 Who, when he had found one pearl of great price, went and sold all that he had, and bought it.

47 Again, the kingdom of heaven is like unto a net, that was cast into the sea, and gathered of every kind:

48 Which, when it was full, they drew to shore, and

g Prov. 2 : 4, 5....h Phil. 3 : 7, 8....i Isa. 55 : 1; Rev. 3 : 18....j Prov. 3 : 14, 15 ; 8 : 11....k ch. 22 : 10.

(Luke 13 : 6–9; Rom. 2 : 4), and is an inspiration of patience to us in our intermixture with iniquitous and ensnaring men. *Incidentally* it teaches the following lessons: All good influences come from Christ; all evil influences come from Satan. The world is Christ's kingdom, the ungodly are in revolt against their king. The difference between the children of God and of the wicked one is, *in appearance*, nothing, the tares are undistinguishable from the wheat; it is in reality radical, they spring from different seeds and different sowers; it is manifested in the fruit, the one is health-giving, the other poisonous; and in the end, one is for the granary, the other for the furnace. The intermixture of good and evil men in life is a part of God's plan; all attempts, whether by religious persecution or monastic seclusion, to interfere with it, are disastrous failures. Evil influence is propagated secretly at night; grows rankly without cultivation. Every good sowing in church, in Sabbath school, in the home circle, is followed by evil sowing, wherefore we must watch alway for tares. The certainty of a coming divine judgment; the terribleness and the finality of the divine punishment of sin. Finally, the parable is historically illustrated in (*a*) the history of the Fall; God sowed good seed, the devil dropped the seed of an evil ambition, the fruit was poison; (*b*) the history of the Jewish nation, in which God sowed good seed by the hand of Moses and the prophets, the devil tares by the influence of apostate kings and false prophets and idolatrous nations, the end was national death; (*c*) the history of the early church, in which the devil was still busy sowing tares (Acts 13 : 10; 1 Cor. 1 : 11, 12; Gal. 5 : 7, 8; 1 Tim. 4 : 1–3); (*d*) in the history of the post-apostolic church, into which the devil introduced false doctrines, ecclesiastical ambitions, heathen idolatries; (*e*) in the history of the Reformation, in which with much good seed was sown also the seed of Socinianism, Antinomianism, and modern Rationalism. The evil of attempting to uproot the tares is illustrated by the history of all religious persecution; whether of the Reformers by the hierarchy, or of the Puritans by the Church of England, or of the Baptists and Quakers by the Puritans. The practical lesson to every individual disciple is, Be patient towards all men.

44–46. Parables of Hid Treasure and the Pearl. These two parables, uttered to the disciples, not to the multitude (verse 36), go together. They represent different phases of the same truth; each helps to interpret the other. Combined, they teach the general lesson that the kingdom of heaven must be seized and appropriated by each individual for himself. "It is not merely a tree overshadowing the earth, or leaven leavening the world, but each man must have it for himself, and make it his own, by a distinct act of his own will."—(*Trench.*) Neither does God redeem the whole world of humanity by one general act of grace, but finds and purchases each soul unto himself by a special act of love. The features of the story in each case are taken from the common life in the East. Owing to war, robbers, and the absence of modern methods of investing property, such as banks, stock, bonds, etc., it was customary in the East for men to bury a part of their wealth in the ground, keeping the secret sacredly. In case of war, such burials were very frequent. A forced flight, sudden death, or other accident, would often prevent its removal. Hence the discovery of hid treasure in the East is, even at the present day, an occurrence not extraordinary. That such hiding was common in O. T. times is illustrated by Job 3 : 21; Prov. 2 : 4; Jer. 41 : 8. The pearl, too, was held in higher estimation in ancient times than at present. The merchantman and caravan were frequently seen by the sea of Galilee, which was on the highway of commerce between the far East and the Mediterranean Sea.

Interpretation. Both parables bear a double meaning: (1.) In the human race was hid a treasure, viz., the faithful and elect to be gathered out of all nations. Christ discovered it; for the joy that was set before him, endured the cross, despising the shame, and, though he was rich, for our sakes became poor, that he might purchase the field—the world—and so procure the treasure—his church hidden in it. Through the world he still goes, seeking in human souls pearls, which, by his own grace, he makes goodly, and ransoming each one, which, by the price he pays, and by its own inestimable value in the eyes of divine love, is a "pearl of great price." Thus Christ's estimate of the value of the kingdom of God, and his sacrifice of all for it, is an inspiration to us. For (2) that kingdom is a treasure hidden from the eyes of those whom the god of this world hath blinded, but which, being suddenly revealed, inspires the finder with

sat down, and gathered the good into vessels, but cast the bad away.
49 So shall it be at the end of the world: the angels shall come forth, and sever the wicked from among the just;
50 And shall cast them into the furnace of fire: there shall be wailing and gnashing of teeth.
51 Jesus saith unto them, Have ye understood all these things? They say unto him, Yea, Lord.

1 ch. 25 : 32. ... m verse 42.

joy; it is a pearl of great price, whether measured by what its cost is to Christ, or by its value to the possessor; and this treasure, this pearl, is worth all else, is possessed only by him who forsaketh all to become Christ's disciple (Luke 14 : 33). (3.) The points of contrast in the parables are not accidental. The two represent different types of experience; the first, a man who, without earnest seeking, finds, as it were by accident, the truth and life that is in Christ; the second, the seeker after truth in various quarters (goodly pearls in many markets), who finds in Christ the one thing needful (the one pearl of great price), which costs all that he hath. Nathaniel and the Samaritan woman illustrate the first, Paul and the Ethopian eunuch (Acts 8 : 27) the second. (4.) Other points in the parable have been noted, c. g., The treasure hid in the field is compared to the truth hid in the external church (Trench, Alford), or in the Holy Scriptures (Jerome, Augustine); the joy that inspires the finder is the inspiration which enables him to sell all that he hath, and is a hint that Christian self-sacrifice is gainful and should be joyful; his hiding the treasure is thought to typify the young Christian's tremulous anxiety lest he lose the new-found life, or possibly his first inclination at concealment till he has measured the reality and value of his experience. Unnecessary difficulty has been occasioned by doubts concerning the morality of the course of the finder in the first parable. But Christ no more commends his course by using it, as an illustration, than he commends the merchant who devotes his life to getting goodly pearls, or the unjust judge (Luke 18 : 1-7), to whom he compares God. No difficulty need be experienced by the fact that the obtaining of the kingdom of God is compared to a purchase. This is a common symbol in the Scripture (Prov. 23 : 23; Matt. 25 : 9, 10; Rev. 3 : 18), and is interpreted by such declarations as the exhortation of Isaiah to "buy without money and without price" (Isaiah 55 : 1, 2), and such experiences as those of Paul, who counted all things but loss for the excellency of the knowledge of Christ Jesus (Phil. 3 : 7, 8).

47-50. Parable of the Drag-net. The drag-net, or seine (Gr. σαγήνη), is one of small depth but great length; Trench says that some of these seines on the coast of Cornwall are half a mile long. One side is kept close to the bottom by weights, the other is buoyed up by corks or bladders; thus, when spread, it stands in the water like a wall. Having been spread, the fishermen draw it at both ends to the land, enclosing in it every fish not small enough to escape through its meshes. Then the separation takes place, and the useless fish are thrown away, while the good are kept for the market.

Interpretation. The all but universal interpretation of the commentators is as follows: The net is the church, the fishermen are the ministry, the gathering out of the sea is the gathering into the visible church of both good and evil, the landing of the fish and the selection of the good is the day of judgment. Thus this parable is only a repetition, in a different form, of the parable of the tares. From this interpretation I dissent, because (a) it makes the central feature of the parable the present work of the ministry, while Christ's own interpretation makes the fishing a mere incident, the separation of the fish the central feature; (b) it represents the fishermen as the ministry, while Christ declares that they represent the angels; (c) it represents the church as gathering, not *out of* the world by moral lines, but *a part of* the world by mere geographical lines, and the contents of the church (the net) in nowise different morally from that of the world at large (the sea beyond); (d) it gives no significance to the drawing to the shore, and on the contrary, represents only the church as subject to the judgment of God; (e) it repeats the parable of tares, and is thus an anticlimax in a series which otherwise possesses a true progress and development of the truth from the beginning to the close. I should hesitate to dissent from the whole current of thought in this matter, were it not that the ordinary interpretation was evidently originally adopted for controversial reasons, to silence the Donatists, who demanded a rigid discipline in the church, and has since been accepted by each new commentator, apparently on the authority of preceding writers, with little or no original investigation. To me the interpretation, which I find substantially in *Arnot* (to whose treatise on the parables the reader is referred for a careful and candid discussion of the subject), appears more consonant, both with the meaning of the parable and the course of the entire series. The sea is the world; out of it, by unseen but invisible influences, all humanity, good and evil, large and small, old and young, are drawn steadily, and despite their forebodings and struggles to escape, to the shore of eternity. Not until that shore is reached can the kingdom of God be fully disclosed; then the angels, who come with Christ

52 Then said he unto them, Therefore every scribe *which is* instructed unto the kingdom of heaven, is like unto a man *that is* an householder, which bringeth forth out° of his treasure *things* new and old."

53 And it came to pass, *that* when Jesus had finished these parables, he departed thence.

54 And^p when he was come into his own country, he taught them in their synagogue, insomuch that they were astonished, and said, Whence hath this *man* this wisdom, and *these* mighty works?

55 Is not this the carpenter's son? Is not his mother called Mary? and his brethren, James, and Joses, and Simon, and Judas?

56 And his sisters, are they not all with us? Whence then hath this *man* all these things?

57 And they were offended^q in him. But Jesus said

n Prov. 10 : 21 ; 15 : 7 ; 18 : 4 . . . .o Cant. 7 : 13 . . . .p Mark 6 : 1, etc. ; Luke 4 : 16, etc . . . .q Isa. 49 : 7 ; 53 : 3 ; John 8 : 49.

in his glory to judge the world (Matt. 25 : 31), separate the good from the bad, gathering the former into the many mansions (vessels) and casting the latter away. On verse 50, see note on verse 42, above.

This interpretation renders this parable a fitting climax in the series of seven. The Sower represents the work of Christ and the hindrances it meets in the human heart; the Tares point to the true cause of these hindrances, evil influences set at work by the evil one; the Mustard Seed gives assurance of the final victory of Christ, in the growth of the great tree from a small seed; the Leaven points out the method of that growth—secret, silent, by permeation, by agitation; the Treasure and the Pearl teach that only by a joyful choice of Christ, as a chief good, can any one come into the kingdom: and the Drag-net points out its final consummation, after death the inevitable lot, and in the judgment the inevitable test, of the whole human race. Each parable, too, receives an illustration in an historical epoch of the church. The apostolic church was the greatest of all the seed times of the church; in the ages immediately following grew up, in corruptions of life, doctrine, and worship, tares, and, by persecution, the R. C. church attempted, in vain, to distinguish between the tares and the wheat, and to destroy the one and leave the other; the little seed grew, and still grows on, more and more overshadowing all the earth; the leaven secretly, but by perpetual agitation, penetrates society; in that agitation, and in part because of it, hundreds and thousands of souls find the hid treasure; and in this later age, in which knowledge is increased, when many run to and fro seeking it, many obtain the pearl of great price, worth all else; till at last the end shall come, when all humanity shall be drawn from the sea of time to the shore of eternity, and the final and inevitable judgment shall take place.

51, 52. CLOSE OF THE PARABLES. Compare with these verses Mark 4 : 34, "When they were alone he expounded all things to his disciples." **Have ye understood?** (Greek συνήκατε), i. e., with the heart. Compare verse 19 above and note, and Romans 10 : 9. **Scribe.** The scribes were the theological teachers of the age. See notes on Matt. 2 : 4.

The spirit of Christ's question is that of a father or teacher, who makes sure that his explanation has been understood. The answer is not one of undue self-confidence; though it is not to be supposed that the disciples understood the whole significance of these parables, still less the prophetic meaning which is involved in them. "Their reply must be taken as spoken from their then standing-point, from which little would be seen of that inner and deeper meaning which the Holy Spirit has since unfolded."—(*Alford.*) The parable of the householder which follows is interpreted by the contrast between Christ himself and the Scribes, the theologians and professional teachers of Judaism (Matt. 7 : 29, and note). They, like their modern antitypes, taught by rote what they learned from the teachings of their predecessors, and in unvarying routine, without any living experience of the truth. Christ declares that the Christian scribe must bring forth out of his own treasure, *i. e.*, his own heart experiences (compare Matt. 12 : 35), things both new and old, neither despising the old because it is old, nor rejecting the new because it is new. The contrast is not merely between the Old Testament and the New Testament, nor between old and new forms of truth, but between old and familiar disclosures, and new experiences and apprehensions of the truth. It is interpreted and applied by the charge of Robinson the Puritan pastor to his Puritan flock on the occasion of their embarking for New England: "I charge you before God and his blessed angels that you follow me no farther than you have seen me follow the Lord Jesus Christ. The Lord has yet more truth to break out of his Holy Word. I cannot sufficiently bewail the condition of the Reformed churches, who are come to a period in religion and will go at present no further than the instruments of their reformation. Luther and Calvin were great and shining lights in their times, yet they penetrated not into the whole counsel of God." Our preaching should be not a mere repetition and amplification of Christ's precepts, but, like that of St. Paul, rooted in Christ, yet with its own stalk and branches. "We must not content ourselves with old discoveries, but must be adding new." "Laying up is in order to laying out, for the benefit of others."—(*Matthew Henry.*)

53-58. CHRIST REJECTED AT NAZARETH. Alford and Olshausen regard this incident as

unto them, A prophet is not without honour, save in his own country, and in his own house.

58 And he did not many mighty works there, because of their unbelief.

identical with that more fully narrated in Luke 4 : 14–29. In this they differ from most harmonists, and for reasons that appear to me inadequate (see notes on Luke). Mark gives a more accurate note of time than Matthew, and interposes between the parables and the rejection at Nazareth the account of several miracles. If we suppose his chronological order to be correct, the reference here to the "mighty works" will be explained by these miracles.

54. **His own country**, i. e., Nazareth and the region about, see Matt. 2 : 23. **Synagogue**. For account of Jewish Synagogue see note on Matt. 4 : 23. **Astonished**. At the fact, the method, and the effect of his teaching, see Matt. 7 : 29.

55. **Carpenter's son**. Mark (6:2) says *the carpenter*. This, and the Jewish custom which required every father to teach his son a trade, whatever pursuit in life he might eventually follow, indicates that Christ worked in his earlier years at the carpenter's trade with his father. That carpentering was a real art and well advanced is evident, both from the structures erected, e. g., the Temple and the palace of Solomon and Herod, and from the tools employed. There are references in Scripture to the rule, the measuring line, the plane, the compass, the saw, the awl, and the hammer and nails. **His brethren**. See note below. **Joses**. The Sinaitic manuscript has *John*, the Vatican has *Joseph*.

57. **Offended in him**. Stumbled at him. To them he was a stone of stumbling. They recognized to a certain extent his wisdom and his power—observe wisdom, not learning—but they were too much prejudiced by what they supposed they knew of him, and his parentage,

and his education, to receive his teaching. The question here put by the Nazarenes was subsequently put by the Judeans (see John 7 : 15 and note). Observe that Christ is himself a perpetual rebuke of the spirit of caste, whether of family, or station, or of culture; for he was in appearance the son of a carpenter, in reality a carpenter, and in culture, humanly speaking, without the learning of the schools of his day. Observe, too, that the test of a religious teacher is, not the endorsement or certificate of the schools, which Christ did not possess; nor personal popularity, which Christ did not always possess; but real, permanent spiritual power and fruitfulness, as an instructor in righteousness. **In his own house**. See John 7 : 5.

58. **He did not many mighty works**. The Greek word (δύναμις) signifies literally *power*, or *strength*. Here it is equivalent to works such as would manifest the divine power. Mark's language is singular: He *could* there do no mighty works; he adds, however, that Christ "laid his hands upon a few sick folks and healed them;" see note there. **Because of their unbelief**. The object of his miracles, then, was not to convince wilful skeptics of his divine authority; if it were, he would have done the most miracles where the unbelief was strongest. To use the miracles as an argument for the divine authority of Christianity, with those who deny its authority and reject its teachings, is to misapprehend their purport and aim. They are the seal of his divine authority, to those who are morally and spiritually ready to receive the truth, but need for it some external sanction (see John 14 : 10, 11).

BRETHREN OF THE LORD.

Brethren of our Lord are mentioned ten times in the N. T. (see references below). The question how we are to understand these references is one which is generally regarded as difficult; albeit, the difficulty has been enhanced, if not absolutely created, by dogmatic and theological considerations. I shall give in this note, briefly, (1) the Scripture references; (2) a statement of the three principal opinions concerning them; (3) the reasons which have led to the view that the term brethren signifies cousins; (4) the grounds of the opinion which I believe to be the correct one.

1. *Scripture references*. In Matt. 12 : 46, Mark 3 : 31, and Luke 8 : 19, we have an account of an endeavor by the mother and brethren of Jesus to interrupt Christ's preaching, and get him away from the multitude, on account of their fears for his personal safety, and their failure to appreciate and sympathize with his divine enthusiasm (compare Mark 3 : 21). In Matt. 13 : 55 and Mark 6 : 3 we have a reference by the Nazarenes to his brethren, in connection with his reputed father, and his real mother. In John 2 : 12 it is stated that Jesus and his mother and brethren went to Capernaum for a short time. In John 7 : 3, 5, 10, the brethren are introduced alone as urging Jesus to go up into Judea, and show himself and his works at Jerusalem; and it is distinctly stated that his brethren did not believe on him. In Acts 1 : 14 they are represented as meeting with Mary and the twelve for prayer, after the ascension and before the descent of the Holy Spirit. In 1 Cor. 9 : 5 Paul refers to them in language which implies a distinction between them and the twelve. In Gal. 1 : 19 he refers to James, the

Lord's brother, as though he were an Apostle. Those are all the passages in the N. T. which refer directly to brethren or sisters of the Lord.

(2.) *Theories of interpretation.* These are three; (*a*) that the term brethren is synonymous with cousins; that the brethren and sisters of our Lord were children of Mary's sister, and Lange supposes adopted by Mary into her own family; (*b*) that they were children of Joseph by a former wife, and so regarded as the brethren of Jesus, though not so in reality; (*c*) that they were younger brothers and sisters, true children of Joseph and Mary.

(3.) *Arguments for the cousin theory.* (*a.*) The term brother is sometimes used in the East to designate a more distant lateral relationship, as the term son is used to designate a more distant lineal relationship (Gen. 11:27, w. 13:6, and 14:16; 29:12-15). The hypothesis that these brethren were cousins or other relations of Jesus is therefore not impossible. (*b.*) Their names appear to identify the brethren of the Lord with certain of his Apostles. Their names are given as James, Joses (Joseph? John? see note above), Simon and Judas. Three of Christ's Apostles bore respectively the names of James, Simon and Judas. James, the Apostle, had also a brother Joses (Mark 15:40) and a brother Judas (Luke 6:16). (*c.*) James, the Lord's brother, is distinctly classed by Paul with the Apostles (Gal 1:19). (*d.*) Christ would not at his death have commended his mother to John (John 19:26, 27), nor would that disciple have taken her to his own home to live, if she had at the time other children living, for they would have been her natural protectors. (*e.*) It is derogatory to the character of Mary and to the dignity of our Lord to suppose that children were born to her subsequent to the birth of Jesus. This last argument is, I suspect, the real foundation of the cousin theory. The whole R. C. doctrine of Mariolatry rests upon the doctrine of her perpetual virginity, and the feeling which underlies that doctrine exists also in many Protestant minds in a modified form.

(4.) *Arguments against the cousin theory.* (*a.*) The term brethren is never used *in the N. T.* to signify a wider relationship than true brothers; though its use in a metaphorical sense, *e. g.* Matt. 12:49, is not uncommon. The O. T. references, given above, do not justify us in depriving it in the N. T. of its natural and normal meaning. (*b.*) The more general term kinsman (Greek συγγενής), though of frequent use in the N. T. (Mark 6:4, Luke 1:36, 58; 2:44; 14:12; 21:16; John 18:26; Acts 10:24; Rom. 9:3; 16:7, 11, 21), and the more precise designations of cousin (Greek ἀνεψιός), and sister's son (Gr. υἱὸς τῆς ἀδελφῆς), (Acts 23:11; Col. 4:10) are never used in respect to the brethren of the Lord. (*c.*) In every instance in the Gospels they are mentioned in connection with Jesus' mother, and in such a manner as to imply that they were part of Mary's household; while there is nothing to imply that they were either children of Joseph by a former marriage, or adopted children. (*d.*) In John it is distinctly stated that Jesus' brethren did not believe in him, while it is as distinctly stated in a preceding chapter that the twelve did believe in him, despite the withdrawal of other disciples (Compare John 6:66-69 with 7:3-5). (*e.*) In Acts the brethren are said to have met *with* the twelve, and cannot therefore be confounded with or regarded as in part making up the number of the twelve. (*f.*) The language of Luke 2:7 (Comp. Matt. 1:25 and note), "she brought forth her first-born son," *implies* that other children were subsequently born to Mary. (*g.*) The only Scripture argument for doubting that they were true brethren of the Lord is the identity of the names of three of them with those of three of the Apostles, James, Simon, and Judas. But the frequency with which these names occur in Jewish families takes all weight from this consideration. Josephus mentions twenty-one Simons, seventeen Joses, and sixteen Judases; and in the apostolic lists are two Simons, two Judases and two Jameses. The fact that James, the Lord's brother, is called an Apostle (Gal. 1:19), does not indicate that he was one of the twelve, for Paul and Barnabas are also called Apostles (Acts 14:14). That title belongs not merely to the twelve, but to those who were living and personal witnesses of Christ's resurrection (1 Cor. 9:1; 15:8, 9). That Christ commended his mother to the keeping of John does not prove, and hardly implies that there were not other children, who, since they were then unbelievers, were not in sympathy with their mother, and who also may have been without means to provide for her comfort.

For myself I can find no other reason for taking the language of the N. T., concerning the brethren of our Lord, in any except its natural sense, save a feeling, which I believe to be essentially false, that it somehow derogates from the dignity of Mary and of Jesus, to suppose that she lived in the marital relation subsequent to Christ's birth. Such a feeling, even if well-grounded, would certainly be no basis for the interpretation of Scripture; but it is not well-grounded. On this point Dr. Schaff's remarks are well worth pondering: "Neither his nor her honor require the *perpetual* virginity after his birth, unless there be something impure and unholy in the marriage relation itself. The latter we cannot admit, since God instituted marriage in the state of innocence in Paradise, and St. Paul compares it to the most sacred relation existing, the union of Christ with his church. And the Apostles and Evangelists, who are certainly much safer guides in all matters of faith

CHAPTER XIV.

AT that time* Herod the tetrarch heard of the fame of Jesus;
2 And said unto his servants, This is John the Baptist: he is risen from the dead; and therefore mighty works do show forth themselves in him.
3 For Herod had laid hold on John, and bound him, and put *him* in prison for Herodias' sake, his brother Philip's wife.

---

* Mark 6 : 14 ; Luke 9 : 7, etc.

---

and religious feeling than even fathers and reformers, seem to have had no such feeling of repugnance to a real marriage between Joseph and Mary. It may be regarded as another proof of the true and full humanity and the condescending love of our Saviour, if he shared the common trials of family life in all its forms, and moved a brother among brothers and sisters, that he might be touched with a feeling of our infirmities." See on this subject the Introduction to Epistle to James, and *note* on The Apostles, their lives and characters, Matt. ch. 10, p. 147.

Ch. 14 : 1-12.—THE DEATH OF JOHN THE BAPTIST.—THE TESTIMONY OF A GUILTY CONSCIENCE (verse 2).—THE WAGES OF FAITHFUL PREACHING (Compare 2 Cor. 11 : 22-27)—FEAR OF PUBLIC OPINION IS A POOR SUBSTITUTE FOR THE FEAR OF GOD (verses 5 and 9).—THE DIFFERENCE BETWEEN DANCING, AND THE DANCE (verse 6 with chap. 11 : 17).—THE DANGER OF VOLUPTUOUSNESS.—A BAD PROMISE IS BETTER BROKEN THAN KEPT.—THE POWER FOR EVIL OF A WICKED WIFE AND MOTHER.—JESUS THE REFUGE OF THE AFFLICTED AND PERSECUTED (verse 13).

For parallel accounts see Mark 6 : 14-29, and Luke 3 : 19, 20 ; 9 : 7-9. Luke does not relate the death of John. Mark gives some particulars omitted here. Josephus (Ant. 18 : 5) gives more fully the history of Herod's marriage to Herodias. The facts in the case, necessary to an understanding of this narrative, are these: Herodias, the grand-daughter of Herod the Great, through his favorite wife Mariamne, was an ambitious, designing, unprincipled woman. She married Herod Philip, son of Herod by another Mariamne, and heir apparent to the throne. But Philip was disinherited by his father's will, and the kingdom was divided between Antipas, Archelaus, and a second Philip; Antipas, the Herod mentioned here, being Tetrarch of Galilee and Perea (see note on Luke 3 : 1, and map ther.). He married the daughter of Aretas, king of Petra, but being brought into company with Herodias, the wife of his half brother Philip, he divorced his own wife, and married Herodias, who abandoned her husband for the purpose. The king of Petra, indignant at the affront put upon him, declared war against Herod Antipas. John the Baptist, during the preparations for this war, denounced the Tetrarch for this crime, which had plunged the province into such difficulties, as well as for his other tyrannies (Luke 3 : 19), and Herod, fearing the influence of his preaching, arrested him and cast him into prison.

Subsequent to the assassination of the Baptist, described in this chapter, Herod Antipas was totally defeated, and his army destroyed by Aretas, an event which the Jews interpreted as a divine punishment upon Herod for John's death. Later in his life, Herod, instigated by Herodias, went with her to Rome to obtain the title of king, and to complain of Agrippa, his nephew, for assuming it, was banished by Caligula to Lyons in Gaul, whence he removed to Spain, where he died, his wife sharing his exile with him. The Scripture references show him to have been tyrannical (Luke 3 : 19), cunning (Luke 13 : 31, 32), voluptuous, and superstitious. He is the Herod to whom Christ was sent by Pilate during the Passion week (Luke 23 : 6-11), and his conduct there agrees with his character as represented here. See for full history of John's imprisonment and death *Abbott's Jesus of Nazareth*, chapter 21.

1. At that time. At this period of Christ's ministry. Mark gives what is the most probable chronological order. Subsequent to the parables by the sea-shore (Mark 4 : 1-35), followed certain miracles (Mark 4 : 35—6 : 6), and the commission of the twelve (Mark 6 : 7-13), recorded by Matthew more fully in Chapter 10. Their itinerant ministry added to Christ's fame and brought it to the ears of Herod. **Tetrarch.** Properly the governor of the fourth part of a country; but also used to designate a tributary ruler whose authority and position were not sufficient to justify the title king. Herod Antipas is generally and properly called Tetrarch, though also entitled "king" here, in verse 9, and in Mark 6 : 14, 22.

2. Therefore, *i. e.*, because he is risen from the dead. **Mighty works are at work in him.** (Greek, δυνάμεις ἐνεργοῦσιν.) During his life John wrought no miracles (John 10 : 41). Herod supposed that his resurrection had clothed him with new power. This opinion was shared by others (Matt. 16 : 14 ; Mark 8 : 28). Luke says (Luke 9 : 7-9) that Herod was perplexed, and implies that his belief in John's resurrection was imbibed from others.

3. Laid hold. Arrested; compare for meaning, Matt. 21 : 46 ; 26 : 4, 50, where the Greek is the same. This arrest of John the Baptist had taken place nearly a year previous (Matt. 4 : 12). Andrews places the arrest of John the Baptist in April, A.D. 28, his death in the winter of A.D. 29. **Prison.** In the castle of Macherus, as we learn from Josephus. For description of it, see note on Matt. 11 : 2.

4 For John said unto him, It* is not lawful for thee to have her.
5 And when he would have put him to death, he feared the multitude, because they counted him as a' prophet.
6 But when Herod's birthday was kept, the daughter of Herodias danced before them, and pleased Herod.
7 Whereupon he promised with an oath to give her whatsoever she would ask.
8 And she, being before instructed of her mother, said, Give me here John Baptist's" head in a charger.

9 And the king was sorry:" nevertheless, for the oath's" sake, and them which sat with him at meat, he commanded *it* to be given *her*.
10 And he sent, and beheaded John in the prison.
11 And his head was brought in a charger, and given to the damsel: and she brought *it* to her mother.
12 And his disciples came and took up the body, and buried* it, and went and told Jesus.
13 When Jesus heard of *it*, he' departed thence by ship into a desert place apart: and when the people had heard *thereof*, they followed him on foot out of the cities

† Lev. 18 : 16 ; 20 : 21....t ch. 21 : 26 ; Luke 20 : 6....u Prov. 29 : 10....v Jud. 11 : 31, 35 ; Dan. 6 : 14-16....w Jud. 21 : 1 ; 1 Sam. 14 : 28 ; Ecc. 5 : 2....x Acts 8 : 2....y ch. 10 : 23 ; 12 : 15 ; Mark 6 : 32, etc. ; Luke 9 : 10, etc. ; John 6 : 1, 2, etc.

4. Unto him. These words are omitted by the Sinaitic manuscript. It is uncertain whether John's reproof was a private and personal one, or was a public denunciation, before the people, of the crime of their prince. **It is not lawful.** Because the wife of Herod Antipas was still living, the husband of Herodias was still living, and Herodias and Herod Antipas were relatives within the degrees of consanguinity, within which marriage was forbidden by Lev. 18 : 11 ; for Herodias was a grand-daughter of Herod the Great, and Antipas was a son of Herod the Great, though by another wife. Lev. 18 : 16 directly forbids marriage to a brother's wife, *i. e.*, while the brother is living.

5. Because he feared the multitude. He also stood in awe of John, recognizing in him a prophet, and in many respects yielding to his counsel (Mark 6 : 20). It is a reasonable deduction from Mark's language that Herod Antipas was not without some conscience, but was under the influence of his wife, who was more resolute and more wicked than himself.

6. Herod's birth-day was kept. By a great feast to the nobility of Galilee (Mark 6 : 21). **The daughter of Herodias.** By her previous husband Philip, her name was Salome. She subsequently married another Herod, Philip the tetrarch of Trachonitis, and subsequent to his death, Aristobulus, the brother of Agrippa (Josephus' Ant. 18 : 5, 4). **Danced before them.** It was in the East, even more than with us, a disgrace for a woman to enter such a scene of carousing as characterized the king's feast (compare Esther 1 : 10-12). The dance was and still is sensual and exciting. The maiden carries her own instrument with her, and accompanies herself. Only the professional dancer, whose position is inferior to that which she occupies here, will ordinarily prostitute her womanhood to the entertainment of such an assemblage (see *Thomson's Land and Book*, 2 : 345). But the entertainment was adapted to please the voluptuous king, who was pleased, not shamed, by the dishonorable accomplishment and exhibition of his adopted daughter.

7. He promised with an oath to give her whatsoever she would ask. Mark adds, Unto the half of my kingdom. "Why marvel? Since even now, after the coming in of so high a wisdom, for a dance sake, many of these effeminate young men give up their very souls, and that without constraint of any oath."—(*Chrysostom*.)

8. And she being urged on by her mother (Gr. προβιβασθεισα). Not, as in our English version, *before instructed*. This is not the proper significance of the Greek, and it appears from Mark 6 : 24, that after the dance she went out and asked her mother, What shall I ask? before preferring the demand. She was not in the conspiracy, but was made the instrument of it. **Charger.** A wooden trencher or dish, on which food was served up. In Luke 11 : 39, the same word is rendered *platter*.

9. Sorry. Both because he feared the people (verse 5) and the reproaches of his own conscience (Mark 6 : 20). But he feared the ridicule of those that sat at meat with him more. He was not true king in his own court. Note the difference between *sorrow* and *repentance*, and the worthlessness of sorrow that does not lead to repentance.

12. Went and told Jesus. Observe that the death of John the Baptist appears to have put an end to the doubts and jealousies which his disciples entertained concerning Jesus during the Baptist's life. Observe, too, that it was sorrow which drove them to Christ, to whom they came not while their own teacher was with them. When the deprivation of our earthly teachers brings us to the heavenly, it is gain, not loss.

On this whole incident the reflection of Chrysostom is worth pondering, "She looked to be concealed after this and to hide her crime (by the death of her accuser). But the very contrary was the result ; for John's cry was heard the more loudly thereafter." "The more thou dost dissemble a sin, the more thou dost expose it. Sin is not hidden by the addition of sin, but by repentance and confession."

13-27. THE FEEDING OF FIVE THOUSAND.—WALKING ON THE SEA.—See Mark 6 : 30-56 ; Luke

14 And Jesus went forth, and* saw a great multitude, and was moved with compassion* toward them, and he healed their sick.
15 And when it was evening, his disciples came to him, saying, This is a desert place, and the time is now past; send the multitude away, that they may go into the villages, and buy themselves victuals.
16 But Jesus said unto them, They need not depart; give ye them to eat.
17 And they say unto him, We have here but five loaves, and two fishes.
18 He said, Bring them hither to me.
19 And he commanded the multitude to sit down on the grass; and took the five loaves and the two fishes, and, looking up to heaven, he blessed, and brake; and gave the loaves to *his* disciples, and the disciples to the multitude.
20 And they did all eat, and were filled: and they took up of the fragments that remained twelve baskets full.*
21 And they that had eaten were about five thousand men, beside women and children.
22 And straightway Jesus constrained his disciples to get into a ship, and to go before him unto the other side, while he sent the multitudes away.
23 And when he had sent the multitudes away, he* went up into a mountain apart to pray; and when the evening was come, he was there alone.
24 But the ship was now in the midst of the sea, tossed with waves: for the wind was contrary.
25 And in the fourth watch of the night Jesus went unto them, walking on the sea.
26 And⁴ when the disciples saw him walking on the sea, they were troubled,* saying, It is a spirit; and they cried out for fear.
27 But straightway Jesus spake unto them, saying, Be*ⁿ* of good cheer; it is I, be not afraid.
28 And Peter answered him and said, Lord, if it* be thou, bid me come unto thee on the water.
29 And he said, Come. And when Peter was come down out of the ship, he walked on the water, to go to Jesus.
30 But when he saw the wind boisterous, he was afraid; and beginning to sink, he cried, saying, Lord, save me!ʰ
31 And immediately Jesus stretched forth *his* hand,¹

a ch. 9 : 36 ; 15 · 32....a Heb. 4 : 15....b 2 Kings 4 : 1-7....c Mark 6 : 46....d Job 9 : 8 ; John 6 : 19....e Luke 24 : 37....f Acts 23 : 11 ; g Phil. 4 : 13....h Ps. 69 : 1, 2 ; Lam. 3 : 57....i Ps. 138 : 7.

8 : 10-17; John, ch. 6; and see notes on John. Comparing these accounts, the course of events appears to have been as follows:—Jesus commissioned his disciples (Matt. 10) to preach the gospel in the villages, while he preached in the cities. This combined preaching extended his fame and brought it to the ears of Herod, who believed Jesus to be John the Baptist risen from the dead. This fact came to the knowledge of Jesus about the time that his disciples returned from their commission (Mark 6 : 30, 31); he therefore called them to leave their work and the multitude, and with them departed from the western and populous shore of the sea of Galilee to a plain at the foot of the mountain east of Bethsaida, a town on the north banks of the sea of Galilee where the Jordan enters the sea (consult map). The people followed Jesus on foot, and from his retirement among the mountains he saw them gathering on the plain. The throng was doubtless increased by the fact that the Passover was nigh, and pilgrims were on their way to Jerusalem to celebrate it (John 6 : 3-5). Jesus thereupon descended the mountain, and spent the day in teaching them and healing them (Mark 6 : 34 ; Luke 9 : 11), and toward evening (Matt. 14 : 15) fed them with the five loaves and two small fishes. In their enthusiasm, the people would have made him king (John 6 : 15); whereupon Jesus directed the disciples to take to their boat and row along the coast to Bethsaida, where he would meet them, i. e., Bethsaida Julias, not another Bethsaida on the western coast, as has sometimes been imagined (see note on Mark 6 : 45). One of those winds which often sweep down the valley of the Jordan from the Lebanon, struck the disciples' boat, and swept it out into the lake. It was as they were rowing back to meet their Lord, according to appointment, that he came forth to meet them "swift walking on the wave." They then completed their journey, and arrived at the land of Gennesaret, on the western shore, where Christ performed the miracles referred to here in verses 34-36 and in Mark 6 : 53-56, and on the day following preached the sermon which John alone records (John 6 : 22-71), in which he disclosed something more definitely of his approaching death, which led many of his Galilean followers to forsake him (John 6 : 66), and which constituted the close of his public ministry in Galilee. For notes on the miraculous feeding of the multitude and the subsequent walking on the sea, with the sermon which followed, see John chap. 6. Luke describes the feeding of the five thousand, but not the walking on the sea. This feeding is not to be confounded with that of the four thousand (Matt. 15 : 32-39), which took place later in Christ's ministry.

28-31. PETER ATTEMPTS TO WALK ON THE WATER. Peculiar to Matthew. This incident entirely negatives the hypothesis of Bleek, that perhaps Jesus was on the land, and the disciples in the storm and darkness thought him to be on the sea. Of course there was no room for misapprehension in the case of Peter. The incident itself is generally regarded as an illustration of Peter's great faith. To me the lesson appears quite different. Zealous, but impetuous and self-confident, the same spirit which led Peter into the court of the High Priest at the time of Christ's trial—a certain rash willingness to go into danger, a certain thoughtless scorn of it, a certain subtle and yet unconscious vanity in the exhibition of his own faith and courage—led him now to wish to show his faith by walking on the wave. But he only showed his fear. Christ walked on the wave for a purpose, to come to his disciples whom otherwise he could not reach; and he fell not; Peter walked on the wave for

and caught him, and said unto him, O thou of little faith, wherefore didst thou doubt?"

32 And when they were come into the ship, the wind ceased.

33 Then they that were in the ship came and worshipped him, saying, Of a truth thou art the Son of God.

34 And when they were gone over, they came into the land of Gennesaret.

35 And when the men of that place had knowledge of him, they sent out into all that country round about, and brought unto him all that were diseased:

36 And besought him that they might only touch the hem of his garment: and as many as touched were made perfectly whole.

CHAPTER XV.

THEN came to Jesus scribes and Pharisees, which were of Jerusalem, saying,

2 Why do thy disciples transgress the tradition of the elders? for they wash not their hands when they eat bread.

3 But he answered and said unto them, Why do ye also transgress the commandment of God by your tradition?

4 For God commanded, saying, Honour thy father and mother: and, He that curseth father or mother, let him die the death.

5 But ye say, Whosoever shall say to his father or his mother, It is a gift, by whatsoever thou mightest be profited by me;

6 And honour not his father or his mother, *he shall be free*. Thus have ye made the commandment of God of none effect by your tradition.

7 Ye hypocrites! well did Esaias prophesy of you, saying,

8 This people draweth nigh unto me with their mouth, and honoureth me with *their* lips: but their heart is far from me.

---

j James 1 : 6....k Ps. 107 : 29....l Dan. 3 : 28; Luke 4 : 41; John 1 : 49; 6 : 69; 11 : 27; Acts 8 : 37; Rom. 1 : 4.....m Mark 6 : 53.....n ch. 9 : 20; Num. 15 : 38; Mark 5 : 10 ; Luke 6 : 19; Acts 19 : 19 ....o John 6 : 37.....p Mark 7 : 1, etc....,q Col. 2 : 8, 20; Tit. 1 : 14.....r Ex. 20 : 12; Deut. 5 : 16.....s Ex. 21 : 17; Lev. 20 : 9.....t Deut. 27 : 16.....u Isa. 29 : 13.

---

no other purpose than the pleasure of doing a great deed, and demonstrating, perhaps to himself even more than to others, that he dared attempt it; and he would have sunk but for his Saviour's presence. It was a useless miracle for which Peter asked; the result was an exhibition, not of his strength, but of his weakness. That Christ did not regard Peter's act as an exemplification of faith is evident from his rebuke, "O thou of little faith." And the lesson appears to me to be, True faith never attempts wonders for the sake of doing them. It relies on God for every thing in time of need, but *never seeks or manufactures occasions for marvelous experiences or exhibitions of faith*. It is noteworthy that the Gospels narrate the failures in miraculous power and in faith in understanding of Christ (comp. Matt. 16 : 10, 11, 23; 17 : 16; Mark 9 : 10-29) as no book of myths would do.

32, 33. They that were in the ship. Alford thinks the crew are designated. But there is nothing in the account to indicate that there was any crew. The disciples were fishermen, and would have probably managed their own boat. Mark says they were sore amazed, and wondered, "for they considered not the miracle of the loaves; for their heart was hardened." But this language is not severer than some words of condemnation uttered by Christ directly to the twelve, *e. g.*, Matt. 16 : 8, 9; Luke 24 : 25. **Thou art the Son of God.** Compare Matt. 8 : 27. There a similar quelling of the storm led only to the expression, "What manner of man is this?" Here the answer is afforded to that question. This is the first time that Jesus is so called by men in the Synoptic Gospels. If we compare the expression with Peter's declaration of faith, "Thou art the Christ, the Son of the living God" (Matt. 16 : 16), we may find in his experience here, the seed of his faith there. Observe that this miracle is regarded by the disciples as an evidence of Christ's divine nature and authority, and that he does nothing to indicate that they are under any misapprehension.

34-36. Miracles in the Land of Gennesaret. Peculiar to Matthew and Mark 6 : 53-56. John, however, gives a hint of it in his expression: "After these things," *i. e.*, after the sermon at Capernaum, which followed the feeding of the five thousand, "Jesus walked in Galilee" (John 7 : 1). The chronological order is somewhat uncertain. It is probable, however, that the account here and the parallel one in Mark is of a tour throughout Galilee, more or less protracted, following the miracle of the feeding and the sermon at Capernaum, which was his last discourse in that city; that during this tour the rebuke of the Pharisees, narrated in the next chapter, was uttered; and that shortly thereafter Jesus left Galilee, and retreated with his disciples into the coasts of Tyre and Sidon, as narrated in chap. 15 : 21.

The land of Gennesaret. A plain lying along the north-western shore of the Sea of Galilee. It is stated by Drs. Robinson and Porter to be about three miles long and one broad. Stanley makes it much larger; but, of course, its bounds are indeterminate, and one writer probably includes what the other excludes from the plain. Though now covered with thorn-bushes, it gives evidence of having once possessed a marvelous fertility. Tiberias, Magdala, Chorazin, and Capernaum were situated on or near this plain, which was watered by four mountain springs, which at that time the heats of summer seldom if ever impoverished. **Hem of garment.** See notes on Mark 5 : 27.

Ch. 15 : 1-20. Eating with Unwashed Hands. Peculiar to Matthew and Mark 7 : 1-23. The account is fullest in Mark. See notes

Ch. XV.] MATTHEW. 193

9 But in vain they do worship me, teaching *for* doctrines,ᵛ the commandments of men.
10 And he called the multitude, and said unto them, Hear, and understand:
11 Notʷ that which goeth into the mouth defileth a man; but that which cometh out of the mouth, this defileth a man.
12 Then came his disciples, and said unto him, Knowest thou that the Pharisees were offended, after they heard this saying?
13 But he answered and said, Every plantˣ which my heavenly Father hath not planted, shall be rooted up.
14 Let them alone: theyʸ be blind leaders of the blind. And if the blind lead the blind, both shall fall into the ditch.
15 Then answered Peter, and said unto him, Declare unto us this parable.
16 And Jesus said, Are ye also yet without understanding?

17 Do not ye yet understand, that whatsoever entereth in at the mouthᶻ goeth into the belly, and is cast out into the draught?
18 But those things which proceed out of the mouth come forth from the heart; and they defile the man.
19 Forᵃ out of the heart proceed evil thoughts, murders, adulteries, fornications, thefts, false witness, blasphemies:
20 These are *the things* which defile a man: but to eat with unwashen hands defileth not a man.
21 Thenᵇ Jesus went thence, and departed into the coasts of Tyre and Sidon.
22 And, behold, a woman of Canaan came out of the same coasts, and cried unto him, saying, Have mercy on me, O Lord, *thou* son of David! 'my daughter is grievously vexed with a devil.
23 But he answered her not a word.ᵈ And his disciples came, and besought him, saying, Send her away; for she crieth after us.

ᵛ Col. 2 : 22....ʷ Acts 10 : 15; Rom. 14 : 14, 20; 1 Tim. 4 : 4; Titus 1 : 15....ˣ John 15 : 2, 6....ʸ ch. 23 : 16; Luke 6 : 39....ᶻ Luke 6 : 45; James 3 : 6....ᵃ Gen. 9 : 5; 8 : 21; Prov. 6 : 14; 24 : 9; Jer. 17 : 9; Rom. 3 : 10-19; Gal. 5 : 19-21; Eph. 2 : 3; Titus 3 : 3....ᵇ Mark 7 : 24....ᶜ Luke 18 : 38, 39....ᵈ Ps. 28 : 1; Lam. 3 : 8.

---

there. The time and occasion are uncertain; probably during the tour throughout Galilee referred to in the last verses of the preceding chapter, and more fully described in Mark 6 : 53-56, and hinted at in John 7 : 1. The Scribes and Pharisees came from Jerusalem (Mark 7 : 1), perhaps on their return from the Passover mentioned in John 6 : 4. With this passage should be compared the analogous teaching, on a different occasion, in Luke 11 : 37, &c.

12-14. These verses are found only in Matthew. The *plant* is a common symbol in Scripture of teaching, both true and false, (Matt. 13 : 3-8, 24-30; Mark 4 : 26-29; John 15 : 1, 2). Here the declaration is that any teaching, however erroneous, which God has not inspired, shall not abide; the moral is the same as that of the parable of the tares (Matt. 13 : 37-43 and notes); the principle the same as that substantially promulgated by Gamaliel to the Sanhedrim (Acts 5 : 38, 39). **Let them alone.** This seems at first a singular counsel respecting the teachers of error. It is, however, different from, Let the error alone, or, Let the pupils of error alone. Christ very rarely entered into direct controversy with false teachers. I think in no single instance did he invite to or provoke a controversy with them. He devoted himself to the affirmative work of preaching the truth, and, for the most part, let the preachers of error alone. And God has rooted up their plants. Christ is, in this respect, an example to the modern Christian teacher in dealing with modern antagonisms to Christianity. The best corrective of Rationalism and Romanism is the preaching of an affirmative and practical Christianity. **Fall into the ditch.** Observe that Christ's disciples had been assailed for eating with unwashed hands, because this was in the eyes of the Pharisees an uncleanness. Christ's response to his disciples embodies the idea that the guidance of the Pharisees will lead directly to the foulest uncleanness.

Ch. 15 : 21-28.—THE SYRO-PHŒNICIAN WOMAN.—FAITH ILLUSTRATED; IT IS EARNEST, IMPORTUNATE, HUMBLE.

This incident follows immediately after Christ's last tour through Galilee. It is recorded only here and in Mark 7 : 24-30. The account is fullest here, but Mark adds some significant facts, chiefly the intimation that Jesus' object in going into the heathen territory, was to secure the rest which he could not obtain, even among the mountains of his own land.

21. Thence. From Galilee. **Into the coasts of Tyre and Sidon.** For description of this region see note on Matt. 11 : 21. Whether he went into the Phœnician territory or only to the borders of it has been questioned. The phrase here employed (Greek εἰς τὰ μέρη) occurs in Matthew 2 : 22, and 16 : 13; also in Mark 8 : 10, and Acts 2 : 10, and in all of these cases indicates going into the territory. The context sustains that interpretation here; he left Galilee and went into Phœnicia to secure rest. Mark 7 : 24, adds that he entered into a house, and would have no man know it; but he could not be hid.

22. A woman of Canaan. Mark describes her more particularly. She was a *Greek* or Gentile, *i. e.* in language and religious education, and a *Syro-Phœnician*. There were Phœnicians in Africa, known as Liby-Phœnicians, and in Syria known as Syro-Phœnicians. She belonged to the latter; was probably one of a mixed race, in which the blood of the Syrians and Phœnicians mingled, and therefore doubly despised by the Jews. The term Canaan was the older title of the country, and the inhabitants were successively termed Canaanites and Phœnicians, as the inhabitants of England were successively called Britons and Englishmen. Matthew used the older term, Mark the later. **From the same coasts coming out, cried unto him.** Not, as in our version, *came out of the same coasts*. She was

24 But he answered and said, I am not sent but unto the lost sheep of the house of Israel.
25 Then came she, and worshipped him, saying, Lord, help me!
26 But he answered and said, It is not meet to take the children's bread, and to cast it to dogs.
27 And she said, Truth, Lord: yet the dogs eat of the crumbs which fall from their masters' table.
28 Then Jesus answered and said unto her, O woman, great is thy faith: be it unto thee even as thou wilt. And her daughter was made whole from that very hour.

a woman of Canaan *from* (ἀπό) the same territory, and *came out* to meet Jesus probably from her house or village. **Have mercy on me.** The suffering of the child is the burden of the mother. Her prayer is for mercy for herself, so clearly is she identified with her daughter. Observe, she does not ask him to *come* and heal, as the nobleman in John 4 : 49, and the ruler in Matt. 9 : 18. Her faith shows itself in the very outset. Compare the similar faith of the centurion in Matt. 8 : 8, 9, and observe that in both cases it was manifested, not by an Israelite, but by a Gentile. **Son of David.** Evidently the woman had some knowledge of the Old Testament, and its prophecies of a Messiah. She may have been a proselyte. **Grievously vexed with a devil.** Literally *very evil deviled*, and so rendered in one of the old versions. On the nature of demoniacal possessions see note at close of chap. 8, page 85.

23. **Send her away.** Dismiss her. The language does not indicate whether by healing or by giving a positive refusal to heal. The reasonable implication, however, is that they had endeavored to drive her away, as was done in other parallel cases (Matt. 19 : 13; Luke 18 : 39), but in vain. They recognized Christ's object to be retirement, an object which her presence and petitions were sure to defeat.

24. **I am not sent but unto the lost sheep of the house of Israel.** Compare note on Matt. 10 : 6. Here, however, Christ defines his mission, not that of his disciples; but only the limits of his own personal and earthly ministry. It was not till after his death that the vail was rent, which shut out all but the high priest from the Holy of Holies—and by his death that he saves all who come unto him whether Jew or Gentile. James Morison gives well the reason for his declining to extend his earthly mission to Gentile races: "To have spread out his ministry farther during the brief period of his terrestrial career, would simply have been to have thinned and weakened his influence. Whatever might have been gained *extensively* would have been lost intensively." Compare Romans 11 : 12–17, where the implication is that the rejection of Christ by the Jews was, in the Providence of God, the precursor of the preaching of the Gospel to the Gentiles. It must come to the world either through the Jews, or despite the refusal of the Jews to receive it. Compare also Matt. 21 : 42, 43, where the implication is the same.

25. **Then came she.** Hitherto she had followed him in the way; now she came, as Mark more particularly describes, to the house where he was. **And worshipped him.** Rather *reverenced* him. See note on Matt. 8 : 2, where the original verb is the same.

26. **It is not meet.** Not, It is not *allowable* (ἔξεστιν), though some manuscripts give this reading, but, It is not *appropriate* (καλός). This is the reading of the Received Text, of the Sinaitic manuscript, and the undoubted reading in Mark 7 : 27. Mark adds an important sentence, which both explains this declaration and gives the key to the mother's reply. Christ says, "Let the children *first* be filled; for it is not meet," etc. This language implies that there is food in the Gospel for the Gentile as well as for the Jew, but that the Gospel should *begin* with Israel. It is clear from this that Christ did not teach that the Gentiles were to be despised and outcast, and did not intend to be so understood. **And cast it to the pet dogs.** The Greek here (κυνάριοι) signifies a little dog; is here probably equivalent to house or pet dog, in contradistinction to the dogs of the street, (κύων), which in the East are mostly without masters, and roam the towns and cities in packs, and feed upon offal and even corpses. The word which I have rendered "pet dogs," is used only here and in Mark 7 : 27, 28. Its use, coupled with the intimation that the Gentiles are to be fed but not at *first*, gives an indefinable but important color to the whole incident, which has been generally overlooked.

27. **Truth, Lord: for the pet dogs eat of the crumbs which fall from the table of their masters.** Observe, that she acquiesces heartily in Christ's declaration: it is not fit that the dogs be fed *before* the children; that she gives the reason: *because* they feed from that which the children cast away or pass by in indifference; and that she recognizes in the Israelites the masters, in spiritual things, of the Gentiles. from whose table the Gentiles are to be fed, for she says not, The table of the master, but The table of their masters (τῶν κυρίων αὐτῶν). Our English version, *Yet the dogs feed*, implies a contrast between his statement and hers. The original (καὶ γάρ) implies that she gives, in her statement, a reason for her assent to his. It is not needful to deprive the children to supply the

CH. XV.]   MATTHEW.   195

29 And Jesus departed from thence, and came nigh unto the sea of Galilee; and went up into a mountain, and sat down there.
30 And great multitudes came unto him, having with them *those that were* lame, blind, dumb, maimed, and many others, and cast them down at Jesus' feet; and he healed them :ᵏ
31 Insomuch that the multitude wondered, when

j Mark 7 : 31....k Ps. 103 : 3 ; Isa. 35 : 5, 6

dogs. So it is not needful to deprive Israel of its blessing in order to give me the blessing I crave: what they have cast away I seek. It would be different if I asked you to leave Israel to preach and to heal in Phœnicia.

28. Compare the language of Mark (7 : 30), "And when she was come to her house, she found the devil gone out, and her daughter laid upon the bed."

MEANING OF THIS INCIDENT. In interpreting this incident we are to remember certain facts which the commentators, as well as the skeptical critics, have sometimes forgotten. (*a*.) Jesus departed from Galilee, not to continue his ministry, but to rest from it. To have complied with the mother's request would have defeated his purpose; did defeat it, so that he straightway retreated again from the coasts of Tyre and Sidon into the mountains of Galilee, and thence into the region about Cæsarea Philippi (Mark 15 : 29 ; 16 : 13). (*b*.) He knew by a perfect spiritual insight just what measure of trial the woman could bear, so that the test, which would have been hazardous if attempted by another, was not so when used by him. (*c*.) The presumption that the tone of his voice, and the manner of his utterance, gave to his words a different impression from that which they bear in the simple reading of them, is not unreasonable, in the light of the result to which they led. The interpretation of this incident, which regards Christ as having repelled and rebuffed the woman, treated her with an appearance of Jewish contempt as a dog, and yielded at the last to her importunity, in spite of his original apparent, if not real intention, I cannot accept because (*a*), so interpreted, the incident stands absolutely isolated ; there is no other case in the Gospels in which Christ refused help to the suffering and the needy. (*b*.) It contravenes his whole spirit ; there is no other in which he indicated any sharing or appearance of sharing in the prejudice which treated Gentiles as dogs; on the contrary, his ministry in Galilee was begun by a public rebuke of that prejudice (Luke 4 : 25, 26), a rebuke subsequently repeated at Capernaum (Matt. 8 : 10-12). (*c*.) The language of the narrative itself does not, when carefully studied, confirm this impression—the impression of one hard to be entreated. His use of the distinctive word "little or pet dogs," his intimation of mercy to the Gentiles in the phrase "Let the children *first* be filled," (Mark 7 : 27), and the woman's method of taking up his reply, not taking exception to his statement, but making his declaration, It is not fitting to take the children's bread and cast it to the pet dogs, a reason for her own, Truth, Lord, *for* the pet dogs eat of the crumbs, all look toward a different tone and spirit in the whole scene. It appears then to me that Christ intended his language as a rebuke to the disciples, not to the mother; that her quick intuition read in his tone what they failed to read in his words; that her ready repartee is the language of awakened hope, not the last despairing cry of a crushed and broken heart ; that he neither intended to repel her nor, in fact, did so; but, knowing her faith, intended to draw forth its expression as a lesson to his as yet untaught disciples, to whom this woman of an apostate race was but a Gentile dog. In other words, I conceive that he spoke in the manner which we sometimes use with children, when we intend to grant their request yet hold them off, and make pretence of finding reason why it should not be granted, for the purpose of trying their earnestness. His very commendation, Great is thy faith, I take to be a recognition of her spiritual appreciation of his love, which his disciples did not then and have not always since comprehended as well as she did.

29-39. THE FOUR THOUSAND FED. The events which follow, up to and including chapter 18, describe a period of apparent retirement, spent partly in Galilee, partly north of Galilee in the districts about Cæsarea Philippi. Matthew does, indeed, record some public miracles, as the one here, and Mark adds more that Matthew omits ; but it is noticeable that there is no intimation here, or anywhere after this, of any considerable preaching of the Gospel in Galilee. On the other hand, Christ's endeavor to remain in retirement is not only clearly stated by Mark (9 : 30), but is also indicated, less clearly, in the fact that our Lord's miracles are performed apart from the multitude (Mark 7 : 33 ; 8 : 22-26), and are accompanied by injunctions of secrecy (Matt. 9 : 30; Mark 7 : 36 ; 8 : 26). He goes, too, from one district to another, as if seeking repose, which the throng deny him (Matt. 15 : 29, 30, 39 ; 16 : 1, 4 ; Mark 7 : 29, 27). So marked is this change in his ministry, that his disciples taunt him with his concealment (John 7 : 2-5). This period, up to his departure from Galilee, mentioned in Matthew 19 : 1, to fulfill the ministry, more fully described by John, is devoted chiefly to instructing his disciples respecting the

196 MATTHEW. [Ch. XVI.

they saw the dumb to speak, the maimed to be whole, the lame to walk, and the blind to see: and they glorified the God of Israel.

32 Then¹ Jesus called his disciples *unto him*, and said, I have compassion on the multitude, because they continue with me now three days, and have nothing to eat: and I will not send them away fasting, lest they faint in the way.

33 And^m his disciples say unto him, Whence should we have so much bread in the wilderness, as to fill so great a multitude?

34 And Jesus saith unto them, How many loaves have ye? And they said, Seven, and a few little fishes.

35 Andⁿ he commanded the multitude to sit down on the ground.

36 And he took the seven loaves and the fishes, and° gave thanks, and brake *them*, and gave to his disciples, and the disciples to the multitude.

37 And they did all eat, and were filled: and they took up of the broken meat that was left seven baskets full.

38 And they that did eat were four thousand men, beside women and children.

39 And he sent away the multitude, and took ship, and° came into the coasts of Magdala.

CHAPTER XVI.

THE Pharisees also with the Sadducees came, and tempting, desired him that he would shew them a sign^a from heaven.

---

l Mark 8 : 1, etc....m 2 Kings 4 : 43, 44....n ch. 14 : 19, etc....o 1 Sam. 9 : 13; Luke 22 : 19; 21 : 20....p Mark 8 : 10....q ch. 12 : 38, etc.; Mark 8 : 11, etc.; Luke 11 : 16; 12 : 54-56; 1 Cor. 1 : 22.

Kingdom of God, and embraces warnings against the leaven of the Pharisees (16:1-12), the full disclosure of his own divinity (16:13-20), accompanied by clearer prophecies of his death and resurrection (16:21-28), the manifestation of his glory in the transfiguration (17:1-8), and instructions respecting faith, humility, and forgiveness and kindness (ch. 17:19 to ch. 18:35). The account of the miracles of healing here referred to, as well as of the feeding of the four thousand, is fullest in Mark; see notes there (Mark 7:31-37; 8:1-9).

29. It is evident from the fact that *after* the feeding Christ took ship to come into the coasts of Magdala, which was on the western and populous side of the sea, that he came at first into the eastern coasts. Mark adds that he came through the coast of Decapolis, a district chiefly on the eastern shore. See note there. **Went up into a hill country.** Not a particular mountain, as might be supposed from our version, but up into the hill district east of the sea of Galilee; for the most part then, as now, wild and uninhabited. **Sat down there.** That is, stopped there. *Sit* is sometimes thus used in the N. T. as equivalent to *dwell* or *abide*, *e. g.* Matt. 4 : 16; Luke 1 : 79; Acts 14 : 8.

30. Cast them down. A graphic indication of their haste and eagerness.

31. The maimed to be whole. Tischendorf omits this clause. Alford retains it. It does not imply that any missing members were restored. The word rendered *maimed* signifies literally bent or *crooked*, and nothing more is necessarily involved than a restoration of vitality to a before useless member, as from paralysis. The word applies particularly to the hands, as the word lame to the feet. In no recorded instance did our Lord create members which were missing. Even his miraculous powers Christ did not put forth, says Olshausen, without internal law or order. In this respect, it may be added, his miracles differ from the mere prodigies of the *pseudo* wonder-workers. Mark (7:31-37) gives an account of a particular miracle, the healing of one who was deaf and had an impediment in his speech.

God of Israel. The Pharisees accused Jesus of blasphemy under a statute (Deut. 13:1-4) which punished with death all attempts to divert the allegiance of the people from Jehovah to other gods, and subsequently condemned him to death on the ground that he had thus attempted to divert the allegiance of the people to himself. Observe the refutation of his charge here; their reverence for the God of Israel was increased, not lessened. It is still charged that the doctrine of the divinity of Christ leads to idolatry, the substitution of a hero worship for the worship of a Divine Spirit. In fact, Christianity has produced the highest and most intelligent and spiritual worship of the Infinite and Invisible God (compare John 5 : 23).

32-39. This miracle of the feeding of the four thousand, not to be confounded with the feeding of the five thousand before described by Matthew, is more fully described by Mark 8 : 1-9. See notes there. It is not mentioned by the other two Evangelists. The only material variation in the two accounts is in the description of Christ's subsequent departure from the eastern shore. Matthew says he *came into the coasts of Magdala*, that is, its environs. Mark says he came into *the parts of Dalmanutha*. Neither place is elsewhere mentioned in the N. T. Magdala or Magadar is undoubtedly identical with the modern El-Mejdel. It is situated on the western coast of the sea of Galilee. See map. It was probably the birth-place, and gave the cognomen to Mary Magdalene, that is, Mary of Magdala. Dalmanutha was either identical with it, being only another name for the same place, or a village in the immediate vicinity.

Ch. 16 : 1-4. DEMAND OF A SIGN.—OUR DUTY: TO STUDY THE SIGNS OF THE SPIRITUAL SEASONS.—THE ANSWER TO MODERN SKEPTICISM; THE SIGNS OF THE PRESENT TIMES.

Peculiar to Matthew and Mark 8 : 10-12; fuller here. An analogous demand had been previously made and compliance refused. For there is no reason for identifying this account with that given by Matthew, in chapter 12 : 38-40.

2 He answered and said unto them, When it is evening, ye say, *It will be* fair weather; for the sky is red.
3 And in the morning, *It will be* foul weather to day, for the sky is red and lowering. O *ye* hypocrites! ye can discern the face of the sky; but can ye not *discern* the signs of the times?
4 A wicked and adulterous generation seeketh after a sign; and there shall no sign be given unto it, but the sign of the prophet Jonas.ʳ And he left them, and departed.
5 And when his disciples were come to the other side, they had forgotten to take bread.
6 Then Jesus said unto them,ˢ Take heed, and beware of the leavenᵗ of the Pharisees and of the Sadducees.

ʳ Jonah 1 : 17....ˢ Luke 12 : 1....ᵗ 1 Cor. 5 : 6-8; Gal. 5 : 9; 2 Tim. 2 : 16, 17.

The Jews believed that false gods could work signs on earth, but only the true God could give a sign from heaven. It is not at all strange that the Pharisees and Sadducees should repeat their demand for such a sign, nor that Christ should reply, as before, by referring them to his future resurrection, as typified by the miraculous rescue of Jonah. That this was the second demand of this sort is incidentally confirmed by the touching allusion, in Mark, to the effect which their resolute unbelief produced on the mind of Jesus: He sighed deeply in his spirit. Observe that in Christ, skepticism, even the most obdurate, awoke pity rather than indignation or a spirit of controversy. "He pities and bewails them, as incurably diseased."—(*Chrysostom.*)

2, 3. A figure analogous to that employed in these verses is to be found in Luke after the words, He answered and said unto them, are omitted in several of the best manuscripts, including the Vatican and the Sinaitic. Tischendorf omits them. This figure is not found, either, in Mark's account. But the internal evidence of genuineness is conclusive to my mind. I can easily imagine that an early copyist might, with Strauss, think the passage "totally unintelligible;" but I cannot as readily believe that any one should have had the genius to conceive and interpolate it.

Lowering. Gloomy, with an aspect analogous to that of one who lowers his brows in depression or anger. **Ye can discern the face of the sky.** The Jews were curious in observing the face of the heavens, and the temperature of the air, from which they believed they could discern the prospects of the season. Thus, from the direction which the smoke took on the last day of the feast of the Tabernacles, they undertook to foretell the quantity of the rain for the ensuing year. **Signs of the times.** The original word (*καιρῶν*) rendered *times*, signifies properly *an appointed* or *set time*. It is used in this sense in John the Baptist's preaching, "The time is fulfilled" (Mark 1 : 15), and in this sense here, Christ's question is, Cannot ye discern the signs or tokens of the time appointed, by symbol and prophet in the O. T., for the coming of the Messiah?—in the overthrow of the throne of Herod and the subjection of Israel to Rome, in the degradation, political and moral, of the realm, in the coming of John the Baptist in the spirit of Elijah, and in the miracles wrought for the blessing of the people in fulfillment of such prophecies as that of Isaiah 61 ; 1–3.

The word miracle in the N. T. is generally a translation of the Greek word (*σημεῖον*) here rendered *sign*; for the miracle is always a sign or token of the divine presence and power. Observe then two practical lessons to ourselves in Christ's reply here. It is the duty of Christians to study the signs of God's seasons in church and state, and adapt their work accordingly. The answer to modern skepticism is not chiefly the miracles of the past, *i. e.* the signs of divine power in the first century, but the signs of divine presence and power in our own times. Christ never employs miracles to overthrow unbelief; in employing the argument from them for that purpose we do not use them as Christ used them. Compare note on Matt. 13 : 58.

Ch. 16 : 5–12. WARNING AGAINST THE LEAVEN OF FALSEHOOD.—THE DANGERS OF FALSE TEACHING AND PERNICIOUS INFLUENCE.—THE DUTY OF WATCHFULNESS.—FORMALISM, RATIONALISM, WORLDLINESS, ARE SINS AKIN TO EACH OTHER.

Peculiar to Matthew and Mark 8 : 13–21. The latter account is more graphic and minute. The same caution against the leaven of the Pharisees was repeated on another occasion. See Luke 12 : 1.

5. To the other side. From the western and populous side of the Sea of Galilee to the north-eastern shore. Immediately after this conversation they went, perhaps to get bread, to Bethsaida (Mark 8 : 22) which is situated at the entrance of the Jordan into the lake (see map). **To take bread.** Rather *loaves*. Mark with characteristic particularity adds that "neither had they in the ship with them more than one loaf." The loaf was a thin cake or cracker, made of flower and water or milk, ordinarily mixed with leaven and left to rise, and baked in the oven. It was generally about a finger's breadth in thickness. Three were not too much for a meal for a single person (Luke 11 : 5), and one was considered barely sufficient to sustain life. It is one of these crackers or cakes that is intended by the phrase "morsel" in 1 Sam. 2 : 36, and "piece" in Jer. 37 : 21. Two hundred were not a great supply for a company. See 1 Sam. 25 : 18 ; 2 Sam. 16 : 1.

6. Take heed and beware. A double in-

7 And they reasoned among themselves, saying, *It is* because we have taken no bread.
8 *Which* when Jesus perceived, he said unto them," O ye of little faith, why reason ye among yourselves, because ye have brought no bread?
9 Do ye not yet understand, neither remember the five" loaves of the five thousand, and how many baskets ye took up?
10 Neither the seven" loaves of the four thousand, and how many baskets ye took up?
11 How is it that ye do not understand, that I spake *it* not to you concerning bread, that ye should beware of the leaven of the Pharisees and of the Sadducees?
12 Then understood they how that he bade *them* not beware of the leaven of bread, but of the doctrine of the Pharisees and of the Sadducees.

u ch. 6 : 30 ; 9 : 26 ; 14 : 31....v ch. 14 : 19, etc....w ch. 15 : 34, etc....x ch. 15 : 1-9.

junction. *Be on the watch* for secret errors and evil influences, and *guard yourselves* against them. **Leaven.** This answered to the yeast of modern times. It is in the Bible a symbol of a secret, subtle and pervasive influence; generally of an evil character. Compare 1 Cor. 5:6–8 and notes on Matt. 13:33. **Of the Pharisees and of the Sadducees.** Mark omits *of the Sadducees* and substitutes *of Herod*. The Pharisees were the formalists of the first century, the Sadducees the rationalists, the Herodians the unprincipled and worldly politicians. The leaven against which Christ warns his disciples is that of formalism and pretence, of sneering unbelief, and of the craft and cunning of worldliness. Compare his characterization of Herod in Luke 13 : 32.

7. They reasoned among themselves, etc. Great care was taken by the Pharisaic canons what leaven was to be used and what not ; *e. g.* whether heathen leaven might be employed, is the subject of rabbinical discussions. The disciples thought that Christ reproved them for their carelessness in forgetting to provide bread, lest they corrupt themselves by using bread mixed with the Pharisees' leaven. The incident indicates the spiritual dullness of the disciples (compare Luke 22 : 38), and **refutes the idea of one school of modern rationalists, that many of the spiritual ideas of the Gospels originated with the Evangelists and were imputed by them to Christ.** So far from originating any, they could not even understand his. Observe the indication that, in their ordinary travels, they provided themselves with food, the injunction of Matt. 10 : 9, 10 being purely temporary in its application; and also that in their travels our Lord depended on the disciples to provide the necessary food for their journey. (Compare John 4 : 8).

8. Which when Jesus knew. Perhaps from observation, perhaps by that immediate knowledge of the heart of which the N. T. affords so many illustrations (Mark 2 : 8 ; Luke 5 : 22 ; 6 : 8). **O ye of little faith.** Observe the implication as to the meaning of the word faith, as Christ uses it. Not **here**, Ye of small belief, limited creed, or even defective spirit of trust; but Ye of little spiritual perception. Compare for Scripture significance of faith 2 Cor. 4 : 18 and Hebrews 11 : 1. To this report of Christ's rebuke, Mark makes an important addition. See Mark 8 : 17, 18. He also gives the questions below respecting the two miracles more fully than Matthew. See Mark 8 : 19–21. Observe the fact indicated in the account there, that the disciples remembered definitely the two miracles, and the exact number of baskets of fragments left, but did not learn their spiritual lessons. A striking illustration of "having eyes, yet seeing not."

9–10. Do ye not understand, neither remember the five loaves of the five thousand, and how many traveling baskets (κοφινους) **ye took up? neither the seven loaves of the four thousand, and how many grain baskets** (σπυριδες) **ye took up?** Observe that Christ distinctly refers to two miracles of feeding ; that he discriminates between them by his reference to the "five loaves of the five thousand" and the "seven loaves of the four thousand," and by referring to the different kinds of baskets used. This contrast corresponds exactly to the two accounts (compare notes on Mark 8 : 1-10 and John 6 : 1-13), and to the recollection of the apostles who (Mark 8 : 19-20) respond to Christ's question that in one case they gathered up twelve *traveling* baskets, in the other seven *grain* baskets. It is impossible in the face of this testimony to believe that the account of both miracles is derived from the same event, if we attach any credence to the Evangelist's narratives.

SPORTA.   COPHINUS.
(Grain Basket.)   (Traveling Basket.)

The two accompanying illustrations show the difference in kind between the baskets used on the two occasions. The Cophinus is taken from an engraved gem ; the Sporta from the statue of a young fisherman in the Royal Neapolitan Museum. The *Sporta* was commonly used by the Romans as a provision basket ; the *Cophinus* was used by the Jews as a kind of traveling basket. The scholars are not agreed as to which was the larger ; perhaps there was no generic difference in size.

11. The best critics give, by a slight change in

13 When Jesus came into the coasts of Cæsarea Philippi, he asked his disciples, saying, Whom[y] do men say that I, the Son of man, am?

14 And they said, Some say that thou art John the Baptist; some, Elias; and others, Jeremias, or one of the prophets.

y Mark 8:27; Luke 9:18, etc....a ch. 14:2; Luke 9:7-9.

reading and punctuation, a different rendering to this verse, which should read: "**How is it that ye do not understand that I spake not to you concerning bread? But beware of the leaven of the Pharisees and of the Sadducees.**" Christ does not explain; but he chides their dullness, then repeats his warning, and leaves them to study out its meaning for themselves, which they do.

12. But of the teaching of the Pharisees and of the Sadducees. Not merely the *doctrine*, that is, the things taught, but the *teaching*, which includes the spirit and method. Luke, in his account of Christ's use of the same symbol on another occasion (Luke 12:1), gives Christ's own interpretation, "Beware ye of the leaven of the Pharisees, *which is hypocrisy*."

In considering the practical significance of this teaching, observe that (1) Christ rebukes his disciples, not for a fragrant dereliction, but for a lack of spiritual perception; (2) he teaches in enigma, and requires them to study out its meaning for themselves; (3) their dullness to perceive the spiritual meaning of his teaching was akin to that of the Pharisees, for which he had just before rebuked them (verses 1-4), and both spring from the same source, lack of spiritual life and consequently spiritual perception; (4) false teaching and pernicious influences are ranked by our Lord together and compared to leaven, because subtle, unobserved, and pervasive; (5) the false doctrine of the Sadducees, the worldly spirit of the Herodians, and the religious formalism of the Pharisees are classed together; (6) the disciples are warned to be on the watch against evil teaching in the very quarters where the nation looked and had a right to look for its religious, philosophical, and political leaders.

Ch. 16:13-20. PETER'S CONFESSION OF CHRIST.—THE FALSE AND THE TRUE CONCEPTION OF JESUS CONTRASTED: A PROPHET; THE MESSIAH.—THE SECRET OF ALL TRUE SPIRITUAL KNOWLEDGE: THE TEACHING OF THE SPIRIT OF GOD (1 Cor. 2:10).—THE SECRET OF ALL STABILITY IN CHRISTIAN CHARACTER: FAITH IN A LIVING AND LIFE-GIVING CHRIST. THIS MAKES EVERY POSSESSOR A PETER.—THE FOUNDATION OF THE CHRISTIAN CHURCH: LIVING FAITH IN A LIVING SAVIOUR.—HOW TO MAKE THE CHURCH STRONG AGAINST THE GATES OF HELL: A REVIVAL OF THIS LIVING FAITH BY RECEIVING THE SPIRIT OF GOD.—THE POWER OF THE CHRISTIAN IN THE KINGDOM OF GOD: POWER TO BIND AND LOOSE, i. e., TO WALK IN THE PERFECT LAW OF LIBERTY.—NECESSITY OF CAUTION IN PREACHING THE TRUTH: PREACH ONLY WHAT THE PEOPLE ARE TRULY PREPARED TO HEAR (John 16:12).

This significant and solemn colloquy is recorded by Mark (8:27-30) and Luke (9:18-21), though less fully than here. Matthew alone gives the blessing of Christ pronounced on Peter in verses 18 and 19. John, who wrote his Gospel to make clear his Lord's divinity (John 20:31), omits this incident altogether. The omission is an indication that he wrote with the other Gospels before him, and supplied only what they lacked. The time is correctly indicated in the course of the narrative here. It was after Christ had closed his public ministry in Galilee, and was seeking repose with his disciples for the purpose of imparting to them especial instruction in the principles of his kingdom.

13. When Jesus came into the region of Cæsarea of Philippi. There were two Cæsareas in Palestine; one on the coast, midway between Joppa and Mount Carmel, the other north of Galilee at the head waters of the Jordan, about four miles east of Dan, the northernmost town of the Holy Land proper (see map). It was termed *Cæsarea* in honor of Augustus Cæsar, the great patron of the Herodian family, to whom the great temple erected here by Herod was dedicated, and *Philippi*, i. e. of Philip, to distinguish it from the other Cæsarea and in honor of Herod Philip the tetrarch (Matt. 14:1, and note), who made it the site of his villas and palaces. It is probably to be identified historically with the Baal-gad under Mount Hermon, which marked the northern boundary of Joshua's conquest (Joshua 11:17). Here, subsequently, was erected a sanctuary to the heathen god Pan, which gave to the town the new name of Paneas, which still lingers in the modern appellation Banias. This sanctuary of Pan was constructed in a cave in the rock (*Stanley's Sinai and Palestine*, p. 390); Greek inscriptions on the face of the rock, testifying to the former existence of this sanctuary, still remain. Above this sanctuary, and on the cliff itself, Herod built the white marble temple in honor of Augustus. It is conjectured, not unreasonably, that Christ's colloquy with his disciples took place within sight of this temple; that he referred indirectly to the temple thus founded on a rock, yet not to abide. From this same cliff burst forth, in rivulets, which just below unite in a single stream, the waters which constitute the higher source of the Jordan.

Asked his disciples. Apparently the twelve only. **Whom do men.** Luke says, *the people* (Greek ὄχλος), that is, the common people, the multitude, as distinguished from the Scribes and

15 He saith unto them, But whom say ye that I am?
16 And Simon Peter answered and said,[a] Thou art the Christ, the Son of the living God.
17 And Jesus answered and said unto him, Blessed art thou, Simon Bar-jona: for flesh[b] and blood hath not revealed it unto thee, but[c] my Father which is in heaven.
18 And I say also unto thee, That thou art Peter,[d]

a ch. 14 : 33 ; Ps. 2 : 7 ; John 1 : 49 ; Acts 9 : 20 ; Heb. 1 : 2, 5....b 1 Cor. 2 : 10 ; Gal. 1 : 16 ; Eph. 2 : 8....c 1 John 4 : 15 ; 5 : 20....d John 1 : 42.

the Pharisaic leaders. **That the Son of man is.** This is the reading of the best manuscripts. The Son of man in the N. T. always signifies the Messiah. According to one interpretation, and one which the reading I have given seems to sustain, the question would be, what sort of a person do the public think the expected Messiah to be. But our English version evidently represents the spirit of the question more accurately: What estimate do the public put upon me, the Messiah? For (a) the question is thus reported by both Mark and Luke, where there is no doubt as to the reading, and (b) Christ's second question to his disciples, Whom say ye that I am? shows that he inquires not merely into the commonly received doctrine respecting the Messiah, but into the public opinion, and into his disciples' opinion, respecting himself. Why does he ask this question? To lead his disciples on to a confession of their own higher faith. If one is uncertain respecting the divine character of Jesus Christ, let him, as here, compare that with other hypotheses, and by a comparison reach the truth.

14. **They said, Some, John the Baptist.** This was the opinion of Herod, who thought John whom he had beheaded was risen from the dead (Matt. 14 : 2). **Others, Elijah.** Malachi (4 : 5) had prophesied that Elijah the prophet should come before the great and dreadful day of the Lord, a prophecy fulfilled by the advent of John the Baptist. See Matt. 11 : 14, and note. Some of the people thought Jesus fulfilled this prophecy, and looked forward to the coming of another Messiah. **And others, Jeremiah, or one of the prophets,** i. e. "that one of the *old prophets is risen again*" (Luke 9 : 19). Jeremiah is placed first, because in Jewish canon he was placed first among the O. T. prophets.

16. **And Simon Peter answered.** His original name was Simon or Simeon. The appellation Peter was given him by our Lord, when he first and but temporarily joined Jesus at the ford of Bethabara (John 1 : 40, 41). Chrysostom characterizes him as the "mouth of the apostles and the leader of the apostolic choir." But there is nothing to indicate here that he spoke for them; rather impulsively and ardently, he gave instant expression to his own conviction. Observe his language; not, I say that thou art, nor, We say that thou art, but Thou art. He expresses not an opinion, but an assured and certain fact. **Thou art the Christ.** That is, the *Messiah*, literally *the Anointed*. See note on the names of Jesus, p. 21. **The Son of the living God.** Mark says simply *Thou art the Christ;* Luke, *The Christ of God.* The phrase *living God* was common among the Jews, not merely to distinguish Jehovah from idols (Josh. 3 : 10 ; Acts 14 : 15 ; 1 Thess. 1 : 9), but also to indicate his character as a personal Being, who enters into sympathetic relations with the soul of man, and by the warmth of his own life imparts to the needs of the human soul. (Psalm 42 : 2 ; 84 : 2 ; 2 Cor. 3 : 3 ; 1 Tim. 4 ; 10). It is thus peculiarly appropriate as a designation of Christ, who is the highest manifestation of this personal, living, and life-giving character of our God.

17. **Happy art thou, Simon, son of Jonas.** The meaning of Jonas is *dove*. Some of the commentators see in this an allegorical meaning—Simon, son of the Dove, that is, child of the Holy Spirit. Others think that it recalls his earthly origin in contrast with the spiritual blessing conferred upon him. I should rather regard it simply as an emphatic address, as in John 21 : 15-17, "Simon, son of Jonas, lovest thou me." Such an employment of the double name is common with us in emphatic address. Why peculiarly happy? A similar confession of faith had apparently been made before; by the disciples when Jesus quelled the storm on the lake of Galilee (Matt. 14 : 33), and by Nathaniel on his first meeting with Christ (John 1 : 49). Christ himself answers the question. **For flesh and blood hath not revealed it unto thee, but my Father which is in Heaven.** The previous expressions of faith were produced by wonder, and were founded on extraordinary displays of power or knowledge, which are of *themselves* very inadequate foundations on which to build such a faith. Peter's language here was the expression, in calmness, of a settled conviction, which was produced by a disclosure of the divine character of Christ to the spiritual apprehension of the disciples, by the direct influence of the Spirit of God. True spiritual blessedness consists not in a merely intellectual belief, but in the spiritual apprehension of Christ's divine character. Compare Matt. 11 : 27 ; 1 Cor. 2 : 5 ; Gal. 1 : 15, 16. *Flesh and blood* was a phrase in common use among the rabbis to designate man in contradistinction to God. Here, it is equivalent to anything human, *i. e.*, Christ declares, No power or faculty of man, in yourself or others, has imparted this knowledge to you. Compare 1 Cor. 15 : 50 ; Gal. 1 : 16 ; Ephes. 6 : 12 ; Heb. 2 : 14. Observe the implication of a direct disclosure of the truth by the Spirit of God to the soul. Observe, too, that whilst modern theology

and upon this rock I will build my church; and the gates of hell shall not prevail against it.

19 And I will give unto thee the keys of the kingdom of heaven; and whatsoever thou shalt bind on earth,

e Eph. 2 : 20; Rev. 21 : 14... f Ps. 9 : 13... g Isa. 54 : 17... ch. 18 : 18.

attributes the work of revelation and inspiration to the Holy Spirit, it is here attributed to the Father; one of the many indications that the N. T. makes no such clear philosophical distinction between the three Persons of the Trinity as were later made.

18. Thou art a rock and upon this rock. There is here a play upon the words which it is impossible to preserve fully in the English. The Greek word Peter signifies rock, though there is a difference in the form of the word as Christ uses it; in the first clause of the sentence he employs the masculine form (πέτρος, *petros*), in the latter clause the feminine form (πέτρα, *petra*). Some scholars have drawn important doctrinal conclusions from this variation (see notes below); but the grounds for so doing are very slight. The ordinary form is feminine. In applying the word to a man, Jesus would naturally change it to the masculine form.

I will build my church. The word (ἐκκλησία) here rendered *church*, means, etymologically, *something called together;* it stands in the Septuagint or Greek version of the O. T. for the Great Congregation, or Jewish House of Parliament or Congress, a body half way between a representative gathering and a mass meeting, probably sometimes one and sometimes the other. (Numb. 14 : 1-5, 10; 27 : 18-23; 1 Kings 8 : 1-5; 1 Chron. 13 : 1-8; Psalm 22 : 22). "In the N. T. it most frequently occurs in the sense of an assemblage of Christians generally" (*Kitto*); and if it ever signifies a definite ecclesiastical organization, with officers and spiritual or ecclesiastical powers, this is a secondary meaning, and one which the Apostles could not have attached to it at this time, *when no such organization existed.* Here it is simply equivalent to *my called, i. e.* those called out of the world to represent visibly among men Christ's invisible kingdom; in other words, his entire inorganic body of professed disciples.

The gates of Hades shall not prevail against it. On the meaning of the word hell or Hades (here ᾅδης), see note on Matt. 5 : 22. The phrase *gates of Hades* may be regarded as here equivalent to the forces of the kingdom of death sallying out from its gates, as from a fortified city, to attack the Kingdom of Christ, represented in its Great Congregation; or we may conceive the metaphor to be drawn from the attempt of an enemy to hold captives in a walled city, but without effect, the gates being unable to keep them in their captivity. Thus the gates of Gaza did not prevail against Samson (Judges 16 : 1-3). This appears to me to be the better interpretation. Thus the metaphor involves a promise of immortality, both to the Christian and the Church. Death seems to capture and carry captive the Christian, and so to destroy the Church; but the gates of Hades are powerless to hold the captives, and through the death portal they that seem to be captured enter into the assembly and church of the first-born in heaven (Hebrews 12 : 22, 23). Of the fulfillment of this promise, historical illustrations are afforded by the deliverance of Peter from death (Acts 12 : 1-11), by the resurrection of the Saints at the death of Christ (Matt. 27 : 52), but most of all by the resurrection of Jesus himself as a first-fruits (1 Cor. 15 : 20).

THE FOUNDATION OF CHRIST'S CHURCH. This and the following verse have given rise to volumes of bitter controversy. I shall treat them separately, on account both of their difficulty and their importance. The principal interpretations of this verse are the following:

I. *The ordinary Roman Catholic view;* that Christ declares his purpose to found a great ecclesiastical organization; that this organization was to be built upon Peter and his successors as its true foundation; that they were to represent to all time the authority of God upon the earth, being clothed, by virtue of their office, with a continuous inspiration, and authorized by the word, and fitted by the indwelling Spirit of God, to guide, direct, illumine, and command the disciples of Christ, with the same force and effect as Christ himself. This view is untenable for the following reasons: (*a.*) Christ does not, as we have seen, refer to a definite ecclesiastical organization by the word church (ἐκκλησία), and would not be so understood by his disciples. (*b.*) Peter was not by nature rock-like; he was, on the contrary, characteristically impulsive and unstable. (See note on Simon Peter, pp. 103, 110.) There must be, therefore, some other significance in the words, Thou art a rock, which the Romish interpretation loses. (*c.*) Neither he nor the other disciples understood that Christ invested him with any such authority and position. He did not occupy any such place in the church while he lived. In the first council at Jerusalem (Acts 15 : 7-11) he was simply an adviser, the office of chief, or President, being apparently held by James; Paul withstood Peter to his face as no disciple ever withstood Christ, or would have withstood his acknowledged representative (Gal. 2 : 11-14); and throughout the N. T. the apostles are all treated as co-equals (Matt. 18 : 1; 19 : 28; 23 : 8; John 15 : 1-3; Rev. 21 : 14). (*d.*) There is neither here nor anywhere else in the N. T. any hint of the appointment of a successor to Peter, or of any authority in him to appoint a successor, or of any such authority vested in any of the apostles, or exercised or assumed to be exercised by any of them. (e.) The N. T. throughout, and the O. T. in all its prophecies, recognizes Christ as the chief corner-stone, the foundation on which the Kingdom of God can alone be built (1 Cor. 3:11; Ephes. 2:20). (f.) Mark and Luke omit from their account this utterance of Christ; if it really designated Peter as the foundation of the visible church, and was thus essential and not incidental to the right understanding of the whole incident, it would not be omitted from their accounts.

II. *Various Protestant views.* Of these the chief are the following: 1. That the church was built upon Peter, because he was the first to make it known, as to the Jews on the day of Pentecost (Acts 2:14-36) and subsequently to the Gentiles (Acts, ch. 10). But this view is untenable because (a) the words are too solemnly spoken, and too significant, to be reduced to a mere promise of personal priority in time in preaching the Gospel; (b) according to this view Peter was a builder of the church, not its foundation; and (c) even as a builder he was less a founder than Paul, or perhaps even John and James. 2. That Christ does not refer to Peter, but to his declaration, Thou art the Christ, the Son of the living God, i. e. he declares the rock on which he will build his church is not Peter, but the doctrine of the divinity of Jesus Christ, to which Peter has given expression. But this is untenable because (a) it ignores Christ's play upon the words *Petros* (πέτρος), Peter, and *petra* (πέτρα), rock; (b) the church is not represented in the N. T. as built upon any doctrine, but upon living souls (see Scripture references below, III, b); (c) in fact churches which have retained this doctrine in their creed, the Roman Catholic for example, have become corrupted and Christless in their life. 3. That Christ refers to himself, as in the prophecy of John 2:19, "Destroy this Temple, and in three days I will build it up." Those who hold this view assert that the Rock is throughout the Bible a symbol of God or of Christ (Deut. 32:4, 31; 1 Sam. 9:2; Psalm 92:15; Isaiah 26:4, marg.; 44:8, marg.; 1 Cor. 10:4); that the change in the Greek from the masculine form *Petros* (πέτρος), Peter, to the feminine *petra* (πέτρα), rock, indicates a change in meaning, which Christ may have further interpreted by pointing to himself; that the form of his language indicates such a change, since he does not say "upon *thee*," but "upon this rock." Thus they regard Christ's language as equivalent to, Thou art a piece of rock, and upon the Rock Christ Jesus, from which thou dost derive thy rock-like character, I will build my church. I regard this view untenable because (a) it fails fairly to interpret the play upon the words Peter (πέτρος, *petros*) and rock (πέτρα, *petra*); (b) it contravenes the spirit of the figure, in which Christ, by the words, I will build my church, represents himself as the builder, not as the foundation; (c) it fails to harmonize with the context, in which Christ promises to give to Peter, because of his faith and his place in the church, the keys of the kingdom of heaven. (d.) A careful examination of other passages will indicate that Christ is represented as the Rock on which the church is to be built, only in so far as he is embodied in the life and the faith of his disciples.

III. *The view which I believe to be the correct one* is as follows: That which makes Simon to be in truth a Peter (*a rock*) is his vital faith in Jesus as the Christ, the Son of the living God. Every one who possesses a like faith is, according to the measure of his faith, a Peter, that is, a rock, and Christ builds his church on this rock, that is, on this living experience of faith in the Christ, the Son of the living God, inspired in the hearts of men by the Spirit of God. If this living faith be wanting, neither a whole college of apostles and their successors, nor the most orthodox creed, nor the most unquestioning belief in the divinity of the historic Christ, can sustain the church. Christ's words, then, as I understand them, might be paraphrased thus: *Now*, taught the fundamental truth of the Christian system, not by flesh and blood, but *by my Father which is in heaven*, thy nature is changed, thy native instability is taken away, and henceforth *thou art Peter, a rock; and upon this rock*, this character thus divinely transformed by the renewing of the Spirit (Rom. 12:2) and made strong by a vital faith in the Son of the living God, *I will build my church*, the assembly of my disciples, whose faith is to stand, not in the wisdom of men, but in the power of God. This living faith in Christ, not an ecclesiastical order, nor a correct creed, nor natural strength of character, shall be the basis of my church, which shall be built *out of* living men, and *upon* their living faith in me, as their Messiah and the Messiah of the world. (Compare 1 Cor. 1:27-31; 7:5; 1 Thess. 1:5; 1 Pet. 2:5.) This view I believe to be the correct one, because (a) it accords with the character of Peter, who was not stable by nature, but derived all his true strength from a vital faith in Jesus Christ; (b) it accords with other passages of Scripture, which represent the church as built of living hearts, and upon Christ as embodied in the faith and life of his disciples (Ephes. 2:20-22; Gal. 2:9; 1 Pet. 2:4-6; Rev. 21:14); (c) it accords with the subsequent historical fulfillment of this promise, which has proved that the church is strong and stable, just in the proportion in which its members possess a vital faith in Jesus Christ, and are made Peters (*rocks*) by this their divinely begotten faith in their Head; (d) it embodies whatever

shall be bound in heaven; and whatsoever thou shalt loose on earth, shall be loosed in heaven.

20 Then¹ charged he his disciples, that they should tell no man that he was Jesus the Christ.

1 Mark 8 : 30.

of truth there is in the other interpretations; the superficial truth in the Roman Catholic view, which seizes the letter, but ignores the spirit; and the deeper truth of the more common Protestant view, which perceives correctly that the doctrine of Christ is the foundation of Christianity as a system of doctrines, and Christ is the foundation of his church as a living organism, but which has failed to recognize the significance of the letter, and so has failed to get Christ's full meaning; (c) it is incidently confirmed by Peter's words in 1 Pet. 2 : 4–6, which indicate his understanding of Christ's teaching here, and which certainly point not to himself, but to a vital faith in Christ as the foundation of the Christian Church. In Lange on Matthew, Dr. Schaff's notes, the reader will find a statement of the views of the different commentators. He will be interested to observe that the fathers, Augustine, Jerome, Chrysostom, and others, make either Christ or Peter's confession of a faith in Christ, the rock, not Peter himself; and that the last of the three views I have given above is substantially sustained, by Calvin and by the best modern scholars. Among them may be mentioned Lange, Schaff, Olshausen, De Wette, Meyer, Stier, and Brown.

If this interpretation be correct, the passage teaches—(1.) That the only condition of membership in the visible church which Jesus Christ recognized is vital faith in himself, wrought by the indwelling Spirit of God, neither moral life nor doctrinal belief being adequate without; for of those who possess this faith he declares he will construct his Great Congregation, his visible church. (2.) The condition of true power in the church is always vital faith in Jesus Christ, in the hearts of its members, without which neither ecclesiastical order nor doctrinal accuracy is of any efficacy. The first step, therefore, toward a revival of power in the church, is always the revival of this living faith in the hearts of both minister and people, by seeking and receiving in docility the teaching of the Spirit of God.

19. And I will give unto thee the keys of the kingdom of heaven, etc. In considering the meaning of this confessedly enigmatical and hotly contested passage, the candid student must bear in mind two canons of criticism: *first*, in interpreting Bible metaphors, we must ascertain how the hearers would have understood the metaphorical language; *second*, any principle which we find stated in the Bible in enigmatical or ambiguous language, we may generally expect to find stated elsewhere in the Bible in simpler and more perspicuous language. For essential truths do not depend upon isolated passages, still less upon such as are confessedly difficult of interpretation. Applying the first principle, the following facts must be noted: (1.) This verse is not a gift, but a promise of a gift: *I will give.*

ANCIENT KEY.

(2.) The key, in the East, was a symbol of authority, was made long, with a crook at one end, so that it could be worn round the neck as a badge of office. To this use of the key reference is had in the phrase, "The government shall be upon his shoulder" (Isaiah 9 : 6), and in the promise to Eliakim, "The key of the house of David I will lay upon his shoulder" (Isaiah 22 : 22). (3.) The phrase "kingdom of heaven" in the Gospels never means the visible, external, organic church, and rarely, if ever, the future state in contrast with the present, but the reign of God in the individual soul, or in the community. (See note on Matt. 3 : 2.) The "keys of the kingdom of heaven" do not, then, symbolize power to admit or exclude from the earthly church, or from heaven, but *power in the life of allegiance to God, i. e.* in the Christian life. (4.) The word *bind* (δέω) is never used in the N. T. as a metaphor for condemnation, or fastening guilt upon the soul, but is used metaphorically for binding the individual by laws, as in Rom. 7 : 2; 1 Cor. 7 : 27, 39; and the word *loose* (λύω) is never used as a symbol for pardon or deliverance from sin, but always, either literally of unbinding or dissolving, as in Mark 1 : 7; 2 Pet. 3 : 10, 11, 12, or metaphorically of the relaxing or dissolving of a law, as in Matt. 5 : 19 (where, see note); John 5 : 18; 7 : 23; 10 : 35; 1 Cor. 7 : 27. The words "*bind*" and "*loose*" had also this well established significance among the Jewish rabbis, being nearly equivalent to "prohibit" and "permit." Lightfoot gives a number of illustrations; one will here suffice. "They do not send letters by the hand of a heathen on the Sabbath, no, nor on the fifth day of the week. Yea, the school of Shammai *binds* it (prohibits it) even on the fourth day of the week; but the school of Hillel *looseth* it (permits it)." (5.) The declaration of Christ is not *whomsoever* thou shalt bind and loose, but *whatsoever* (ὅ ἂν) thou shalt bind and loose. Applying these facts, this verse will read thus: I will give thee *authority* (the keys) in the *Christian life* (the kingdom of heaven); and whatsoever thou shalt *prohibit thyself* (bind) on earth shall be *prohibited* (bound) in heaven; and whatsoever thou shalt *permit thyself* (loose) on earth shall be *permitted* (loosed) in heaven.

Two questions remain to be asked and answered: *First*, On whom is this gift bestowed? Certainly not on Peter and his successors in office, for neither here nor anywhere else in the N. T. is there any hint that he had either office or successors. In Matt. 18: 18 it is conferred certainly on all the twelve; and since it is there coupled with instructions concerning forgiveness, and a promise concerning prayer, which are of universal application, it may safely be regarded as not confined to them, but bestowed on all who possess that divinely inspired faith in Christ the Son of the living God, which (see note on preceding verse) made Simon, son of Jona, a Peter, a rock. *Second*, Are there any parallel passages to this promise, as thus interpreted? Confessedly there are none which sustain the papal interpretation. The supposed power of the pope to admit to and shut out from heaven rests solely on this one verse, though John 20: 23 (see note there) is cited in support of his power to remit or retain sin. On the other hand, the right of the individual Christian to rely daily upon the personal help of a living Saviour, and to be governed in his life, not by laws and rules and regulations, but by the in-dwelling Spirit of God, illuminating and inspiring his conscience, is abundantly confirmed by other passages of Scripture. See for example John 8: 32, 36; Rom. 7: 6; 2 Cor. 3: 17; 5: 7; Gal. 3: 25; 4: 7, 31; 5: 1, 16, 18; Col. 2: 14-16, 20-22. It may be objected that this interpretation amounts to a repeal of all law, and a declaration of personal infallibility in every Christian. To which I reply that the language is not more absolute in terms than is that of such promises as, "Whatsoever ye shall ask the Father in my name he will give it you," which, by common consent, we limit by other declarations of Scripture, common sense, and by our own experience. Fairly interpreted, the promise of the *keys* gives not license to the individual to be without law, but it gives him liberty and power in his Christian life to follow the guidance of the Spirit of God, not sure that he will make no mistakes, but sure that there is no condemnation for them that "walk after the Spirit" (Rom. 8: 1).

I understand, then, the promise of the keys to be made to Peter as the possessor of a living faith in Jesus as the divine Messiah, and through him to all who, by a like faith, are endued with a like strength of character, not natural but God-given, and I would paraphrase it thus: To my disciples I will give authority in their spiritual life, so that they shall no longer be bound by rules and regulations like those of the Pharisees or of the Mosaic code, but whatsoever, under the inspiration of a living faith in me, they shall prohibit themselves, God will prohibit, and whatsoever, under that inspiration, they shall permit themselves, God will permit; for they shall have the mind of the Spirit. If I have read this passage aright, it is the spiritual Magna Charta of the disciples of Christ, and its conversion into an engine of ecclesiastical oppression must be accounted one of the most notable among the many perversions of Scripture.

The other principal interpretations of this verse may be classified as follows: 1. *The papal;* that the power of the keys was given to Peter and his successors in office, and confers upon the pope, and through him upon the bishops and other clergy deriving their power from him, authority to admit to or shut out from the kingdom of heaven. 2. *The ecclesiastical;* that this power is given to Peter and the twelve, and to their successors in office, the clergy of the Christian church, and that it confers upon the Christian ministry, or upon the Christian church through the ministry, the power of the keys, whatever that may be, some regarding it as simply a power of teaching, and by teaching opening the kingdom of heaven (Luke 11:52), some the power of discipline, of opening and shutting the door of the visible church on earth, some of true admittance and exclusion from the heavenly kingdom, given to the apostles but retained by the modern ministry, "only conditionally, viz., on the supposition of true repentance and living faith, which the clergy cannot perfectly discern, since the gift of trying the spirits has ceased."—(*Olshausen.*) 3. *The historical;* that it was given only to Peter and his co-disciples, that it conferred on them the power of opening the doors of the kingdom by their preaching, or of binding and relaxing the Jewish laws by their inspired decisions, or of retaining and remitting sin; and the following passages are cited among others in illustration of its exercise. Acts 2: 38-41; 3: 1-8; 5: 1-10; 8: 21; 10: 41-48.

20. That they should tell no man. Both because they were themselves not yet fully instructed, and because the people were not prepared to hear and receive the truth. The Messiahship of Jesus was perfected by his death and resurrection, and on the fact of the resurrection the apostles, Peter pre-eminently, based their subsequent public proclamation that Jesus was the Christ. (Acts 2: 32-36.)

16: 21-28. CHRIST'S TEACHING CONCERNING SELF-SACRIFICE.—"FROM THAT TIME FORTH:" CHRIST ADAPTS HIS TEACHING TO THE FAITH OF HIS HEARERS; AFTER THEIR DECLARATION OF HIS DIVINITY COMES HIS PROPHECY OF HIS SUFFERING.—THE IMPETUOSITY OF LOVE MAY LEAD INTO SIN.—THE TRANSITION FROM THE FULLNESS OF FAITH TO WORLDLINESS ILLUSTRATED BY PETER.—THE SAME DISCIPLE IS AT ONE MOMENT A ROCK,

CH. XVI.]   MATTHEW.   205

21 From) that time forth began Jesus to shew unto his disciples, how that he must go unto Jerusalem, and suffer many things of the elders and chief priests and scribes, and be killed, and be raised again the third day.
22 Then Peter took him, and began to rebuke him, saying, Be it far from thee, Lord this shall not be unto thee.

23 But he turned, and said unto Peter, Get thee behind me, Satan;[k] thou art an offence unto me;[l] for thou savourest not the things that be of God, but those that be of men.
24 Then said Jesus unto his disciples, If any[m] man will come after me, let him deny himself, and take up his cross, and follow me.

j Luke 9 : 22 ; 18 : 31 ; 24 : 6, 7 ; 1 Cor. 15 : 3, 4....k 2 Sam. 19 : 22....l Rom. 14 : 13....m ch. 10 : 38 ; Mark 8 : 34 ; Luke 9 : 23 ; 14 : 27 ; Acts 14 : 17 ; 1 Thess. 3 : 3.

AT THE NEXT, A STONE OF STUMBLING.—THE CAUSE OF SPIRITUAL APOSTACY: "THOU REGARDEST NOT THE THINGS THAT BE OF GOD, BUT THOSE THAT BE OF MEN."—CHRIST OUR MODEL OF RESISTANCE TO EVIL: INSTANT, EARNEST, RESOLUTE.—CROSS TAKING AND CROSS BEARING ARE THE CONDITIONS OF FOLLOWING CHRIST.—THE NATURE OF TRUE CHRISTIAN SELF-DENIAL.—TWO IMPORTANT QUESTIONS: WHAT PROFIT IN BARTERING ONE'S LIFE FOR THE THINGS THAT SHOULD MINISTER TO IT? HOW CAN A LOST LIFE BE RECLAIMED?—THE CERTAINTY OF COMING JUDGMENT A WARNING TO THE IMPENITENT, AN INSPIRATION TO THE CHRISTIAN.—OUR PRIVILEGE: WE SEE THE GLORY OF THE SON OF GOD IN HIS KINGDOM.—Compare Luke 10 : 24.

Given by Mark (8 : 31-38 ; 9 : 1) and Luke (9 : 22-27). But the latter says nothing of Peter's rebuke and Christ's reply.

21. From that time forth began Jesus to shew. This is the first clear prophecy, by Christ, of his crucifixion, though it was intimated in his sermon at Capernaum on the True Bread (John, ch. 6). But the disciples could not receive the doctrine of his death, and did not until history confirmed it. (See Mark 9 : 32 ; Luke 9 : 45 ; 18 : 34). Observe the regular development in his teaching. First, he simply proclaims "The kingdom of heaven is at hand" (Matt. 4 : 17); then he explains the principles and laws of that kingdom in the Sermon on the Mount; then in the parables by the sea (Matt. ch. 13), he sets forth in figures the nature of its progress and the obstacles it will encounter; but not until, by no direct word of his, but by gradual acquaintance with him, the disciples have come to the full faith that he is the Messiah, the Son of God, does he begin to foretell to them his cross. **He must go.** Not because he could not escape, but because it was the way ordained for the fulfilment of his work. Luke 24 : 26 ; Acts 3 : 18. **Elders, Chief Priests, and Scribes.** The *elders* were leaders in the Jewish nation. Their office dates from the patriarchal era. Their age gave them their authority as counsellors and leaders; hence their name. So the modern term Sheik means old man, and the shiek's age is the ground of his authority. These elders exercised certain not very well defined political functions; were organized by Moses into a body, somewhat resembling our Senate (Numb. 11 : 16, 17 ; compare Josh. 9 : 18-21 ; Jer. 26 : 10-16); but existed as a recognized class of men before his time (Exod. 3 : 16 ; 4 : 29). From among them were chosen the governors of districts (Deut. 31 : 28) and local magistrates (Deut. 19 : 12 ; 21 : 3 ; 22 : 15 ; Ruth 4 : 9, 11 ; 1 Kings 21 : 8). From them were selected certain representatives of the lay element in the Sanhedrim, the supreme court of the Jewish nation in the time of Christ. The *chief priests* were the heads of the priestly courses; the *scribes* were the Jewish rabbis, the writers and teachers of the law. Christ's language here represents the Sanhedrim, which was composed of these three classes, laymen, priests, and teachers (see note on Matt. 2 : 4), and constituted the tribunal before which he was tried, and by which he was condemned to death (Matt. 26 : 57, 59).

22. Then Peter took him. Apparently one side. For Mark says Christ spoke that saying openly, as though to contrast with the conference between Christ and Peter which followed; and adds that after Peter's rebuke Christ turned about and looked on his disciples. Luther translates, *Peter took him to himself*.—**Rebuked him.** The Greek (ἐπιτιμάω) signifies literally, to *adjudge*, hence to find fault with. Peter's impulse was founded on a love for Christ which could not bear the thought of his rejection and crucifixion. But it was the disciple's duty to listen to, not to instruct the Master. **Be it far from thee.** Literally, *Mercy on thee!* that is, *God be merciful to thee, God forgive thee*, for this speech. It was an exclamation of strong dissent, seemingly of impatient dissent. Compare for its significance 1 Chron. 11 : 19, where in the Septuagint or Greek version the language is the same, and would be literally rendered, "God forgive me the doing of this thing." **This shall not be to thee.** Peter assumed that he "knew better and could ensure his Divine Master against such an event. It is this spirit of confident rejection of God's revealed purposes which the Lord so sharply rebukes."—(*Alford.*) It is the same spirit which made the cross of Christ a stumbling-block to the Jews and to the Greeks foolishness (1 Cor. 1 : 23), and which leads modern philosophy to reject the N. T. doctrine of a suffering God; and the cause of this rejection is always the same, namely, regarding "not the things that be of God, but those that be of men."

23. But he turned, *i. e.* away from Peter and back to the disciples. Compare Mark 8 : 33. —**Get thee behind me, Satan.** On which

25 For° whosoever will save his life shall lose it; and whosoever will lose his life for my sake shall find it.

26 For what is a man profited, if he shall gain the whole world, and lose his own soul? or° what shall a man give in exchange for his soul?

o John 12 : 25 ; Ex. 4 : 14. . . .o Ps. 49 : 7, 8.

Gavazzi says that the church which is founded on Peter as its rock is a Satanic church. The word Satan signifies adversary. Peter was the adversary of Christ in that he employed his friendship, not to strengthen him for the day of trial, but to dissuade him from it. He unconsciously repeated the temptation presented by the devil in the wilderness. Observe here Christ's illustration of the spirit of his teaching to the disciples, in ch. 10 : 36, 37. Observe, too, that our best friend becomes our worst enemy when he employs his friendship to tempt us to evil, and notice the spirit in which Christ resists the solicitations of such friendship.—**An offence unto me.** The original word (σκανδαλον) here employed, is literally a *trap stick*, *i. e.* a bent stick on which the bait is fastened, and against which the animal strikes and springs the trap. Hence it is used in the N. T. as a metaphor to designate anything which tends to lead one into moral or spiritual ruin. See note on ch. 5 : 29. To Christ Peter is such a trap-stick, who would be, if Christ yielded to him, a baited lure to trap him into sin. Contrast Peter's quiet acceptance of this rebuke with the resistance and anger of Judas Iscariot in John 12 : 47, with Luke 22 : 3, 4. Compare the spirit of John and James when rebuked by our Lord. Luke 9 : 54-56. See Prov. 27 : 6.

Thou art regarding not the things of God, but those of men. Contrast with verse 17 above. In accepting Christ, despite his apparent lowly origin and his really humble career, Peter showed his appreciation of spiritual things; in rejecting the idea of a suffering Messiah he showed that he still retained the earthly idea of greatness, as *power*, rather than the divine idea of greatness, as *love*. (See Exod. 33 : 18, 19 ; Psalm 103 : 8, 13,&c.). The original word rendered *savourest* (φρονεω) expresses the action of the mind, heart and will; it is more than thinking, since that involves only the idea of intellectual activity. Its significance will be indicated to the English reader by comparing the use of the same verb in Rom. 8 : 5, *Do mind* the things of the flesh ; Rom. 12 : 16, *Mind* not high things ; Phil. 2 : 5, *Let* this *mind* be in you which was also in Christ Jesus.

24. Then said Jesus unto his disciples. Also publicly and to the multitude (Mark 8 : 34). The rebuke was private, the teaching public—a lesson to the ministry. Preaching should be practical, but not personal.—**If any man wills to come after me.** That is, will make this his purpose.—**Let him renounce himself.** The Greek verb here (απαρνεομαι) rendered *deny*, is used in describing Peter's denial of his Lord (Matt. 26 : 34, 35). The Latin translation is *abnego*, from which comes our verb abnegate. He must *renounce* self as his master, and *accept* Christ as his master. Christian self-denial consists, not in self-inflicted suffering, nor in sacrificing particular interests, but in *disowning self-interest as the motive of life* and substituting therefor the will of God and the welfare of men.—**And take up his cross.** Luke adds *daily* (Luke 9 : 23). Observe, *his own cross*, not some other man's. Compare Heb. 12 : 1, Let us run with patience the race that is set *before us*. Observe too, on the one hand, that the Christian is not merely to bear the inevitable cross laid upon him, but to *take up* the cross voluntarily ; and on the other, that Christian cross-bearing consists not in assuming penances and inventing self-sacrifices (Col. 2 : 23), but in disowning allegiance to one's self and substituting therefor allegiance to God, thus following Christ's example (John 5 : 30 ; 6 : 38. Compare Gal. 2 : 20 ; Col. 3 : 3). The self to be disowned is interpreted by Rom. 8 : 13. The connection between this and the preceding verse is clear: Not only must you accept the doctrine of a suffering Messiah, if you are to be my disciple you must possess my spirit of willing self-sacrifice for love's sake.

25. Whosoever is determined to save his life shall lose it; but whosoever is willing to lose his life for my sake shall find it. In the original Greek there is a difference between the first and second clause of this verse which the English version does not preserve, but which the above translation may indicate to the English reader. On the spiritual significance of this aphorism see note on Matt. 10 : 39.

26. For what shall it profit a man if he shall acquire the whole world and lose his own life ; or what shall a man give as a ransom for his life ; *i. e.* if it is lost. The word (ψυχη) here rendered *soul*, is the same translated *life* in the preceding verse, and should be so rendered here. The contrast is not between gaining this world and losing the next ; nor exactly between acquiring material and sacrificing spiritual interests ; but between gaining that which is external to one's self and losing one's own character and life in the process. Luke gives it more clearly, *For what is a man advantaged if he gain the whole world and lose himself, or be cast away*. This bargain is made by every man who

27 For° the Son of man shall come in the glory of his Father, with his angels, and ᵈ then he shall reward every man according to his works.
28 Verily I say unto you, There ʳ be some standing here, which shall not taste ˢ of death, till they see the Son of man coming in his kingdom.

CHAPTER XVII.

AND after¹ six days Jesus taketh Peter, James, and John his brother, and bringeth them up into an high mountain apart.
2 And was transfigured before them: and his face

p Dan. 7 : 9, 10 ; Zech. 14 : 5 ; Jude 14....q Rev. 22 : 12....r Mark 9 : 1....s Heb. 2 : 9....1 Mark 9 : 2, etc.; Luke 9 : 28, etc.

barters physical health for luxuries he cannot enjoy, or intellectual culture for means to purchase books and pictures which he cannot appreciate, or affection for money to buy everything for wife and children but love, or worst bargain of all, spiritual life for earthly prosperity. Compare Luke 12 : 16–21 ; 1 Tim. 6 : 9–12, and Eccles., especially chaps. 1 and 2. The second clause of the verse is not, as it appears to be in our version, a repetition of the first clause ; it enforces the argument by a consideration of the irreparable loss when the life of the soul is lost. When a man's life has been spent, what can he give as a ransom or price to get its return? is Christ's question. See Psalm 49 : 7. All other loss can be repaired ; a lost life can never be regained.

27. The connection is this : The self-denial of the present is but temporary, and works out a far more exceeding and eternal weight of glory (2 Cor. 4 : 17). The reference in this verse is certainly not to the transfiguration which follows, nor to the destruction of Jerusalem, nor to the spiritual coming at Pentecost, for neither of these were the *coming of Christ with his angels,* nor *in the glory of his Father.* These phrases point distinctly to the last judgment. Not less do the words which Mark here adds, " Whosoever therefore shall be ashamed of me and of my words, in this adulterous and sinful generation, of him also shall the Son of man be ashamed when he cometh in the glory of his Father with his angels" (Mark 8 : 38).—**According to his works.** Greek (πρᾶξις) *praxis,* from which comes our word practical. It is here rather *working* than *works.* The *character* is judged, but *by the conduct.* For illustration of this declaration see Matt. 7 : 21 ; 25 : 31–46 ; Rev. 21 : 8. And observe that men are never represented in the N. T. as judged at the last day according to their opinions, but according to their lives.

28. The transition between this and the preceding verse is more noticeable in both Mark and Luke than here. Compare the phraseology there. There is a contrast between the coming, referred to in v. 27, in the glory of the Father, when Christ will become subject to the Father (1 Cor. 15 : 28), and the coming in his own kingdom, referred to in v. 28. That the reference in this latter verse is not to the final judgment is evident (*a*) because Christ did not know when that event would take place (Mark 13 : 32) ; and (*b*) because he seems to imply that those who saw it should taste death after that

coming. The reference is to the spiritual coming to establish his kingdom in the power of the Holy Ghost at the day of Pentecost. See this position fully stated in note on chapter 10 : 23, where the different interpretations are given.

Ch. 17 : 1–9. THE TRANSFIGURATION.—THE DIVINE TESTIMONY TO THE DIVINE NATURE OF JESUS CHRIST. —THE REALITY AND CHARACTER OF THE SPIRIT WORLD. —THE TRANSIENT AND THE PERMANENT IN CHRISTIAN EXPERIENCE.—SEE THOUGHTS BELOW.

The account of this event is given also by Mark (9 : 2–8) and Luke (9 : 28–36). It is referred to distinctly and directly by Peter (2 Peter 1 : 16–18) and perhaps by John (John 1 : 14). *The place* is uncertain. Not Mount Tabor, the legendary site, for a fortified town occupied its top. Probably not Mount Hermon, which has been suggested, for the scene at the foot of the mountain the following day indicates that Christ and the twelve were in a Jewish, not a heathen neighborhood. (See verse 17, and the reference to the Scribes in Mark 9 : 14). The most probable supposition assigns as the site of the transfiguration, one of the hills environing the Sea of Galilee. *The time:* after Christ's Galilean ministry had come to an end. He had pronounced the woes against the cities by the sea (Matt. 11 : 20–24), had withdrawn with his disciples to the coasts of Tyre and Sidon, and thence to Cæsarea Philippi (Matt. 15 : 21 ; 16 : 13), had received from them their recognition of his divine character and mission, and had foretold to them his approaching death (Matt. 16 : 14–28). Then, to strengthen their faith, he gives them a glimpse of his glory. Observe that this is not afforded to the multitude, nor even to all the twelve, nor even to the three most intimate disciples until after their faith in him has been established and declared. For he will not have their faith rest on external evidence ; though he will by it support and strengthen them. So our clearest experiences of Christ's spiritual glory come, not in our first acquaintance with him, but after living with him as our Saviour. *The hour:* the night. For he had gone up into the mountain to pray (Luke 9 : 28) as he was accustomed to do by night (Matt. 14 : 23, 24 ; Luke 6 : 12 ; 21 : 37 ; 22 : 39) ; the apostles were heavy with sleep (Luke 9 : 32), and did not descend until the next day (Luke 9 : 37). Moreover, the transfiguration, especially as Luke describes it, would hardly have been recognizable, certainly not so marked, by day.

did shine as the sun,[a] and his raiment was white as the light.

3 And, behold, there appeared unto them Moses and Elias, talking with him.

4 Then answered Peter, and said unto Jesus, Lord, it is good for us to be here: if thou wilt, let us make here three tabernacles; one for thee, and one for Moses, and one for Elias.

---

a Rev. 1 : 16.

---

1. After six days. That is, subsequent to the prophecies of Christ's death recorded in the previous chapter. All the evangelists give this note of time. Luke says, *about an eight days:* possibly he includes both the last day of the preceding conversation, and the day of the transfiguration; or his language *about* (ώσεί) may be taken to indicate that he is not and does not claim to be definite.—**Peter, James, and John his brother.** They were Christ's only companions in Gethsemane (Mark 14 : 32-42), and there, as here, they were heavy with sleep. They alone witnessed the resurrection of Jairus' daughter (Mark 5 : 37; Luke 8 : 51). Why was this privilege accorded to them above the others? We can only answer, because it seemed good in their Lord's sight. (Compare John 21 : 22 ; Rom. 9 : 11). All Christ's disciples do not now share the same experience of his glory.—**High mountain.** The site is wholly unknown. See above. He went up *to pray* and *as he prayed* was transfigured (Luke 9 : 29). So at his baptism the heavens opened and the dove descended, *as he was praying* (Luke 3 : 21 ; compare Acts 7 : 55, 56 ; Rev. 1 : 10).

2. And was transfigured before them. The nature of the transfiguration is indicated by the description which follows, and yet more definitely by the accounts of Mark and Luke. His face shone as the sun; his garments became white "*as the light*" (Matt.), *i. e.* luminously white, "*as no fuller on earth can white them*" (Mark), *i. e.* with a supernatural whiteness; "*white and glistering*" (Luke), *i. e.* flashing. The same Greek word (έξαστράπτω) in Luke rendered *glistering*, is used in Nahum 3 : 3 to describe spears glittering in the sun, and in Ezek. 1 : 7 to describe the brightness of the living creatures who "sparkled like the colour of burnished brass." The transfiguration then consisted, apparently, in a luminous appearance which pervaded the whole face and figure of Jesus (compare Exod. 34 : 29, 30). As Christ took on him human nature and condition for converse with man, so here, it appears to me, he is represented as taking on the form and condition of the spirits, for the purpose of communion with the spiritual world. Observe that it took place *before them, i. e.* the disciples, not during their sleep. They saw, not only Christ after he was transfigured, but also the process of the change, as it came over him. It is true, Luke's account, in our English version, implies that they were asleep, and were wakened out of it to behold the glory (Luke 9 : 32). But the original does not justify this interpretation. See notes there.

3. There appeared unto them. That is, to the disciples. The implication is, that they not only saw the appearance, but recognized, in the persons, Moses and Elijah. How this recognition was afforded, is not stated; perhaps by a subtle spiritual power of recognition. We often appear to ourselves to recognize in dreams persons we have never seen ; why may not the soul, in special spiritual conditions, possess a similar power of recognizing, in reality, unknown persons? That Moses and Elijah were recognized, *at the time*, by the apostles, is evident from Peter's proposition (verse 4).—**Talking with him.** Luke gives the subject of the conversation: "His decease which he should accomplish at Jerusalem." It is worthy of note that Elijah did not die, but was translated, and that Moses' death was shrouded in peculiar mystery (2 Kings 2 : 11; Deut. 34 : 6). Dr. Brown's comment here is important : "They speak not of his miracles, nor of his teaching, nor of the honor which he put upon their Scriptures, nor of the unreasonable opposition to him, and his patient endurance of it. They speak not of the glory they were themselves enshrouded in, and the glory which he was so soon to reach. Their one subject of talk is his *decease* which he was going to accomplish at Jerusalem. One fancies that he might hear them say, Worthy is the Lamb that *is* to be slain."

4. Then answered Peter. The foremost to speak ; awe silences the rest, but not him. Compare with his characteristic impetuosity here, the incidents recorded in John 20 : 5, 6 ; 21 : 7. Luke gives the explanation of his speaking. He spake "as they (*i. e.* Moses and Elijah) were departing," evidently to hinder their departure, and induce them to remain.—**It is good for us to be here.** It often appears to the Christian to be good to abide with Christ in spiritual exaltation. But such hours are rare, and meant to be. It is better to descend and go about with Christ doing good. The one is often *our wish*, the other is *his will*.—**Let us make.** The better reading appears to be *I will make.* It is, at all events, an offer of service for the honor of Christ.—**Three tabernacles.** Rather booths, *i. e.* huts of the branches of the trees, such as Jacob made for his cattle (Gen. 33 : 17), and Jonah for a temporary shelter (Jonah 4 : 5). At the feast of the tabernacles, the Jews dwelt for a time in such booths, to remind them of their sojourn in the

5 While he yet spake, behold, a bright cloud overshadowed them: and, behold, a voice out of the cloud, which said, This is my beloved Son, in whom I am well pleased; hear ye him.
6 And when the disciples heard it, they fell on their face, and were sore afraid.
7 And Jesus came and touched them, and said, Arise, and be not afraid.

8 And when they had lifted up their eyes, they saw no man, save Jesus only.
9 And as they came down from the mountain, Jesus charged them, saying, Tell the vision to no man, until the Son of man be risen again from the dead.
10 And his disciples asked him, saying, Why then say the scribes that Elias must first come?

v ch. 3 : 17; Mark 1 : 11; Luke 3 : 22; 2 Pet. 1 : 17....w Isa. 42 : 1, 21...x Deut. 18 : 15, 19; Acts 3 : 22, 23; Heb. 1 : 1, 2; 2 : 1-3....
y Dan. 10 : 10, 18; Rev. 1 : 17....z ch. 11 : 14; Mal. 4 : 5, 6.

wilderness (Lev. 93:49; Neh. 8:15,16). Luke says that Peter spake "*not knowing what he said*," and Mark gives the explanation "*for they were sore afraid.*" In other words, his was not a well-considered proposition, to retain the spirits in earthly tabernacles, but an ardent expression inspired by awe and spiritual ecstasy commingled.

5. Behold, a bright cloud overshadowed them. The language of the English version in Luke would leave the impression that all, including the disciples, entered this cloud; but such is not the significance of the original (see Luke 9:34, and note). Christ, Moses, and Elijah are alone represented as entering into the cloud, which separated them from the disciples' sight, and out of this cloud the voice spake to the disciples. By the disciples such a luminous cloud would be instantly accepted as a symbol of the divine presence. It is represented in the Scripture as the habitation or chariot of God (Psalm 97:2; 104:3; Isaiah 19:1; compare 1 Tim. 6:16). A bright cloud, the Shechinah, is throughout the O. T. dispensation employed as a symbol of God's presence, being very generally entitled "the glory," or "the glory of the Lord." It appeared first to Moses in the bush, burning but not consumed (Exod. 3:2); led Israel through the wilderness (Exod. 13:21, 22); rested on Mount Sinai when Moses went up for conference with God (Exod. 19:9, 18; 24:16); filled the tabernacle on its completion (Exod. 40:34, 35); appeared from time to time as an accompaniment of special communion with God (Exod. 16:7, 10; 33:7-11; Numb. 14:10; 16:19, 42; 20:6). After the death of Moses, just previous to which it is seen (Deut. 31:15), it disappears from Jewish history to reappear at the dedication of Solomon's temple (1 Kings 8:10). Ezekiel describes its solemn departure from Israel (Ezek. 10:4, with 11:23), but prophecies its return (Ezek. 43:2,4), to which also there appear to be references in the other prophets (Isaiah 4:5; Zech. 2:10). This symbol of the "glory of the Lord" appeared to the shepherds at the time of Christ's birth (Luke 2:9), and received Christ at his ascension (Acts 1:9). Since then it has disappeared again from earth, but will surround him at his second coming (Matt. 24:30; 26:64; Mark 13:26; 14:62; Luke 21:27; Rev. 1:7; 14:14), and will receive the ascending saints (1 Thess. 4:17; Rev. 11:12, compare Rev. 10:1).—**A voice out of the cloud.** A voice directly communicating the divine will was a common accompaniment of the appearance of the Shechinah. See Exod. 33:9, and other references above.

This is my beloved Son. Thus a triple testimony confirms the faith of Peter and the disciples declared in the previous chapter—Moses, the lawgiver, Elijah, the prophet, and the appearance and voice of God. The phrase "beloved Son" is applied to no one in the N. T. but to Jesus. Compare Matt. 3:17, and note. Observe also the implied contrast between Moses and Elijah the servants, and Christ the Son of God.—**Hear ye him.** A gentle rebuke to Peter. There are times when the highest duty is not to speak, even in praise of Christ, but simply to be still and know the Lord. See Psalms 4:4; 46:10; Luke 10:39-42. Observe the implication that the law and the prophets both point to and prepare for Christ. The sum of their teaching to us is, Hear ye Him.

6, 7. Peculiar to Matthew. Observe that fear is the common effect in the human mind of any experience which brings near to us the invisible world (Judges 13:20; Ezek. 1:25), and that Christ's reassuring message is, *Be not afraid* (Luke 2:9, 10; Matthew 14:27; 28:4,5; Rev. 1:17).

8. They saw no man save Jesus only. Moses, the representative of the law, and Elijah, of the prophets, depart; Christ the Son, abides. Compare Hebrews 3:5, 6.

9. Vision (Greek ὅραμα). This word is sometimes simply equivalent to sight or things seen (Acts 7:31), sometimes it indicates a spiritual ecstasy or trance, or rather that which appears in the trance state (Acts 11:3; 10, 17), sometimes an experience which may have been wrought through a dream (Acts 16:9; 18:9). Here Christ's direction is simply equivalent to, Tell what you have seen to no man. It leaves the question whether the sight had been afforded in a dream, a trance, or a natural condition, to be determined by other considerations. Luke states that "they (the disciples) kept it close and told no man in those days;" but he does not give the reason for their silence. Mark adds that they questioned one with another "what the rising from the dead should mean," one of the many indications in the N. T. that they did not understand, or at least did not accept, his prophecies of his death, nor comprehend his prophecies of his resurrection.

11 And Jesus answered and said unto them, Elias truly shall first come, and restore all things.
12 But I say unto you, That Elias is come already, and they knew him not, but have done unto him whatsoever they listed. Likewise shall also the Son of man suffer* of them.
13 Then the disciples understood that he spake unto them of John the Baptist.

a ch. 16 : 21.

Both events, though foretold, were entirely unexpected to them. Compare Luke 18 : 34.

LESSONS OF THE TRANSFIGURATION. Many attempts have been made to explain away this incident; as that it is a legend growing out of the glory of Christ's person and teaching, or a dream of Peter, induced by a thunder-storm, the cloud or mist pervaded by electric light being mistaken by the half-wakened disciple for the Shechinah, or that it narrates an experience in a trance, analogous to that of Peter described in Acts, ch. 10. No one, however, can doubt that the writers intended to be understood as narrating a real occurrence. That it could not have been a dream is evident, because it was experienced simultaneously by three, and while they were fully awake (Luke 9 : 32, and note). There is no incident in the Bible of a trance experienced by three simultaneously; but we know too little of what a trance is to speak definitely on that hypothesis. The reality of the conversation of Jesus with Moses and Elias is assured; that, in order to become cognizant of it, the disciples were thrown into a trance is possible, but is nowhere indicated in the narrative. These *quasi* explanations grow out of the assumption either that there is no spirit-world, or that it can never hold communion with this world, two errors which it is the express purpose of this incident to correct.

It appears to me to teach the following lessons: *Directly* (1) that Jesus is the Christ, the Son of the living God. It follows the testimony of Peter to his Lord's divinity; confirms that faith; gives it directly the divine sanction; implies the sanction of the law and the prophets. (2.) The reality and something of the nature of the spirit world. I hesitate to interpret its teachings concerning the nature of an existence which is *necessarily* beyond our clear apprehension. This incident, however, appears to me to *indicate* that the state intermediate death and the judgment is not one of unconscious existence; that the departed dwell in glorified bodies (though Paul appears in 1 Cor. 15 : 44, 51-53, to imply that the glorified body is raised up at the general resurrection); that they are, like the angels, ministering spirits (Heb. 1 : 7); that communication between the other world and this is possible, though exceptional; that the immortal life is not exclusively future, but has already commenced. *Indirectly* it teaches the relation between high ecstatic experience and practical piety. The former are occasional, exceptional, transient, confined to the few; the latter is for all times, for all places, for all persons. But three ascend the mountain with Christ, and they cannot abide there; the many throng him in the valley, and none are denied his presence.

Ch. 17 : 10-13. QUESTION CONCERNING ELIJAH.—THE MESSAGE AND MESSENGER OF GOD ARE OFTEN UNRECOGNIZED.

Elias is the Greek form of the word Elijah. Alford gives the connection of the disciples' question with the preceding incident. "The occasion of this inquiry was that they had just seen Elijah withdraw from their eyes, and were enjoined not to tell the vision. How should this be? If this was not the coming of Elijah, was he yet to come? If it was, how was it so secret and so short?" The prophecy of Elijah's coming, as a forerunner to the Messiah, is in Mal. 4 : 5. On this prophecy and its fulfillment by John the Baptist, see note on Matt. 11 : 14.

11. Elijah indeed cometh. Not *shall first come*, but *is coming*—the tense is present, not future.—**And shall restore all things.** Observe, it is of a *restoration*, not of a *new creation*, Christ speaks. John the Baptist attempted a reformation of Judaism, and he was himself a restoration of the extinct order of prophets and the last of that order. This reformation of Judaism was the preparation for Christianity. Certain of the commentators look for a second coming of Elijah, personally, as a preliminary to the second coming of Christ. Do they also expect a second restoration of Judaism? But this would involve the undoing of what has been done, in the establishment of the larger and freer religion of Jesus Christ. Old things are passed away, and are not to be restored; all things are become new. I do not here consider the vexed question of Christ's second coming. But it seems to me that the language here, and in the succeeding verse, gives no countenance to and is scarcely reconcilable with the second coming of Elijah. However, on all unfulfilled prophecies I speak with diffidence.

12. Elijah is come already. James Morison renders *The coming of Elijah is already past*. **And they knew him not.** They did not recognize in John the Baptist the fulfilment of the prophecy of the coming of Elijah.—**But have done unto him whatsoever they listed.** The account of his martyrdom is given in Matt. 14 : 6-12, Mark 6 : 21-29. The murder was per-

14 And^b when they were come to the multitude, there came to him a *certain* man, kneeling down to him, and saying,
15 Lord, have mercy on my son; for he is lunatic, and sore vexed: for ofttimes he falleth into the fire, and oft into the water.
16 And I brought him to thy disciples, and they could not cure him.
17 Then Jesus answered and said, O faithless and perverse generation! how long shall I be with you! how long shall I suffer you? bring him hither to me.
18 And Jesus rebuked the devil, and he departed out of him; and the child was cured from that very hour.
19 Then came the disciples to Jesus apart, and said, Why could not we cast him out?
20 And Jesus said unto them, Because of your unbelief:^c for verily I say unto you, If^d ye have faith as a grain of mustard seed, ye shall say unto this mountain, Remove hence to yonder place, and it shall remove; and nothing shall be impossible unto you.

21 Howbeit, this kind goeth not out, but by prayer and fasting.
22 And while^e they abode in Galilee, Jesus said unto them, The Son of man shall be betrayed into the hands of men;
23 And they shall kill him, and the third day he shall be raised again. And they were exceeding sorry.
24 And when they were come to Capernaum, they that received tribute *money* came to Peter, and said, Doth not your master pay tribute?
25 He saith, Yes. And when he was come into the house, Jesus prevented him, saying, What thinkest thou, Simon? of whom do the kings of the earth take custom or tribute? of their own children, or of strangers?
26 Peter saith unto him, Of strangers. Jesus said unto him, Then are the children free.
27 Notwithstanding, lest we should offend^f them, go thou to the sea, and cast an hook, and take up the fish that first cometh up; and when thou hast opened his mouth, thou shalt find a piece of money; that take, and give unto them, for me and thee.

---

b Mark 9 : 14, etc. ; Luke 9 : 37, etc. ....c Heb. 3 ; 19....d ch. 21 : 21; Mark 11 : 23; Luke 17 : 6; 1 Cor. 13 : 2....e ch. 16 : 21; 20 : 17–19; Mark 8 : 31; 9 : 30, 31; 10 : 33; Luke 9 : 22; 18 : 33; 24 : 6, 26, 46.....f Rom. 14 : 21; 15 : 1-3; 2 Cor. 6 : 3.

petrated by Herod. Here it is imputed to the Scribes and Pharisees, because their influence was adverse to John, and perhaps because, if they had recognized and received him, Herod, who feared the people, would have feared to perpetrate the murder.

14-21. HEALING OF THE DEMONIAC BOY. Recorded also in Mark 9 : 14–29, and Luke 9 : 37–43. The account is fullest in Mark. See notes there. But observe the transition from the scene of glory to the scene of suffering, and the reason why it would not have been good for Christ and the three disciples to have remained above in tabernacles, on the mountain; because so they would have left the suffering uncared for.

22, 23. CHRIST'S PROPHECIES OF HIS DEATH. Recorded also in Mark 9 : 30–32; Luke 9 : 43–45. See note on ch. 16 : 21.

Ch. 17 : 24-27. DEMAND OF TRIBUTE, AND CHRIST'S REPLY.—THE CHURCH OF CHRIST IS A FREE CHURCH. IT IS SUPPORTED BY VOLUNTARY OFFERINGS, NOT BY COMPULSORY TAXATION.—IT IS BETTER TO SUBMIT TO AN UNJUST DEMAND, THAN, BY RESISTING, TO DO AN ACT OF SEEMING WRONG.

Peculiar to Matthew. Whether this incident occurred at the time indicated by its place in this chapter is uncertain. The temple tribute, here referred to, was generally paid at the time of the Passover, and that leads to the hypothesis that Matthew has inserted it here, out of its place, because of its connection with the other teachings of Christ, in these chapters, concerning himself as the Son of God, and the Church as the representative of the kingdom of God. But the tax was not always promptly paid. Payment was indeed so irregular, that Lightfoot says that the receivers of the tribute had before them two chests placed, one of which received the tax of the current year, the other the tax of the year past.

24. Capernaum. The demand was made at Capernaum, because it was the residence of both Jesus and Peter. The wandering life of our Lord and his disciples had perhaps prevented the demand from having been made before.—**Tribute.** A mistranslation, and an unfortunate one; for it at once conveys the idea of a tax to the Roman government. The true rendering is, *Doth not your master pay the didrachm* (two drachmas), or half shekel, a sum equivalent to about thirty cents of our money. This was a tax levied annually on all Israelites, for the support of the Temple, the morning and evening sacrifice, the incense, wood, shew-bread, scape-goat, &c.

25. Jesus anticipated him. That is, Jesus, knowing what had passed between Peter and the tribute takers, spoke, before Peter had opportunity to speak to him on the subject.—**Of whom do the kings of the earth take custom** (*taxes on goods*) **or tribute** (*the poll tax*)? **of their own sons or of other men?** The contrast is not between the citizens of the State and foreigners or strangers, for taxes were paid by all citizens, but between the children of the royal family, who were exempt from taxation, and the rest of the people. For significance of the word here rendered *strangers*, see Luke 16 : 12; Romans 14 : 4; 15 : 20, where it is rendered *another man*.

26. This is not a mere re-statement of Peter's declaration, equivalent to *Then are the children of the kings free;* but an application of the principle to the question of paying the Temple tax, and is equivalent to, On this principle, the children of God are free from taxes for the support of his kingdom.

27. Lest we should scandalize them; by refusing to pay the tax, an act liable to be totally misunderstood, and charged to impiety or religious indifference.—**And when thou hast opened his mouth, thou shalt find.** But not necessarily in his mouth, perhaps in the stomach where valuables are often discovered by fishermen.—**A piece of money.** Literally a tetradrachm (four drachmas) or stater (Greek στατήρ). The language of our Lord defines the

TETADRACHM OR STATER.

coin which should be discovered, and which would be of exactly the right amount to pay the tax for the two. The stater, which answered to the Hebrew shekel, was equivalent to about sixty cents of our money. **For me and thee.** It is a noticeable fact that Christ never ranks himself with his disciples. His language here is not *for us*, but *for me and thee*, as elsewhere it is not *Our Father*, but "my Father and your Father, my God and your God" (John 20:17).

SIGNIFICANCE OF THIS INCIDENT. The first tabernacle was constructed wholly by voluntary offerings (Exod. 35:5). Subsequently, the amount to be paid yearly by each one for the Tabernacle or Temple was fixed at a half shekel (Exod. 30:12-15), which was accepted as a ransom, for the soul of the giver, unto the Lord. Still no provision was made for compelling payment, if it were refused, and it seems to have remained in the nature of a voluntary gift. But in subsequent history there was a bitter conflict between the Sadducees and the Pharisees, upon the question whether this should be regarded as a free-will offering or made compulsory. The Pharisees, who advocated the latter position, carried their point; and so great was the conflict and their triumph, that they kept the anniversary as a kind of half festival. After the destruction of Jerusalem the tax was continued by Vespasian, but was applied to the uses of the Temple of the Capitoline Jupiter (Josephus' Wars, 7:6, § 6). This temple tax was called for by the temple tax-gatherer, from Jesus. He is uncertain whether this new Rabbi will acknowledge or repudiate the tax, will class himself with the Pharisees or Sadducees. Peter, knowing his Lord's principle to fulfill all the obligations of the law (Matt. 3:15; 5:17; 23:3), answers at once that his Master will pay it. Christ replies: The children of a king are not liable to compulsory taxation for their father's support. My followers are children of the Great King. They are not, therefore, to be *compelled* to pay a specified sum for the support of his house and worship. Their offerings must be free-will offerings. Thus Christ stamps with his disapproval all systems which make the church of Christ depend for support on ecclesiastical taxation of any kind, and declares that it must be supported by the free-will offerings of the children of God. This he has declared before by implication (Matt. 10:10, and note). This is the basis on which the church was subsequently placed by the apostles (Acts 2:45; 4:34; 1 Cor. 16:1, 2; 2 Cor. 9:1,7). The incident has been misinterpreted by some of the older commentators, who mistook the tribute referred to for the tax payable to the Roman government—an error which is refuted, both by the original Greek, and by the general scope of the incident. It has been misunderstood by many of the English and the continental commentators, who have been generally committed to a State church, and averse to see in the N. T. anything inconsistent with the support of such a church by church rates. They have accordingly generally regarded it as simply a personal claim by Christ to be free, because he is the Son of God. But that he signifies the freedom of all his followers from ecclesiastical tax, and the support of his church by free-will offerings, is evident because (*a*) he declares not, Then *am I* the Son of God free, but then are *the children* free; (*b*) he emphasizes this declaration by providing payment for Peter as well as for himself; (*c*) this accords (see references above) with other parallel teachings of the N. T.; (*d*) it accords with the fact that a half shekel tax was a ransom paid for the soul (Exod. 30:12), and that the souls of the children of God are ransomed once for all by Christ. Trench says, "This (liberty) plainly is not true concerning dues owing to God; none are so bound to render them as his '*sons*.'" But this is an exact begging of the question, or rather a direct repudiation of the teaching of Christ and the apostles, which is, that all the law is included in love, and that no *compulsory* dues can take the place of a free-will offering. For a fuller statement of this interpretation see E. H. Plumptre in *Smith's Bible Dictionary*, article *Tribute*. The Lord provides the money, however, "lest we *should scandalize them.*" James Morison gives the explanation well: "leading them to think, perhaps, that he was opposed to the temple-service, or that he was churlish in his disposition, or that in his heart, the true state of which is often revealed by money transactions, he was irreverent toward God." And Plumptre draws aright the lesson from his compliance. "It is better to comply with the payment, than to startle the weak brethren, or run counter to feelings that deserve respect, or lay an undue stress on a matter of little moment."

CHAPTER XVIII.

A T the same time came the disciples unto Jesus, saying, Who is the greatest in the kingdom of heaven?

2 And Jesus called a little child unto him, and set him in the midst of them,
3 And said, Verily I say unto you, Except ye be converted,ᵇ and become as little children,ⁱ ye shall not enter into the kingdom of heaven.

g Mark 9 : 33, etc. ; Luke 9 : 46, etc. ; 22 : 24, etc....h Ps. 51 : 10-13 ; John 3 : 3... .i 1 Cor. 14 : 20 ; 1 Pet. 2 : 2.

Ch. 18 : 1-14. DISCOURSE CONCERNING GREATNESS IN THE KINGDOM OF HEAVEN.—CHRIST'S USE OF OBJECT TEACHING (V. 2).—LESSONS TO BE LEARNED FROM A LITTLE CHILD.—CONVERSION ILLUSTRATED (V. 3).— HUMILITY ILLUSTRATED (V. 4).—TO RECEIVE CHRIST, RECEIVE ONE OF HIS LITTLE ONES (V. 5).—TO OFFEND CHRIST, TEMPT ONE OF HIS LITTLE ONES (VS. 6-9).—THE NEEDY ARE NEAREST TO GOD'S THRONE (V. 10).—REDEEMING LOVE ILLUSTRATED (VS. 11-14).

PRELIMINARY NOTE. This eighteenth chapter of Matthew contains instructions concerning the Kingdom of God, which were given to the twelve alone. It may be divided into three sections. In the first (verses 1-14) Christ warns his disciples against ambition and self-seeking, and counsels them against leading astray humbler and feebler disciples; in the second (verses 15-20) he tells them what course the disciple is to pursue toward the wrong-doer; in the third (verses 21-35) he illustrates and enforces the duty of personal forgiveness. The conference appears to have taken place at Capernaum and in the house (Mark 9 : 33), possibly the house of Peter, who resided there. Verses 1-9 have their parallel in Mark 9 : 33-50, and Luke 9 : 46-50. The rest of this chapter is peculiar to Matthew. Some of the aphorisms contained in it are, however, found elsewhere in Christ's teaching, and some points here hinted at are more fully treated by our Lord at other times (see notes below). Matthew connects the instructions given in this chapter by the particles "moreover" (verse 15) and "then" (verse 21); but these do not always, in N. T. usage, indicate a close chronological connection; and though it is not improbable that this chapter constituted one discourse, delivered to the disciples at one time, it is by no means certain that Matthew has not gathered here instructions imparted at different times, but all during the same general period of Christ's ministry, and relating to the same general theme.

1. At the same time. Literally, *In the same hour.* That is, apparently, immediately subsequent to the incident narrated in the previous chapter. According to this account the disciples came to Christ with the question, Who is the greatest? According to Mark (9 : 33) they had engaged in a dispute who should be the greatest, i. e., who should hold the chief offices in the political kingdom which they supposed Christ had come to establish. Christ asked them the subject of their controversy, and they held their peace, being probably ashamed of it. Townsend's explanation of the seeming inconsistency is reasonable. This is, that certain of the disciples had claimed pre-eminence, as James and John did later, that Jesus asked them of their dispute, that they were ashamed to reply, and that then the other disciples preferred the question, Who is the greatest ? Matthew has given only this question and Christ's answer; Mark has narrated the circumstances which led to it. Similar disputes continued, in spite of the teaching given here, down almost to the time of Christ's death. (Matt. 20 : 20, 21, 24 ; Luke 22 ; 24.)—**Who is the greatest.** Literally, *greater*, i. e., than the rest. The language is in the original, as in the English, in the present tense ; but the question probably had a future meaning. Their question was not, What elements of character make true greatness? who of us *is* greatest? but, Who of us shall occupy the highest place in your coming kingdom? It was the question of the ecclesiastic, not of the true Christian disciple. "Peter was always the chief speaker, and already had the keys given him; he expects to be lord chancellor, or lord chamberlain of the household, and so to be the greatest. Judas had a bag, and therefore he expects to be lord treasurer, which, though now he comes last, he hopes will then dominate him the greatest. Simon and Jude are nearly related to Christ (but query as to this statement, see pp. 111, 112), and they hope to take the place of all the great officers of state, as princes of the blood. John is the beloved disciple, the favorite of the Prince, and therefore hopes to be the greatest. Andrew was first called, and why should not he be first preferred ?"—(*Matthew Henry.*)

2. And Jesus called a little child to him. Evidently, from the language employed (the Greek is *παιδίον*, the diminutive), it was a young child ; evidently from his *calling* it, not a mere infant.—**And set him in the midst of them.** A striking illustration and an incidental endorsement of object teaching in morals. The O. T. prophets, Ezekiel especially, often employed the same method.

3. Except ye be converted. For the meaning of the word (στρέφω) here rendered *converted*, see Luke 7 : 9. Jesus "turned him about," i. e., he was going in one direction and turned about so as to face in the other direction, Acts 7 : 39, "our fathers * * * in their hearts *turned back* again into Egypt," i. e., from following and serving Jehovah turned back to

4 Whosoever therefore shall humble himself[j] as this little child, the same is greatest in the kingdom of heaven.

5 And whoso shall receive one such little child[k] in my name, receiveth me.
6 But whoso shall offend[l] one of these little ones

[j] Luke 14:11; Jas. 4:10....[k] ch. 10:42....[l] Mark 9:42; Luke 17:1, 2.

worship the golden calf which was an image of the Egyptian bull, Acts 13:46, "seeing ye judge yourselves unworthy of everlasting life, we *turn* to the Gentiles." These passages indicate the meaning to be attached to the word here rendered *convert* (στρέφω), which always signifies a radical and complete change, in method, spirit, or course. Here it is, Unless you be turned entirely away from this spirit of self-seeking you cannot enter the kingdom of heaven, much less be greatest in it. The verb is in the passive mood; it is not, Except ye turn, but, Except ye *be* turned, thus indicating that the turning of the disciples, to be effectual, must be by a higher power than their own.

[The Greek student should also observe that the tense here is not the future, but the aorist, and represents neither an act completed in the past time, i. e., it is not equivalent to, Except ye *had been* converted, nor one to be effected in the future, Except ye *shall be* converted, but one *past and continuing*. Except ye be *continually* turned back from this spirit of self-seeking, and *continually* take on the spirit of a little child. Parallel is John 15:6, If a man abide not in me he *is* cast forth, neither *has been* nor *will be*, but *is in the state of* a branch broken from the vine. See Buttmann's N. T. Gr. § 137, p. 198; Winer's N. T. Greek, § 40, 5, b, p. 277.]

And become as little children. "Not foolish (1 Cor. 14:20), nor fickle (Eph. 4:14), nor playful, but childlike (Matt. 11:16); as children we must desire the sincere milk of the word (1 Pet. 2:2); be careful for nothing, but leave it to our heavenly Father to care for us (Matt. 6:31); be harmless and inoffensive, and void of malice (1 Cor. 14:20); governable and under command (Gal. 4:2); and what is here chiefly intended, we must be humble as little children."—(*Matthew Henry*.) See also 1 Pet. 1:14. (See note on next verse.) Observe that elsewhere manhood is set before us as our aim (Eph. 4:13). The sense in which childhood is a pattern to us is well given by Chrysostom. "For such a little child is free from pride, and the mad desire of glory, and envy, and contentiousness, and all such passions, and having many virtues,—simplicity, humility, unworldliness,—prides itself on none of them; having a twofold severity of goodness; to have these things and not to be puffed up about them."

4. Whosoever therefore shall humble himself as this little child. This interprets the preceding verse, and points out the respect in which we are to become as little children; and it is in turn further interpreted by the addition in Luke (9:48), *He that is least among you all, i. e. who is willing to be least in rank and dignity, the same shall be great*. Humility is not thinking meanly of one's self, but being willing, even with great powers, to take a lowly office and perform seemingly menial and insignificant and not honored service. The first is not characteristic of childhood, the latter is. Christ's own example is the best interpretation of his teaching; for an interpretation of this precept, therefore, see Phil. 2:5-8. Compare Phil. 4:12, and Christ's symbolic repetition of this teaching in the washing of the disciples' feet, John 13:3-5, 12-15.

5. And whoso shall receive one such little child. These words are to be taken in their most natural signification, He who, for Christ's sake, receives a little child to his heart, receives Christ, and that irrespective of any faith in or love for Christ in the child's experience. Compare Matt. 10:40-42.—**In my name.** Literally, *upon my name, i. e.* upon the ground of my name, out of consideration to me, and for my sake.—**Receiveth me.** Observe that the true way to receive Christ is to receive, into our hearts, for Christ's sake, those who need the hospitality of our sympathies, as the way to serve Christ is by serving the needy and suffering (Matt. 25:40).

At this point in Christ's instructions occurred a significant interruption and Christ's response, for account of which see Mark 9:38-41 and notes there. On the passage up to this point Calvin observes that the disciples were guilty of a double fault, first in laying aside anxiety about their present warfare to discuss future reward, a fault allied to the vain curiosity of those who now neglect terrestrial duties for celestial speculations, whose condition is as if a man who was about to commence a journey made enquiries where a lodging-place was situated, but did not move a step; the second in striving with wicked ambition to excel each other, instead of rendering mutual assistance. Matthew Henry observes that if Christ ever intended to teach the primacy of Peter, the occasion was afforded by the disciples' question, Who is the greatest? whereas his answer emphatically disallows any primacy. And Chrysostom, with characteristic quaintness, says, "We are not able to attain so much as unto their faults, neither do we ask *who is greatest in the kingdom of heaven;* but who is greatest in the earthly kingdom, who is wealthiest, who most powerful."

6. But whoso shall offend. Cause to stumble or fall into sin. See note on Matt. 5:29.

MATTHEW. 215

which believe in me, it were better for him that a millstone were hanged about his neck, and *that* he were drowned in the depth of the sea.
7 Woe unto the world because of offences! for^m it must needs be that offences come; but woe^n to that man by whom the offence cometh!
8 Wherefore,^o if thy hand or thy foot offend thee, cut them off, and cast *them* from thee: it is better for

thee to enter into life halt or maimed, rather than, having two hands or two feet, to be cast into everlasting fire.
9 And if thine eye offend thee, pluck it out, and cast *it* from thee; it is better for thee to enter^p into life with one eye, rather than, having two eyes,^q to be cast into hell fire.
10 Take heed that ye despise not one of these little

m 1 Cor. 11 : 19 ; Jude 4....n Jude 11....o ch. 5 : 29, 30 ; Mark 9 : 43, 45....p Heb. 4 : 11....q Luke 9 : 25.

—**Which believe in me.** The Greek preposition (εἰς) *in*, when employed, as here, respecting the feelings, signifies the end or aim towards which they reach. Here the meaning is, Whose faith reaches out after me as its chief good. For experience indicated by the phrase, compare Phil. 3 : 13, 14. In the N. T. we are said to believe *in* (εἰς) Jesus Christ, but never to believe *in* (εἰς) any prophet, apostle or other human teacher, one of the numerous minor indications of Christ's superhuman character. "We believe Paul, but we do not believe *in* Paul."—(*Augustine.*)—A **millstone.** Literally, an *ass' millstone.* The larger mills were turned by asses, the smaller ones by hand. The Greek here (μύλος ὀνικός,) signifies the former kind of stone.—**Cast into the depth of the sea,** *i. e.* the open or deep sea, remote from land. This method of capital punishment was practised by the Egyptians, Greeks, and Romans, and possibly occasionally by the Jews.

7. Woe unto the world. The language may be read as that either of lamentation or of denunciation. Compare Matt. 23 : 15, 16, with Mark 13 : 17. Perhaps the feeling here represented is a commingled one.—**Because of temptations.** Literally, *traps.* See note on Matt. 5 : 29 ; 16 : 23.—**For it must needs be that temptations come.** This truth is set forth as an additional warning. The disciple must not forget that there is no possibility of avoiding temptation, and must therefore always be on his guard both for himself and others. The language might imply nothing more than that, as life is constituted, temptations are unavoidable. Compare for use of the same word rendered here *needs be* (ἀνάγκη), Luke 14 : 18 ; 23 : 17, where no absolute compulsion is indicated. But in another place (Luke 17 : 1), Christ uses even stronger language : *It is impossible but that offences will come.* The question at once occurs, Why is it impossible ? This question carries the mind directly back to the origin of evil ; it belongs to philosophy, not to biblical interpretation. Christ makes no attempt to answer it here, or elsewhere. Personally, I count it one of the insoluble problems of the universe.—**But woe to that man by whom the temptation cometh.** But if temptations be a necessity, why is he blameworthy who produces them ? This is a question which the commentators and theologians discuss ;

Christ does not, either here or elsewhere. He simply sets the two facts side by side ; the inevitableness of temptation ; the personal responsibility and sin of the tempter. The one is ratified by our observation ; the other by our personal consciousness. It is observable that Christ's method here is in general the biblical method, which frequently sets forth seemingly conflicting truths in strong terms, and often in close juxtaposition, but nowhere offers explanations to harmonize them. See, for examples, Acts 2 : 23 ; Rom. 9 : 14-23 ; Phil. 2 : 12, 13 ; 2 Pet. 1 : 4, 5, 10.

8-9. The connection is this. So great is the evil of becoming a cause of temptation to others or to yourself, that it is better to cut off the most innocent or even useful exercise of a God-given power, than so to use it as to lead yourself or others into sin. See the same aphorism, with a slighty different connection, in Matt. 5 : 29, 30, and note there. In the original the use of the article makes stronger the contrast than in our version, which should read, "Enter into *the* life * * * than be cast into *the* fire everlasting." On the phrase hell-fire (verse 9), see note on Matt. 5 : 22. Mark adds a description of it in the words, "Where their worm dieth not, and the fire is not quenched" (Mark 9 : 48). He also adds two verses not given by Matthew or Luke. See Mark 9 : 49, 50.

10. Take heed. (ὁράω.) A word of caution of frequent use in the N. T., and indicating a subtle temptation against which the Christian must watch. Compare Matt. 16 : 6 ; Luke 12 : 15 ; 1 Thess. 5 : 15.—**That ye despise not one of these little ones.** Not merely *one of these children,* but one of these *little ones ; i. e.* any one who is insignificant and unimportant. Compare Matt. 10 : 42 ; 11 : 11. The caution is administered to the spirit that seeks a high place in the church, a caution not to look down with contempt upon the weak in faith, the poor in knowledge, or in grace, or in station. Compare for the application of the principle, Rom. 14 : 1-3, 13, 15. The word here rendered *despise* (καταφρονέω) is literally to *think down upon,* or as we should say, *look down upon.*

For I say unto you that their angels, *i. e.* their guardian angels. With *possibly* two exceptions (Acts 12 : 15 ; Rev. 22 : 8, 9) the term *angel* (ἄγγελος) is never used in the N. T. to designate a departed spirit, which is always rendered by another word (πνεῦμα or ψύχημα). In some in-

ones; for I say unto you, That in heaven their angels do always behold* the face of my Father which is in heaven.

11 For the Son of man is come to save that† which was lost.

12 How think ye? If° a man have an hundred sheep, and one of them be gone astray, doth he not leave the ninety and nine, and goeth into the mountains, and seeketh that which is gone astray?

13 And if so be that he find it, verily I say unto you, he rejoiceth more of that *sheep*, than of the ninety and nine which went not astray.

14 Even so it is not the will of your Father which is in heaven, that one† of these little ones should perish.

15 Moreover, if thy" brother shall trespass against thee, go and tell him his fault between thee and him alone: if he˟ shall hear thee, thou hast gained thy brother.

---

r Acts 12 : 15....*s* Ps. 17 : 15....*t* ch. 1 : 21; Luke 9 : 56; 19 : 10; John 3 : 17; 10 : 10; 12 : 47; 1 Tim. 1 : 15....*u* Luke 15 : 4, etc....
v 2 Pet. 3 : 9....*w* Lev. 19 : 17; Lu. 17 : 3....*x* Jas. 5 : 20.

---

stances both *angel* (ἄγγελος) and *spirit* (πνεῦμα) are used in such connection as to indicate very clearly that they are not synonymous (Acts 23 : 8, 9). Etymologically the word means *messenger*, and it is sometimes so rendered in the N. T. (Matt. 11 : 10; Luke 7 : 24, 27). Usually it is employed to designate celestial beings, who are represented as the messengers of God (2 Kings 19 : 31; Psalm 91 : 11, 12; Heb. 1 : 13, 14). Here are intended the celestial messengers who are allotted as the special guardians of God's children. Not their *departed spirits* after death, but their *guardian angels* while they live are represented as nearest the throne.

Do always behold the face of my Father. That is, they always have direct and immediate access to God. The picture is interpreted by the usage of courts, where certain special favorite officers always have access to the throne (1 Kings 10 : 8; Esther 1 : 14; Jer. 52 : 25). Without pressing the language, which is seemingly metaphorical, as all language descriptive of the spiritual world must be, it evidently implies (1) the doctrine of guardian angels, *i. e.* that angels are not only in general the ministering servants of God, but that special angels are allotted as the special guardians and attendants of individuals (compare Psalm 91 : 11, 12; Acts 27 : 23); and (2) that the weakest and feeblest of God's flock, not merely the *children*, but the little ones, in intellectual and spiritual power and in ecclesiastical position and earthly honor, have the readiest and nearest access to God; in other words, that weakness and want, not greatness, constitute the strongest appeal to him. And with this idea consorts the entire passage. Stier's note, though somewhat fanciful, is beautiful: "Here is Jacob's ladder planted before our eyes: beneath are the little ones; then their angels; then the Son of man in heaven, in whom alone man is exalted above the angels, who, as the Great Angel of the covenant, cometh from the Presence and Bosom of the Father; and above Him again the Father Himself and His good pleasure."

11. For, the Son of man is come to save that which was lost; *i. e.*, the celestial messengers of the weak are always before the face of God, *because the very office of redeeming love is to save the lost*, those that cannot save themselves. Observe the implication (1) that the world is lost, undone, beyond all human help;

(2) that the object of Christ's coming was not to teach or to legislate, but to *save*. Compare John 1 : 13; 3 : 14–17. This verse is wanting in the Vatican and Sinaitic MSS., and is omitted by Griesbach, Lachmann, Tischendorf and Tregelles. But it is found in the great body of MSS. both uncial and cursive, and in all the old versions, the Vulgate, Syriac, Armenian and Ethiopic. Alford retains it. It is found also in Luke 19 : 10, where its authenticity is undoubted.

12, 13. This parable is expanded in Luke 15 : 4–6. See notes there. The proper rendering of verse 12 is, *Doth he not leave the ninety-nine upon the mountain?* It is not the strong and safe that need care, but the weak and feeble. The strong expression of verse 13 is not to be weakened by any such modification as that of James Morrison, "In the calm depth of his soul there is a settled satisfaction in the possession of the 99, which is ninety-nine times deeper than the emotion which is stirred into activity by the recovery of the one." The words of Christ are not to be thus shorn of their meaning. The highest joy, recognized in the Bible, as existing in heaven or on earth, is the joy, not of *possessing*, but of *saving* a soul. Compare Isaiah 53 : 11; Luke 15 : 7, 10; Heb. 12 : 2; Psalm 147 : 11; Micah 7 : 18; Zeph. 3 : 17.

14. The language of the original appears to me to be even stronger than that of our version.— **So there is not a will in the presence of your Father in heaven that one of these little ones should perish.** Not only it is not *his* will; but he will not permit such a will *in his presence*. This verse alone ought to be sufficient as a refutation of the doctrine that God chooses some souls for destruction, in order to show forth his glory.

Ch. 18 : 15-20.—CHRIST'S PRECEPTS FOR THE SETTLEMENT OF QUARRELS.—THE POWER OF UNITED CHRISTIAN FAITH.

15. Moreover. This conjunction connects what follows with what proceeds. Christ has before warned us from offending against others; he now tells us what we are to do when others sin against us. Calvin traces the connection clearly and well. "Christ enjoins his disciples to forgive one another, but to do so in such a manner as to endeavor to correct their faults. It is

16 But if he will not hear *thee, then* take with thee one or two more, that in the mouth of two or three witnessesʸ every word may be established.

17 And if he shall neglect to hear them, tell *it* unto the church: but if he neglect to hear the church, let himˢ be unto thee as an heathen man and a publican.

y Deut. 19 : 15; 2 Cor. 13 : 1....s Rom. 16 : 17; 1 Cor. 5 : 5-5; 2 Thess. 3 : 6, 14.

necessary that this be wisely observed; for nothing is more difficult than to exercise forbearance toward men, and at the same time not to neglect the freedom necessary in reproving them."—**If thy brother.** Not merely *fellow-Christian.* Since God is the Father of the whole human race, it is treated in Scripture as one family, and all men as brethren. Compare Matt. 5 : 22-24; 7 : 3-5; Hebrews 8 : 11; James 2 : 15; 1 John 2 : 10. Evidently, from these and parallel passages the instructions here are not necessarily limited to the case of church members who offend.—**Shall trespass against thee.** Christ does not tell the church how it is to treat one who apostatizes from the faith or from a holy life; but the individual Christian how he is to treat one who has personally sinned against him. True, some MSS., including the Sinaitic and the Vatican, omit *against thee,* as does Tischendorf and Lachmann, but the ordinary reading is the better one. The omission was probably for the purpose of giving an ecclesiastical meaning to the passage. —**Go and convince him between thee and him alone.** Privately as possible, that you may not have his pride arrayed against you. For the spirit in which this should be done compare Gal. 6 : 1. In how many cases should we be ashamed of having taken offence, in the very attempt to speak of it; in how many more, would such a kindly conference end all trouble.—**If he shall hear thee.** Not, as Chrysostom, "if he should be persuaded that he has done wrong;" but, literally, "*if he shall hear thee,*" *i. e.* if, as we say, he is willing to listen to reason; if he is ready for a Christian conference and mutual explanations.—**Thou hast gained thy brother.** Brotherliness is represented as something too valuable to be easily cast away. The idea is not, thou hast saved a brother from sin and death, but thou hast personally gained his brotherly affection. The original verb (κερδαίνω) always carries with it the idea of a personal gain. Compare Matt. 16 : 26; 25 : 17, 20, 22; Phil. 3 : 7.

16. But if he will not hear. Observe, not, if you cannot convince, but, *if he will not hear, i. e.,* if he refuses to enter into conference, in the spirit of concession and conciliation, so that you cannot thus gain your brother. —**Then take with thee one or two.** "If possible," says Wesley, wisely, "men whom he esteems and loves."—**That upon the mouth of two or three witnesses every word,** *i. e.* between you and him, in your endeavors for a reconciliation,—**may be established.** Observe the object of this second going.

It is not, primarily, that they may convince him, but that there may be no room to doubt afterwards which of you sought reconciliation and which of you resisted it. Observe, too, that this proceeding is not as a foundation for inflicting punishment, but for the sake of the offender's amendment and a restoration of fellowship.

17. And if he shall refuse to hear them. Still observe the condition; not, if he refuse to yield to them, but if he *refuse to hear, i. e.* to enter cordially into their and your spirit of reconciliation. The same word in the Septuagint in Esther 3 : 3, is rendered *transgress.* It carries with it the idea of a contemptuous disregard.—**Tell it to the church.** That is, to the assembly of Christ in which you are in fellowship, that they may understand and justify your position. On the meaning of the word (εκκλησία) here rendered *church,* see note below, and notes on Matt. 16 : 18.—**But if he refuse to hear the church.** If he resists their endeavors for a mutual reconciliation between the two.—**Let him be unto thee.** Unto thee, *not unto the church.* There is nothing said here, and nothing implied, as to any withdrawal of fellowship by the church. It is not even implied that the offender is in the church.—**As a heathen man and a publican.** With whom the Jews had no intercourse (Acts 10 : 28; compare John 4 : 9). There is no suggestion of proceedings for punishment, either by the individual or the church. The direction is simply tantamount to this: If, after all your efforts, you cannot secure reconciliation, then *you may have nothing more to do with him.* That Christ does not justify the feeling of scorn and hate with which the Jews generally regarded the heathen and publican is clear from the parable which follows (vs. 21-35). But he does recognize the fact that exigencies in life sometimes arise which call for a complete separation from wilful wrong-doers.

OF DEALING WITH AN OFFENDING BROTHER. These verses are frequently referred to as containing "the general principles on which church discipline should be carried on." Is this interpretation correct? I think not, for the following reasons: (*a.*) At the time these directions were given no Christian church was organized, and the disciples did not anticipate the organization of one. They believed that Christ was about to set up a temporal kingdom in which they were to share. They could not, therefore, have understood this to be a rule of ecclesiastical discipline. (*b.*) The word (εκκλησία) here rendered *church,* etymologically signifies *that which is called out,* and

18 Verily I say unto you, Whatsoever* ye shall bind on earth, shall be bound in heaven; and whatsoever ye shall loose on earth, shall be loosed in heaven.

19 Again I say unto you, That if two of you shall agree on earth as touching any thing that they shall ask,ᵇ it shall be done for them of my Father which is in heaven.

a ch. 16 : 19; John 20 : 23; Acts 15 : 23–31; 2 Cor. 2 : 10....b Mark 11 : 24; John 16 : 24; 1 John 5 : 15.

so an *assembly*, and is so sometimes rendered in our version (see Acts 19 : 32, 39, 41). In the O. T. (Septuagint or Greek version) it represents the Great Congress or Jewish Parliament (see note on Matt. 16 : 18). In the N. T. "the word most frequently occurs in the Christian sense of an assemblage of Christians generally, 1 Cor. 11 : 18," (*Kitto's Bib. Cyc.*); see also, Rom. 16 : 5; 1 Cor. 16 : 19. Here, certainly, it indicates not an ecclesiastical organization, still less the rulers or authorities in such an organization, but an assemblage of the people of God, and is defined by verse 20. See note there. (*c*.) Nowhere else does Christ give any rules for the conduct of ecclesiastical affairs; nothing respecting the number or nature of church officers, the mode of their appointment or election; their length of service; their authority. It must be regarded as remarkable if, leaving all other ecclesiastical questions to be determined by his followers, he should give particular rules for the determination of disciplinary proceedings in the church. (*d*.) The context relates wholly to personal relations and personal duties; the preceding verses are a warning against tempting the weak and feeble into sin; the following verses are an exposition of the duty of personal forgiveness. We should not naturally look in such connection for rules of ecclesiastical procedure. (*e*.) The language throughout is inconsistent with the ecclesiastical interpretation. The direction is given, not to the church, but to the individual. "If *thy* brother shall trespass *against thee*;" the "one or two" are to be taken, as witnesses that the individual has done all in his power to procure a reconciliation; and the *final* result, in the case of one obstinate in refusing reconciliation, is *not church action of any kind*, but only this, that he is to be "*unto thee*," *i. e.* to the person with whom he refuses to be reconciled, as a heathen and a publican. (*f*.) The heathen and publicans were subjected to no penalties of any sort in Judea; religious persecution was utterly foreign to the spirit of their institutions. The Jews simply had no intercourse with them. The command, Let him be *unto thee* as a heathen and a publican, does not therefore justify civil penalties or disabilities of any description, nor call for exclusion from the privileges and fellowship of the church, nor for any public condemnation or general obloquy, nor for any formal act of excommunication, or any ecclesiastical pains or penalties. It simply justifies the individual Christian in ceasing to maintain friendly and personal relations with one who, after this triple endeavor, refuses to live in friendly relations with him. The reader will not understand me as denying the right of the church to discipline members, nor the propriety of pursuing the method here indicated in the case of church discipline; but this passage has not in my judgment, any direct bearing on ecclesiastical proceedings, and certainly does not constitute a law for their conduct. But the reader ought to be advised that most commentators take a different view, and regard these precepts as directions for the administration of ecclesiastical discipline. Lightfoot and Alford might perhaps be regarded as exceptions, though their views are not very clear. "The business here is not so much concerning the censure of the person sinning as concerning the vindication of the person reproving."—(*Lightfoot*.) "That the church (ἐκκλησία) cannot mean the church as represented by her rulers, appears by verses 19, 20, where *any* collection of believers is gifted with the power of deciding in such cases. Nothing could be further from the spirit of our Lord's command than proceedings in what were oddly enough called 'ecclesiastical' courts."— (*Alford*.)

I understand then Christ's directions here to be simply this: If a brother man has wronged you, do not give up his brotherly love at once. First, try by personal conference to secure reconciliation; if he will not be reconciled, take a friend or two to witness that you have done what you can to be reconciled; if he refuses to listen to them, tell your Christian brethren of the difficulty; and if their intervention is in vain, then and only then are you justified in having nothing to do with him. In our ordinary intercourse with each other, how often we reverse these directions, say of one who has offended us, I owe him no grudge, but I want nothing more to do with him, and after our decision tell the church and the neighbors our version of the quarrel as our justification. "If," says John Wesley, speaking of Christ's directions here, "if this be the way to take, in what land do the Christians live?" Compare with this passage Matt. 5 : 21–26.

18. Observe that here the power of the keys (what that is I have considered in note on Matt. 15 : 19, which see) is conferred on all the disciples, for there is nothing whatever to indicate that the promise is not as universally applicable as the directions given in the preceding verse, and the promise in the verses which follow. The term *heaven* here is used as in Matt. 21 : 25, and is

20 For where two or three are gathered together* in my name, there am I in the midst of them.
21 Then came Peter to him, and said, Lord, how oft shall my brother sin against me, and I forgive him? till seven times?
22 Jesus saith unto him, I say not unto thee, Until seven times; but, Until seventy times seven.
23 Therefore is the kingdom of heaven likened unto a certain king, which would take account of his servants.

*John 20 . 19; 1 Cor. 5 : 4. ...d Mark 11 : 25; Luke 17 : 4; Col. 3 : 13. ...e Rom. 14 : 12.

---

used in the same sense as in that passage, and in Matt. 16 : 19, *loosed in heaven* being nearly equivalent to *loosed by God*. The promise may be paraphrased thus: Whatever, under the guidance of the Spirit of God, you do, shall be ratified by your Father in heaven.

19. Again I say unto you that if two of you shall agree. Literally, shall *symphonize* or sound together. The original Greek verb (συμφωνέω) is one from which comes our word symphony, and carries with it a concealed metaphor: Shall accord as musical instruments in symphony.—**Concerning anything that they shall ask.** Language could hardly be stronger. The Greek is, *Concerning everything whatsoever ye shall ask.*—**It shall be done for them by my Father.** It is impossible to reconcile this promise with any theory of prayer which denies that prayer is really influential with God. Compare with it Matt. 21 : 22; Mark 11 : 24; John 14 : 13, 14; 15 : 7, 16; 16 : 23, 24, which indicate the condition of such prayer as may claim this promise. Illustrations of the fulfillment of the promise in this and the succeeding verse are afforded by Acts 1 : 14 with 2 : 1–4, and Acts 12 : 5, 12. An illustration of a misapprehension of Christ's meaning and of his refusal of a request presented by two of the apostles, who were agreed, is afforded by Mark 10 : 35. Comparing these passages, and I have purposely referred only to the words of Jesus, it is evident that his promise is not absolute and unconditional, but that the fundamental condition of the spirit of all true prayer, is implied, viz., trust in and submission to the higher will and wisdom of our heavenly Father. And indeed this is hinted at by the language of this verse, Anything that they shall *ask*, since asking always implies a recognition of the right to refuse; and still more is this implied in the verse which follows, which gives the reason for the promise. Why shall such power be given to the disciples? *Because* where two or three are gathered in Christ's name he is in their midst to inspire and direct their petitions. Compare Rom. 8 : 26.

20. For where two or three are gathered together in my name. "Not collecting themselves promiscuously in their own name, or according to their own devices, or for their own glory, much less in a spirit of strife and division; but with yearnings of love to me and of union with me; in the manner appointed by me, in the unity of my church, and in obedience to my law, and for the furtherance of my glory."—(*Wordsworth*.) For the meaning of "*in my name*" compare John 14 : 13; 15 : 7. Chrysostom's note on the connection of the 19th and 20th verses with what precedes is important. "Having declared the evils consequent on strife, he now displays the blessings of unity. They who are of one accord do prevail with the Father as touching the things they ask, and they have Christ in the midst of them."—**There am I in the midst of them.** Compare Matt. 28 : 20. Later theology has contrived no better definition of a church than this verse affords: The gathering of Christ's disciples, united in Christ, and with him in their midst. Observe that neither here, nor anywhere else in the Gospels, is there any implication that his being in the midst of such an assembly, bringing with him the powers conferred here in verse 18, and in Matt. 28 : 19, 20, to baptize and preach, is dependent upon any church order, ordained ministry, apostolic successors, special rites, ceremonies, or creeds, or anything of the kind. It seems also to me that wherever Christ is, there by a reasonable implication is the right to proclaim him, whether by words, as in preaching, or by rites and symbols, as by baptism and the Lord's Supper.

Ch. 18 : 21–35. PARABLE OF THE UNMERCIFUL SERVANT.—THE DUTY OF FORGIVENESS; THE NATURE OF FORGIVENESS; THE MOTIVE OF FORGIVENESS.—See Thoughts below.

21-22. Then came Peter to him. For further instruction as to the duty of forgiveness inculcated in the preceding verses. He wanted a specific rule limiting the obligation of forgiveness. The Rabbis limited it to three repetitions of an offence. Peter, with a glimmering idea that the rule should be enlarged, proposed seven as the limit. Christ's reply "seventy times seven" (not as James Morison, and some others, seventy-seven) refuses to assign any limit. Living in a kingdom of grace, we are to exercise it as we depend upon it, *without limitation*. On the meaning of the word forgive (ἀφίημι), see note on Matt. 6 : 12.

23. Therefore is the kingdom of heaven likened. *Therefore, i. e.* because it is a kingdom of forgiveness, founded on the forgiveness of God to us, the unforgiving cannot abide in it. "As certainly as there is no kingdom of God without the forgiveness which we receive, so certainly there is no kingdom of God without the

24 And when he had begun to reckon, one was brought unto him, which owed him ten thousand talents:
25 But forasmuch as he had not to pay, his lord commanded him to be sold,^f and his wife, and children, and all that he had, and payment to be made.
26 The servant therefore fell down, and worshipped him, saying, Lord, have patience with me, and I will pay thee all.
27 Then the lord of that servant was moved with compassion,^g and loosed him, and forgave him the debt.
28 But the same servant went out, and found one of

f 2 Kings 4 : 1 ; Isa. 50 : 1. . . .g Ps. 78 : 38.

---

forgiveness which we bestow."—(*Dräseke*.)— **Unto a certain king.** Literally, *a man, a king.* And because any comparison of the divine kingdom with the human kingdom is and must be imperfect, this parable must not be pressed in details, as has been done by some commentators. —**Which would take account of his servants.** The Greek (δοῦλος) signifies primarily slaves, but not so here, for the debtor was to be sold into slavery to pay the debt. In an Oriental despotism the subordinates of a king are in fact, though not in form, his slaves, their property and life being subject to his will. By the servant mentioned in the next verse Christ depicts, I judge, the chief of some province, who has defaulted in his accounts. The account-taking does not answer to the last judgment, for after that there is no opportunity for the condemned to exercise or abstain from mercy to his fellows. Arnot gives the true interpretation well: "So the King Eternal in various ways, and at various periods, takes account of men, especially of those who know his word, and belong externally to his church," as by "a commercial crisis, a personal affliction, a revival," or, let me add, those heart-searchings that come without explicable cause on almost all men at some period in their life.

24. One was brought to him. He did not come willingly.—**Which owed him ten thousand talents.** The talent was a weight, not a coin; the value it represented would therefore necessarily depend upon the purity of the coinage. The Hebrew (silver) talent is variously estimated from $1750 to $2250, the gold talent as high as $35,000. Ten thousand is used in the N. T. as a general expression for a great number (1 Cor. 4 : 15; 14 : 19). The original might be rendered here *innumerable.* The Sinaitic MSS. has simply "many" (πολλάς). Trench affords illustrations of the amount indicated, by comparing it with other sums mentioned in the Scripture and in secular history. 10,000 talents is the amount which Haman estimated would be derived from the destruction of the whole Jewish people (Esther 3 : 9). In the construction of the tabernacle 29 talents of gold were used (Exod. 38 : 24); David prepared for the temple 3000 talents of gold, and the princes 5000 (1 Chron. 29 : 4-7); the queen of Sheba presented to Solomon 120 talents (1 Kings 10 : 10); the king of Assyria laid upon Hezekiah 30 talents of gold (2 Kings 18 : 14); and in the extreme impoverishment to which the land was brought at the last, 1 talent of gold was laid upon it by the king of Egypt (2 Chron. 36 : 3). Harpalus, satrap of Babylonia and Syria, carried off with him 5000 talents when he fled to Athens from the wrath of Alexander. With 10,000 talents Darius sought to buy off Alexander from prosecuting his campaign in Asia. The same sum was imposed as a fine by the Romans on Antiochus the Great after his defeat. Alexander the Great, at Susa, paid the debts of the whole Macedonian army with 20,000 talents. The amount here represents the magnitude of the debt which the sinner owes to God, and the hopelessness of ever paying it. For interpretation of the metaphor of *debt*, here and elsewhere in N. T. employed, see Matt. 6 : 12, and note.

25. Had not to pay. Equivalent to, *had nothing with which to pay.* Compare Luke 7 : 42. The implication is plain; man has nothing with which to make good his accounts with God.— **His Lord commanded him to be sold.** Apparently the debtor could be sold for debt under Jewish law (Lev. 25 : 39) and perhaps his family with him (verse 41; compare 2 Kings 4 : 1; Neh. 5 : 1, 5 : Isaiah 50 : 1 ; Amos 2 : 6; 8 : 6). Under the denunciations of the practice by the later prophets this selling of debtors disappeared from Judea. The imagery of the parable is probably taken from Oriental despotisms, where the rights of the individual are utterly ignored. It cannot be spiritually applied. We sell ourselves to sin, but are ransomed from the voluntary servitude by God (Rom. 6 : 16-18).

26. Worshipped him. *Did him reverence.* See Matt. 2 : 2, and 8 : 2 and notes. Observe, however, that it is not said that the other servant worshipped his fellow-servant.—**Lord, have patience with me and I will pay thee all.** A promise impossible of fulfilment. Luther explains this as the voice of mistaken self-righteousness. Trench regards it simply as "characteristic of the extreme fear and anguish of the moment." Observe, there is no confession of wrong, no appeal for help. The experience typified is not that of penitence, but only of fear. It is interpreted by the histories of Pharaoh (Exod. 9 : 27, 28 ; 10 : 16, 17, etc.), Saul (1 Sam. 15 : 24, 25, 30), Ahab (1 Kings 21 : 27), Belshazzar (Dan. 5 : 9), and Felix (Acts 24 : 25).

27. Observe, how much greater the gift than the request. Compare Ephes. 3 : 20. The fact that the king grants a remission of the debt, yet sub-

his fellowservants which owed him an hundred pence; and he laid hands on him, and took *him* by the throat, saying, Pay me that thou owest.

29 And his fellowservant fell down at his feet, and besought him, saying, Have⁸ patience with me, and I will pay thee all.

30 And he would not; but went and cast him into prison, till he should pay the debt.

31 So when his fellowservants saw what was done, they were very sorry, and came and told unto their lord all that was done.

32 Then his lord, after that he had called him, said unto him, O thou wicked servant, I forgave thee all that debt, because thou desiredst me:

33 Shouldest not thou also have had compassion on thy fellowservant, even as I had pity on thee?

34 And his lord was wroth, and delivered him to the tormentors, till he should pay all that was due unto him.

35 So¹ likewise shall my heavenly Father do also unto you, if ye from your hearts forgive not every one his brother their trespasses.

---

b verse 26.... i Luke 19 : 22.... j ch. 6 : 12 ; Prov. 21 : 13 ; Jas. 2 : 13.

---

sequently enforces its payment (verse 34), has occasioned the commentators some perplexity. But this accords with Oriental despotism, which would recognize in such a remission nothing that could not be revoked at will; and it accords with the divine pardon, which is *offered* to all the world, but is *effectual* only to such as accept it. And he who refuses to bestow grace refuses *by that act* to enter the kingdom of grace. The very object of this parable is to show that every man must choose between mercy and justice.

28. Went out. "He is said to go out, because in the actual presence of his lord he could scarcely have ventured on the outrage which follows."—(*Trench*.) Arnot gives the spiritual interpretation well. "The moment of close dealing between God and the soul has passed. The man goes out from that solemn and searching communion. He has not been converted; he has only been frightened."—**A hundred pence,** *i. e. denarii*, a small silver coin equal to about 18 cents. The debt, therefore, was equal to $18. The contrast intended between our sins against God and our neighbors' sins against us is clear. "Though thou continually pardon thy neighbor absolutely, for all his sins, as a drop of water to an endless sea, so much, or rather much more, doth thy love to man come short in comparison with the boundless goodness of God, of which thou standest in need."—(*Chrysostom*.)—Laid **hands on him and took him by the throat, saying, Pay me if thou owest anything.** This (εἰ τι not ὅ τι) is the proper reading. It does not intimate a doubt whether anything be due, but is the strong expression of one who exacts to the utmost every debt. The picture is realized daily in the hardness of professing Christians to the unfortunate as well as the guilty. "Those who get most mercy give the least; and cruelty is hatched under the wings of tenderness."—(*Dräseke*.)

29, 30. "The one besought for 10,000 talents, the other for 100 pence; the one his fellow-servant, the other his lord; the one received entire forgiveness, the other asked for delay, and not so much as this did he give him."—(*Chrysostom*.) This creditor's sin we repeat when we hold resentment against an offender until he makes atonement and reparation. What is this but demanding that he pay the debt?

31. Were very sorry. But the lord was *wroth* (verse 34). In us sin should awaken, predominantly, sorrow, which in God awakens indignation.—**And came and told their lord all.** The first resort of the Christian against oppression is prayer (Exod. 3 : 7 ; James 5 : 4).

32, 33. The lord now calls him "wicked servant," and is "wroth" with him; but not before. Observe the ground on which Christ bases our duty of forgiveness: I forgave thee all that debt. "The sin with which he (the servant) is charged is, not that *needing mercy* he refused to show it, but that *having received mercy* he remains unmerciful still."—(*Trench*.)

34. The picture is interpreted by the usages of the East, where torture is used, even at the present day, to compel debtors to confess to acquisitions which they are suspected of hiding. In both Greece and Rome torture was used as a punishment and as a means of compelling confession, but apparently not in prosecutions for debt.—**Till he should pay all.** This certainly does not imply, it rather negatives, the idea of a future restoration. "When the Phocæans, abandoning their city, swore that they would not return till the mass of iron which they plunged into the sea, returned once more upon the surface, this was the most emphatic form they could devise of declaring that they would never return; such an emphatic declaration is the present."—(*Trench*.) Similarly Alford: "The condition would amount, in the case of the sum in the parable, to perpetual imprisonment;" and Chrysostom: "That is forever; for he will never repay."

35. Their trespasses, is omitted from the best manuscripts. On the verse, see note on Matt. 6 : 12.

THOUGHTS ON THE PARABLE. I. The *parallel*. The Eternal King constantly calls us to account (Luke 16 : 2), in providences and heart-searchings, which compel us to confess our inability to meet his just demands (Job 25 : 4 ; Psalm 130 : 3 ; 143 : 2 ; Rom. 3 : 22). On our cry for forbearance he proclaims the Gospel of full and free forgiveness (Rom. 1 : 24,

CHAPTER XIX.

AND it came to pass, *that* when Jesus had finished these saying, he departed^k from Galilee, and came into the coasts of Judæa beyond Jordan:
2 And great multitudes followed him; and he healed them there.
3 The Pharisees also came unto him, tempting him, and saying unto him, Is it lawful for a man to put away his wife for every cause?
4 And he answered and said unto them, Have ye not read, that he^l which made *them* at the beginning, made them male and female,
5 And said, For^m this cause shall a man leave father and mother, and shall cleave to his wife; and they twain shall be one flesh?

k Mark 10 : 1; John 10 : 40....l Gen. 1 : 27; 5 : 2; Mal. 2 : 15....m Gen. 2 : 24; Eph. 5 : 31.

25; 1 John 1 : 8, 9); so soon as we go out from the consciousness of the divine examination we forget that we depend on mercy, and become inexorable and exacting to our fellow-men. Thus we prove ourselves no citizens of the kingdom of grace, and call down upon ourselves the same justice we have meted out to others. II. *The lessons.* The parable teaches directly: (1) the duty of consideration and forbearance toward honest but unfortunate debtors, one generally overlooked; (2) the duty of forgiveness, which must be continuous and long-suffering (verse 22), full and free, like the Lord's (verse 27; compare Ephes. 4 : 32, and Matt. 6 : 12 and note), and from the heart (verse 35); but is consistent with rebuking and convincing of sin (verse 15), even as the Lord rebukes and convinces us; for verses 15-17 and this parable interpret each other, and are to be taken together; and (3) the incentive to forgiveness, viz., the fact that God has forgiven us (verse 31). *Indirectly*, it teaches the accountability of every soul to God (verse 23; compare John 3 : 18); the hopelessness of accounting to him and our dependence on his forgiving love; the fulness and freeness of his forgiveness (verse 27); the smallness of all transgressions against us compared with ours against God (verse 24 with verse 28); the feeling which all uncharitableness should awaken in our hearts—sorrow; the first step we should take to redress it—prayer (verse 26); and consequently patience and self-restraint toward the wrong-doer; and the finality of the last judgment, and the hopelessness of a future restoration for those who, by their conduct in this life, have cast away God's mercy (verse 34). More than this it appears to me cannot be fairly deduced from the parable. Its great lesson is well summed up by Chrysostom: "Two things doth Christ require here; both to condemn ourselves for our sins and to forgive others; and the former for the sake of the latter."

Ch. 19 : 1, 2. Mission in Perea. The harmony of the three Gospels, at this point, becomes peculiarly difficult. The most probable opinion appears to be this: Christ left Galilee and went up to Jerusalem, where he prosecuted the ministry described in John, chaps. 7—10; from the mob at Jerusalem he escaped to Perea, that part of the Holy Land east of the Jordan, whose ministry is described in general terms by these two verses, and by the parallel ones in Mark 10 : 1, and 10 : 40-42. Of this ministry, Luke gives the only full account, in chaps. 14—18; but the incidents and instructions here, and in the next chapter to verse 16, probably belong to the Perean ministry. See Harmony in Introduction. If this opinion be correct, a number of months elapsed between the close of the last chapter and the beginning of this.

Ch. 19 : 3-12. CHRIST'S LAW OF MARRIAGE AND DIVORCE.—THE ORIGIN OF MARRIAGE—DIVINE; THE NATURE OF MARRIAGE—ONE LIFE IN THE FLESH; THE DURATION OF MARRIAGE—THE LIFETIME; FOR WHOM MARRIAGE IS INTENDED—THE WHOLE HUMAN RACE; THE THREE EXCEPTIONS TO THE GENERAL LAW OF MARRIAGE—(1) THOSE CONGENITALLY INCAPACITATED; (2) THOSE AFFLICTED WITH INCAPACITY; (3) THOSE PRACTISING VOLUNTARY CONTINENCE FOR RELIGIOUS REASONS.

3. Tempting him. Our Lord was in the dominion of Herod Antipas, who had slain John the Baptist for publicly condemning the tetrarch's illegal divorce and illicit marriage. See notes on Matt. 14 : 1-12. Perhaps they hoped to secure Christ's arrest by Herod. It was possibly in this connection that, under pretense of friendship, they warned him to flee from Herod (Luke 13 : 31).—**For every cause.** In Greece, the husband might dismiss his wife without ceremony; in Rome, either party could dissolve the marriage tie at pleasure. No judicial decree, and no interference of any public authority, was required (*Smith's Dictionary of Antiquity*, art. Divortium). Cicero dismissed Terentia after thirty years of married life. Cato the younger divorced his wife that he might give her to a friend. The laws of Moses (Deut. 24 : 1-4) provided that the husband might divorce his wife, "because he hath found some uncleanness in her," by giving a bill of divorce setting forth the reason. This must be in writing and given in the presence of witnesses (see note on Matt. 1 : 19). Grave discussions had taken place among the Rabbis as to the proper interpretation of this statute. The school of Shammai denied the right of divorce except for adultery; the school of Hillel asserted the utmost latitude of divorce. The latter appears to have been the prevalent view. "He that desires to be divorced from his wife for any cause whatsoever," says Josephus, "and many such cases arise among men, let him in writing give assurance that he will never use her as his wife any more, for

6 Wherefore they are no more twain, but one flesh. What therefore God hath joined together, let not man put asunder.
7 They say unto him, Why did Moses then command to give a writing of divorcement, and to put her away?
8 He saith unto them, Moses, because of the hardness of your hearts, suffered you to put away your wives: but from the beginning it was not so.

9 And I say unto you, Whosoever shall put away his wife, except it be for fornication, and shall marry another, committeth adultery: and whoso marrieth her which is put away doth commit adultery.
10 His disciples say unto him, If the case of a man be so with his wife, it is not good to marry.
11 But he said unto them, All men cannot receive this saying, save they to whom it is given.
12 For there are some eunuchs, which were so born

a 1 Cor. 7 : 10....o Deut. 24 : 1; Isa. 50 : 1....p ch. 5 : 32; Luke 16 : 18....q Prov. 19 : 13; 21 : 9, 19.

by these means she will be at liberty to marry another husband."—(*Ant.* IV : 8, § 23.)

4-6. Mark says he first asked them, What did Moses command you? they replied by a reference to Deut. 24 : 1-4; he then quoted the account of the creation and the contemporaneous institution of marriage. The two versions are not inconsistent. Thus we may suppose that Christ referred them to Moses' law, meaning the original law given in Genesis; they replied by referring to the later statute in Deuteronomy; he then explained his original question, What did Moses command you? by referring them distinctly to Genesis; whereupon, as represented here (verse 7), they asked his explanation of Deut. 24 : 1-4. For the interpretation of Christ's argument, see note below. Observe, however, here, how he who came to *fulfil* the law (Matt. 5 : 17), in this case goes back of the permission of the civil law, enacted because of the hardness of the people's hearts, to the original and divine intent of marriage, as interpreted in the very act of creation. **Made them male and female,** *i. e.*, in the very act of creation, God embodied the idea of marriage. Observe how the unity of the two is implied in the language of Genesis. "In the image of God created he him; male and female created he them" (Gen. 1 : 27). And again, "Male and female created he them; and blessed them, and called *their* name Adam (Gen. 5 : 2).—**And said** (Gen. 2 : 24). This was said not by Adam, as Alford, but by the inspired historian, and is his divinely inspired conclusion from the whole account of creation.—**Shall be one flesh.** That is, as Stier, "one within the limits of their united life in the flesh, for this world; beyond this limit the marriage is broken by the death of the flesh." The Greek and Roman idea of marriage, was a union of feeling and affection; hence it was dissoluble at the will of the parties, when that union was severed by incompatibility or contention. And this philosophy underlies the modern free divorce idea, miscalled free-love. According to Scripture, however, marriage consists not in the unity of the spirit and soul, but in the fact that the wedded pair become one flesh, *i. e. one in their earthly relations and life.* Hence marriage ceases at death (Matt. 22 : 30), though the spiritual union does not; hence, too, the earthly relation may be formed where there is no union of soul, as with a harlot (1 Cor. 6 : 16). Hence it is not dissoluble by a mere cessation of mutual sympathy, any more than the blood relations of brother and sister, or father and child, can be so dissolved. The one relation is as permanent as the other, though one is formed voluntarily, the other involuntarily.— **What therefore God has joined together let not man put asunder.** This is not, as often quoted, equivalent to *Those whom*, by his blessing on the marriage, God has joined together, but, as the context shows, Since God, in the very act of creation, showed the divine purpose to be the joining in one earthly life of male and female, let not man, by his act, break or loosen the bond.

7-8. See note on verse 3 above. The reference is to Deut. 24 : 1-4. For other O. T. laws bearing on this subject see Deut. 22 : 21-23; Numb. ch. 5; compare note on Matt. 1 : 19. Observe the difference between the Pharisees' language and Christ's. They ask, Why then did Moses *command?* He replies, *Moses suffered.* The original Greek verb (ἐπέτρεπε), rendered *suffered*, is literally "throw upon," *i. e.* he throws upon you the responsibility of breaking the divine bond, because the hardness of your hearts rendered it impossible to enforce it by civil legislation. This verse is a key to much of the Mosaic legislation, which did not reflect the divine will concerning human character and condition, but only so much of the divine will as could be enforced by civil government. Some commentators regard the phrase, *hardness of your hearts*, equivalent to harshness in the marriage relations. The more general sense of sinfulness appears preferable. The Greek compound word (σκληροκαρδία) occurs only here and in Mark 10 : 5, and 16 : 14.

9. These words were uttered by Christ to his disciples alone in the house (Mark 10 : 10-12). They are so explicit that it appears amazing that any who accept Christ's authority should have attempted to explain them away. **Fornication** (πορνεια) is properly not merely adultery, but harlotry. So Milton; and his labored attempt to prove that any ineradicable incompatibility is a just cause of divorce renders his testimony all the more important: "In the Greek and Latin sense, by fornication is meant the common prostitution of the body for sale." The word fornication (Latin *fornication*) is derived from *fornix*, a

from *their* mother's womb: and there are some eunuchs, which were made eunuchs of men: and there be eunuchs, which have made themselves eunuchs for the kingdom of heaven's sake.* He that is able to receive *it*, let him receive *it*.

13 Then were there brought unto him little children,

r 1 Cor. 7 : 32.

harlot, primarily a cell or vault, such being the customary abodes of the harlots of Rome. That the Greek word (πορνεία) signifies properly harlotry is equally evident from its derivative (πόρνη) a harlot, and that it is not merely synonymous with adultery (μοιχεία) is clear from its use in conjunction with that word in the N. T. (*e. g.* Matt. 15 : 19 ; Mark 7 : 21). I would not press this difference here except to point out that Christ in giving the law, which is *not for the state but for the individual disciple*, does not in words even recognize adultery, except in its grossest forms, as a ground adequate for dissolving the marriage tie. Milton refers to the metaphorical use of fornication in the Scripture to designate unfaithfulness toward God (Numbers 15 : 39 ; Psalm 73 : 26, 27 ; Jer. 3 : 6-13), as an evidence that wilful disobedience or distrust or "intractable carriage of the wife to the husband" is a Scriptural cause of separation. Rather it stamps on all alienation from God, and joining to idols or the world, God's severest condemnation. But Milton's tracts on this subject are marvels of theological special pleading. I should rather draw from Jer. 3 : 14 a lesson of the duty of husband or wife, to endeavor at first to reclaim even an unfaithful spouse, before seeking divorce. To suppose that lustful imaginations, which are defined by Christ in Matt. 5 : 28 as adultery *in the heart*, is included in the fornication here indicated as a ground of divorce, is to take away from this passage all significance. How can we judge of the imaginations of another's heart?

And whoso marrieth the divorced doth commit adultery. There is some doubt whether these words have not been added. Tischendorf omits them; Alford retains them. The same principle is however enunciated in Matt. 5 : 32 and Luke 16 : 18, where the reading is undoubted. Does this forbid the marriage of the *innocent* party after separation on account of fornication? The Roman Catholic church forbids such marriage; the Protestant and Greek churches allow it. Christ appears to me to condemn only (1) marriage to any one who has been divorced for any other reason than fornication; or (2) divorced for his or her own infidelity. The principle, and indeed the language, applies equally to either sex.

10. If marriage is truly for better for worse, if from it there is no release, then the disciples think one had better not take the hazard of it. They express in words what some express by their lives.

11. Not all can receive this saying, *i. e.*, your saying. It is not good to marry.—**Save to whom it has been given.** The tense indicates not a gift *to be* bestowed, but that *has been* bestowed; and the reference is not to spiritual grace of self-restraint, to be given to the saint in answer to prayer, but to a native constitutional character belonging to the few, who therefore are not impelled to marriage.

12. The Lord distinguishes three classes who would receive this saying, and would abstain from marriage: (1) those incapacitated from birth for the marriage relation; (2) those incapacitated by subsequent action of men; this incapacity being in the East inflicted, sometimes as a punishment, sometimes on servants, who were in consequence admitted to the harem, from which all other men were excluded; (3) those who, in order to better perform special work in the kingdom of God, voluntarily practise absolute continence. For it is impossible to believe that Christ means that a literal self-mutilation can ever be a religious act; though Origen is said to have so understood the passage, and in his youth to have "committed the unnatural deed which forever disqualified him for marriage." (*Schaff* in Lange on Matt. 19 : 12.) The passage certainly *does* imply that celibacy may be in certain exigencies and certain individuals a virtue, practised for good reason for the sake of better serving in the kingdom of God; it as certainly *does not* imply any general duty of celibacy in any class, or that the celibate's spiritual condition is, by reason of his celibacy, higher than that of others. On the contrary, it implies that marriage is the rule and celibacy is the exception. The priests of the O. T. married; Peter certainly, other of the apostles probably, were married; marriage is employed in both O. T. and N. T. as the type of God's union with his people; and forbidding to marry is declared to be characteristic of the apostasy of later times. The student may consult to advantage the following passages as bearing on this subject: Lev. 21 : 14; Matt. 8 : 14; Acts 21 : 8, 9; 1 Cor. 7 : 1, 2; 9 : 5; 1 Tim. 3 : 2; 4 : 3; Heb. 13 : 4.

OF CHRIST'S LAW OF DIVORCE. In considering the significance of this passage it must be remembered that Christ, neither here nor anywhere else, propounds laws for the state, but, in contrast with the laws of Moses, principles for the individual disciple (*see notes on* Matt. 5 : 17, 37, 48). Only by implication can any rules for incorporation in civil legislation be deduced from this

Cн. XIX.]   MATTHEW.   225

that he should put *his* hands on them, and pray: and the disciples rebuked them.
14 But Jesus said, Suffer⁴ little children, and forbid them not, to come unto me; for of such⁵ is the kingdom of heaven.

15 And he laid *his* hands on them, and departed thence.
16 And behold, one came, and said unto him, Good Master, what good⁶ thing shall I do, that I may have eternal life?

⁴ Mark 10 : 14; Luke 18 : 16, etc.....⁵ ch. 18 : 3....⁶ Mark 10 : 17; Luke 10 : 25 ; 18 : 18.

passage. Bearing this in mind the course of Christ's argument may be thus summed up: God instituted marriage in the act and by the very fact of creation, in that he made man male and female, and ordained them to live together as *one flesh, i. e.* in one confluent earthly life. This ideal was never realized; and Moses, adapting his civil laws to the actual condition of the Jews, did not attempt by civil penalties to prohibit the dissolution of the marriage tie, but threw on them the responsibility of dissolving it, subject to certain conditions, enacted for the better protection of the wife. This civil law does not modify the obligation of the original divine institution, which forbids any child of God from sundering the marriage tie except for the one crime of adultery. For most marriage is desirable; the only exceptions being those who are by nature or by subsequent maltreatment incapacitated, or who practise celibacy for special religious reasons. Modern legislation may *perhaps*, " because of the hardness of men's hearts," permit a legal separation for other causes than adultery; for it is the primary function of the State not to make men conform to the divine ideal, but to restrain them in so far as is necessary for mutual protection; but the true Christian can never permit it for himself. His duty is always patience, gentleness, forbearance.

Ch. 19 : 13-15. CHRIST BLESSES LITTLE CHILDREN.—CHRIST'S LOVE FOR CHILDREN.—THE CHILDREN'S LOVE FOR CHRIST (Mark 10 : 16).—THE RIGHT OF BRINGING CHILDREN TO CHRIST.—THE SIN OF HINDERING THEIR COMING, BY WORD OR EXAMPLE.—THE CONDITION OF ENTERING THE KINGDOM OF HEAVEN : A CHILD-LIKE SPIRIT (Mark 10 ; 15).

Mark 10 : 13-16, and Luke 18 : 15-17 give some additional particulars. Compare with this incident Matt. 18 : 1-4 and notes there. It is a suggestive if not a significant fact that this blessing of little children follows immediately after the above discussion concerning marriage.

13. **Little children.** Luke says *infants*. The English reader will get the true significance by comparing the following passages, where the same Greek word (βρέφος) is used, as that rendered *infants* in Luke : Luke 2 : 12, 16 ; Acts 7 : 19 ; 2 Tim. 3 : 15 ; 1 Pet. 2 : 2. It is evident from a comparison of these passages that children too young to receive instruction, or to understand what was being done for them, were included among the " little children " brought to Jesus.

There is not the least reason to suppose that they were brought to be healed. Lange says that it was customary for children to be brought to the presidents of the synagogues for blessing. To the disciples this seemed a superstitious fancy, and an intrusion on the more serious labors of our Lord.

14. **But Jesus said.** Mark adds that he *was much displeased.*—**Let the little children alone, and hinder them not from coming to me.** The language of rebuke in the original is stronger than in our version. The above rendering may help to give to the English reader its tone. For the meaning of the word here rendered *suffer* (ἀφίημι), the student may advantageously compare Mark 14 : 6 ; 15 : 36 ; John 12 : 7, where the verb is the same.—**For of such is the kingdom of heaven.** Not merely of those who possess a child-like disposition, though this is included, and is expressly stated in Mark and Luke, " Whosoever shall not receive the kingdom of God as a little child shall not enter therein;" but *of such little children,* both because out of them grow up the citizens of that kingdom, and because they are themselves, in their childhood, members of it.—**Kingdom of God** is certainly not here equivalent to church, as Mr. Barnes asserts, if by that he means the ecclesiastical organization. Does Christ mean, by his next sentence, as reported in Mark 10 : 15, that the adult must receive the church as a little child in order to be received into it? Christ's meaning is interpreted by his language in Matt. 12 : 30 (see note there). There are two kingdoms, one of darkness the other of light, one of good the other of evil, one of Satan the other of God, in which every person is of necessity; for there is no third kingdom. The children belong in the Lord's kingdom, until they voluntarily depart from it, to enter, by deliberate sin, the kingdom of Satan.

15. **Laid hands on them.** This was a common mode of benediction among the Jews. Gen. 48 : 14 ; Numb. 27 : 18 ; Deut. 34 : 9 ; Acts 8 : 17 ; 19 : 6.

NOTE ON CHRIST'S BLESSING OF THE CHILDREN. This passage is fragrant with the love of Christ for little children, see Mark 10 : 14, " he was much displeased ;" and their love for him, see Mark 10 : 16, " he took them up in his arms;" for little children do not willingly go to every stranger. It teaches (1) his sympathy for and with children ; (2) our right to bring children

17 And he said unto him, Why callest thou me good? *there is* none good but one, *that is*, God: but if thou wilt enter into life, keep the commandments.

18 He saith unto him, Which? Jesus said, Thou shalt do no murder, Thou shalt not commit adultery, Thou shalt not steal, Thou shalt not bear false witness;

v Exod. 20 : 13; Deut. 5 : 17, etc.

to him for blessing, and this before they can understand anything concerning him or his truth; (3) that they are members of Christ's kingdom, are so regarded by him, and are to be so regarded by us, and this *irrespective of any parental faith*, for there is no declaration here of parental faith, nor is it even stated that these children were brought by their parents, much less that they were received for their parents' sake; (4) that such as die before they have wandered out of God's kingdom into the kingdom of Satan are certainly saved, since they are "of the kingdom of heaven;" (5) as Alford, that "not only may the little infants be brought to him, but in order for us who are mature to come to him, we must cast away all (?) that wherein our maturity has caused us to differ from them and become like them" (compare, however, Matt. 18 : 1-4 and notes there); and (6) it condemns all conduct on the part of the church, the teacher, or the parent, which tends to repress, chill, or check the enthusiasm of childhood for Christ and darken its simple faith in him. But it certainly *does not* teach (1) that children are by nature, and without a spiritual change, *true children of God*, in the face of such explicit declarations as John 3 : 5, 6; nor (2), except by a very doubtful implication, that they should be members of the visible earthly church; nor (3) that they are proper subjects of baptism. The last is argued for by Alford. But surely the question whether the rite of baptism is properly employed for the consecration of children, or only as a symbol of self-consecration, is not in the remotest degree touched on here.

Ch. 19 : 16-22. THE RICH YOUNG RULER.—THE GREAT QUESTION: WHAT SHALL I DO TO INHERIT ETERNAL LIFE?—THE UNIVERSAL CONSCIOUSNESS WHICH ENFORCES IT: THE CONSCIOUSNESS OF SPIRITUAL LACK.—THE DIVINE ANSWER: FORSAKE ALL AND FOLLOW ME (Luke 14 : 33).—See Lessons below.

This incident is recounted also in Mark 10 : 17-22 and Luke 18 : 18-23. The three accounts should be carefully compared by the student. The time and place are uncertain; probably in Perea, on Christ's last journey to Jerusalem. The instructions which follow, in Matt. 20 : 16, are called forth by this incident, and should be studied in connection with it.

16. And behold one. A young man (verse 20) and a ruler (*Luke*), *i. e.* probably of a synagogue. See for description of office, Matt. 4 : 24.— **That I may have eternal life.** The form of his question indicates that he had been an auditor of Jesus Christ, and that the Master's teachings had taken deep hold on him. He asks not for the kingdom of heaven, which might mean an earthly kingdom, but for *eternal life*, which certainly includes the idea of immortality beyond the grave.

17. Why callest thou me good; none good but one, God. The Sinaitic and Vatican with some other manuscripts have here, *Why askest thou me concerning the good; one is the good*. This reading is adopted by Alford, De Wette, Meyer, Olshausen, Lange, Schaff, indeed by most scholars, and is sustained by Griesbach, Tischendorf, Lachmann, and Tregelles. In the face of such unanimity I hesitate to express a doubt. But I am not convinced that the reading of the Received Text is erroneous. For (1) Mark and Luke have the question as we have it in our English version, and there is no variation of reading in their accounts. We must then either suppose that Matthew has misreported the incident, or that Christ asked the double question, "Why askest thou me concerning the good? One is the Good. Why callest thou me good? None is good but one, God." And in spite of some attempt (see *Schaff* in Lange) to make this appear reasonable, I think it will strike the ordinary reader as forced and artificial. (2.) The question, as reported in the modified reading, forms no answer to the young man's question. This will clearly appear, if we put question and answer plainly, as proposed by the modified reading:—*Young man:* "What good thing shall I do?" *Christ:* "Why askest thou me concerning what good thou shalt do? There is only one good Being." If this means anything it is, in such a connection, an intimation that the effort to be good is useless, since God alone is the Good One. Dr Brown has shown, and I refer the curious student to his pages, that there is at least a respectable authority for the Received Text; and on the whole, considering that this is the indubitable reading in Mark and Luke, it appears to me to be the most probable one. In brief, I incline to the opinion that this is one of the very few cases in which internal evidence, which is here very strong, should be allowed to counterbalance external evidence, which is here somewhat conflicting.

Admitting the reading of the Received Text, how are we to interpret it? Is it true, as claimed by some commentators, that Jesus here "disclaims his own title to such a character as many of his disciples have attributed to him, that of uncreated perfection?"—(*Livermore*.) This, it appears to me, wholly misses the spirit of Christ

19 Honor thy father and *thy* mother; and, Thou shalt love thy neighbor as thyself.
20 The young man saith unto him, All these things have I kept from my youth up: what lack I yet?
21 Jesus said unto him, If thou wilt be perfect, go *and* sell that thou hast, and give to the poor, and thou shalt have treasure in heaven: and come *and* follow me.
22 But when the young man heard that saying, he went away sorrowful: for he had great possessions.

* w Lev. 19 : 18.... x Luke 12 : 33; 16 : 9; Acts 2 : 45; 4 : 34, 35; 1 Tim. 6 : 18, 19.... y John 12 : 26....1 Tim. 6 : 9, 10.

throughout this interview. He does not rebuke the young man for employing what was nothing more than the language of respect by any pupil to a teacher. The term Master was of itself no proof of allegiance. The Pharisees used it. (Matt. 19 : 38.) Christ probes the young man's faith with a question whose meaning may be thus interpreted. Why call you me Good Master? There is but one Good, namely God. Do you employ the phrase as Nicodemus (John 3 : 2)? or, as the twelve disciples, do you recognize in me a divine Master in truth, whose word is law? And to this question the young man makes no response. Then Christ probes him with a second test. To those who see in this question a repudiation of the divinity of Jesus Christ, Stier replies, "Either, There is none good, but God; Christ is good; therefore Christ is God; or, There is none good, but God; Christ is not God; therefore Christ is not good." There is no answer to this but to deny the sinlessness of Christ.—**If thou wilt enter into life, keep the commandments.** The Greek verb rendered *keep* (τηρέω) carries with it the idea of watchfulness; keep, as one keeps a prisoner committed to his charge. Compare Matt. 27 : 36, 54, and Prov. 4 : 23, where the verb is the same.

18. He saith unto him, Which? Jesus saith unto him, The following. Observe, Christ only mentions the laws which govern men's relations to each other. There is nothing said of the first four of the ten commandments, nothing of, Thou shalt love the Lord thy God. Does Christ then teach that obedience to the *moral* law, without love for God, or faith in him, suffices for eternal life? To so read his words would be to miss their whole spirit. He throws the young man back upon himself, compels him to give the inventory of his own moral goodness, and then to confess his own sense of lack. An ordinary teacher would have endeavored to convince him of his need; Christ compels him to confess it.

20. All these things have I kept. Not the language of self-conceit, for Mark adds that "Jesus beholding him loved him," but the sincere expression of one who had carefully observed the requirements of the moral law, and judging of his life from his own standpoint, could see in it no specific disobedience. He is thus the type of a very common character, one which is scrupulous in life, yet finds no true peace of mind in obedience. Compare for parallel, Paul's experience in Phil. 3 : 4-6.—**From my youth up.** These words are omitted by the best manuscripts, and by Alford and Tischendorf.—**What lack I yet?** For parallel to this experience and interpretation of it see Luke 15 : 14; for Scripture answer to it see Rom. 3 : 23, and Heb. 12 : 15. The Greek scholar will observe that the verb rendered in these passages respectively *lack, to be in want, come short,* and *fail,* is the same (ὑστερέω).

21. In considering the practical lesson of this direction bear in mind, (1.) Its connection, well given by Lord Bacon, "But sell not all that thou hast, except thou come and follow me; that is, except thou have a vocation, wherein thou mayest do as much good with little means, as with great." (2.) The fact that the test was not an unusual one. The disciples had abandoned their all to follow Christ (Matt. 4 : 22; 9 : 9; 19 : 27). If this ruler was to be *with* them he must be one *of them,* in his voluntary poverty. (3.) The principle, which is for all time. Not all disciples are required to abandon their property, any more than all are required to abandon their business with James and John and Matthew (1 Cor. 7 : 17, 20, 24); but all are required to hold their property and use their industry for Christ, and subject to his orders, as interpreted by his providence, for both to be ready to give him an account (Matt. 25 : 14-30). There is nothing in the incident, fairly interpreted, to justify the assertion that Christ condemns the possession or the acquisition of wealth.

22. He went away sorrowful. Mark expresses very graphically, in the original, the change in his countenance. *But he, saddened at the saying, went away grieved.* This young man is never referred to again in the N. T.; for the conjecture that he is to be identified with Lazarus is certainly without evidence, it appears to me without probability. That he may have subsequently become a disciple is possible; there is no intimation of such a result in the N. T.

LESSONS OF THE INCIDENT. They lie in a consideration of the *character, consciousness,* and *lack* of this young man. In *character* he was exemplary (verse 20), loveable (Mark 10 : 21), with religious culture and position (Luke 18 : 18), and he was an earnest, reverential seeker, in public, of eternal life, from Christ (comp. Mark 10 : 17). His *consciousness* was of a lack, which neither wealth, honors, amiability, moral life, religious education, position and labors, nor all combined, could

23 Then said Jesus unto his disciples, Verily I say unto you, That a rich man shall hardly enter into the kingdom of heaven.
24 And again I say unto you, It is easier for a camel to go through the eye of a needle, than for a rich man to enter into the kingdom of God.
25 When his disciples heard *it*, they were exceedingly amazed, saying, Who then can be saved?
26 But Jesus beheld *them*, and said unto them, With men this is impossible; but with*a* God all things are possible.

27 Then answered*b* Peter, and said unto him, Behold, we have forsaken all,*c* and followed thee: what shall we have therefore?
28 And Jesus said unto them, Verily I say unto you, That ye which have followed me, in the regeneration, when the Son of man shall sit in the throne of his glory, ye*d* also shall sit upon twelve thrones, judging the twelve tribes of Israel.
29 And*e* every one that hath forsaken houses, or brethren, or sisters, or father, or mother, or wife, or

<small>a 1 Tim. 6 : 9, 10....a Ps. 3 : 8; 62 : 11; Zech. 8 : 6....b Mark 10 : 28; Luke 18 : 28 ...c Phil. 3 : 8....d ch. 20 : 21; Luke 22 : 28–30; 1 Cor. 6 : 2, 3; Rev. 2 : 26....e Mark 10 : 29, 30; Luke 18 : 29, 30; 1 Cor. 2 : 9.</small>

satisfy. His *lack* was the love and faith that holds all things as *from* God (James 1 : 17), uses all *for* God (Mark 25 : 14–30), and obeys the divine command whithersoever it leads. Lacking this "one thing needful," he lacked all, and went away sorrowful.

Ch. 19 : 23–30. DISCOURSE CONCERNING RICHES.—EARTHLY WEALTH A HINDRANCE TO HEAVENLY GLORY.—THE IMPOSSIBLE WITH MAN NOT DIFFICULT WITH GOD.—THE CHRISTIAN'S RECOMPENSE.

The rest of this chapter and the parable which constitutes the first sixteen verses of the chapter following, are closely connected, and constitute one discourse, growing out of the preceding incident. Parallel to this chapter, to its close, are Mark 10 : 23–31, and Luke 18 : 24–30.

23–26. With these verses should be carefully compared Mark 10 : 23–26. From this comparison it appears that Christ, seeing the young man go away sorrowful, says, as here, A rich man shall hardly, *i. e.* with difficulty, enter the kingdom of heaven. The disciples express their astonishment at this saying, as the world has since, and Christ at once repeats and interprets it (Mark 10 : 24), Children, how hard is it for them that trust in riches to enter into the kingdom of God. Then follows the emphatic metaphor of verse 24 here (Mark 10 : 25) : It is easier for a camel to go through the eye of a needle than for a rich man (*i. e.* as already explained, one who trusts in riches), to enter into the kingdom of God. The apostles' question, which follows, Who then can be saved? (verse 25) is not equivalent to, *If it is so hard for the rich, how can the poor enter?* but, Since, though few men are rich, all men trust in riches, *i. e.* have faith in them, how can any enter. Observe the emphatic teaching of verse 26, that salvation is with men impossible, *i. e.* by the power of men (compare John 1 : 13), and the strong assertion that the salvation of *all*, even by implication of those who have made their trust in riches, is possible with God. Attempts have been made to explain away the force of the metaphor of the camel and the needle's eye, as (1) by reading for camel, cable (for κάμηλος, κάμιλος), a reading invented to soften Christ's language; (2) by the assertion that the small gate to the walled city, for foot passengers, was called the eye of a needle, a statement for which I can find no adequate authority. The natural interpretation of the phrase is the correct one. It is used to express, not the difficulty, but the impossibility of entering the kingdom of heaven by human power or skill. Parallel to this expression are similar aphorisms among the rabbis; *e. g.* "Just as soon will an elephant pass through the spout of a kettle" (*Roberts*), or "'Perhaps thou art one who can make an elephant pass through the eye of a needle,' *i. e.* who speaks things that are impossible."—(*Lightfoot.*) On the whole teaching compare Prov. 30 : 8, 9; 1 Tim. 6 : 9, 10, 17. In Luke 12 : 16–21, Christ explains what he means by "them that trust in riches."

27. Christ had just promised to the young man, if he forsook all and followed him, "treasures in heaven" (verse 21). No such promise had ever been made to the twelve. Hence Peter's question. "The '*all*' which the apostles had left was not in all cases contemptible. The sons of Zebedee had hired servants (Mark 1 : 20), and Levi could make a great feast in his house. But whatever it was, *it was their all.*"—(*Alford.*)

28. This verse is peculiar to Matthew. Like all unfulfilled prophecies it is difficult of interpretation. The grammatical construction is itself not clear. The verse may be read either, *Ye which in the regeneration have followed me shall * * * sit upon twelve thrones*, or, *Ye which have followed me shall in the regeneration * * * sit upon twelve thrones.* I think the latter reading is preferable and assume it here to be the correct one; the difference is not, however, very important. Without undertaking a full discussion of the teaching implied in the verse it may suffice here to remark, (1) that the promise refers to a future coming of Christ. The phrase *When the Son of man shall sit in the throne of his glory* describes a future coming in glory, in contrast with the incarnation which was a coming in humiliation. Christ sometimes employs the phrase *Coming of the Son of man*, or its equivalent, to designate the spiritual coming at Pentecost (see

children, or lands, for my name's sake, shall receive an hundred-fold, and shall inherit everlasting life.

30 But many *that are* first shall be last; and the last *shall be* first.

CHAPTER XX.

FOR the kingdom of heaven is like unto a man *that is* an householder,^f which went out early in the morning to hire labourers into his vineyard.

2 And when he had agreed with the labourers for a penny^a a day, he sent them into his vineyard.

3 And he went out about the third hour, and saw others standing idle in the marketplace,

4 And said unto them, Go ye also into the vineyard, and whatsoever is right, I will give you. And they went their way.

5 Again he went out about the sixth and ninth hour, and did likewise.

---

f ch. 19 : 16 , 21 : 31, 32; Mark 10 : 31, Luke 13 : 30; Gal. 5 : 7 , Heb. 4 ; 1....g Cau. 5 : 11, 12,...h ch. 18 : 28.

Matt. 10 : 23 and note), but by the phrase *Coming in his glory*, or, *in the glory of his Father*, I think he always refers to a second coming (Matt. 16 : 27, 28, where the two comings are contrasted, see note there; Matt. 25 : 31; Mark 8 : 38; 10 : 37, 13 : 26; Luke 9 : 26; 21 : 27; compare Matt. 26 : 64; John 1 : 51). (2.) The term *regeneration* (παλιγγενεσία) is ambiguous. It occurs in the N. T. only here and in Titus 3 : 5, and in the latter passage refers to a spiritual change wrought in the heart by the Spirit of God. But it appears to me hardly doubtful, that the disciples would have understood Christ here to refer to that new order which is to be established at the second coming of the Messiah, when all old things will pass away, and all things will become new, and which is referred to in Isaiah 65 : 17 ; 66 : 22; Acts 3 : 21 ; 2 Pet. 3 : 13; Rev. 21 : 5. (3.) The promise here made to the twelve, *Ye also shall sit upon the twelve thrones, judging the twelve tribes of Israel*, paralleled by the similar promise in Luke 22 : 28-30, is upon its face simply a personal promise to them; but elsewhere are to be found promises, apparently to all the saints, of sharing with Christ, in a manner which is not explained, in his office of Judge and King, Dan. 7 : 22; 1 Cor. 6 : 2, 3; Jude 14, 15; Rev. 3 : 21; 20 : 4. (4.) Whatever else this promise may mean, it certainly imports the possession of a celestial office of great trust, dignity, and importance. That we can safely undertake to define its meaning with greater particularity, I doubt. (5.) The other interpretation of this verse, given by both Chrysostom and Lightfoot, is that Christ refers to his spiritual coming at Pentecost, and that the prophecy is nearly equivalent to, When I come in spiritual glory and power, ye, by your spiritual life, or by your doctrine, shall condemn the Jewish nation, which will reject me and my Gospel. But for the reasons given above this appears to me to be untenable.

29. Mark and Luke both give this promise, which is not merely to the twelve, but to all disciples, to "every one that hath forsaken," &c. Mark gives it more fully, "He receiveth (the aorist tense in Mark, signifying not a promise to be fulfilled in the future but one continually fulfilled) an hundredfold, *now in this time, houses and brethren and sisters, and mothers, and lands, with persecutions*. The words underscored are peculiar to Mark. On the interpretation of the promise observe (1) it cannot possibly have been literally understood, for that would involve a multiplying of mothers, an impossibility, and would take away all significance from the important qualifying clause, *with persecutions*, since the loss of houses and lands, and of earthly friends, constitutes the very essence of persecution. Nor (2) is it possible to suppose that Christ means that in the new heaven and the new earth these shall be multiplied, for Mark expressly says, "*now, in this time*." Nor (3) does it mean, as Mr. Barnes interprets it, " the loss shall be compensated or made up" by the possession of "the pardon of sin, the favor of God, peace of conscience," &c., for this constitutes the "*everlasting life*" which begins on earth but continues in heaven, and which is promised in addition to "the hundredfold." The promise is parallel to that of Matt. 5 : 5 (see note there), and is fulfilled because (*a*) Christianity has operated as a general law to enhance the earthly prosperity of the race, to make wealth more general and more secure, and affections less liable to sundering through despotism, quarrels, or death ; (*b*) friends are multiplied and friendships made sweeter and more sacred by Christianity, especially among those who heartily accept and practically show forth Christ in their daily life ; (*c*) the spirit of true religion in the soul enhances a hundredfold the true and high enjoyment of earthly possessions and affections; no one can enjoy the earth as he who accepts it as God's gift of love (compare 1 Cor. 3: 21-23) ; (*d*) those who have been called to fulfill *literally* the condition of *forsaking all* for Christ, have as a rule enjoyed life's prosperities; *e. g.* there are few children better provided for in all that makes life desirable than those of our foreign missionaries. This verse is utterly irreconcilable with the spirit of asceticism in the Christian, and equally so with the idea that Jesus Christ sanctioned voluntary mendicancy, in any form.

30. This is the text of the following parable, and appears again at its close (Matt. 20 : 16). The connection is this : But, all those that forsake their all shall receive all compensation ; not you apostles alone, or even pre-eminently, for, **Many first shall be last, and last first.**

Ch. 20 : 1-16. THE PARABLE OF THE LABORERS.—THE CALL OF CHRIST; A CALL TO CHRISTIAN WORK

6 And about the eleventh hour he went out, and found others standing idle, and saith unto them, Why stand ye here all the day idle?

7 They say unto him, Because no man hath hired us. He saith unto them,¹ Go ye also into the vineyard; and whatsoever is right, *that* shall ye receive.

8 So when even was come, the lord of the vineyard saith unto his steward, Call the labourers, and² give them *their* hire, beginning from the last unto the first.

9 And when they came that *were hired* about the eleventh³ hour, they received every man a penny.

10 But when the first came, they supposed that they should have received **more**: and they likewise received every man a penny.

11 And when they had received *it*, they murmured against the goodman of the house,

12 Saying, These last have wrought *but* one hour, and thou hast made them equal unto **us**, which have borne the burden and heat of the day.

13 But he answered one of them, and said, Friend, I do thee no wrong: didst not thou agree with me for a penny?

14 Take *that* thine *is*, and go thy way: I will give unto this last even as unto thee.

l Prov. 19:15; Ecc. 16:49; Acts 17:21; Heb. 6:12....j Ecc. 9:10; John 9:4....k Luke 10:7....l Luke 22:40-45....m Luke 15:29, 30.
...n ch. 22:12....o John 17:2.

(compare Luke 5:10).—THE BUSIEST WORLDLING IS AN IDLER.—GOD'S PROMISE TO THE CHRISTIAN: WHATEVER IS RIGHT I WILL GIVE (compare 1 John 1:9).—BUT ONE EXCUSE FOR IDLENESS: NO OPPORTUNITY FOR LABOR (v. 7).—GOD'S SHORT ANSWER TO ALL CRITICISM ON HIS PRESENT PROVIDENCE AND HIS FINAL JUDGMENT: IT IS LAWFUL FOR ME TO DO WHAT I WILL WITH MINE OWN. —"THE KINGDOM DEMANDS WORKERS; HIRELINGS IT DISDAINS."—"NOT, HOW MUCH HAST THOU DONE? BUT, WHAT ART THOU NOW? WILL BE THE GREAT QUESTION OF THE LAST DAY."—"WORK IS THE MEANS, MAN THE END."

This parable is peculiar to Matthew. Tischendorf and Alford both omit from verse 7 the words "And whatsoever is right that shall ye receive," and Tischendorf rejects also from verse 16 the last clause. See note below on that verse. For the meaning of the word **Friend** in verse 13 compare Matt. 22:12; 26:50, which give a solemn significance to its use. The Greek word (ἑταῖρε) is different from that employed as an indication of intimacy, as in John 15:14. With these exceptions there is nothing in the original which is not adequately represented in our English version. There are, however, but few parables that have received more diverse interpretations. The curious reader will find them collated in Trench on the Parables. The difficulties have been enhanced, if not created, by ignoring the context, and by endeavoring to find a spiritual parallel for every incident and allusion in the story. Without giving space to these conflicting opinions, I shall indicate here what appear to me to be the main lessons inculcated.

LESSONS OF THE PARABLE. *The story.* This needs very little explanation. The ordinary Jewish working-day lasted from sunrise to sunset. Taking this to be equivalent to from 6 A.M. to 6 P.M., we have the third, sixth, ninth, and eleventh hours respectively equivalent to 9 A.M., 12 M., 3 P.M., and 5 P.M. The custom of waiting in a market-place for employment is common at the present day in all countries where laborers are many and employers few. The penny, here *denarius*, equaled in value eighteen cents. That it was a fair day's wages is implied here. It was the pay of a Roman soldier at or a little before this time. Compare Luke 10:35. The payment of the wages at sundown agrees with Jewish custom, founded on and enforced by the laws of Moses, Deut. 24:15.—*The parallel.* The householder (οἰκοδεσπότης) unmistakably represents God (Matt. 10:25; 13:27; 21:33); the vineyard is a not unfrequent symbol of his kingdom, or his church in the unecclesiastical sense of that word (Isaiah 5:1, 7; Jer. 12:10; Matt. 21:28, 33, etc.; Luke 13:6, etc.); he calls us to Christian labor, in *his* vineyard, *i. e.* both with and for him (1 Cor. 3:9). The first whom he calls, and who enter into a bargain, so much work so much pay (verse 2), represent those who enter into a covenant of works, and give their Christian zeal and activity for an expected reward; the second who make no bargain, but trust all to the Master (verses 4, 7), those who enter his service, counting it their simple duty and trusting the recompense of reward to his good pleasure (Heb. 10:35, 36; see Rom. 4:4, 5; 2 Cor. 5:14); the day represents the earthly life, not of the individual but of the race, for at evening comes the accounting, *i. e.* the judgment at the end of the world. The reward is the heavenly inheritance, the eternal life, the crown of righteousness promised to all who truly love and faithfully serve him; those who object to this view, because it makes eternal life a matter of wages, not a free gift, forget that Christ constantly uses this term *reward*, here rendered *hire* (μισθός), to designate the saint's heavenly inheritance (Matt. 5:12; 6:1; 10:41, 42; Mark 9:41; Luke 6:23, 35; compare 1 Cor. 3:8, 14; Rev. 22:12). All who enter the vineyard are, it appears to me, true disciples of Christ, and all receive the reward; the murmuring (verse 11), therefore, represents not the spirit with which any will finally receive God's allotment, since none of the disciples of Christ will murmur at His dispensation of the heavenly inheritance, but the spirit which too often prevails among the disciples upon earth, who virtually think their hard labour entitles them to large reward, and who in their thoughts complain at the divine allotments of this earthly life. Dr. Brown, however, suggests that one object of the parable is to teach, "that men who have wrought in Christ's service all their days, may, by the spirit which they manifest at last, make it too evident that, as

15 Is it not lawful for me to do what I will with mine own? Is⁴ thine eye evil, because I am good?

16 So⁵ the last shall be first, and the first last: for⁶ many be called, but few chosen.

p Rom. 9 : 15-24; James 1 : 18,...q ch. 6 : 23; Deut. 15 : 9....r ch. 19 : 30...s ch. 22 : 14; 2 Thess. 2 : 13; James 1 : 23-25.

between God and their own souls, they never were chosen workmen at all." This is unquestionably an important truth (compare Matt. 7 : 22, 23; 25 : 41-46), but it does not appear to me to be the truth which this parable is intended to teach. See below on ver. 16.—*Lessons.* To understand these the parable must be taken in its connection. The rich young man has gone away sorrowful, choosing present riches rather than treasures in heaven (chap. 19 : 22). Peter, who has forsaken all for Christ, asks what he and his co-disciples are to have therefore, and Christ replies with the promises of chap. 19 : 28, 29, and then adds the caution, "Many first shall be last, and the last first," of which this parable is an interpretation, and from which it ought not to be separated by the chapter division. Its *primary* application is to the apostles, for whom Peter had asked the question. Because called to labor in the burden and heat of the day, in an era when labor involved large self-sacrifice and persecution, the apostles were not, on that account, entitled to claim any higher reward than those who came later, and who served, in their time, with equal fidelity. It applies *secondarily* to all who enter the kingdom of God, whether early or late in life, whether to do abundant labor or to do very little, *provided they enter when first called*, and labor faithfully according to their opportunity. It applies *spiritually* to all in his kingdom, and teaches that (1) men are not paid in proportion to the amount or the burdensomeness of the work done, and (2) that the spirit which labors for wages and expects a return for its sacrifice and services is the last in the kingdom, though in the amount of its sacrifice and service it may be first, and the spirit that does what God assigns to be done, leaving all to him, is the first in God's kingdom, though in sacrifices borne and services accomplished it may be last. *Incidentally* are the following lessons : (1.) God calls us ; we do not first choose him or apply first to him (verse 1 ; compare John 15 : 16). "Every summons to a work in the heavenly vineyard is from the Lord."—(*Trench.*) (2.) All without God's vineyard are idlers (verse 6) ; "the greatest man of business in worldly things is a mere idle gazer, if he has not yet entered on the true work which alone is worth anything, or gains any reward."—(*Stier.*) (3.) There is to be a final accounting for the children of God as well as for the world (verse 8; compare Luke 19 : 14, 15, 27). (4.) God calls us to account, but will not submit to be called to account and judged by us, an attempt we often make in our theological and philosophical discussions (verse 15; compare Rom. 9 : 19, 20). (5.) It gives no promise or hope of eternal life to those who reject the Gospel until their death-bed, because none can take encouragement from the eleventh hour laborer, except those who to the question, Why stand ye here idle ? can reply, No man hath hired us. *Each laborer went to work at the first call.* (6.) Nor does it militate against the doctrine, elsewhere taught in Scripture, of degrees, both of reward and punishment (Matt. 25 : 20-23; Luke 12 : 47, 48 ; 1 Cor. 3 : 14, 15), for though each man received a penny, yet to each the penny was what he would make of it. "The last go home, each with a penny in his pocket and astonished glad gratitude in his heart ; their reward accordingly is a penny and *more.* The first, on the contrary, go home each with a penny in his pocket, and corroding discontent in his soul ; their reward accordingly is *less* than a penny."—(*Arnot.*) God himself is the Christian's reward (Gen. 15 : 1), and is to each soul what the soul has capacity to receive. Even upon earth we can see that the joy of God's presence is much to some and little to others. (7.) Nor does it imply that heaven is given as wages for labor ; on the contrary, it teaches the reverse. Like the parable of the unjust judge Luke 18 : 1-5), it teaches by contraries. It is as if Christ said, to the bargaining spirit represented by Peter's question, Even if the kingdom of God were one of mere work and wages, many last would be first and first last. There is a curious parallel to and yet contrast with this parable in a rabbinical one quoted by Lightfoot, where there is the same employment, a similar apparent inequality in payment, the same murmuring, but a very different response. "The King saith to them, He hath labored more in those two hours than you in the whole day." It is curious that some Christian commentators have interpreted Christ's parable thus, and so have made it confirm that very spirit of legalism which it condemns.

16. The first clause of this verse is used elsewhere by Christ (Luke 13 : 30), where he evidently distinguishes between the first called, the Jews, who are yet finally rejected, and the last called, the Gentiles, who are finally accepted. But here and in chap. 19 : 30, the reference is evidently to two classes of disciples, as interpreted above. The last clause of the verse is wanting in the Sinaitic and Vatican manuscripts, and is omitted by Tischendorf. It is retained by Alford. If not an addition by a copyist its interpretation here is difficult. It appears again in Matt. 22 : 14, where clearly the distinction is between those who are invited by the Gospel but are not prepared for

17 And Jesus going up to Jerusalem, took the twelve disciples apart in the way, and said unto them,
18 Behold, we go up to Jerusalem; and the Son of man shall be betrayed unto the chief priests and unto the scribes, and they shall condemn him to death,
19 And shall deliver him to the Gentiles, to mock, and to scourge, and to crucify *him*: and the third day he shall rise again.
20 Then came to him the mother of Zebedee's children, with her sons, worshipping *him*, and desiring a certain thing of him.
21 And he said unto her, What wilt thou? She saith unto him, Grant that these my two sons may sit, the one on thy right hand, and the other on the left, in thy kingdom.
22 But Jesus answered and said, Ye know not what ye ask. Are ye able to drink of the cup that I shall drink of, and to be baptized with the baptism that I am baptized with? They say unto him, We are able.
23 And he saith unto them, Ye shall drink indeed of my cup, and be baptized with the baptism that I am baptized with; but to sit on my right hand, and on my left, is not mine to give, but *it shall be given to them* for whom it is prepared of my Father.
24 And when the ten heard *it*, they were moved with indignation against the two brethren.
25 But Jesus called them *unto him*, and said, Ye know that the princes of the Gentiles exercise dominion over them, and they that are great exercise authority upon them.
26 But it shall not be so among you: but whosoever will be great among you, let him be your minister:
27 And whosoever will be chief among you, let him be your servant:
28 Even as the Son of man came not to be ministered unto, but to minister, and to give his life a ransom for many.
29 And as they departed from Jericho, a great multitude followed him.
30 And, behold, two blind men, sitting by the way side, when they heard that Jesus passed by, cried out, saying, Have mercy on us, O Lord, *thou* son of David!
31 And the multitude rebuked them, because they should hold their peace: but they cried the more, saying, Have mercy on us, O Lord, *thou* son of David!

32 And Jesus stood still, and called them, and said, What will ye that I shall do unto you?
33 They say unto him, Lord, that our eyes may be opened.
34 So Jesus had compassion *on them*, and touched their eyes: and immediately their eyes received sight, and they followed him.

CHAPTER XXI.

AND when they drew nigh unto Jerusalem, and were come to Bethphage, unto the mount of Olives, then sent Jesus two disciples,
2 Saying unto them, Go into the village over against you, and straightway ye shall find an ass tied, and a colt with her: loose *them*, and bring *them* unto me.
3 And if any *man* say ought unto you, ye shall say, The Lord hath need of them; and straightway he will send them.
4 All this was done, that it might be fulfilled which was spoken by the prophet, saying,
5 Tell ye the daughter of Sion, Behold, thy King cometh unto thee, meek, and sitting upon an ass, and a colt the foal of an ass.
6 And the disciples went, and did as Jesus commanded them,
7 And brought the ass, and the colt, and put on them their clothes, and they set *him* thereon.
8 And a very great multitude spread their garments in the way; others cut down branches from the trees, and strawed *them* in the way.
9 And the multitudes that went before, and that followed, cried, saying, Hosanna to the Son of David! Blessed *is* he that cometh in the name of the Lord: Hosanna in the highest!
10 And when he was come into Jerusalem, all the city was moved, saying, Who is this?
11 And the multitude said, This is Jesus, the prophet of Nazareth of Galilee.
12 And Jesus went into the temple of God, and cast out all them that sold and bought in the temple, and overthrew the tables of the moneychangers, and the seats of them that sold doves;
13 And said unto them, It is written, My house shall be called the house of prayer; but ye have made it a den of thieves.

---

heaven, and those who are prepared and so are among the chosen people of God. But here the context seems to forbid such an interpretation. It has been suggested that the term *chosen* is used here in a different sense, equivalent to *choice ones*, so that the meaning is, There are many disciples, but few that are pre-eminent in their calling. This is certainly a possible meaning, but it is not sustained by any parallel passage in the N. T., the term *chosen* or *elect* (*εκλεκτις*) never having this significance, unless Rev. 17 : 14 be an instance. I incline to the opinion, which is as old as Calvin, that the sentence does not belong here.

17-31. CHRIST GOES UP TO JERUSALEM. INCIDENTS ON THE WAY. There is nothing to connect the remaining incidents in this chapter with those which immediately precede. They all occurred on the occasion of Christ's going up to Jerusalem to the last Passover and to his Passion and death. Luke's account of this journey (Luke 18:31 to 19:28) is the fullest, though he omits the petition of the sons of Zebedee. Mark (10:32-34) gives the account of Christ's prophecy of his death more fully than Matthew, and (10:35-45) the account of the petition of the sons of Zebedee in almost the same form. For notes on those two incidents see Mark; for notes on the healing of the blind men see Luke.

Ch. 21: 1-22. TRIUMPHAL ENTRY INTO JERUSALEM. There is some uncertainty as to the order of events here narrated. Certainly the impression produced by Matthew's narrative is that all occurred on the same day. Mark, however, (11:11) states that Christ entered the Temple and "when he had looked round about upon all things, and now the eventide was come, he went out unto Bethany with the twelve;" and he gives the cleansing of the Temple on the following day. And this is probably the correct chronology. See note on Mark 11 : 1.

1-11. An account of this triumphal entry is given also in Mark 11 : 1-11, Luke 19 : 29-44, and

14 And the blind and the lame came to him in the temple; and° he healed them.
15 And when the chief priests and scribes saw the wonderful things that he did, and the children crying in the temple, and saying, Hosanna° to the son of David! they were sore displeased,
16 And said unto him, Hearest thou what these say? And Jesus saith unto them, Yea; have ye never read, Out^p of the mouth of babes and sucklings thou hast perfected praise?
17 And he left them, and went out of the city into Bethany; and he lodged there.
18 Now in the morning as he returned into the city, he hungered.
19 And^q when he saw a fig tree in the way, he came to it, and found nothing thereon, but leaves only, and said unto it, Let no fruit grow on thee henceforward for ever. And presently the fig tree withered^d away.
20 And when the disciples saw *it*, they marvelled, saying, How soon is the fig tree withered away!
21 Jesus answered and said unto them, Verily I say unto you, If^s ye have faith, and doubt not, ye shall not only do this *which is done* to the fig tree, but also if ye shall say unto this mountain, Be thou removed,^t and be thou cast into the sea, it shall be done.
22 And all things whatsoever ye shall ask^u in prayer, believing, ye shall receive.
23 And^v when he was come into the temple, the chief

John 12 : 12-19. It is fullest and most graphic in Luke. See notes there.

12, 13. This casting of the traders out of the Temple, narrated also in Mark 11 : 15-19, and Luke 19 : 45-48, is not to be confounded with that recorded in John 2 : 13-17 at the commencement of Christ's ministry. It is not at all strange that, scourged from the Temple, they should, in less than three years, have returned again to corrupt it. History is full of parallels. Compare Matt. 12 : 43-45 and note. The Temple was cleansed but not filled by the indwelling of the Spirit of God. For the symbolical significance of this purification of the Temple see notes on John 2 : 13-17.

14. Peculiar to Matthew, who alone gives any account of miracles being wrought at this time.

15, 16. This incident of the participation of the children of the Temple in the greeting to Christ is also peculiar to Matthew. In the Jewish as in the Roman Catholic service, children took part in the service of song. It was probably these children who caught the public enthusiasm, and joined in the chorus of Hosanna to the Son of David. The incident marks the height which the enthusiasm reached. Christ's rebuke of the chief priests should be studied by those who would check Christian enthusiasm in children at the present day. Christ's reference, *Have ye never read?* is to Psalm 8 : 2. The Greek word (καταρτίζω) here translated *perfected*, is rendered in Matt. 4 ; 21 *mending*, in Gal. 6 : 1 *restore*; it is more literally *Thou restorest praise*. True praise of God had perished from the Temple; in the mouths of these children of the Temple it was being restored. So every babe is, in his innocence, a restorer of the praise of God to the earth. Compare Matt. 18 : 4; Mark 10 : 15.

17-22. The account of the cursing of the fig-tree is given only here and Mark 11 : 12-14, 20-26. It is fullest in Mark. See notes there.

Ch. 21 : 23-46. Chaps. 22 and 23. CHRIST'S LAST PUBLIC DISCOURSES—TUESDAY, 4th APRIL, A.D. 30.

The teachings contained in the rest of this chapter and in chapters 22 and 23, were all given publicly in the Temple on Tuesday. They constitute the close of Christ's public ministry. Parallel to Matthew's report here is Mark 11 : 27 to end of chap. 12; and Luke, chap. 20. With these accounts should be read John 12 : 20-50, which repeats nothing given in the other Evangelists, but appears to report other instructions which were given on the same occasion. Matthew's account of the public teachings of this eventful day is much the fullest; Mark (12 : 41-44) and Luke (21 : 1-4), however, give the account of the widow and two mites, which Matthew omits, and John (12 : 20-36) gives the interview with the Greeks which no other Evangelist gives. The fact that John, whose general record of Christ's Judean ministry is so full, says almost nothing of the teachings of this day, is one of the many indications that he wrote with the other Gospels before him, and in part to supply what they lacked.

In studying in detail the teachings contained in this and the two following chapters, their general character and aim must not be forgotten. Tuesday, the 4th day of April, was by far the most eventful in the life of Christ, prior to his passion and death. On the evening of that day, and for that day's utterances, not at his more formal trial, he was condemned to die. When he first entered the Temple it was evident that systematic plans had been formed to silence him (Luke 19 : 47, 48). Pharisees, Sadducees and Herodians united against him; assumed to be his disciples; mingled their questions with those of honest enquirers; endeavored to entrap him into answers that should arouse popular prejudice or embroil him with the Roman government; plied him with flatteries; and praising his boldness and independence, sought to cajole him (Matt. 22 : 16; Mark 11 : 27; 12 : 13, 14; Luke 20 : 20, 21). Hitherto, Christ had either openly refused or successfully evaded all such questions. He now pursued a different course; sought to draw out the hierarchy; made plain to all the people the ineradicable antagonism between him and the priesthood; and closed with a solemn and terrible denunciation of them (Matt. 21 : 32; 22 : 21, 29-32; 23 : 13-36), which yet

priests and the elders of the people came unto him as he was teaching, and said, By[w] what authority doest thou these things? and who gave thee this authority.

24 And Jesus answered and said unto them, I also will ask you one thing, which if ye tell me, I in like wise will tell you by what authority I do these things.

25 The baptism of John, whence was it? from heaven, or of men? And they reasoned with themselves, saying, If we shall say, From heaven; he will say unto us, Why did ye not then believe him?

26 But if we shall say, Of men; we fear the people; for[x] all hold John as a prophet.

27 And they answered Jesus, and said, We cannot tell. And he said unto them, Neither tell I you by what authority I do these things.

28 But what think ye? A certain[y] man had two

---

w Exod. 2 : 14. ... x ch. 14 : 5. ... y Luke 15 : 11, etc.

---

ended in an outcry of infinite pathos, of divine pity and compassion (23 : 37-39). This commingled denunciation and lamentation constituted Christ's farewell to Judaism—the culmination of his ministry, the first word of whose earliest public and recorded discourse had been 'Blessed,' and to the graciousness of whose first sermons all had borne glad testimony (Matt. 5 : 3; Luke 4 : 22). See *Abbott's Jesus of Nazareth*, chap. 28, pp. 402-404, from which this note is condensed.

Ch. 21 : 23-27. FIRST ATTACK ON CHRIST.—HIS AUTHORITY QUESTIONED. See Lessons below.

Mark (11 : 27-33) and Luke (20 : 1-8) give the account of this interview in almost the same words. Christ was *walking* (Mark) and *preaching the Gospel* (Luke), *i. e.* telling the people the good news of the coming kingdom of God.

23. Into the Temple. The outer court of the Temple, the court of the Gentiles (see notes on John 2 : 14-17) was a convenient gathering place of the people, and during the Passover week would be thronged. Here Christ and his apostles often preached (John 7 : 14; 8 : 2; Acts 3 : 4; 5 : 14, 21, etc.).—**The chief priests.** That is, the leaders of the priesthood. See note on Matt. 2 : 4.—**The elders of the people.** These were laymen. See note on Matt. 16 : 21. Mark and Luke add *scribes*; these were the theologians of Judaism. Lange and Alford suppose this to have been an official delegation from the Sanhedrim. That is certainly possible, but by no means clear. I should think it more probable, from Matt. 22 : 15, that prior to the time there referred to, the efforts to entangle Christ were individual and extemporized.

These things. This includes his whole ministry. He had neither the authority of a rabbi to teach, nor of a priest to cleanse the Temple. There is significance in the vagueness of the language, *these things*. They were unwilling to specify the cleansing of the Temple, and so seem publicly to justify its pollution.—**And who gave thee this authority?** This question interprets the other, and indicates their object, viz., authority on which they could found a charge of blasphemy. They thus sought by indirection, what on his trial the high priest sought by a direct question. See Matt. 26 : 63, 64.

25. The baptism of John. "Meaning thereby, the whole office and teaching of which the baptism was the central point and seal,"—(*Alford*.)—**From heaven.** Equivalent here to *from God.*—**And they reasoned among themselves.** In a conference aside. Surely it is a strain upon the narrative to suppose that they returned to the Sanhedrim, and that a formal consultation was there held. As to the Evangelist's source of knowledge, it may have been, as Alford supposes, Nicodemus or Joseph of Arimathea; is it not more probable to have been our Lord himself, who knew what was in man and read even their unuttered thoughts?—**Why did ye not then believe him?** Generally, accept him and his mission. How far they were from doing this is evident, from Christ's charging them with the murder of John the Baptist (Matt. 17 : 12 and note). What gives special point to this inquiry, however, is John the Baptist's testimony to Christ (John 1 : 6, 7, 29, 34; 3 : 31). If they believed John was a prophet they could not question the authority of Christ.

26. We fear the people. Luke adds: *all the people will stone us.* "Seest thou a perverse heart. In every case they despise God, and do all things for the sake of men."—(*Chrysostom.*)—**For all hold John as a prophet.** Compare Luke 7 : 27.

27. We cannot tell. Literally, *we do not know*. "They were caught in a rough alternative, and could extricate themselves only by a step of desperation—a confession of ignorance, and that of hypocritical (pretended?) ignorance."—(*Lange*.) They assumed to judge of Christ's authority; he compelled them to confess publicly their inability to judge of the authority of John the Baptist. Their utter want of moral principle, their supreme and even unconcealed indifference to the truth stands out nowhere more clearly than in these last days of Christ's ministry. Compare Matt. 22 : 15; Luke 20 : 20; John 11 : 47-50.—**Neither tell I you.** "An answer, not to their outward words, *We know not*, but to their inward thoughts, We will not tell."—(*Alford*.)

LESSONS. One may admire in this incident the skill with which Christ confounds the enemies of truth. It illustrates (*a*) Christ's refusal to submit his claims to the decision of inimical skeptics; (*b*) the unity of divine truth; one cannot accept a part and reject a part, *e. g.* accept John the Baptist and reject Christ; (*c*) the hypocrisy of much that appears to be religious investigation; (*d*) the right of a religious teacher

sons; and he came to the first, and said, Son, go work to-day in my vineyard. 29 He answered and said, I will not; but afterward[a] he repented, and went. 30 And he came to the second, and said likewise. And he answered and said, I go, sir; and went not. 31 Whether of them twain did the will of *his* father?

They say unto him, The first. Jesus saith unto them, Verily I say unto you, That the publicans and the harlots go into the kingdom of God before you. 32 For John came unto you in the way of righteousness, and ye believed him not; but the publicans[b] and the harlots[b] believed him: and ye, when ye had seen *it*, repented not[c] afterward, that ye might believe him.

[a] 2 Chron. 33:12, 13; 1 Cor. 6:11; Eph. 2:1-13....a Luke 3:12....b Luke 7:37, etc....c Rev. 2:21.

to answer a fool according to his folly, *if he has the ability so to do*.

Ch. 21:28-32. PARABLE OF THE TWO SONS.—THE TEST OF PIETY IS PRACTICE, NOT PROFESSION.

This parable is peculiar to Matthew. The story is of a small vineyard, which the father works with the aid of his own family only. In other respects it corresponds to the parable of the laborers (Matt. 20:1-16). The owner of the vineyard represents God; the two sons, two types of character; the vineyard itself, the world, which is God's field (Matt. 13:38); and the command the call of God to his children, which is a call to become co-workers with him (1 Cor. 3:9). Compare notes on Matt. 20:1-16.

28. How seems it to you? That is, what do you think yourself of the case I put to you? Analogous to this appeal is Isaiah 1:18; analogous to our Lord's method here, is Nathan's with David (2 Sam. 12:1-12). It incidently indicates to the religious teacher how, by indirection, to approach a sacred conscience.

29. He * * * said, I will not. This is the language of flagrant, open, and audacious sin. Compare Luke 15:12; 19:14. The character and experience described are represented in such passages as Prov. 1:24; Jer. 2:25; 44:16. —But afterwards regretted it and went. The Greek word (μεταμέλομαι) here rendered *repent* should not be so translated. It occurs in the N. T. only here and in verse 32 below, and in Matt. 27:3; 2 Cor. 7:8; Heb. 7:21. It differs from the word (μετανοέω), more generally rendered *repent;* that word signifies a change of purpose, this, rather regret. See note on Matt. 3:2. Here, however, though the idea of regret is prominent, the result, a change of mind, is involved in the narrative.

30. He * * * said, I sir. There is an air of alacrity and of *quasi* self-assurance in the original, which our version hardly retains. Morison paraphrases it, "You may depend upon *me* sir." The character and experience described are depicted in such passages as Isaiah 29:13; Ezek. 33:31; Matt. 15:8; Rom. 2:17-23; Titus 1:16.

31, 32. Publicans and harlots. For a description of the Publican see note on Matt. 9:9. For description of the Pharisees, here referred to in the words "before *you*," see note on Matt. 3:7. Publicans and harlots had accepted Christ and enrolled themselves among his disciples (Matt. 9:9; Luke 7:29,37-50; 15:1, 2; 19:2, 3, 10).—Go into the kingdom of God before you. An intimation that the way was still open, so that the Pharisees might follow on if they would. —In the way of righteousness. Preaching *obedience* as the way of life, which was the radical doctrine of Pharisaism, but preaching a very different kind of obedience, viz., compliance with the moral not with the mere ceremonial law (see Luke 3:10-14). John the Baptist came upon their own ground, yet they believed not.—When ye had seen it, regretted not, that ye might believe him. That is, they had no *such* regret as led to a practical belief in John, and practical compliance with his instructions.

LESSONS. These two sons represent, not the Gentiles and the Jews, as interpreted by some of the earlier commentators, nor the Publicans and Pharisees, as usually interpreted by the later commentators, but *those Publicans* who regretted their open and flagrant sinfulness, and commenced a life of obedience, and *those Pharisees* who endeavored to cover a life of real disobedience by a pretence of compliance with the law. The first son indicates only Publicans who, like Matthew and Zaccheus, forsook their sins to follow Christ; the second son does not indicate Pharisees who, like Nicodemus, Joseph of Arimathea, and Paul, forsook their sins to follow him. In its modern application the parable teaches, not that there is more hope for a flagrant sinner than for a virtuous man, but that the flagrant sinner *who forsakes his sins*, enters the kingdom of heaven before the orthodox and moral man, *who clings to his sins*. The first son is commended, not *because of the daring wickedness of his reply*, but *because he regretted it and showed his regret by his action*. "What comfort will it afford to the lost to reflect that they went openly to perdition, in broad day-light, before all men, and did not skulk through by-ways, under pretence that they were going to heaven."—(*Arnot*.) On the other hand the second son is *not condemned for his answer*, but *in spite of it*, and because, having promised obedience, he refused to render it. The lesson of the parable is then exactly the lesson of Matt. 7:21-27. *Incidentally* it opens the door of hope to all, even the least and the lowest. "Who was more wretched than Matthew? But he became an Evangelist. Who worse than Paul? But he became an apostle. * * *

33 Hear another parable: There was a certain householder, which*d* planted a vineyard, and hedged it round about, and digged a winepress in it, and built a tower, and let it out to husbandmen, and went into a far country:
34 And when the time of the fruit drew near, he sent his servants*e* to the husbandmen, that they might receive the fruits of it.
35 And*f* the husbandmen took his servants, and beat one, and killed another, and stoned another.
36 Again, he sent other servants more than the first: and they did unto them likewise.
37 But, last of all, he sent unto them his son, saying, They will reverence my son.
38 But when the husbandmen saw the son, they said

d Ps. 80 : 8-16; Sol. Song 8 : 11, 12; Isa. 5 : 1-7; Jer. 2 : 21; Mark 12 : 1; Luke 20 : 9, etc.... *e* 2 Kings 17 : 13, etc.... *f* ch. 5 : 12; 23 : 34-37; 2 Chron. 36 : 16; Neh. 9 : 26; Jer. 25 : 3-7; Acts 7 : 52; 1 Thess. 2 : 15; Heb. 11 : 36, 37; Rev. 6 : 9.

Rahab was a harlot, yet was she saved; and the thief was a murderer, yet he became a citizen of Paradise; and while Judas being with his Master, perished, the thief being on a cross, became a disciple."—(*Chrysostom*.) The whole parable illustrates Matt. 19 : 30.

Ch. 21 : 33-46. THE PARABLE OF THE WICKED HUSBANDMEN.—THE ACCOUNTABILITY OF NATIONS TO GOD.—THE PUNISHMENT OF GODLESS AND UNFAITHFUL NATIONS.

This parable was a part of the Temple instruction on the day which constituted the close of Christ's public ministry. It is reported also in Mark (12 : 1-12) and Luke (20 : 9-19). It was spoken to all the people (Luke) and therefore personally applied to all, not merely, as some of the commentators have supposed, to their religious leaders.

33. Hear another parable. Confounded by the previous parable and its application, those who came to perplex Christ (verse 23) would have withdrawn; he recalls them.—**There was a certain householder which planted a vineyard.** Judea was formerly a land of vineyards; these were constructed on its hills, which were often terraced to the summit. From the earliest settlement by the Israelites it was famous for its grapes (Numb. 13 : 23; Isaiah 16 : 8-10; Jer. 48 : 32). The *hedge* was sometimes a stone wall, sometimes a true hedge of thorns; this last, if formed, as is common in the East, of the prickly aloe, was an effectual protection against wild beasts (Psalm 80 : 12, 13; Sol. Song 2 : 15). The *wine-press* was dug in the earth or hewn out of the solid rock. It consisted of two vats, at different elevations, the grapes being trodden out in one; the other receiving the juice. The *tower* was a place of shelter for watchmen who guarded the fruit of the vineyard; it was also used for storing the fruit. It is customary in the East, as in Ireland and in other parts of Europe, for the owner to let out his estate to *husbandmen, i. e.* tenants, who pay him an annual rent, either in money, or, as apparently in this case, in kind. The attempt to find a spiritual parallel for the hedge, and wine-press and tower, appears to me unnatural and far-fetched. But Chrysostom's remark is worth nothing. "Observe his great care and the excessive idleness of these men. For what pertained to the husbandmen he himself did, the hedging round about, the planting of the vineyard, and all the rest." The sources of national prosperity, not only with the Jews, but with all nations, come from God. To preserve and ripen what he has given is alone left to man.

And went abroad. "By his going into a far country he means his great long-suffering."—(*Chrysostom*.) But it seems to me he means more than this. Christ repeatedly represents God as appearing to withdraw from the earth, that he may test the fidelity and obedience of his children (Matt. 24 : 48; 25 : 14; Luke 19 : 12). I should rather say this represents and partially explains "the eternal silences," God's seeming absence.

34. And when the time of the fruit drew near. By the Mosaic law the fruit of the trees was not to be eaten for five years after planting. This reasonable provision, though based on religious grounds, gave the tree opportunity for maturing before use (Lev. 19 : 23-25). But the analogy is not to be pressed. All time is the time of fruit with the individual and with the nation. God continually seeks for fruit (Luke 13 : 7; John 15 : 2, 5, 8).

35, 36. Such scenes of violence as are here described (verses 35, 36), have been common, not only in the East, but even in Ireland, and they have not been unknown even in this country, *e. g.* in the days of the anti-rent controversy in N. Y. State. "For an abundant historical justification of this description, and as showing that the past ingratitude of the people is not painted here in colors a whit too dark, see 1 Kings 18 : 13; 19 : 14; 22 : 24-27; 2 Kings 6 : 31; 21 : 16; 2 Chron. 24 : 19-22; 36 : 15, 16; Jer. 20 : 1, 2; 37 : 15; and also Acts 7 : 51-55; 1 Thess. 2 : 15; Heb. 11 : 36, 37."—(*Trench*.) Compare also Matt. 23 : 34-37; Mark and Luke give this description of the treatment of the servants somewhat more graphically.

37. In Luke the lord of the vineyard is represented as saying, *What shall I do?* a picture of human perplexity, representing the grief of the Heavenly Father over his rebellious children. Mark's report of Christ's language is noticeable. He says, *Having yet therefore one son, his well-beloved.* Christ thus discriminates clearly between himself, the *Son*, and the prophets who were but *servants* (compare Heb. 3 : 5, 6).—**They will respect my son.** "So also elsewhere he saith,

Cн. XXI.]   MATTHEW.   237

among themselves, This is the heir :ᵍ come, let us kill him, and let us seize on his inheritance.
39 And theyʰ caught him, and cast *him* out of the vineyard, and slew *him.*
40 When the lord therefore of the vineyard cometh, what will he do unto those husbandmen?
41 They say unto him, He will miserably destroy¹ those wicked men, and will let out *his* vineyard unto other¹ husbandmen, which shall render him the fruits in their seasons.

42 Jesus saith unto them, Did ye never read in the scriptures, Theᵏ stone which the builders rejected, the same is become the head of the corner: this is the Lord's doing, and it is marvellous in our eyes?
43 Therefore say I unto you, The kingdom¹ of God shall be taken from you, and given to a nationᵐ bringing forth the fruits thereof.
44 And whosoever shall fallⁿ on this stone shall be broken: but on whomsoever it shall fall, itᵒ will grind him to powder.

g Heb. 1 : 1, 2.... h Acts 2 : 23; 4 : 25–27....i Ps. 2 : 4, 5, 9; Zech. 12 : 2...j Luke 21 : 24; Rom. 9 : 26; 11 : 11....k Ps. 118 : 22; Isa. 28 : 16; 1 Pet. 2 : 6, 7....l ch. 3 : 12....m Isa. 26 : 2....n Isa. 8 : 14, 15....o Heb. 2 : 2, 3.

If perchance, they will hear (Ezek. 2 : 5), not being ignorant, but lest any of the obstinate should say that his prediction necessitated their disobedience."—(*Chrysostom.*) Perhaps this is all. Yet it seems to me that this language of Scripture, of constant appeal to the will of man, shows that God recognizes a real freedom of will, which theologians and philosophers have sometimes denied. The way was still open for them, so that they might respect and listen to the Son, though God foreknew their rejection of him. Compare Acts 2 : 23.

38, 39. This is the heir. That the Pharisees recognized in Christ the divine Messiah is not probable; that they did recognize his miraculous power is certain from John 3 : 2; 11 : 47–50; and the latter reference indicates that if they did not recognize in him the Messiah it was due to willful prejudice.—**Seize on his inheritance.** That which engendered the bitter hostility of the priests and scribes to Christ, was the fact that his teaching threatened to destroy their influence and power. They considered the nation their property; and they slew the Son that they might hold it for themselves (John 11 : 48; 12 : 19).—**Cast him out of the vineyard.** The commentators notice that Christ was delivered over to the Gentiles to be slain (John 18 : 28), and was crucified without the gate (John 19 : 17; Heb. 13 : 11, 12). But neither fact appears to me to be indicated here. Mark reverses the order of Matthew's language and says, *Killed him and cast him out of the vineyard.*

41. Miserable fellows! miserably will he destroy them. (κακοὺς κακῶς ἀπολέσει αὐτούς.) The language of indignation is far stronger in the original, of which I give, as nearly as possible, a literal translation, than in our English version. The Pharisees did not perceive the drift of his parable, or perhaps this was the answer of the people, and "*God forbid*" (Luke 20 : 16) was their involuntary response to the popular expression. To this their response, reported only by Luke, Christ replies with the quotation from the O. T. of the next verse, thus confirming the lesson of his parable.

42. This quotation is from Psalm 118 : 22. From the same Psalm, ver. 26, was taken the song sung by the people on Christ's triumphal entry into Jerusalem, two days before (Matt. 21 : 9). The date and occasion of that Psalm are uncertain, and to what the Psalmist referred in the proverbial phrase here quoted, is therefore also uncertain. Mr. Barnes' interpretation appears to me rational. "We are not to suppose that this Psalm had original reference to the Messiah; but it is applicable to him, and it is used, here and elsewhere, merely to show them how the principle was found in their own writings, that one who was rejected, like a stone unfit to be worked into any part of a building, *might* he in reality so important, that it would be laid yet at the very corner, and become the most valuable stone in the edifice—that on which the whole superstructure would rest."

The head of the corner refers *not* to the highest point or coping of the wall, but to the corner-stone, laid at the foundation, binding together the two walls; on it the whole superstructure, in a measure, rests. There are four corner-stones, but in large buildings one is generally laid with ceremony, as the first step in the true structure of the edifice. Christ is declared elsewhere in the N. T. to be the corner-stone of his church. See Acts 4 : 11; 1 Cor. 3 : 11; 1 Pet. 2 : 6, 7; compare Isaiah 28 : 16; Zech. 4 : 7; and especially Ephes. 2 : 20–22, where Christ's office in binding together Jew and Gentile in one spiritual edifice is portrayed.—**Marvellous.** Because the rejected stone is become the corner-stone. The superstructure also is largely made up of stones rejected by the world's builders. Compare Acts 4 : 13; 1 Cor. 1 : 26, 27.

43. Given to a nation producing the fruits thereof. Not any particular nation, nor the Gentiles generally, but God's peculiar people, his chosen nation out of all lands. See Acts 15 : 14; 1 Pet. 2 : 9; Rev. 5 : 9.

44. Trench gives well the meaning of this enigma. "They fall on the stone who are offended at Christ in his low estate (Isaiah 8 : 14; 53 : 2; Luke 2 : 34; 4 : 29; John 4 : 44); of this sin his hearers were already guilty. They on whom the stone falls are those who set themselves in self-conscious opposition against the Lord; who, knowing what he is, do yet to the end oppose themselves to him and to his kingdom. These shall not merely fall and be broken; for one might recover himself,

45 And when the chief priests and Pharisees had heard his parables, they perceived that he spake of them.
46 But when they sought to lay hands on him, they feared the multitude, because theyᵖ took him for a prophet.

CHAPTER XXII.

AND Jesus answered and spake unto them again by parables, and said,
2 Theᑫ kingdom of heaven is like unto a certain king, which made aʳ marriage for his son,

p Luke 7 : 16 ; John 7 : 40.... q Luke 14 : 16.... r Rev. 19 : 7, 9.

---

though with some present harm, from such a fall as this; but on them the stone shall fall as from heaven, and shall grind them to powder." Compare Matt. 12 : 32 and note. The verb here rendered *grind to powder*, is literally *winnow*, and here implies both *making* chaff of them and *scattering* them as chaff to the winds of heaven. Compare Dan. 2 : 35; to which Christ perhaps intends a reference. Observe the *implication* that there is no possibility of restoration, an implication adverse directly to the restoration of the Jews as a nation, and indirectly to the restoration of a lost soul after judgment. "Mercy has lighted this premonitory fire. The Lord sends out foreshadowings of judgment to drive from their unbelief, those who refuse to yield to gentler means."—(*Arnot.*)

45, 46. According to Mark, after this parable, "They *i. e.* the Pharisees left Christ and went their way." They subsequently sent disciples as spies to assume an air of honest inquirers and so entrap him. Matt. 22 : 15 and note.

LESSONS OF THE PARABLE. The vine (Psalm 80: 8-16; Jer. 2 : 21; Ezek. 15 : 1-6; 19 : 10) and the vineyard (Isaiah 5 : 1-7; 27 : 2, 3) are employed in the O. T. as symbols of the Jewish nation. See also Matt. 20 : 1; and John 15 : 1. The parallel between this parable and those in Psalm 80 : 8-16 and Isaiah 5 : 1-7 is so striking, that it is not improbable that Christ and his auditors had one or both of those passages in mind. But a radical difference is noticeable. In the Psalms the hedges are broken down and the vineyard ravaged by wild beasts, *i. e.* the Jewish nation was desolated by the heathen; in Isaiah the vineyard brings forth wild grapes, *i. e.* the Jewish nation produced no good fruit. Here the *vineyard is fruitful*, but the husbandmen will not render up the fruits. In the O. T. the kingdom of God and the Jewish nation are treated as identical; in the N. T. the vineyard is the *kingdom of God*, and is to be taken *from the nation*, and given to one bringing forth the fruits thereof.

The *householder* then represents God; the *vineyard* the kingdom of God (see note on verse 33), the *hedge*, and *winepress*, and *tower*, the various advantages conferred by God upon the Jewish people (Rom. 9 : 4); the *husbandmen*, not the religious leaders of the people, but the people themselves, who were intrusted with the kingdom, and who should have brought forth the fruits of righteousness in themselves, and in their children,

each generation cultivating the succeeding generation; the *going into a far country*, is the seeming withdrawal of God from the earth into the realm of the silent and the unseen; the *servants* are the prophets sent to the nation from time to time, and shamefully ill-treated; the *Son* is Christ, the last appeal of a merciful God to an unfaithful nation; *the coming of the Lord of the vineyard* is primarily God's coming in the destruction of Jerusalem, when the nation was destroyed, and the kingdom taken from Israel and given to *the nation bringing forth the fruits thereof, i. e.* the elect of all lands. The *practical lessons* of the parable to our own times are as follows: The real foundation of national prosperity is found in God's gifts; every nation is accountable to God, as a nation, and for its national use of its privileges and position; the seeming indifference and real watchfulness of God; the certainty of a coming judgment, in time for the nation, in eternity for the individual; the total destruction of the unfaithful nation, illustrated by history, and illustrating the doom of the individual; and the finality of that doom, enforced by the result of the final judgment in this parable, as expressed in the words, "Grind them to powder." Verse 42 indicates that Christ is the foundation of national life, as well as of Christian and church life, and verse 43 that the continuance of national prosperity is conditioned on practical righteousness.

Ch. 22 : 1-14. PARABLE OF THE WEDDING FEAST.—GUILT IS INDIVIDUAL AND PERSONAL.—THE GREATEST SIN; THE REJECTION OF THE GOSPEL.—THE FALSE PROFESSOR OF RELIGION: HE PROFESSES CHRIST, BUT DOES NOT PUT ON CHRIST.—See analysis below.

ANALYSIS.—This parable, which is peculiar to Matthew, has been sometimes confounded with that of the Great Supper in Luke 14 : 15-24. We must believe either that Christ employed substantially the same figure more than once in his ministry, though with variation both in imagery and in application, or else that we have here two different reports of the same parable. The former opinion appears to me the better one. The parallel between the two discourses is very clear. In both there is a supper, to which the guests first invited decline to come; in both their places are filled up by a throng invited from the streets. But the difference is more marked than the resemblance. That parable was delivered in

Ch. XXII.] MATTHEW. 239

3 And° sent forth his servants to call them that were bidden to the wedding: and they would not come.
4 Again, he sent forth other servants, saying, Tell them which are bidden, Behold, I have prepared my dinner; my oxen and *my* fatlings *are* killed, and all things *are* ready: come unto the marriage.
5 But they made light¹ of *it*, and went their ways, one to his farm, another to his merchandise:

o Ps. 69 : 11 ; Jer. 25 : 4 ; 35 : 15 ; Rev. 22 : 17.....*t* Ps. 106 : 24, 25 ; Prov. 1 : 24, 25 ; Acts 24 : 25 ; Rom. 2 : 4.

---

a Pharisee's house, this in the Temple; that before the enmity of the leaders had been fully developed, this as a warning of their danger; that represented simply a supper given by a certain man, this a wedding-feast given by a king on the marriage of his son; in that the guests simply absent themselves, in this they maltreat the servants sent to invite them; in that they simply are shut out from the supper, in this they are destroyed, and their city burned with fire; that is addressed to the remark of a bystander, Blessed is he that shall eat bread in the kingdom of God, and points out how in all ages, and in all communities, Christian and Jewish, the actual invitation to eat bread in that kingdom is disregarded, and portrays the reasons in the three excuses assigned, this is closely connected with the preceding parable, and sets forth in a new light, and from a different stand-point, the judgment against the Jewish nation for its rejection of the Lord. In brief, that parable emphasizes the Gospel invitation, the fact of judgment and condemnation is subordinate and incidental, this emphasizes the judgment and condemnation, the Gospel invitation is subordinate and incidental. That illustrates the grace, this the judgment of the Lord. It is not derogatory to Christ to suppose that he employed this parable twice; it is rather a token of the skill of the Great Teacher that he uses substantially the same picture to teach lessons which in modern theology have often been represented as incongruous if not inconsistent. The student should compare with this parable that in Luke and the notes there.

This parable is closely connected with the preceding one—The Wicked Husbandmen. It is unfortunate that the two are separated by a chapter division. The two teach the same lesson, the rejection of Christ by the Jews, God's chosen people, and their rejection and destruction in consequence. But that represents God as coming to demand fruits, this to bring a gift; that represents the nation as determined not to account for its trust, this as determined not to receive grace; that is drawn from the O. T., this is redolent of the N. T.; that deals with the Jewish nation *as a nation*, for the husbandmen conspire and act together (ch. 21 : 38), this deals with individuals *as individuals*, each one declines for himself the king's invitation, some being simply indifferent, others open in their enmity (verses 5, 6) ; that again represents the calling of a new nation to whom the kingdom of God shall be given (ch. 21 : 43), this represents that in this new call each soul shall give account of itself, and none shall abide in the kingdom of heaven without personal preparation, the wedding-garment (verse 12). That therefore teaches the unity, responsibility and judgment of nations, this distributes that responsibility, and allots that judgment to the individual.

2. **The kingdom of heaven is likened unto a man king** (see note on Matt. 18 : 23) **who would make a wedding feast for his son.** The wedding festivities in the East are often protracted for several days, sometimes for an entire week or more (Gen. 29 : 27 ; Judges 14 : 12. See notes on John 2 : 1, etc., and Matt. 25 : 1). The word rendered *marriage* in this verse is the same translated *wedding* in the next. It properly signifies the wedding feast. "The two favorite images under which the prophets of the Old Covenant set forth the blessings of the New, and of all near communion with God, that of a festival (Isaiah 25 : 6 ; 65 : 13 ; Sol. Song 5 : 1), and of a marriage (Isaiah 61 : 10 ; 62 : 5 ; Hos. 2 : 19 ; Matt. 9 : 15 ; John 3 : 29 ; Eph. 5 : 32 ; 2 Cor. 11 : 2), meet and interpenetrate each other in the marriage festival here."—(*Trench.*) The fact that the guests, *i. e.* the disciples of Christ, constitute Christ's bride, exemplifies the fact that no figures borrowed from human life are adequate fully to illustrate spiritual truth. Even in the parable we only see through a glass darkly. For parallel passages of Scripture, see Prov. 9 : 3–5 ; Zeph. 1 : 7, 8 ; Luke 22 : 18, 30 ; Rev. 19 : 7. Observe, that the Bible by the symbol of the feast represents the religious life as one of joyousness, and by the symbol of the marriage as one of a most sacred and intimate fellowship with God. Observe, too, that the espousal takes place on earth; the marriage is completed in heaven.

3. It is not uncommon in the East, when the feast is ready, to send a notice to those that have been invited (see Est. 5 : 8 ; 6 : 14). Observe here the implication that the O. T. was an invitation to the feast, to which the N. T. was the second summons, with the declaration, All things are ready. Compare Gal. 4 : 4.

4. An attempt is made by some commentators to find a parallel in the N. T. for this double sending, *e. g.*, that the first sending is by John the Baptist and the earlier ministry of the twelve during the lifetime of the Lord, the second by their preaching subsequent to Pentecost. I should rather see in it only a testimony to the long-suffering and patience of God, in repeating

6 And the remnant took his servants, and entreated *them* spitefully, and slew *them*.
7 But when the king heard *thereof*, he was wroth: and he sent forth his armies, and destroyed those murderers, and burned up their city.
8 Then saith he to his servants, The wedding is ready, but they which were bidden were not worthy.
9 Go ye therefore into the highways, and as many as ye shall find, bid to the marriage.
10 So those servants went out into the highways, and gathered together all, as many as they found, both bad and good: and the wedding was furnished with guests.
11 And when the king came in to see the guests, he saw there a man which had not on a wedding garment:
12 And he saith unto him, Friend, how camest thou in hither, not having a wedding garment? And he was speechless.
13 Then said the king to the servants, Bind him hand and foot, and take him away, and cast *him* into outer darkness: there shall be weeping and gnashing of teeth.

a 1 Thess. 2 : 15....v Dan. 9 : 26; Luke 19 : 27....w ch. 10 : 11, 13; Acts 13 : 46; Rev. 3 : 4; 22 : 14....x ch. 13 : 47....y Zeph. 1 : 12....
z Ps. 45 : 14; Isa. 61 : 10; 2 Cor. 5 : 3; Eph. 4 : 24; Rev. 16 : 15; 19 : 8....a Jer. 7 : 28....b Isa. 52 : 1; Rev. 21 : 27....c ch. 8 : 12.

and re-repeating the Gospel message, as I should see in the end of the parable a justification for refusing to cast pearls before the swine that trample them under-foot and turn again to rend the giver.—**All things are ready.** See note on Luke 14 : 17.

5, 6. In the parable in Luke the excuses of those that decline are given more fully. See notes there. Observe the two classes here. First are the indifferent, **They made light of it**, literally, *But they caring not;* the same word is rendered *neglect* in Hebrew 2 : 3, which illustrates the character of these hearers. The second are the open enemies of the King (verse 6). These two classes, the indifferent and the openly opposed, indicate nearly the whole Jewish nation.—The first class again are divided into two classes: **They went their ways, one to his farm, the other to his commerce.** *Merchandise* is admissible here as a translation only in the sense of "The act or business of trading." The original (*emporia from emporos, traveler*) signifies literally, a *journey for traffic.* Thus it here indicates, the *labor*, not the *results*, of acquisition. One was absorbed by his possession, the other by his getting. "The first would *enjoy* what he already possesses; the second would acquire what is as yet only in anticipation. The first represents the rich; the second those that would be rich (1 Tim. 6 : 9, with 17)."—(*Trench*.)
Entreated them spitefully and slew them. Neglect of the invitation we can understand, but why this murdering of the king's heralds? A royal feast often possesses a political significance. Thus it has been supposed that the feast recorded in Esther, ch. 1, is identical with the great gathering called when Xerxes (Ahasuerus) was planning his Greek expedition. A refusal to attend such a feast would be significant of rebellion, which some might carry further than others. For the historical fulfillment of this as a prophecy of the Jewish maltreatment of the apostles, see Acts 4 : 3; 5 : 18, 40; 7 : 58; 8 : 3; 12 : 3; 14 ; 5, 19; 16 : 23; 17 : 5; 21 : 30; 23 : 2; 1 Thess. 2 : 2, 14-16. Arnot gives well the practical application: "In our own day, it does not require extraordinary sagacity to perceive the same spirit in the relish and readiness with which certain classes catch up a cry against any one who, not ashamed of the Gospel of Christ, has discharged his commission in full."

7. The armies of the earth are God's armies, by whom he executes punishment on ungodly nations (Deut. 28 : 49, &c.; Isaiah 10 : 5, 6; Jer. 51 : 20-23). The direct reference here is, of course, to the destruction of Jerusalem by the Roman legions. Observe that only the *murderers* are destroyed; those who simply rejected the invitation are only rejected from the supper. Compare Luke 14 : 24 with 19 : 27. I would not press this, except so far as it indicates a gradation in the divine punishments.

8. Not worthy. Compare Acts 13 : 46. Those that refuse God's grace, whatever the excellence of their character, are the *unworthy;* those that show themselves ready to receive it are the *worthy*, whatever the natural poverty of their character. Luke 18 : 10-14.

9, 10. The highways. More literally the *confluences of the ways, i. e.*, the open squares and market-places where the people would naturally assemble. Observe, the invitation is to be extended without discrimination, and all both *bad* and *good* are to be brought to the feast. There is no condition of coming to Christ, but *just to come.* The bad are invited *that they may be made good* (1 Cor. 6 : 9-11; Eph. 2 : 1-5). "The beautiful words of Augustine on Christ's love to his church may find here their application, 'He loved her foul that he might make her fair.'"—(*Trench*.) Compare Jer. 3 : 1-14. Of the "good," Nathaniel and Cornelius are illustrations (John 1 : 47; Acts 10 : 1, 2, 4, 22; compare Luke 8 : 15); of the "bad," Matthew and Zaccheus and Saul of Tarsus (Matt. 9 : 9; Luke 19 : 2, 8; Acts 9 : 1, 2; 1 Tim. 1 : 13-16).

11-13. It is a custom at the present day in the East for the host to present his guests with robes of honor. A story is told in Trench, of a vizier slain for failing to wear such a robe, his failure being accounted a mark of disrespect. It is certain that robes were an important part of Oriental wealth (Josh. 7 : 21; Judges 14 : 12; James 5 : 2), and were often given as marks of peculiar favor (Gen. 41 : 42; 45 : 22; 1 Sam. 18 : 4; 2 Kings 5 : 5; Dan. 5 : 7; Esther 6 : 8), and, probably, were frequently given out on State

14 For⁴ many are called, but few *are* chosen.
15 Then⁶ went the Pharisees, and took counsel how they might entangle him in *his* talk.
16 And they sent out unto him their disciples, with the Herodians, saying, Master, we know that thou art true, and teachest the way of God in truth, neither carest thou for any *man;* for thou regardest not the person of men.
17 Tell us therefore, What thinkest thou? Is it lawful to give tribute unto Cæsar, or not?

d ch. 7 : 14; 20 : 16; Luke 13 : 23, 24... e Mark 12 : 13, etc.; Luke 20 : 20, etc.

occasions to all guests. The symbolic meaning of the wedding garment has been a subject of discussion, some Protestant writers having insisted that it represents faith, the Romish writers that it represents charity. Christ gives no interpretation. Here he simply teaches that though all, both bad and good, are invited, no one will be allowed in the heavenly kingdom who is not prepared for the company and the occasion. In what that preparation consists, and how procured, he does not here teach. But other passages in Scripture answer these questions. Our own righteousness is as filthy rags (Isaiah 64 : 6); these God takes from us that he may clothe us with garments of salvation (Luke 15 : 22; Isaiah 61 : 10), which are washed white in the blood of the Lamb (Rev. 7 : 14). These we put on when we put on the Lord Jesus Christ by faith, in baptism (Rom. 13 : 14; Gal. 3 : 26, 27), which we do, not merely by a belief in Christ, but by such a personal reception of him, that we lay off the old man and put on a new man in Christ Jesus (Eph. 4 : 24; Col. 3 : 10-14). Without these garments of holiness, the free gift of God (Rev. 3 : 18), none can enter heaven (Rev. 16 : 15). The wedding garment, then, is neither charity nor faith, but the righteousness of the saints (Rev. 19 : 8), *i. e.*, that radical change in character and life wrought by the spirit of God, through faith in Jesus Christ, without which no man can see the Lord (Heb. 12 : 14). To be without a wedding garment, implied that the man thought his usual attire good enough for the king's wedding; he thus represents those who profess to follow Christ, but who think themselves good enough as they are, and do not seek from him that new birth without which no man can see the kingdom of heaven. The lesson, then, of this incident on the wedding garment is that no one can enter heaven except through humility and a change of nature, that we must not only accept Jesus Christ openly, but put on the Lord Jesus Christ, and that there is discrimination in God's kingdom, but to be exercised by the king, not by his servants (Matt. 13 : 29, 30), and at the door of the feast, not in the invitation.

Friend. The word so rendered here (ἑταῖρος), appears only here and in Matt. 11 : 19; 20 : 13; and 26 : 50. See note on Matthew 20 : 13.—**Speechless,** literally *gagged.* That he had no answer to make shows clearly that it was not beyond his power to be properly attired. The spiritual significance Arnot puts well. "The judgment will be so conducted that the condemned will be compelled to own the justice of their sentence."—**Servants.** The Greek word translated *servants,* in verse 13, is not the same as that rendered *servants* in verse 3. The one are the messengers of the Gospel, the other are the angels. Compare Matt. 13 : 39, 40.—**Outer darkness.** See note on Matt. 8 : 12.

14. This verse is the text of the parable. The **many called** include, first, the entire Jewish nation, who are not chosen, because they refuse the Gospel invitation; second, the Gentiles, of whom they alone are chosen who see and seek in the kingdom of God that in which it consists, "righteousness and peace, and joy in the Holy Ghost." Rom. 14 : 17.

Ch. 22 : 15-22. CONCERNING TRIBUTE TO CÆSAR.—THE GROUND AND THE LIMITATION OF THE DUTY OF OBEDIENCE TO CIVIL GOVERNMENT.

This incident is also given by Mark (12 : 13-17), and Luke (20 : 20-26). It occurred in the Temple, during the last day of Christ's public teaching.

15. Took counsel. That is, held a consultation; no official meeting, as of the Sanhedrim, is indicated. Their previous attempt (Matt. 21 : 23) appears to have been without concert or preparation. Luke describes more fully their object: "They sent forth spies, which should feign themselves just men, that they might take hold of his words, that so they might deliver him unto the power and authority of the governor," *i. e.*, the Roman governor Pilate.

16. Their disciples. Concealing themselves, and sending persons who should be unknown to Jesus,—**With the Herodians.** These are mentioned only here and in Mark 12 : 13, etc., and Mark 3 : 6. The reference to the leaven of Herod in Mark 8 : 15 contains perhaps an indirect allusion to them. They are not described by Josephus or any contemporary writers. Their character can only be conjectured from their name. They were probably a political rather than an ecclesiastical party, the adherents of the Herodian family, who were the creatures of Cæsar. The Herodians, therefore, would have been ready to prefer an accusation against any one who counselled refusal to pay the Roman tax.—**Master, we know, etc.** They purported to be true inquirers, to desire counsel, and by flattery sought to draw him on to a repudiation of the Roman tax. To them is applicable the proverb which Alford quotes;

18 But Jesus perceived their wickedness, and said, Why tempt ye me, ye hypocrites?
19 Shew me the tribute money. And they brought unto him a penny.
20 And he saith unto them, Whose is this image and superscription?
21 They say unto him, Cæsar's. Then saith he unto them, Render[f] therefore unto Cæsar the things which are Cæsar's, and unto God[g] the things that are God's
22 When they had heard these words, they marvelled, and left him, and went their way.

f ch. 17 : 25, 27 ; Rom. 13 : 7....g Mal. 1 : 6-8 ; 3 : 8-10.

The devil never lies so foully as when he tells the truth. Compare with their language here their characterization of Christ on other occasions, e. g. John 7 : 12 ; 8 : 48 ; 9 : 16.

17. Is it lawful to give tribute unto Cæsar, or not? Mark adds the still more direct question: *Shall we give, or shall we not give?* Cæsar was the official name of the Roman emperor. The reigning Cæsar was Tiberius. The *tribute*, literally *census money, i. e.* poll tax, was paid by every Jew. It was inquisitorial, followed a careful taking of the census, in which every man was obliged to report his family, his property and his income (see note on Luke 2 : 1), and was extremely odious to the Jews, who counted it a badge of their national degradation (compare note on Matt. 9 : 9). Its payment was resisted by some, especially among the Galileans, not only on political but also on religious grounds. Deut. 17 : 15 might have been regarded as a *quasi* justification for their resistance. The revolt referred to in Acts 5 : 37 (see note there) appears to have been caused by this tax.

18. But Jesus perceived their wickedness. Luke characterizes it more clearly as *craftiness*, Mark as *hypocrisy*.—**Why tempt ye me, hypocrites?** "Jesus shows them that he is *true*, as they had said."—(*Bengel*.)

DENARIUS—A PENNY.

19, 20. Show me the tribute money. Literally, the *coin of the census, i. e.* the coin in which the tribute is paid.—**They brought unto him a penny.** Literally, a *denarius*, a Roman coin equal to about seventeen cents of our money. The annexed cut shows the image and superscription referred to. By requiring them to bring him the coin he compels them to answer, tacitly, their own question; for the Jewish rabbis taught that, "wheresoever the money of any king is current, there the inhabitants acknowledge that king for their lord."—(*Lightfoot*.) By accepting the Roman coinage they accepted the Roman government and all the consequent responsibilities and obligations.

21. Render unto Cæsar. Rather here, *give back to Cæsar*. Compare for similar use of the same verb (ἀποδίδωμι), Luke 4 : 20 ; 9 : 42. They ask, Is it lawful to *give*, he replies, *give back*. Since they accepted in the coinage of Cæsar the benefits of his government, they were bound to *give back* a recompense in tribute.—**The things that are God's.** Not the temple tribute merely, but all things. As the acceptance of Cæsar's government involves the duty of tax-paying to him, so the acceptance of every good and perfect gift from above involves the duty of supreme allegiance to God.

LESSONS OF THIS INCIDENT. *The problem.* The enquirers appeared to be honest disciples (Luke 20 : 20), approached Christ with the language of respect (verse 16) and with a question on which the nation was divided. If Christ replied, Pay tribute, he would render himself obnoxious to the people, who, *without exception*, expected to be delivered from the Roman yoke and Roman taxation by the Messiah. If he answered, Pay not, he would involve himself with the Roman government, and afford a real ground for the false accusation afterwards preferred against him (Luke 23 : 2). The latter answer the Pharisees hoped to elicit from Christ.—*Christ's solution.* He compels the questioners to expose their own inconsistency. They accept in the coin of Rome the Roman government. So long as they do this they are bound to give back support to it. For so long as the citizen accepts the benefit of a government he owes it allegiance and obedience. At the same time Christ affords both the ground and the limitation of this obedience. The powers that be are ordained of God. Because we are to render to God the things that are God's we are to render to Cæsar the things that are Cæsar's, for Cæsar is of God ; but when Cæsar requires what God forbids we are to disobey. For illustration of the duty of obedience to human law, see Rom. 13 : 1-7 ; 1 Cor. 7 : 21-24 ; Ephes. 6 : 5-8 ; Col. 3 : 22-25 ; 1 Pet. 2 : 13-17.—For illustration of the duty of disobedience, under the higher law of allegiance to God, see Dan. 3 : 18 ; 6 : 10 ; Acts 4 : 19 ; 5 : 29. Certain of the commentators see in Christ's answer here a solution of the much-vexed question of Church and State. But I am unable to see how it has anything more than a remote bearing on that problem.—*Spiritual lesson.* This Dean Alford suggests. It can hardly have been recognized by

23 The[b] same day came to him the Sadducees, which[i] say that there is no resurrection, and asked him,
24 Saying, Master, Moses said, If a man die, having no children, his brother shall marry his wife, and raise up seed unto his brother.
25 Now there were with us seven brethren: and the first when he had married a wife, deceased, and, having no issue, left his wife unto his brother:
26 Likewise the second also, and the third, unto the seventh.
27 And last of all the woman died also.
28 Therefore, in the resurrection, whose wife shall she be of the seven? for they all had her.

29 Jesus answered and said unto them, Ye do err, not[k] knowing the scriptures, nor the power of God.
30 For in the resurrection they neither marry, nor are given in marriage, but are as the angels[l] of God in heaven.
31 But as touching the resurrection of the dead, have ye not read that which was spoken unto you by God, saying,
32 I[m] am the God of Abraham, and the God of Isaac, and the God of Jacob? God is not the God of the dead, but of the living.
33 And when the multitude heard *this*, they were astonished[n] at his doctrine.

[b] Mark 12 : 18, etc. ; Luke 20 : 27, etc.... [i] Acts 23 : 8.... [j] Deut. 25 : 5 ; Ruth 1 : 11.... [k] John 20 : 9.... [l] ch. 18 : 10 ; 1 John 3 : 2....[m] Exod. 3 : 6, 15, 16 ; Heb. 11 : 16.....n ch. 7 : 28 ; Mark 12 : 17.

the auditors, but it is perhaps none the less involved, though indirectly, in the second clause of Christ's reply. "Man is the coinage and bears the image of God (Gen. 1 : 27); and this image is not lost by the fall (Gen. 9 : 6; Acts 17 : 29; James 3 : 9). We owe then ourselves to God ; and this solemn duty is implied, of giving ourselves to Him, with all that we have and are."

Ch. 22 : 23-33. THE SADDUCEES SILENCED.—THE SCRIPTURE PROVES THE RESURRECTION.—FAITH IN GOD'S OMNIPOTENCE REMOVES ALL DIFFICULTIES.

This conference is reported also in Mark 12 : 18-27, and Luke 20 : 27-40.—See the latter passage and notes there.

23. The Sadducees. The materialists and infidels of the first century. They denied not merely the resurrection of the body, but also the immateriality and immortality of the soul (Acts 23 : 8). For brief statement of their history and opinions, see note on Matt. 3 : 7.—**Which say.** Rather, *saying;* i. e. they came for the very purpose of arguing the point with Jesus.

24-28. The law referred to is recorded in Deut. 25 : 5, 6. For illustration of its exercise see Ruth, chap. 4. The case here proposed was doubtless an imaginary one, invented for the purpose of presenting an objection to the doctrine of a future life. An illustration of the spirit of much modern theological controversy.

29. Not knowing, i. e. not understanding. Two frequent causes of religious error are here hinted at : first, a failure to understand the Scripture, which we often read, as they did, either superficially and carelessly, or blinded by our theological prejudices ; second, a failure to realize the power of God, it being a common error of theological and philosophical reasoning to limit the divine power to those forms of exercise with which we are acquainted. Observe the fact that the Bible expressly rests the doctrine of the resurrection on the exercise of *divine power* (Acts 26 : 8 ; Rom. 4 : 17 ; 6 : 11 ; 1 Cor. 6 : 14).

30. Compare Luke 20 : 34-36 which gives the reply more fully. For a consideration of the Bible idea of marriage see notes on Matt. 19 : 4-6. This declaration does not imply that the angels are the spirits of the departed ; on the contrary, it discriminates between the two, for it compares the one to the other. Nor does it imply that there is no recognition of friends in heaven and no perpetuation of friendship. Nor does it involve the literal resurrection of the earthly body ; on the contrary, it implies a radical difference between the celestial and the terrestrial body. (Compare 1 Cor. 15 : 42-44, 50.) But Christ declares that as in heaven there will be no more death (Luke 20 : 36), so there will be no succession and renewal of life, which is the main object of marriage ; hence the physical relation of marriage will not continue to exist ; and that alone constitutes the difficulty in the case proposed.

31, 32. Christ refers the Sadducees, not to the teaching of the later prophets, but to Moses whom they had cited. And he carries them back to God's covenant with Israel as a nation, entered into at the burning bush (Luke 20 : 37 ; Exod. 3 : 6). Observe that both here and there the language is in the present tense, I *am* the God of Abraham, etc. Thus the covenant, which rendered the Jews God's peculiar people, is itself called to witness to the resurrection of the dead. Christ's use of this passage is inconsistent with the idea of an intermediate unconscious state, and equally so with the position of those who maintain that the doctrine of the resurrection of the dead is not taught in the earlier books of the O. T. Christ shows that it is not only taught there, but is inwrought into the very structure of the teaching, and asserts that the Sadducees fail to recognize it only because they know not the Scriptures. A comparison of Christ's language here with Rom. 14 : 9, Christ is "Lord both of the dead and the living," affords a striking illustration of the *verbal* contradictions which are not infrequent in Scripture. But the contradiction is *merely verbal ;* the argument there really confirms the argument here ; for Paul cites Christ's death and *resurrection*, as an evidence that he is the Lord of those that die, who are also raised from the dead that he may be their Lord. Luke repeats Christ's practical deduction, which is the same as Paul's : "All live to him." See Luke 20 : 38 and note, and compare Rom. 14 : 8.

34 But when the Pharisees had heard that he had put the Sadducees to silence, they were gathered together.
35 Then° one of them, *which was* a lawyer, asked him *a question*, tempting him, and saying,
36 Master, which *is* the great commandment in the law?
37 Jesus said unto him, Thou⁹ shalt love the Lord thy God with all thy heart, and with all thy soul, and with all thy mind.
38 This is the first and great commandment.
39 And the second *is* like unto it,⁴ Thou shalt love thy neighbour as thyself.

o Luke 10 : 25, etc. ... p Deut. 6 : 5 ; 10 : 12. ... q Lev. 19 : 18.

33. Doctrine. Rather, teaching; here certainly not *what* he taught, for the doctrine of the resurrection was generally accepted among the people, but the *manner* in which he confirmed it and confounded those who opposed it.

Ch. 22 : 34-40. THE GREAT COMMANDMENT.—CHRIST'S CREED : LOVE.—CHRIST'S DEFINITION OF PIETY AND PHILANTHROPY.

Parallel to this is Mark 12 : 28-34. The account is not given by Luke or John. But an incident analogous is found in Luke (10 : 25, *etc.*), where Christ, in answer to a further inquiry, defines by a parable what is a *neighbor*, and also interprets the nature of true love. The two passages should be studied together. That the two are not different reports of the same incident is evident, because : that reported by Luke (a) occurs earlier in Christ's ministry ; (b) probably in Perea ; (c) the *inquirer* gives the summary of the law ; (d) Christ's object is to humble a self-righteous inquirer. This occurs (a) at the close of Christ's ministry; (b) in Jerusalem ; (c) Christ gives the summary of the law ; (d) his purpose is the rebuke of Pharisaic dialectics, and the inculcation of love as the essence of true religion.

34. That he had put the Sadducees to silence. Literally, *had muzzled the Sadducees*. In this victory over their opponents they exulted. Observe, the Sadducees, though probably not convinced, were silenced ; they could make no reply.

35. A lawyer. That is, one versed in the rabbinical laws ; a Jewish theologian. In Mark he is called a *scribe*. The latter phrase appears to have been an official designation of a recognized teacher ; the former an unofficial designation of one learned in Jewish laws, both scriptural and traditional.—**Tempting him.** He subsequently accepted Christ's answer heartily (Mark 12 : 32-34). It does not follow that he was an honest inquirer in the beginning. I judge that he was neither a caviller, nor a disciple, but one curious to see what reply Christ would make to one of the puzzling theological problems of the day.

36. Compare Mark's language (Mark 12 : 28). The question was a common one. Some Pharisees asserted that the Sabbath commandment was first in importance ; others, the law against idolatry ; others put first the rabbinical rules respecting ablutions.

37. Thou shalt love the Lord thy God, etc. The language of this verse is not that of mere emphatic iteration. Each word has its own peculiar significance. The *heart* is the seat of the affections and emotions. God calls not merely for obedience, but for *love*. Compare Prov. 23 : 26 ; Jer. 3 : 14. The word *soul* should rather be rendered *life*. This is unquestionably the primary significance of the Greek ($\psi\upsilon\chi\eta$), which is derived from a verb meaning to breathe. It signifies the *vital principle*, and in the N. T. generally, either physical life, as in Matt. 2 : 20 ; Acts 20 : 24 ; 27 : 10 ; or all that is embodied in our word *life* in its deeper significance. It would generally be better translated by the word *life*. Thus, What shall it profit a man to gain the whole world and lose his own soul ? is really, Lose his own *life*, that to which the world should minister (see note on Matt. 16 : 25) ; Ye shall find rest unto your *souls*, is, Rest unto your lives, *i. e.* in your whole experience. Here the command is, Love with thy whole *life*, *i. e.*, love must not only manifest itself in feeling, it must rule the whole life, by ruling its source and springs. "The reason must be a reason acting in the spirit of love ; the conscience must be a conscience acting in the atmosphere of love ; the taste must be a taste acting in the spirit and atmosphere of love—love to God and love to man. The appetites and passions, and every other faculty, in all their power and variety and versatility, may act, but they will act as steeds that feel the one rein, which goes back to the hands of the one driver, whose name is Love."—(*Henry Ward Beecher*.) John 14 : 15, 23 ; 2 Cor. 5 : 14 ; 1 John 2 : 5 ; 4 : 16, illustrate this command. The *mind* embraces the intellectual powers and activities, whether employed in study, in business, or in social activity. A supreme love toward God must be the inspiration of the whole mental life, and furnish its purpose. Parallel to this is Prov. 12 : 5 ; Psalm 119 : 15, 97 ; 2 Cor. 10 : 5 ; Phil. 1 : 9. Mark adds, with all thy *strength*. That is, the love must be one of enthusiasm and power, not a sentiment, but a working *force*. Parallel to this is Eccles. 9 : 10 ; Rom. 12 : 11 ; Eph. 6 : 6, 7 ; Col. 3 : 23. The commandment is quoted by Christ from Deut. 6 : 4, 5.

39. Like unto it. Because love is always the same in character, whether it goes out

40 On these two commandments hang all the law and the prophets.
41 While the Pharisees were gathered together, Jesus asked them,
42 Saying, What think ye of Christ? whose son is he? They say unto him, *The Son* of David.
43 He saith unto them, How then doth David in spirit call him Lord, saying,
44 The LORD said unto my Lord, Sit thou on my right hand, till I make thine enemies thy footstool?
45 If David then call him Lord, how is he his son?
46 And no man was able to answer him a word; neither durst any *man*, from that day forth, ask him any more *questions*.

toward God or toward man; and because neither can exist without the other. True piety and morality can never be divorced. Piety without morality is superstition; morality without piety is conventional and insincere. Compare 1 John 4 : 7, 8, 20.—**Thy neighbour as thyself.** On, Who is my neighbour? see Luke 10 : 25 and James 1 : 27. Observe that self-love is not wrong, when it is mated to and balanced by love to others. Observe, too, that the command here goes farther than the Golden Rule (Matt. 7 : 12), though one interprets the other; that affords a measure of conduct; this calls for that love which can alone inspire right conduct. The precept is quoted from Lev. 19 : 18.

40. Remember that Christ came to fulfill the law and the prophets (Matt. 5 : 17 and note); he here, therefore, declares the end of his mission, viz., the inspiration of love toward God and man. Love is the highest of the graces (1 Cor. ch. 13), the fulfillment of the law (Rom. 13 : 9, 10; Gal. 5 : 13, 14), the test and measure of Christian experience (1 John 3 : 14). Neither a ceremony, a creed, nor an emotional experience, but love, is the heart of the religion of Jesus Christ. It is by love, as Christ defines it here, that the soul lives in harmony with God; by love, as Paul defines it in 1 Cor. ch. 13, that he is to live in harmony with his fellow-men; and by love that he is to secure harmony in himself. "There is but one pilot from the cradle to the grave—there is but one pilot from this world to the next—and his name is Love."—(*Henry Ward Beecher*.) But this love is not merely an emotion, or sentiment, or an impulse, but a principle, which seated in the *heart*, rules the *life*, inspires the *mind*, and imparts *strength* to the whole man. Observe, that the religion of Jesus Christ does not call for the suppression of man's powers, but for the highest conceivable inspiration and activity of the whole being, under the summer influence of love, and this the highest conceivable form of love, love received from and going out to God.

Ch. 22 : 41-46. THE PHARISEES BAFFLED.—THE DIVINITY OF THE MESSIAH PROVED FROM THE OLD TESTAMENT.

This incident is recorded also in Mark 12 : 35-37 and Luke 20 : 41-44. Compare Mark's account.

42. What think ye of the Messiah? The word Christ is not a proper name, but a title. The question is not, What think ye of me personally? but, What think ye of the Messiah whom all are expecting? See note on names of Jesus, page 21.—**The Son of David.** This was the common opinion, and it was true (Luke 1 : 32; Rom. 1 : 3), but not the whole truth. It was not generally believed by the Jews that the Messiah should be divine. Jesus was condemned for blasphemy in calling himself the Son of God (Matt. 26 : 63-65). In this colloquy he proves out of the Scripture that the Messiah of prophecy was to be the Son of God.

43. In spirit. Mark's language is yet more clear, *By the Holy Ghost:* "a weighty declaration by our Lord of the inspiration of the prophetic Scriptures."—(*Alford*.)

44. The quotation is from Psalm 110. It is one frequently referred to in the N. T. as prophetic of the Messiah (Acts 2 : 34, etc.; 1 Cor. 15 : 25; Heb. 1 : 13; 5 : 6; 7 : 17, 21; 10 : 13). It is evident, from its use here and in these passages, that it was generally so regarded by the Jews. The language of the verse cited (ver. 1) is unambiguous. "There was not any one on earth in the time of David to whom it could be applicable; any one whom he would call his "Lord" or superior. If, therefore, the Psalm was written by David, it must have referred to the Messiah, to one whom he owned as his Superior, *his* Lord, *his* Sovereign."—(*Barnes*.)—**Sit thou on my right hand.** A place of the highest honor (1 Kings 2 : 19; 1 Sam. 20 : 25; Matt. 20 : 21).—**Till I make thine enemies thy footstool.** Alford and Tichendorf, instead of footstool, read *under thy feet*. Putting the feet on captives taken in war was a common Oriental method of symbolizing complete triumph over them (Joshua 10 : 24; 2 Sam. 22 : 41). Parallel to this promise is 1 Cor. 15 : 25 and Heb. 10 : 13.

46. Neither durst any one from that day forth ask him any more. That is, for the purpose of caviling. His disciples asked him questions subsequently (Matt. 24 : 3; 26 : 22; John 14 : 5); and the effect of these instructions on the common people was not to repel, but to attract them (Mark 12 : 37).

CHAPTER XXIII.

THEN spake Jesus to the multitude, and to his disciples,
2 Saying, The*w* scribes and the Pharisees sit in Moses' seat:
3 All therefore whatsoever they bid you observe, *that* observe and do; but do not ye after their works; for*x* they say, and do not.
4 For they bind heavy burdens,*y* and grievous to be borne, and lay *them* on men's shoulders; but they *themselves* will not move them with one of their fingers.

w Mal. 2:7.... *x* Rom. 2:21-23.... *y* Acts 15:10.

Ch. 23. CHRIST'S FAREWELL DISCOURSE IN THE TEMPLE.—PHARISAISM DESCRIBED. IT IS BURDENSOME AND UNSYMPATHETIC (2–4), OSTENTATIOUS (5–7), A HINDRANCE TO TRUE RELIGION (13), AVARICIOUS AND HYPOCRITICAL (14), ZEALOUS FOR SECT BUT NOT FOR SOULS (15), INGENIOUS BUT CORRUPT IN CASUISTRY (16–22), SCRUPULOUS IN CEREMONIALS, INDIFFERENT TO TRUE LIFE (23, 24), SCRUPULOUS IN EXTERNAL MORALITY, INDIFFERENT AS TO THE SPIRIT (25–28), SELF-RIGHTEOUS AND SELF-CONFIDENT (29–31), APPLAUDED BY MEN, CONDEMNED BY GOD (32–39).

This chapter constitutes the closing public address of Christ. After delivering it he departed from the Temple, and gave no more instruction except privately to his own disciples. (Matt. 24:1.) It is one discourse; the attempt to interpret it as a series of fragments collected by Matthew, requires no other refutation than the simple reading of the discourse. On other occasions (Luke 11:42-54 and 13:33-35) some of the same thoughts and almost the identical expressions here recorded were used. But we must either suppose that Christ not infrequently repeated the same or substantially the same discourse on different occasions, or we must give up all reliance on the historical trustworthiness of the Evangelists as reporters. Matthew alone gives this discourse fully; Mark (12:38-40) and Luke (20:45-47) give a suggestion of it. It stands at the close of Christ's public ministry, and is its consummation as the Sermon on the Mount is its inauguration. The burden of this, as of that, is a warning against the irreligion of Judea's religious teachers; but that is affirmative, this denunciatory, that points out the right way, this is a solemn condemnation of the wrong way. The whole discourse is an illustration of the precept, Abhor that which is evil (Rom 12:9), and of the "wrath of the Lamb" against all unrighteousness, and interprets a phase of Christ's character, and therefore of God's character, which modern sentimental philosophy is fond of ignoring, his passionate and vehement abhorrence of sin. Christ's example is in all things a pattern for his followers; and his spirit of indignation we are to imbibe, as well as his spirit of patient, long-suffering love. This philippic, therefore, is a sufficient justification for the disciple, when the occasion demands a similar disclaimer and denunciation of ecclesiastical oppression and hypocritical pretence. Yet its peculiar commingled character should be observed; it is both a philippic and a lament, the language of vehement indignation and poignant sorrow. Terrible in its invective, it ends in an outcry of infinite, divine pathos and compassion. The discourse is by its construction naturally divided into three parts: (1) warnings against the spirit of ostentation which characterized the Scribes and Pharisees (verses 1-12); (2) solemn denunciation of their hypocrisy (verses 13-33); (3) conclusion and farewell to the temple and Jews (verses 34-39).

1. Luke says *In the audience of all the people,* thus emphasizing the fact that it was a public discourse, Christ confutes the Pharisees in colloquy, then denounces their ostentation and hypocrisy.

2-4. Scribes and Pharisees. See notes on Matt. 3:7; 5:20—**Sit in Moses' seat.** Because members of the Jewish Sanhedrim or Council (see note on Matt. 2:4) which claimed to have originated in Moses' appointment (Numb. 11:17, 24) and which was the sole political representative of Jewish nationality. The word *seat* here is equivalent to our word *bench,* as in the phrase "The judicial bench;" and the meaning is not, "Do all things which they, as successors of Moses, out of his law, command you to observe;" it is not an endorsement of them as *teachers,* but a direction to obey their commands as Jewish magistrates. Compare note on Matt. 22:15-22, p. 264, and ref. there. That this does not impose, as the Roman Catholic commentators claim, a duty of implicit obedience to church authorities, whatever their character, is evident from Matt. 16:6. Observe, however, that the bad example of a religious teacher is no excuse for not following what is right in his instructions, and that generally Christ's method of emancipating the soul from oppressive laws, whether ecclesiastical or political, is not by direct attack on the laws, but by such a general development of the soul as makes it superior to and eventually free from them. See note on Matt. 5:19.—**For they say and do not.** Compare Rom. 2:18-24, and contrast 1 Cor. 4:16; 11:1; Phil. 3:17.—**Heavy burdens.** By their minute and exacting ritualism. For illustration of its character see notes on Matt. 12:2; and Mark 7:2.—**But they will not move them.** Not, it seems to me, They are indifferent and neglectful of their own laws; this does not seem to have been the case; but, Though rigorous in making laws, they proffer no sympathy or help to those that struggle to fulfill them. There is this characteristic difference between the religion of Jesus

Ch. XXIII.] MATTHEW.

5 But* all their works they do for to be seen of men: they make broad their phylacteries,ᵃ and enlarge the borders of their garments,

6 Andᵇ love the uppermost rooms at feasts, and the chief seats in the synagogues,

7 And greetings in the markets, and to be called of men, Rabbi, Rabbi.

* ch. 6 : 1-18. ...ᵃ Num. 15 : 38. ...ᵇ Mark 12 : 38, etc.; Luke 11 : 43, etc.

Christ and all false religions and all corruptions of Christianity. The latter only enact laws; the former comes to impart *power*. See John 1 : 12; Rom. 8 : 3, 4; 2 Tim. 1 : 7.

5. In this and the two following verses Christ exposes the motives of the righteousness of Pharisaism, viz., desire of applause. Compare Matt. 6 : 1-18.—**They make broad their phylacteries.** These were strips of parchment, on which were written four passages of Scripture, viz., Exod. 13 : 2-10; 11-17; Deut. 6 : 4-9; 13-22. These were placed in a box of black calfskin and bound on the arm or forehead. The custom grew out of a literal interpretation of Deut. 6 : 8 and Exod. 13 : 9, but seems to have originated during the captivity. Minute regulations are given in the rabbinical books as to methods of wearing, &c. A similar practice is alluded to by Chrysostom as prevalent in his day: "So many of our women now wear the Gospels hung from their necks." Our cut illustrates one of these

PHYLACTERY IN USE.
From Jessup's "Women of Arabia."

phylacteries in use. They are employed even now in Mohammedan countries, the inscriptions being taken from the Koran. The phylactery is worn by modern Jews only on special occasions. What the Pharisees made broad was the case, not the parchments within.

And enlarge the borders of their garments. The ordinary outer garment of the Jews was a quadrangular piece of cloth, to each of the four corners of which, in conformity with Numb. 15 : 38, 39, and Deut. 22 : 12, a tassel was attached, as shown in the accompanying illustration. Each tassel had a conspicuous thread of deep blue to symbolize the heavenly origin of the commandments, of which it was intended to serve as a reminder. The whole edge of the garment appears also to have been fringed, the ends of the threads composing the woof being left. Illustrations of the sacredness attached to

FRINGED GARMENT.

this fringe and tassels are afforded by Matt. 9 : 20; 14 : 36; Luke 8 : 44. The object of the original commandment, Chrysostom gives well, in comparing the wearing of this fringe to the binding of a thread round the finger as a reminder. These rebukes of Christ applied to our own time, condemn the spirit, however manifested, which assumes a peculiar dress for the purpose of making a show of piety.

6, 7. **And love the first places at feasts.** Not *rooms* in the modern and common sense of the term, but *the chief seats* at the table. Every seat had, according to its locality, its peculiar dignity. See Luke 14 : 7, note.—**And the chief seats in the synagogues.** At the upper end of the synagogue stood the ark or chest containing the Book of the Law. This portion of the synagogue answered to the chancel in a modern church. Near it were the *chief seats*, which were usually occupied by the elders of the synagogue. Compare with Christ's condemnation of the Pharisees here, James 2 : 2, 3.—**And greetings in the market-places.** As manifestations of the reverence of their fellow-men. On the form of Jewish salutation see note on Luke 10 : 4.—**And to be called Rabbi.** A title of respect given by the Jews to their religious teachers, and often addressed to our Lord without rebuke, being often translated *Master*. (Matt. 26 : 25, 49; Mark 9 : 5; 11 : 21; John 1 : 38; 3 : 2, 26; 4 : 31; 6 : 25, &c.) To it very nearly answers in significance our modern title, *Doctor*. Its use is thought to have arisen about the time of Herod the Great. There were degrees of honor in the title, Rabbi being considered higher than Rab, and Rabban

8 But be not ye called Rabbi: for one is your Master, even Christ; and all ye are brethren.
9 And call no man your father upon earth; for one is your Father, which is in heaven.
10 Neither be ye called masters: for one is your Master, even Christ.
11 But he that is greatest among you, shall be your servant.

c Jas. 3 : 1....d ch. 6 : 9....e ch. 20 : 26, 27.

than Rabbi. The Pharisees, though they loved it, assumed to be indifferent to it. Lightfoot quotes the rabbinical motive, Love the work, but hate the title.

8. But be not ye called Rabbi: for one is your teacher. The best manuscripts omit from this verse the words *even Christ*, and give a different word for *Master* from that rendered Master below in verse 10. (Here it is διδάσκαλος, there it is καθηγητής.) Verses 8-10 then, literally rendered, will read thus: "*But be not ye called Rabbi; for one is your Teacher, and all ye are brethren. And call no one your father upon the earth; for one is your Father, the Heavenly. Neither be ye called leaders; for one is your Leader, Christ.*" That by the "teacher" is intended the Holy Spirit is indicated by Prov. 1 : 23; Jer. 31 : 33, 34; John 14 : 26; 16 : 13, 14; 1 Cor. 2 : 13; 1 John 2 : 20. If so, "we have God in his Trinity, here declared to us as the only Father, Leader (Rom. 7 : 19), and Teacher of Christians, the only One, in all these relations, on whom they can rest or depend. They are all *brethren*; all substantially equal — *none by office or precedence nearer to God than another; none standing between his brother and God*."—(*Alford.*) Observe, in confirmation of this, how Christ separates himself from man and ranks himself with God, who is our only leader. (Ephes. 5 : 3.)

9. And call no man your Father upon earth. The title of "Father" appears to have been given in early times to priests and prophets (Judges 17 : 10; 18 : 19; 2 Kings 6 : 21; 13 : 14) and in later times, even by Paul, to the members of the Sanhedrim (Acts 22 : 1). In its ordinary use it carried with it a recognition of paternal authority in spiritual things, the Jewish Rabbi being regarded, as is the Roman Catholic priest of to-day, as an *authority* in matters of faith and conscience.—**And all ye are brethren.** Compare Ephes. 3 : 15; Rev. 1 : 9; 22 : 9.

10. Neither be ye called leaders: for one is your Leader, even Christ. The Pharisees all claimed to accept the Old Testament as a divine authority; but they were divided into schools or sects, under human leaders, as the School of Hillel and the School of Shammai, and the zealous among them were more anxious for the triumph of their school than for the elucidation of the truth.

Respecting the application of these three precepts to our own times, observe (1) that it is not the mere use of the words *Rabbi*, *Father*, and *Leader*, which Christ condemns, but the spirit of strife and vainglory which leads to their use; (2) that the three prohibitions are not mere reiterations of the same prohibition in different forms, but condemn essentially different though cognate faults; (3) that those faults are as truly manifest in modern Christian usages as in ancient Jewish usages. The first prohibition, "*Be not ye called Rabbi,*" forbids all ecclesiastical titles given and received *for the mere sake of honor*, and indicating no real office. In direct violation of its spirit, and almost in direct violation of its letter, is the custom of conferring the title Doctor of Divinity on clergymen. I concur heartily with Mr. Barnes' note on this point. "This title (Rabbi) corresponds with the title Doctor of Divinity as applied to ministers of the Gospel: and, so far as I can see, the spirit of the Saviour's command is violated by the reception of such a title, as really as it would have been by their being called Rabbi. It makes a distinction among ministers. It tends to engender pride and a sense of superiority in those who obtain it, and envy and a sense of inferiority in those who do not; and the whole spirit and tendency of it is contrary to the simplicity that is in Christ." The title Reverend is legitimate only as a convenient method of indicating *the office* of pastor or minister. But this prohibition does not seem to me to forbid such inartificial titles as are the *natural and spontaneous expressions of respect and affection, e. g.,* "Pastor Harms," "Father Taylor," nor such as indicate a real office, *e. g.,* "Bishop Simpson," "Dean Alford." The second prohibition, *Call no man your Father*, forbids the exercise of *spiritual authority over the conscience* by pope, priest, or pastor, and equally forbids the disciples of Christ from submitting to such authority. It condemns both the ambition in priest and pastor which seeks authority over the conscience, and the spiritual indolence in laymen which yields to such claims in order to avoid the necessity of personal search for the truth. This prohibition is interpreted by such passages as Rom. 14 : 4, 10, 12; 1 Pet. 5 : 3; Gal. 2 : 5; 2 Cor. 10 : 1. In direct violation of both its letter and spirit is the Roman Catholic custom of giving to the priests the title of "Father," and submitting to the exercise of a paternal authority in spiritual things. And observe that it is the *apostles*, whose successors the priests claim to be, who are forbidden the title to the spiritual authority which the priests have assumed. The third prohibition, *Neither be ye called leaders*, forbids the formation of schools and sects, which look not directly to

12 And^f whosoever shall exalt himself, shall be abased; and he that shall humble himself, shall be exalted.

13 But woe unto you, scribes and Pharisees, hypocrites! for ye shut up the kingdom of heaven against men: for ye neither go in *yourselves*, neither suffer ye them that are entering to go in.

14 Woe unto you, scribes and Pharisees, hypocrites! for ye devour widows' houses,^g and for a pretence make long prayer: therefore ye shall receive the greater damnation.

15 Woe unto you, scribes and Pharisees, hypocrites; for ye compass sea and land to make one proselyte ! and when he is made, ye make him twofold more the child^h of hell than yourselves.

---

f Prov. 15 : 33 ; Jas. 4 : 6, ...g 2 Tim. 3 : 6 ; Tit. 1 : 11, ...h John 8 : 44 ; Acts 13 : 10 ; Eph. 2 : 3.

Christ as the *only Leader*, but to subsequent human teachers as leaders. It is interpreted by 1 Cor. 1 : 12, 13. In direct violation of its letter and spirit is the organization of the disciples of Jesus Christ into schools of theology under human leadership, as followers of Luther, Calvin, Wesley, Campbell, &c. This does not differ in any respect from the division of the Pharisees into the schools of Hillel and Shammai, which our Lord here rebukes.

11, 12. Verse 12 is an aphorism which occurs several times in Christ's teaching. (Luke 14 : 11 ; 18 : 14). On its significance see note on Matt. 18 : 4. Here it is interpreted by the preceding verse ; he humbles himself who makes himself the servant of others (1 John 3 : 16). The double declaration of the two verses is interpreted by history. Even in secular things we no longer regard as great those who have made the world serve them—as Alexander the Great, Gregory the Great, and our own "railroad kings ;" but those who have well served their generation—as Washington, Luther, and Stephenson.

13-33. This portion of Christ's discourse denounces three classes of sins which in different forms exist to-day as in Christ's day : (1) A semblance of religious zeal accompanying real worldliness and selfishness (verses 13-15) ; (2) A subtle casuistry, busying itself in distinctions that are conventional, false, and immoral (verses 16-22) ; (3) A scrupulous regard for external rites and ceremonies, accompanied with a supreme indifference to the heart and life (verses 23-33).

13. Because ye shut the kingdom of heaven in the face of men; not merely *against* them, but in their faces as they are about to enter in, by taking away the key of knowledge (Luke 11 : 52). This the Pharisees did (1) by denying the Scripture, which is a key to the kingdom of heaven, to the common people, as the priests of the middle ages did subsequently (for to read the Scripture without note or comment was regarded as dangerous for the unlearned in the time of Christ as in the time of Luther) ; (2) by perverting it and substituting traditions for it, thus shutting out the people from that knowledge of Christ which the Scripture affords (Mark 7 : 9-13 ; John 5 : 39) ; (3) by their evil and misleading example (Matt. 23 : 3). This the Roman Catholic Church did in almost precisely the same manner. This is still done whenever, in the pulpit or the Sabbath-school, the subtleties and technicalities of a metaphysical theology are substituted for the simple exposition and application of the Gospel, or the teachings of Scripture are made of none effect by the lives of professing Christians. Compare Lev. 19 : 14 ; Isaiah 57 : 14.

14. This verse is omitted from the best manuscripts; Tischendorf, Tregelles, Lachmann and Alford all omit it. It has probably been inserted here from Mark 12 : 40 and Luke 20 : 47, where it is unquestionably genuine. The Pharisees were scrupulous as to hours of prayer, as were subsequently the Christians in the early Church. (See note on Matt. 6 : 5-15, p. 61.) It was a rabbinical proverb, Long prayers make a long life. An instance which illustrates this verse is given by Josephus in Antiq. 18 : 3, 5 : "These men persuaded Fulvia, a woman of great dignity, and one that had embraced the Jewish religion, to send purple and gold to the Temple at Jerusalem ; and when they had gotten them they employed them for their own uses, and spent the money themselves." A similar power has been exercised from a very early period by the Roman Catholic priests, especially over women ; and this to such an extent, and at so early a date, that Justinian passed ordinances forbidding the clergy to inherit possessions ; these were revived in England in the statutes of Mortmain, which forbid any bequests for charitable or ecclesiastical uses. It was by their assumed sanctity that the Pharisees, as the priests, obtained their influence over women. Christ's denunciation applies to all who make their religion a cloak for covetousness (1 Thess. 2 : 5).

15. Go about sea and land to make one proselyte. It is significant that the word here is in the original exactly that used respecting Christ in Matt. 4 : 23, Jesus *went about* all Galilee ; but the object of our Lord's going about was to heal the sick and proclaim the glad tidings of the Gospel, the object of the Pharisees going about was to increase the number of their adherents. The difference between religious and proselyting zeal is just this : one is for God and humanity, the other is for one's self, one's school, or one's sect. In Smith's Bible Dictionary, art. *Proselytes*, is given an account of the methods employed by the Pharisees in pros-

16 Woe unto you, *ye* blind guides, which say, Whosoever shall swear by the temple, it is nothing; but whosoever shall swear by the gold of the temple, he is a debtor.
17 *Ye* fools, and blind! for whether *is* greater, the gold, or the temple that sanctifieth the gold?
18 And, Whosoever shall swear by the altar, it is nothing; but whosoever sweareth by the gift that is upon it, he is guilty.
19 *Ye* fools, and blind! for whether *is* greater, the gift, or the altar that sanctifieth the gift?
20 Whoso therefore shall swear by the altar, sweareth by it, and by all things thereon.
21 And whoso shall swear by the temple, sweareth by it, and by him that dwelleth therein.
22 And he that shall swear by heaven, sweareth by the throne of God, and by him that sitteth thereon.
23 Woe unto you, scribes and Pharisees, hypocrites! for ye pay tithe of mint, and anise, and cummin, and have omitted the weightier *matters* of the law, judgment, mercy, and faith: these ought ye to have done, and not to leave the other undone.

i ch. 15 : 14....j Ps. 94 : 8....k Ex. 29 : 37; 30 : 29....l 2 Chron. 6 : 2; Ps. 26 : 8....m ch. 5 : 34; Ps. 11 : 4; Isa. 66 : 1....n Luke 11 : 42....o ch. 9 : 13; 1 Sam. 15 : 22; Jer. 22 : 15, 16; Hos. 6 : 6. Mich. 6 : 8.

elyting, which recalls the more familiar methods of the Jesuits. "When they had power they used force; when they had not power they resorted to fraud. They appeared as soothsayers, divines, exorcists, and addressed themselves especially to the fears and superstitions of women." The proselytes are divided in the rabbinical books into two classes. The proselytes of the gate, a phrase derived from Exod. 20 : 10, were such heathen as dwelt in the land of Israel, or even out of it, and who, without submitting to circumcision or any other part of the ceremonial law, feared and worshipped the true God. Of such we probably have examples in Luke, ch. 7; Acts, ch. 10; John 12 : 20; Acts 13 : 42; and it is generally believed that the phrases "religious proselytes" (Acts 13 : 43), "devout Greeks" (Acts 17 : 4), and "devout men" (Acts 2 : 5) refer to this class. The proselytes of righteousness were circumcised and baptized, and took upon them the whole Jewish law and its observances. These were rare, and it is to these, doubtless, Christ here refers. Such a proselyte could but be made worse by his *pseudo* conversion; he was "a disciple of hypocrisy merely, doubly the child of hell, condemned by the religion he had left, condemned again by that which he had taken."—(*Alford*.)

Twofold more the child of hell than yourselves. The Pharisees taught that no heathen could become a member of the Jewish nation except he were "born again" (see note on John 3 : 3). Jesus here asserts that the proselyte of the Pharisees is born from below, not from above. "Out of bad heathen they were made worse Jews."—(*Erasmus*.) And the reason was, not merely because those who were the most zealous proselytizers were most indifferent to moral and spiritual life, but, as Meyer, because "Experience proves that proselytes become worse and more extreme than their teachers." The warning applies to all attempts to add *numbers* without *spiritual life* to the church, school, or sect. Of the effect of such endeavors Jesuit missions afford a mournful illustration.

16-22. The gold of the temple (verse 16). Possibly the ornaments of the temple, but more probably the sacred treasure, made up of gifts devoted to the temple by the worshippers. Thus the Pharisees made the gift to the temple, which was in reality a gift to the ecclesiastics (see note on verse 14) more sacred than the temple itself—**He is guilty** (verse 18) should be rendered *He is bound*. The word is the same rendered *He is debtor* in verse 16.

The precise nature of the Pharisaic precepts here condemned is largely a matter of surmise. It is clear, however, that by nice casuistical distinctions the Pharisees made vows and oaths of none effect. The modern application is to all casuistry the object or effect of which is to lessen the sense of obligation to the law of God. Of a like casuistry in the Jesuit fathers, Pascal in his "Provincial Letters," gives numerous illustrations. These permitted miserliness, envy, falsehood, private revenge, duelling, and even assassination, on grounds as frivolous as those which Christ here exposes. The application to oaths of all forms, is also apparent. The appeal, however framed, is never to an inanimate thing, but to God, either directly, or through one of his attributes, or to some one as a witness in the place of God. To release, therefore, from an oath, because it is by the temple rather than by the gold, or by the altar rather than by the gift, is folly, not only because it reverses the true order of relative importance (verse 17-19) but also because it ignores the fact that every oath, however phrased, is really an appeal to God (verses 21, 22). Compare Matt. 5 : 33-36 and notes.

23. Ye pay tithe of mint and anise and cummin. Under the Mosaic law the tenth of all produce belonged to Jehovah and must be offered to him in kind, or redeemed with money (Lev. 27 : 30-33). The *mint*, our modern mint, the *anise*, probably the modern dill, and the *cummin*, were all insignificant plants used for sauces, or for perfume; the dill or anise was also used as a medicine. These were, according to the letter of the law, liable to tithe, for it required "the seed of the land" as well as "the fruit of the tree." And our Lord does not condemn but impliedly approves the Pharisees' scrupulousness in paying the tithe of these herbs. What he condemns is the conscience that pretends to be scrupulous in matters of insignificant detail, and is indifferent

24 *Ye* blind guides! which strain at a gnat, and swallow a camel.
25 Woe unto you, scribes and Pharisees, hypocrites! for*p* ye make clean the outside of the cup and of the platter, but within they are full of extortion and excess.
26 *Thou* blind Pharisee! cleanse first that *which is* within the cup and platter, that the outside of them may be clean also.

27 Woe unto you, scribes and Pharisees, hypocrites! for ye are like unto*q* whited sepulchres, which indeed appear beautiful outward, but are within full of dead *men's* bones, and of all uncleanness.
28 Even so ye also outwardly appear righteous unto men, but within ye are full of hypocrisy and iniquity.
29 Woe unto you, scribes and Pharisees, hypocrites! because ye build the tombs of the prophets, and garnish the sepulchres of the righteous,

p Mark 7 : 4, etc....q Luke 11 : 44; Acts 23 : 3.

in matters of real importance. The modern application is to the spirit which is scrupulous in ritualistic observance and indifferent to the weightier matters of the law as interpreted below.— **And have neglected**, not *merely* omitted but dismissed from mind; **the weightier matters of the law**, not the more *burdensome* but the more *important* requirements: **judgment, mercy, and faith**. By *judgment* is meant, not justice, *i. e.* "giving to all their just dues" (*Barnes*), for the original word (κρίσις) never bears this significance in the N. T.; but *spiritual discrimination*. Our English version exactly represents the spirit of the original. The Pharisees by their casuistry showed an utter lack of capacity to judge of moral and spiritual things. Compare Luke 12 : 57; John 7 : 24. *Mercy* is the exercise and manifestation of sympathy and goodwill to all mankind, especially the suffering and the sinful, precisely the opposite of the proud and uncharitable disposition of Pharisaism. See note on Matt. 5 : 7, and for illustrations of their lack of mercy see Luke 7 : 39; John 8 : 3–5. *Faith* is not equivalent here to fidelity, as some of the commentators interpret it. So to render it is to miss entirely the spiritual meaning of Christ's words. Our English version renders the original correctly. The whole passage is interpreted by Micah 6 : 8, and Hosea 12 : 6. *Clear spiritual discernment, love to one's neighbor, humble trust in God*— these are the important matters of the law. Compare 1 Tim. 1 : 5.— **These ought ye to have done.** Observe that Christ does not condemn scrupulousness in small matters, but demands that which is higher. The way to emancipate the conscience from bondage is not to denounce unnecessary scruples, but to fill the soul with a larger and higher idea of the religious life.

24. Blind guides which strain out a gnat. The word *at* before strain was originally a printing error for *out*, which first appeared in King James' version in 1611, and has been faithfully copied ever since. To strain *at* a gnat represents the stomach rising as it were against the little insect, but kept down by a *strain* or vigorous effort. To strain *out* a gnat is to pass the water or wine through a strainer before drinking, to purify it of insects. This is a common practice in the East, and it was done by the Pharisees to avoid partaking anything ceremonially unclean (Lev. 11 : 23, 41, 42). The Hindoos have a similar proverb: Swallowing an elephant and being choked with a flea. The camel was also ceremonially unclean, because it did not divide the hoof (Lev. 11 : 4). "It is not the scrupling of a little sin that Christ here reproves; if it be a sin though but a gnat, it must be strained out; but the doing of that, and then swallowing a camel. In the lesser matters of the law to be superstitious, and to be profane in the greater, is the hypocrisy here condemned." —(*Matthew Henry.*)

25, 26. Ye make clean the outside of the cup and platter. There is perhaps a reference to the scrupulousness of the Pharisees in the washing of their dishes, etc., to avoid ceremonial pollution (see Mark 7 : 2-5, note). The meaning of the metaphor is clear; Pharisaism is always solicitous for the external appearance, and indifferent to the inner spirit. Compare Matt. 15 : 19, 20.— **But within they are full of extortion**, *i. e.* ravening, covetousness, greed, **and excess**, self-indulgence. Of the opposite spirit, Paul in 1 Cor. 9 : 27 affords an illustration. These two words suggest the two characteristic vices of Pharisaism, ancient and modern—a spirit of covetousness, and a spirit of self-indulgence, covered by a pretence of virtue and piety.

26. Christ indicates the only true method of radical reformation, from within working outward, not from without working inward. Religion is the preparation for morality, not morality for religion. But only God can cleanse that which is within (Psalm 51 : 7, 10; Ezek 36 : 25, 26; John 3 : 3, 5).

27, 28. Whitewashed sepulchres. The Jews whitened the sepulchres annually with lime or chalk that all might know that the place was unclean and to be avoided. For this practice Ezek. 39 : 15 was cited. Dead bodies were unclean according to the Mosaic law, and the touch of them defiled (Num. 5 : 2, 6-8). In Luke 11 : 44 an analogous but different figure is used. There the Pharisees are compared to concealed graves, with which the people come in contact and by which they are defiled, unconsciously—**Are full of hypocrisy and lawlessness.** (Greek ἄνομία.) Pretending to be scrupulous in his obedience to the law, the Pharisee is oblivious

30 And say, If we had been in the days of our fathers, we would not have been partakers with them in the blood of the prophets.
31 Wherefore ye be witnesses unto yourselves, that ye are the children of them which killed' the prophets.
32 Fill ye up then the measure of your fathers.
33 Ye serpents, ye generation' of vipers! how can ye escape the damnation of hell?
34 Wherefore, behold, I send unto you prophets, and wise men, and scribes: and *some* of them ye shall kill and crucify; and *some* of them shall ye scourge in your synagogues, and persecute *them* from city to city:
35 That upon you may come all the righteous blood shed upon the earth, from the blood of righteous Abel unto the blood of Zacharias son of Barachias, whom ye slew between the temple and the altar.

---

r Acts 7 : 52 ; 1 Thess. 2 : 15..., *s* Gen. 15 : 16 ; 1 Thess. 2 : 16 ...t ch. 3 : 7..., *u* Acts 7 : 59....v Acts 5 : 40 ; 2 Cor. 11 : 24, 25....w Heb. 11 : 37....x Lam. 4 : 13 ; Rev. 18 : 24... y Gen. 4 : 8....z 2 Chron. 24 : 20, 21.

---

of its character (Matt. 5 : 17, 20, 22, &c.) and of its object, the development of love (Rom. 13 ; 8; Gal. 5 : 14 ; 1 Tim. 1 : 5). That soul is truly lawless which is without the spirit of love. "Such are men now also, decking themselves indeed outwardly, but full of iniquity within. * * * If one should tear open each man's conscience, many worms and much corruption would he find, and an ill-savor beyond utterance; unreasonable and wicked lusts I mean, which are more unclean than worms."—(*Chrysostom.*)

29-31. Because ye repair the tombs of the prophets, and decorate the monuments of the righteous. That is, this is your only mode of honoring them, in lieu of observing their words, imbibing their spirit, or imitating their lives. Thus Herod the Great, a monster of cruelty (see note on Matt. 2 : 1), rebuilt the sepulchre of David.—**And say, if we were in the days of our fathers we would not be partakers with them.** The language of self-confidence; very like much modern language concerning the bigotry and intolerance of past ages. Whenever, instead of chiding ourselves for our present faults, we exult because we do not repeat the faults of the past, we subject ourselves to Christ's condemnation here.—**Wherefore ye witness to yourselves that ye are the children of them that killed the prophets.** Compare Luke 11 : 47, 48. Certainly, building the tombs and decorating the monuments of the murdered did not indicate an approval of the murderers. I can only understand this passage thus: By calling the murderers your fathers you testify that you are their children, and by building the tombs of the murdered prophets you testify to their guilt in murdering the prophets. Of this guilt, as shown in the parable of the wicked husbandmen (Matt. 21 : 37-39), and in the following verses of this discourse, they were partakers. The spirit of Pharisaism honors the martyrs of past ages and repeats its persecutions in the present.

32. Fill ye up then the measure of your fathers. The language both of prophecy and of terrible irony and invective. Somewhat analogous in spirit is the language of Eccles. 11 : 9. This whole discourse (see verse 35 and note) is founded on the responsibility of nations *as nations*, and of the race *as a race*. If by act or acquiescence we ratify the sins of past eras we fill up its measure of guilt, and render ourselves accountable therefor.

33. Compare the language of John the Baptist, Matt. 3 : 7 and note. Observe, however, the difference. There it is, *Who hath warned you to flee?* a door seems still to be left open; here it is, *How can ye escape?* the door is shut.

34. Wherefore. The words, It is written, must be understood. In the analogous discourse reported in Luke the hiatus is supplied, Therefore, saith the wisdom of God, behold, &c. (Luke 11 : 49). Christ does not say, Because of your blood-guiltiness I send prophets and wise men that you may kill them, but, Because of your blood-guiltiness one of your own prophets has described your character in these words. But we do not find in the O. T. any passage which answers exactly to Christ's language here. Alford, Olshausen and Stier refer to 2 Chron. 24 : 18-22. "The words in our text are not indeed," says Alford, "a citation, but an amplification of verse 19 there—a paraphrase, giving the true sense of what the wisdom of God intended." There is in the apocryphal book, 2 Esdras, 1 ; 30-33, a passage which answers remarkably to the present. It is as follows: "I gathered you together as a hen gathereth her chickens under her wings: but now what shall I do unto you? I will cast you out from my face. When ye offer unto me, I will turn my face from you: for your solemn feast days, your new moons, and your circumcisions have I forsaken. I have sent unto you my servants the prophets, whom ye have taken and slain, and torn their bodies in pieces, whose blood I will require of your hands, saith the Lord. Thus saith the Almighty Lord, your house is deserted, I will cast you out as the wind doth stubble."—**Prophets and wise men and Scribes.** *Prophets* are the inspired teachers of the Jews; *wise men*, those who possess natural or acquired wisdom, *e. g.* Solomon; *Scribes*, those who simply copy and teach the wisdom of others. "In these last the character is for the most part acquired; in *wise men*, innate; in *prophets*, inspired."—(*Bengel.*)—**Crucify.** There is perhaps a reference to the crucifixion of Christ. Subsequently many of his followers were crucified; but in general, crucifixion appears to have been a heathen not a Jewish mode of pun-

36 Verily I say unto you, All these things shall come upon this generation.
37 Oᵃ Jerusalem, Jerusalem, *then* that killest the prophets, and stonest them which are sent unto thee, how often would I have gatheredᵇ thy children together, even as a hen gathereth her chickens under *her* wings, and ye would not!
38 Behold, your house is left unto you desolate.ᶜ
39 For I say unto you, Ye shall not see me henceforth, till ye shall say,ᵈ Blessed *is* he that cometh in the name of the Lord.

a Luke 13 : 34.... b Deut. 32 : 11, 12 ; Psalm 91 : 4.... c Zec. 11 : 6.... d ch. 21 : 9 ; Psalm 118 : 26.

ishment.—**Scourge in your synagogues.** There is abundant evidence that the synagogue was a place both of trial and of punishment. (Matt. 10 : 17 ; Acts 22 : 19).

35. So that upon you may come all the righteous blood which is being poured out upon the earth. The verb is in the present and represents this bloody stream as still flowing. It should come on them, because by slaying the Son they became participators in the crimes of those who had slain the heralds, because the guilt of murder lies not in the *amount* of blood shed, but in the *spirit* which sheds it, and because the nation is treated here, as in the parable of the wicked husbandmen (Matt. 21 : 33-46 and notes), as a unit. The language is figurative, and represents the stream of innocent blood, flowing from the days of Abel, as coming upon and whelming the Jews in condemnation. Compare Matt. 27 : 25 ; Acts 5 : 28.—**Unto the blood of Zacharias, son of Barachias.** For different explanations of this verse see Lange on this passage. It is hardly doubtful that it refers to the Zacharias mentioned in 2 Chron. 24 : 20-22. He was slain "in the court of the house of the Lord" by the *people*, and dying, cried, "The Lord look upon it and require it." It is true that this Zacharias was the son of Jehoida, not of Barachias, who was the father of Zechariah the minor prophet. But the Sinaitic manuscript omits the words "son of Barachias," as does Tischendorf, and it is not improbable that the phrase was added by an early copyist, who mistook this Zacharias for Zechariah. Luke does not have the addition "son of Barachias." It is true also that Zacharias was not the last martyr in the O. T. history ; but his martyrdom was one of the most notable. Concerning it the Jews had a saying that the blood was never washed away until the temple was burned at the captivity. In the arrangement of the Hebrew canon of the O. T. it was narrated last, though chronologically that of Urijah (Jer. 26 : 23) was later.—**Between the temple,** *i. e.* the inner holy of holies, **and the altar,** *i. e.* of burnt-offering, which stood outside, in the priests' court. Two Greek words are used in the N. T. both of which are rendered in our version, Temple. The word used here (ναός) generally signifies the innermost court or holy of holies.

36. All these things shall come upon this nation. On the true meaning of the word (γενεά) here rendered *generation*, see note on Matt. 24 : 34. The meaning of the verse is that all their crimes were treasured up and should return in punishment upon the Jewish nation. Compare Rom. 2 : 5.

37. That killest the prophets. See 1 Kings 18 : 4 ; Neh. 9 : 26 ; Jer. 2 : 30 ; 26 : 23.—**And stonest them which are sent unto thee.** See Matt. 21 : 35 ; John 10 : 31, 39 ; Acts 7 : 58 ; 21 : 31 ; 22 : 22, 23. The earthly ambassador is inviolable ; observe how God's ambassadors have been treated.—**How often would I have gathered thee together.** To protect from impending danger and destruction. This Christ sought to do, not only in his earthly life, and by his preaching in Jerusalem (comp. Acts 1 : 8), but by Divine messages and providences in the earlier history of the Jews. The verse is an indirect testimony to the divinity of Christ. For a similar figure used concerning God, see Psalms 17 : 8 ; 57 : 1 ; 61 : 4 ; 91 : 4.—**I would * * * ye would not.** God's will for our salvation may be defeated by our will resisting it. Compare Prov. 1 : 24, 25 ; Ezek. 18 : 32.

38. Behold your house. The temple : God's house no longer.—**Desolate.** Literally *desert.* The church is desolate when God departs ; so is the soul, the temple of God, when godless.

39. Till ye shall say. Not *except* ye shall say, for the original will not bear that meaning, but *until ye shall say.* Alford sees in this a reference to such prophecies as Hosea 3 : 4, 5 ; Zech. 12 : 10 ; 14 : 8-11. It certainly *looks toward* a spiritual conversion of the Jews, a time when Jew as well as Gentile shall recognize whosoever cometh in the name of the Lord. Compare Rom. 11 : 11, 15, 26 ; Phil. 2 : 10, 11.

Ch. 24. CHRIST'S DISCOURSE ON THE LAST DAYS.—THE PREPARATION : TRIBULATION (5-7) ; PERSECUTION (9) ; SECTARIAN CONFLICTS (10) ; FALSE TEACHING (11) ; APOSTACY (12) ; UNIVERSAL DIFFUSION OF THE GOSPEL (14).—THE TYPE : THE DESTRUCTION OF JERUSALEM (15-22).—THE GREAT DANGER OF THE CHURCH : FALSE CHRISTS AND FALSE SCHEMES OF REDEMPTION (23-27).—THE HOUR : NOT UNTIL JUDGMENT SHALL BE COTERMINOUS WITH CORRUPTION (28).—THE FINAL COMING : MANIFEST, GLORIOUS, RECOGNIZED BY ALL (29-31) ; IMMEDIATELY AFTER THE TRIAL PERIOD, AS SUMMER FOLLOWS SPRING (32, 33) ; CERTAIN (34, 35) ; SURPRISING (36-39) ; SEPARATING COMPANIONS (40, 41).—PRACTICAL LESSONS : THE DUTY OF WATCHFULNESS (42-44),

AND FIDELITY (45-47); THE DANGER OF UNBELIEF AND LAPSE INTO SIN (48-51).

PRELIMINARY NOTE.—Mark (ch. 13) and Luke (21:5-33) both report this discourse. John gives no account of it, but his report of Christ's last words to his disciples (ch. 14-16), which were also prophetic, should be studied in connection with this chapter. The unfulfilled prophecies are the most difficult portions of Scripture, and this, the most definitely prophetic of our Lord's discourses, is confessedly one of the most difficult.

The Problem.—After the death of Jesus Christ, the violence of the Jewish people and their intestine feuds, of which, even in the Gospels, we get glimpses, rapidly increased. Friends were alienated, families broken up, and a man's worst foes were those of his own household. Brigandage, imposture, and assassinations were rife. Even the Temple was not a place of safety. The high priest was slain while performing public worship. The priests quarrelled, openly and shamelessly, over the tithes. At length, possessed by a seeming frenzy, the Jews broke into open revolt against the Romans, seized on the most important posts in the country, and inflicted a severe though temporary defeat on the Roman arms. Vespasian and Titus were sent to chastise them back to submission. In the spring of A. D. 70, when the city was crowded with the multitudes who came up to the feast of the Passover, Titus surrounded Jerusalem with his legions. Within, the people were divided into factions, and fought with one another. The horrors of famine were added to those of riot, pillage, murder, and siege. According to the accounts of Josephus, which are not altogether trustworthy, but which constitute our chief source of information, awful prodigies added terror to the scene: a comet hung above the city; a bright light shone in the Temple; the immense Temple gates swung open of their own accord; armed squadrons were seen in the heavens. The Jews themselves, given over to madness, profaned the Temple, setting up as high priest an ignorant rustic. At length, after five months of a siege which has no parallel in its commingled horrors of famine, internal feuds, and external assault, the city was taken by storm, the Temple was set on fire and consumed, and the walls of the city were demolished. Of the Jews, the aged and infirm were killed; the children under seventeen were sold as slaves; the rest were sentenced, some to the Egyptian mines, some to the provincial amphitheatres, some to grace the triumph of the conqueror. For fuller descriptions of this siege the reader is referred to the Bible Dictionaries, to Milman's *History of the Jews*, and to Josephus' *Wars of the Jews*. See also note on verse 21 below. The question to be determined respecting this twenty-fourth chapter of Matthew, and it is one on which the ablest scholars are not agreed, is this: *How far are its prophecies to be regarded as fulfilled in and by this siege and destruction of Jerusalem and the consequent dispersion of the Jews?*

Hints toward its Solution.—The student may obtain some light from a consideration of the following facts: (*a.*) The discourse is elicited by the question of verse 3. The disciples, who had anticipated that Christ's kingdom was immediately to appear, awed by Christ's solemn denunciation of the Jewish nation (chap. 23:37-39), and his solemn assertion of the destruction of the Temple (verse 2), but still supposing that the destruction of Jerusalem, the coming of the Messiah, *i. e.* the public manifestation of Jesus as the Messiah, and the end of the world, were to be contemporaneous, desire to know when this will be accomplished. (*b.*) Though Christ's discourse is elicited by this question, he does not satisfy their curiosity. On the contrary, he asserts in express terms that no man knows the day or the hour (verse 36), makes this assertion of their ignorance the ground of the practical exhortation to "watch" (verse 42), and even asserts his own ignorance of it (Mark 13:32, note). (*c.*) His object is practical, not theoretical; he speaks not to inflame the imagination, nor to gratify curiosity, but to enforce the duty of patience, fidelity, and watchfulness. And whatever difficulty there may be in understanding the prophetic meaning of the discourse, there can be none in understanding and applying its practical and spiritual instructions. (*d.*) It thus resembles all unfulfilled prophecy. For the object of prophecy is not to give us foreknowledge, but 1st, to inspire with hope and incite to courage, and 2d, to give such outlines of future events as, *when fulfilled*, shall become evidences of the truth of God's word. "I have told you," says Christ, "before it come to pass, that, *when it is come to pass*, ye might believe." (John 14:29, comp. Luke 24:8; John 2:22; 16:4; Isaiah 48:5; Jer. 44:29). (*e.*) History is itself in God's hands prophetic. The partial fulfilment becomes an historical prophecy of a further fulfilment; in this case the judgment of God on Jerusalem and the Jewish nation, is itself a prophecy of God's final judgment on all who reject the Messiah of the world, and is indeed the beginning of his judgment of the nations, the end of which is not yet. To this chapter the words of Lord Bacon are peculiarly applicable: "Divine prophecies, being of the nature of their author, with whom a thousand years are as one day, are not punctually fulfilled at once, but have springing and germinant accomplishment throughout many ages." (*f.*) The interpretation of this discourse depends largely on the meaning given to certain verses in it, especially to the metaphor in verse 28, the confessedly poetic language of verses 29-31, and the word *generation* in verse 34. See notes below. Fully recognizing the difficulty of the subject, doubting whether Christ's prophecy here can ever be perfectly apprehended until its fulfilment becomes its interpreter, I suggest the following analysis as a key to the discourse.

Analysis.—The question (verse 3): When will occur the destruction of the Temple, thine own glorious manifestation as the Messiah, and the end of the world? *Christ's response.* Do not imagine that the kingdom will immediately appear. Be not deceived by the claims of false Messiahs. There must first be a period of tribulation, the travail out of which the kingdom shall be born (4-8), a period of persecution from without, and schism, apostacy, and false doctrine within (9-12), to be accompanied by the preaching of the Gospel throughout the habitable globe (13, 14). The length of this period no one knows save the Father; not even the Son (Mark 13 : 32). When, therefore, you see the fulfilment of Daniel's prophecy (Dan. 9 : 27 ; 12 : 11), do not imagine that the end has come, and abide in Jerusalem. Flee; for terrible will be the suffering of that time (15-22). Do not, then, allow false reports of the coming of the Messiah to mislead you. For his coming will be in such a manner that it cannot be questioned (23-27). Nor shall judgment stop at Jerusalem. Wherever there is corruption, thither the executioners of God's judgment will hasten (28). Immediately after this period of travail and world-judgment, i. e., without any intervening sign or note of preparation, will come the Son of man to judge the world (29-31), even as summer follows spring (32, 33). But though Jerusalem is destroyed, the Jewish race shall abide, a living testimony to the truth of my words (34, 35). But the day and hour of their fulfilment no man knoweth (36). It will be sudden (37-41). Wherefore watch, be faithful, be always ready, looking for the appearance of your Lord (42-51), who will come to judge not only the world, but the church, condemning those who have lived in it without divine grace (ch. 25 : 1-13), without spiritual thrift and industry (ch. 25 : 14-30), and without practical benevolence and beneficence to their fellow-men (ch. 25 : 31-46).

Other Views.—I summarize the other principal interpretations of this passage. They are almost as numerous as the commentators, but they may be classified conveniently as follows:

1. *The rationalistic:* that Christ himself supposed that the judgment would follow immediately upon the destruction of Jerusalem, and so taught. This view is not only inconsistent with belief in the divine or even the inspired character of Christ, it is also inconsistent with and refuted by the very terms of the discourse. Analogous to this is the view of so Evangelical an interpreter as Olshausen, that "Jesus did intend to represent his coming as contemporaneous with the destruction of Jerusalem and the overthrow of the Jewish polity," because "it should be considered every moment *possible*, and that believers should deem it every moment *probable*." In other words, that Christ taught what he knew to be error for the sake of a moral effect, for this seems to me to be the practical result of this interpretation.

2. *The semi-rationalistic:* that the Evangelists misapprehended the tenor of Christ's discourse, interpreted it according to their own preconceived ideas, and so represented Christ as teaching that the destruction of Jerusalem and the final judgment were to be contemporaneous. So Neander interprets it: "It is easy to explain, how points of time which he kept apart, although he presented them as counterparts of each other, without assigning any express duration to either, were blended together, in the apprehension of his hearers, or in their subsequent repetitions of his language." It is true that this discourse was perhaps heard only by Peter, James, John, and Andrew (Mark 13 : 3), in which case our reports are not from ear-witnesses, and there may be omissions. But it is impossible to suppose that they are such as materially to alter the sense, and yet believe that Christ's promise of inspiration to his disciples (John 14 : 26 ; 16 : 13) has been fulfilled.

3. *The historical:* that Christ's discourse relates wholly to the destruction of Jerusalem; that the language of verses 29-31 is poetic and figurative, and amounts only to this, that "there would be nothing wanting to indicate the greatness of the events that were at hand, that the violent commotions and terrible calamities which were coming would be accompanied by extraordinary signs and portents that attend all great occurrences."—(*Furness.*) This view is not only sustained by such writers as Professor Norton and J. H. Morison (Unitarian), but also by such Evangelical divines as Mr. Barnes and Drs. Jacobus, Owen, Brown, and Adam Clarke. It is the view of Lightfoot and of some other of the older divines. In the notes which follow, especially on ver. 29-31, I state the grounds on which this opinion is based, and some of the reasons which appear to me to be conclusive against it. A still more serious objection is this: The object of this whole discourse is the closing exhortation to fidelity and watchfulness (verses 42-51), which Christ expressly declares is for all his disciples, not merely for the twelve (Mark 13 : 37) ; and it is not the *past* destruction of Jerusalem, but the *future destruction of the world and coming of Christ*, possible at any day or hour, which alone affords a ground for this exhortation.

CHAPTER XXIV.

AND ᵃ Jesus went out, and departed from the temple: and his disciples came to *him* for to shew him the buildings of the temple.

2 And Jesus said unto them, See ye not all these things? Verily I say unto you, There ᶠ shall not be left here one stone upon another, that shall not be thrown down.

3 And as he sat upon the mount of Olives, the disciples came unto him privately, saying, Tell us, when shall these things be? and what *shall be* the sign of thy coming, and of the end of the world? ᵍ

4 And Jesus answered and said unto them, Take ʰ heed that no man deceive you.

ᵃ Mark 13:1; Luke 21:5....f 1 Kings 9:7; Jer. 26:18; Luke 19:44,...g 1 Thess. 4:1, etc....h Col. 2:18; 2 Thess. 2:3.

---

4. *Other interpretations:* these are numerous, such as (1) that the whole discourse relates exclusively to the end of the world, and that the destruction of Jerusalem is only incidentally and indirectly alluded to, a more complete destruction being yet to come, perhaps by an earthquake; (2) that the discourse may be divided into three parts which answer respectively three questions put by the disciples, *e. g.*, verses 1-14 relating to the second coming of Christ, 15-28 to the destruction of Jerusalem, 29-51 to the end of the world; (3) that Christ pictures the two events without regard, as it were, to perspective, the first, the destruction of Jerusalem, occupying the foreground, the last, the end of the world, the background, with no intimation of the eras that intervene; (4) that he separates them, but that his declaration "*Immediately* after the tribulation of those days" (verse 29), is to be read in the light of the declaration that with God a thousand years are as one day, the intervening period being in his sight a small matter. It would make these notes too cumberous and perplexing to explain and refute these views in detail. The grounds of the *historical* interpretation are to some extent indicated in the notes. None of the other views appear to me at all tenable, except the one here adopted. This substantially agrees with the interpretation of Lange, Pressense, Howard Crosby, Alford, Calvin, James Morison, and Chrysostom, though no two of these agree in all details.

1. His disciples came to him. As he was going out of the Temple (Mark 13:1).—**The buildings of the Temple.** Few buildings in ancient or modern times have equalled in magnificence Herod's Temple. With its outbuildings it covered an area of over nineteen acres, was built of white marble, was forty-six years in building (John 2:20), and employed in its construction ten thousand skilled workmen. The accompanying illustration is from H. W. Beecher's *Life of Christ.*

The disciples were amazed and perplexed by Christ's public prediction of its destruction (Matt. 23:36-39; Luke 19:43, 44). And well they might be, for the fortifications of Jerusalem and its natural advantages rendered it so apparently impregnable, that after its fall Titus, the captor, is reported by Josephus (*Wars of Jews*, 6:9, 1) to have said, "It was no other than God who ejected the Jews out of these fortifications. For what could the hands of men, or any machines do, toward overthrowing these towers?"

2. There shall not be left here one stone upon another. This prophecy has been so literally fulfilled, the walls being demolished by order of Titus, that Josephus says, "There was left nothing to make those who had come hither believe it had ever been inhabited." Of the Temple proper not a vestige remains. It was built, however, upon an immense platform, partly composed of natural rock, partly of immense masonry. This platform is still standing, and some look for its future demolition by an earthquake.

3. Mount of Olives. This was over against Jerusalem, and directly opposite the Temple, which was therefore in full view. See map of Jerusalem, chap. 26, page 277.—**The disciples came unto him.** Mark (13:3) specifies their names, Peter, James, John, and Andrew; and the language implies, but does not necessarily prove, that these were the only ones to whom this discourse was delivered.—**Tell us when shall these things be,** *i. e.*, the destruction of Jerusalem.—**And what shall be the sign of thy coming.** Not of his second coming, for though Christ had foretold his crucifixion, the disciples did not understand his saying (Mark 9:32; Luke 9:45), but the sign of his *public manifestation as the Messiah*. This they were momentarily expecting (Luke 19:11; Acts 1:6).—**And of the end of the world.** Not merely of the Jewish dispensation, though the Greek is perhaps capable of being so rendered. Christ had in public discourse alluded to the end of the world in connection with his own appearance as the Messiah (Matt. 13:39, 40, 49). The disciples, supposing that the destruction of Jerusalem, the overthrow of Judaism, the manifestation of Jesus as the Messiah-King, and the end of the world, would be contemporaneous, asked when they would occur, and what would be the sign of their approach. One principal object of Christ's discourse is to correct their misapprehension. Calvin interprets well their probable state of mind: "Having been convinced that, as soon as the reign of Christ should commence, they would be in every respect happy, they leave warfare out of the account, and fly all at once to a triumph." He also emphasizes the practical lesson: "No man wishes to sow the seed, but all wish to reap the harvest before the season arrives."

THE TEMPLE OF HEROD—RESTORED BY FERGUSSON.

The temple is shown surrounded by its courts and outer wall, as it is supposed to have been in the time of Christ, while Zion, enclosed by its walls, crowded with towers, as described by Josephus, forms the background.

5 For many shall come in my[1] name, saying, I am Christ; and shall deceive many.
6 And ye shall hear of wars,[j] and rumours of wars; see that ye be not troubled: for all *these things* must come to pass, but the end is not yet.

7 For[k] nation shall rise against nation, and kingdom against kingdom: and there shall be famines, and pestilences, and earthquakes, in divers places.
8 All these *are* the beginning of sorrows.

i Jer. 14: 14. .... j Dan. xi. .... k Hag. 2: 21, 22.

4, 5. Take heed. This is the text of this discourse, and to it Christ constantly recurs. Compare verses 13, 23-25, 42-44. "We ought not to inquire into future and final events, through curiosity, but from a desire to fortify ourselves."—(*Bengel.*) I add that curiosity halts ever unsatisfied at this chapter; but the spiritual desire for practical warning and admonition is abundantly satisfied.—**That no man deceive you.** The Jews, from such prophecies as Isaiah 54: 13; Jer. 31: 34; Mal. 4: 2, expected that after the Messiah came they would enjoy immunity from false doctrine. Jesus here warns his disciples to be still on their guard against it. —**For many shall come in my name.** Literally *upon my name, i. e.,* as Wordsworth interprets it, "standing upon it and usurping it." That by *In my name* Christ does mean, As my disciples, is evident from the following clause of the sentence.—**Saying, I am the Messiah,** *i. e.,* taking the title and claiming the authority of the Messiah. Buck, in his Theological Dictionary, gives a list of twenty-nine false Christs, though he includes such persons as Mahomet in his list. The last of these was as late as the seventeenth century. It is evident that this prophecy was not completely fulfilled prior to the destruction of Jerusalem. The warning is equally applicable to our own day. What was Joseph Smith, the founder of Mormonism, with his impious claim to be prophet, priest, and king, but a false Messiah?

6, 7. And ye shall hear of wars and rumors of wars. A seeming anti-climax, but a real climax. The rumors of an expected invasion are often more dreadful than the invasion itself. Those who can do so, should read Dr. Schaff's graphic note descriptive of his personal experience in Gettysburg during the civil war (Lange on Matt. 24: 6).—**Be not troubled.** That is, be not apprehensive that the end of the world is yet. Compare 2 Thess. 2: 2.—**The end is not yet.** Luke's language is yet more explicit, *These things must come to pass; but the end is not immediately* (Luke 21: 9, note). The end here is not equivalent to, The end of the Jewish dispensation. When the words stand, as here, without qualification or interpretation, they generally mean in the N. T. "*The end of the world.*" Comp. 1 Cor. 15: 24; 1 Pet. 4: 7.

For nation shall rise against nation, etc. Luke's description (21: 10, 11) is yet more detailed and specific. In the period intervening this prophecy and the destruction of Jerusalem, there were serious disturbances, (1) at Alexandria, A. D. 38, in which the Jews as a nation were the especial objects of persecution; (2) at Seleucia, about the same time, in which more than fifty thousand Jews were killed; (3) at Jamnia, a city on the coast of Judæa, near Joppa. Many other such national tumults are recorded by Josephus. See especially *Wars of the Jews* 2: 17; 18: 1-8.—**Famines and pestilences.** A great famine, prophesied in Acts (11: 28) occurred A. D. 49, and another in the reign of Claudius, and mentioned by Josephus (*Antiq.* 3: 15, 3). A pestilence, A. D. 65, in a single autumn carried off 30,000 persons at Rome.—**Earthquakes.** Between this prophecy and the destruction of Jerusalem there were (1) a great earthquake at Crete, A. D. 46 or 47; (2) one at Rome, A. D. 51; (3) one at Apamia in Phrygia, A. D. 53; (4) one at Laodicea in Phrygia, A. D. 60; (5) one in Campania; (6) one in Jerusalem, A. D. 67, described in Josephus (*Wars of the Jews* 4: 4, 5). I take this list from Alford's Commentary. It is, however, evident that the prophesies of these verses (5-8) are not peculiarly applicable to the period immediately preceding the destruction of Jerusalem. The prophecy of *wars and rumors of wars* applies with still greater force to the campaigns of Charlemagne, the wars between the Popes and the German emperors, the conflicts between Napoleon I. and the allied armies, the more recent wars between France, Italy, Austria, and Germany, the various civil wars which have devastated England, particularly the wars of the Roses and the Revolution under Cromwell, and in our own country the American Revolution and the Civil War; to many of these is equally applicable the declaration that "nation shall rise against nation." Of *famines, pestilences,* and *earthquakes* there have been more remarkable instances since than before the destruction of Jerusalem, and instances in which the Christian church has suffered far more severely. I understand Christ's language here to be an admonition to expect a long period of conflict and trial before the end will appear, a prophecy which history has both interpreted and fulfilled.

8. All these are the beginning of travail (ὠδίν). Not merely of *sorrows*, but of *that labor pain of the world, out of which the kingdom of God is to be born.* The figure is not infrequent in the N. T. (see Rom. 8: 22; 1 Thess. 5: 3); and

CH. XXIV.] MATTHEW. 259

9 Then¹ shall they deliver you up to be afflicted, and shall kill ᵐ you; and ye shall be hated of all nations for my name's sake.
10 And then shall many be ⁿ offended, and shall betray one another, and shall hate one another.

11 And ᵒ many false prophets shall rise, and shall deceive ᵖ many.
12 And because iniquity shall abound, the love of many shall wax ᵠ cold.

l Luke 21 : 12....m John 16 : 2; Acts 7 : 59....n ch. 13 : 21....o 2 Pet. 2 : 1; 1 John 4 : 3....p 1 Tim. 4 : 1....q Rev. 3 : 15, 16.

it is one full of the brightness of hope. The world's anguish is itself a prophecy of the future birth of the kingdom of righteousness.

9–13. Then. "During this period, not after, these things have happened."—(*Alford*.)—**Shall they deliver you up.** The language is impersonal; it is equivalent to, You shall be delivered up.—**And ye shall be hated of all nations for my name's sake.** Compare with this warning the blessing which accompanies it (Matt. 5 : 11, 12). Both warning and promise are applicable to all Christ's disciples to the end of time. Compare John 15 : 18-21; 16 : 1-4.—Then, *i. e.*, during this period of persecution, and because of it.—**Many**, within the Church of Christ, **shall be offended**, *i. e.*, stumbled, entrapped, caused to fall into sin. See Matt. 5 : 29; 16 : 24 and notes.—**And many false prophets shall arise**, *i. e.*, false religious teachers, pretending to have a divine mission and to be entrusted with a divine message. Compare Matt. 7 : 15-20 and notes.—**And because iniquity shall abound**, in the world without, **the love**, both toward God and man, **of many**, within the church, **shall wax cold.** "It is the nature of love to burn."—(*Bengel*.) The danger to the church in a time of the general prevalence of iniquity is coldness of love and worldliness of spirit; a danger which peculiarly threatens in the present era.

These verses indicate four dangers which will assail the church: persecution from without (verse 9); apostasy, schism, and controversy within (verse 10); false doctrine (verse 11); and worldliness and consequent backsliding (verse 12). Each of these dangers came in a small measure upon the Apostolic church before the destruction of Jerusalem. The disciples were subjected to persecution, and some of its leaders were *killed* (Acts 7 : 59, 60; 8 : 3, 4; 12 : 2, etc.). They were *hated* by the Gentiles as well as by the Jews (Acts 10 : 19-22; 19 : 23; 28 : 22; 1 Pet. 2 : 12; 3 : 14). Some were *offended*, and fell away (2 Tim. 4 : 10). There were *schisms* and *controversies* within the church (1 Cor. 1 : 11-13), and *false teachers* (1 Tim. 1 : 6, 7; 2 Tim. 3 : 6-8), and *coldness* and *worldliness* (1 Tim. 6 : 9, 10, 17-19; 2 Tim. 4 : 10; James 2 : 2-6). In further illustration of the fulfilment of these prophecies the student may profitably consult the following passages: Acts 20 : 30; Rom. 16 : 17, 18; 2 Cor. 11 : 13; Gal. 1 : 7-9; Col. 2 : 17-end; 1 Tim. 6 : 3-5, 20, 21; 2 Tim. 2 : 18; 2 Pet. 2; 1 John 2 : 18, 22, 23, 26; 4 : 1, 3; 2 John 7. But these were only the beginning of travail in the church.

And in her history, subsequent to the destruction of Jerusalem, the reader must look for a larger fulfilment. The persecutions of the Christian church constantly increased in violence up to the days of Constantine. By the edicts of Diocletian, all Bibles were ordered to be destroyed, all ecclesiastics to be thrust into prison, all Christians to be compelled by torture to sacrifice to the gods, and all the contumacious to be put to death. Mr. Lecky, who is certainly not inclined to exaggerate these Roman persecutions, thus describes some of the afflictions to which the early Christians were subjected: "We read of Christians bound in chairs of red-hot iron, while the stench of their half consumed flesh rose in a suffocating cloud to heaven; of others who were torn to the very bone by shells or hooks of iron; of holy virgins given over to the lust of the gladiator or to the mercies of the pander; of two hundred and twenty-seven converts sent on one occasion to the mines, each with the sinews of one leg severed by a red-hot iron, and with an eye scooped from its socket; of fires so slow that the victims writhed for hours in their agonies; of mingled salt and vinegar poured over the flesh that was bleeding from the rack; of tortures prolonged and varied through entire days."—(*History of European Morals*, Vol. I : 497.) That the disciples were *hated* is abundantly illustrated by Gibbon. They were charged with licentiousness, incest, and human sacrifice (*Gibbon's Rome*, II : 11). Tacitus calls the Christians "a race of men hated for their crimes." Many in the church were *offended*, so many that the church was subsequently seriously divided on the question whether such apostates and recusants might be received back again into the fold. The *internal conflicts*, of party against party in the church, is abundantly illustrated in its subsequent history, in the terrible persecutions inflicted by the Roman Catholic Church upon Protestants, surpassing in severity and extent any ever inflicted by the heathen, in the controversies in the Roman Catholic Church itself between the rival popes and between the Jansenists and Jesuits in France, and in the Protestant Church even down to our own day, between different sects. From *false teachers* and from *coldness and worldliness*, the church has always suffered, certainly to a greater degree in these latter days than in the Apostolic era. Observe, too, that, though every age has, in some degree, all of these tribulations, yet,

13 But⁵ he that shall endure unto the end, the same shall be saved.
14 And this gospel of the kingdom shall be ⁶ preached in all the world for a witness unto all nations: and then shall the end come.

15 When ye, therefore, shall see the abomination of desolation, spoken⁷ of by Daniel the prophet, stand in the holy place, (whoso readeth, let him understand:)
16 Then let them which be in Judæa flee into the mountains:

r Rev. 2 : 10....s ch. 28 : 19; Rom. 10 : 18; Rev. 14 : 6....t Dan. 9 : 27; 12 : 11.

historically, each age is characterized by its own peculiar form of tribulation, and that they follow each other in consecutive order, as indicated in Christ's language here. First comes the period of peril from without, that of Imperial persecution; next that of schism and conflict within, that of the Roman Catholic persecutions and of the ecclesiastical conflicts between Roman Catholic, Greek, and Protestant communions, and the sectarian strife between the Protestant churches. This has well-nigh passed; and we are now in the age of "false prophets," an age which, with liberty of speech, brings within the church itself much false doctrine; an age which produces a bishop-Colenso) who denies the inspiration of the Scripture, and a professor of theology (Strauss) who denies the existence of a personal God, the immortality of the soul, and the reality of religion as a vital experience. Is it a mistake to conclude that the dangers to the church in the future lie, not in any recurrence of religious persecutions, or of denominational conflicts, but in false prophets, and still more in an era, yet to be developed, of abounding iniquity without, and consequent coldness and worldliness within the church?

13, 14. He that shall endure to the end. Not he that endures to the end of the Jewish economy shall be saved in the destruction of Jerusalem, nor he that endures to the end of the world shall be saved in the day of judgment, but he that endures to the end of the period of trial, *whatever that in his case may be*, shall be saved by and through his endurance of the appointed discipline (Ephes. 6 : 13; Rev. 2 : 7, 11, 17, etc.; 2 : 14). Compare the more explicit language of Luke 21 : 19 and note. Mark (13 : 9-11) and Luke (21 : 12-15) report Christ's practical directions to the disciples how to *endure* the trial hour when it comes.—**And this good news of the kingdom shall be heralded in the whole habitable globe.** Not merely throughout Palestine. The Greek word here employed (οἰκουμένη) never has that signification in the N. T. It may mean, either the then known world (Luke 2 : 1; Acts 11 : 28; 24 : 5), or the entire globe (Rev. 3 : 10; 12 : 9; 16 : 14). I think here the latter meaning is included.—**For a testimony unto all nations.** A testimony to them of Christ's redemption; a testimony *against* such as reject it. Compare note on Matt. 8 : 4. It is true that the Gospel was preached, in the greater part of the then known world, before the destruction of Jerusalem. But the prophecy here, as in the preceding verses, is, I think, more far-reaching. "*The apostasy of the latter days*, and the *universal dispersion of missions*, are the two great signs of the end drawing near."—(*Alford*.) Observe that Christ does not say that the Gospel will be received *by* or even *among* all nations, only that it will be proclaimed *to* them. The standard will be set up; allegiance may not be paid to it. But this certainly indicates that an increased Christian activity in the church and increased triumphs of the Gospel will be contemporaneous events with the coldness, conflicts, and apostacy foretold in the preceding verses.—**And then shall come the end,** *i. e.*, the end of the period of trial and judgment, and so the end of the world.

15. When ye therefore shall see the abomination of desolation, *i. e.*, the abomination that makes desolate, **spoken of by Daniel** (Dan. 9 : 27; 12 : 11), **stand in a holy place**, not in the Holy of holies, the words here used are never employed in the N. T. to signify the Holy of holies or inner Temple; nor is it, as in the English version, *The* holy place, but, as I have translated it above, *A* holy place. Mark gives as an equivalent expression, *Standing where it ought not.*—**Whoso readeth, let him understand.** This is generally regarded as an admonition of the Evangelist, added to emphasize Christ's warning. If this surmise be correct, the Gospel of Matthew must have been written not long prior to the destruction of Jerusalem, for the object of this addition is to enforce Christ's caution to the disciples, to make good their escape from the doomed city.

The connection of this verse appears to me to be this: Daniel had prophesied of an abomination of desolation which should precede the "consummation," *i. e.*, the final coming of the Messiah as king. The disciples, imbibing the erroneous ideas of their time, would suppose that the Messiah's coming would immediately follow this sign, and with mistaken faith might remain in Jerusalem, awaiting there an expected divine deliverance. Christ, so far from confirming this error, carefully corrects it. *Therefore,* he says, *i. e., because there is to be a long period of tribulation and judgment preceding the end of the world,* when ye see the sign spoken of by Daniel, do not imagine that the end is come, and so abide in the city: flee upon the mountains. And in the following verses, to verse 22, he en-

17 Let him which is on the housetop not come down to take any thing out of his house :
18 Neither let him which is in the field return back to take his clothes.
19 And ⁿ woe unto them that are with child, and to them that give suck in those days !
20 But pray ye that your flight be not in the winter, neither on the sabbath day :
21 For ᵛ then shall be great tribulation, such as was not since the beginning of the world to this time, no, nor ever shall be.

ᵘ Luke 23 : 29. . . . ᵛ Dan. 12 : 1.

forces this admonition by a vivid description of the peril. The admonition was not in vain. Not a single Christian is known to have perished in the siege of Jerusalem. What is *the abomination which makes desolate referred to here and in Daniel*, it is not easy to determine. The commentators generally suppose it to refer to the standards of the Roman army, which contained heathen emblems, and the direction to be equivalent to that of Luke 21 : 20 : *When ye shall see Jerusalem compassed with armies, know that the desolation thereof is nigh*. But the Roman eagles had been seen in and about Jerusalem for many years. Others refer the words to the internal desecration of the Temple by the Zealots. In either case there can be no doubt that Alford is correct in saying : " Whatever it was, it was a definite, well marked event, for the flight was to be immediate, on one day (not on the Sabbath), and universal, from all parts of Judea." When this sign appeared, whatever it was, the disciples were not to think the Messiah was at hand ; they were to flee.

16-18. These verses contain directions for the flight of the Christians.—**Into the mountains.** Rather, upon the mountains, *i. e.*, to a refuge beyond them. It is said by Eusebius that at the siege of Jerusalem the Christians fled to Pella, a city on the northernmost boundary of Perea.—**On the housetop.** The Jewish roof is flat, is a common resort, and is a natural point of observation in time of peril (Isaiah 22 : 1). It is said that one may run from one part of Jerusalem to another, and even to the city gates, along these flat roofs of the houses. But I should regard this and the next verse not as a command to flee in any particular manner, but simply as a warning against delay. They that were on the housetop were not to return to take anything with them ; they were to go unencumbered.—**His clothes.** Literally his *cloak* (ἱμάτιον). This was an outer garment not used in work, but the almost necessary accompaniment of every Jewish traveler. It was a shawl or blanket, made of wool and of a square or oblong square form, fastened round the neck or on the shoulder by a brooch, and usually worn as an outside mantle over the tunic or undergarment. It was thrown off or left at home during work (John 13 : 4) ; but was used at night as a wrapper, and would seem to the disciples almost indispensable in such a flight. But they were not to turn back even for

THE CLOAK.

so important an article. The exigency would be too urgent ; the peril too great.

19, 20. Hindrances within their control they were not to permit, from hindrances beyond their control they were to seek deliverance by prayer ; a hint as to the use and the limitation of prayer. They were to pray that the flight might not be *in the winter*, that thus they might avoid the additional exposure and suffering ; nor *on the Sabbath day*, because they would thus meet with impediments from without, such as the shutting of the gates of cities, or from their own Sabbath scruples, from which the Jewish Christians were not wholly freed, and which forbade traveling further than a Sabbath day's journey (about one mile), and also because to flee from Judea on the Jewish Sabbath might subject them to the enmity and persecution of the Jews, who would in consequence regard them as both traitors and heretics.

21. For then shall be great tribulation. Luke describes it more in detail (Luke 21 : 24), and the ancient prophecies with still more terrible particularity (Deut. 28 : 49-57 ; Dan. 12 : 1). Josephus (*Wars of the Jews*, B. 6) gives an account of the horrors of this unparalleled siege. According to him there were slain 1,100,000 Jews ; 97,000 were taken captive, many of whom were subsequently tortured and slain ; the prisoners captured during the siege were crucified in such numbers that " room was wanted for the crosses, and crosses wanted for the bodies ;" the famine within devoured the people " by whole houses and families," and was so terrible that the prophecy of Deuteronomy was literally fulfilled ; one mother killed, roasted,

22 And except those days should be shortened, there should no flesh be saved: but ʷ for the elect's sake those days shall be shortened.
23 Then ˣ if any man shall say unto you, Lo, here *is* Christ, or there ; believe *it* not.
24 For ʸ there shall arise false Christs, and false prophets, and ᶻ shall shew great signs and wonders;

insomuch that, if ᵃ *it were* possible, they shall deceive the very elect.
25 Behold, I have told you before.
26 Wherefore if they shall say unto you, Behold, he is in the desert: go not forth: Behold, *he is* in the secret chambers; believe *it* not.
27 For as the lightning ᵇ cometh out of the east, and

w Isa. 65 : 8, 9. .... x Deut. 13 : 1, 3. .... y ver. 5 : 11. .... z 2 Thess. 2 : 9-11; Rev. 13 : 13. ... a John 10 : 28, 29. ... b Zec. 9 : 14; Luke 17 : 24, etc.

and ate her own child (*Wars of the Jews*, 6 : 3, 4). The language of Josephus in narrating the events singularly resembles the language of Christ in prophesying them: "No other city," says he, "ever suffered such miseries, nor did any age, from the beginning of the world, ever breed a generation more fruitful in wickedness than this was." And again: "If the miseries of all mankind from the creation were compared with those which the Jews then suffered, they would appear inferior." See Preliminary Note.

22. And except those days should be shortened there should be no flesh saved. Greswell, (and Alford quoting from him,) refers to several causes which combined to shorten the siege of Jerusalem: (1.) Herod Agrippa had begun to fortify the walls of Jerusalem against any attack, but was stopped by orders from Claudius (A. D. 42 or 43). (2.) The Jews being divided into factions among themselves, totally neglected any preparations to stand a siege. (3.) The magazines of corn and provisions were burnt just before the arrival of Titus. (4.) Titus arrived suddenly, and the Jews voluntarily abandoned parts of the fortifications. (5.) Titus himself confessed that he owed his victory to God. See note on verse 1. But while this is the primary meaning of the promise, viz., that the providential shortening of the siege should give escape to some, there is also included the large significance which Lange attaches to the words, The destruction of Jerusalem is a beginning of God's judgment on the nations; but he cuts short the judgment, and waits, that by his long-suffering he may save (Isaiah 30 : 18; Rom. 2 : 4; 2 Pet. 3 : 9). The student should observe Luke's language here, which clearly implies an interval between the consummation of the destruction of Jerusalem and the end of the world: Jerusalem shall be trodden down of the Gentiles, *until the times of the Gentiles be fulfilled* (Luke 21 : 24 and note).

23-25. Then. During the times of trouble just described.—**If any shall say to you, Lo, here is the Messiah, or there; believe not.** Unbelief, then, is sometimes a duty. —**For there shall arise false Christs.** See note on verse 5.—**And false prophets.** See note on verse 11 and on Matt. 7 : 15-20.—**And shall shew great signs and wonders.** Josephus tells us that the false Christs and prophets appeared as magicians, promising to work miracles. The language here is precisely the same used of the miracles wrought by Moses (Acts 7 : 36), by the Apostles (Acts 2 : 43; 4 : 30; 5 : 12; 6 : 8; Rom. 15 : 19; 2 Cor. 12 : 12; Hebrews 2 : 4), and by Christ (John 4 : 48; Acts 2 : 22). *The mere presence of prodigies, then, is of itself no evidence of revelation or inspiration;* they must accompany truth, which, by its inherent character and blessed fruit, gives divine sanction to the miracle. And the lack of this truth-teaching distinguishes the *pseudo* miracles of the false prophets of Judaism, of the priests in the middle ages, and of modern spiritualism, from those of the Bible. Compare Deut. 13 : 1-3.—**So that they shall deceive, if it were possible, the very elect.** So perfect will be the imposture. But it will not be possible (John 6 : 39; 10 : 28; Rom. 8 : 38, 39; 2 Tim. 2 : 19; 1 John 5 : 18).

In these verses Christ recurs to the warning with which he began his discourse (verses 4, 5). The disciples are not to confound the destruction of Jerusalem with the end of the world; reports of the coming of the Messiah will be current, but are not to be believed. Of such false Christs we have accounts in Josephus. "The nearer the Jews were to destruction, the more did these impostors multiply, and the more easy credit did they find with those who were willing to have their miseries softened by hope."—(*Kenrick.*) See also Josephus' *Wars of the Jews*, 2 : 13, 4-7, and Acts 21 : 38. But while the primary application of the warning is to the destruction of Jerusalem, its application to later times is made clear by other passages of Scripture. See 2 Thess. 2 : 8-12; 1 Tim. 4 : 1-3; 2 Tim. 3 : 1-5; Rev. 13 : 14; 19 : 19-21. Rightly understood "they will preserve the church firm in her waiting for Christ, through even the awful troubles of the latter days, unmoved by enthusiasm or superstition, but seeing and looking for Him who is invisible."—(*Alford.*)

26. In the desert——in the secret chambers. According to Josephus, impostors fulfilled both these predictions, some drawing the people off into the desert, others concealing themselves in secret hiding-places in the city.

27. As the lightning * * * so shall also the coming of the Son of man be. This cannot refer to the preaching of the Gospel of Christ by the Apostles, as Calvin interprets it, for Christ distinctly declares elsewhere that the

shineth even unto the west; so shall also the coming of the Son of man be.

28 For wheresoever ⁶ the carcase is, there will the eagles be gathered together.

29 Immediately after the tribulation of those days shall ᵈ the sun be darkened, and the moon shall not give her light, and the stars shall fall from heaven, and the powers of the heavens ᵉ shall be shaken,

30 And then shall appear the sign of the Son of man ᶠ in heaven: and then shall all the tribes of the earth mourn, and they ᵍ shall see the Son of man coming in the clouds of heaven, with power and great glory.

31 And he shall send his angels with a great sound ʰ of a trumpet; and they shall gather together his elect ⁱ from the four winds, from one end of heaven to the other.

c Job 39 : 30;...d Isa. 13 : 10; Ezek. 32 : 7; Amos 5 : 20; Acts 2 : 20; Rev. 6 : 12....e 2 Pet. 3 : 10.....f Dan. 7 : 13; Rev. 1 : 7....
g ch. 16 : 27; Mark 13 : 26; Luke 22 : 69....h 1 Thess. 4 : 16.....i Zec. 14 : 5.

---

kingdom of God shall come in the Gospel without observation (Luke 17 : 20, 21); nor to the destruction of Jerusalem, as some of the modern commentators interpret it, for the Son of man was not recognized in that event by the Jews, and the very point of this declaration is that Christ's coming shall be recognized universally. It can only refer to his final coming in judgment; and the connection is this: Be not deceived by false Messiahs, for when I come it will be in such a form that no one can doubt or question, it will be sudden, public, manifest to all; observe, not merely *as the lightning*, but *as the lightning when it shines from the East even unto the West, i. e.*, when the whole heavens are aglow with its light.

28. For. The best manuscripts omit this word. And the omission makes a material difference in the connection, and therefore in the probable interpretation.— **Wheresoever the carcass is, there will the eagles be gathered together.** The vultures were reckoned by the ancients as belonging to the eagle family, and are probably referred to here. The true eagle feeds readily on carrion (see *Goodrich's Nat. Hist.*, Vol. II, p. 38), but is a solitary bird, while the vultures congregate in great numbers. The history of the interpretation of this verse is a curiosity. The Fathers and, following them, Calvin and Wordsworth, understood it, *Wherever Christ is, there will his saints and angels gather*, an interpretation which is not consistent with the context, nor congruous with other passages of Scripture, and which is revolting to good taste. The modern commentators generally understand it, *Where the Jewish nation is, there will the Roman armies*, whose national standard was the eagle, *be gathered*. But this interpretation does not harmonize with the context. Dr. Crosby renders it, *False Christs will gather where there is a false people*. But the false Christs are themselves the product of the false people. In this, as in so many other passages, the Bible is its own best interpreter. The metaphor is one employed in the O. T., where the *eagle*, or in more general terms, *the bird of prey*, represents foreign armies called by God to execute his judgment on a corrupt nation (Deut. 28 : 49; Lam. 4 : 19; Hosea 8 : 1; Habakkuk 1 : 8). Christ's language here, then, is equivalent to, Judgment will not be inflicted on Jerusalem alone; that will not be the end; wherever there is corruption, there will be inflicted the judgments of God. This truth is illustrated in the destruction of Jerusalem, but not less surely and strikingly in the overthrow of Greece and Rome, in the decay of Spain, in the desolations visited on France, and in our own civil war.

29-31. Immediately, not merely suddenly, the Greek word (εὐθέως) is not capable of that translation.—**After the tribulation of those days.** That is, not immediately after the destruction of Jerusalem, but immediately after the period of travail and judgment above described in verses 4–14, and again referred to in verses 23–28. The end of the world and manifestation of the Messiah as king shall follow this period of tribulation *at once*, with no other sign and no intervening period, as the summer follows the spring (verses 32, 33).

Shall the sun be darkened * * * The rest of the language of this and the two succeeding verses is undoubtedly poetic. We cannot conceive that a sign in the heavens should be seen or a trumpet be heard simultaneously on both sides of a round globe. Those who regard this twenty-fourth chapter as a prophecy simply of the destruction of Jerusalem, understand the language here as a poetic and figurative description of the calamities to fall upon Judea. According to their view these expressions are interpreted as follows: *The sun shall be darkened, and the moon shall not give her light* is equivalent to, Those shall be dark days, and in support of this are cited, Isaiah 13 : 10; 24ᵃ: 23; 34 : 4; 50 : 3; 60 : 19, 20; Ezek. 32 : 7; Joel 3 : 15, where similar language is employed in describing earthly judgments of God upon sinful cities, as Babylon, Tyre, etc.; *Then shall appear the sign of the Son of man in heaven* is not, The sign shall appear in heaven, but a sign shall appear testifying that the Son of man is in heaven, this sign being the destruction of Jerusalem; *Then shall all the tribes of the earth mourn* means that all the inhabitants of Palestine shall experience great sorrow at the desolation of their land and the destruction of their Holy City; *And he shall send his angels with the sound of a trumpet*, is equivalent to, Then shall he send his messengers (the word here rendered *angel* is sometimes translated messenger, Mark 1 : 2; Luke 7 : 24; 9 : 52), with the trum-

32 Now learn a parable of the fig tree: When his branch is yet tender, and putteth forth leaves, ye know that summer *is* nigh:
33 So likewise ye, when ye shall see all these things, know that it is near, *even* at the doors.

34 Verily I say unto you, this generation shall not pass till all these things be fulfilled.
35 Heaven and earth shall pass away, but my words shall not pass away.

---

j Luke 21 : 29. ... k Jas. 5 : 9. ... l Ps. 102 : 26 ; Isa. 51 : 6.

---

pet of his Gospel to call together unto his church the true disciples of Christ, or, He shall send his guardian angels to preserve the elect from the calamities falling upon the Jews. The student may find this view in brief in Lightfoot, and more fully in J. H. Morison, Adam Clarke, and Owen, and something of it in Barnes, who appears, however, not to be fully satisfied with it. To me it appears utterly untenable for the following reasons: (*a*.) The Apostles, who were looking for a majestic manifestation of the Messiah as their king, could not have so understood Christ's language here, and it is ordinarily safe to assume that Christ meant his words to be taken in the sense in which his auditors would naturally have taken them. (*b*.) They did not so understand him; for metaphors, unmistakably borrowed from Christ here, are used by the Apostles, especially Paul, in describing the last judgment (2 Thess. 1 : 7; 1 Cor. 15 : 52; 1 Thess. 4 : 15-17; comp. John 11 : 52). I am unable to see why the same principle of interpretation which converts Christ's sublime description of the last days into a poetic description of the destruction of Jerusalem, would not expunge from the N. T. all its prophecies of Christ's second coming and the final judgment, by looking for their fulfilment in other terrible national calamities. (*c*.) The common reader would certainly not understand Christ's language here to be applicable to the destruction of Jerusalem, and the Bible was intended for ordinary readers. *Interpretations which contradict the common understanding are to be received with great hesitation.* (*d*.) Christ himself employs almost the same language in other connections, where it cannot be doubted that he refers to his final coming to judge the world (Matt. 25 : 31; 26 : 64; Mark 14 : 62). (*e*.) The inhabitants of Palestine did not in any sense *see* in the destruction of Jerusalem the Son of man coming; on the contrary, he is unrecognized by the great body of the Jews to the present day. (*f*.) Christ did not through his Apostles gather together the elect from the four winds of heaven; on the contrary, they were scattered abroad to the four winds of heaven, in the persecutions which immediately preceded, and in those which accompanied the destruction of Jerusalem, and went everywhere preaching the Gospel (see Acts 8 : 1, 4 ; 11 : 19). I then understand that Christ here refers to his second coming to judge the world, a coming that will be sudden, and that will be accompanied by such signs and portents that there can be no possible mistake concerning his appearing. I do not here consider the question whether there is to be a pre-millennial coming of Christ prior to the last judgment. If so, the evidence must be found elsewhere in Scripture. There is nothing in this prophecy to indicate it.

32, 33. As we judge from the presence of certain signs in nature, that spring is over and summer is nigh, so we are to judge when the advent of the Messiah is at hand, by no miraculous signs and portents, but by the development and progress of the world's travail and judgment, as described in the preceding verses. Compare Matt. 16 : 3.

34. This nation shall not pass, till all these things be fulfilled. Of course, if the English version is correct here, and Christ declares that all this prophecy is to be fulfilled before the *then generation passed away*, this verse would leave but one alternative; we should be compelled to believe, either that the Lord himself thought the destruction of the world would follow immediately on the destruction of Jerusalem, and this in the face of his distinct refusal to indicate when the former event would occur (verse 36), and his emphatic assertion that he did not know (Mark 13 : 32), and his careful and repeated warnings against that error (verses 4, 5, 15, 23 and notes); or that he refers in this chapter only to the destruction of Jerusalem, an interpretation which it appears to me does violence to the plain meaning of verses 29-31. But if we read this verse, as I have translated it above, then the marvellous if not miraculous preservation of the Jewish *nation*, though dispersed through all lands, and persecuted through all these ages, is a perpetual and living testimony to the truth of Christ's prophecy. On the question whether the original word rendered *generation* in this verse can be properly rendered *nation* I transcribe, modifying it so as to make its references intelligible to the English reader, the note of Dean Alford. "As this is one of the points on which the rationalizing interpreters lay most stress, to show that the prophecy *has failed*, it may be well to show that the original (γενεά) has in Hellenistic Greek the meaning of a *race or family of people*. For this purpose see Jer. 8 : 3 (Septuagint); compare Matt. 23 : 36 with verse 35, and observe that the then living generation did not slay Zacharias, so that the *whole people* are addressed. See also Matt. 12 : 45, where the sense absolutely requires that the meaning of *nation* should be attached

36 But ᵐ of that day and hour knoweth no *man*, no, not the angels of heaven, but my Father only.
37 But as the days of Noe *were*, so shall also the coming of the Son of man be.
38 For as in the days that were before the flood, they were eating and drinking, marrying and giving in marriage, until ⁿ the day that Noe entered into the ark,
39 And knew not, until the flood came, and took them all away; so shall also the coming of the Son of man be.
40 Then shall two be in the field; the one shall be taken, and the other left.
41 Two *women shall* be grinding at the mill; the one shall be taken, and the other left.

m Zec. 14 : 7 ; 1 Thes. 5 : 2.... n Gen. 6 : 2.

to the word. See also Matt. 17 : 17 ; Luke 17 : 25 ; 16 : 8. In the latter passage, 'The children of this world are *in their generation* wiser than the children of light,' the word *generation* is predicated both of the children of this world and of the children of light, and evidently not used literally of an age of men. Compare also Acts 2 : 40 ; Phil. 2 : 15. In all these passages *generation* (γενεά) is equivalent to *nation* (γένος), or nearly so ; having, it is true, a more pregnant meaning, implying that the character of one *generation* stamps itself upon *the race*, as here in this verse also." That is, here the prophecy is not merely that the Jewish nation, *as a nation*, should not pass away, but also that it *should not lose its national characteristics ;* amid all the changes of time it should remain unchanged ; and this prophecy has been wonderfully fulfilled in the unparalleled history of the Jews.

35. This verse is wanting in the Sinaitic manuscript. Tischendorf omits it. Alford retains it. It unquestionably belongs to the discourse, and is found in Mark 13 : 31 and Luke 21 : 33. Parallel to it is Matt. 5 : 18. The physical universe is temporal and transient ; truth is eternal and immutable. The one is continually passing away before our eyes ; the other, like its divine author, is "the same yesterday, to-day, and forever." Compare 2 Cor. 4 : 18 ; and on the certainty of coming judgment, here specially referred to, Deut. 33 : 34 ; Jer. 2 : 22 ; Rom. 2 : 5.

36. But of that day. This phrase "*that day*," when used absolutely, as here, generally signifies in the N. T. the day of judgment, the great day, the consummation of all others. See for examples, Matt. 7 : 22 ; Luke 10 : 12 ; 1 Thess. 5 : 4 ; 2 Tim. 1 : 12, 18 ; 4 : 8. So the book of revelation is called the Bible, *i. e.*, *The* Book, or the Scriptures, *i. e.*, *The* Writings. Here the context as well as the general N. T. usage forbids the idea of any other reference than to the day of judgment, when heaven and earth shall pass away.—**Knoweth no one, no, not the angels in heaven.** Mark (13 : 32) makes the important addition *nor the Son.* See note there. Observe here, however, that the whole of the rest of this chapter is based on this assertion of ignorance concerning the coming of the day of judgment, and that it is therefore clear, (1) that Christ does not confound the destruction of Jerusalem with the end of the world, nor intend to tell his disciples when the end will be ; (2) that all schemes of interpretation of prophecy which assume to predict the day, are in direct conflict with Christ's solemn assertion that it is not known to man, nor to the angels in heaven, nor even to himself.

37-39. The rest of this chapter is peculiar to Matthew. But the same truth—the necessity of constant watchfulness—is enforced in language analogous, and with the same or similar illustrations, in other discourses of our Lord reported in Luke 12 : 41-45 ; 17 : 26-37. Compare Christ's language there and here. Christ here employs the deluge as an illustration of the suddenness and certainty of the coming judgment. In Luke 17 : 28-30 he adds a reference to the destruction of Sodom and Gomorrah.—**Noe.** The Greek form of Noah.—**The coming of the Son of man.** The same word *coming* (παρουσία) is used here, as in verses 3 and 27 above. Nearly all critics are agreed that *here* Christ refers to his second coming in the day of judgment ; why not there ? Observe the parallel : In the days before the flood the people had warning of the impending judgment (1 Pet. 3 : 19), but did not know the day or the hour, neglected the warning, and gave themselves up, in disregard of it, to luxury and self-indulgence ; and when the flood came, preparation was too late. Observe, too, that eating, drinking, and marrying are right, but to give the life up to them is wrong ; and that luxury and seeming security are precursors of danger and doom. Alford notices the implication that wine and its effects existed prior to the fall of Noah (Gen. 9 : 20), and that Christ indirectly confirms the O. T. account of the flood.

40, 41. Then shall two be in the field, laboring together. Saints and sinners shall be commingled to the last. Compare Luke 17 : 34.—**One is taken.** Not shall be ; the verb is in the present tense. Christ, as it were, stands in the midst of and sees the events he is describing. The word rendered *taken* is literally *taken to* or *with another.* The event is interpreted by John 14 : 3, and yet more clearly by 1 Thess. 4 : 17 : "Then we which are alive and remain, shall be caught up together with them in the clouds, to meet the Lord in the air." Evidently this is not to be confounded with the flight mentioned in verses 16-18 ; that is *voluntary escape*, this is *divine deliverance.*—**Two grinding at the**

42 Watch° therefore; for ye know not what hour your Lord doth come.
43 But know this, that if the goodman of the house had known in what watch the thief would come, he would have watched, and would not have suffered his house to be broken up.
44 Therefore be ye also ready: for in such an hour as ye think not, the Son of man cometh.

45 Who then is a faithful and wise servant, whom his lord hath made ruler over his household,ᵖ to give them meat in due season?ᵍ
46 Blessed *is* that servant, whom his lord, when he cometh, shall find so doing.
47 Verily I say unto you, that he shall make him rulerʳ over all his goods.

o Luke 12:39, 40; Rev. 3:3; 16:15.... p Jer. 3:15.... q ch. 13:52.... r ch. 25:21.

mill. The mills of the ancient Hebrews probably differed but little from those at present in

AN EASTERN MILL.

use in the East. These consist of two circular stones, about eighteen inches or two feet in diameter. The upper stone has a hole in it, through which the grain passes. The mill is worked by women, the lowest servants, or captives (Exod. 11:5; Judg. 16:21), who are usually seated on the bare ground (Is. 47:1, 2), facing each other. Both hold the handle, and pull *to* or push *from*, as men do with the cross-cut saw.

The preceding verses set forth the certainty (verse 35), the unexpectedness (verse 36), and the suddenness (verses 37-39) of the coming judgment; these set forth its closeness in separating those commingled on earth. " It will be a surprising and a separating day."—(*Matthew Henry*.) Compare chapter 25:31-33. Alford says of these verses, " Nor do they refer to the great judgment of 25:31, for then (verse 32) *all* shall be summoned:—but they refer to the millennial dispensation and the gathering of the elect to the Lord *then.*" Whether there is or is not to be such a millennial dispensation prior to the final judgment I do not here discuss. It seems to me, however, that there is nothing here to indicate a double coming of Christ. In both passages a separation is described, though in different language and with different metaphors.

42. Watch therefore. Not for the day of judgment, for no watching will give the disciples a knowledge of its approach; but, in constant expectancy of its coming (2 Pet. 3:12), be watchful over yourselves, that ye may be always ready.

That this is Christ's meaning is clear from parallel exhortations to watchfulness. We are to watch and pray lest we enter into temptation (Matt. 26:41; Mark 14:38), accompanying our watching with faith (1 Cor. 16:13), thanksgiving (Col. 4:2), sobriety (1 Thess. 5:6; 1 Pet. 4:9), and purity (Rev. 16:15); see also note to Parable of ten virgins (ch. 25:1-13, p. 229). Observe (1) that the ignorance of the disciples concerning the *day*, as some manuscripts have it, or the *hour*, as others have it, of Christ's coming, is the basis of the exhortation to watchfulness; (2) that the exhortation is given not only to the twelve, but to all Christ's disciples to the end of time (Mark 13:37); and (3) that the connection clearly implies that the previous verses refer to Christ's second coming, not to the destruction of Jerusalem. Watch *therefore;* wherefore? Not because destruction *did* come unexpectedly on Jerusalem, but because it *will* come unexpectedly on the world.

43, 44. But ye know this. The verb may be rendered either in the imperative or the indicative mood. The idea is the same in either case: Ye do not know the day of Christ's coming; but ye know the duty and the necessity of constant watchfulness.—**If the master of the house.** Not any particular person; this verse is a parable in brief.—**In what watch.** The Jewish night was anciently divided into three watches, the first or "beginning of the watches" (Lam. 2:19) lasting from sunset to 10 P. M., the middle watch (Judges 7:19) lasting from 10 P. M. to 2 A. M., and the morning watch (Exod. 14:24; 1 Sam. 11:11) lasting from 2 A. M. till sunrise. But under the Romans the watches were increased in number to four (Matt. 14:25; Mark 13:35 and note).—**The thief would come.** Elsewhere in the N. T. Christ's coming is compared to that of a thief (1 Thess. 5:1-10; Rev. 3:3; 16:15), because (1) it is sudden, (2) to those whose treasure is all earthly, it is destructive. To such his coming, whether in death or in judgment, leaves nothing (Luke 19:20).—**And would not have suffered his house to be broken up.** Literally *dug through*. The houses of the East were often built of sun-burnt brick, clay, earth, or even loose stones, through which it was easy to make an opening.—**Be ye also ready.** In Matt. 6:19, 20, Christ tells us how to be ready.

45-47. In Luke 12:42-46 a similar parable is

48 But and if that evil servant shall say in his heart, My lord delayeth his coming ;
49 And shall begin to smite *his* fellow-servants, and to eat and drink with the drunken;
50 The lord of that servant shall come in a day ᵃ when he looketh not for *him*, and in an hour that he is not aware of,
51 And shall cut him asunder, and appoint *him* his portion with the hypocrites: there ᵇ shall be weeping and gnashing of teeth.

a 1 Thess. 5 : 3 ; Rev. 3 : 3 . . . . b chap. 25 : 30.

given in answer to Peter's question, Speakest thou this parable unto us, or even unto all? Here it answers the same unuttered question. **Whoever is the faithful and wise servant** shall receive the reward ; whoever is the evil servant shall receive punishment. Compare with this parable Mark 13 : 34-37.—**Who then is a faithful and wise servant ?** Faithful *to* his lord and so *in* his daily duty ; wise, *i. e.* prudent, foreseeing, looking for the coming of his lord. Compare Prov. 22 : 3 ; 27 : 12.—**Whom his lord hath placed over his servants.** Not merely the pastor, bishop, or apostle is here designated. Whoever, by reason of genius, position, or wealth, has influence or control over others is in so far placed over them, and is accountable to his Lord for the administration of his trust.—**To give them meat.** The object God has in making some men *rulers*, is that they may feed others. The great are to be the servants of the feeble. Compare Luke 22 : 26 ; 1 Cor. 14 : 12 ; 1 Pet. 5 : 2, 3.—**In the season.** That is *now*, while the season for doing good lasts. Compare Gal. 6 : 9, 10 and note.—**He shall place him over all his possessions.** Compare Rev. 2 : 26 ; 3 : 21. But how can each servant be placed over all God's possessions ? Alford answers the question well : " That promotion shall not be like earthly promotion, wherein the eminence of one excludes that of another,—but rather like the diffusion of love, in which, the more each has, the more there is for all." So each saint owns all God's possessions, even now (1 Cor. 3 : 21, 22).

48-51. But and if that evil servant shall say in his heart. The worst skepticism is that which lurks *in the heart* of the professed disciple, not that which openly assails the church from without.—**My lord.** Observe, he is a professed disciple of the Lord (comp. verses 10, 12).—**Delayeth his coming.** A frequent cause of apostacy in the church is practical unbelief in the second coming of Christ. Compare Rom. 2 : 4 ; 2 Pet. 3 : 3-12.—**Shall begin to smite * * * and to eat, etc.** The two forms of sin most common to those in high places, oppression and self-indulgence.—**Shall cut him asunder.** A punishment practised among both ancient Hebrews and other nations (1 Sam. 15 : 33 ; 2 Sam 12 : 31 ; Dan. 2 : 5 ; 3 : 29 ; Heb. 11 : 37).—**And shall appoint his portion,** *i. e.* his fellowship (Rev. 21 : 8), **with the hypocrites.** See note on chap. 6 : 2, and compare Rev. 21 : 27 ; 22 : 15.—**There shall be weeping and gnashing of teeth.** See note on chap. 8 : 12. In this verse is one of the incidental evidences that the metaphors of Scripture cannot be literally interpreted. *Cutting asunder* indicates destruction ; *weeping and gnashing of teeth*, a living in suffering. Neither can be regarded as indicating here anything more than a terrible and final punishment.

Observe the contrast between the good and the evil servant. The good servant is *faithful*, to his lord and in his trust ; *prudent*, in watching for his lord's coming ; *beneficent*, using his power as a trust, for others ; *patient*, in continuing his well-doing till the coming of his lord ; and his blessing is an enlarged honor, and a grander sphere of activity in the future. The evil servant becomes a *practical disbeliever* in Christ's second coming, uses his power to *oppress* his fellow-servants, and to *gratify himself*, finds his *companions* with the self-indulgent, not with the self-denying ; and to him judgment comes *suddenly* (Matt. 7 : 26, 27), *unexpectedly, without warning*, and with *terrible and final condemnation*, that separates him from the saints, and allots his portion with sinners. Compare Ezekiel, chap. 34 ; and observe the illustration of the evil servant in the corrupt and worldly among the ministry in all ages and all branches of the church.

Ch. 25. CHRIST'S DISCOURSE ON THE LAST DAYS CONCLUDED.

PRELIMINARY NOTE.—This chapter is peculiar to Matthew. It contains a description of the judgment, first in the parable of the ten virgins (1-13), second, in that of the talents (14-30), third, in a description which is pictorial, but not parabolic (31-46). A question requires statement, if not answer, before entering on the interpretation of the chapter in detail. The millenarian commentators, *e. g.*, Stier, Olshausen, Alford, hold that the millennium intervenes between the judgment described in the two parables (1-30) and that depicted in the closing section of this chapter (31-46). According to this view Christ first comes, selects his faithful followers (the wise virgins, the industrious servants), who reign with him for a thousand years. At the expiration of this time he comes again, to judge the rest of mankind according to their works, and this is the judgment described in verses 31-46. In support of this view reference is had to Rev., chap. 20, and to 1 Thess. 4 : 16, 17, with 2 Thess. 1 : 7-10. It is also said that it is the doctrine of the Scripture that the world of unbelievers is to be judged *according to its works* (Eccles. 3 : 17 ; 12 : 14 ; Matt. 16 : 27 ; Rom. 2 : 6 ; 1 Cor. 3 : 13 ; Rev. 20 : 12, 13 ; 22 : 12) ; that from this judgment believers are delivered by faith in Christ, so that they shall not come into judgment (John 3 : 18 ; 5 : 21 ; 1 Cor. 11 : 31), but shall themselves judge the world (Matt. 19 : 28 ; 1 Cor. 6 : 2, 3). It is further argued that a distinction between the two judgments is indicated here ; that in the first two parables only the professed followers of Christ are judged ; that in the first one the condemned virgins are not only professed, but real disciples, who are waiting for their Lord, with lamps lighted and filled with oil ; that in the closing picture of the last judgment Christ represents in the "all nations" gathered before him only the world of non-believers, including the heathen, whom he distinguishes from his own brethren (ver. 40), who have already entered with him into glory, and that he renders the judgment wholly upon the ground of works, not of faith, which excludes the idea that true believers in him are among those there assembled for judgment.

Whether there is such a distinction between Christ's pre-millennial and final coming I do not here discuss. For the significance of the passages which are supposed to support that view, see notes on them, especially Rev. chap. 20. It must suffice to say (1) that Christ evidently recognizes here but one *public and manifested* appearing of the Son of man (chap. 24 : 21, 39, 44, 50 ; 25 : 1, 13 ; especially comp. chap. 24 : 30, 31 with 25 : 31) ; (2) that whatever selection of the saints takes place prior to the judgment will therefore *apparently* take place in an unrecognized manner, may be taking place now ; (3) that there is but one true judgment-day, and that the judgment of all mankind will be conducted upon the same general principles ; a part will not be judged by one standard and a part by another, for the servants as well as the non-believers will be judged according to their works (Matt. 7 : 21-23 ; 24 : 45-51 ; John 5 : 28, 29 ; 2 Cor. 5 : 10 ; Gal. 6 : 8). And that this is not inconsistent with the doctrine that they will be saved by faith and not by works is apparent from John 15 : 2, 4, 6 ; Ephes. 2 : 10 ; James 2 : 17, 18 ; for good works are the fruits of faith (Heb. chap. 11). Whether we can, from the unfulfilled prophecies of Scripture, frame a more definite system of last things, I at present doubt. Alford himself, who lays down the millenarian view as interpreted above very positively in the first edition of his commentary, in a later edition qualifies his strong assertion. "Having now entered," he says, "on the deeper study of the prophetic portions of the N. T., I do not feel the same confidence in the exegesis I once did as to prophetic interpretations here given of the three portions of this chapter 25. But I have no other system

to substitute, and some of the points here dwelt on seem to me as weighty as ever. *I very much question whether the thorough study of Scripture prophecy will not make me more and more distrustful of all human systematizing, and less willing to hazard strong assertion on any portion of the subject.*" With the spirit of this self-distrust and doubt I most heartily concur. The practical lessons of the unfulfilled prophecies are plain ; their full prophetic meaning I am more and more persuaded can be interpreted only by their fulfillment.

Ch. 25 : 1-13. PARABLE OF THE TEN VIRGINS.— DAILY GRACE ESSENTIAL TO FUTURE GLORY.

PRELIMINARY NOTE.—To understand this parable, some acquaintance with marriage ceremonies as they formerly existed among the Jews, is necessary. This, fortunately, it is not difficult to obtain ; for not only ancient literature describes them very fully, but the Eastern marriage ceremonies of the first century have remained substantially unchanged.

The betrothal was itself a much more solemn act than with us, and was often accompanied by a public ceremonial. Usually a period of twelve months intervened between the betrothal and the wedding ceremony, during which time the bride-elect continued to live with her friends, and all communications between herself and the bridegroom were carried on through the medium of a "friend of the bridegroom" (John 3:29). No religious ceremonies appear to have been performed at the wedding, but it is thought that some formal ratification of the betrothal took place, with an oath ; to this custom there may be an allusion in Ezek. 6 : 8 and Mal. 2 : 14. The essential feature in the wedding ceremony consisted in taking the bride to her future husband's home. Throughout the day preceding this ceremony, both parties fasted, confessing their sins, and seeking forgiveness. It is thought, also, that the bride prepared herself for the wedding ceremony by a bath, taken, as it certainly is in modern times, with some pomp, and as an important part in her share of the wedding ceremonial (Ruth 3 : 3 ; Ezek. 23 : 40 ; Ephes. 5 : 26, 27). This is now usually done on the preceding day. When the evening of the wedding day arrived, the bridegroom, attired in wedding apparel (Isaiah 61 : 10), of which a peculiar nuptial head-dress was a characteristic, set out, at a fixed hour, accompanied with his companions, known as "children of the bride-chamber" (Matt. 9 : 15), to bring the bride either to her new home, or to some other place appointed for her reception. It would appear from some modern accounts, that sometimes the bride is brought to the house of the bridegroom, who remains there to receive her. This marriage procession was, and still is, the essential feature in the Eastern wedding ; and it gave a peculiar significance to the Hebrew phrase, to "take a wife." It was a symbol of capture, which in a ruder form is still preserved among some barbarous tribes in Africa, and among the modern Arabs, with whom the capture and removal of the bride is accomplished with considerable show of violence. The bride, attired in her bridal costume (Jer. 2:32), awaited the arrival of the bridegroom. This costume, when she was a maid, was always white (Rev. 19:7, 8), often richly embroidered (Ps. 45:14); essential parts of it were a wreath of myrtle on the head, or, according to some authorities, a chaplet, gold or gilt; a peculiar girdle encircling her waist, and a white veil (Gen. 24:65) not only concealing her face, but completely covering her person. This last was regarded as a symbol of her submission to her husband (1 Cor. 11:10). With her maids she joined the procession, which

A MODERN MARRIAGE PROCESSION IN JERUSALEM.

then marched back through the streets to the appointed place, where a feast was prepared for the company. Music, torches, and every demonstration of joy accompanied the train. The former, produced largely by small drums, and tambourines, is described, in accounts of the modern procession, as of a very extraordinary description. Often gymnasts or others accompany these processions, in the modern ceremony, performing their feats of dexterity before an admiring throng. The accompanying illustration, from the pencil of Mr. A. L. Rawson, is an exact reproduction of such processions, as they may be seen to-day in the streets of Jerusalem. As the procession neared the bridegroom's house it was joined by other friends of the bride and groom, swelling its tumult and accompanying it to its destination. When this was reached the procession entered, including the invited guests; the door was then closed, and no one arriving subsequently was permitted to enter (vers. 10-12, note). The marriage contract was then signed, and the party sat down to the feast. At the close of the meal came the nuptial benediction, pronounced according to a prescribed form, by the bridegroom himself; if the bride were a virgin, parched corn was distributed among the guests; and the marriage ceremony was concluded by conducting the bride, in state, to her bed-chamber. The accompanying festivities, however, lasted for days, sometimes for a fortnight. For Scripture illustrations of marriage ceremonies, see Gen. ch. 24; Judges, ch. 14; Ruth, ch. 4; and John 2:1-10.

The general lesson of this parable appears to me to be plain, though it has sometimes been missed, and oftener not clearly stated. The ten virgins go forth with their lamps lighted to meet the bridegroom. They thus represent professing Christians, in whom the light of piety has been really, or at least in appearance, lighted. All slumber and sleep while the bridegroom tarries. The sole distinction between them is that five have oil with which to replenish their lamps, and five have not. Oil was used in the Jewish economy to burn in the lights of the temple, and to anoint both kings and priests. It was thus a symbol of divine grace (Psalm 45:7, 8; Acts 10:28; Heb. 1:9). By anointing with oil the king became the

CHAPTER XXV.

THEN shall the kingdom of heaven be likened unto ten virgins,ᵘ which took their lamps, and went forth to meet the bridegroom.ᵛ
2 And fiveʷ of them were wise, and five were foolish.
3 They that *were* foolish took their lamps, and took no oilˣ with them;
4 But the wise took oilʸ in their vessels with their lamps.
5 While the bridegroom tarried, they all slumbered¹ and slept.

<small>u Ps. 45 : 14 ; Ch. 5 : 8, 9 ; 2 Cor. 11 : 2. ... v John 3 : 29. ... w chap. 22 : 10 ; Jer. 24 : 2-9. ... x Is. 48 : 1. ... y 1 John 2 : 20. ... z 1 Th. 5 : 6.</small>

Lord's anointed. It is by the grace which this oil symbolized that we are made kings and priests unto God. The chief lesson of the parable, then, I take to be this: It is not enough to experience religion once for all, and to join, even with a real experience, the professed band of Christ's followers. Our prayer must be for daily grace, as for daily bread. And those who have been content merely to light their lamps, without providing a supply of oil, *i. e.*, to *begin a Christian life without recognizing their continual dependence upon God for continual supplies of grace*, will at the last find the door of his kingdom shut against them. Thus the distinction is not between those who merely profess and those who really possess religion, but between those who are content with one experience and those who recognize their need of continuous supply of divine grace. The Galatians were foolish virgins (Gal. 3 : 1 ; 5 : 4, 7). The parable emphasizes and is interpreted by such passages as John 15 : 4-6, etc.; 2 Tim. 2 : 1 ; Heb. 4 : 16 ; 12 : 15, 28 ; 2 Pet. 3 : 18. Parallel to it is the lesson of the manna, which had to be gathered day by day (Exod. 16 : 19-21). Thus, too, this parable emphasizes the soul's dependence on God, the next parable the soul's duty to God; this our need, that our obligation; this measures us by what we receive, that by what we do; this is Calvinistic, that is Arminian. It would not be safe to conclude that any souls really lighted from on high will apostatize and forever fall away. The parable represents the virgins *as they appear to the bystander*, the disciples as they appear to the world. The event alone shows who have oil with their lamps and who have not. For other lessons of the parable, see the notes in detail. Mr. Arnot calls attention to the striking contrast between the insignificance of the story and the solemn sublimity of its lesson. "A few country girls arriving too late for a marriage, and being therefore excluded from the festival, is not in itself a great event; but I know not any words in human language that teach a more piercing lesson than the conclusion of this similitude."

1, 2. Then shall the kingdom of heaven be likened unto. *Then* connects the following parable with the preceding chapter. The discourse is all one. It is in the second coming of Christ that the kingdom of heaven is like this story of the virgins.—**Ten virgins.** No special significance attaches to the number. It was a usual number in a marriage procession. Nor any to the fact that virgins are mentioned. In all ages of the world virgins have been chosen as bridesmaids. The Roman Catholic deduction in favor of professed virginity deserves to be mentioned only as a warning against that literal interpretation of details, which is by no means confined to Roman Catholic interpreters. The deduction of Alford and Olshausen that both the wise and the foolish are true disciples of Christ, appears to me to be equally unfounded. If all had not been represented as virgins the picture would have been false to real life.—**Five of them were wise and five were foolish.** For the meaning of this contrast compare Matt. 7 : 25-27; 24 : 45; 2 Pet. 1 : 5-9. Observe that in the Scripture godliness is always represented as wisdom, and ungodliness as folly (Psalm 14 : 1 ; Prov. 9 : 35, 36; Ephes. 5 : 15).

3, 4. These verses mark the only contrast between the two classes. See Preliminary Note. Observe that in the outset no distinction is *visible* between the wise and foolish virgins; both have lamps burning, but the wise have the lasting supply of oil (grace), the foolish have not. So in the church no visible line separates those whose light is fed by their own resolution from those whose dependence is a continual supply of daily grace from God. The Jewish lamp was a shallow vessel filled with oil. The wick floated

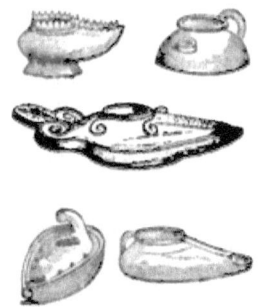

ASSYRIAN LAMPS.
(From originals in British Museum.)

on the oil. Our illustration represents some lamps exhumed in the Assyrian excavations. The originals are in the British Museum. Others almost exactly like these have been recently dis-

[Cн. XXV.] MATTHEW. 271

6 And at midnight^a there was a cry^b made, Behold, the bridegroom cometh; go ye out^c to meet him.
7 Then all those virgins arose, and trimmed their lamps.
8 And the foolish said unto the wise, Give us of your oil; for our lamps are gone out.^d
9 But the wise answered, saying, Not so; lest there be not enough for us and you; but go ye rather^e to them that sell, and buy for yourselves.
10 And while^f they went to buy, the bridegroom came; and they that were ready went in with him to the marriage: and the door was shut.^g
11 Afterward came also the other virgins, saying,^h Lord, Lord, open to us.

a Rev. 16: 15....b 1 Thess. 4: 16....c Am. 4: 12....d Luke 12: 35....e Isa. 55: 1, 6....f Am. 8: 12, 13....g Heb. 3: 18, 19; Rev. 22: 11....h chap. 7: 21-23; Heb. 12: 17.

covered in Jerusalem. In the marriage procession such lamps were placed on sticks, and thus converted into torches. In separate vessels, oil was carried with which to replenish the lamps.

5. While the Bridegroom tarried. In this there is a hint that the Lord would not come immediately, nor so soon as his church expected him. The same hint is given in chap. 24: 48. Observe that there the wicked servant thinks the Lord delays, so watches not for his coming; here the foolish virgin thinks he is coming immediately, so makes no provision of oil; an indication that a sinful heart can find in directly contrary beliefs excuses for the same real neglect.—**They all slumbered and slept.** Literally, *nodded and fell asleep*. The fact is hardly to be spiritually pressed. If at all, it seems to me that Calvin, and following him, Arnot, give the key to its true meaning. "Disciples in the body cannot be occupied always and only with the expectation of their Lord's appearing. Sleep and food, family and business, make demands on them as well as on others, demands which they cannot and should not resist. If the coming of the Bridegroom be delayed till midnight the virgins must (naturally will) slumber; this is not a special weakness of individuals, it is the common necessity of nature."—(*Arnot*.) And observe the implication, if the Christian has grace in his heart, he is always ready, though asleep; if not, he is unready, though he were wakeful and seemingly watching. Not *what death finds us doing*, but *how death finds us furnished, is the important question*.

6, 7. At midnight. Observe the implication here, which underlies the instruction of the previous chapter, that the coming of the Lord will be unexpected.—**There was a cry made.** Either by watchers more wakeful, or by the first of the approaching procession. Parallel to this cry is the "great shout" and "the voice of the archangel," which shall accompany the descent of the Lord. (1 Thess. 4: 16).—**Trimmed their lamps.** "The hand lamp naturally was small and would not contain a supply of oil for many hours. The trimming itself implied two things, an infusion of fresh oil, and removal of whatever had gathered round, and was clogging the wick. For the last purpose a little instrument, often hung by a slender chain from the lamp itself,

pointed, for the removal of the snuffs from the flame, and with a little hook at the side by which the wick, when need was, might be drawn further out. This instrument is sometimes found, still attached to the bronze lamps, discovered in sepulchres."—(*Trench*.) One of these instruments is to be seen in the annexed cut, hanging just above the lamp. The illustration is copied from a Roman bronze.

8, 9. Gone out. Literally *going out*. The apparent piety which is not furnished with constant supplies of divine grace may seem bright in life, but fails in the hour of trial, especially of death.—**Not so.** In the Greek the negative is expressed much more emphatically: *By no means* (μὴ ποτε). Observe the significance of (1) the request: *Give us of your oil*. "How fondly in such a crisis the empty lean on the full."—(*Arnot*.) (2.) The answer: *Not so; lest there be not enough for us and you*. In this answer they show their wisdom. No one can supply grace for another's need. Incidently there is here a witness against the Roman Catholic doctrine of works of supererogation, *i. e.*, that the saints accumulate a store of good works from which the church may draw for those who have no merit of their own. Comp. Psalm 49: 7; Rom. 14: 12; 1 Pet. 4: 18. (3.) The counsel: *Go ye rather to them that sell, and buy for yourselves*. This was the best advice possible; but it was too late to comply with it. At midnight the stores would be shut. The opportunity for purchasing, which the foolish had enjoyed in common with the wise, was now past. Alford's interpretation of the language here, *Go to them that sell*, as "no mean argument for a *set and appointed ministry* and moreover for a *paid ministry*," appears to me a curious illustration of the literalism that misinterprets. Surely the ministry are not shopkeepers to *sell* the grace of God. The interpretation of this direction is to be found in Isaiah 55: 1 and Rev. 3: 18. God alone dispenses divine grace; and the very point of the parable here is that one disciple cannot supply another.

12 But he answered and said, Verily I say unto you, I know you not.
13 Watch *therefore, for ye know neither the day nor the hour wherein the Son of man cometh.
14 For *the kingdom of heaven is as a man travelling into a far country, *who* called his own servants, and delivered unto them his goods.
15 And unto one he gave five talents, to another two, and to another one; to every man according to his several ability; and straightway took his journey.

Hab. 1 : 13....j chap. 24 : 42, 44 ; Mark 13 : 33, 35 ; Luke 21 : 36....k Luke 19 : 12, etc....l Rom. 12 : 6 ; 1 Cor. 12 : 4, etc.; Eph. 4 : 11.

10–12. Mr. William Ward in his "View of the Hindoos," quoted in Trench, gives an account of an Oriental wedding, which illustrates the figure here. "After waiting two or three hours, at length, near midnight, it was announced, as if in the very words of the Scripture, Behold the bridegroom cometh, go ye out to meet him. All the persons employed now lighted their lamps, and ran with them in their hands to fill up their stations in the procession. Some of them had lost their lights and were unprepared ; but it was then too late to seek them, and the cavalcade moved forward to the house of the bride. * * * The bridegroom was carried in the arms of a friend, and placed upon a superb seat in the midst of the company, where he sat a short time, and then went into the house, the door of which was immediately shut, and guarded by Sepoys. I and others expostulated with the door-keepers, but in vain." Observe the significance of the spiritual lesson. The foolish virgins are now in earnest, but it is too late. "The salvation of the soul depends, not on frightened earnestness in the moment of departure, but on faith's calm closing with Christ, before the moment of departure comes."—(*Arnd.*)

The door was shut. Christ is the door (John 10 : 7, 9), and *now* stands open to all who will come unto the Father by him (Acts 2 : 39), the door which admitted Aaron after his idolatry, David after his adultery, Peter after his denial, Saul of Tarsus after his persecution of the church. But this door does not stand open forever (Luke 13 : 24, 25).
—**Afterward came also the other virgins.** Not having obtained the oil, but without it, yet hoping for admission notwithstanding. This at least is the implication of the narrative, for the shops would be closed at midnight—and of the parable, for its object is to teach that divine grace must be sought *now*, while it is to-day (Heb. 3 : 15). "They came looking for mercy when now it was time for judgment."—(*Augustine.*) To the marriage-feast (heaven), none are admitted without light (holiness), which can be sustained only by oil (divine grace), (Eph. 5 : 5 ; Heb. 12 : 14). "The door was shut, as much for the security and joy, without interruption of those within, as for the lasting exclusion of those without (Gen. 7 : 16 ; Rev. 3 : 12).—(*Trench.*) In Rev. 21 : 25, 27, the gates of the heavenly city are represented as always open, and the implication is that those who are without are excluded by no external or arbitrary barrier, but by their own nature and spirit.

Comp. Rev. 22 : 11, 15.—**I know you not,** *i. e.*, recognize you not as bridesmaids. Comp. Matt. 7 : 23, and note ; also 2 Tim. 2 : 19. He will not know those at the last who knew not him in life. Comp. Matth. 10 : 32, 33, and note.

13. Watch therefore ; for ye know neither the day nor the hour. The words, *Wherein the Son of man cometh*, are omitted by the best manuscripts. But they undoubtedly interpret aright the meaning of the verse. This carries us back to Matt. 24 : 42, and connects the parables of this chapter with the warnings of the previous chapter. Thus the admonition to watchfulness is the text of the whole discourse ; and this and the following parable both emphasize and interpret that admonition. Watch, that divine grace fail you not, is the lesson of this parable ; Watch, that your own powers and opportunities are not neglected or misused, is the lesson of the parable of the talents.

Ch. 25 : 14–30. PARABLE OF THE TEN TALENTS.— DILIGENCE IN DUTY ESSENTIAL TO FUTURE GLORY.

This parable is peculiar to Matthew. Mark 13 : 34–35 contains an abbreviated form of it. Luke 19 : 11–27 contains an analogous parable, that of the ten pounds, which has sometimes been confounded with this, but is different in structure, and was uttered on a different occasion. The central teaching of this parable is clear. Its primary application is to his immediate disciples. Our Lord, when he ascended up on high, gave various gifts to them, adapting his divine grace to their natural capacities (Eph. 4 : 8–12), and for their use of these gifts of the Spirit, he here teaches them they must give account on his return. Secondarily it applies to all his disciples throughout all time ; for all are his servants and receive their all from him, and for their use of it must give account to him. Thirdly it applies to all men ; for all receive their native capacities and their opportunities, their characters and their circumstances, from God ; he bestowes them not as a *gift*, but as a *trust ;* and for their use thereof they will be called to account. The sin against which Christ admonishes his disciples here is not that of the unjust steward (Luke 16 : 1), for here there is no wasting of goods ; nor that of the prodigal (Luke 15 : 13), for here there is no riotous living ; nor that of the unmerciful servant (Matt. 18 : 28), for here is no indifference to humanity ; nor that of the evil servant (Matt. 24 : 49), for here there is neither excess nor oppression. Our Lord

16 Then he that had received the five talents went and traded with the same, and made *them* other five talents.
17 And likewise he that *had received* two, he also gained other two.
18 But he that had received one, went and digged in the earth, and hid his lord's money.
19 After a long time,ᵐ the lord of **those servants** cometh, and reckonethⁿ with them.
20 And so he that had received five talents, came and brought other five talents, saying, Lord, thou deliveredst unto me five talents; behold, I have gained beside them five talents more.
21 His lord said unto him, Well done, *thou* good and faithful servant: thou hast been faithful over a few things, I will make thee rulerᵒ over many things: enter thou into the joy of thy lord.
22 He also that had received two talents, came and said, Lord, thou deliveredst unto me two talents: behold, I have gained two other talents beside them.
23 His lord said unto him, Well done, good and faithful servant: thou hast been faithful over a few things, I will **make** thee ruler **over** many things: enter thou into the joy of thy lord.
24 Then he which had received the one talent, came, and said, Lord, I knew thee that thou art an hard man,ᵖ reaping where thou hast not sown,ᵠ and gathering where thou hast not strawed

m ch. 24 : 48. ... n ch. 18 : 23, 24. ... o Luke 12 : 44; 22 : 29; Rev. 3 : 21. ... p Job 21 : 15. ... q Jer. 2 : 31.

admonishes us that non-use is a sin as truly as misuse, neglect as truly as flagrant disobedience. The whole parable pivots on the words *unprofitable servant*, and it is one of solemn warning, not only to every church-member, but also to every person, who is so living as neither to grow in grace himself nor to edify others. "The warning here is for those who *hide* their talent, who, being equipped of God, for a sphere of activity, do yet choose, in Lord Bacon's words, 'a goodness solitary and particular, rather than generative and seminal.'"—(*Trench*.) The same lesson is enforced by the parable of the barren fig-tree (Luke 13 : 6–9). For comparison of this with preceding parable see Preliminary Note on the Parable of the Ten Virgins, above. For special lessons here see notes below.

14, 15. A man traveling into a far country. By this is figured primarily the seeming withdrawal of Christ from his church, and secondarily, the seeming withdrawal of God from all direct participation in human affairs. See Matt. 21 : 33, note.—**His own servant.** Rather slaves. These among the Romans were not only employed in the usual domestic offices and in the labors of the field, the mines, and the factory, but also as factors or agents for their masters in the management of business, and were often entrusted with property to a large amount.—**Five talents.** The Hebrew (silver) talent is variously estimated at from $1500 to $2250, the gold talent as high as $55000. See for fuller account of it, note on Matt. 18 : 24. The amount, therefore, here represented is considerable. Its spiritual significance is partially conveyed by our English use of the word talent, as equivalent to power or capacity, especially mental, a use which has grown out of this parable. But it also includes powers which are external, as well as those which are inherent in the character, and therefore wealth and position. Chrysostom gives the meaning well. "The talents here are each person's ability, whether in money, or in teaching, or in what thing soever."—To every man according to his several ability. If there be any lesson in this it is not that grace is given according to the measure of faith, for faith is the gift of God, nor that grace is adapted to the natural ability, for there is no real distinction between natural and supernatural ability, all are from God. In human life we grade our trusts according to the natural ability of the recipient; God gives to different men in different measures, as it pleases him, but always grades his gifts, so that ability and opportunity go together. "No one is burdened beyond his ability (Exod. 4 : 10–12) ; therefore he is justly compelled to render an account."—(*Bengel*.) Also, there is a difference in endowments and therefore in requirements (Rom. 12 : 16; 1 Cor. 12 : 4–31; Ephes. 4 : 7–12). Observe the teaching in these passages, as in this parable, that there are *no absolute gifts; all are trusts,* to be employed in God's service for the edification of his church (1 Cor. 14 : 12).

16, 18. Traded with them. Literally *labored with them,* i. e., he added to them by his own industry. Whoever, in allegiance to his divine Master, and by his diligent use of God's gifts, adds to the spiritual value of his own character (1 Pet. 1 : 5–10), or to the true welfare of his fellowmen (Rom. 15 : 2; 1 Cor. 14 : 12), fulfills the part of a faithful servant. The result is gain to God, a true addition to God's wealth.—**Digged in the earth.** A common method of hiding treasure in the East. Matt. 13 : 44–46, and note.

19-23. After a long time. A hint that the second coming of Christ would not take place immediately. Compare Matt. 24 : 48 ; 25 : 5, note. Observe (1) the language of the servants, *Thou* deliveredst unto me five talents ; behold I have gained beside them (literally *upon them*). In Luke it is "Thy pound hath gained five pounds." Both statements are true. All gain in spiritual things is both ours and God's; whether in personal experience (1 Cor. 15 : 10; Phil. 2 : 12, 13) or in Christian work (John 15 : 5; 1 Cor. 3 : 9) we are co-laborers with God. His talent makes a gain; yet we also make it, but always *upon* his talents, i. e., by their means. (2.) The language of the Lord. He commends not the acquisition but the fidelity. "Faithfulness, not success, is rewarded."—(*Alford*.) And the reward conferred is a larger sphere of labor: "I will make thee ruler over many things." This is yet clearer in Luke : "Have thou au-

25 And I was afraid,' and went, and hid thy talent in the earth: lo, *there* thou hast *that is* thine.
26 His lord answered and said unto him, *Thou* wicked* and slothful servant, thou knewest that I reap where I sowed not, and gather where I have not strawed:
27 Thou oughtest therefore to have put my money to the exchangers, and *then* at my coming I should have received mine own with usury.

28 Take therefore the talent from him, and give *it* unto him which hath ten talents.
29 For unto ' every one that hath shall be given, and he shall have abundance: but from him that hath not shall be taken away " even that which he hath.
30 And cast ye the unprofitable servant into outer darkness:" there shall be weeping and gnashing of teeth.

r Prov. 26 : 13; Rev. 21 : 8....*s* ch. 18 : 32; Job 15 : 5, 6; Luke 19 : 22; Jude 15....*t* ch. 13 : 12; Mark 4 : 25; Luke 8 : 18; 19 : 26. ..
u Luke 10 : 42... *v* ch. 8 : 12.

---

thority over ten cities." This principle of reward is constantly illustrated in this life, where fidelity in the smaller sphere leads to the larger one. But it receives its fulfillment in the other life, where reward is not merely kingly honors, but kingly responsibility and labor. (2 Tim. 4 : 8; Rev. 2 : 10. Comp. Heb. 1 : 14.) And it is illustrated here in the closing sentence, "Enter thou into the joy of thy Lord," whose joy was and is in doing good. Matt. 18 : 13, note. Observe Leighton's comment on this promised reward: "Here some drops of joy enter into us; there we shall enter into joy, as vessels put into a sea of happiness."

24-27. The spiritual significance of this servant's report and his Lord's answer appears to me to be this: One of the most common causes of spiritual inactivity and indolence is a morbid fear of making mistakes, of losing the one talent in trading instead of increasing it, of doing harm rather than good by work. And this is founded on a false conception of God as a hard master, who calls to rigorous account for the *results* of our work, whereas he calls us to account only for the *purposes* that animate us (Rom. 8 : 1; 2 Cor. 8 : 12). To this spirit Christ replies in effect, If it were as you imagine, God a hard and exacting master, this should make you afraid of neglect and indolence, for he will call you to account for non-use as well as for misuse. The foundation of the fear here rebuked is want of faith. The slothful servant does not recognize that he is to work *in* God as well as for God. Illustrating it by contraries is Augustine's prayer: "Give what thou dost command, and command what thou wilt." Observe, however, the implication in the Lord's rebuke, "Thou wicked and slothful servant." The excuses which men offer for idleness, whether to others or their own consciences, are false; the real reason is spiritual sloth.

One talent. There is a significance in the fact that it is the servant with one talent who is idle, which Chrysostom puts well: "Let no man say, I have but one talent, and can do nothing; for thou canst even by one approve thyself. For thou art not poorer than that widow (1 Kings 17 : 12); thou art not more uninstructed than Peter and John, who were both unlearned and ignorant men (Acts 4 : 13)."—**Money-changers.** These were men who carried on a business midway between modern banking and modern pawnbroking. They took money on deposit and loaned it out on interest, paying interest themselves to the depositors. Their interest varied from ten to thirty-six per cent.; its average was from twelve to eighteen per cent.—**Usury. Interest.** This does not determine the rightfulness of the taking of usury, or even of interest. Christ simply employs the common affairs of life as an illustration, without, however, passing judgment on the principle involved in them. Taking usury was common among the Greeks, but the Jews were forbidden to take it from their brethren (Exod. 22 : 25; Lev. 25 : 36; Deut. 23 : 19), but might take it from foreigners (Deut. 23 : 20). The spiritual significance of the language of verse 27, "Thou oughtest, therefore, to have put my money to the exchangers," is not quite clear. Alford's interpretation and application is reasonable and noteworthy: "The machinery of religious and charitable societies in our own day is very much in the place of the money-changers. Let the subscribers to them take heed lest they be not in the degraded case of this servant, even if his excuse had been genuine."

28, 29. The principle here enunciated is illustrated continually in life. It is embodied in the proverb, "Drawn wells are never dry," and in the aphorism of the wise man in Prov. 11 : 24. Non-use leads to death. The limb used is strengthened, disused becomes weak. By exercise the mental faculty acquires strength, by indolence loses power. Even money can increase only by being used for others' benefit. But these illustrations point to the final fulfillment of the principle, in the day when the indolent will find both his *power* and his *opportunity* for doing good forever taken away from him (John 9 : 4).

30. See Matt. 8 : 12, note, where the bearing of this language on the doctrine of future punishment is considered. Observe that the same condemnation is visited on the *unprofitable* servant as on the guest without a wedding garment (Matt. 22 : 13), the hypocrites (chap. 24 : 51), and the workers of iniquity (Luke 13 : 27, 28). Compare with the teaching of this parable the parable of the fig tree (Luke 13 : 6-9), that of the vineyard (Isaiah 5 : 1-7), and the injunction of 1 Tim. 4 : 14, "Neglect not the gift that is in thee;" and observe that the smaller the apparent gift, the more reason for its careful and diligent cultivation, development, and use.

Ch. XXV.] MATTHEW. 275

31 When ʷ the Son of man shall come in his glory, and all the holy angels with him, then shall he sit upon the throne of his glory:
32 And before ˣ him shall be gathered all nations; and he shall separate ʸ them one from another, as a shepherd ᶻ divideth *his* sheep from the goats:

33 And he shall set the sheep on his right hand,ᵃ but the goats on the left.
34 Then shall the King say unto them on his right hand, Come, ye blessed ᵇ of my Father,ᶜ inherit the kingdom ᵈ prepared ᵉ for you from the foundation of the world:

w ch. 16:27; 19:28; Dan. 7:13; Zec. 14:5; Mark 8:38; Acts 1:11; 1 Thess. 4:16; 2 Thess. 1:7; Jude 14; Rev. 1:7....z Rom. 14:10; 2 Cor. 5:10; Rev. 20:12....y ch. 13:49; Ezek. 20:38....z Ps. 78:52; John 10:14, 27....a Heb. 1:3....b Ps. 115:15....c Rom. 8:17; 1 Pet. 1:4....d 1 Thess. 2:12; Rev. 5:10....e 1 Cor. 2:9; Heb. 11:16.

Ch. 25 : 31-46. THE LAST JUDGMENT DESCRIBED.—THERE IS NO TRUE PIETY WITHOUT PRACTICAL PHILANTHROPY; NO TRUE PHILANTHROPY WITHOUT PIETY.

These verses constitute a pictorial and dramatic but not parabolic description of the last judgment. Nowhere else does Christ describe definitely that event. The passage clearly teaches the following great truths: (1) That there will be a final judgment; (2) that it will come with the final appearing of our Lord at the end of the world; (3) that it will consist, not of a trial, but of a public announcement of the divine judgment, founded upon the trial which life affords; (4) that it will be public—before all nations and all angels, i. e., all created beings known to us to exist; (5) that it will result in a public separation of all men into two distinct classes, not into a great variety of grades; (6) that this separation will be based, not on our creeds, our forms and ceremonies, or our religious professions, but on our practical charity to our fellow-men; (7) that the decisions of this judgment will be final, unappealable, and irreversible. See notes below, both for elucidation of these lessons and consideration of others not so clear. On the general relation of this description to preceding parables, see Preliminary Note.

31-33. When the Son of man shall come in his glory. Compare the language of description in chap. 24 : 30, 31. The event described is apparently the same; an incidental evidence that neither the destruction of Jerusalem nor a millennial coming prior to the last judgment is there described.—**Then shall he sit—and before him shall be gathered.** The language, *when* he shall come * * *then* he shall sit, points to a definite occasion of public judgment, *at the second and public coming of Christ*, but not necessarily a *day* in the limited sense of that term. True, "It is not implied that we shall all be gathered before him at one and the same moment" (*J. H. Morison*), but it is implied that it shall be a definite occasion, and when Christ comes in his glory (Matt. 13:40; Acts 11:31; Rom. 2:16; 1 Cor. 4:5).—**All angels—all nations.** "How great publicity."—(*Bengel*.) The term *all nations* is limited by the millenarian commentators to the heathen, or at least the non-believing world. See Preliminary Note to this chapter. It is certainly capable of this interpretation, since the term (ἔθνος) is most frequently used in the N. T. to signify the Gentiles in contradistinction to the Israelites, and is frequently rendered *Gentiles* (Acts 4:27), and sometimes *heathen* (Acts 4:25). But it is sometimes used distinctively of the Jews (Luke 7:5; John 11:48, 50; Acts 10:29), and sometimes includes them with the Gentiles (Matt. 26:19; Luke 24:47), and it is therefore certainly capable of the meaning which our English version here gives to it. And this meaning appears better to accord with the description elsewhere given of the last judgment (Eccles. 12:14; 2 Cor. 5:10; Rev. 20:12, 13).—**He shall separate them one from another.** Compare Ezek. 34 : 17. Observe, the separation is not into a great variety of grades, which merge into one another; it is into two well-defined classes. This description cannot be reconciled with the conception that the other world will be one simply of development, into which all men will enter at the stage of progress reached here, to pass by a process of education into the next higher class. There are but two classes, though there may be grades of character and condition in both. Observe, too, that there is a real separation between the righteous and the wicked on earth, but it is not made apparent till the judgment-day. Then the gulf between them is fixed forever (Matt. 13:37, note; Luke 15:28).

34. Then shall the King say. Christ is the King, whose kingdom shall be then manifested when he comes to judge the world (John 5:27; Rom. 14:9; Rev. 19:6,7).—**Come.** We come to Christ both for salvation here and for glory hereafter; we come that we may be with him where he is (John 14:3; 17:24).—**Ye blessed of my Father.** Not, Ye that are to be blessed, but Ye that *have been* blessed; the perfect participle is used. They are blessed because all the fruits of true love which men *apparently* produce are *really* fruits of the Spirit (1 Cor. 3:6; 1 John 4:7, 12).—**Inherit the kingdom prepared for you.** The kingdom of which Christ is King, and which consists in righteousness, peace, and joy in the Holy Ghost (Rom. 14:17). We enter it fully when we come where there is no more sin or temptation (Rev. 21:27). We inherit it because it is God's free *gift* (Rom. 6:23), and is given only to those who, being born again, are the children, and therefore the heirs, of God (John 3:3, 5; Rom. 8:16, 17; Gal. 4:6, 7).—**From the foundation of the world,** *i. e.,* so prepared in the councils of

35 For I was an hungred, and ye gave me meat: I was thirsty, and ye gave me drink: I was a stranger, and ye took me in:
36 Naked, and ye clothed me: I was sick, and ye visited me: I was in prison, and ye came unto me.
37 Then shall the righteous answer him, saying, Lord, when saw we thee an hungred, and fed *thee?* or thirsty, and gave *thee* drink?
38 When saw we thee a stranger, and took *thee* in? or naked, and clothed *thee*?
39 Or when saw we thee sick, or in prison, and came unto thee?
40 And the King shall answer and say unto them, Verily I say unto you, Inasmuch as ye have done *it* unto one of the least of these my brethren, ye have done *it* unto me.

f Isa. 58:7; Ezek. 18:7...g 1 Pet. 4:9; 3 John 5...h James 2:15, 16...i James 1:27...j 2 Tim. 1:16; Heb. 13:3...k Prov. 19:17; Mark 9:41; Heb. 6:10.

divine love; not actually made ready, for Christ went that he might prepare a place for us (John 14:2).

35, 36. For. These verses give the reason why those on the right hand are accepted. They are a N. T. exposition of Prov. 19:17, "He that hath pity on the poor lendeth to the Lord." Comp. 1 Tim. 6:17-19; 1 John 3:16-18; ch. 4, and Scripture references given below. And observe that every element in this description is illustrated by Scripture.—**I was a hungered and ye gave me to eat.** See 1 Kings 17:10-15; Ruth 2:14-17.—**Thirsty and ye gave me drink.** Matt. 10:40-42.—**I was a stranger and ye treated me hospitably.** The word here rendered *took in* is the same rendered in Deut. 22:2 and Josh. 2:18 *bring in*, and in Judges 19:15, 18, *took in*, and *receive*. For illustration of the spirit of hospitality see Numb. 10:29 with 1 Sam. 15:6; 30:11, 12; Acts 28:1, 2.—**Naked and ye clothed me.** Acts 9:36-39.—**I was sick and ye visited me,** more literally, *looked after me*. For illustration see Luke 7:2, 3; 10:30-37.—**In prison and ye came to me.** Jer. 38:7-13; 2 Tim. 1:16, 17.

Respecting these verses observe (1) in Chrysostom's language, "How easy are these injunctions. He said not, I was in prison and ye set me free; I was sick and ye raised me up again; but *ye visited me* and *ye came unto me.*" (2.) No reference is made to spiritual help. The case is one in which the less includes the greater, as the promise of reward to one who gives a cup of cold water, includes a promise for all larger service. Even the lowest forms of philanthropy, if they are the offspring of true love, have their reward. (3.) A real personal service is indicated, one involving some sacrifice of time and property. (4.) He that does these things has the spirit and follows the example of Christ, for we were hungry and he gives us to eat (John 6:30-35), thirsty and he gives us drink (John 4:14; 6:55, 56), strangers from the promise and he receives us to himself (Ephes. 2:18, 19), naked and he clothes us (Rom. 13:14; 2 Cor. 5:3; Gal. 3:27; Rev. 3:18), sick and he visits us with redeeming love (Psalm 147:3; Jer. 3:22; Hosea 14:4; Luke 1:68, 78; Heb. 2:6), in prison and he comes to us, shares our prison fare, and so ransoms and delivers us. (Rom. 8:1, 2, 3; Heb. 2:9, 10.)

37-39. Most of the commentators regard this as the language merely of humility. But ignorance that whatever we have done for our fellow-men has been done in and for Christ is not Christian humility. It argues, on the contrary, a defective Christian experience. "Such an answer (as that here given) it would be impossible for them to make, who had done all distinctly with reference to Christ, and for his sake, and with his declaration of chap. 10:40-42, before them."—(*Alford*.) Nor is it necessary to suppose, from this language, that only the heathen are represented as here in judgment; though that they are included, and will be accepted if they have endeavored to live according to the law of God as interpreted by their conscience, is clearly declared by Paul in Rom. 2:7-11. The plain teaching of the passage is this, that not only those who have in this life recognized Christ as their Lord and Master will be accepted by him, but also those who have never done so and yet have actually imbibed his spirit and followed his example, in the consecration of their lives to their fellow-men; for they give thereby evidence that they are the children of God, born of the Spirit of God, blessed of the Father (verse 34, note), though the full disclosure of his grace they may not apprehend until they recognize their King in the day of judgment. With this accords a host of other passages of Scripture. Deut. 15:7; Job 29:13-16; 31:16-23; Psalm 112:9; Isaiah 58:7-11; Ezek. 18:7, 16; Dan. 4:27; Luke 11:41; Acts 10:31; Heb. 6:10; 13:16; James 1:27; 1 John 2:10; 3:14; chap. 4. It does not conflict with the doctrine that no man can enter the kingdom of God unless he is born again; but it recognizes love to man as the best outward evidence of the new birth (1 John 4:7). It does not conflict with the doctrine that all men are saved by Christ; but it recognizes the truth that they may be saved by a Redeemer whose redemption they did not understand. But observe, that "it is not the *works*, *as such*, but the *love* which prompted them, that love which *was their faith*—which felt its way, though in darkness to him who is love—which is commended" (*Alford*); and that when Christ is, in the day of his glory, fully disclosed to them, they recognize him as their *Lord*.

40. Inasmuch as, *i. e.,* just in so far as, ye have done it unto one of the least of

CH. XXV.]   MATTHEW.   277

41 Then shall he say also unto them on the left hand, Depart¹ from me, ye cursed, into everlasting ᵐ fire, prepared ⁿ for the devil and his angels:
42 For I was an hungred, and ye gave me no meat: I was thirsty, and ye gave me no drink:
43 I was a stranger, and ye took me not in: naked, and ye clothed me not: sick and in prison, and ye visited me not.

44 Then shall they also answer him, saying, Lord, when saw we thee an hungred, or athirst, or a stranger, or naked, or sick, or in prison, and did not minister unto thee?
45 Then shall he answer them, saying, Verily I say unto you, Inasmuch° as ye did *it* not to one of the least of these, ye did *it* not to me.
46 And these ᵖ shall go away into everlasting punishment: but the righteous into life eternal.

l Luke 13 : 27....m ch. 13 : 40, 49 ; Rev. 14 ; 11....n Jude 6 ; Rev. 20 : 10....o Zec. 2 : 8 ; Acts 9 : 5....p Dan. 12 : 2 ; John 5 : 29.

these my brethren. Primarily, his disciples (Matt. 12 : 50; Hebrews 2 : 11), but, secondarily, any one of the great family of man, **Ye have done it unto me.** "Let us then take heed not to neglect any, nor to apply ourselves out of natural inclination more to one than to another, but to those whom either the Providence of God sends us, or in their necessity obliges us to prefer."—(*Quesnel*.)

41. Depart from me. As the reward of the saints is to be forever with the Lord (1 Thess. 4 : 17), so the punishment of the wicked is everlasting exile from his presence (2 Thess. 1 : 9). The language is that of intense moral aversion; and it implies the hopelessness of the doom. For how can the sinner *without God*, redeem himself from his sin? (John 15 : 5)—**Ye accursed.** Under the Jewish law persons or things might be devoted to Jehovah, by vow, in which case they became his irrevocably, and could not be redeemed. Cattle were put to death (Lev. 27 : 26–29). Out of this custom grew the devotion to death, as a punishment, of an individual (Exod. 22 : 20), or an idolatrous city (Deut. 13 : 12, etc.; comp. Deut. 7 : 24, etc.; 3 : 6; Josh. 6 : 17, etc.; 10 : 28, etc.; 11 : 11). Such persons or things were pronounced *accursed*. The reference here is to this Jewish custom. Those on the left of the judge are metaphorically described as *devoted to death*, and *beyond the hope of redemption*.—**Into everlasting fire prepared for the devil and his angels.** Fire may be a symbol of purification, which it certainly is not here, or of destruction, or of torment. The language here conveys apparently the latter shade of meaning. Comp. Rev. 19 : 20; 20 : 10. Observe the implication of the personality of the devil. How could a fire be prepared for abstract evil, or for the sinful propensities of the heart? Contrast this verse with verse 34. *Come—depart; Blessed—cursed; the kingdom—everlasting fire*. Observe, too, another and important contrast. "Blessed *of my Father*: but not Cursed of my Father, because all man's salvation *is of God*, all his condemnation *from himself*. The kingdom prepared *for you*, but the fire which has been prepared for *the devil and his angels, not for you*; because there is election to life, but there is no reprobation to death; a book of life, but no book of death; no hell *for* man because the blood of Jesus has purchased life for all; but they who will serve the devil must share with him in the end."—(*Alford*.) On the word *everlasting*, see note at close of chapter, verse 46.

42-45. Observe there is here no charge of positive oppression, only of neglect. Comp. Luke 16 : 19–25. But, as in verses 37–39, the less includes the greater. "How severely shall they be punished who take away the goods of others, when those are punished after this manner, who only refuse to give what is their own."—(*Quesnel*.) Observe, too, the significance of their ignorance, which is real, not pretended. They were unconscious that their inhumanity was also impiety. They would have shown honor to the king if they had recognized him; but he measures their character by their treatment of his subjects.

46. And these shall go away into everlasting punishment: but the righteous unto life everlasting. On this verse volumes have been written, and on its interpretation the best scholars are not fully agreed. Referring the student to larger treatises for an investigation of verbal criticism, it must suffice here to say, (1.) That the same Greek word is used in both clauses of the sentence, rendered in the one "eternal," in the other "everlasting," and that, therefore, presumptively, the punishment threatened is as lasting as the life promised. (2.) That the etymology of the word here rendered *everlasting* is in dispute; some scholars find its origin in two Greek words (ἀεὶ ὤν, αἰών), *ever being*, in which case our word *everlasting* is an almost literal translation; others trace its etymology to a word (ἀω) signifying *to breathe*, and so find its equivalent to be primarily a life, a generation, hence an age or cycle of years. The former etymology is adopted by the majority of modern scholars. (3.) The word certainly does not always signify in the Scripture eternity. Of its application to a period of time which was really limited the following passages from the O. T. (Septuagint) are illustrations: Gen. 17 : 8; 48 : 4; Lev. 16 : 34; Numb. 25 : 13; Hab. 3 : 6. In the N. T. it is used also of time limited, in Rom. 16 : 25; 2 Tim. 1 : 9; Titus 1 : 2, where the phrase *since* or *before the world began* would be literally *since* or *before the time ages*, i. e., the beginning of the cycle of time; see also Philemon 15, Thou shouldest receive him, i. e., the fugitive Onesimus, forever, though here the idea of receiving

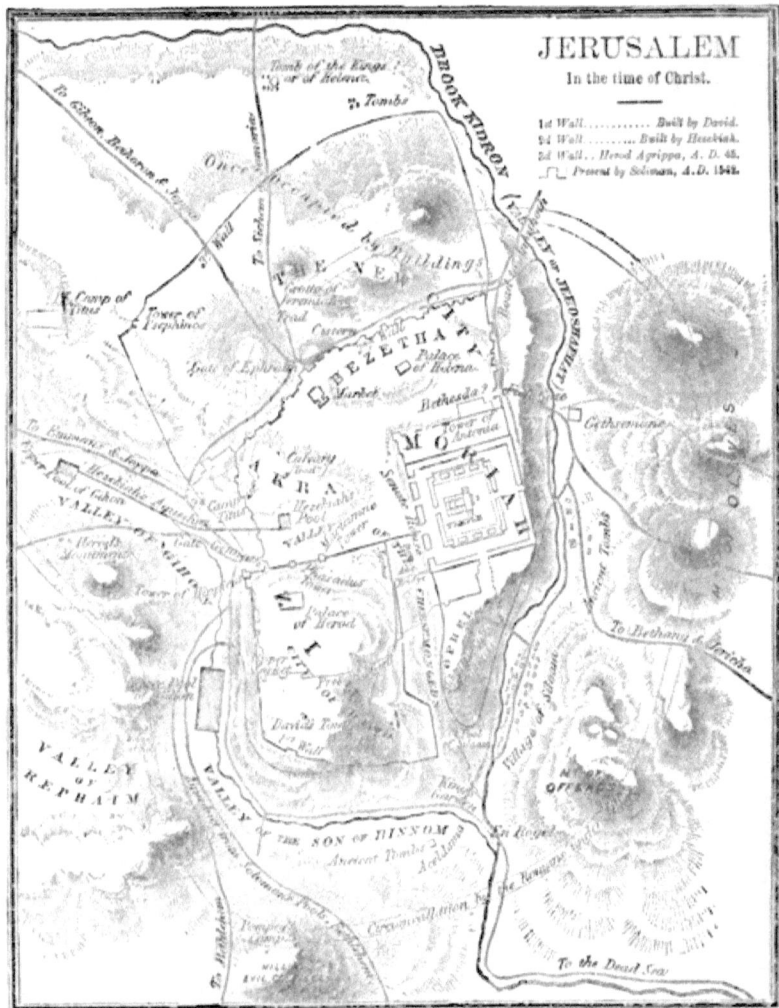

The accompanying map presents the supposed sites in the city of Jerusalem. They are, however, largely hypothetical. The city is built on two hills, environed on either side by valleys, that of the Hinnom and that of the Kedron; a third valley, that of the Cheesemongers, penetrates the heart of the city, dividing it into two parts. This valley is now largely filled up with debris, produced by the frequent sieges to which the city has been subject. It is reasonably certain that the ancient Temple stood where the Mosque of Omar now stands, i. e., on the eastern hill, known in Scripture as Mount Moriah, and the palace of Herod on the opposite hill, Mount Zion. Across the valley of Jehoshaphat, over against Jerusalem, is the Mount of Olives. Somewhere in that valley, or on the western slope of that mount, was the garden of Gethsemane. Over the mountain, about two miles away, was Bethany, the house of Mary, Martha, and Lazarus. Christ, with his disciples, coming from Jericho, by the road marked on this map, entered Jerusalem in triumph on Saturday (ch. 21 : 6-11) by one of the eastern gates; every night he retreated from the city to Bethany, or perhaps to solitude on the Mount of Olives; and from this mountain he overlooked the city with his disciples at the time of the prophecy contained in Matt., ch. 24 (see ver. 3). The other localities of the Passion Week are quite uncertain. I believe, however, that the trial before the Sanhedrim took place in or adjoining the Temple (Luke 22 : 66, note), and the trial before Pilate at the Tower of Antonia (John 18 : 28, note). The place of execution and burial is unknown; it is hardly possible that it can be the traditional site, which is indicated on this map. See Matt. 27 : 33, note.

CHAPTER XXVI.

AND it came to pass, when Jesus had **finished all** these sayings, he said unto his disciples,
2 Ye know ᵃ that after two days is *the feast of* the passover, and the Son of man is betrayed to be crucified.

3 Then assembled together the chief priests, and the scribes, and the elders of the people, unto the palace of the high priest, who was called Caiaphas,
4 And consulted ʳ that they might take Jesus by subtilty, and kill *him*.
5 But they said, Not on the **feast** *day*, lest there be an uproar among the people.

q Mark 14 : 1, etc. ; Luke 22 : 1, etc. ; John 13 : 1, etc. . . . *r* Psalm 2 : 2.

---

the slave in a Christian covenant and fellowship, to be literally ever-during, may be embodied. Of the other 66 times in which the word occurs in the N. T., it is 51 times used in describing the blessedness of the saints, 3 times is applied to the Gospel, 3 times to God or his attributes, 3 times (2 Cor. 4 : 18 ; 2 Thess. 2 : 16 ; Heb. 6 : 2), where the word *everlasting* unquestionably correctly represents it, and 6 times it is applied to future punishment. Thus it will be seen that the ordinary usage of the N. T. justifies the translation here, *everlasting*. (4.) In *all* Scripture usage, I think without exception, the word *indicates a period of time as long as the existence of the object spoken of.* The Jewish nation, as long as it preserved its organic existence, possessed the Holy Land, and the priesthood service (Gen. 17 : 8 ; Lev. 16 : 34). So the Gospel was a mystery from the beginning of the world's existence (2 Tim. 1 : 9). If this be true, then whenever this word is predicated of the soul's condition it signifies one, whether of life or of death, of blessedness or of punishment, as lasting as the soul. (5.) There is nothing in this verse to indicate the nature of the punishment threatened. The question whether it consists in ever-during life in suffering, or real soul-destruction, must be solved, if at all, by reference to other Scripture. The phrase *everlasting punishment* implies that the *result*, not the *punishment*, will be everlasting, as the phrase *eternal judgment* (Heb. 6 : 2) signifies not a judgment lasting eternally, but one having eternal results. (6.) The reward promised is *life eternal*, and this signifies not merely existence, which might or might not be a boon, but the highest and noblest activity of the soul, in all its God-given powers, and this *eternal*, *i. e.*, with no fear of decadence, infirmity, or lapse into sin.

Ch. 26 : 1-16. PREPARATION FOR THE CRUCIFIXION.— IN THE HEARTS OF THE DISCIPLES ; BY THE ENEMIES OF CHRIST ; BY THE UNCONSCIOUS PROPHECY OF LOVE'S OFFERING ; BY THE TREACHERY OF AN APOSTLE.— THOUGH FOREWARNED OF SORROW, WE ARE NOT ALWAYS FOREARMED AGAINST IT (ver. 1, 2, with Luke 21 : 21, 26).—MEN LOVE DARKNESS RATHER THAN LIGHT, BECAUSE THEIR DEEDS ARE EVIL (ver. 3-5 ; comp. John 3 : 19, 20).—THE TRUE DISCIPLE RARELY KNOWS THE TRUE VALUE OR MEANING OF HIS OWN LIFE (ver. 6-13).—CHRIST COULD NEVER BE CRUCIFIED BY THE WORLD BUT FOR TREACHERY IN HIS OWN CHURCH (ver. 14-16).

In these verses Matthew groups several incidents that point to the crucifixion. They are four in number : (1) verses 1, 2, Christ's prophecy of the crucifixion ; (2) verses 3-5, the conspiracy of the Jewish authorities ; (3) verses 6-13, Mary's unconscious preparation for the Lord's burial by anointing him ; (4) verses 14-16, Judas' agreement to betray his Lord. Whether these events occurred in the order here narrated is uncertain. See note on verses 6-16 below. From this point the passion of our Lord properly begins. His mission as a prophet merges in his mission as a sacrifice ; his words are pregnant to the last, as his soul has suffered from the beginning. But it is as the Sufferer rather than as the Teacher he appears in the remaining scenes of his life.

1, 2. When Jesus had finished all these sayings. The discourse contained in chapter 23 was the last delivered by Christ in public. That contained in chapters 24 and 25, and those reported by John in chapters 14-16, were delivered only to the apostles, the former, perhaps, to but four of them (Mark 13 : 3).—**Ye know.** Because he had previously foretold his passion.— **After two days is the Passover, and the Son of man is betrayed** (the present tense, with a future force ; see Mark 9 : 31, note) **to be crucified.** Whether the Jewish Passover took place on Thursday, on the evening of which the Lord's Supper was instituted, or on Friday, the day on which our Lord was crucified, is confessedly one of the most difficult questions in N. T. chronology. So far as this verse affords a note of time at all, it appears to me to sustain the former view. If this prophecy was spoken immediately at the close of the discourse reported in chapters 24 and 25, *i. e.*, on Tuesday evening, the Passover Supper would come on Thursday evening. Alford thinks, on the contrary, that this is a solemn declaration that "the deliverance of our Lord to be crucified and the taking place of the Passover strictly coincided," because Christ says, "After two days is the Passover, and the Son of man is betrayed to be crucified." But he apparently forgets that the *betrayal* took place on the evening of the day preceding the *crucifixion* ; so that if the betrayal and the Passover coincided, the Passover and the Lord's Supper also coincided. See on the whole question, Note on the Lord's Supper, below.

6 Now when Jesus was in Bethany, in the house of Simon the leper,
7 There came ᵃ unto him a woman having an alabaster box of very precious ointment, and poured it on his head, as he sat *at meat*.

8 But when his disciples saw *it*, they had indignation, saying, To what purpose *is* this waste?
9 For this ointment might have been sold for much, and given to the poor.

ᵃ John 11 : 1, 2 ; 12 : 3.

3-5. Then assembled together the chief priests, etc. That is, the Sanhedrim (Matt. 2 : 4, and note). Presumptively this conference was held on Tuesday night, at the close of Christ's public denunciation of the Jewish leaders (chapter 23).— **The high priest, called Caiaphas.** The high priest was originally the highest religious officer in the land, and held office for life; but at this time was appointed and removed by the Roman government at will, so that in 107 years the office had been filled with 27 appointees. He was the head of the Sanhedrim, and exercised some political and judicial as well as ecclesiastical functions. Caiaphas was a son-in-law of Annas (John 18 : 13), with whom he seems to have in some way shared the duties of the office (Luke 3 : 2 and note). His character, as a wily and unscrupulous politician, is indicated by his counsel respecting Jesus (John 11 : 49-51), and by his conduct during the subsequent trial of Jesus (Matt. 26 : 57-68, notes). Peter was at a later period brought before him and Annas (Acts 4 : 6). He was appointed high priest 27 A. D., and was removed 36 or 37 A. D. Nothing is known of his history subsequent to his deposition.

5. But they said, Not during the feast. Not merely the feast-day, *i. e.*, the day on which the Passover was sacrificed and eaten, but at any time during the festal season, which lasted for seven days. On these occasions Jerusalem was thronged with pilgrims. Christ was popular with the Galileans, and the leaders feared an attempt by them at resistance. Perhaps such an attempt would have been made, but for the fact that Christ discountenanced it (verses 52-54).

6-16. The anointing of Jesus by Mary, and the subsequent treachery of Judas.— This anointing is also described by Mark (14 : 3-10) and John (12 : 2-8). For general exposition see notes on John 12 : 1-8. From his account it appears to have taken place at the house of Lazarus and his sisters Mary and Martha, and to have been performed by Mary, who poured the ointment on Christ's feet as well as on his head. It is not to be confounded with the anointing mentioned in Luke 7 : 36-50, though this has been done. There is nothing in common between them, except the name of the householder, Simon (Luke 7 : 40); and this was a very common name in Palestine. The occasion, the time, the parties, and the spiritual significance, are all different. The repetition of the incident is not at all strange. "An act of this kind, which had been once commended by our Lord (as in Luke), was very likely to have been repeated, and especially at such a time as six (?) days before the Last Passover, and by one anointing him for his burial."—(*Alford*.) The time when this anointing here described took place is uncertain. John's account apparently indicates six days before the Passover, *i. e.*, probably Friday preceding the crucifixion. And this is the view of Townsend, Andrews, Alford, J. H. Morison, and others. These writers suppose that Matthew inserts the account out of its chronological order, because Judas Iscariot's treachery is closely connected with his complaint of Mary's extravagance, and Christ's rebuke of him (John 12 : 4, 7). Matthew and Mark apparently indicate two days before the Passover, *i. e.*, on the Tuesday night preceding the crucifixion. This is the view of Robinson, Geo. W. Clark, and Dr. Hackett (*Smith's Bib. Dict.*, vol. ii., p. 1372, note). This view appears to me the more probable one, for, (1) the note of time is not definite or conclusive in either of the Evangelists; (2) the immediate occasion of Judas's treachery seems to have been the rebuke administered at this supper (comp. verse 14 here with John 12 : 4, 7); (3) if his plan was formed four days before, why was it not earlier executed? (4) the discourses of Christ's prophesying the overthrow of Judaism, his own crucifixion, and a long period of trial preceding his second coming (chap. 24), might well prepare the mind of Judas, if his adhesion to Christ was largely induced by earthly ambition, for the temptation of avarice and ambition, combined with resentment. But without some previous disappointment and bitterness of soul, such as would be produced by the final overthrow of all his hopes of preferment, it is difficult to understand how he should have been incited to his treachery.

6, 7. Bethany. A village about two miles east of Jerusalem (John 11 : 18), being on the other side of the Mount of Olives. See map, p. 238. It was the home of Mary and Martha, where Christ was wont to visit when in Jerusalem (Luke 10 : 38-41; Matt. 21 : 17; Mark 11 : 11, 12). It was the scene of the resurrection of Lazarus (John, ch. 11), and of Christ's own ascension (Luke 24 : 50). It is not mentioned in the O. T.—**Simon the leper.** Nothing is known of him. Whether the father, or the husband of one of the sisters, or a more distant relative, is merely matter of conjecture. He is not mentioned in the other incidents referring to

Ch. XXVI.] MATTHEW. 281

10 When Jesus understood *it*, he said unto them, Why trouble ye the woman? for she hath wrought a good work upon me.
11 For ye ᵗ have the poor always with you; but meᵘ ye have not always.
12 For in that she hath poured this ointment on my body, she did *it* for my burial.
13 Verily I say unto you, Wheresoever this gospel shall be preached in the whole world, *there* shall also

this, that this woman hath done, be to d for a memorial of her.
14 Then oneᵛ of the twelve, called Judas Iscariot, went unto the chief priests,
15 And said *unto them*, What will ye give me, and I will deliver him unto you? And they covenantedʷ with him for thirty pieces of silver.
16 And from that time he sought opportunity to betray him.

ᵗ Deut. 15 : 11.... u John 14 : 19; 17 : 11.... v ch. 10 : 4.... w ch. 27 : 3; Zech. 11 : 12, 13.

this family; hence the surmise that he was dead. He could not at this time have been a leper, and living in the house, for in that case he could not have received guests.—**A woman.** Mary, the sister of Martha and Lazarus (John 12 : 3).

8, 9. His disciples. The complaint appears to have originated with Judas (John 12 : 4), but may have been caught up and echoed by the others.—**For much,** John and Mark specify the cost, 300 pence (denarii), equal to $54, but equivalent to nearly a year's wages of an ordinary laboring man (Matt. 20 : 2, note).

11. Ye have the poor always with you. Mark adds significantly: "Whensoever ye will, ye may do them good."

13. The promise of this verse is given by Mark, but not by John. On it Alford well remarks, "This announcement is a distinct prophetic recognition by our Lord, of the existence of *written records*, in which the deed should be related; for in no other conceivable way could the universality of mention be brought about."

14–16. Judas Iscariot, *i. e.*, probably Judas of Kerioth, a town of Judea (Josh. 15 : 25). On his character and the explanation of his treachery, see notes on chap. 27 : 3-10.—**Chief priests,** *i. e.*, heads of the priestly courses. Matt. 2 : 4, note.—**Thirty pieces of silver,** *i. e.*, thirty shekels, equal to about eighteen dollars. It was

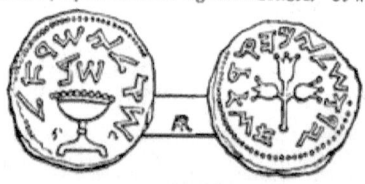

A SHEKEL.

the sum fixed to be paid in case of the killing of a slave by an ox (Exod. 21 : 32. Comp. Lev. 27 : 3). The exact sum to be paid for Christ's betrayal was a subject of prophecy (Zech. 11 : 12, 13). The smallness of the sum forbids the idea that Judas was incited only by avarice, unless the thirty shekels be regarded merely as earnest money; and this hypothesis appears untenable, for no more appears to have been paid to him. The language in Zechariah and in Matt. 27 : 3, indicate that the thirty shekels was the price *paid*, not an

earnest to bind the bargain. Whether the priests actually paid him the money at this time, or only agreed to pay it, is not clear from the original, which is literally, *They placed to him thirty shekels.* This may mean that they actually delivered it to him, as is indicated by Zechariah, or that they put it to his credit, on condition of his fulfillment of his promise. The latter agrees better with the accounts in Mark (14 : 11) and Luke (22 : 5). In the latter passage the word rendered *covenanted* is different from that employed here, and signifies a covenant or agreement.

Ch. 26 : 17–25. PREPARATIONS FOR THE LAST PASSOVER.

Of the institution of the Lord's Supper, and the concurrent events, we have four accounts, viz., Matt. 26 : 16–30; Mark 14 : 12–25; Luke 22 : 7–30, and 1 Cor. 11 : 23–25. John gives no account of the Lord's Supper, but is the only one who reports the contemporaneous feet-washing, and the discourses of Jesus in connection with the Supper. That he omits all mention of the Supper, and reports what the other Evangelists do not mention, is an incidental indication that he wrote with the other histories before him, and in part for the sake of supplying what they omitted. A harmonized narrative of the four Gospels is confessedly difficult, Alford thinks "impossible." It is at best but hypothetical. The most probable hypothesis combines these accounts as follows: Christ gives two of his disciples directions as to the preparation of the Passover supper for himself and the twelve (Mark 14 : 12-16; and Luke 22 : 7-13, notes); when the even is come he goes with the twelve to the place prepared for them, where an unseemly strife occurs as to which shall be greatest (Luke 22 : 24-30, notes); this Christ rebukes by washing the feet of the disciples (John 13 : 1-20, notes); all then take their places at the table (Matt. 26 : 20); Christ prophecies his betrayal (Matt. 26 : 21-25; Mark 14 : 18-21; Luke 22 : 21-23; John 13 : 21-30, notes); Judas learning that his treachery is known, goes out to complete it (John 13 : 27-30, notes). The Supper, which has been interrupted by this incident, now goes on and ends with the institution of the Lord's Supper at the close of the Passover feast (Matt. 26 : 26-29, notes; Mark 14 : 22-25; Luke 22 : 19, 20; 1 Cor. 11 : 23-25). After, or during, this meal Christ gives his disciples the instruc-

17 Now a the first *day* of the *feast of* unleavened bread, the disciples came to Jesus, saying unto him, Where wilt thou that we prepare for thee to eat the passover?
18 And he said, Go into the city to such a man, and say unto him, The Master saith, My time is at hand; I will keep the passover at thy house with my disciples.
19 And the disciples did as Jesus had appointed them; and they made ready the passover.

20 Now when the even was come, he sat down with the twelve.
21 And as they did eat, he said, Verily I say unto you, that one of you shall betray me.
22 And they were exceeding sorrowful, and began every one of them to say unto him, Lord, is it I?
23 And he answered and said, He b that dippeth *his* hand with me in the dish, the same shall betray me.

x Exod. 12 : 6, 18. . . . y Ps. 41 : 9 ; 55 : 12, 13.

tions and utters for them the prayer recorded in John, chaps. 14–17 inclusive.

17. Now the first of the unleavened bread. That is, the first *day,* viz. Thursday the 14th day of Nisan. The feast of the unleavened bread, or the Passover, properly began on the 15th of Abib or Nisan, and lasted seven days. But the preceding day, the 14th, was the one appointed for the slaying of the lamb, and on the evening of that day the paschal supper was eaten (Exod. 12 : 6 ; Lev. 23 : 5). It was, therefore, termed the first day of the feast. See note on Lord's Supper below, § 1. —**The disciples came to Jesus.** The movement for the observance of the Passover originated, therefore, with them. The directions were given to two of them only, Peter and John (Luke 22 : 7–13).—**Where wilt thou that we prepare the Passover?** The Scripture directions for the preparation of the Passover are contained in Exod. 12 : 1–11, 14–20, but are modified by Deut.

fuller in Mark (14 : 12–16) and Luke (22 : 7–13). See notes on Luke.—**My time is at hand.** Peculiar to Matthew. Its meaning can hardly be other than, The time for my passion and death (John 7 : 6).

20. When even was come. The lamb must be killed "in the evening" (Exod. 12 : 6), or, as it is rendered in the margin in Exodus, "between the two evenings," a phrase interpreted by the rabbis as equivalent to between the declining and the setting sun, *i. e.,* between 3 P. M. and 5 P. M., or between sunset and deep twilight. The former was the more general view. Deut. 16 : 6 specifies more accurately, "about the going down of the sun." The paschal supper followed, on the same night (Exod. 12 : 6).—**He sat down with the twelve.** Literally, *Reclined with the twelve.* The supper appears to have been originally taken standing (Exod. 12 : 11); but whether the direction so to take it was intended except for the Israelites at the time of the exodus, is uncertain. It was not observed in Christ's time. The reclining posture had been borrowed from other nations long prior (Amos 6 : 4), probably from the Babylonians and Syrians (Esther 1 : 6, 8 ; 7 : 8). In taking their places in the manner indicated in the annexed cut, John reclined next to Christ on one side ; thus he might easily rest his head on the Master's bosom (John 13 : 25). **Judas** sat near Christ, probably on the other side, for Christ reached to him a sop or morsel (John 13 : 26).

16 : 5, 6. The guest-chamber was already prepared (Mark 14 : 15), and the lamb had probably been previously selected for the sacrifice (Exod. 12 : 10). The other preparations would consist of making ready the unleavened bread, the bitter herbs, etc. Jewish custom required that the Passover be celebrated, if not within the city walls, at least within the distance of a Sabbath day's journey, *i. e.,* about three-quarters of a mile.

18, 19. The account of this direction and the apostle's compliance is not found in John. It is

Observe that only the twelve participated with Christ in this supper. The proprietor of the house was probably at the same time partaking the Passover in another room with his own family. On Passover week every Jew in Jerusalem extended the hospitality of his house to these strangers. Our Lord and the twelve were a full paschal company ; ten persons were the minimum number. Luke (22 : 24–30, notes) gives an account of a strife among the disciples which should be greatest, probably a contention which should have the places of honor at the table, in

CH. XXVI.]   MATTHEW.   283

24 The Son of man goeth as it is written ᵃ of him; but woe unto that man by whom the Son of man is betrayed ! it had been good for that man if he had not been born.

25 Then Judas, which betrayed him, answered and said, Master, is it I ? He said unto him, Thou hast said.
26 And as ᵇ they were eating, Jesus took bread, and blessed *it*, and brake *it*, and gave *it* to the disciples, and said, Take, eat ; this is my body.

ᵃ Ps. 22 : 1, etc. ; Isa. 53 : 3, etc. .... ᵇ 1 Cor. 11 : 23, etc.

which case it doubtless preceded the supper, and was followed by Christ's washing of the disciples' feet (John 13 : 1–20, notes) in rebuke of their contention.

21–25. An account of Christ's prophecy of his betrayal is given by all the Evangelists, but most fully by John 13 : 21–25 ; see notes there.

22. Unto him. Not merely, as Alford, To each other. They both inquired among themselves (Luke 22 : 23), and of Christ.—**Lord, is it I ?** Their language expresses in the original a much stronger negation than in our version. *Surely not I, Lord ?* Compare their strong assertion that they will not deny him (ver. 35). To their questioning Christ makes no response. John then asks more quietly, Who is it ? (John 13 : 23–25).

23. This answer, apparently given only to John (John 13 : 25, 26), does not designate the betrayer to the disciples. According to the Jewish ritual the administrator in the course of the supper dipped the bitter herbs in a prepared sauce, and passed the dish to the rest. This Christ now did. His reply to the question of John was simply an emphatic reiteration of his previous declaration (John 13 : 19), "He that eateth bread with me hath lifted up his heel against me." That it did not designate the traitor to any of the disciples is clear from John 13 : 28 ; Judas alone perceived that his treachery was known to Christ.

24. This verse is not found in John. In slightly different forms it appears in Mark and Luke. Compare with it Acts 2 : 23, and Matt. 18 : 7, note. Observe the incidental confirmation of the doctrine elsewhere taught, that for the finally lost soul there is no redemption. It could not with truth be said of one, It had been good for that man if he had not been born, if the temporary punishment of his sin was to be followed by his final redemption, and his glorious realization, at last, of the image of God.

25. Alford supposes that these words, which are peculiar to Matthew, are "an imperfect report of what really happened, viz., that the Lord dipped the sop and gave to Judas, thereby answering the general doubt, in which the traitor had impudently presumed to feign a share." I should rather think that Judas, thunderstruck by the sudden unveiling of his secret purpose, was at first silent ; that when he recovered himself he sought to hide his confusion by repeating the question, or rather denial, of the other disciples, and that, in the intense excitement of the scene, they neither noticed his question nor

Christ's reply. Jesus added, "That thou doest do quickly," on which Judas left the room. That he was not present during the institution of the Lord's Supper appears to me, from a comparison of the narratives, to be the most probable hypothesis ; but John, who alone mentions that Judas left the room, says nothing whatever concerning the institution of the Lord's Supper.—**Thou hast said.** A form of affirmative, equivalent to Thou hast said correctly. Compare chap. 27 : 11 and Exod. 10 : 29. The spirit and aim of this disclosure is thus well hinted at by Chrysostom : "He said not, Such an one shall betray me ; but 'one of you,' so as again to give him power of repentance by concealment. And he chooseth to alarm all for the sake of serving this man." Christ's tender treatment of Judas, throughout, is one of the most touching and significant facts in his life. Was it not also in part his purpose to drive the traitor from the room ? Not until after Judas departs does Jesus open his heart to the disciples in the discourse preserved by John.

Ch. 26 : 26–30, THE LORD'S SUPPER.—A MEMORIAL, A PARABLE, AND A PROPHECY.—IT IS A MEMORIAL OF CHRIST AS A GIFT, AND CHRIST AS A SACRIFICE.—IT IS A PARABLE OF THE TRUE NATURE OF CHRISTIANITY, CHRIST IN US.—IT IS A PROPHECY OF FUTURE GLORY, PERFECT COMMUNION WITH CHRIST, PERFECT COMMUNION OF SAINTS. SEE NOTE ON LORD'S SUPPER BELOW.

PRELIMINARY NOTE. The account of the institution of the Lord's Supper does not differ materially in the three Synoptics, Matthew, Mark 14 : 22–25, Luke 22 : 14–20, and in 1 Cor. 11 : 23–25. Luke, however, mentions a cup before the supper, which is not mentioned by the other Evangelists (Luke 22 : 17). The Rabbinical books give detailed instructions for the observance of the feast of the Passover. It is very doubtful whether the ritual therein prescribed was observed in Christ's time. But the following general rules respecting the Passover throw some light on Christ's administration of the supper described by Paul and the Evangelists. No uncircumcised male (Exod. 12 : 48) was admitted. Women partook of the feast. Usually not less than ten nor more than twenty sat down to the table. The father or head of the family acted as master of the feast. The guests reclined at the table (verse 20, note). The supper was commenced with a blessing asked by the head of the family ; he next passed a cup of wine, referred to in Luke 22 : 17, and the bitter herbs (Exod. 12 : 8), which were eaten either with or without being dipped in the prepared sauce. This was the sop referred to in John 13 : 26. Then the unleavened bread was passed, whereupon one of the children asked the meaning of the ceremonial ; this was explained by the father in accordance with Exod. 12 : 26, 27. It was at this distribution of the bread that Christ imparted a new significance to the Passover, by departing from the original and Jewish ritual, and declaring that the bread was henceforth a memorial of his death, not of the Jewish national deliverance (Matt. 26 : 26). A psalm was then sung—Psalms 113, 114—and the lamb was carved and eaten. This was followed by a third and fourth cup of wine, or wine and water, and one or the other of these was the cup which Christ blessed and declared to be a symbol of his blood (see ver. 27). The supper was then closed by chanting Psalms 115-118, the hymn mentioned here in verse 30.

26. As they were eating. Compare Mark 14 : 22. This clearly indicates that the Lord's Supper was instituted *during the progress of the Paschal Supper*, not as a separate ordinance at its close. See note on the Lord's Supper below. Nor is it inconsistent with the statement in Luke 22 : 20, 1 Cor. 11 : 25, that he took the cup "after supper," for the third and fourth cup of the Passover were taken at the close of supper, and this language merely distinguishes the cup here mentioned from the one with which the supper began, which is mentioned only by Luke (22 : 17). —**And blessed.** Some manuscripts have here "Gave thanks." But the reading of the Received Text is preferable. This blessing of the bread would include giving thanks, but it would also embrace the invocation of the divine blessing upon the bread. Comp. 1 Sam. 9 : 13. The language is precisely the same as that used in Matt. 14 : 19, Mark 6 : 41, and there is as little reason for supposing that it involves a mystical charge in the one case as in the other, that is, no reason at all. It was customary for the father at the distribution of the bread to pronounce the benediction, "Blessed be he who causeth bread to grow out of the earth." But, says Grotius, "not so much for the old creation, rather for the new, for which he came into this world, he pours out prayer and renders thanks to God for the redemption of the human race, as though it were already accomplished."—**And brake.** The bread that was broken was a round cake or cracker of unleavened bread. See Mark 8 : 6 for illustration. Throughout the entire Passover week no leavened bread was allowed in the house (Exod. 12 : 8, 15). The administration of the Lord's Supper was subsequently termed the "breaking of bread" (Acts 2 : 42; 1 Cor. 10 : 16). In the breaking and distribution of bread to others is there not symbolized, not only our covenant and communion with Christ, but also our duty of breaking and distribution to others what we receive from him? Is there not also significance in the fact that he passed by the lamb, which in the future history of the church it would often be inconvenient and sometimes impossible to provide, and took, as the symbol of his body, bread, which can always be obtained ?

Take, eat ; this is my body. Luke adds, "which is given for you" (22 : 19); Paul, "which is broken for you" (1 Cor. 11 : 24); and both add, "This do in remembrance of me." The bread, then, is (1) a symbolic reminder that Christ is God's unspeakable gift to us (John 3 : 16; 2 Cor. 9 : 15) ; (2) that the gift is perfected only in that he is *broken* for us (John 3 : 14; 10 : 15; 19 : 39); (3) that it is efficacious only as we *partake* of him, *i. e.*, receive him into ourselves, so that he becomes one with us, as he is one with the Father (John 17 : 23), as the bread when eaten becomes part of our nature, and so the sustainer of our life. Concerning the proper interpretation of Christ's declaration, "*This is my body*," from which the Romanists deduce the doctrine of transubstantiation, it must suffice here to note briefly, (1) that it is incredible that the apostles, with their Lord sitting before them in bodily form, should have understood Christ to mean literally that the bread was his body ; and we are to understand Christ as they would have understood him ; (2) that his language here closely conforms to that of the Jewish ritual. When the lamb was passed the master was asked by one of the children, "What is this?" and the father replied, "This is the body of the lamb which our fathers ate in Egypt." Christ uses, but modifies, the same formula. Does any one suppose the lamb slain in Egypt was miraculously multiplied through all the subsequent ages? (3) that Christ, in the fuller discourse reported in John, chap. 6, which is a prophetic interpretation of this supper, carefully guards his disciples against the literalism into which the Romish church has fallen. In verse 63 he distinctly declares, "The flesh profiteth nothing," and gives the explanation that the spirit, received by receiving his words, can alone impart life ; (4) that the same literalism would make havoc of the symbolism of both the O. T. and the N. T. Let the student consider the effect of its application, for example, to the following passages : Gen. 15 : 1 ; Psalm 31 : 3 ; 84 : 11; John 10 : 7, 11 ; 1 Cor. 10 : 4. The sacred writers commonly employ the verb "to be" as equivalent to the verb "to represent ;" *e. g.*, "The three branches *are* three days" (Gen. 40 : 12, 18); "These bones *are* the whole house of Israel" (Ezek. 37 : 11); "The field *is* the world, the good seed *are* the children of the kingdom, the tares *are* the children of the wicked one" (Matt. 13 : 38); "The seven stars *are* the angels, the seven candle-

CH. XXVI.]　　　　　　　　MATTHEW.　　　　　　　　285

27 And he took the cup, and gave thanks, and gave it to them, saying, Drink ye all of it ;
28 For this is my blood of the new testament,[b] which is shed for many for the remission of sins.
29 But I say unto you, I will not drink henceforth of this fruit of the vine, until that day when I drink it new with you in my Father's kingdom.[c]
30 And when they had sung an hymn, they went out into the Mount of Olives.

b Jer. 31 : 31. . . . c Isa. 95 : 6.

sticks *are* the seven churches" (Rev. 1 : 20). The key-note to the interpretation of the supper and Christ's language respecting it is well given by James Morison : "The supper is a parable to the eye, the touch, the taste." See below, note on the Lord's Supper, § 4.

Whether Christ ate of the bread and drank of the wine has been a matter of some discussion. There is no clear answer to the question in the account. Chrysostom apparently thinks he did, Alford that he did not. James Morison suggests that "He was, as it were, giving himself to his disciples. To have given himself to himself would have been to have either ignored or perplexed the profound significance of the ordinance." On the contrary, Luke implies his participation (See Luke 22 : 15, 18, note). But if he did not participate, this would be no reason why the modern administrator should not partake. "Although in one sense he represents Christ blessing, breaking, and distributing, in another he is one of the disciples, examining himself, confessing, partaking."—(*Alford.*) Christ's language here, "Take, eat," is also quite inconsistent with the Romish doctrine that the Lord's Supper is a continuous sacrifice of Christ. "He bids his disciples *take;* and therefore it is he alone that offers. What the papists contrive, as to Christ's offering himself in the Supper, proceeded from an opposite author. And certainly it is a strange inversion, when a mortal man, who is commanded to take the body of Christ, claims the office of offering it; and thus a priest, who has been appointed by himself, sacrifices to God His own Son."—(*Calvin.*)

27. And he took the cup. *After supper* (Luke 22 : 20 ; 1 Cor. 11 : 25). It was, therefore, the third or fourth cup as described above, at the close of the Supper, and after the bitter herbs, the unleavened bread, and the lamb had been eaten. Of the form of the ancient cups we give three illustrations—two of them Egyptian drinking-cups, such as are still used in Egypt ; the other, an ancient Roman wine - cup.—**And gave thanks.** The Communion should be an occasion, as the sacrifice of Christ should be for us an inspiration, of thanksgiving (Psalm 116 : 13 ; Rev. 5 : 6, 9). From the Greek verb here rendered gave thanks (εὐχαριστέω, eucharisteo) comes one of the names frequently given to the ordinance, the Eucharist.—**And gave it to them.** The Romish church in the administration of the Supper, distributes only the bread to the laity, and confines the cup to the priest. The Romish writers do not claim direct Scripture authority for such a distinction, but they assert that the bread is "the body and blood and soul and divinity of Jesus Christ entire," so that there is no necessity for participating in his blood also. They cite Luke 24 : 30 and Acts 2 : 42, in support of the doctrine that participation in the bread alone is sufficient to constitute a full and true communion. Of the direction here, *Drink ye all of it,* they say that the command was given to the apostles only, and therefore applies only to the priests. The argument proves too much. For only the apostles were admitted to the original supper, so that the same reasoning would exclude the laity altogether; and if one kind suffices for the laity, by a parity of reasoning it suffices for the priesthood, and the cup might be abolished entirely.—**Drink ye all of it.** "Why, concerning the bread, did he say simply that they should eat; but, concerning the cup, that all should drink? It is as though he designed to counteract the cunning of Satan" (*Calvin*), *i. e.* by guarding against the error which he foresaw would be subsequently introduced into the church.

28. For this is my blood. See verse 26, note, and below note on Lord's Supper, § 4. Up to this time the blood of bulls and of goats had represented Christ's blood; henceforth the simple wine of this memorial supper should represent it (Hebrews 9 : 13, 14).—**Of the new covenant.** Alford and Tischendorf both omit the word *new* here. But in Luke its presence is undoubted. Therefore, the ordinary reading undoubtedly correctly represents Christ's words.—**Which is**

ROMAN WINE-CUP.　　　EGYPTIAN CUPS.

shed. He speaks by anticipation, but in the present tense, because his passion has already truly begun.—**For many.** In a sense for *all,* in that all may accept and become partakers of the new covenant (Rev. 22 : 17) ; not for all, in that all will not accept nor become partakers (Rev.

22:15). Parallel to the *many* here are the many of Rom. 5:19; Hebrews 9:28, and the great host of Rev. 5:11.—**For the remission of sins.** Not, as James Morison, "a condensed way of expressing remission of the penalty due to sin," but, literally for the remission, *i. e.*, the putting away of sin. The blood of Jesus not only secures pardon (Acts 5:31), but cleanseth from all sin (1 John 1:7). The object of his death is that we may have eternal life (John 3:14-16), and be redeemed from all iniquity (Titus 2:14). Observe Christ's solemn and emphatic endorsement by the very institution of the Lord's Supper, (1) of the O. T. doctrine of sacrifices, *i. e.*, of salvation through the shedding of blood; (2) the N. T. doctrine that the sins of the world are put away by Christ, not merely through the influence of his life, teachings and example, but by *his blood, poured out for a sinful world.* As by the bread he emphasizes the truth that our spiritual life depends on our receiving his spirit into our hearts, so, by the wine, he emphasizes the truth that his covenant or promise of grace depends on the pouring out of his blood, *i. e.*, on him as a sacrifice for our sins (Matt. 20:28; John 12:24, 32, 33; 15:13; Rom. 3:25; 5:6, 8, 10; 1 Cor. 15:3; Hebrews 9:12, 16, 26, 28; 10:10, 19; 1 Pet. 2:24; 1 John 1:7; Rev. 1:5; 5:9). As to the contrast between the Old and New Covenants, see Gal. 4:21-31; Hebrews 8:9-13; 10:16-18, and compare Deut. 28:1; 30:16, with Rom. 7:25; 8:1. But in the O. T. the promise of salvation from sin was, as it is in the N. T., to penitence and faith. See Rom. chap. 4; Isaiah 55:7.

29. This fruit of the vine. This language is used *after the blessing has been pronounced* on the cup, showing evidently that it still contained wine simply, and that the language "This is my blood" is to be interpreted as symbolical.—**Drink it new.** Not drink *new* wine, but drink it anew. (The Greek is not νέον but καινόν.) The new heavens and the new earth shall have a new memorial of God's love in Christ. Observe (1) that the Lord's Supper is a prophecy as well as a parable; has a future as well as a commemorative aspect; looks back to the Passover, forward to the marriage supper of the Lamb; (2) that as the Lord's Supper superseded the Passover, so the heavenly supper will supersede the earthly memorial. Luke (chap. 22:18) reports similar language to that used here; but in connection with the cup before the Supper. Perhaps the words were repeated.

30. And when they had sung an hymn. Literally, *when they had hymned.*—Psalms 113, 114, 115, and 116, were ordinarily chanted at the Jewish Passover; the first two during, the last two at the close of the service. These were probably the Psalms now chanted.—**They went out into the Mount of Olives.** Luke adds, "as he was wont," *i. e.*, during this passion week.

Compare John 8:1. This may have been for solitude simply, or also in part for safety. He went directly to the Garden of Gethsemane. Before going out to the Mount of Olives, Christ uttered a part at least, if not all, of the discourses reported in John, chaps. 14-16, and the prayer in John, chap. 17.

NOTE ON THE LORD'S SUPPER.—Several questions relating to the proper interpretation of the account of the Lord's Supper, as given by the Evangelists, we consider together here. The theological and ecclesiastical questions respecting the proper mode of observance of the rite in our churches of to-day, it does not come within the province of a commentary to discuss, except incidentally.

1. *Time of observance.* There is no doubt that the Lord's Supper was instituted on Thursday evening, the day before the crucifixion. Between that day and the resurrection, which took place on the first day of the week (Matt. 28:1), two full days, Friday and Saturday, intervened. But whether it was observed on the evening of the Passover supper, or on the evening preceding, *i. e.*, whether Thursday or Friday evening was the time observed by the Jewish people as the Passover, is a serious question. This question is of no particular importance, except that the supposed discrepancy between John and the three Synoptic Gospels has been made the occasion of assault on the credibility of the gospel narratives. I shall here state very briefly the difficulty, and what I believe to be the true solution. For a fuller exposition the student is referred to Robinson's *English Harmony of the Gospels*, VIII, §§ 133-158, Intro. note, and Andrews' *Life of Our Lord*, pp. 423-460.

The feast of the Passover properly began on the 15th and lasted to and including the 21st day of Nisan (Numb. 28:17), thus making a feast of seven days. But the Jews calculated their feast days, including the Sabbath, from the sunset of the day preceding. Thus the feast of the Passover strictly began on the evening of the 14th of Nisan. On that day the lamb to be eaten was slain between three and five o'clock in the afternoon, and on the evening of the same day the supper, prescribed in Exod. 12:17-20, was eaten in the various households (Exod. 12:6; Lev. 23:5; Numb. 9:3-5; Deut. 16:6). This was not strictly of a festival character. The unleavened bread, the bitter herbs, the dress and attendant circumstances (Exod. 12:8-11), all reminded the nation of their bitter bondage in Egypt. "It was," says Lightfoot, "a thing rubbing up the remembrance of affliction, rather than denoting gladness and making merry." After this supper, a memorial of the fearful night when the dead lay in every house of Egypt, followed the more joyous festivities which rendered the week one of national rejoicing. The rites which characterized this week are described in Numbers 28 : 18-25, and Lev. 23 : 4-8. There were also introduced by the Jews, subsequent to the institution of the Passover, voluntary offerings, which were called Khagigah or Chagigah. These more joyous offerings were usually presented on the 15th of Nisan, the day succeeding the supper proper. These facts interpret both the difficulty and the solution. The three Synoptists unquestionably represent Christ as eating the true Passover with his disciples. Matthew says that on the first day of the unleavened bread (verse 17) the disciples came to Christ for directions respecting preparations for the Passover, i. e., the Passover supper. Mark and Luke are still more definite. "The first day of unleavened bread when they killed the Passover," says Mark; "when the Passover must be killed" is Luke's language. It would be almost impossible to designate more distinctly the 14th day of Nisan, when the lambs were slain in the temple, to be eaten in the households that same evening. "Philologically considered there cannot be a shadow of doubt but that Matthew, Mark, and Luke intended to express, and do express in the plainest terms, their testimony to the fact that Jesus regularly partook of the ordinary and legal Passover meal on the evening after the 14th of Nisan, at the same time with all the Jews."—(*Robinson*.)

John's Gospel, on the other hand, has been taken to indicate that the meal described by the Synoptists must have been taken before the Passover supper, i. e., on the evening of the 13th of Nisan. And Alford, who offers no explanation of the supposed discrepancy, declares in strong terms that "the narrative of John not only does not sanction but absolutely excludes" the other supposition, i. e., that the Lord's Supper and the paschal supper were contemporaneous. The references in John's Gospel which are supposed to sustain this assertion are the following : John 13 : 1, "Now *before* the feast of the Passover" when Jesus knew that his hour was come; John 18 : 28, "They themselves (the Jews) went not into the judgment hall (on Friday morning, the day of the crucifixion) lest they should be defiled; but that they might eat the Passover;" John 19 : 14, "It was the preparation of the Passover, about the sixth hour," a phrase which occurs in describing the trial before Pilate on Friday forenoon; John 13 : 29, "Buy that we have need of against the feast," words supposed to have been uttered by Christ to Judas during the Lord's Supper, and therefore to indicate that the feast was still future. Referring the reader, for fuller interpretation, to these passages and the notes upon them, it must suffice here to say (1) that while the Synoptists generally mean by "the Passover" (το πασχα) the feast of the paschal lamb, John generally uses the same term to embrace the festivities of the entire week; (2) that John wrote after the destruction of Jerusalem and the end of Judaism as the divine religion, and, therefore, it might be expected that he would write with less precision of language concerning Jewish rites and ceremonials; (3) that if we believe, as I think we have abundant reason for believing, that John wrote with the Synoptists before him, and to supply what they omitted, it is difficult to conceive that he would have left what appears to be a glaring contradiction between his account and theirs, if we assume that by the word "passover" in John 18 : 28, and 19 : 14, he means the paschal supper; (4) that there is no contradiction whatever, if we understand by his use of that term the festivities of the Passover week, which did not, as we have shown, strictly begin until the 15th of Nisan. As to the argument of Alford that the law forbade the Jews departing from their house after the paschal meal before morning (Exod. 12 : 22), whereas Christ and his apostles went out at the close of the supper, the answer is that, in point of fact, this prohibition, even if intended to be observed in the subsequent memorial services, which is doubtful, was in Christ's time no longer observed. As to the argument that, according to Rabbinical law, a trial and execution could not take place on a feast day, the sufficient reply is that many of the rules of the Rabbinical law were violated by the proceedings in the trial and crucifixion of Jesus. I judge, then, with Robinson, that "there is nothing in the language of John, or in the attendant circumstances, which upon fair interpretation requires or permits us to believe, that the beloved disciple either intended to correct or has in fact corrected or contradicted, the explicit and unquestionable testimony of Matthew, Mark, and Luke," and with Andrews, that "there is no discrepancy between the Synoptists and John. The Lord ate the true paschal supper at the appointed time,—the time when it was eaten by the Jews in general, on the evening following the 14th of Nisan," i. e., as we should say, on the evening of the 14th. For an opposite view, see Farrar's *Life of Christ*, Appendix, Excursus X. That the Lord's Supper was partaken on the evening of the Jewish Passover is maintained by Robinson, Andrews, Kitto, Smith, Eddy, Newcome, and apparently Lightfoot ; it is doubted or denied by Pressensé, Milman, Ellicott, Townsend, Alford, Neander, and Farrar.

2. *Relation of the Lord's Supper to the Passover.* The question whether our Lord simply adopted and modified the paschal supper, or at its close instituted a new and independent Christian ordinance, is a matter of debate. It is important only in throwing light on the significance of the ordinance. The paschal supper was a family

rather than a church ordinance, was observed in the home circle, the father administered it, and originally killed the lamb himself, though a later law required the sacrifice to be performed at the temple (Deut. 16 : 1-6). Matthew and Mark in their account of the Lord's Supper both say "As they were eating Jesus took bread" (see ver. 26; Mark 14 : 22). Luke and Paul both say that he took the cup "after supper" or "when he had supped" (Luke 22 : 20; 1 Cor. 11 : 25). Some eminent scholars, among whom may be mentioned Dr. Conant of this country, and Dr. Brown of Scotland, following Calvin, regard the Lord's Supper as entirely separate from the paschal feast and instituted at its close. The more general opinion is that the words "after supper" or "when he had supped" indicate simply that the cup referred to was the third or fourth in the paschal supper, which was taken toward the close of the feast; and that as Jesus adopted but gave new significance to baptism, so he employed the paschal feast, but gave a new meaning to it. This substantially appears to be the view of Lightfoot, Lange, Ellicott, Stanley, Alford, Andrews, and Barnes: and this appears to me the better view. This view is also sustained, indirectly, by Paul's reference to Christ as our Passover in 1 Cor. 5 : 7.

3. *Did Christ intend this Supper as a permanent Church Ordinance?* The language of the Evangelists is not conclusive on this question. His words, "This do in remembrance of me" (Luke 22 : 19; 1 Cor. 11 : 24, 25) might mean simply, Hereafter keep the Passover feast, as long as it is observed, in remembrance not merely of the Jewish national deliverance, but of the new and grander covenant in my blood. The command is not *in words* more specific or significant than the command in John 13 : 14, 15, to wash one another's feet. But the subsequent practice of the apostles (Acts 2 : 42, 46, 20 : 7), and still more the fact that directions for the Lord's Supper were made a matter of special revelation to Paul (1 Cor. 11 : 23), seem to make it clear that Christ intended the ordinance for a perpetual one, and that his apostles so understood it. Whether it was intended to be strictly a *church* ordinance, and confined to members of the visible church, is another question, and one on which the record of its institution throws no light.

4. *Significance of the Lord's Supper.* The Roman Catholic interpreters, taking literally Christ's words, "This is my body," "This is my blood" (verses 26, 28), hold that Christ's sacrifice is a continuous one; that by the blessing of the priest the bread and wine are now converted into the "body and blood and soul of our Lord Jesus Christ;" that hence the consecrated elements "contain Jesus Christ himself, the fountain of all grace, and become, if worthily partaken, the pre-eminent means of grace, ministering to the spiritual nature, and preparing the body for the glorious change of the resurrection of the last day." The objections to this view are, (1) that it violates the fundamental rule of Scripture exegesis, in not taking the words of Jesus Christ in the sense in which they would have been understood by his hearers at the time; (2) it represents the sacrifice of Christ as continuous, while the Scripture declares it to have taken place once for all (Heb. 9 : 28; 10 : 12-18); (3) it represents the need of man to be a participator in Christ's body and blood, whereas what man needs is a participation in Christ's spirit, without which we are none of his (Rom. 8 : 9); (4) it rests on the assertion of a continuous miracle, viz., the change of bread and wine into flesh and blood, while confessedly there is nothing to indicate such a change; the bread is still in appearance and in chemical constitution bread, and the wine is still wine; and thus the very essence is wanting of a true miracle, which is an *external and sensible sign* of a spiritual truth or a divine authority. See note above on verse 26.

In studying the true significance of this supper, note the following facts: (1.) Its simplicity. It is instituted as the disciples are eating; out of the materials of the supper; without a prescribed form or ritual; with no other preparation than love in Christ for his disciples, and in the disciples for Christ. (2.) Historically it is connected with the Passover, which prefigured and interprets it. Thus it memorializes our deliverance from the bondage of sin by the death of Christ, who is our Passover (Rom. 8 : 2; 1 Cor. 5 : 7). (3.) It prophetically points to the future marriage supper of the Lamb (ver. 29; Mark 14 : 25). (4.) The bread and wine enter into and become part of our flesh and blood, and so the support of our life. It is Christ *in us* who is the hope of glory (Rom. 8 : 9; Gal. 2 : 20). (5.) The wheat must be bruised and broken, and the grape crushed and bleeding, before we can eat the bread or drink the wine. It is by the death of Christ that we have life (see above, ver. 28, note; Gal. 3 : 13; 1 Pet. 4 : 1; Rev. 5 : 6). Compare, for Christ's own interpretation of this supper, John 6 : 26-65. Observe especially, in its bearing on transubstantiation, verse 63.

5. *Method and conditions of observance.* These are evidently not to be determined by the *example* of Christ; for the original supper was taken in a private house, an upper chamber, at night, around a table, reclining, women excluded, only the ordained apostles admitted. None of these conditions are maintained to-day by any Christian sect. If the conditions are determined by Christ's *words*, these prescribe no form, give no hint who shall administer, and prescribe no condition of participation but a loving remembrance of Christ himself (Luke 22 : 19; 1 Cor. 11 : 24, 25). And

31 Then saith Jesus unto them, All ye shall be offended because of me this night: for it is written,⁴ I will smite the shepherd, and the sheep of the flock shall be scattered abroad.

32 But after I am risen again,⁵ I will go before you into Galilee.

33 Peter answered and said unto him, Though all men shall be offended because of thee, yet will I never be offended.

34 Jesus said unto him, Verily I say unto thee, That this night, before the cock crow, thou shalt deny me thrice.

35 Peter said unto him, Though I should die with thee, yet will I not deny thee. Likewise also said all the disciples.

---

d Zec. 13 : 7. .... e ch. 28 : 7, 10, 16.

---

with this agrees the words of Paul (1 Cor. 11 : 27–29), where he defines eating unworthily to be eating without "discerning the Lord's body," *i. e.*, as the context shows, like an ordinary supper, and without remembrance of the Lord.

Ch. 26 : 31–35. PROPHECY OF PETER'S DENIAL.—LET HIM THAT STANDETH TAKE HEED LEST HE FALL.

The four Evangelists record Christ's prophecy of Peter's denial; Mark 14 : 27–31; Luke 22 : 31–38; John 13 : 36–38. The prophecy appears to have been twice uttered—once before the supper, of which Luke and John give a report, once after the supper, of which Matthew and Mark give a report. Luke's account must be compared with Matthew's in order to understand Peter's spirit. He had been warned of his danger, and had resented the warning; it is now repeated, but is still resented. The proverb, "Forewarned is forearmed," is true only of watchful souls.

31. Then. After the supper, but not necessarily after they had left the room.—All ye shall be offended. Caused to stumble and fall into sin. Compare Matt. 11 : 6, note. Christ is sometimes a cause of stumbling; and a rock of offence; so the Christian will be at times in the course of duty.—For it is written. The reference is to Zech. 13 : 7, which Henderson translates as follows: "Awake, O sword! against my Shepherd, and against the man who is united to me, saith Jehovah of Hosts; smite the shepherd, and the sheep shall be scattered." The sword is simply an emblem of death by any instrument (Exod. 5 : 21; 2 Sam. 12 : 9 with 2 Sam. 11 : 24). It is therefore an appropriate emblem of the crucifixion. The prophecy itself is difficult; but that it refers to Christ is evident, (*a*) because Christ is the only Shepherd who can be described as "the man who is united to God;" (*b*) because Christ here explicitly applies it to himself.—I will smite the shepherd. Not merely, as Bengel, "God is said to smite Jesus, since he delivered him to be smitten." Throughout the N. T. Christ is represented as offered up by his own Father or by himself, though it is also explicitly declared that he was slain by wicked men (John 3 : 16; Rom. 5 : 8; Heb. 7 : 27; 9 : 14, 28; comp. John 18 : 11; Acts 2 : 23).

32. I will go before you into Galilee. For fulfillment of this prophecy see Matt. 28 : 7; Luke 24 : 7; John, chap. 21. The connection and significance is well given by Quesnel: "The sheep forsake the shepherd, but he forsakes not his sheep."

33. Peter answered, * * * I will never be offended. Christ had previously warned Peter of his peculiar danger: "Satan hath desired to have you, * * * but I have prayed for thee" (Luke 22 : 32), and Peter had resented the idea that he needed the Lord's prayers. Now, when Christ warns all of their danger, Peter should have been the first to heed the admonition, but is the most outspoken in resenting it. His self-confidence has not been weakened by the previous warning; only experience can weaken it. "Where he should have prayed and said, Help us, that we be not cut off, he is confident in himself and saith, 'Though all men should be offended in thee, yet will I never.'"—(*Chrysostom*.)

34. Jesus said unto him. Mark (14 : 30) gives probably his exact words: "Verily (see Matt. 5 : 18, note) I say unto thee, That this day, even in this night, before the cock crow twice, thou shalt deny me thrice." The first cock-crow is at midnight, but inasmuch as few hear it, the cock-crowing is generally put for the *second* crowing, *i. e.*, the early dawn. Matthew's language here, "before the cock crow," is thus equivalent to Mark's "before the cock crow twice;" by both the early dawn is indicated. In fact, the cock was heard to crow twice during the thrice repeated denials of Peter (Mark 14 : 68, 72).—Deny me. Disown me as Master and Lord. Comp. Luke 22 : 34.

35. Peter said unto him, Even if it should bind me to die with thee yet would I not disown thee. His language in the original is stronger than that of our English version.—Likewise also said all the disciples. They were inspired by Peter's enthusiasm, and imbibed his self-confidence.

There is a right Christian confidence, but it rests on the presence and power of the Lord (Phil. 4 : 13; 2 Tim. 1 : 12); and upon a consciousness of personal weakness (2 Cor. 12 : 9, 10). Peter's rested on his own courage and fidelity, and failed him in the hour of trial. "A man's willingness is not sufficient unless he receive succor from above; but, we gain nothing by succor from above, if there be not a willingness on our own part."— (*Chrysostom*.) Comp. Phil. 2 : 12, 13.

36 Then cometh Jesus with them unto a place called Gethsemane, and saith unto the disciples, Sit ye here, while I go and pray yonder.

37 And he took with him Peter and the two sons of Zebedee, and began to be sorrowful and very heavy.

f Mark 14 : 32, etc. ; Luke 22 : 39, etc. ; John 18 : 1, etc.

Ch. 26 : 36–46. CHRIST'S AGONY IN GETHSEMANE.—CHRIST'S NATURE, EXPERIENCE, AND OFFICE ILLUSTRATED; HE TAKES ON HIM NOT MERELY THE APPEARANCE BUT THE REALITY OF MANHOOD; BECOMES A SYMPATHIZING HIGH PRIEST; IS TEMPTED IN ALL POINTS LIKE AS WE ARE YET WITHOUT SIN (Phil. 2 : 7, 8; Hebrews 2 : 16–18; 4 : 15, 16).—CHRIST'S LOVE FOR US ILLUSTRATED; THE AGONY OF GETHSEMANE IS THE AGONY OF A SUFFERING LOVE.—THE SINFULNESS OF SIN ILLUSTRATED; BY THE EXPERIENCE OF HORROR IT PRODUCES IN CHRIST.—THE CHRISTIAN'S CONFLICT ILLUSTRATED; THE BATTLE BETWEEN THE WILLING SPIRIT AND THE WEAK FLESH; THE ARMAMENT, PRAYER; THE VICTORY, CALM ACQUIESCENCE IN THE DIVINE WILL.

This inexplicable experience is recorded by Matthew, Mark (14 : 32–42), and Luke (22 : 39–46). John (18 : 1) mentions going into the garden, but not the agony, an indication that he wrote with the other Evangelists before him, and in part to supply what they had omitted. Luke, alone, (verses 43, 44) mentions the appearance of the angel strengthening Christ and the bloody sweat; otherwise, the three accounts are substantially the same. The verbal differences, especially in their reports of the prayer, are noteworthy and instructive; "Shewing us, even in this solemn instance, the comparative indifference of the letter when we have the inner spirit."—(*Alford.*) Observe the inconsistency of these accounts with the modern mythical theory of the origin of the Gospels. Such a struggle would never

GARDEN OF GETHSEMANE: JERUSALEM IN THE BACKGROUND.

be invented and imputed to the God-man, by his adherents. Even Celsus (2d century) and Julian (4th century) held it up for contempt as an evidence of weakness and fear; and Renan and Schenckel endeavor, in vain, to reconcile it with their conception of the character of Jesus as merely a lofty and noble man.

36. Then; probably about midnight; **cometh Jesus to a place called Gethsemane.** The word is Hebrew, and means *oil-press*.

38 Then saith he unto them, My soul is exceeding sorrowful, even unto death: tarry ye here, and watch with me.

39 And he went a little farther, and fell on his face, and prayed, saying, O my Father, if it be possible, let this cup pass from me! nevertheless, not as I will, but as thou *wilt*.

g Ps. 116 : 3; Is. 53 : 3, 10; John 12 : 27.... h Heb. 5 : 7....i ch. 20 : 22....j John 5 : 30; 6 : 38; Rom. 15 : 3; Phil. 2 : 8.

Wordsworth comments on its significance as an emblem of trial, distress, and agony, and refers to Isaiah 63 : 3; Lam. 1 : 15; Joel 3 : 13. Comp. Rev. 14 : 20. It was a garden, *i. e.*, an orchard, outside of Jerusalem, east of the brook Cedron, on the slope of the Mount of Olives beyond, and was a spot where Christ and his disciples were wont to resort (John 18 : 1; Luke 22 : 39). Its location cannot be identified with certainty. Our illustration shows the traditional site, which is enclosed with a low wall covered with white stucco, and comparatively recently erected. A series of rude pictures are hung along the wall, representing different scenes in Christ's passion. The place is under the control of the Roman Catholic priesthood. If not the genuine garden, which is very doubtful, it is in the same general locality, and the olive-trees are of very great antiquity, and so decayed as to require to be propped up to prevent being blown down by the wind.—**Sit ye here while I go and pray yonder.** Compare the language of Abraham in Genesis 22 : 5, "Abide ye here with the ass, and I and the lad will go yonder and worship." "Jesus, priest and victim, lays himself on the altar, with Abraham's faith and Isaac's resignation."—(*Stier.*)

37. Peter and the two sons of Zebedee. James and John. They had been witnesses of his transfiguration (Matt. 17 : 1) and of one of his greatest miracles (Mark 5 : 37). "Jesus Christ imparts his sorrow and heaviness of heart to those whom he loves the most."—(*Quesnel.*)—**Began to be very sorrowful and dejected.** So great was his sorrow now, that all which he had previously endured was as nothing ; now, as for the first time, he *began* to experience sorrow. Mark says that he was "*sore amazed*," and the original, which is aptly rendered, implies that the disclosure of the sorrow came upon him, if not literally as a surprise, at least with new and unexpected force. Luke (22 : 44) says he was "in an *agony*," *i. e.*, a conflict, for this is the literal meaning of the original. Combining these accounts we have a hint of the elements which entered into this mystical experience. There was a *conflict*, *i. e.*, between his dread of the impending Passion, and his desire to accomplish it. (Luke 12 : 50; John 12 : 27, 28) ; a bitter *sorrow*, the secret of which we may partially conjecture, but is not and cannot be fully interpreted to us ; a *dejection*, produced by the seeming failure of his earthly mission, the rejection of him by his nation, the dullness of spiritual vision, even in his disciples ; and a sense of *surprise* and *horror* in the full and unexpected disclosure made in that hour of the burden he must bear. See LESSONS OF GETHSEMANE below.

38. My soul is exceeding sorrowful, even unto death. A proverbial expression indicating the severity of the suffering. Comp. Jonah 4 : 9. But here it is not hyperbolic. Certainly it is not to be interpreted as Bengel, "Such sorrow might have driven an ordinary man to suicide." The sorrow itself was, if not alleviated, sufficient to cause death ; it brought him to death's door. "Our Lord's whole inmost life must have been one of continual trouble of spirit. He was a man of sorrows and acquainted with grief. But there was an extremity of anguish now, reaching even to the utmost limit of endurance, so that it seemed that more would be death itself."—(*Alford.*) Rather, more *would have caused death*, as is indicated by the bloody sweat produced by what he endured. See Luke 22 : 44, note.—**Tarry ye here and watch with me.** Not because "in the abasement of his humanity he regarded them as some comfort to him." The hunger of the human soul for sympathy and love is not a part of its abasement. It is in the O. T. attributed to God (Jer. 3 : 14; 31 : 20; Ezek. 33 : 11; Hosea 11 : 8) and here to the God-man. In his struggle with the powers of darkness he desired the fellowship of friends.

39. And he went a little further ; about a stone's cast (Luke). The distance would not exceed forty or fifty yards, if so much ; the disciples might therefore catch the leading words of Christ's prayer before drowsiness overpowered them. This separation from his disciples was because he would be alone. "When some great necessity urges us, because the fervor of prayer is more fully indulged when we are alone, it is useful for us to pray apart. And if the Son of God did not disregard this aid, it would be the greatest madness of pride in us not to apply it for our own advantage."—(*Calvin.*)—**And fell on his face.** Mark says, "on the ground ;" Luke says, "he kneeled down."—**And prayed, saying, * * * Let this cup pass from me.** The cup is in the O. T. an emblem both of the mercy (Psalm 23 : 5), and of the wrath (Psalm 75 : 8; Isaiah 51 : 22; Jer. 25 : 15–17; Ezek. 23 : 33) of God ; generally, the latter. The cup which Christ drinks, of sorrow, becomes the cup of our salvation (Psalm 116 : 13; Matt. 26 : 27, 28). To him it is wrath, to us it is mercy.

In studying this prayer of our Lord, compare the accounts in the three Evangelists.

40 And he cometh unto the disciples, and findeth them asleep, and saith unto Peter, What! could ye not watch with me one hour? 41 Watch,ᵏ and pray, that yeˡ enter not into temptation;ᵐ the spiritⁿ indeed *is* willing, but the flesh *is* weak.

k Mark 13 : 33 ; 14 : 38 ; Luke 22 : 40 ; Eph. 6 : 18 ; Rev. 16 : 15....l Pr. 4 : 14, 15...m Rev. 3 : 10....n Is. 25 : 8, 9 ; Rom. 7 : 18–25 ; Gal. 5 : 17.

MATTHEW.	MARK.	LUKE.
Oh my Father, *if it be possible*, let this cup pass from me; nevertheless, not as I will, but as thou wilt.	Abba, Father, *all things are possible* unto thee: *take away* this cup from me; nevertheless, not what I will, but what thou wilt.	Father, *if thou be willing*, remove this cup from me; nevertheless, not my will, but thine be done.

Observe (1) the variation in expression. Matthew says, "If it be possible;" Mark, "All things are possible;" Luke, "If thou be willing." If it was not possible, this was only because God, in his supreme wisdom, did not will to remove the cup, *i. e.*, because the Divine will could not be carried out except by Christ's Passion and death. The spirit of the prayer is seen by combining the accounts thus: Father, all things are possible to thee; if thou canst accomplish thy Divine purposes and let this cup pass from me, remove it. Observe (2) the spirit of the prayer as embodied in all these accounts. (*a.*) Its simplicity and brevity illustrate his own instructions (Matt. 6 : 7, 8). We need not suppose that the report is a verbatim one; but it certainly exhibits the essential character of this prayer. (*b.*) Its trustfulness. In the address Abba, Father, and the expression of confidence in the Father's power, All things are possible unto thee. Nothing depends on Judas, Caiaphas, or Pilate; all on God (comp. verse 53; John 19 : 11). (*c.*) Its earnestness and outspokenness of petition, "Take away this cup." Before his Father he pours forth his desire without hindrance. Comp. Heb. 4 : 16. (*d.*) Its supreme petition. Not as I will, but as thou wilt. This is not merely the language of submission, but of petition; he does not merely say, If not as I will, then as thou wilt, but, Do not what I will, *rather* what thou wilt. *But* (πλην) is an adversative particle signifying a positive preference for the petition which follows. Thus he negatives the erroneous notion of prayer, viz., that it is the means by which the wish of man determines the will of God, "Not as I will;" and teaches the true office of prayer, viz., to change the will human into the will divine. See a sermon by F. W. Robertson on Matt. 26 : 39. The commentators see in this prayer a plain refutation of the Monothelite heresy, which held but one will in the Lord Jesus. "The distinction is clear and marked by our Lord himself. In his *human* soul he willed to be freed from the dreadful things before him; but this human will was overruled by the inner and divine purpose, the will at unity with the Father's will."—(*Alford.*) Similarly Calvin, Ryle, and others. But, in the same sense and to the same extent, the experience of Paul (Rom. 7 : 15–17), and of every Christian, shows two wills. Such metaphysical refinements on Scripture belong not to the spirit of little children, with which we are to receive this and all the mysteries of the kingdom of grace (Matt. 18 : 3). The experience of Christ is to be interpreted, so far as it can be interpreted at all, by our own lesser but analogous conflicts. "It is not inconsistent with the spirit of prayer that Christ here asks a thing that is impossible to be granted to him; for the prayers of believers do not always flow on with uninterrupted measure to the end, do not always maintain a uniform measure, are not always arranged even in a distinct order, but on the contrary are involved and confused, and either oppose each other or stop in the middle of the course, like a vessel stopped by tempests, which, though it advances towards the harbor, cannot always keep a straight and uniform course, as in a calm sea."—(*Calvin.*)

40. And he cometh unto the disciples. That is to the three, Peter, James, and John.—**And findeth them asleep.** "Sleeping for sorrow" (Luke). Observe, they forget sorrow in sleep, Christ conquers it by prayer. Compare with the world's forgetfulness of sorrow the Christian's victory over it, Rom. 5 : 3 ; 8 : 35–39. —**Unto Peter.** Who had just boasted that he would never forsake his Lord, yet forsook him at the very entrance-door of his Passion.—**One hour.** Not to be taken literally. There is nothing definite to indicate the time spent in the garden. Andrews supposes that they reached it about midnight, and the arrest took place between one and two in the morning. Certainly considerable time elapsed between the arrest and daylight.

41. Watch and pray. Observe the double command. Some watch without praying, some pray without watching. Corresponding to this is Paul's direction in Phil. 2 : 12, 13.—**That ye enter not into temptation.** Contrast James 1 : 2, "Count it all joy when ye fall into divers

42 He went away again the second time, and prayed, saying, O my Father, if this cup may not pass away from me, except I drink it, thy will be done.
43 And he came and found them asleep again: for their eyes were heavy.
44 And he left them, and went away again, and prayed the third ᵒ time, saying the same words.

45 Then cometh he to his disciples, and saith unto them, Sleep on now, and take *your* rest; behold, the hour is at hand, and the Son of man is betrayed into the hands of sinners.
46 Rise, let us be **going**: behold, he is at hand that doth betray me.

o 2 Cor. 12 : 8.

temptations." It is a joy to us to be brought involuntarily into circumstances that try our faith, and so give us new disclosures of our Saviour's power and grace; it is a sorrow to us when we enter into temptation voluntarily, and so entertain it with the will. Thus to enter into temptation is to enter into sin.—**The spirit indeed is eager, but the flesh is weak.** The reference is unmistakably to Peter's eager declaration that he was ready to suffer imprisonment and death with Christ (Luke 22 : 33). Thus Christ looks mercifully upon their strong desire, and so pardons their weak performance. It is, however, true that our Lord himself illustrates this saying. "At that moment he was giving as high and pre-eminent example of its truth as the disciples were affording a low and ignoble one. He, in the willingness of the spirit, yielding himself to the Father's will to suffer and die, but weighed down by the weakness of the flesh; they, having professed, and really having, a willing spirit to suffer with him, but, even in the one hour's watching, overcome by the burden of drowsiness."—(*Alford*.) Observe in this contrast the lesson for us. In both Christ and the disciples there is a willing spirit, in both weakness of the flesh. But in Christ the spirit conquers the flesh, and he is victor; in the disciples the flesh conquers the spirit, and they are defeated. "Not every one that saith unto me Lord, Lord," the willing spirit, "but he that doeth the will of my Father," whose flesh obeys the will, "shall enter into the kingdom of heaven" (Matt. 7 : 21).

42. He went away again and prayed the second time. "More earnestly," says Luke, who adds the account of the bloody sweat (Luke 22 : 41, note). Observe the change in the prayer which Mark and Luke do not indicate. The continuance of the trial he accepts as God's answer to the petition, "Let this cup pass from me;" he now asks only, "Thy will be done." The wish to be relieved from the Passion is subdued; the will to fulfill the Father's will is supreme. At what time the angel appeared to him, strengthening him, as described in Luke 22 : 44, is uncertain. I should agree with Alford in placing it after the first prayer, and considering the change in the form of petition, which Matthew alone notes, as due to that gracious interposition. His prayer was heard and answered, as was Paul's (2 Cor. 12 : 8-10).

43, 44. And he left them. Observe that he makes no attempt to arouse them the second time.—**Saying the same words.** Mark uses the same language in describing the second prayer. Matthew's account is, apparently, the most specific of the three. Luke does not mention the third prayer.

45, 46. Sleep on henceforth. Not merely *now*. The language implies that the opportunity for watchful sympathy with the Master has forever passed. He will make no further demands upon their sympathies.—**Rise, let us be going.** The language of the next verse indicates that the Temple officers, with Judas, were already approaching the garden, and the instant arousal of the disciples was essential to their safety. The seeming contradiction of the two directions has given rise to various explanations. The best, because the simplest and most natural, is that which interprets them as the expression of inflections of feeling. The direction to "Sleep on" is uttered in semi-soliloquy, "partly in bitterness, partly in reproach, partly in a kind of irony, partly in sad earnest." The direction, "Rise; let us be going," is a practical command, uttered directly to the disciples, to arouse them to the danger at hand. The one is a gentle reproach for past neglect; the other is a kindling command for the present exigency. The moral significance of the two is admirably drawn out by F. W. Robertson, in a sermon, which embodies them in two sentences: "The irreparable past; the available future."

LESSONS OF GETHSEMANE.—The mystery of Gethsemane is a subject for reverent study, not for full interpretation. No theology can explain Christ's character, no psychology can fathom his experience. No one may enter into the mysteries of his experience of grief; but no one who loves his Lord can pass it by uncontemplated. In studying it, beware of any interpretation which professes to afford a complete explanation. Such interpretations are either extra Scriptural, or anti-Scriptural; they either deny the agony, because it is inconsistent with Christ's divine nature, or belittle it, by explanations inconsistent with the heroism of his human nature. Reverently recognizing the incomprehensible mystery of this agony, we may yet discern in it clearly certain facts and lessons. In deducing them I quote in part from my *Jesus of Nazareth*, chap. 31, where I have endeavored to give a fuller analysis of this experience. (1.) *A real spiritual struggle with temptation is described.* The language of the Evangelists is explicit. Christ is sorrowful, dejected, surprised, in an agony. See verse 37, note. Other incidents in his life indicate analogous though lesser struggles with temptation (Matt. 4 : 1-11, note, p. 40 ; Luke 19 : 50 ; John 12 : 27 ; 16 : 32). The Epistle to the Hebrews, referring unmistakably to this experience, describes it as a real spiritual conflict. Heb. 5 : 7 declares that Christ *suffered* being tempted, *i. e.*, temptation really entered into his soul (Heb. 2 : 18 ; comp. 4 : 15). (2.) *The nature of the conflict is indicated.*—This was not between two wills, the human and the divine; the conception of two wills in one person is not found in Scripture, and is a hypothesis of later theology, to account for the person and experience of Christ. All such extra-Scriptural psychology is to be regarded with distrust. Christ intimates the nature of the conflict as one between the flesh and the spirit, the natural desire to escape the anguish of the Passion, and the higher spiritual purpose to fulfill, at whatever cost, the mission given him by the Father (ver. 41, note). Thus it is partially interpreted by the analogous conflicts in Christian experience. But the contrast between our partial and his perfect victory is noteworthy. See, for examples, the cases of Moses (Exod. 4 : 1-17), Gideon (Judges, chap. 6), Elijah (1 Kings 19 : 1-14), David (Psalms 42, 43, 73, 77, etc.), Jeremiah (1 : 4-10, 11 ; ch. 4, etc.), Jonah (chap. 4), Paul (Rom. 7 : 15-25). (3.) *Some hints of the elements in Christ's agony are given or may be reverently surmised.* (*a.*) Jesus was in the prime of manhood; life was just opening before him; his soul was eager for work, and conscious of rare capability to perform it; his death was the end of all human hope of achievement. (*b.*) Into this one hour was crowded by prevision the combined horrors of the Passion, its cruelty, its shame, its physical torment, its spiritual tortures. "His flesh with all its capacities and apprehensions, was brought at once into immediate and simultaneous contact with every circumstance of horror and pain that awaited him (John 18 : 4); which is never the case with us. Not only are the objects of dread gradually unveiled to our minds, but hope is ever suggesting that things may not be so bad as our fears represent them."—(*Alford.*) (*c.*) To his own anguish was added that of others vicariously borne: his mother's grief, his disciples' dejection and dispersion, the doom of his country (Luke 19 : 41-44), which he had vainly striven to succor and save (Matt. 23 : 37), and the future perils, persecutions, conflicts, and defeats of his church—all seen in instantaneous vision. (*d.*) The torment of unloving hearts added torture—the kiss of Judas, the denial of Peter, the desertion by all the disciples save one, the cry "Crucify him, crucify him," coming from those for whom he died, and all this a prophecy of future betrayals, denials, crucifixions. "He saw the seeming fruitlessness of his sacrifice; he saw his cross despised by some, ignored by many more; he heard the story of his love repeated in a thousand pulpits by cold lips, and falling in a thousand congregations on dull ears." (*e.*) The sense that all was voluntarily borne, might have been easily escaped, might still be escaped. He laid down his own life; no man took it from him (verse 53 ; John 10 : 18). Was he not throwing away a life which duty as well as instinct demanded he should preserve? (*f.*) The Tempter added subtle suggestions of evil, hinted at (John 14 : 30) but unreported. "He who employed in the wilderness all his arts of flattery, employed in the garden all his inconceivable enginery of malice." Such seems to me to be some of the human elements of anguish and conflict which enter into this hour; but they alone do not interpret it. For (4.) *There was an element in that conflict which we can never fully appreciate.* Of this, the later writers, Paul especially, gives some hint, but in language which the heart rather than the reason must interpret (Rom. 8 : 3 ; 2 Cor. 5 : 21 ; Gal. 3 : 13). To Christ "death as the punishment of *sin*, bore a dark and dreadful meaning, inconceivable by any of us, whose inner will is tainted by the love of sin. Psalms 40 : 12 ; 38 : 1-10."—(*Alford.*) "To see as in the revelation of an instantaneous vision the dark deeds and darker thoughts of generations past and generations yet to come ; to turn from the setting sun of the past to the rising sun of the future, and alike in the night and in the morning horizon of history see only written the deep damnation of a lost world ; and then to feel the dark pall of this accursed load settling strangely down upon the soul—a soul whose divine purity trembled with unutterable horror at the lightest thought of sin—this, infinitely more than human experience, is incapable of any other interpretation than that which it receives from the superhuman agony of him who, for our own sakes, endured it." (5.) *The method of Christ's conflict and the secret of his victory.* By his experience he explains and qualifies his teaching: "Sufficient for the day is the evil thereof." He looks intently and courageously on the future; he summons all his powers to consider it and equip himself for it; he pours forth in full freedom of prayer his wish, "Let this cup pass from me;" he compels that wish to yield to the supreme purpose of his life, "Thy will be done;" and he receives the gracious answer by the presence of the angel strengthening him to do that will (Luke 22 : 43; comp. Heb. 5 : 7). (6.) *The completeness of Christ's victory.* He did not cease the struggle until he had conquered; once ended it was never renewed. In all the terrible scenes of the Passion which ensued, he never wavered, hesitated, faltered, or showed signs

47 And while he yet spake, lo, Judas, one of the twelve, came, and with him a great multitude, with swords and staves, from the chief priests and elders of the people.

48 Now he that betrayed him gave them a sign, saying, Whomsoever I shall kiss, that same is he; hold him fast.

49 And forthwith he came to Jesus, and said, Hail, Master; and kissed him.

p Acts 1 : 16. ...q Ps. 28 : 12. ...r 2 Sam. 3 : 27 ; 20 : 9 ; Ps. 28 : 3.

of fear. At the last he not only endured the cross, but despised the shame (Heb. 12 : 2). For a fuller study of the spiritual significance of Gethsemane I may refer the reader to Abbott's *Jesus of Nazareth*, from which I have quoted in this paragraph.

Ch. 26 : 47-56. BETRAYAL AND ARREST OF JESUS.—CHRIST INTERPRETS AND EXEMPLIFIES HIS OWN TEACHING; OF NON-RESISTANCE TO VIOLENCE (Matt. 5 : 39-41); OF LOVE TO ENEMIES (Matt. 5 : 44); OF CHEERFUL FULFILMENT OF THE DIVINE WILL (Matt. 6 : 10; 7 : 21; 12 : 50).

The arrest of Jesus is described by the four Evangelists, Mark 14 : 43-52 ; Luke 22 : 47-53 ; John 18 : 2-12. Matthew and John were eye-witnesses; Mark is thought to have derived much of his information from Peter ; Luke's account is briefer than the others. John alone mentions the falling of the guard to the ground. Here, as throughout his Gospel, there are evidences that he wrote to supply what the other Evangelists omitted. The witnesses of this event had just been aroused from sleep; their eyes were still heavy ; they were surprised, terrified, confused ; the discrepancies in their accounts are those of independent narrators ; they are not irreconcilable, but the exact order of events narrated is somewhat hypothetical. I think it to have been substantially as follows : Christ's prayer is broken in upon by the tramp of the approaching guard, and the gleaming of their lights as they issue from the gate of the city; their approach, observed across the intervening brook Cedron, he interprets as God's final answer to his prayer—it is the divine will that he should drink the bitter cup. He proceeds to the entrance of the garden and arouses his disciples (ver. 46); Judas, who leads the band, draws near to kiss Jesus according to the pre-arranged signal; is abashed by the Lord's reproachful question, "Betrayest thou the Son of man with a kiss ?" and makes no reply (ver. 49, 50; Luke 22 : 48); the band share his confusion, and under the influence of the superhuman majesty of our Lord, fall backward (John 18 : 4-6) ; the disciples emboldened, ask permission to resist (Luke 22 : 49); and Peter, more impetuous than the rest, does not wait for an answer, but initiates the attack (ver. 51; John 18 : 10) ; Christ rebukes him (ver. 52-54) ; heals the wounded servant (Luke 22 : 51) ; and demands of the officers that they let the disciples go their way (John 18 : 8) ; the disciples, forbidden to resist, interpret this as a hint to escape,

and flee (ver. 56) ; at the same time the officers, who have recovered from their momentary awe, proceed to bind Jesus (John 18 : 12), disregarding his dignified remonstrance against being treated as a thief (ver. 55). For a full understanding of all the elements in this midnight scene all the accounts should be carefully compared, but especially Matthew and John. See notes here and on John.

47. And while he yet spake. He had barely time to arouse the disciples before Judas arrived ; not improbably their arrival awakened the eight, who were sleeping at or near the entrance to the garden.—**Judas, one of the twelve, came.** There is a solemn significance in the fact that the three Synoptists all note that the betrayer was "one of the twelve." John (18 : 1) explains Judas' knowledge of Christ's retreat.—**And with him a great multitude.** A comparison of the various accounts shows the composition of this multitude. There were, (1) a police force from the temple. They are called in John 18 : 3, "officers from the chief priests and Pharisees," in Luke 22 : 52, "captains of the Temple." These were a portion of the Temple police, a strictly Jewish force, composed of Levites, and frequently referred to both in O. T. and N. T. history (2 Kings 11 : 9 ; John 7 : 32 ; Acts 4 : 1-3). These were all armed with "staves," answering to the modern policeman's baton ; (2) a Roman force, furnished probably at the request of the Sanhedrim, by the Roman authorities. This is the "band" referred to in John 18 : 3-12. They were armed with a peculiar short sword, one-edged, defined here and in Mark as a *machæra* (μάχαιρα). Our illustration, from an engraved gem, indicates its probable character ; (3) ser-

THE MACHÆRA.

vants of the high-priest (ver. 51), who accompanied the band, perhaps to assist in the arrest, perhaps merely led by curiosity and that contagion of malice which induced their subsequent persecution of Jesus (ver. 67 ; Mark 14 : 65) ; (4) certain of the priests and elders in person, to make sure of the consummation of the arrest (Luke 22 : 52). The force was provided with lanterns and torches (John 18 : 3, note) to search in any dark places in the garden. Judas preceded the guard (Luke 22 : 47).—

50 And Jesus said unto him,ᵃ Friend, wherefore art thou come? Then came they and laid hands on Jesus, and took him.
51 And, behold, one of them which were with Jesus stretched out *his* hand, and drew his sword, and struck a servant of the high priest's, and smote off his ear.
52 Then said Jesus unto him, Put up again thy sword into his place: for* all they that take the sword, shall perish with the sword.
53 Thinkest thou that I cannot now pray to my Father, and he shall presently give me more than twelve legions of ⁿ angels?
54 But how then shall the scriptures be fulfilled, that ᵛ thus it must be?

a Ps. 41:9; 55:13.... *i* Gen. 9:6; Ezek. 35:15, 6; Rev. 13:10.... *n* ch. 4:11; 2 Kings 6:17; Dan. 7:9.... *v* Luke 24:26, 46

From the chief priests and elders. Mark adds "the scribes." Probably by this description is intended the Sanhedrim, the chief judicial and legislative body of the Jews (see Prel. Note, p. 258.), though their act, in planning and ordering the arrest, may have been informal and unofficial. Comp. John 7:50, 51, where Nicodemus protests against a similar course of action, as illegal.

48, 49. Gave them a sign. That is, had given them the sign previously. It was necessary, inasmuch as in the darkness Christ might be confounded, by the officers, with the disciples. The whole account indicates anxiety lest he should escape as he had done before (John 7:45, 46; 8:59; 10:39).—**Hold him fast.** Mark (14:44, note) says, "Lead him away securely." This fear of a rescue affords a singular evidence of the moral incapacity of Judas to understand the character of Jesus. The guards evidently shared his apprehensions or they would not have bound Jesus. But it is not so strange as the misapprehension of the eleven, who actually asked permission to attempt such a rescue (Luke 22:49).

49, 50. Hail, Rabbi; and kissed him. The kiss was a customary salutation amongst near relatives and friends, both in patriarchal and later times. (Gen. 27:26, 27; 29:11, 13; 33:4; 45:15; Exod. 4:27; 2 Sam. 15:5; 19:39; Rom. 16:16; 2 Cor. 13:12; 1 Thess. 5:26; 1 Pet. 5:14). The treacherous kiss of Judas recalls that of Joab (2 Sam. 20:8, 10).—**Comrade.** Not *"friend."* (ἑταῖρε not φίλος.) Christ never sacrificed *truth* to courtesy or conventionalism. This word, mistranslated "friend," occurs in the N. T. only here and in Matt. 20:13; 22:12; it conveys reproach.—**Wherefore art thou come?** This is not asked for information, but as an appeal to the conscience of Judas. He replies with the treacherous kiss. Christ responds with a final appeal, "Judas, betrayest thou the Son of man with a kiss?" (Mark), but receives no answer. These are his last words to the apostate disciple. The incident recorded by John 18:4-9, I regard as occurring after this conference with Judas, who was in advance of the rest, and before the final seizure of Jesus by the band.

51. One of them which were with Jesus. Mark's language is still more indefinite; he says a "by-stander." John alone gives the name of the assailant, Peter, and of the assailed, Malchus. The hypothesis is reasonable that the other Evangelists concealed the names, in order not to involve their co-disciple in danger from the Jewish authorities. John did not write until after the destruction of Jerusalem, when the Jewish authorities had no longer power to avenge this assault. We may reasonably surmise that Malchus was one of the foremost to lay hands on Jesus, and that Peter aimed the blow at his head, but was too impetuous to be sure-aimed. Christ healed the wound inflicted (Luke 22:51). Before this assault some of the disciples asked permission to resist (Luke 22:49), but Peter did not wait for the Lord's answer. The sword (μάχαιρα, *machœra*) was the short one-edged sword of which we have given an illustration above.

52-54. Peculiar to Matthew. Parallel to these verses is John 18:11; "Put up thy sword into his sheath: the cup which my Father hath given me, shall I not drink it?" Observe, the sword is Peter's, not his Lord's; *thy* sword, not mine; and the place of the Christian's sword is its sheath, from which he may draw it only at the divine command.—**All they that take the sword shall perish with the sword.**—Not a command, as Alford interprets it; so rendered it is self-contradictory, and would even justify Peter, who meant that Malchus, who had taken the sword of injustice, should perish by the sword of a just resistance and retribution; not an unqualified and absolute assertion, for it is not true of all, and the right to bear and use the sword is elsewhere distinctly recognized in the N. T. (Rom. 13:4); but the statement of a general law, that violence begets violence, and that those who are most ready to resort to physical force for self-protection, are the most liable to suffer from it, while non-resistants are the least sufferers, a truth abundantly illustrated by the history of the Friends.—**Twelve legions of angels.** One each for Christ and the eleven. A legion, in the Roman army organization, consisted of 6000. Compare Christ's declaration here with John 10:18 and with the language of his prayer in Gethsemane. The choice was still open to him to escape the Passion, to conquer his foes by force. But so he could not become the conquerer of the world by the patience of love. His submission was not a passive acquiescence in the inevitable, but a supreme choice to fulfill the Father's mission in the Father's way.—**But how then shall the Scriptures be ful-**

55 In that same hour said Jesus to the multitudes, Are ye come out, as against a thief, with swords and staves for to take me? I sat daily with you teaching in the temple, and ye laid no hold on me.

56 But all this was done, that the scriptures *w* of the prophets might be fulfilled. Then all the disciples forsook him, and fled.

w Gen. 3 : 15; Ps. 22 : 1, etc.; 69 : 1, etc.; Isa. 53 : 3, etc.; Lam. 4 : 20; Dan. 9 : 24, 26; Zech. 13 : 7; Acts 1 : 16.

filled? That is, How shall the divine will be fulfilled? for the Scriptures are the reflection of that will, and they had clearly disclosed that the world was to be conquered, not by irresistible might, but by suffering love (Isaiah ch. 53). The act of Peter exemplifies the folly of misdirected zeal. It was the only circumstance which could give any color to the charges afterward brought by the priests against Jesus before Pilate (Luke 23 : 2, 5). Peter carries out in action the spirit which Christ had before rebuked in him (Matt. 16 : 22, 23) and in his co-disciples James and John (Luke 9 : 54–56).

55. Are ye come out as against a thief? Judas had cautioned the guard to lead Jesus away securely (Mark 14 : 44), and when they finally arrested him they bound him (John 18 : 12). This indignity, it appears to me, probably called forth the remonstrance of this verse. Compare the language of Luke 22 : 52, 53.—**I sat daily with you teaching in the Temple.** The offence with which he was charged was one of teaching, not of robbery or violence; it was open, public, unconcealed, and the time to arrest him was the time of his teaching; he had neither hid himself nor surrounded himself with his followers for self-protection; the indignity of this midnight arrest was, therefore, gratuitous.

56. That the writings of the prophets might be fulfilled. Whether these words were uttered by Christ or added by Matthew, is uncertain. The fact that they are found subsequently in Mark's account renders the former hypothesis preferable. For prophecies referred to, consult marg. ref.—**And they all forsook him and fled.** But Peter, and probably John, only for a little way. Finding they were not pursued, they turned and followed the band to the high priest's house (John 18 : 15).

Ch. 26 : 57–68. TRIAL OF JESUS BEFORE CAIAPHAS AND THE COUNCIL.—WICKED ENDS BEGET WICKED INSTRUMENTS.—CHRIST SOUGHT MAN'S LIFE; MAN SOUGHT CHRIST'S DEATH.—THE COMMON CAUSE OF SLANDER (ver. 61, with John 2 : 19, 21).—THE BEST ANSWER TO SLANDER—SILENCE (ver. 63).—CHRIST'S SOLEMN TESTIMONY TO HIS OWN DIVINE NATURE AND MISSION (ver. 64).—" DESPISED AND REJECTED OF MEN " (ver. 67, 68).

PRELIMINARY NOTE.—*Harmony of the narratives.* The N. T. certainly records three, possibly four, distinct judicial or quasi-judicial examinations of Jesus prior to his crucifixion. The contrast in the four Gospel narratives appears from the following tabular view. Matthew and Mark differ only verbally.

Matt. 26 : 57 to 27 : 2. Mark 14 : 53 to 15 : 1.	Luke 22 : 54–71.	John 18 : 13–27.
Jesus is led to Caiaphas' palace, the council assembles, witnesses are summoned, a trial proceeds, Jesus is convicted, the denial of Peter occurs, whether at the same time and place is not clear, the conviction is followed by insults and buffetings, and by a second council (27 : 1) to insure the execution of the sentence pronounced; thence Jesus is led away to Pilate.	Jesus is led to the high priest's palace, Peter denies him, he is insulted and buffeted, but no formal trial is reported until at daybreak the Sanhedrim is assembled, and Christ is led to it; the trial takes place, he is convicted and at once conducted to Pilate (23 : 1).	Jesus is taken to the house of Annas, a preliminary examination ensues, whether at the house of Annas or Caiaphas is not clear; during this preliminary examination, the denial by Peter takes place, and thence Christ is led to Pilate. There is no report of a formal trial by the Sanhedrim.

It is evident from a comparison of these reports that with our imperfect knowledge we cannot be certain as to the order of the events described, and equally evident that there is no necessary or irreconcilable inconsistency. Some scholars suppose that the examination reported in John 18 : 19–23 took place before Annas, was followed by an informal trial in the palace of Caiaphas (Matt. 26 : 57–54), succeeded by a formal trial at daybreak (27 : 1), the latter being described by Luke (22 : 66–71); others suppose that Jesus was sent at once from Annas to Caiaphas, that the preliminary examination described in John took place in the palace of Caiaphas while the Sanhedrim was assembling, was followed by a second examination before the Council reported by Matthew, which was in turn succeeded by a formal trial and sentence hinted at in Matthew 27 : 1, but more fully reported in Luke 21:66-71; still others suppose, and this appears to me the more natural and probable supposition, that Matthew, Mark and Luke report, though in a different form, the same proceedings, and that the real order of events was probably substantially as follows: Christ was first led to the house of Annas, the leading spirit of the priestly party; thence *at once* to the house of Caiaphas, where the examination described by John took place, and the denial by Peter, recorded by all the Evangelists; meanwhile the Sanhedrim had assembled, and the formal trial was had as described by Matthew, Mark and Luke, though whether in the palace of Caiaphas or the council-chamber adjoining the Temple (Luke 22:66, note) is uncertain, as is also the question whether the buffetings and insults took place after the formal condemnation as implied by Matthew, or during the preliminary examination as implied by Luke, or twice. According to this view the meeting of the Sanhedrim referred to in Matthew 27:1, was not a trial but a private conference to determine on the necessary measures to secure the execution of the death sentence agreed upon. The reasons for this opinion will partly appear in the notes hereafter. See especially on ver. 59; ch. 27:1; Luke 22:67-70; John 18:24.

The trial. The court convened to try Jesus Christ was the Sanhedrim or Sanhedrin. The origin of this assembly is traced in the Mishna to the seventy elders whom Moses associated with him in the government of Israel (Numb. 11:16), but this is doubtful. It is now more generally thought to have arisen subsequent to the Macedonian supremacy in Palestine. It consisted of chief priests; that is, the heads of the twenty-four priestly classes; scribes, that is, rabbis learned in the literature of the church; and elders, who were chosen from amongst the most influential of the laity. Hence a common designation in the N. T. is "chief priests and scribes," or "elders and chief priests and scribes," or "chief priests and elders" (Matt 2:4; 16:21; 27:1). Jewish tradition puts the number of members at seventy-one. The high priest usually presided; the vice-president sat at his right hand. The other councillors were ranged in front of these two in the form of a semicircle. Two scribes or clerks attended, who on criminal trials registered the votes, one for acquittal, the other for condemnation. The *place* in which the sessions of the Sanhedrim were ordinarily held was, according to the Talmud, a hall called *Gazzith*, supposed to have been situated in the south-east corner of one of the courts near the Temple building. The language of Luke (22:66, note) indicates that the trial of Jesus was held in this council-chamber. The Sanhedrim had lawful and exclusive jurisdiction in all cases where capital punishment could be inflicted, although the power of inflicting capital punishment had been taken from them by the Romans (John 18:31, note). If, as I suppose, this trial took place after Peter's denial, the hour is fixed by the cock crowing at about four o'clock; the day Friday, April 7, A.D. 30.

Methods of procedure. The Jewish methods of judicial procedure are fully given in the Rabbinical books. Their rules constitute an elaborate and on the whole a merciful code. The court could not be convened by night; the accused could not be condemned on his own confession; two witnesses were necessary to secure sentence of death; these witnesses must be examined in the presence of the accused; he had the opportunity of cross-examination; a perjurer was liable to the penalty which would have been visited in case of conviction upon the prisoner; the latter had a right to be heard in his own defence; a verdict could not be rendered on the same day as the trial, nor on a feast-day; the discovery of new evidence, even after the preparations for execution had commenced, entitled the condemned to a new hearing. These rules were utterly disregarded in this trial. The letter of the law forbidding night trials was observed (Luke 22:66), but its spirit was violated by a midnight examination and a hasty trial in the twilight of the dawn. A quorum of the court was present, but it was convened with haste so great, and with notice so inadequate, that one at least of the most influential friends of Jesus had apparently no opportunity to participate in its deliberations (Luke 23:51; 22:70, and Mark 14:64). Witnesses were summoned, and discrepancies in their testimony were noted; but the just and reasonable rule requiring the concurrent testimony of two was openly and almost contemptuously disregarded. An opportunity was formally offered Jesus to be heard in his own behalf, but no adequate time was afforded him to secure witnesses or prepare for his defence, and the spirit of the court denied him audience, though its formal rules permitted him a hearing. Finally, all other means of securing his conviction having failed, in violation alike of law and justice, he was put under oath and required, in defiance of his protest, to bear testimony against himself. The law requiring a day's deliberation was openly set aside, and with haste as unseemly as it was illegal, the prisoner was sentenced and executed within less than twelve hours after his arrest, within less than six after the formal trial.

The sentence and its significance. The crime of which Jesus Christ was accused and found guilty, and for which he was sentenced to death by the Sanhedrim, was blasphemy (see ver. 65. Comp. John 19:7). This was a well recognized and clearly defined crime among the Jews. It con-

57 And ˣ they that had laid hold on Jesus led *him* away to Caiaphas the high priest, where the scribes and the elders were assembled.

58 But Peter followed him afar off, unto the high priest's palace, and went in, and sat with the servants, to see the end.

59 Now the chief priests, and elders, and all the council, sought false witness against Jesus, to put him to death:

60 But found none: yea, though many false witnesses came, *yet* found they none. At the ʸ last came two false witnesses,

x Mark 14 : 53, etc. ; Luke 22 : 54, etc. ; John 18 : 12, etc. . . . y Ps. 27 : 12 ; 35 : 11.

sisted of any act which tended to turn the **hearts** of the people from Jehovah, who was both their God and their King. This was not only irreligion, but treason, and was punishable with death (Exod. 22 : 20; Numb. 25 : 1–5; Deut. 13 : 1–5; 18 : 9–20; see Matt. 12 : 32, note). Illustrations of this crime and its fruits are afforded by Numbers 16 : 1–40; 1 Kings 18 : 17–40. Jesus was accused of blasphemy because he had proclaimed himself to be equal with God, and had claimed and received divine honors. To this accusation there were but two possible defences; one that he had made no such claim, the other that he was indeed the Jehovah of the O. T. manifested in the flesh, and being a new revelation, the supplement and completion of the old. On this trial he took the latter course. Put under oath, called on to declare in the most solemn manner his position and claims, he asserted that the charge that he had proclaimed himself the Son of God was true, and that the assertion itself was true. Thus his declaration (ver. 64, note) of his Divine Sonship constitutes Christ's solemn testimony to himself, uttered at the momentous crisis of his life, under the solemn sanction of an oath, in the course of judicial proceedings, in the presence of the highest council of the realm, in the far more sacred presence of God and his recording angels, at the peril of his life, and with a clear comprehension of the meaning which not only priests and people would attach to it, but with which it would be forever invested by humanity. If it had not been true it would have been blasphemy. "It is not easy," says one of America's most distinguished jurists, Prof. Greenleaf, "to conceive on what ground his (Christ's) conduct could have been defended before any tribunal, except upon that of his superhuman character. No lawyer, it is conceived, would think of placing his defence upon any other basis." See, for a fuller description of the trial and a fuller statement of this question and the Scripture passages bearing upon it, Abbott's *Jesus of Nazareth*, chaps. 33, 35.

57. Led him away to Caiaphas. First, however, to Annas, by whom he was sent to Caiaphas (John 18 : 13, 24). He was the son-in-law of Annas, was appointed high-priest by the Roman Procurator about 27 A. D., held the office during the whole administration of Pilate, was deposed 36 or 37 A. D. He had predetermined the death of Jesus (John 11 : 50). Both Annas and Caiaphas were creatures of the Roman court; both belonged to the Sadducaic party; both, that is, were openly infidel concerning some of the fundamental truths of the Hebrew faith.—**Were assembled.** In preparation for the trial. They had planned the arrest (Matt. 26 : 3–5, 14, 15), and had furnished the temple guard to consummate it (John 18 : 3).

58. Peter followed him afar off. This has been the text for many a denunciation of Peter; but he could not have followed in any other way. His fault, if any, was for following at all.—**Unto the courtyard of the high-priest.** Not the *palace*, but the open courtyard around which the palace was built (ver. 69, note).—**To see the end,** *i. e.*, what the end would be. Curiosity, not devotion, led him into danger.

59. All the council. This seems to indicate that Matthew is describing a meeting of the entire Sanhedrim, and hence probably the formal and official trial of Jesus. If so, the preliminary examination before Caiaphas, and Peter's accompanying denial of his Master (John 18 : 15–27), took place between ver. 58 and 59 here, and Matthew goes back from his description of the trial to describe subsequently, and out of its chronological order, Peter's denials (ver. 69–75).—**To put him to death.** Not to ascertain the truth, but to destroy one whom they considered a personal enemy, was this trial conducted (John 5 : 18 ; 7 : 19, 25 ; 8 : 37, 40 ; 11 : 50).

60. But found none. That agreed together. Two witnesses were required by Jewish law for conviction (Deut. 19 : 15; John 8 : 17 ; 2 Cor. 13 : 1). The charge against Jesus of declaring himself the Son of God and so making himself equal with God (John 10 : 33) was one which it was impossible to substantiate by any witnesses outside the immediate circle of Christ's disciples, for his ministry had been one of singularly commingled boldness and caution—boldness in the truths he uttered, caution in the methods of his utterance. He never publicly proclaimed himself the Messiah. He forbade the evil spirits from announcing his character (Mark 1 : 34). He received the confession of his disciples, but refused to permit them to repeat it to others (Matt. 16 : 20). Interrogated by the Jews whether he was the Christ, he had refused a direct reply, and had referred them to his works (John 10 : 24, 25, note). He had given the same response to the public questioning of John's disciples. In most of his later ministry

61 And said, This *fellow* said,ᵃ I am able to destroy the temple of God, and to build it in three days.
62 And the high priest arose, and said unto him, Answerest thou nothing? What *is it which* these witness against thee?
63 But⁴ Jesus held his peace. And the high priest answered and said unto him, I adjureᵃ thee by the living God, that thou tell us whether thou be the Christ,ᶜ the Son of God.
64 Jesus saith unto him, Thou hast said; nevertheless I say unto you, Hereafterᵈ shall ye see the Son of man sitting on the right handᵉ of power, and coming in the clouds of heaven.

ᵃ John 2 : 19-21....a chap. 27 : 12, 14; Isa. 53 : 7....b 1 Sam. 14 : 25, 28; 1 Kings 22 : 16....c chap. 16 : 16; John 1 : 34....d Dan. 7 : 13; John 1 : 51; 1 Thess. 4 : 16; Rev. 1 : 7....e Ps. 110 : 1; Acts 7 : 55.

---

he had veiled his meaning in parables, which revealed the truth to honest inquirers, but hid it from his foes. "Probably no two witnesses could be found out of the ranks of the disciples who had ever heard out of his own lips an avowal of his Messiahship." (Andrew's *Life of Christ*, p. 501.) In John 4 : 26 and 9 : 37, the declaration of his Messiahship was made to docile believers if not to actual followers.

61. **I am able to destroy the Temple of God**, etc. Observe in reference to this charge, (1) that Christ had not said so, he had said (John 2:19) that the Jews would destroy the temple, which he would restore; (2) that they understood, at least partially, that he had referred to his own body (Matt. 27 : 40, 63); (3) that in their testimony these false-witnesses did not agree (Mark 14 : 59); the nature of their discrepancy is, perhaps, indicated by the variations in the testimony as reported by Matthew and Mark; (4) even if he had used the words attributed to him they would have formed no ground for a death-sentence. The charge illustrates the growth of calumny. "False evidence takes up some truth; and a great calumny can often be made by no great change of words."—(*Bengel.*) Observe, too, that Scripture imputes falsehood to those who pervert the truth as well as to those who invent a lie.

62, 63. **And the high-priest arose.** Angered by the failure of the prosecution and by the stinging rebuke of Christ's silence. By that silence he eloquently condemned the prejudice of the court and declared his own conviction of the uselessness of defending himself before it.—**Jesus held his peace.** The best answer to wilful calumny is ordinarily silence.—**I adjure thee by the living God.** An ordinary formula of administering an oath. (*See* Gen. 24 : 3, John's Bib. Archæology.) By this act, therefore, the high-priest put Christ under oath to testify concerning his own claim and character. The high-priest's action was illegal, since by Rabbinical laws the accused could not be condemned on his own confession. Comparing Luke's account (22 : 67-71) it appears that Christ first protested against the illegality, that his protest was overborne by a clamorous demand from all the members of the court, and that to this demand Christ acceded by giving the testimony recorded in the following verse. Thus he literally fulfilled his declaration, "I lay down my life; no man taketh it from me, but I lay it down of myself" (John 10 : 17, 18.)—**The Messiah, the Son of God.** These phrases are not used by the high-priest as synonymous. In Luke's account they are represented as embodied in two questions (Luke 22 : 67, 70). The O. T. prophets indicate that the Messiah was to be in a peculiar sense the Son of God (Psalm 2 : 7; 45 : 6, 7; Isaiah 7 : 14; 9 : 6; Micah 5 : 2). But it is clear from Jewish Rabbinical writings, from the treatment accorded to Jesus, and from the ready facility with which false Christs were at this time and a little later received by the Jews, that they did not generally believe that their Messiah would be other than a great prophet and a king, coming to achieve victory for the nation. The demand of the high-priest here is, therefore, twofold. He asks: Dost thou claim to be the Messiah? Dost thou claim to be the Son of God? To both questions Christ replies, using language singularly explicit in defining the sense in which he claims to be the Son of God. The language of the succeeding verse utterly forbids our interpreting this phrase when applied to Christ as parallel to its use when applied to ourselves, *e. g.*, 1 John 3 : 1.

64. **Thou hast said.** A Jewish form of affirmation equivalent to "I am" (Mark 14 : 62). It is found also in ordinary Greek; *e. g.*, "Thou thyself, said he, sayest this, Oh Socrates" (*Xenophon's Memorabilia*, Book III.) A simple assent to the question in the case of the Jewish oath sufficed (see Numb. 5 : 22). Christ, however, adds a solemn declaration of his future coming as a divine Judge. —**Nevertheless.** Rather, *more than that* (πλήν), *i. e.*, not only am I the Messiah and the Son of God, but I shall come hereafter to judge the world.—**Hereafter.** Literally *henceforth*, *i. e.*, from this time forward, including also, the far future. The time of Christ's humiliation draws to its end, and with his resurrection commences his era of glory and power, consummated at the judgment-day (1 Cor. 15 : 24-28).—**The Son of Man.** A common appellation of the Messiah, borrowed by Christ from Daniel and used by him to designate himself (see Matt. 10 : 23, note).—**On the right hand of power.** Equivalent to "power of God" (Luke 22 : 69). "The Hebrews often called God, Power."—(*Bengel.*) Comp. Psalm 110 : 1. —**And coming in the clouds of heaven.** For judgment (Matt. 25 : 31; John 5 : 27). Observe the contrast in this verse between the present and

CH. XXVI.]　　　　　　　　MATTHEW.　　　　　　　　301

65 Then the high priest rent his clothes, saying, He hath spoken blasphemy; what further need have we of witnesses? behold, now ye have heard his blasphemy.
66 What think ye? They answered and said, He is guilty of death.ᶠ

67 Thenᵍ did they spit in his face, and buffeted him; and others smote *him* with the palms of their hands,
68 Saying, Prophesy unto us, thou Christ, Who is he that smote thee?

f Lev. 24 : 16 ; John 19 : 7. . . . g Isa. 50 : 6.

the future. They now sitting to judge him, he will then sit to judge them; they are now strong and he apparently weak, then he will sit on the right hand of power and they will call in vain on the mountains and rocks to hide them (Rev. 6 : 16). "As the Passion advances, its amazing *contrasts* grow in affecting interest. The Deliverer in bonds; the Judge attainted; the Prince of Glory scorned; the Holy One condemned for sin; the Son of God as a blasphemer; the Resurrection and the Life sentenced to die. The Eternal High-Priest is condemned by the high-priest of that year."—(*Stier.*) On the significance of Christ's testimony here to himself, see Prel. Note.

65. **Then the high-priest rent his clothes.** This was a common Jewish sign of grief. Of rending clothes at hearing blasphemy, see an illustration in 2 Kings 18 : 37; 19 : 1. Lightfoot quotes from the Rabbinical books the rule "when witnesses speak out the blasphemy which they heard, then all, hearing the blasphemy, are bound to rend their clothes." The rending of clothes was ordinarily forbidden to the high-priest (Lev. 10 : 6), but the prohibition probably applied only to private mourning. His act here may have been a natural expression of abhorrence at what he sincerely regarded as language of blasphemy. More probably it was a simulated and theatrical expression for the purpose of producing an effect upon the court.—**He hath spoken blasphemy.** By claiming to be the Son of God. On the nature of blasphemy under the Jewish law, see Prel. Note and ref. there.—**He is liable to death.** The Jewish law made it a capital offence to turn the people away from allegiance to the true God (Deut. 13 : 1-5). Of this Christ was accused, and for this condemned to die (John 19 : 7). In fact, however, the doctrine of the divinity of Christ has not weakened but strengthened the allegiance of the human race to the Father (John 14 : 6 ; Phil. 2 : 11). Quesnel's practical commentary on this sentence is noteworthy. "The Author of Life, and Life eternal itself, is then judged worthy of death; and can we complain after this of the injustice of human judgments as to ourselves?"

67, 68. **Buffeted him.** The original (κολαφίζω) signifies to strike with the fist.—**Smote him with the palms of their hands.** The original (ῥαπίζω) signifies in Scripture usage to strike a flat blow with the back or the palm of the hand, or with a staff. Comp. Matt. 5 : 39, where the verb is the same.—**Saying, Prophesy unto us.** They had first blindfolded him (Luke 22 : 64). These indignities were inflicted, not by the members of the court, but by the servants (Mark 14 : 65; Luke 22 : 64), who doubtless reflected in a meaner way the vindictive spirit of their masters. Luke represents them as preceding, Matthew and Mark as following, the sentence of the court. The former appears to me more probable. The blow struck by the officer of the high-priest, and narrated by John only (ch. 18 : 22), is distinct from these indignities. Chrysostom notes the evident truthfulness of the Evangelical narratives, which conceal nothing of the apparent humiliation of their Lord. Such is not the nature of a myth. He eloquently portrays the indignity : "For what could be equal to this insolence? On that Face, which the sea, when it saw it, had reverenced, from which the sun, when it beheld it on the cross, turned away his rays, they did spit, and struck it with the palms of their hands, and smote upon the Head; giving full swing in every way to their own madness."

Ch. 26 : 69-75. DENIALS OF OUR LORD BY PETER.—THE DANGER OF SELF-CONFIDENCE (Prov. 11 : 2).—THE GROWTH OF SIN ILLUSTRATED (James 1 : 14, 15).—See Thoughts below.

PRELIMINARY NOTE.—The denial of our Lord by Peter is recorded by the four Evangelists, Mark 14 : 66-72; Luke 22 : 54-62; John 18 : 15-17, 25-27. I believe that they all occurred as indicated in John's account, during an informal examination of Jesus in the house of Caiaphas. For greater distinctness, the three Synoptists have described it disentangled from this contemporaneous examination. If this supposition be correct, it preceded the formal trial of Jesus by the Sanhedrim, as is indicated by Luke, though narrated subsequently by Matthew and Mark. The four accounts are varied in their details, and scholars are not agreed in respect to their true order. Any harmony is of necessity hypothetical, though I believe with Dean Alford that "if for one moment we could be put in possession of all the details as they happened, each account would find its justification, and the reasons of all the variations would appear." The following tabular statement will facilitate the student in comparing these four narratives :

FIRST DENIAL.

Matthew 26 : 69-75.	Mark 14 : 66-72.	Luke 22 : 54-62.	John 18 : 15-27.
And Peter sat without in the hall, and a maid came to him, saying, "Thou also wast with Jesus of Galilee." But he denied before them all, saying, "I know not what thou sayest." And when he had gone out into the porch,	And as Peter was down in the hall, there cometh one of the maids of the high-priest; and when she saw Peter warming himself, she looked upon him and said, "Thou also wast with Jesus the Nazarene." But he denied, saying, "I know not, neither understand I what thou sayest." And he went out into the porch, and the cock crew.	And when they had kindled a fire in the midst of the hall, and were set down together, Peter sat down among them. But a certain maid beheld him as he sat by the fire, and earnestly looked upon him, and said, "This man was also with him." And he denied, saying, "Woman, I know him not."	Another disciple, who was known to the high-priest (probably John), came into the hall, leaving Peter at the gate without. He spoke to the maid who kept the gate, and she admitted Peter. And she saith to him, "Art not thou also one of this man's disciples?" He saith, "I am not."

SECOND DENIAL.

Another damsel saw him, and saith to those who were there, "This one also was with Jesus the Nazarene." And again he denied with an oath, "I do not know the man."	And a maid saw him, and began to say to those standing by, "This is one of them." But he again denied it.	And after a short time another (masculine gender) saw him, and said, "Thou art also of them." And Peter said, "Man, I am not."	And the servants and officers, having made a fire of coals because it was cold, stood there warming themselves, and Peter was with them, standing and warming himself. They said, therefore, to him, "Art not thou also one of his disciples?" He denied it, and said, "I am not."

THIRD DENIAL.

And after a while came unto him they that stood by, and said to Peter, "Surely thou also art one of them; for thy speech makes thee manifest." Then began he to curse and to swear, saying, "I know not the man." And immediately the cock crew. And Peter remembered the word of Jesus which said unto him, "Before the cock crow, thou shalt deny me thrice." And he went out and wept bitterly.	And a little while after they that stood by said again to Peter, "Surely thou art one of them; for thou art a Galilean" (and thy speech agreeth thereto is not in the best manuscripts). And he began to curse and to swear, saying, "I know not this man of whom ye speak." And the second time the cock crew. And Peter called to mind the words that Jesus said unto him, "Before the cock crow twice, thou shalt deny me thrice." And rushing out, he wept.	And about the space of one hour after, another (masculine gender) confidently affirmed, saying, "Of a truth this man also was with him; for he is a Galilean." And Peter said, "Man, I know not what thou sayest." And immediately, while he was yet speaking, the cock crew. And the Lord turned and looked at Peter, and Peter remembered the word of the Lord, how he had said unto him, "Before the cock crow, thou shalt deny me thrice." And Peter went out and wept bitterly.	One of the servants of the high-priest (being his kinsman whose ear Peter cut off) saith to him, "Did not I see thee in the garden with him?" Again, therefore, Peter denied. And immediately a cock crew.

If, as is probably the case, John is "that other disciple known to the high-priest" (John 18 : 15, 16), he is the only one of the Evangelists who was an eye and ear witness, and this fact would render it probable that his order is the correct one; though it is not the one usually adopted by the harmonists. May he not have written it in part to correct accounts which were derived at second-hand? Following his account the facts would appear to be as follows: Jesus is led to the palace of the high-priest Caiaphas, where he is subjected to a preliminary and informal examination while the Sanhedrim are assembling; Peter, whose resistance to the guard has rendered him legally liable to arrest and punishment, and who is the only one of the eleven who is so (comp. John 18 : 10 with ver. 26), is admitted to the courtyard of the palace (ver. 69, note) through the influence of John; as he enters, the portress asks him if he is not a disciple, and he denies it; he joins the group

69 Now [b] Peter sat without in the palace: and a damsel came unto him, saying, Thou also wast with Jesus of Galilee.
70 But he denied before *them* all, saying, I know not what thou sayest.
71 And when he was gone out into the porch, another *maid* saw him, and said unto them that were there, This *fellow* was also with Jesus of Nazareth.
72 And again he denied with an oath, I do not know the man.
73 And after a while came unto *him* they that stood by, and said to Peter, Surely thou also art *one* of them; for thy speech bewrayeth thee.

b Mark 14 : 66, etc.; Luke 22 : 55, etc.; John 18 : 16, etc.

about the fire in the centre of the courtyard, is a second time interrogated and a second time denies; he then retreats again to the gateway, is again pressed with the charge, this time by a kinsman of Malchus, and repeats his denial more vehemently than before; just at this juncture Jesus is perhaps led out to trial, his look (Luke 22 : 61) and the crowing of the cock, recalls Peter to himself, and in the confusion incidental to the transference of the prisoner to the council-chamber, he makes good his escape. This order of events seems to me more natural than to suppose, as is ordinarily done, that Peter first denied his Lord in the courtyard, then retreated to the door and repeated his denial, and then returned again to the centre of the yard, courting anew danger and temptation. The order, however, is problematical; the main facts are not. These are, that Peter thrice denied his Lord, the last time at cock crowing, followed his sin by repentance (not, however, mentioned by John), the circumstances exactly fulfilling our Lord s prophecy; and that he fell into his sin from a spirit of self-confidence, from a want of prayer and watching, and from a disregard of his Lord's warning. The variations in the narratives are such as we might expect from independent historians, but it is impossible to reconcile them with the hypothesis that the accounts were dictated by the Holy Spirit to the Evangelists as amanuenses. It is noticeable that Peter was questioned by a number (Mark 14 : 70; John 18 : 25), and Peter's denials were reiterated and vehement; the variations in the language, as reported by the Evangelists, may indicate either that they do not report the exact words used, or that different Evangelists report different phrases employed.

69. Peter was sitting without in the

INTERIOR COURTYARD OF ORIENTAL HOUSE.

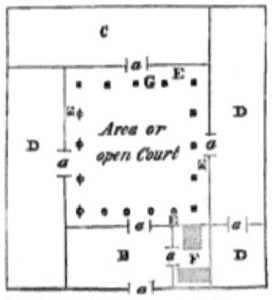

PLAN OF ORIENTAL HOUSE.
a, a. Doors. B. Porch. C. Harem.
D, D. Other rooms. E, E. Galleries between court and rooms. F. Stairs.

courtyard. Of the high-priest's house (Mark 14 : 54). The denials could not, therefore, have taken place in the palace of Annas, unless Annas and Caiaphas occupied the same dwelling. An Oriental house is usually built around a quadrangular interior court into which there is a passage, sometimes arched, from the street, through the front part of the house; this is closed by a heavy folding gate with a smaller wicket for single persons. This entrance is tended by a porter (answering to the French *concierge*) who in this case was a maid (John 18 : 17). In the larger palaces this servant sat in a porter's lodge at the entrance. The courtyard was very generally paved or flagged, and was sometimes ornamented with beds of flowers and was open to the sky. The accompanying cut and plan illustrates this description. Peter entered through the arched gateway *a, a,* warmed himself at an open fire, kindled in the courtyard, in a portable stove (see John 18 : 18, note), from which point he could probably see and partially overhear the preliminary examination of Jesus, taking place in one of the rooms D, D, which frequently open in front upon the courtyard.

70-74. I know not what thou sayest.

74 Then began he to curse and to swear, *saying*, I know not the man. And immediately the cock crew.

75 And Peter remembered the¹ word of Jesus, which said unto him, Before the cock crow, thou shalt deny me thrice. And he went out, and wept bitterly.

¹ verse 34 ; Luke 22 : 31-34.

"A shuffling answer; he pretended he did not understand the charge, and knew not whom she meant by Jesus of Galilee, or what she meant by being with him."—(*Matthew Henry.*)—**Gone out into the porch.** The gateway or vestibule marked in the plan, B.—**With an oath.** Perhaps Peter the fisherman was a profane man, and in the time of temptation the old habit, long cast off, reasserted itself. That he possessed originally the vices common to a seafaring life is perhaps indicated by Luke 5 : 8.—**Thy speech bewrayeth thee.** Makes thee manifest. The Galilean accent was peculiar; the Galileans could not pronounce accurately the gutturals. The kinsman of Malchus, whose ear Peter had cut off, joined his accusers at this time (John 18 : 26). Evidently he was now beset by a throng whose suspicions could not be easily allayed. Comp. the four accounts of this last scene.—**To curse and to swear.** The first word indicates that he invoked imprecations upon himself if his denial were not true. The second word signifies an appeal to the Deity in attestation of his truth. Matthew Henry observes that "we have reason to suspect the truth of that which is backed by rash oaths and imprecations. None but the devil's sayings need the devil's proofs."—**The cock crew.** Mark relates that the cock crowed twice, vers. 68, 72; the others speak only of his crowing once. This accords also with their respective accounts of our Lord's prophecy. "The cock often crows about midnight or not long after; and again always about the third hour or daybreak. When, therefore, 'the cock crowing' is spoken of alone, this last is always meant. Hence the name cock crowing, for the third watch of the night, which ended at the third hour after midnight (Mark 13 : 35). Mark, therefore, here relates more definitely; the others more generally."—(*Robinson.*) The O. T. does not mention the cock, and it is said, on the authority of the Rabbinical books, that no cock was allowed to be kept in Jerusalem. But (1) the Rabbinical books are very doubtful authority on such a matter. They state with tolerable accuracy the rules of the Jewish ritualists, but are poor authority for the practices of the Jewish people; and (2) the cock crowing might have been heard from the hillside outside the walls, over against Jerusalem.

75. Peter remembered the word of Jesus (ver. 34). He was called to himself by the crowing of the cock and by a look from Jesus (Luke 22 : 61).

LESSONS FROM PETER'S DENIAL.—In studying the moral significance of this incident, observe, (1) Peter's temptation, (2) his sin, (3) his repentance. (I.) *His temptation.* He is ardent, impulsive, impetuous, but self-confident, knowing not his own weakness. He is forewarned by Christ, but is blind to his own danger. He follows his Master to the high-priest's palace, not drawn by love to serve his Lord, but by curiosity and perhaps bravado to see the end (ver. 58, note). Because he is self-confident, he does not watch and pray (ver. 40); because he does not watch and pray, he does not foresee the temptation; because he has not foreseen, he enters into temptation. (2.) *His sin.* Observe its development. First was the self-confidence which despised Christ's warning (ver. 35); next the spiritual sloth that permitted sleep while Christ prayed (vers. 40, 43, 45); next the false position in entering the high-priest's palace and joining the enemies of the Lord, *concealing his discipleship;* next his denial of his Lord—first an evasive answer, I know not what thou sayest; then a flat denial, I know not the man; finally perjury added to falsehood, Began he to curse and to swear. (3.) *His repentance.* His conscience was throughout uneasy; the crowing of a cock and the look of his Lord sufficed to recall the forgotten warning, and the recall of the Lord's warning pierced his heart. He "went out into the black night, but not, as Judas, into the darkness of despair. Weeping bitterly, he awaited the dawn of another and a better morning."—(*Lange.*) His repentance he attested (*a*) by the bitterness of his tears; (*b*) by his humble submission to his Lord's subsequent rebuke (John 21 : 15-17); (*c*) by his subsequent courage in confessing Christ in the face of threatened danger (Acts 4 : 8-12, 19); (*d*) by the thoroughness with which he learned the lesson of humility, as illustrated by his own subsequent epistles (see particularly 1 Pet. 1 : 5, 17 ; 3 : 15 ; 4 : 12). And observe that Peter's sin, repentance, and pardon afford to the disciples of Christ a witness of how great is the forgiving kindness of the Lord, and how large his pardoning mercy, even to apostates. Comp. 1 Tim. 1 : 16. Again, contrast (1) *Peter and Jesus.* Jesus, before the high-priest, with the sanctity of an oath, testifies to his divinity, and so surrenders himself to the cross; Peter, before the servants, adds an oath to his denial of the Lord, and so escapes arrest. (2.) *Peter here and elsewhere.* He who was the first to confess Christ the Son of God, was the first to deny him (comp. Matt. 16 : 16). But

CHAPTER XXVII.

WHEN the morning was come, all the chief priests and elders of the people took counsel¹ against Jesus to put him to death.

2 And when they had bound him, they led *him* away, and delivered him² to Pontius Pilate the governor.

3 Then Judas, which had betrayed him, when he saw that he was condemned, repented himself, and brought again the thirty pieces of silver to the chief priests and elders,

4 Saying, I have sinned, in that I have betrayed the innocent blood.³ And they said, What *is that* to us? see thou *to that.*

j Ps. 2 : 2....k ch. 20 : 19....l 2 Kings 24 : 4.

---

even then he rebuked Christ for prophesying his passion (Matt. 16 : 22); no wonder that he now refused to share it. He who drew a sword to resist the guard (John 18 : 10) lacked courage to resist his own fears. He was the most courageous and the most cowardly of the eleven. He who denied now never denied again, but learned well the needed lesson of courage and caution. See ref. above to Acts and 1 Peter. That the old weakness was not, however, at once and forever eradicated, see Gal. 2 : 11, 12. (3.) *Peter and Judas.* Both looked for a temporal Messiah ; both were disappointed by the revelation of a suffering Messiah ; both disowned Him whom they had once followed. But Judas did so deliberately, Peter under a stress of unexpected temptation ; one of his own will, the other despite the purpose of his better self ; one sought refuge from remorse in death, the other from the burden of his sin in the forgiveness of his Lord.

Ch. 27 : 1-10. JESUS IS LED TO PILATE.—REMORSE AND DEATH OF JUDAS.—FALSE REPENTANCE : "A MAN MAY KNOW HIS SIN, CONCEIVE AN ABHORRENCE OF IT, REPENT OF IT, CONFESS IT, RESTORE HIS ILL-GOTTEN GOODS, RETIRE FROM THE OCCASION, AND YET BE A FALSE PENITENT, LIKE JUDAS."—(*Quesnel.*)—INDIVIDUAL RESPONSIBILITY ; EVERY SOUL MUST SEE TO ITS OWN SIN.—SATAN ENTICES US TO SIN, BUT DESERTS US WHEN WE HAVE FALLEN INTO IT.—THE REWARD OF APOSTASY (ver. 5 with Acts 1 : 18).—THE HYPOCRITE'S CONSCIENCE : LAWFUL TO PAY THE PRICE OF BLOOD ; UNLAWFUL TO PUT IT INTO THE LORD'S TREASURY.—THE DEATH OF CHRIST PROVIDES A RESTING-PLACE FOR THE OUTCAST.—A MARVELLOUS PROPHECY, MARVELLOUSLY FULFILLED.—THE PUNITIVE POWER OF CONSCIENCE ILLUSTRATED.

The trial before Pilate is reported by the four Evangelists, most fully by John. See below, on ver. 11-31. The remorse and death of Judas are described only by Matthew ; a different account is given by Peter in Acts 1 : 18, 19. See below, on ver. 6-8.

1, 2. When the morning was come. "This was the time of saying their phylacteries, namely, from the first daylight to the third hour. But where was these men's religion to-day? Did you say your phylacteries this morning, my good fathers of the council, before you came to sit on the bench ?"—(*Lightfoot.*)—**All the chief priests and elders.** Not literally *all*; one, at least, was probably absent (Luke 23 : 51).—**Took counsel to put him to death.** That is, to execute the death-sentence already passed upon him. The language implies, not a formal trial (as Lange, James Morison, Alford, and others), but a private conference to devise means for the execution of the death-sentence. The Jews had not the power under the Roman government of putting to death (John 18 : 31, note), and a charge of blasphemy would be looked on with as much indifference by Pilate in Jerusalem as by Gallio in Achaia (Acts 18 : 12-17). It was therefore necessary to present some other charge, and support it by some plausible evidence. The result of this conference was an accusation of sedition (Luke 23 : 2).—**Pontius Pilate the governor.** The Roman provinces were of two kinds, Senatorial and Imperial. The latter were governed by military officers, who held their office and power at the pleasure of the Emperor. They looked after the taxes, paid the troops, preserved order, and administered a rude sort of justice ; from their decisions there was ordinarily no appeal, except in the case of a Roman citizen. Judæa was an Imperial province ; Pontius Pilate was its governor or procurator, and was directly amenable to the Emperor, Tiberius Cæsar, for his administration. On his character see notes on John (ch. 19 : 16).

3, 4. Judas * * * repented himself. There are two Greek words used in the N. T., both of which are rendered *repent.* They are not quite synonymous ; the one (μετανοέω) signifies literally to *know after*, and hence indicates a change of mind or purpose (Matt. 3 : 2, note) ; the other (μεταμέλομαι) signifies literally, to *care after*, and so to carry a burden of sorrow for the past. The latter is the word used here. The distinction is well stated by Trench : "He who has *changed his mind* about the past is in the way to change everything ; he who has an *after care* may have little or nothing more than a selfish dread of the consequences of what he has done." This appears to have been the state of mind of Judas.—**The thirty pieces of silver.** Thirty shekels, *i. e.*, $18 to $20. The fact that this was all that was returned indicates that it was all that was received ; not merely, as some have supposed, earnest money paid down to bind the bargain (ch. 26 : 15, note).—**I have sinned in that I have betrayed the innocent blood.** This

5 And he cast down the pieces of silver in the temple, and departed, and went and hanged ᵐ himself.
6 And the chief priests took the silver pieces, and said, It is not lawful for to put them into the treasury, because it is the price of blood.
7 And they took counsel, and **bought with them the potter's field, to bury strangers in.**
8 Wherefore that field was called, The field **of blood**, unto this day.
9 Then was fulfilled that which was spoken ⁿ by Jeremy the prophet, saying, And they took the thirty pieces of silver, the price of him that was valued, whom they of the children of Israel did value;
10 And gave them for the potter's field, as the Lord appointed me.

m 2 Sam. 17 : 23 ; Ps. 65 : 23 ; Acts 1 : 18.... n Zech. 11 : 12, 13.

language is inconsistent with the theory that Judas' betrayal was a stratagem to compel Christ to declare himself the Messiah. The word translated sin (ἁμαρτάνω), though literally meaning to err, in the N. T. usage *always signifies moral wrong*, never a mere error in judgment. The Jewish law required the court to receive any new evidence for the accused, even after conviction and sentence. I believe that this was an attempt on Judas' part, under this well-known provision, to offer evidence to the innocence of Jesus, and so secure a reversal of the sentence pronounced against him. In refusing to receive his testimony the court violated its own rule of procedure. Dr. Robinson, it is true, places this testimony of Judas subsequent to the condemnation of Pilate. But he assigns no adequate reason for departing from the order indicated by Matthew, and his hypothesis does not agree with the narrative. This interview between Judas and the court was, apparently, while the court was in session, and in the Temple (vers. 3, 5); and after Jesus was conducted to Pilate, the members of the Sanhedrim, or at least an important portion of them, seem not to have returned to the Temple till they had seen the crucifixion accomplished (vers. 39, 41). I judge, then, that Judas came to the council while they were deliberating how to execute the death-sentence which they had pronounced (ver. 1), and for the purpose of procuring a reversal of that sentence. Observe the significance of his testimony. " Had our Lord been condemned to death on the evidence of one of his own disciples, it would have furnished infidels with a strong argument against Christ and the Christian religion. 'One of his own disciples, knowing the whole imposture, declared it to the Jewish rulers, in consequence of which he was put to death as an impostor and deceiver.'"—(*Adam Clarke.*)—**See thou to that.** Rather, *Thou shalt see to that.* The verb is in the indicative, not the imperative mood. Pilate repeats the same language to the multitude (ver. 24). Both Pilate and the priests are unconscious witnesses to the truth (Ezek. 18 : 4 ; Gal. 6 : 5).

5. In the Temple. The word so rendered (ἱερός), is ordinarily employed in the N. T. to designate the Holy Place which was God's special abode, and which the priests alone might enter (Mark 15 : 38 ; Luke 1 : 9). If this be the meaning here, Judas came to the entrance, and when the money was refused, cast it through the open door into the Holy Place in a rage, and went away. I should think it more probable, with Bengel, that the word here stands for the more general one (ἱερός), usually employed to designate the whole sacred edifice with its outbuildings. Probably the Sanhedrim were still in session in the council-chamber (see Luke 22 : 66, note), and Judas entered during their deliberations to offer his evidence to the innocence of the accused, which, by the rules of Jewish procedure, they were required to receive. —**And departed, and went and hanged himself.** Lange supposes that he first attempted to retire from the world and do penance by a life of solitude, and that not till afterwards did despair drive him to suicide. It is not probable that the consultation as to what should be done with the money, reported in the succeeding verse, took place till after the crucifixion.

6–8. It is not lawful. Because, being blood-money, they regarded it as unclean (See Deut. 23 : 18). "Blind and merciless priests, very careful in laying out Judas' money, but not in the least concerned what will become of his soul."—(*Quesnel.*) Comp. Matt. 23 : 14, 29–33. A strange conscience that pays blood-money without scruple, but scruples to give it to the Lord. But it is better than the modern conscience which takes the devil's money for the devil's work, and is appeased by paying a part into the treasury of the Lord.—**The price of blood.** That is, For blood—the murderer's wages.—**The potter's field.** A place from which clay had been excavated for some well-known pottery, and purchased for so small a price because of its now useless character.—**To bury strangers in.** Possibly, as Alford, for stranger Jews, quite as probably for Gentiles, more probably for both. It was to be a burial-place for the poor and the unknown. The site of this field is unknown; the traditional site is just outside the walls of Jerusalem on the south of Mount Zion. That the "field of blood" should ever have been regarded as a sacred spot is one of the curiosities of Church history. Such, however, is the fact. It was believed in the Middle Ages that the soil of this place had the power of very rapidly consuming bodies buried in it; and in consequence either of this, or of the sanctity of the spot, great quantities of the earth were taken away; among others, by the Pisan Crusaders in 1218, for their

Campo Santo at Pisa, and by the Empress Helena for that at Rome.—**Unto this day.** This expression indicates that some time elapsed between the event and the publication of Matthew's gospel. Comp. ch. 28 : 15.

The account of the death of Judas in Acts 1 : 18, 19, is quite different from that given here. The most common explanation is also the most natural, viz., that Judas hanged himself as described by Matthew, that the cord broke and in the fall he was mangled in the manner described by Peter, that his suicide took place in the field purchased by the priests with the blood money, and from the double circumstance of this purchase and his death it was called the field of blood, and that Peter's expression: "He purchased a field with the reward of iniquity," is a bitter ironical reference to the recompense of Judas' treachery, which would be understood by his hearers, to whom the facts were all well known. "Prof. Hackett, referring to a suggestion that he may have hung himself upon a tree overhanging the valley of Hinnom, says: 'For myself, I felt, as I stood in the valley and looked up to the rocky terraces which hang over it, that the proposed explanation was a perfectly natural one. I was more than ever satisfied with it.' He found the precipice, by measurement, to be from twenty-five to forty feet in height, with olive-trees growing near the edges, and a rocky pavement at the bottom, so that a person who fell from above would probably be crushed and mangled, as well as killed."—(*Andrews.*)

9, 10. Then was fulfilled, etc. There is no such prophecy in Jeremiah. It occurs in Zechariah 11 : 12, 13. Either the Evangelist quoted from memory and made a mistake in his citation (*Alford*), or he referred to Jeremiah because his Book was placed first in the Books of the Prophets (*Lightfoot*), or by a transcriber's error Jeremiah was substituted for Zechariah (*Barnes, James Morison*). In the Greek manuscript, words, proper names especially, were often abridged. Mr. Barnes claims that the change by the transcriber of a single letter *Iriou* (Jeremiah) for *Zriou* (Zechariah), would account for the mistake. The prophecy itself is mystical, and would, I believe, be inexplicable but for its historical fulfillment. It is in these words (Henderson's translation): "And I said to them, If it be good in your eyes, give my reward; and if not, forbear. So they weighed my reward, thirty pieces of silver. And Jehovah said to me, Cast it to the potter, the splendid price at which I was estimated by them! And I took the thirty pieces of silver and cast them into the House of Jehovah to the potter." Apparently the prophet calls for his recompense; the people offer him a contemptible sum; the Lord regards it as offered to himself; and he directs it to be contemptuously rejected by being thrown to the potter in the Temple, a symbolic act which in some way, not now very clear, expressed scorn or contempt. In the fulfillment of this, which was a prophetic act, the same sum, thirty pieces of silver, are paid as the price for the Saviour's blood; the money is returned by the traitor, to the priests in the Temple; the priests, regarding it with abhorrence, refuse to put it into the treasury of the Lord; and it is used for the purchase of a potter's field. The correspondence between the prophecy and its fulfillment is the more striking because of the difference of the circumstances in the two cases. A comparison of the quotation with the original prophecy indicates that it is made from memory; it is not verbally exact.

CHARACTER AND CAREER OF JUDAS ISCARIOT. —The character of Judas Iscariot is an enigma. He is called by Christ to be a disciple, is ordained as an apostle, is sent forth to preach the Gospel, power is conferred on him to work miracles (Luke 6 : 16; Matt. ch. 10), and he is made treasurer of the band (John 12 : 6). He deserts the cause to which he has voluntarily consecrated himself, betrays his Master for the paltry sum of thirty pieces of silver (Matt. 26 : 15, note), personally conducts the guard to Christ's place of retreat, and shows himself both to the Master and his followers as a traitor, thus indicating a nature not only dead to conscience, but indifferent to the just scorn and contempt of his companions. Yet when his treachery is consummated he is filled with remorse at a result which he might easily have anticipated even if Christ had not explicitly foretold it, he endeavors to repair the wrong by a voluntary testimony to the innocence of the accused, returns the money paid him for his treachery, and evinces the bitterness of his remorse by his act of self-destruction. In the interpretation of this enigma two extreme hypotheses have been proposed, each of which appears to me to be false in fact, and to lose the lesson of Judas' life and death. The first supposes him to have joined the disciples solely from worldly and selfish motives, and to have abandoned them solely to secure the proffered bribe. This interpretation of his character is inconsistent with, (1) his selection by Christ, who can hardly be thought to have chosen as an apostle one who was a traitor in thought and feeling from the outset; (2) the smallness of the bribe. This thirty shekels was equal to $18 to $20; making a fair allowance for the difference in values between that age and this, it would be *equivalent* to about $150 of our currency. This sum would hardly of itself constitute an adequate motive for such a deed of infamy, even to the most avaricious; (3) the fact that the offer of betrayal originated with Judas; the bribe was not first proffered to him. (4.) Judas' disappointment, remorse, and return of the bribe. If the money was the sole motive of his treachery, there is nothing to account for this. The second hypothesis regards him as the victim of a delusion rather than the perpetrator of a crime. It supposes that Judas was a sincere, though mistaken and worldly-minded disciple of Jesus; that he believed Jesus to be the long-looked for Messiah; that he was impatient of his Master's delay in publicly declaring himself and inaugurating his Messianic kingdom; that he therefore resorted to a stratagem and contrived Christ's arrest, fully believing that, thus compelled to exert his miraculous powers for his own deliverance, he would assert his Messiahship and set up his kingdom in Jerusalem; and that when the result proved so different and so disastrous, the mistaken disciple was overwhelmed with remorse and despair. See this view, in a modified form, defended in Dr. Clarke's *Commentary on Acts*, ch. 1; he maintains that Judas did not destroy himself, truly repented of his sin, did what he could to undo his wicked act, and that "there is no positive evidence of the final damnation of Judas in the sacred text." This view is inconsistent, (1) with Judas' reception of the bribe. If his treachery were a mere stratagem, surely he might have contrived some other way of accomplishing it. By his compact with the priests, his withdrawal from the Supper table, and his accompanying the band to Gethsemane, he emphasizes his entire separation from the disciples; (2) with his own language, "I have *sinned* in that I have *betrayed* the innocent blood" (ver. 3, note); (3) with the subsequent language of Peter and the disciples respecting him. He "purchased a field with the *reward of iniquity*." "Judas by transgression fell, that he might *go to his own place*" (Acts 1:18, 25); (4) with Christ's language, who designates him as "the son of perdition" (John 17:12) and declares of him that "it were good for that man if he had not been born" (Matt. 26:24). Some light on the true interpretation of Judas' character and career is thrown by a consideration of the following facts: (1.) All the disciples originally expected that an immediate and earthly kingdom would be set up by Christ. This expectation they retained to the last (Matt. 19:27; Luke 19:11). When he disavowed this, many who had followed left him (John 6:66). Thus *in them all* there was a conflict between personal allegiance to their Master, and worldly ambition, strengthened by life-long religious prejudice derived from priestly and Pharisaic teaching. (2.) The name Iscariot (probably *of Kerioth*), indicates that Judas was originally a resident of Kerioth, a town of southern Judea. In that case he was the only Judean among the twelve, and of them all, therefore, the one most likely to be imbued with the Jewish worldly ideas respecting the Messiah's kingdom, with the narrow national prejudices against the admission of Gentiles to the kingdom of God, and with reverence for the priesthood, the Pharisees, and the Jewish church and religion; the one most likely, therefore, to take offence at Christ's distinct renunciation of a temporal kingdom, distinct declaration of a kingdom open to the Gentile nations, and emphatic denunciation of the religion of the priesthood and the Pharisees. (3.) He did not inaugurate any measures for the betrayal of his Master until after Christ's final and public rupture with the hierarchy, his vehement denunciation of the hypocrisy of the Pharisees in his Temple ministry, his declaration (in the parables of the two sons and the wicked husbandmen) that the kingdom would be taken from them and given to the Gentiles, and his prophecy to his own disciples, in language still more distinct, that Jerusalem was to be destroyed, and the kingdom of God founded on its ruins, after the Messiah's death, and only in the far future, at his second coming (Matt., chaps. 21-24). (4.) The immediate occasion of Judas' compact with the priests was Christ's public rebuke, administered at the house of Mary and Martha, and accompanying a still more explicit prophecy of his approaching death (Matt. 26:6-16). I believe, then, that Judas originally followed Jesus, as did the rest, from a mixed motive, partly drawn by personal ambition, partly by a real reverence for Christ and the moral beauty of his teaching; that in all the disciples there was at first a perplexity, and then a conflict between ambition and spiritual love, as the nature of Christ's kingdom was more and more clearly disclosed; that in the eleven Christ conquered, in the twelfth ambition; that, disappointed by Christ's prophecy of his own sufferings and death, and the approaching overthrow of the Jewish temple, priesthood, and religion, and angered by the personal rebuke publicly administered to him, Judas abandoned what seemed to him a failing cause, hoping by his treachery to gain a position of honor and influence in the Pharisaic party; that the thirty pieces of silver constituted not the main, but only an incidental motive; that his treachery brought him, as treachery always does, only the contempt of the priesthood, who used him as their tool and then cast him away; that his conscience was tardily awakened, by his disappointed ambition, to a sense of his fruitless sin and his public ignominy, but not to a sense of his guilt before God or his need of an opportunity for pardon; that thus his experience resembled that of King Saul, not that of the Prodigal Son (1 Sam. 15:30; Luke 15:18, 19; and see ref. below); that by offering a tardy testimony to the innocence of Jesus, and returning the bribe, he endeavored to undo his work, but, could not; and so, rejected by the priests, scorned by the disciples, and scourged

11 And Jesus stood before the governor: and the governor asked him, saying, Art thou the King of the Jews? And Jesus said unto him, Thou sayest.
12 And when he was accused of the chief priests and elders, he answered ⁰ nothing.
13 Then said Pilate unto him, Hearest thou not how many things they witness against thee?
14 And he answered him to never a word; insomuch that the governor marvelled greatly.

o chap. 26 : 63.

by his own conscience, he sought refuge from himself in death. The lessons of his life appear to me to be, (1) that one may be high in Christ's church, but no true disciple, an apostle and an apostate (Matt. 7 : 22; 1 Cor. 9 : 27); (2) the growth of sin—worldliness leads to ambition, ambition to estrangement from Christ, estrangement to apostasy, treachery, and death. Hence the character of Judas is a warning to all worldly professors of religion who endeavor to serve both God and mammon (1 Tim. 4 : 10); (3) the nature of true repentance. In the case of Judas the external signs are not wanting. He confesses his guilt; endeavors, by testifying to the innocence of Jesus, to repair the wrong which he has done; returns the money; proves by his death how deep is his sorrow. But the internal spirit of true repentance is wanting. It is a sense of shame before men, rather than of guilt before God; its poignancy is due rather to the fruitlessness than the enormity of his guilt; it is manifested in remorse for the past, not in any new purpose for the future; and it leads not to a new life in Christ Jesus, but to a despairing death. Repentance is inspired chiefly by conscience, remorse chiefly by pride, avarice, or self-esteem; repentance inspires to a new life, remorse leads to despair and death; repentance seeks forgiveness, remorse oblivion; repentance conducts Peter to Christ, remorse drives Judas from him. See note on Peter's denial of his Lord, p. 264. And for illustrative passages on true and false repentance see the following : True repentance— 2 Sam. 24 : 10; 1 Kings 8 : 46–50; Ezra 9 : 6–13; Neh. 1 : 6, 7; 9 : 33; Psalm 51; Dan. 9 : 5–7; Luke 15 : 17, 18; 2 Cor. 7 : 9–11; false repentance—Gen. 4 : 13; Lev. 26 : 36; Deut. 28 : 65–67; 1 Sam. 15 : 30; Micah 7 : 17; Luke 13 : 28; Rev. 6 : 15–17.

Ch. 27 : 11-31. TRIAL BEFORE PILATE.—THE VALUE OF POPULARITY: THE CROWD GIVES LIBERTY TO THE MURDERER, AND THE CROSS TO THE SON OF GOD.—THE CRIME OF ENVY (18): "LIKE THE WORM, IT NEVER RUNS BUT TO THE FAIREST FRUIT; LIKE A CUNNING BLOODHOUND, IT SINGLES OUT THE FATTEST DEER IN THE FLOCK."—GOD'S MERCY: HE USES EVEN THEIR SUPERSTITION FOR THE RECLAMATION OF THE SUPERSTITIOUS (19).—THE CURSE OF AN APOSTATE AND PERSECUTING CHURCH: IT IS THE CHIEF PRIESTS WHO INCITE THE CRY, CRUCIFY HIM (20).—PASSION CAN GIVE NO REASON FOR ITS DEMANDS: CONVICTED OF INJUSTICE, IT ONLY CRIES OUT THE MORE (23).—THE USELESSNESS OF MERE CEREMONIAL.—NO ONE CAN ESCAPE HIS JUST RESPONSIBILITIES (24).—THE AUDA-CITY AND THE COWARDICE OF CRIME: IT DARES ALL CONSEQUENCES BEFOREHAND, AND TRIES TO EVADE THEM AFTERWARD (25 with Acts 5 : 28).—THE CROWNED SUFFERER: HIS PATIENT SUFFERING CROWNS HIM WITH IGNOMINY HERE, WITH GLORY HEREAFTER (27–29 with Phil. 2 : 6–11).

The trial of Christ before Pilate is reported by the four Evangelists: Mark 15 : 1–23; Luke 23 : 1–25; John 18 : 28 to 19 : 16. Of this trial John gives the fullest account. For consideration of Pilate's character and the practical lessons to be drawn from his course, see notes there. Matthew's account of the mockery by the soldiers (ver. 26-30) is the fullest; and he alone recounts Pilate's wife's dream (ver. 19) and his hand-washing (ver. 24, 25). Mark's account is almost exactly parallel to Matthew's, except some additional information respecting Barabbas. Luke alone gives the accusation preferred by the Jews against Jesus (ver. 2, 3) and the sending of Jesus to Herod (ver. 4-12). Combining the four accounts, the probable order of events seems to be as follows: Jesus is brought before Pilate, who demands the accusation; this demand the priests endeavor to evade (John 18 : 29-32); they then accuse him of sedition (Luke 23 : 2, 3); Pilate examines Christ privately in respect to this charge, and acquits him (John 18 : 33-38); in the clamor of voices which ensues he catches the word Galilee, learns that Jesus is a Galilean, and sends him to Herod (Luke 23 : 4-12); on his return he repeats his declaration of Jesus' innocence, but proposes as a compromise to scourge him (Luke 23 : 13-17); at the same time some among the crowd demand the customary release of a prisoner (Mark 15 : 8), and Pilate proposes to release Jesus to them; while waiting for their response he receives his wife's message (Matt. 27 : 19); the people, being instigated by the priests (Mark 15 : 11), demand the release of Barabbas and the crucifixion of Jesus (Matt. 27 : 20-23; Mark 15 : 11-14; Luke 23 : 18-23; John 18 : 39, 40); Pilate washes his hands in attestation of his own innocence (Matt. 27 : 24), and delivers Jesus to the soldiers, who scourge and mock him (Matt. 27 : 26-30; Mark 15 : 16-19; John 19 : 1-3); he makes two more attempts to save Jesus, by appealing first to the pity and then to the patriotism of the people (John 19 : 4-15), but finally yields to the mob and delivers our Lord to be crucified (Matt. 27 : 31; Mark 15 : 20; Luke 23 : 24, 25; John 19 : 16).

11-14. The governor. Pilate. See above on ver. 2.—**Art thou the King of the Jews?** This examination was preceded by a charge of

15 Now *at that* feast the governor was wont to release unto the people a prisoner, whom they would.
16 And they had then a notable prisoner, called Barabbas.
17 Therefore, when they were gathered together, Pilate said unto them, Whom will ye that I release unto you? Barabbas, or Jesus which is called Christ?
18 For he knew that for envy ᵃ they had delivered him.
19 When he was set down on the judgment-seat, his wife sent unto him, saying, Have thou nothing to do with that ᵇ just man; for I have suffered many things this day in a dream because of him.

20 But the chief priests and elders persuaded the multitude that they should ask ᶜ Barabbas, and destroy Jesus.
21 The governor answered and said unto them, Whether of the twain will ye that I release unto you? They said, Barabbas.
22 Pilate saith unto them, What shall I do then with Jesus, which is called Christ? *They* all say unto him, Let him be crucified.
23 And the governor said, Why, what evil hath he done? But they cried out the more, saying, Let ᵈ him be crucified.

p Mark 15 : 6, etc.; Luke 23 : 17, etc.; John 18 : 39, etc.....q Prov. 27 : 4; Eccles. 4 : 4....r Isa. 53 : 11; Zech. 9 : 9; Luke 23 : 47; 1 Pet. 2 : 22; 1 John 3 : 1....s Acts 3 : 14....t ch. 21 : 38, 39.

sedition, preferred by the priests (Luke 23 : 2, 5). It is more fully reported by John (ch. 18 ; 28-38, notes). Jesus was acquitted.—**He answered nothing.** He first explains to Pilate the nature of his kingdom, and satisfies him that he is innocent of sedition; after that he keeps silence. He will answer honest perplexity, but not willful slander.

15-18. The governor was wont to release unto the people a prisoner. This custom is mentioned in all the Gospels; it is not mentioned in secular history, and its origin is unknown, but its significance is not difficult to understand. "In a conquered country the interests of the government are generally regarded as so distinct from those of the people, that even the punishment of criminals, especially those guilty of political crimes, is regarded as in some sense an injury to the community. A foreign power comes and establishes itself over them, and it is not surprising that even wholesome control should be unpopular, and that the pardon of a state criminal should be regarded as a boon from the authorities—a suitable contribution from the government to the means of rejoicing at a great public festival."—(*Jacob Abbott's Corner-Stone.*)—**Notable.** Rather notorious; the original (ἐπίσημος) is capable of either a good or a bad sense.—**Called Barabbas.** Some manuscripts have here and in the following verse *Jesus Barabbas.* Barabbas means *son of Abba*, or *son of his father.* Pilate's question, then, would be, Whom will ye that I release unto you, Jesus the son of Abba, or Jesus called the Messiah? External evidence does not support this reading, but it is more probable that the word Jesus was omitted by some scribe in the early copies from motives of reverence, than that it was subsequently added. Of Barabbas nothing more is known than what is told in the four Gospels. He was one of a band (Mark 15 : 7), probably their leader, and had committed both robbery and murder in the insurrection in which he had been engaged (Luke 23 : 19; John 18 : 40).—**He knew that,** etc. Probably, therefore, he knew something about Jesus before this time; he had given the band of soldiers for his arrest (John 18 : 3, note), and certainly knew something of the spirit and character of the priests. See note on character of Pilate, John 19 : 16. Observe the indirect testimony to the character of the prosecution of Christ by the priests, and compare their spirit with that of John the Baptist (John 3 : 27, 30). In support of this statement respecting their motives, see John 11 : 48-50.

19. This incident of Pilate's wife's dream is recorded only by Matthew. Nothing is known of her.—**He was set down on the judgment-seat.** Formally to adjudicate the case; the previous examinations had been informal and preliminary. For illustration of judgment-seat see John 19 : 13, note.—**Have thou nothing to do with that just man;** *i. e.,* have no part in the proceedings for his condemnation.—**In a dream.** The Romans had great faith in dreams. Homer declared that "they come from Jove". In obedience to dreams the great Emperor Augustus went begging money through the streets of Rome. They were employed by God throughout the O. T. times for prediction or for warning, but generally either to those who were aliens to the Jewish covenant, as in the cases of Abimelech (Gen. 20 : 3-7), Laban (Gen. 31 : 24), the butler and baker (Gen. 40 : 5), Pharaoh (Gen. 41 : 1-8), the Midianite (Judges 7 : 13), Nebuchadnezzar (Dan. 2 : 1, etc.; 4 : 10-18), the magi (Matt. 2 : 12), Pilate's wife (Matt. 27 : 19); or to God's servants during the periods of their most imperfect knowledge of him, as in the cases of Abraham (Gen. 15 : 12), Jacob (28 : 12-15), Joseph (37 : 5-10), Solomon (1 Kings 3 : 5), and Joseph, husband of Mary (Matt. 1 : 20; 11 : 13, 19, 22). In this case I believe that God, who made use of the star to direct the astrologers to the cradle of Jesus, made use of a dream to warn Pilate from participating in Christ's condemnation.

20-23. While Pilate was receiving this message from his wife and waiting the answer to his question of ver. 17, the chief-priests and elders were busy in the crowd, persuading them what answer to give. That their outcry, Let him be crucified, was vehement and tumultuous, is indicated by ver. 24 and Luke 23 : 23. Observe that Pilate appeals for Christ's release with shrewd-

CH. XXVII.] MATTHEW. 311

24 When Pilate saw that he could prevail nothing, but *that* rather a tumult was made, he took water, and washed *his*ᵘ hands before the multitude, saying, I am innocent of the blood of this just person: see ye *to it*.
25 Then answered all the people, and said, Hisᵛ blood *be* on us, and on our children.
26 Then released he Barabbas unto them: and when he had scourgedʷ Jesus, he delivered *him* to be crucified.
27 Then the soldiers of the governor took Jesus into the common hall, and gathered unto him the whole band *of soldiers*.

28 And they stripped him, and put on him a scarlet robe.
29 And when they had platted a crown of thorns, they put *it* upon his head, and a reed in his right hand: and they bowed the knee before him, and mockedˣ him, saying, Hail, King of the Jews!
30 And they spitʸ upon him, and took the reed, and smote him on the head.
31 And after that they had mocked him, they took the robe off from him, and put his own raiment on him, and ledᶻ him away to crucify *him*.

---

u Deut. 21:6... v Deut. 19:10; Josh. 2:19; Acts 5:28,...w Isa. 53:5; Luke 18:33...r Ps. 69:19, 20... y Isa. 49:7; 50:6; 53:3, 7,...z Numb. 15:35; 1 Kings 21:10, 13; Acts 7:58; Heb. 13:12.

---

ness. *Jesus which is called the Messiah* is an appeal to their patriotism; *What evil hath he done?* to their sense of justice. Comp. his later endeavors, John 19:5, 13, 14. Crucifixion was a Roman punishment, and the erection of a cross on Jewish soil was itself a sign of the national degradation. The demand for crucifixion shows how far passion swayed the mob, who unconsciously fulfilled Christ's own prophecy (John 3:14; 8:28).

24, 25. He could prevail nothing; that is, by persuasion, and he was not willing to hazard a conflict with the mob lest he should be accused to the emperor of indifference to his interests (John 19:12).—**He took water and washed his hands.** The washing of hands as betokening innocence from blood-guiltiness is described in Deut. 21:6-9; and the Jews would therefore have understood this symbolic act. But there is no reason to suppose that Pilate derived it from the Jews. Ablutions were performed in ancient Greece, and probably in Rome, by private individuals, when they had polluted themselves by any criminal action.—**See ye to it.** Rather, *Ye shall see to it.* See note on ver. 4.—**His blood be on us.** But later they complained of the Apostles, that by their preaching "they intend to bring this man's blood upon us" (Acts 5:28). If Pilate's endeavor was to appeal to the priests' dread of divine punishment, by throwing the whole responsibility upon them, it signally failed. The terrible imprecation of this verse was terribly answered in subsequent history, in which the blood of Christ fell upon all who participated in his condemnation and death. Not only was the crucifixion, which the Jews demanded to be inflicted on Jesus, inflicted on myriads of Jews during the siege of Jerusalem, not only were they sold as slaves in great numbers for less than the thirty pieces of silver paid to Judas, but the judgments of God followed significantly the individuals who were most prominent in this crime. "Before the dread sacrifice was consummated, Judas died in the horrors of a loathsome suicide. Caiaphas was deposed the year following. Herod died in infamy and exile, stripped of his procuratorship very shortly afterwards, on the very charges he had tried by a wicked concession to avoid. Pilate, wearied out with misfortunes, died in suicide and banishment, leaving behind him an execrated name. The house of Annas was destroyed a generation later by an infuriated mob, and his son was dragged through the streets, and scourged and beaten to his place of murder."—(*Farrar.*)

26-31. Of this mockery of Jesus by the soldiers Matthew gives the fullest account. Crucifixion was always preceded by scourging.

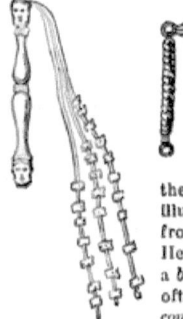

SCOURGES.

The scourge consisted of several chains or thongs of leather with pieces of metal or bone affixed to them which cut at every stroke a bloody furrow in the quivering flesh. Our illustrations are taken, one from an original found at Herculaneum, the other from a *bas-relief*. Scourging itself often produced death. The *common hall*, which Mark in the original more specifically describes as the court-yard (αὐλή), was probably the central court around which the Jewish house was usually constructed. See Matt. 26:69, note. The place I believe to have been, not the palace of Herod as Alford supposes, but the tower of Antonia. See John 18:28, note. The *whole band*, or cohort, which was gathered to join in the mockery, was the tenth part of a legion, embracing from three to six hundred men; but here probably only that portion of the band or cohort which was then actually on service. The *scarlet robe* (χλαμύς), was a short and light mantle originating with the inhabitants of Thessaly or Macedonia, whence it was imported into other parts of Greece, and became a regular equestrian costume of the period. The accompanying illustration, from a Greek vase, will give the reader a better idea of its character than any description. In Mark and John it is described as a "purple robe," but Matthew

SCARLET ROBE.

alone gives in the original its technical name. Both scarlet and purple were worn as marks of pre-eminence and wealth (Luke 15 : 19; Rev. 17 : 4). Alford suggests that this scarlet robe may have been the one in which Herod arrayed Christ. This is possible, but hardly probable. The word in Luke rendered *gorgeous* (λαμπρός), indicates rather a white robe (Luke 23 : 11, note). It is not known with certainty what was the plant employed in making the *crown of thorns*. Matthew calls it the acanthus (ἄκανθα), but neither this nor the traditional plant known as *spina christi* fully answers the conditions of the narrative. Some flexile shrub or plant must be understood, possibly some variety of the cactus or prickly pear. Thorn bushes of various kinds are plentiful in Palestine. Our illustration presents a not uncommon species.

CROWN OF THORNS.

Meyer supposes that the object of the thorn crown was not to occasion pain but "to mock;" but the common conception of the thorns, pressed into a lacerated and bleeding brow, agrees better with the narrative, though not necessitated by it. The *reed* may have been the stalk of any plant, or a true reed, or some instrument made from it. The accompanying illustration represents the *Papyrus antiquorum* or paper reed of the ancients. It grows still in great quantities near the plain of Gennesaret. Other varieties of reeds are found along the Jordan, and elsewhere in Palestine. Arrows, fishing-rods, pens, canes for measuring and other purposes, were made from the reed. A long cane, with a sponge affixed to the end of it for cleansing the ceiling of a room, was a common article of Roman furniture. This may have been the reed here used by the soldiers. This hour of Christ's coronation in mockery has been well described as the hour of Christ's grandeur. "He was King then, and was indeed crowned. No throne was like the steps on which he stood. No imperial person was so august as this derided and martyred Jew. If he had, by a resort to violence, relieved himself, he would have been discrowned. To suffer in sweet willingness; to have the suffering roll to unknown depths and not to murmur—this was to be a king far beyond the ordinary conception of kingship."—(*Henry Ward Beecher's Sermons*, Harper's Ed.)

THE REED.

31. His own raiment. (ἱμάτιον). The cloak described in Matt. 24 : 18, note.

CH. 27 : 32-56. THE CRUCIFIXION.—CHRIST'S MEETING OF DEATH: WITH PERFECT COMPOSURE AND WITH A SOUL ALERT (ver. 34).—THE INSENSIBILITY OF THE HUMAN HEART: ILLUSTRATED IN GAMBLING AT THE FOOT OF THE CROSS (35).—CHRIST IS NUMBERED WITH TRANSGRESSORS. IT IS NO INTOLERABLE HARDSHIP TO BE SO NUMBERED IF GOD AND OUR OWN CONSCIENCE APPROVE US. WE ARE THEN NUMBERED WITH CHRIST (38).—THE TRUE AND THE FALSE TEST OF RELIGION. THE TRUE TEST, THE POWER IT GIVES TO CONFER BLESSING UPON OTHERS; THE FALSE TEST, ITS SUPPOSED POWER TO CONFER BLESSING ON OURSELVES (42).—GOD PERMITS HIS BELOVED TO SUFFER (43), BUT MAKES THEM, WITH CHRIST, MORE THAN CONQUERORS IN SUFFERING.—THE TESTIMONY OF NATURE TO THE DIVINITY OF THE SON OF GOD (45).—SPIRITUAL LONELINESS DOES NOT ALWAYS PROVE THAT GOD HAS WITHDRAWN FROM US. THE TESTIMONY OF CHRIST'S AGONY TO HIS LOVE FOR US, TO THE REAL BURDEN OF SIN TO A SINLESS SOUL (46).—THE WORLD'S MISINTERPRETATION OF CHRIST'S SUFFERINGS. IT CAN NEVER UNDERSTAND HIS CRY (47-49).—BOLDNESS OF ACCESS GIVEN TO GOD IN CHRIST (51).—HE IS OUR RESURRECTION (52, 53). —THE DANGER OF PASSION, PRIDE, AND PREJUDICE, ILLUSTRATED BY THE CHIEF-PRIESTS. THE BEAUTY OF PATIENCE, LONG-SUFFERING, AND LOVE, ILLUSTRATED BY CHRIST.—CHRIST, AS OUR EXAMPLE TEACHES US HOW TO DIE; BY HIS DEATH HE TEACHES US THE DIVINE LOVE, AND THE CURSE OF SIN; IN HIS DEATH HE BEARS OUR SINS THAT WE MAY NO MORE BEAR THEM (2 Cor. 5 : 21; 1 Pet. 2 : 24).

PRELIMINARY NOTE. The crucifixion is recorded by the four Evangelists. Comp. Mark 15 : 21-41; Luke 23 : 26-49; John 19 : 17-30. Matthew and Mark are almost exactly parallel; the differences are only verbal. Luke and John both narrate incidents not recorded by the others.

The most casual reader of the N. T. can hardly fail to notice the severe simplicity of the Evangelical narratives. They could not be more

32 And as they came out, they found a man of Cyrene, Simon by name; him they compelled to bear his cross.

33 And when they were come unto a place called Golgotha, that is to say, a place of a skull,

---

absolutely colorless if they were official reports by Pilate or his subordinates. There is not a single epithet employed to express or excite, either indignation against the crucifiers, or reverence or compassion for the crucified. There is no attempt to deduce any doctrinal conclusion. Simply the facts are stated. Their singular impartiality is of itself a remarkable testimony to their divine inspiration; for the story of the cross has acquired its power in part from the marvelous self-restraint of the historians. They have placed before the world the scene as they saw it; each new generation sees through a clear and colorless atmosphere the Crucified One, undraped with the rhetoric of feeling; His death is eloquent because the story is told without eloquence; and the latest ages can say, Not only our ears have heard, but our eyes have seen the glory of the suffering Lord. Following their example I shall endeavor in these notes simply to give such information as will better enable the student to comprehend the facts. He who believes that the cross of Christ is the enthronement of God, because the supreme display of Divine love for the salvation of sinners, among whom he includes himself, cannot look upon the Crucified One with compassion; nor upon the crucifiers with hate. The admonition of Christ, "Weep not for me," forbids pity; the prayer of Christ, "Father forgive them," forbids wrath. The spirit with which the redeemed in heaven approach the Lamb slain from the foundation of the world (Rev. 5: 12), is that in which we are to approach Him on earth.

Grouping the four narratives, the incidents which they narrate appear to be substantially as follows: An association of women was organized in Jerusalem to alleviate the sufferings of condemned criminals. They followed Jesus to the cross, perhaps are the women referred to in Luke 23: 27, and offered him, before his crucifixion, an anodyne composed of vinegar and gall, called by Mark 15: 23, "wine and myrrh." He declined it because he would not meet death with a stupefied soul. Its object was to deaden his sensibilities (ver. 34; Mark 15: 23). The cross was extended on the ground and Jesus was nailed to it. At this time he uttered the prayer, "Father, forgive them, for they know not what they do" (Luke 23: 34). The clothing of criminals was a perquisite of the Roman soldiers. They sat down at the foot of the cross to divide Christ's garments. His tunic was a seamless robe of fine texture. One of the company produced dice, the Roman medium for gambling, and they commenced to cast lots for the possession of this robe (vers. 35, 36). At a little distance stood a group of Galilean women, among whom was Mary. Jesus, in the midst of his own anguish, did not forget hers, and commended her to the keeping of the beloved disciple (John 19: 26, 27). It was customary to bear before the prisoner, condemned to death, an inscription which designated the crime for which he was condemned. This inscription, written by Pilate in the three languages of the time, that of the court, Latin, that of the Gentile population, Greek, and that of the Jews, Hebrew or Aramaic, was fastened to the cross, above the head of the Divine Sufferer (ver. 37). With him were crucified two brigands (ver. 38, note). Of these one joined in the taunts of the multitude; the other reproached his companion, confessed his sin, and appealed, not in vain, to the Saviour of sinners, for salvation (Luke 23: 39-43). The priests, the soldiers, and those that passed by, taunted the Lord with his seeming impotency and approaching death; but he made no response (vers. 40-44; Luke 23: 35, 37). At length a preternatural darkness, such as often precedes an earthquake, began to gather over the scene. With a cry of agony, full of mystery to us, as it was to those who stood at the cross, he appealed to his God, who seemed to have forsaken him; then cried with a loud voice, clear and full to the last, "It is finished!" and gave up the ghost (vers. 45-50). It was three o'clock (the ninth hour), which was the hour of evening sacrifice. The long-presaged earthquake came. The veil of the Temple was rent, the graves were opened; subsequently many bodies of the saints which slept arose. The sublimity of Christ's death, not less than the portents which accompanied it, wrung from the Roman centurion the confession "Truly this was the Son of God" (ver. 54; Mark 15: 39). To hasten the death of the crucified the soldiers broke the the legs of the two thieves; but seeing that Jesus was already dead, pierced his side, out of which came blood and water (John 19: 31-42). The incidents of the weeping women, Christ's prayer for the forgiveness of his enemies, and the penitent thief, are peculiar to Luke; see notes there. The reply of Pilate to the remonstrances of the priests against his inscription, the women at the cross, and the piercing of Christ's side, are peculiar to John; see notes there. For the incidents peculiar to Matthew or common to the four Evangelists, see notes below.

32. And as they came out. That is, from the city; the place of execution was without the city walls (Heb. 13: 12). This was customary among the Jews (Numb. 15: 35; 1 Kings 21: 13; Acts 7: 58), and also among the Romans.—**A man of Cyrene, Simon by name.** He is described by Mark, 15 : 21, as the father of Alexander and Rufus. It has been supposed by some that they are the persons mentioned in Romans 16 : 13 and 1 Tim. 1 : 20 or Acts 19 : 33, but this is quite uncertain. Nothing more is known with certainty of him; but the hypothesis that he was a Jewish pilgrim from Africa is a reasonable one. Cyrene was a city of Libya, the capital of Cyrenaica; it was founded by a colony of Greeks about b. c. 632; stood on table-land 1,800 feet above the level of the Mediterranean; was at this time a Roman city, and united in government with the not distant island of Crete. That it was the abode of many Jews is indicated by Acts 6 : 9, from which it would appear that the Cyrenian Jews had a synagogue of their own in Jerusalem. Some of the first Christian teachers were Cyrenians (Acts 11 : 20; 13 : 1).—**Him they impressed to bear his cross.** This is the proper translation of the Greek. The Roman officer had official authority to press into the military service, for a special purpose, either horses or men. See note on Matt. 5 : 41. Jesus at first carried his own cross (John 19 : 17), as the convict customarily did; there is no positive authority for what is, however, a reasonable surmise, that, weakened by want of sleep and loss of blood, he was no longer able to sustain it. This opinion is embodied in ancient art, which represents him as sinking beneath the weight of the cross.

33. Golgotha. A Hebrew word, meaning a skull. From its Latin equivalent *calvariæ* comes our English word Calvary, which occurs in the English N. T. only in Luke 23 : 33, where it should be translated "a skull." The signifi-

GOLGOTHA.

cance of the name is uncertain. Some suppose that it was the common place of execution, and that the skulls of those who were executed lay about; others that it was a bare rounded knoll, in form like a skull. This opinion is the sole foundation for the almost universal impression that it was a hill. The location of this place of execution is unknown. There are three hypothetical sites. The first, which is supported by an ancient tradition, is now occupied by the Church of the Holy Sepulchre, indicated in the accompanying cut by the dome to the reader's right. But the ancient traditions are of very small value in determining the Biblical sites; the monks who designate the place of execution and burial, point out with equal certainty the holes in the rock in which the cross was planted! If, as is probable, this site was then, as it is now, within the city walls, it cannot be the true Golgotha. The second hypothesis is that of Mr. Fergusson, who asserts that Golgotha was on Mount Moriah, and that the Mosque of Omar, or Dome of the Rock, to the reader's left in the picture, covers the true site. He designates a cave beneath this dome as the probable burial-place. But this view, which rests mainly on architectural arguments, based on the character of the Mosque of Omar, is not generally accepted by scholars, who are almost unanimous in the opinion that this Mosque occupies the site of the ancient temple. A third theory identifies Golgotha with the mound in the foreground of our illustration, now known as the Grotto of Jeremiah. It is situated about forty rods to the northeast of the Damascus gate. The cave sepulchre beneath is one of the largest in the country, and may have been the burial-place. But of this hypothesis we can only say that there is nothing, except its distance from the tower of Antonia, opposed to it. All that we can *know* of Golgotha is that it was near the city (John 19 : 20), apparently near a public highway (Mark 15 : 29), in the immediate vicinity of one of the gardens

34 They gave him vinegar to drink, mingled ᵃ with gall: and when he had tasted *thereof*, he would not drink.
35 And ᵇ they crucified him, and parted his garments,
casting lots; that it might be fulfilled which was spoken ᶜ by the prophet, They parted my garments among them, and upon my vesture did they cast lots.
36 And sitting down, they watched him there;

a Ps. 69 : 21. ... b Ps. 22 : 18; Mark 15 : 24, etc.; Luke 23 : 34, etc.; John 19 : 24, etc. ... c Ps. 22 : 18.

which surrounded Jerusalem (John 19 : 41), and is, as indicated by Luke's language, "*the* place called the skull," a well-known spot.

34. They gave to him vinegar to drink mingled with gall. Mark says, "wine mingled with myrrh," but the difference is purely verbal. "As the wine used by the soldiers was a cheap, sour wine, little, if at all, superior to vinegar, and as myrrh, gall, and other bitter substances are put for the whole class, there is really no difference in these passages."—(*Alexander*.) It was customary to give a stupefying drink to criminals on their way to execution. This was probably the draught offered to our Lord, perhaps by the women referred to in Luke 23 : 27; see note there. Christ, when he knew from the taste its object, refused to partake, an indication that he deliberately chose to have all his powers alert at this last hour. There is no reason for the belief that it was offered to him twice, or in a spirit of rancor and scoffing.

35, 36. And they (the soldiers) **crucified him.** According to Mark (15 : 25), it was the third hour; that is, 9 A. M.; but this may mean that the third hour had already passed. See John 19 : 14, note.—**And parted his garments casting lots.** Of this, John gives a fuller account. See notes on John 19 : 23, 24.—**That it might be fulfilled.** This clause is omitted by all the best manuscripts and the best scholars. It was probably added in the margin by some ancient harmonist, from John 19 : 24. The reference is to Psalm 22 : 18.—**They watched him there.** This was customary, to prevent the crucified person from being taken down by friends. There were four soldiers (John 19 : 23).

THE NATURE OF CRUCIFIXION. — Crucifixion was used as a punishment by Grecians, Romans, Egyptians, and other nations, but not by the Jews. Its infliction by the Romans was a badge of Israel's servitude. To hang even a corpse upon a tree was accounted among them the greatest indignity (Deut. 21 : 22, 23). The lingering death of the cross rendered crucifixion eminent in cruelty even in that cruel age. Cicero called it a punishment most inhuman and shocking, and wrote of it that it should be removed from the eyes and ears and every thought of man. It was reserved by the Romans for slaves and foreigners. There were three forms of crosses, the first in the shape of the letter X, called the *crux decussata*, or, later, St. Andrew's Cross; one in the form of the letter T, called the *crux commissa*,

THE THREE CROSSES.

or, later, St. Anthony's cross; and third, the Latin cross, or *crux immissa*, like the preceding one, except that the upright beam projected above the horizontal one. There is also the Greek cross, consisting of two pieces of wood of equal length crossing each other at right angles in the centre. That the Latin cross was the one on which Jesus was crucified is indicated by uniform tradition, and by the fact that the inscription was placed upon it over his head. The convict was fastened to the cross, sometimes as it lay upon the ground, sometimes after its erection. In the former case the body was terribly wrenched when the cross was raised and dropped into its place; the concussion often dislocated the limbs. To fasten the sufferer to the cross his hands were nailed to the crosspiece; the feet were sometimes bound, sometimes nailed. That the latter course was adopted in the case of Christ is indicated, though not demonstrated, by Luke 24 : 39, 40. The feet were probably nailed separately, not, as represented in most art, and purely for artistic reasons, with one foot lying over the other and both transfixed with one nail. Lest the hands and feet should not bear the strain, a little wooden pin projected just below the thigh, which afforded the body a partial though painful support. There was no support to the feet, though this is sometimes represented in art. The crucified person was not raised high in air; his feet were but a little above the ground. In this respect the common art representations are not true to the facts.

Thus, with no vital organ directly touched, the victim was left to die. The heat of the Oriental sun, the festering of the undressed wounds, the increased torment produced by every attempted movement to secure relief, the burning fever, the throbbing head, the intense thirst—all combined to make death by crucifixion as horrible as it was protracted. See an elaborate description of it in Farrar's *Life of Christ*, and one more scientifically

37 And set up over his head, his accusation written, THIS IS JESUS THE KING OF THE JEWS.
38 Then were there two thieves crucified with him; one on the right hand, and another on the left.
39 And they that passed by reviled him, wagging their heads,
40 And saying, Thou that destroyest the temple, and buildest *it* in three days, save thyself. If thou be the Son of God, come down from the cross.
41 Likewise also the chief priests mocking *him*, with the scribes and elders, said,

42 He saved others, himself he cannot save. If he be the King of Israel, let him now come down from the cross, and we will believe him.
43 He trusted in God; let him deliver him now, if he will have him; for he said, I am the Son of God.
44 The thieves also, which were crucified with him, cast the same in his teeth.
45 Now from the sixth hour there was darkness over all the land unto the ninth hour.
46 And about the ninth hour Jesus cried with a loud voice, saying, Eli, Eli, lama sabachthani? that is to say, My God, my God, why hast thou forsaken me?

full in Stroud's *Physical Cause of Christ's Death*. So great were the tortures of this lingering death that there are many ancient instances of men who bought with large bribes the privilege of being executed in some other manner, and the death was ordinarily hastened by the wearied executioners, by a thrust with the spear or a blow with the club.

37, 38. Set up over his head his accusation. It was customary to bear before the condemned an inscription which designated his crime, and which was subsequently attached to the cross. Such was this inscription. On the variations in the Evangelists' report of it, see John 19 : 19, 20, notes.—**Two thieves.** Rather, *brigands*, for this is the significance of the original (λησταὶς). It is not improbable that they belonged to the band of which Barabbas was the leader (Mark 15 : 7). Christ's crucifixion between them was a literal fulfillment of prophecy (Mark 15 : 28; Isaiah 53 : 12).

39-43. The three Synoptists mention this mockery; John does not. Three classes are described as participating in it. The passers-by (ver. 39), that is, those casually going to and from the city; the chief priests (ver. 41); and the soldiers (Luke 23 : 36).—**Wagging their heads.** A symbol of derision (Job 16 : 4; Psalm 22 : 7).—**Thou that destroyest the temple * * * save thyself.** The reference is to John 2 : 19, and the language here and in verses 62, 63, indicates that their misrepresentation of his language upon his trial (ch. 26 : 61) was willful.—**He saved others.** Not a real acknowledgment of his saving power; the language is that of bitter irony.—**Himself he cannot save.** An unconscious utterance of the truth, like the accusation preferred against him as "a friend of publicans and sinners." If he had saved himself he could not have saved others (ch. 26 : 53, 54).—**He is the King of Israel!** Not, according to the best manuscripts, *If he be the King of Israel*, as in our English version. The language is that of taunt, and refers to the inscription upon the cross; and its object was, perhaps, in part to turn the edge of its sarcasm against the nation. "Ho! Ho! he is the king of Israel! let him descend from the cross now, and we will believe in him." If he had done so it would have made no difference in their belief, for they resisted the greater miracle of his resurrection (ch. 28 : 14, 15).—**Let him deliver him now if he will have him.** A striking illustration of the false idea of special Providence. Many still think that he who seems to be deserted by God cannot be a son in whom he is well pleased, and that God may always be expected to interfere immediately to save his children from unjust suffering. Observe, by comparison with Psalm 22, written by David at least a thousand years before this time, a singular testimony to the inspiration of prophecy.

44. The brigands also * * * * upbraided him. Luke 23 : 39 gives the language which seems to have been employed only by one. Of the penitence of the other, Matthew and Mark make no mention. The hypothesis that both at first reviled and one afterwards repented, a supposition entertained by some of the older commentators, is much less probable than that Matthew and Mark omit, perhaps are not acquainted with, the incident of the penitent thief, and simply speak of the derision in general terms.

45. From the sixth hour. Twelve o'clock. On the discrepancy between this verse and John 19 : 14, see note there.—**There was darkness over all the land until the ninth hour.** That is, 3 P.M. It is neither necessary nor reasonable to suppose that this darkness enveloped the whole earth. The original (γῆ), here rendered land, is often used in the N. T. for a limited territory (Matt. 2 : 6, 20, 21; 4 : 15; 11 : 24; 14 : 34). The darkness could not have been produced by an eclipse, for the Passover was celebrated at the full moon, when the moon is opposite the sun. It may have been a natural phenomenon, premonitory of the earthquake which followed. Stroud (*Physical Cause of Christ's Death*) gives a number of illustrations of similar phenomena of darkness connected with earthquakes or volcanoes. The fact is mentioned by the three Evangelists, but not by John; and the early fathers appealed to profane testimony in attestation of it. Wordsworth notes the contrast between this darkness and that in Egypt: "Then the Hebrews had light in their dwellings while the rest of Egypt

47 Some of them that stood there, when they heard *that*, said, This *man* calleth for Elias.
48 And straightway one of them ran, and took a sponge, and filled *it* with ᵏ vinegar, and put *it* on a reed, and gave him to drink.
49 The rest said, Let be, let us see whether Elias will come to save him.

ᵏ Ps. 69 : 21.

was dark; but now, when the true Passover is killed by them, they are in darkness, and the light of the Gospel is about to be poured on the Gentile world." It is not possible to misapprehend the solemn significance of this act, representing the sympathy of nature with its crucified Lord; nor necessary to attempt any detailed interpretation, such as that it represented his conflict with the powers of darkness and his present want of heavenly comfort (*Matthew Henry*), or God's detestation of the crime, and his future blinding of the Jewish nation (*Calvin*), or that the death of Christ was the going out of the light of the world (*Adam Clarke*).

46. Jesus when he had cried with a loud voice. Literally a *great* voice, *i. e.*, with the voice still strong, unweakened by approaching death. On the significance of this fact see John 19:34, note.—**Eli, Eli, lama sabacthani.** Quoted from Psalm 22:1. The first two words are Hebrew, the latter two Chaldaic. Mark's language, *Eloi*, is a Syro-Chaldaic form, having the same meaning.—**My God, my God, why hast thou forsaken me?** Dr. Adam Clarke, following Lightfoot, proposes to translate this *To what* (sort *of persons*, understood) *hast thou forsaken me?* thus rendering it simply as an expression of astonishment at the wickedness of his crucifiers; but this appears to me untenable, because, though the language of Mark (εἰς τί με ἐγκατέλιπες) is capable of this translation, the language of Matthew (ἱνατί με, etc.) is not; and it weakens the force of the cry, and reduces it to a mere yielding at last to the taunts which up to this point Christ has borne in a sublime silence. Accepting our English translation as correct, how shall we understand it? Certainly not (*a*) as the outcry "of the humanity of our Saviour and not of his divinity" (*James Morison*); for there is no Scriptural authority whatever for thus discriminating a part of Christ's life and experience as divine and a part as human, a refinement of scholastic theology which deprives both his example and his manifestation of the divine nature of their true meaning and power; nor (*b*) as spoken in our name, and as a lesson for us that we should never despair, even though God hides his face from us (*Wordsworth*). This lesson is sublimely taught by the cry of Christ in this hour. But to suppose that he uttered it *for the purpose*, is to deprive it of all moral power, and to throw over his utterances, even the most solemn and sacred, the suspicion that they are not simple truth, but have been uttered for dramatic effect; nor (*c*) that it is simply "an expression of agony couched in the devout language of Scripture."—(*Furness.*) Doubtless it is this; but Christ would not have taken the language of Scripture if it did not exactly express his experience. These are all evasions, not interpretations of the passage. (*d.*) Nor are we to hold ourselves debarred from all endeavor to understand their meaning.—(*Bloomfield.*) The words are written for our profit, though to be studied in humility, and with a consciousness that the experience which they indicate defies our analysis and transcends our perfect conception. The student may obtain some light in such a study from a consideration of the following facts: (1.) Jesus is represented in the N. T. as subject to the whole experience of spiritual conflict which belongs to man. No philosophy which ignores or eliminates this truth can interpret the temptation, or the agony in Gethsemane, or the cry upon the cross (comp. Matt. 4:1–11; Prel. Note, § 6, p. 39; ch. 28:36–46, note; Lessons of Gethsemane, p. 293). (2.) He is represented in the Prophets (Isaiah 53:5, 6) and the Epistles (2 Cor. 5:21; Gal. 3:13; 1 Pet. 2:24) as taking upon himself the penalty of our sins; and the penalty of sin is represented throughout the Bible as spiritual separation from God (Deut. 32:20; Prov. 1:24–29; Isaiah 64:7; Micah 3:4; 2 Thess. 1:9). (3.) Some help toward an understanding of this cry may be derived from that phase of Christian experience in which, while the intellect still holds fast to its belief in God, the heart *feels* his presence no more, and the soul is in darkness, in spite of its faith in God (comp. Matt. 11:1–6, note; Exod. 17:4; 1 Kings 19:10; Psalm 10:1; Jer. 12:1, 2). (4.) That there was an inward conflict in Christ's soul is indicated by the twofold nature of the cry; "*My God*" indicates an unrelaxed hold on him; "*forsaken me*" indicates a sense of bereavement of the divine presence. If these are inconsistent, the inconsistency repeats itself frequently in Christian experience. (5.) It expresses surprise, as though some new and unexpected anguish had been added to that already borne, and the indication certainly is that a cry which neither the physical anguish nor the taunts of his foes could wring from his lips was wrung by this mysterious agony of separation from his God. (6.) It is the cry of innocence; the lost know that they are forsaken, but know *why*, and do not call on God as *their* God. It was, therefore, *no literal transfer* of the experience of remorse and spir-

50 Jesus, when he had cried again with a loud voice, yielded up the ghost.
51 And, behold, the veil¹ of the temple was rent ᵐ in twain, from the top to the bottom; and the earth did quake, and the rocks rent;
52 And ⁿ the graves were opened; and many bodies of the saints which ᵒ slept, arose,
53 And came out of the graves ᵖ after his resurrection, and went into the holy city, and appeared unto many

l Exod. 26 : 31 ; Lev. 16 : 2, 15 ; 21 : 23 ; 2 Chron. 3 : 14.....m Isa. 25 : 7.....n Isa. 26 : 19 ; 26 : 19 ; Hosea 13 : 14 ; John 5 : 25, 28....o Dan. 12 : 2 ; 1 Thess. 4 : 14.....p 1 Cor. 15 : 20.

itual death which Christ experienced. Compare the evidence of the triumph of his faith in his last utterance, just before death (Luke 23 : 46.)

47–49. This incident is recorded by all of the Evangelists. A comparison of their accounts is instructive, because it indicates the independence and originality of the accounts. The variations forbid the idea of collusion among the writers, or their acquaintance with each other's accounts, or a common origin. They are such as characterize independent and honest witnesses. Luke's account, which is less detailed, is simply that the soldiers offered Christ vinegar in mockery. John says that Christ said, "I thirst," and that the vinegar was offered in consequence; Matthew that it was offered by one, and the rest objected; Mark that he who offered the drink said, Let alone, that is, Let this suffice, and see if Elias will come. From a comparison of these accounts it would appear that Christ followed the exclamation of the preceding verse with an expression of thirst, that the drink was offered by one of the soldiers, in a spirit of commingled pity and contempt, and that the others objected as reported here. Alford thinks that the language here could not have been used by the soldiers, "who knew nothing about Elias." But it is not by any means certain that they did not know the current Jewish belief that the coming of the Messiah was to be preceded by a coming of Elijah (Matt. 16 ; 14 ; 17 : 10). In that case the language here would be partly a misunderstanding of Christ's words and partly a mockery. The

HYSSOP—
Organum maru.

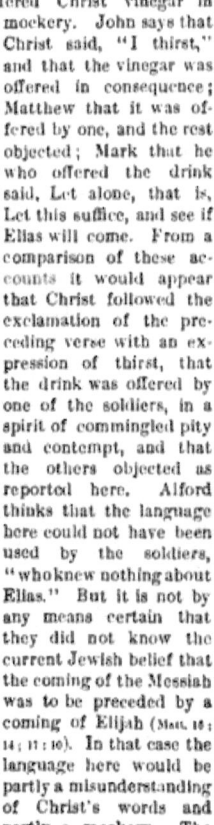

vinegar (*posca*) was a cheap sour wine, mixed with water, which was a common drink, especially for the poorer classes and for soldiers. A vessel filled with it stood near the cross (John 19 : 29), probably belonging to the soldiers, an additional indication that it was offered not by one of the Jews, but by a soldier. The "*reed*" is described by John as the *hyssop*, by many scholars thought to be the caper-plant (Arabic *hysop*), which grows in dry and rocky places and on walls, and is capable of producing a stick three or four feet in length. As the crucified was raised but a little above the ground, such a reed would suffice to reach the sufferer's lips. Dr. Post of Syria, however (*Smith's Bib. Dict.*, Art. *Hyssop*), argues against this supposition, on account of the thorny character of the plant, and proposes in lieu of it the *Organum maru*, which grows on the walls of all the terraces throughout Palestine and Syria, has a slender stem, free from thorns and spreading branches, and ending in a cluster of heads, having a highly aromatic odor, and thus exactly fitted to be made into a bunch for the purposes of sprinkling, for which purpose it was used in O. T. times in purification. He thus thinks this plant, of which we give an illustration from his drawing, best answers the Scripture reference to the hyssop of the Bible (Exod. 19 ; 22 ; Lev. 14 ; 4, 51 ; Numb. 19 : 6, 18 ; 1 Kings 4 : 33 ; Ps. 51 : 7 ; Heb. 9 : 19).

When he had cried with a loud voice. See on verse 46, and Note on Physical Cause of Christ's Death, John 19 : 34. Comparing accounts in Luke and John it appears that he first cried with a loud, *i. e.*, clear, strong voice, "It is finished," then, perhaps, in a more subdued tone, "Father, into thy hands I commend my spirit." — **Yielded up the ghost.** Nothing concerning the voluntary character of his death is fairly deducible from these words, which are simply a common expression for death. See Gen. 35 : 18, where in the Septuagint the language rendered "Her soul was in departing," is substantially the same employed here.

51–53. These incidents are rejected by rationalistic critics as mythical additions to the historical narratives of the crucifixion. There is, however, nothing whatever in the state of the text to throw any doubt over their genuineness. If expunged, it must be wholly, because they are regarded as inherently incredible. Those who believe, as I do, that God is the Lord of Nature, and that he sometimes teaches sublime truths by

54 Now⁹ when the centurion, and they that were with him, watching Jesus, saw the earthquake, and those things that were done, they feared greatly, saying, Truly this was the Son of God.
55 And many women were there, beholding afar off, which ʳ followed Jesus from Galilee, ministering unto him:
56 Among which was Mary Magdalene, and Mary the mother of James and Joses, and the mother of Zebedee's children.

q Mark 15 : 39 ; Luke 23 : 47, etc. . . . r Luke 8 : 2, 3.

a sublime symbolism, will find nothing incredible in the narrative if it is properly comprehended. The only question to such will be, Is it adequately authenticated? The rending of the vail is narrated by the three Synoptists. It might easily have become known through some of the "great company of priests," who early became Christ's disciples (Acts 6 : 7). Apart from such testimony it can hardly fail to have become known. If it did not occur, the story could have been easily and completely refuted at any time prior to the destruction of Jerusalem by the vail itself, and at any time subsequent thereto, and during that generation, by the testimony of living priests. Neander (*Life of Christ*), refers to the later traditions, that a beam over the Temple broke, and that about forty years before the destruction of Jerusalem the Temple doors, though securely locked, suddenly burst open, as affording incidental confirmation of this narrative, from which, perhaps, they sprang. The earthquake and resurrection are peculiar to Matthew. The account of the earthquake accords with and explains the preternatural darkness described by all the Synoptists, and it is incidentally confirmed by the rents and fissures now found in the vicinity of Jerusalem, and indicating volcanic action. But for the resurrection we have only Matthew's testimony, and he does not claim to have been an eye-witness. He does not say the saints appeared to *him*, but to "*many*." It is not referred to by subsequent writers; and its omission by Paul, in 1 Cor. ch. 15, where it certainly would have added strength to his argument if the fact were generally known in the Christian church, is worthy of note. I judge, then, that certainly the rending of the vail, and perhaps the earthquake, is as well authenticated as any event recorded in the N. T.; but that the resurrection is less so. The incidents are confirmed, however, by their religious significance and their accordance with other N. T. teachings. The rending of the vail, which hung before the Holy of Holies (see note below), indicates that in the death of Christ the whole world has access to God; the resurrection, that in his life all his people have resurrection and life eternal. The first is interpreted by Heb. 10 : 19–21, which, with Alford, I believe has a reference to the fact here stated; the other by John 11 : 25. Comp. for both, Rom. 5 : 10.

The vail of the Temple.—This was a vail which hung before the door of the Holy of Holies; the apartment which contained the Ark of the Covenant. This ark, containing the sacred law, and comprising the mercy-seat below the cherubim, was the peculiar shrine of the Godhead. Only the high-priest could enter this apartment, and he but once a year (Exod. 30 : 10; Lev. 16 : 2–19) to sprinkle blood upon the mercy-seat, to blot out the transgressions which the law within the ark was ever charging against the people. The rending of this vail unmistakably indicated that the final sacrifice had been now made, for all time, and that henceforth access to God, through Christ's death, was open to all.—**The earth did quake.** Alford says, "not an ordinary earthquake." What he means, I do not understand. The language implies nothing extraordinary in the earthquake, except in the incidents which accompanied it. The earthquake was to the reverent Jew associated with the presence of God, and regarded as a peculiar token of his power (Judges 5 : 4 ; 2 Sam. 22 : 8 ; Ps. 77 : 18 ; 97 : 4 ; 104 : 32 ; Amos 8 : 8 ; Hab. 3 : 10).—**And the graves were opened.** Graves or sepulchres were commonly made in caves, hewn in the rock; these were broken open by the earthquake.—**Many bodies of holy men.** There is nothing in the language to indicate whether patriarchs and other saints of olden times, or disciples of Christ who had died, as Simeon, Hannah, Zachariah, John the Baptist, and Joseph.—**And coming out of the graves, after his resurrection,** went into the holy city. That is, into Jerusalem. The original is ambiguous, as is my translation, on the point whether the resurrection or only the going into the holy city, was subsequent to Christ's resurrection. The former opinion best accords with 1 Cor. 15 : 23. If we suppose, as I do, with Alford, Wordsworth and the early fathers, that these saints rose with the glorified body (1 Cor. 15 : 51–53), and ascended with their Lord, into heaven, the incident is wholly in accordance with the N. T. doctrine of resurrection, and is indeed a sublime teaching of that doctrine. See 1 Cor. ch. 15, and 1 Thess. 4 : 13–17.

54. The centurion. An officer of the Roman army answering to the captain in our own organization. He commanded a century, answering to our "company," originally a hundred men, subsequently from fifty to a hundred. The annexed cuts present the figures of two centurions from ancient bas-reliefs.—**And they that were with him.** The four soldiers (John 19 : 23) appointed to guard the cross. The feeling of

TWO CENTURIONS.

awe, according to Luke, extended to all the bystanders (Luke 23 : 48). Mark, who says nothing of the earthquake, attributes the centurion's awe to the manner of Christ's death (Mark 15 : 39, note). Doubtless both Christ's personal character and the phenomena of nature which accompanied his death, contributed to produce the impression. Lange notes the triumvirate of Roman soldiers bearing testimony to Christ—the centurion in Capernaum (Matt. 8 : 5–10), the one here mentioned, and Cornelius at Cæsarea (Acts, ch. 10). —**Truly this was a Son of God.** Not *the* Son of God. Neither here nor in Mark is there the definite article. Luke's report is "This was a righteous man," *i. e.*, innocent. It is a gratuitous assumption to presume that the officer was wholly ignorant of the Jewish meaning attached to the term, "Son of God." Two charges had been preferred against Jesus—blasphemy in making himself the Son of God, and sedition against the Roman government. Pilate had publicly and repeatedly acquitted him of the second charge, and the first had been publicly repeated by the priests to Pilate (John 19 : 6, 7). These facts interpret the centurion's testimony here, namely, He is innocent of the crime of sedition (Luke), and is what he claimed to be, a Son of God. But it would be attributing to this Roman soldier a marvelous proficiency in theological knowledge to interpret this as a conscious testimony to the divinity of Jesus Christ, in the modern sense of that term. For similar use of language by a heathen, see Dan. 3 : 25. Sophocles' *Dictionary* refers to the use of this phrase, "Son of God," among heathen writers, as equivalent, or nearly equivalent, to a just or perfect man. Observe that he says not *is* but *was* a Son of God; evidently in his thought the death of Christ was the end. It is worth noticing that the cross had greater effect on the centurion, who was before simply ignorant of and indifferent to Christ, than on the Pharisees, who had the advantage of him in religious knowledge and culture, but had steeled themselves against the truth.

55, 56. The attendance of women at the cross is mentioned by the four Evangelists, but Luke does not give their names, and adds that "all his acquaintance" were there. The disciples, then, were eye-witnesses of the crucifixion. On the proper harmony of Matthew, Mark, and John here, partly depends the question whether the brethren of our Lord mentioned in the N. T. were true brethren or only kinsfolk. See tabular statement and comparison of the accounts, and my conclusion respecting them, on p. 110. Observe that these were not the women referred to in Luke who followed him weeping. *They* were of Jerusalem (Luke 23 : 28); *these* were all Galileans.—**Afar off.** Probably on account of the danger of recognition if they approached too near. Art, which represents them close by, sometimes even embracing the cross, is not true to history.—**Mary Magdalene.** That is, Mary of Magdala. She is described as one out of whom our Lord cast seven devils (Mark 16 : 9). This fact and her presence at the crucifixion and the sepulchre (ver. 61), and our Lord's appearance to her, and her report of his resurrection to the disciples, are all that is known of her. There is no ground whatever for identifying her with the woman that was a sinner, mentioned in Luke 7 : 36–50, and none, therefore, for the popular idea that her early life was profligate. Yet that idea is all but universal. The name is applied to women who have fallen from chastity; institutions for the reformation of such women are known as Magdalene asylums; an order of nuns, in the Romish church, composed chiefly of penitent courtesans, is called Magdalenes, and is dedicated to Mary Magdalene—a curious illustration of the extent to which an entirely groundless idea may gain popular and unquestioned acceptance.—**Mary the mother of James.** Described by John, 19 : 25, as "the wife of Cleophas," elsewhere called Alphæus (Matt. 10 : 3). Cleophas and Alphæus are different Greek forms of the same Hebrew word. The James here mentioned is James the Less, the brother of Joses. Nothing is known of his mother except the information given here and in the accounts of her visit to the sepulchre with Mary Magdalene (Matt. 28 : 1–11; Mark 16 : 1–8; Luke 24 : 1–11).—**The mother of Zebedee's children.** James and John (Matt. 10 : 2). Her name was Salome (Mark 15 : 40); and she is, I believe, to be identified with the one described in John (19 : 25, note) as the "sister of Jesus' mother." Her ambitious request for the preferment of her two sons (Matt. 20 : 20, 21) and her presence at the crucifixion and the sepulchre, are the only references to her in the N. T. Nothing is known of her subsequent history.

57–61. THE BURIAL OF JESUS' BODY. Comp. Mark 15 : 42–57; Luke 23 : 50–56; John 19 : 38–42. John's account is the fullest; see notes there for all that is common to the four Evangelists, and for some account of Jewish burials and

57 When the even was come, there came a rich man of Arimathæa, named Joseph, who also himself was Jesus' disciple:
58 He went to Pilate, and begged the body of Jesus. Then Pilate commanded the body to be delivered.
59 And when Joseph had taken the body, he wrapped it in a clean linen cloth,

60 And laid it in his own new tomb, which he had hewn out in the rock: and he rolled a great stone to the door of the sepulchre, and departed.
61 And there was Mary Magdalene, and the other Mary, sitting over against the sepulchre.
62 Now the next day, that followed the day of the preparation, the chief priests and Pharisees came together unto Pilate,

a Mark 15 : 42, 43 ; Luke 23 : 50–53 ; John 19 : 38. . . . . 1 Isa. 53 : 9.

burial-places. Prior to the burial the soldiers made sure of Christ's death by piercing his side with the spear (John 19 : 34).—**When the even was come.** In Jewish and Grecian reckoning there were two evenings, the first commencing with the declining sun, the second with the setting sun (ch. 26 : 20, note); comp. Exod. 12 : 6, marg. reading, "between the two evenings;" similarly in Numb. 9 : 3 ; 28 : 4. The first evening must be indicated here, for it was *during the preparation*—**A rich man.** Of Arimathea. He is described as a councillor, that is, a member of the Sanhedrim, by Mark and Luke, who give some insight into his character. John says that he was a disciple secretly, for fear of the Jews. Nicodemus came with him, bringing material for anointing the body (John 19 : 39).—**Then Pilate commanded the body to be delivered.** He first assured himself of Christ's death, by inquiring of the centurion (Mark 15 : 44, 45).—**In his own new tomb.** Matthew alone describes it as Joseph's tomb. It was in a garden, and near the place of crucifixion (John 19 : 41). For description and plan of the Jewish tomb see notes on Mark 16 : 3. A comparison of the accounts in the original indicates that this was an artificial excavation in the rock, not cut downward after the manner of a modern grave, but horizontally, after the manner of a modern tomb. For explanation and illustration of the Jewish method of closing the door of such a sepulchre by a circular stone rolled in front of it, see Mark 16 : 3, 4, note.—**The other Mary.** The mother of Joses (Mark 25 : 47). See note on ver. 56, above. From this sorrowful watch they returned home to prepare spices and ointments for the further anointing of Jesus' body (Luke 23 : 55, 56). As they went direct from the place of execution to the grave, they probably knew nothing about the guard given by Pilate; hence, this did not occur to them as a difficulty when they visited the sepulchre to complete the anointing (Mark 16 : 2, 3).

Ch. 27 : 62–66. A GUARD FOR THE SEPULCHRE OBTAINED.—CHRIST CANNOT BE SO ENTOMBED BUT THAT HE WILL RISE AGAIN.—THIS ILLUSTRATED IN PROVERBS: *e. g.*, "TRUTH AGAINST THE WORLD;" "TRUTH CRUSHED TO EARTH WILL RISE AGAIN;" "IT TAKES MANY SHOVELFULS OF EARTH TO BURY THE TRUTH."—ILLUSTRATED IN HISTORY: *e. g.*, THE REFORMATION, THE PURITAN MOVEMENT, THE METHODIST MOVEMENT.

This incident is peculiar to Matthew. It is attacked not only by rationalistic critics, but even given up by Meyer and Olshausen. The objections to the narrative are fairly given and, as it seems to me, adequately answered in Alford's note, which I therefore transcribe. "The chief difficulties found in it seem to be : (1.) How should the chief priests, etc., *know of his having said*, 'in three days I will rise again,' when the saying was hid even from his own disciples? The answer to this is easy. The *meaning* of the saying may have been, and was, hid from the disciples ; but the *fact of its having been said* could be no secret. Not to lay any stress on John 2 : 19, we have the direct prophecy of Matt. 12 : 40, and besides this, there would be a rumor current, through the intercourse of the Apostles with others, that he had been in the habit of so saying. (To this I may add the possible testimony of Judas Iscariot to the priests.) As to the *understanding* of the words, we must remember that *hatred is keener-sighted than love ;* that the raising of *Lazarus* would show *what sort of a thing rising from the dead was to be ;* and that the fulfilment of the Lord's announcement of his *crucifixion* would naturally lead them to look further, to *what more* he had announced. (2.) How should the women, who were solicitous about the *removal* of the stone, not have been still more so about its being sealed, and a guard set? The answer to this is (see notes below), *they were not aware of the circumstance, because the guard was not set till the evening before.* There would be no need of the application before the *approach of the third day*—it is only made for a watch "until the third day" (ver. 64), and it is not probable that the circumstance would transpire that night—certainly it seems not to have done so. (3.) That Gamaliel was of the council, and if such a thing as this, and its sequel (ch. 28 : 11–15) had really happened, he need not have expressed himself doubtfully (Acts 5 : 39), but would have been certain that this was from God. But, first, it does not necessarily follow that *every member* of the Sanhedrim was present and applied to Pilate (see note on ver. 62), or even had they done so, that all bore a part in the bribery of the soldiers (ch. 28 : 12). One who, like Joseph, had not consented to their deed before—and we may safely say that there were others such—would naturally withdraw himself from

63 Saying, Sir, we remember that that deceiver said, while he was yet alive, After³ three days I will rise again.
64 Command therefore that the sepulchre be made sure until the third day, lest his disciples come by night, and ʷ steal him away, and say unto the people,

He is risen from the dead: so the last error shall be worse than the first.
65 Pilate said unto them, Ye have a watch: go your way, make it as sure as ye can.
66 So they went, and made the sepulchre sure, sealing ˣ the stone, and setting a watch.

u John 7 : 12, 47 ; 2 Cor. 6 : 8. ... v ch. 16 : 21 ; 17 : 23 ; 20 : 19 ; Luke 24 : 6, 7 ; John 2 : 19. ... w ch. 28 : 13. ... x Dan. 6 : 17.

further proceedings against the person of Jesus. (4.) Had this been so, the three other Evangelists would not have passed over so important a testimony to the Resurrection. But surely we cannot argue in this way—for thus every fact narrated by *one Evangelist alone* must be rejected—such as the *satisfaction of Thomas* (John 20 : 24–29), which stands in much the same relation, and other such narrations. *Till we know much more about the circumstances under which, and the scope with which each Gospel was compiled, all à priori arguments of this kind are good for nothing.*" (To which add the consideration that Matthew, who wrote for the Jews, among whom the story of the stealing of the body had been circulated (ch. 28 : 15), was the one most likely to afford this explanation and refutation of that rumor.)

62. The day that followed the day of preparation. That is, on the Sabbath. The Jews, who did not hesitate to violate the law in the condemnation of Christ, and even to invoke the Gentile penalty of crucifixion on one of their own nation, would not have hesitated to employ the Sabbath hours, if necessary, to consummate their work. There is no good reason to suppose, therefore, that they waited until Sabbath evening; on the other hand, the guard would not have been set until eve, because there was no danger that the grave, which was near a public highway, would be rifled during the day (see ver. 1 ᵃˢ). So the women, given to them, who came to the sepulchre the next day (Mark 16 : 1–3), may very likely have known nothing of the guard.—**The chief priests and Pharisees.** Not necessarily, nor even probably, a formal meeting of the Sanhedrim. It is not the usual formula used to describe such a meeting. Comp. ch. 26 : 57 ; 27 : 1.

63, 64. After three days I will rise again. The reference is probably to John 2 : 19, which prophecy of Christ's was made directly to the priests and in Jerusalem. This would be interpreted to them by his language in Matt. 12 : 39, 40.—**Lest his disciples come by night.** The guard then would not have been stationed till nightfall, *i. e.*, of Saturday, the Jewish Sabbath.—**And steal him away.** They judged the disciples by themselves. They would not have hesitated to employ such a trick for such a purpose.—**The last error shall be worse than the first.** Observe that they recognize and unconsciously enforce the argument from the resurrection. Granted that Christ rose from the dead, and all that is involved in faith in a supernatural Christianity follows. Observe, too, that they were *sincere* in their belief that Christ and his disciples were deceivers. If they had not, really feared such a deceit, they would not have applied to Pilate for a guard to prevent it. For it is absurd to suppose that they really anticipated the resurrection and thought a Roman seal and guard would prevent it. It is the effect of pride and passion to blind men, not only to the truth, but also to moral qualities in better men ; they are given up to strong delusion *to believe* a lie (2 Thess. 2 : 11).

65, 66. Have ye a watch. The original verb (ἔχετε) may be the imperative or the indicative. It seems better to render it imperative.—(So Meyer and De Wette.) It is not a mere statement that they have a guard—if they had one there was no occasion for the application—but a direction to them to take one. It was evidently a guard of Roman soldiers, but, by Pilate's orders, placed under command of the priests ; and to them the guard reported the resurrection in the first instance (ch. 28 : 11). The term *watch* (κουστωδία) is general, and does not indicate of what number of men it consisted. There is no reason for supposing with Barnes there were sixty, or with Gray that there were four.—**Make it fast, as ye know how.** This is the literal rendition of the original. The guard was given to them, and they were at liberty to take what measures they saw fit to secure the tomb. Thus God's providence ordained that Christ's enemies should furnish a part of the evidence of Christ's resurrection. But for the priests' precaution, their story of a robbery of the tomb might have gained a credence which is now attached to it by no one.—**Sealing the stone.** It was common to seal the doors of tombs with wax or clay (comp. Dan. 6 : 17). Such seals are described by Wilkinson as still found in Egypt. In this case the sealing was probably done by passing a cord across the stone at the mouth of the sepulchre, and fastening it at either end by the sealing clay. On the bearing of this fact on the resurrection of our Lord, see note on the Resurrection of our Lord at close of next chapter

---

Ch. 28 : 1–17. THE RESURRECTION OF JESUS CHRIST.—How ATTESTED: BY SKEPTICAL AND RELUCTANT WITNESSES ; BY THE POWER OF A LIVING AND LIFE-GIVING LORD ; BY THE SABBATH DAY. See NOTE ON

CHAPTER XXVIII.

IN⁷ the end of the sabbath, as it began to dawn toward the first *day* of the week, came Mary Magdalene,ᶻ and the other Mary, to see the sepulchre.

2 And, behold, there was a great earthquake: for the angel of the Lord descended from heaven, and came and rolled back the stone from the door, and sat upon it.

y Mark 16 : 1 ; Luke 24 : 1, etc. ; John 20 : 1, etc. . . . . z ch. 27 : 56.

RESURRECTION OF OUR LORD BELOW.—WHAT IT ATTESTS: THE DIVINE NATURE OF CHRISTIANITY (Acts 2 : 22–24); THE PRESENT POWER OF CHRIST (Rom. 5 : 11), THE FUTURE LIFE OF THE BELIEVER (1 Cor. 15 : 20–23).—IF WE FOLLOW THE COMMANDS OF LOVE, GOD WILL ROLL AWAY ALL STONES. Comp. MARK 15 : 3.— THE RISEN CHRIST BRINGS FEAR TO FOE AND JOY TO FRIEND (ver. 4, 5).—WHOEVER TRULY SEEKS CHRIST NEED NOT FEAR, THOUGH AT FIRST HE DOES NOT FIND HIM.—THE SEPULCHRE IS ALWAYS EMPTY; THE BELOVED HAVE ARISEN (Luke 24 : 5; John 11 : 26).—THE MESSAGE OF THE GOSPEL INSPIRES THE BEARER WITH ALACRITY (ver. 8).—THE OBDURACY OF WILFUL UNBELIEF (ver. 11–15; comp. Luke 16 : 31).—SKEPTICISM IS NOT MODERN: IT HAS BEEN IN THE CHURCH FROM THE BEGINNING (ver. 17).

Of the Resurrection we have accounts materially different, though not inconsistent, in the four Evangelists, and some additional particulars from Paul, in 1 Cor. 15 : 3–8. On the apparent discrepancies and real harmony of the Evangelical accounts see Note on Resurrection of our Lord, p. 330. Of the four Evangelists Matthew gives the briefest and least detailed account. He wrote the Gospel, possibly in Hebrew, probably for Jewish converts (see Intro., p. 43), and appears to have only narrated enough of the circumstances connected with Christ's resurrection to explain and neutralize the Rabbinical story that the body had been stolen. In this he succeeded; this report is no longer current even in Jewish literature (see below on vers. 11–15). He alone reports this attempt to explain away the resurrection.

1. In the end of the Sabbath, as it began to dawn toward the first of the week. There is some difficulty respecting the construction of the original Greek here, but none respecting its substantial meaning. It is literally, *In the end of the Sabbath, in the dawning toward the first of the Sabbath.* The latter phrase, *The first of the Sabbath*, is equivalent to The first day after the Sabbath, the Hebrews being accustomed to designate the days of the week in this manner, as The first of the Sabbath, The second of the Sabbath, etc. The first clause may be rendered *At the end of the Sabbath* (so Lightfoot and Alford), or *After the Sabbath* (so Olshausen, De Wette, Norton, Robinson, Crosby and others), and this better represents the meaning, as the Jewish Sabbath extended from nightfall to nightfall. The time was probably just between night and sunrise (comp. Mark 16 : 2 with John 20 : 1). The latter clause of the verse here, In the dawning of the first day of the week, defines the first clause, In the end of the Sabbath, which otherwise might be taken to mean at nightfall of the Sabbath.—**Came Mary Magdalene and the other Mary.** That is, the mother of Joses (Matthew 27 : 56, note). Salome was with them (Mark 16 : 1); perhaps others (Luke 24 : 1).—**To contemplate the sepulchre.** This appears to be the meaning of the original here. It was an errand of sorrowful love, easily interpreted by our common experience of grief. They also proposed to complete the anointing of the body (Mark 16 : 1), which they could not lawfully do on the Sabbath.

2. And behold there was a great commotion. This is the literal meaning of the word (σεισμός), rendered earthquake. It is rendered *tempest* in Matt. 8 : 24. It is not necessary to understand an earthquake in the ordinary sense of that term. Probably it was a purely local and supernatural disturbance, for the purpose of opening the grave, though possibly an after-trembling, following the earthquake of the crucifixion. Such after-convulsions are not uncommon. There is no good authority for the rendering of the marginal reading of our Bibles, "There *had been* an earthquake." The verb (ἐγένετο) is in the imperfect tense. Whether the women were witnesses of this commotion is another matter. It seems to me clearly, from Mark 16 : 2–4, Luke 24 : 2, and John 20 : 1, that the stone had been rolled away *before they arrived;* and from John 20 : 11–15 that they could not have witnessed the commotion and the first angelic appearance.—**An angel from heaven.** Not *the* angel, a term used in the Old Testament generally, if not always, to designate a particular person, and, as I believe, Jesus Christ himself. Here and in ch. 1 : 20 and 2 : 13, the definite article is wanting, and the translation should be, as in ch. 2 : 19, *an* angel. On the Scripture teaching concerning angels see Luke 1 : 11. All the Gospels unite in representing angelic appearances at the tomb, though they differ in their descriptions. See page 330, Note on the Resurrection of our Lord, § 1. Mark and Luke describe the persons as "men," according to the appearance; Matthew and John as angels, according to the reality. That there were two angels is clear from John's more minute account (John 20 : 12), confirmed by Luke (chapter 24 : 4). Matthew and Mark mention only one angel, perhaps because they knew

3 His countenance was like lightning, and his raiment white as snow:
4 And for fear of him the keepers did shake, and became as dead men.
5 And the angel answered and said unto the women, Fear not ye: for I know that ye seek Jesus, which was crucified.

6 He is not here; for he is risen, as he said. Come, see the place where the Lord lay.
7 And go quickly, and tell his disciples that he is risen from the dead; and, behold, he goeth before you into Galilee; there shall ye see him: lo, I have told you.
8 And they departed quickly from the sepulchre,

a Ps. 104 : 4; Ezek. 1 : 4-14; Dan. 10 : 6; Rev. 1 : 14-16....*b* Heb. 1 : 14....*c* Ps. 105 : 3, 4....*d* ch. 27 : 63... *e* Luke 24 : 34; 1 Cor. 15 : 4....*f* vers. 16, 17.

only of one, not getting the details fully, perhaps because one was prominent as the speaker. Comp. similar discrepancy between Matt. 8 : 28 and Luke 8 : 27, and again, Matt. 20 : 30 with Luke 18 : 35. —**Rolled back the stone.** The grave was not opened by the commotion or earthquake, but the commotion or earthquake accompanied the rolling back of the stone. It is not necessary to suppose that the resurrection accompanied the earthquake. "It was not for Him, to whom (John 20 : 19, 20) the stone was no hindrance, but for the women and the disciples that it was rolled away."—(*Alford*.) Also to emphasize the fact of resurrection, which else might have been thought a trick of legerdemain, perpetrated by the disciples. For plan of tomb with its door of stone see Mark 16 : 3.—**And sat upon it.** As a symbol of the completeness of the victory over death, as the conqueror might sit on the prostrate form of his foe, which is here represented by the sealed door of the tomb.

3, 4. **His countenance was like lightning.** That is, in its vivid brightness. Comp. Exodus 34 : 29, 30; Matthew 17 : 2; Rev. 1 : 14. —**His raiment white as snow.** A symbol of purity and of fellowship with God. Rev. 3 : 4, 5, 18; 4 : 4; 6 : 11; 7 : 9-13. There is some significance in the fact that in all these cases in Revelation the white robe is the dress not of an angel proper, but of a departed saint. Coupling this fact with the statements in Mark and Luke, may we not reasonably suppose that these were the spirits of men, possibly the Moses and Elijah who had appeared on the Mount of Transfiguration with their Lord? If so, they bore an additional testimony to the resurrection.—**And for fear of him the keepers;** that is, the Roman guard mentioned in the preceding verse.—**Did shake with fear, and became as dead;** apparently swooned away with their terror.

5-7. **The angel answered.** To the unspoken fear of the women.—**Unto the women.** It is a reasonable hypothesis that Mary Magdalene, believing that the sepulchre had been rifled, ran back to the city at once (John 20 : 1, 2) to report the fact to the disciples, and was not present at the interview which followed. This not unreasonable supposition harmonizes the account here with that in John. If Mary Magdalene received the tidings of the resurrection from the angels, she would not have addressed the supposed gardener as she did, with entreaty for a return of the body (John 20 : 15).—**Fear not ye.** The pronoun *ye* is emphatic. To these disciples the resurrection of their Lord was no cause for fear, but for rejoicing. So his final coming will be cause of terror to the unbelieving, but not to his own followers. Comp. Psalm 98 : 8, 9 with Rev. 1 : 7. Observe how the shepherds are cautioned against fear in the birth of Christ (Luke 2 : 10), and the disciples on his appearance to them in trouble (John 6 : 20), and in the hour of his resurrection.—**For I know that ye seek Jesus the crucified.** Whoever is honestly and earnestly seeking Jesus the crucified need not fear, even *though he has not consciously found him* (Psalm 105 : 3). Observe that to the angel he is, as to the redeemed in heaven, the Lamb as it were slain (Rev. 5 : 6; 7 : 9).—**For he is risen.** The women then had not seen him rise.—**As he said.** Luke's report is fuller (ch. 24 : 6, 7). For Christ's prophecies of his resurrection see Matt. 16 : 21; 17 : 23.—**Come, see the place where the Lord lay.** Emphatic; not *your* Lord, in which case it might merely mean master or seignior; but *the* Lord (ὁ κύριος). With the definite article this word is in the Gospels equivalent to God. See Matt. 1 : 22; 5 : 33; Luke 1 : 6. They were to come into the tomb and see for themselves that he was not there.—**Tell his disciples.** Especially Peter (Mark 16 : 7).—**He goeth before you.** This language does not imply a literal traveling by Christ. The angel refers to the Lord's last prophecy of his resurrection, which contained a promise couched in almost these very words (Matt. 26 : 32).—**I have told you.** Another and further assurance of the truth of this unexpected glad tidings.

8. **They departed quickly from the sepulchre.** Compare with this and the next clause Mark's language: "They fled from the sepulchre."—**With fear and great joy.** Fear at the sight, joy at the word. The experience was a commingled one; the contradiction is one common in experience. The fear and trembling (Mark 16 : 8) was that not of terror so much as of awe and excitement, such as is often produced by unexpected and astonishing news. It illustrates and is illustrated by Phil. 22 : L

with fear and great joy, and did run to bring his disciples word.
9 And as they went to tell his disciples, behold, Jesus met them, saying, All hail.ᵍ And they came and held him by the feet, and worshipped him.
10 Then said Jesus unto them, Be not afraid: go tell my brethren,ʰ that they go into Galilee, and there shall they see me.
11 Now when they were going, behold some of the watch came into the city, and shewed unto the chief priests all the things that were done.
12 And when they were assembled with the elders, and had taken counsel, they gave large money unto the soldiers,
13 Saying, Say ye, His disciples came by night, and stoleⁱ him *away* while we slept.
14 And if this come to the governor's ears, we will persuade him, and secure you.
15 So they took the money, and did as they were taught: and this saying is commonly reported among the Jews until this day.
16 Thenʲ the eleven disciples went away into Galilee, into a mountain where Jesus had appointed them.

g John 20 : 19 .... h Heb. 2 : 11 .... i ch. 27 : 64. ... j ch. 26 : 32 .... k ch. 16 : 28.

—**Did run to bring his disciples word.** This accords with Luke 24 : 9 ; comp. John 20 : 18. Mark, on the contrary (16:18), says, "Neither said they anything to any man." Alford regards all attempts to reconcile this discrepancy as futile; similarly, DeWette and Meyer. I should understand Mark to mean that they said nothing to any one on the way. So James Morison following Grotius. Apart from the other Evangelists it would be quite incredible to suppose they said nothing respecting this angelic appearance to their co-disciples; and this notwithstanding the explicit direction to tell them. Observe in their haste here to tell the story of the resurrection, an illustration of the spirit which should always actuate the disciples of Christ (Ephes. 4 : 15).

9, 10. As they went to tell his disciples. These words are wanting in the best manuscripts, and are omitted by Tischendorf, Lachmann, Tregelles, and Alford. There is, therefore, nothing to indicate that this interview took place at this time. It is not narrated by any other of the Evangelists, and their narratives indicate, if taken alone, that the women bore no other message to the disciples than that which they received from the angels. John (20 : 11-18), whose account of the resurrection is the fullest, reports an appearance of our Lord to Mary Magdalene, one of these women; it occurs, however, after she had brought the disciples word that the body had been removed, and after John and Peter had visited the tomb and found it empty. Here, too, the women are represented as clasping our Lord's feet; there Mary Magdalene is represented as forbidden to touch her Lord. It is not impossible that Matthew here embodies, in a briefer and more imperfect form, the facts which John has told more fully and accurately.—**Be not afraid.** See above, note on ver. 5.—**Go tell my brethren.** So called for the first time by Christ; because he is the first-fruits of the dead (Heb. 2 : 9-11). He previously had declared that whosoever does the will of God the same is my brother, but he never before employed the term in direct address to his disciples.

11-15. This report is peculiar to Matthew, whose brief account of the resurrection was, perhaps, written chiefly for the purpose of counteracting the report of the Pharisees.—**When they were going.** While the women were hastening to announce the Gospel of the resurrection to the disciples, the soldiers were going to report it to the Pharisees; the one to publish it for the world's redemption, the other to conceal and counteract it. Satan was as quick to silence the Gospel as the disciples to proclaim it.—**When they were assembled with the elders.** The language does not imply a formal meeting of the Sanhedrim, but rather a secret meeting of the special enemies of Christ.—**If this be testified to before the governor.** Not merely, as our English version would indicate, If he happens to hear about it, but, If you are officially accused before him.—**Until this day.** We learn from Justin Martyr that this report was current among the Jews when he wrote, *i. e.*, in the second century. It has been supplanted by the modern Jewish legend, that some of the Jews, disguising themselves as disciples, and mourning with them, remained after they had departed, rifled the tomb of the body of Christ, subsequently exhibited it to the people, and then buried it in Golgotha, the ground of which they thoroughly plowed, that the corpse might never be discovered. The original legend is revived in a modified form by Renan, in "*The Apostles.*" He recognizes that the Jewish story is self-contradictory. "We can scarcely admit that those who so bravely believed that Jesus had risen again, were the very ones who had carried off the body;" but he supposes that, "It is possible that the body was taken away by some of the disciples, and by them carried into Galilee. The others, remaining at Jerusalem, would not have been cognizant of the fact." On the inherent unreasonableness of all such attempted explanations, see below, Note on the Resurrection of our Lord.

16, 17. The eleven disciples went away into Galilee. The original does not indicate that they went at this time. On the contrary, it would appear from John 20 : 26, that they remained in Judea at least a week after the resur-

17 And when they saw* him, they worshipped him: but some doubted.
18 And Jesus came and spake unto them, saying, All¹ power is given unto me in heaven and in earth.
19 Go ⁿ ye therefore, and teach* all nations, baptizing them in the name of the Father, and of the Son, and of the Holy Ghost;
20 Teaching ᵒ them to observe all things whatsoever I have commanded you: and, lo, I ᵖ am with you alway, *even* unto the end of the world. Amen.

l ch. 11 : 27 ; Ps. 2 : 6 ; 89 : 19 ; 110 : 1-3 ; Isa. 9 : 6, 7 ; Dan. 7 : 14 ; Luke 1 : 32 ; John 17 : 2 ; Rom. 14 : 9 ; Eph. 1 : 20, 21 ; Heb. 2 : 8 ;
l Pet. 3 : 22 ; Rev. 11 : 15....m Mark 16 : 15....n Isa. 52 : 10 ; Rom. 10 : 18.... o Acts 2 : 42 ; 1 Cor. 11 : 2.... p ch. 18 : 20 ; Rev. 1 : 18.

rection. Of the appearances in Galilee we have three accounts—the brief one here, the fuller account in John, ch. 21, and the reference by Paul in 1 Cor. 15 : 6, 7, which is probably to an appearance in Galilee. He says, "He was seen of above five hundred at once;" and Galilee was the home of most of Christ's disciples. There is nothing in Mark or Luke to indicate any appearance in Galilee.—**Into a mountain where Jesus had appointed them.** Probably, in some unreported conference or message. The site of this mountain is wholly unknown.—**And seeing him they worshipped him.** Comp. Rev. 5 : 6-14 ; 7 : 9-11 ; and observe that worship is refused by the angel in the book of Revelation (ch. 22 : 8, 9).—**But some doubted.** Not doubted whether they should worship him ; nor some of the eleven doubted whether he had risen. The language describes in general terms the state of skepticism in the early church, which could be overcome only by repeated appearances and invincible proofs. Those that saw worshipped, but some of the great body of disciples were doubtful. Such an one was Thomas until he had seen (John 20 : 24, 25). See Note on Resurrection of our Lord, p. 320, etc.

Ch. 28 : 18-20. CHRIST'S COMMISSION TO HIS CHURCH. —IT COMES FROM AN ALMIGHTY KING AND REQUIRES AN AGGRESSIVE MINISTRY.—IT DEFINES CHRISTIANITY AS A UNIVERSAL RELIGION ADAPTED TO ALL NATIONS, AND A CIVILIZING RELIGION, THE SECRET OF ALL TRUE NATIONAL LIFE.—IT DESCRIBES THE DUTY OF THE CHURCH, TO MAKE DISCIPLES OF ALL NATIONS ; AND ITS INSTRUMENTS, BAPTISM AND TEACHING.—IT INTERPRETS BAPTISM AS INITIATION INTO A NEW LIFE IN THE TRIUNE GOD ; AND THE THEME, THE AUTHORITY AND THE OBJECT OF CHRIST'S TEACHING : THE THEME IS THE GOSPEL ; THE AUTHORITY, THE COMMANDS OF CHRIST ; THE OBJECT, PRACTICAL OBSERVANCE OF HIS WORDS. —IT DISCLOSES THE SECRET OF THE POWER OF THE CHURCH : A REALIZING SENSE OF THE PERPETUAL PRESENCE OF ITS LORD.—IT DEFINES THE PERIOD WHEN ITS WORK WILL CEASE, WHEN REDEMPTION IS CONSUMMATED.

This commission is given in a different form in Mark (16 : 9-20), but the authority of the passage is doubtful. See note there. A different commission is reported by John (20 : 21-23). Comp. also Luke 24 : 46-49. The passage here is one which sustains a doctrine of verbal inspiration, *i. e.*, it indicates that not only the thoughts of the sacred writer were inspired, but, in at least some instances, even his choice of words ; for the full understanding of this commission can be obtained only by a careful study of it word by word. Unfortunately, our English version does not always preserve the accurate signification of the words. In the notes here I simply endeavor to give the English reader the meaning of the original, as interpreted by parallel passages of Scripture, without entering into the doctrinal discussions which have been waged concerning it. The time when this commission was given is uncertain. The place appears, from the connection here, to have been Galilee ; Mark, on the contrary, connects it with the Ascension, which took place from the Mount of Olives (Acts 1 : 12).

18. Spake unto them, *i. e.*, to the eleven ; for there is no evidence to connect it with the appearance to the five hundred, reported only by Paul (1 Cor. 15 : 6, 7). Thus, on its face, this is a purely personal commission to those whom Christ had before selected and ordained. But that it extended beyond them is clear from verse 20, for they have not remained till the end of the world to claim the promise of that verse. There are two interpretations— one, that it embraces the Apostles and *their successors in office*, and hence is a commission and a promise confined to the clergy. But there is no hint here, nor anywhere else in our Lord's sayings, of any successors to the Apostles. The other interpretation is that it is given to the Apostles as the germ and representative of the universal church, and this view is sustained by the considerations : (1.) That the command is not more explicitly limited to the eleven than the commission to observe the Lord's Supper, which by universal consent extends to all the disciples. (2.) By the usage of the early church. With this commission fresh in their minds the Gospel was preached, not by a clerical order, but by all the disciples (Acts 8 : 14 ; 11 : 19). (3.) That the command itself, by its necessary implication, lays the duty of preaching on all disciples, since they are to be taught to do *all things which Christ has commanded the Apostles*, and this includes the command to preach. "Teaching them to observe all things whatsoever I have commanded you makes *them* into *you*, as soon as they are made disciples."—(*Alford.*) (4.) This interpretation best accords with the spirit, if not with the letter of Christ's other instructions, which lay on all disciples the duty of manifesting the Gospel to the world (Matt. 5 : 13-16 ; Mark 4 : 21 ; Luke 10 : 1 ; comp. Rev. 22 : 17).

All power is given unto me in heaven and in earth. The English language contains no adequate equivalent for the word rendered *power* (ἐξουσία). It embraces the ideas of both *power* and *authority*—power coupled with right. It here indicates Christ as the true Lord and King both of nature and of life, human and angelic. For the significance of this declaration comp. Dan. 7 : 14; Rom. 14 : 9; Ephes. 1 : 20–23; Col. 2 10; Heb., chap. 1; 1 Pet. 3 : 22; Rev. 5 : 12, 13. But observe that the language here (*is given*) implies that this power is derived from the Father, is not inherent in the Son. Phil. 2 : 9 indicates that it was in part given to him after and in consequence of his voluntary humiliation, and 1 Cor. 15 : 27, 28 that it is held in subjection to the Father. Observe, too, that the power given to Christ is alleged by him as a reason, not for *subduing*, but for *teaching* all nations. His power is exercised in patience, long-suffering, and love—a power whose highest exemplification is the cross, "to the Jews a stumbling-block and to the Greeks foolishness, but to them which are called the power of God and the wisdom of God." It is the authority and power of love (1 Cor. 1 : 23, 24; comp. Col. 1 : 11).

19. Go ye therefore. Therefore is not in the best MSS. "It is probably a gloss, but an excellent one."—(*Alford.*) It expresses the real connection between the verses, though in the original that connection was probably implied, not expressed. It is because all power is given to Christ that his disciples are to go forth to fulfill this command, strong in the assurance of his presence to the end. Observe in the command *Go forth* a clear designation of the duty of an aggressive ministry. The original (πορεύομαι) signifies a going from place to place. It is best interpreted by the practice of the early disciples, who "went everywhere, preaching the word." It marks a contrast between the new religion and the Jewish, which was intolerant of all other religions, and made no effort at extension among the Gentiles; and the Roman religion, which was tolerant of all other religions, because indifferent, and therefore made no effort to supplant them. Whenever the church sits down content with past conquests, and becomes simply conservative, employing all its energies to preserve and strengthen within its own communion what is already gained, it violates the spirit of this injunction, which requires it to go out into the streets and lanes, and bring in the poor and the maimed and the halt and the blind (Luke 14 : 21).

Disciple all nations. The rendering of our English version is unfortunate, since it employs the same word here and in the next verse to translate two different Greek vowels. The one which I have substituted, following Drs. Conant, Crosby, and others, though perhaps in-elegant English, is a literal rendition of the original. The command is not, *Teach and baptize*, with the added explanation in verse 20 respecting the things to be taught, but, *Make disciples of all nations*, with the added explanation how this is to be done, viz., by baptizing and teaching. Observe that the command to make disciples of *all nations* implies, (1) That Christianity is a universal religion, not merely one of the religions of the world from which, with others, we, in this later day, are to select an eclectic and universal religion; (2) that it is adapted to all nations and all classes (Rom. 1 : 14), a claim which history has abundantly justified, but which was urged by early opponents as a conclusive objection to it; (3) that not a natural development, but obedience to the principles inculcated by Jesus Christ, constitutes the secret of true civilization among all nations, and thus that Christian missions are the mother of civilization; (4) that from all nations the members of Christ's church triumphant are to be gathered to God by obedience to this commission (Rom. 10 : 11–13; Rev. 7 : 9). This command removes the limitations put upon the apostles by their first commission (ch. 10 : 5, note), and shows that it was there temporary only, and it accords with Christ's explicit declarations concerning his mission (Matt. 8 : 11; 13 : 38, note). It marks the beginning of the fulfillment of his prophecies during the last days of his ministry in Jerusalem (Matt. 21 : 43; 22 : 8–10). Henceforth the kingdom of God is to be taken from the Jews and given to a nation bringing forth the fruits thereof. That the disciples at first hesitated to receive uncircumcised Gentiles into the church, notwithstanding this commission (Acts 11 : 2; 15 : 5; Gal. 2 : 12), ought not to surprise any one who considers how strong were the Jewish prejudices against the Gentiles (Acts 22 : 21, 22), and how slow even the apostles were to apprehend the full import of Christ's words (Mark 9 : 39; Luke 16 : 34).

Baptizing them into the name of the Father, the Son, and the Holy Ghost. Not, as in our English version, *In* the name (ἐν τῷ ὀνόματι), but *into the name* (εἰς τὸ ὄνομα). The significance of the phrase is best learned by referring to other parallel passages, *e. g.*, Matt. 3 : 11, I baptize you *in* (ἐν) water *into* (εἰς) repentance; Acts 2 : 38, Be baptized *upon* (ἐπὶ) the name of Jesus Christ *into* (εἰς) the remission of sins; Romans 6 : 3, So many of us as were baptized *into* (εἰς) Christ Jesus were baptized *into* (εἰς) his death; 1 Cor. 10 : 2, And were all baptized *into* (εἰς) Moses in the cloud and in the sea. Comp. 1 Cor. 1 : 13; 12 : 13. These are the principal passages which throw light on the use of the words here employed, and they indicate that to baptize *into* signifies, in N. T. usage, the *end and aim of bap-*

tism. The disciples of John by baptism were brought into repentance, and later the disciples of Jesus into the remission of sins, and into a participation with the death of Christ, as explained in the succeeding verse (Rom. 6 : 4), and the Jews, by their passage of the Red Sea, entered into the Mosaic dispensation, *i. e.*, into the national life and the covenant with God which Moses inaugurated. Interpreting Scripture by Scripture, it would appear that Christ's command here is not, as Dr. Conant, Meyer, De Wette, and others render it, Baptize with reference to the name of the Father, the Son, and the Holy Ghost, that is, Baptize in water and with this formula; but, Bring all nations into covenant and spiritual relations with the Triune God, as by baptism John brought his disciples into repentance, and by the passage of the Red Sea the Jews were brought into a new national life under Moses. In other words it appears to me that Christ *does not here command water baptism of any description*, except by implication. He commands, not the sign, but the thing signified. If we render baptize *immerse*, then the meaning will be, Immerse the nations in the Triune God, so that in him they shall live and move and have their being; or if we understand baptism to be simply a sign of purification and consecration, the meaning will be the same. The nations are to be purified from their old false faiths, and consecrated to God, the Father, Son, and Spirit. That the disciples understood that they were to use water baptism as a sign of this immersion in God, or this consecration to and covenant with Him, is indicated by their subsequent practice, which also, however, indicates that they did not understand that Christ here prescribed a formula of water baptism, for they are not recorded ever to have used it. The ordinary apostolic form was, In the name of Jesus (Acts 2 : 38; 8 : 16; 10 : 48; 19 : 5; 22 : 16). Observe the significance of the phraseology here, in its bearing on the truth that the Father, the Son, and the Holy Ghost constitute one only true God. The language is not, In the *names* plural, but, In the *name* singular. Notice, too, that it is not by acceptance of God merely, that the nations are to be made disciples (deism is not Christianity), but by accepting God as revealed in the Father by creation and providence, in the Son by his earthly life, sufferings and death, and in the Holy Spirit in his constant spiritual presence in the hearts of the children of God.

On the meaning of the word baptize (βαπτίζω), it must suffice to say here, in addition to what I have already said (Note on the Baptism of Jesus by John, p. 35), that after a careful study I am not satisfied that in the N. T. it *necessarily implies* immersion, still less complete submersion (see Mark 7 : 4, note; 1 Cor. 10 : 2), and that in my judgment the Scripture form of baptism, if the Scripture fixes on any form, must be determined by other considerations than the meaning of this word. The best authorities for the student to consult for the Baptist view of this question are Baptism in its Modes and Subjects, by Alexander Carson, and The Meaning and Use of Baptism philologically and historically investigated, by Dr. T. J. Conant. The latter, after a careful and exhaustive list of passages in classical literature, the Scripture, and the church Fathers in which the word occurs, embodies his conclusions as follows: "The ground-idea expressed by this word is, *to put into or under water* (or other penetrable substance), *so as entirely to immerse or submerge;* this act is always expressed in the literal application of the word, and is the basis of its metaphorical uses. This ground-idea is expressed in English, in the various connections where the word occurs, by the term (synonymous in this ground-element), *to immerse, immerge, submerge, to dip, to plunge, to bathe, to whelm.*" For the opposite view the student may consult advantageously four volumes by Rev. J. W Dale, entitled respectively, Classic Baptism, Judaic Baptism, Johannic Baptism, and Patristic Baptism. His conclusion he thus rather vehemently states: "Dipping the body into water is not, nor (by reason of a double impossibility found in the meaning of the word, and in the divine requirement) can it be, *Christian baptism.* That Christian baptism is a water dipping is a novelty unheard of in the history of the church for fifteen hundred years. This idea is not merely an error as to the mode of using the water (which would, comparatively, be a trifle), but it is an error which sweeps away the substance of the baptism without leaving a vestige behind. It is a sheer and absolute abandonment of the baptism of inspiration, which is a baptism *into Christ*—into the name of the Father, and of the Son, and of the Holy Ghost, and the substitution for it of a dipping into water, which has no more place in the Scriptures than the English W has a place in the alphabet of the Greek Testament." On the meaning of the phrase, *In the name of the Father*, etc., see *Rob. Lex.*, art. ὄνομα. "The name of God, of Christ (τὸ ὄνομα τοῦ θεοῦ, τοῦ κυρίου τοῦ χριστοῦ), is a paraphrase for God himself, Christ himself, in all their being, attributes, relations, manifestations." Similarly Dr. Schaff: "The *name* signifies the meaning and essence of the subject as *revealed*, the copy or expression of the Being. In this case the name implies all that belongs to the manifestation of the Triune God in the Gospel, his titles, attributes, and works of creation, redemption, and sanctification." (Comp. Matt. 10 : 41, 42; 19 : 21; 18 : 5–20; 19 : 29, etc.)

20. Teaching them. Contrast this command with that given to the twelve in ch. 10 : 7. Then they were simply to go as heralds to announce that the kingdom of God was drawing nigh (see note there); henceforth they are to become instructors in the whole system of truth taught by Jesus Christ. Observe, then, that the mission of the ministry is not merely to herald the Gospel, but to teach its principles as a system of truth; that only he who is in some sense an instructive preacher fulfills this command; that whenever the ministry thwart intellectual development they are not Christ's ministry; and that implicitly the seal of Christ's condemnation is set on all preaching, which appeals merely to the imagination or the emotions, i. e., which is sensational rather than instructive. Alford lays stress on the fact that in this commission baptism precedes preaching: "It will be observed that in our Lord's last words, as in the church, the process of ordinary discipleship is from baptism to instruction, i. e., admission in infancy to the covenant and growing up into observing all things." But surely the doctrine of infant baptism cannot fairly be deduced from the fact that in this commission Christ places baptism before instruction. As little can we deduce the doctrine that baptism should be administered only on an intelligent profession of faith, from the fact that Christ puts the discipling of all nations before baptism. In fact, in the practice of the Apostles, partial instruction preceded baptism, but not complete instruction in all things commanded by Christ (see Acts 2 : 41; 17 : 32, 33). It is, however, a fair deduction from the language here, that no one is prepared to receive instruction in the things which Christ has commanded, till he has been spiritually baptized, i. e., brought into covenant relations with, and personal allegiance to the Triune God. Submission to God precedes instruction in the mysteries of God's kingdom. Comp. John 3 : 3; 1 Cor. 2 : 7, 8.—**To observe all things whatsoever I have commanded you.** Observe, (1) *The theme of the Christian ministry*, Whatsoever Christ has commanded. Their duty is simply to expound and apply Christ's commands; their magazine is not the traditions or creeds of the church, but the New Testament; for the Epistles are but the logical development and application of truths the germs of which are all to be found in the Gospels. This commission is inclusive; nothing that Christ has commanded may be omitted from the instructions of the church (Acts 20 : 27). It is exclusive; it shuts out from the pulpit ministry all purely secular science and philosophy (1 Cor. 1 : 17; 2 : 4; Rev. 22 : 18, 19). The power of the church is the greatest when its ministry is most simply and truly scriptural. Every revival of religion has accompanied a restoration to the heart of the church of the partially forgotten word of God. (2.) *The authority of the Christian ministry*. It is based on the commands of Christ. The church is to teach what he has *commanded*. It is, therefore, to teach with authority, as he did (Matt. 7 : 29, note), but with *his* authority, not with its own; the authority of the Scripture, not of ecclesiastical councils and decrees. (3.) *The object of the Christian ministry*. To bring men into subjection, not to the church, or its creed, or its ministry, but to Christ himself; "To observe all things whatsoever I have commanded you." On the meaning of the word (τηρέω), rendered *observe*, see Matt. 19 : 17, note. The church is to teach men, not merely to *do* Christ's commandments, but to *keep watch over them*, as a guard over his prisoner, and this includes attentive study of the instructions of Christ, watching with prayer against temptation to insure obedience to the commands of Christ, and watching for the fulfillment of Christ's prophecies. Comp. Matt. 25 : 13; 26 : 41; John 14 : 15, 21-24.

And lo. Literally *behold*. The word is emphatic, and imports the stress which Christ laid, and which the church should lay on the promise which follows. But it is also a command to the church to keep in her sight her spiritually-present Lord. For it is only as she *beholds* the presence of her Lord with her, watching her fidelity, knowing her transgressions, measuring her life, as well as ever proffering to her needed grace and strength, that she is or can be kept pure, and strong, and hopeful, and loving. He is ever in the midst of the seven candlesticks (Rev. 1 : 13), but whether to inspire or to condemn, depends on whether he is there *beheld* by his church. His realized presence is the only explanation of the success of the church of the Apostolic age, the only ground on which it can base an expectation of success in the present or the future.—**I am with you.** Observe the significance of the present tense. To the disciples he appeared to be removed by his death. To their apprehension he replies, not I shall be, but, *I am* with you. His true presence with his church now begins. He is still the "*I am*" of his church (Exod. 3 : 14; John 8 : 58), a perpetually-present Saviour. Comp. with this promise, John 14 : 20-23, and 20 : 22, 23. But observe that it is both a promise and a warning. He is present to rebuke and chasten, as well as to guide, and guard, and inspire (Rev. 3 : 19). For interpretation of this declaration, study the whole of the Epistles to the seven churches of Asia (Rev. chaps. 2 and 3).—**All the days** (πάσας τὰς ἡμέρας). Not merely *alway*. It is a *daily* presence which is promised, not a fitful coming and going, but an abiding (John 15 : 4); a presence, too, in all days, and never even in the darkest to be forgotten.—**Unto the end of the world.** Rather, *Unto the consummation of the cycle*, not merely till the physical world comes to an end, but till the era and work of redemption is completed. The original (συντελεια) signifies not merely the *end*, as of a period of time, but the *completion*, as of a specific work. Comp. Matt. 13 : 39, 40, 49. The Redeemer will remain with his church (1 Cor. 3 : 9) till the work of redemption is finished; then, when it can say with its Lord, "It is finished" (John 19 : 30), it will rise with him to be forever with the Lord (John 17 : 24; 1 Thess. 4 : 17). Then he will not be with us—we shall be with him.

It is not strange that some early copyist should have given fervent expression to the feeling with which the church received this command and promise of the Lord, in the added Amen, which is no part of the original text, but which should ever be the answer of church universal to the gracious words of her Master.

NOTE ON THE RESURRECTION OF JESUS CHRIST.

1. *Harmony of the Gospel Narratives.* The accounts of the resurrection are contained in Matt., ch. 28; Mark, ch. 16; Luke, ch. 24; and John, chs. 20 and 21. For the authenticity of Mark 16 : 9-20 and John, ch. 41, see notes there. The discrepancies in these accounts constitute an argument of rationalistic writers for believing them to be mythical or legendary. The student will readily perceive the nature of these discrepancies in the Evangelical narratives by comparing the following summary of their accounts, arranged in parallel columns for that purpose:

Matt., ch. 28.	Mark, ch. 16.	Luke, ch. 24.	John, chs. 20, 21.
Toward dawn of the first day of the week Mary Magdalene and another Mary come to the sepulchre. An earthquake has occurred, the stone has been rolled away, and the watchmen have swooned with terror. An angel announces to the women the resurrection of Jesus; and they depart to tell the other disciples, meet Jesus on the way, and worship him. He bids them tell the disciples to go to Galilee, where they shall see him. Subsequently the eleven meet him there, and receive their commission. Meanwhile the soldiers, bribed by the Jews, report that the tomb was rifled by the disciples.	*At the rising of the sun* on the first day of the week, the two Marys *and Salome* come to the sepulchre to anoint the body of Jesus; they find the stone rolled away, and a young man (angel?) in the tomb. This young man announces the resurrection of Jesus, and bids them tell the disciples to go into Galilee, where they shall see Jesus. They depart and *say nothing to any man,* because they are afraid. The same day Jesus himself appears to Mary Magdalene, who tells the mourning disciples; but they believe not. He afterward appears to two who are walking into the country (comp. Luke, ch. 24), and who report the appearance to the disciples, but are not believed. Afterward he appears to the eleven as they sit at meat. He gives them their commission and is received up into Heaven.	Early in the morning of the first day of the week the women, including the two Marys, come to the sepulchre and find the stone rolled away. They enter and are perplexed to find the tomb vacant. *Two men* appear to them and announce the resurrection. They return and report it to the rest, but are not believed. *Peter,* however, goes to the sepulchre, finds it vacant, and wonders at the fact. The same day Jesus appears to two disciples during their walk to Emmaus, who return and report the appearance to the eleven. While they are together Christ appears and takes meat with them. He leads them out to Bethany and thence ascends into Heaven.	While *it is yet dark Mary Magdalene* comes to the sepulchre, finds the stone removed, returns, reports to Peter *and John,* who come together to the sepulchre. Peter enters first, then John; they find the sepulchre empty, and go away perplexed. Mary stands without the sepulchre weeping, looks in, sees *two angels,* who speak to her. She answers them, hears a voice without, supposes the speaker to be the gardener, until, at the pronunciation of her name, she discerns the Lord. She reports the facts to the disciples. The same evening Christ appears to them, Thomas being absent, and breathes on them, imparting the Holy Ghost. After eight days he appears again, and convinces Thomas of his resurrection, and subsequently appears to the disciples, in Galilee.

Comparing these four accounts, the following facts are observable: (1.) No one Evangelist gives more than a partial account of the events which occurred between the resurrection and the ascension; the discrepancies, so-called, are largely due to the fact that each narrative is partial and incomplete, and none narrate facts narrated by the others. (2.) We cannot with any certainty construct a perfect harmony out of these accounts, i. e., we cannot be sure of the exact order of the events variously narrated by the different Evangelists. (3.) Though there are discrepancies, such as we might expect in the narrative of such events, penned by truthful and independent writers, each narrating only what he saw, or what he learned from trustworthy and independent witnesses, *there are no contradictions, i. e.,* no fact is stated by one writer which is denied by another, or is irreconcilable with the statement made by another. (4.) In respect to the substantial facts, *viz.,* the death, the burial, the resurrection, on the morning of the third day, first discovered at or about daybreak, and followed by numerous appearances to different witnesses, and at different times, all the Evangelists agree. (5.) The principal discrepancies are the following: The time of the visit to the tomb by the women is described by Mark as sunrise, by John as "while it was yet dark"; *two* angels are described as at the tomb by Luke and John, *one* by Matthew and Mark; an appearance to all the women is described in Matthew, an appearance to Mary alone in Mark and John, and no answering appearance in Luke. In Mark the women say nothing to any man, in the other three Evangelists they tell the disciples. These are, I believe, all the discrepancies of any moment. They are none of them of a character to invalidate the truthfulness of the concurrent testimony to the essential facts. Most of them are easily explicable; for explanations see notes on the various passages; all, I believe, would be explicable if we knew all the facts. (6.) Finally, while a harmony of these accounts is possible, any harmony, constructed in our imperfect knowledge of the events, is necessarily hypothetical. With this explanation I embody what appears to me to be a probable order of the events, as recorded by the four Evangelists, supplemented by Luke in Acts 1 : 1, 2, and Paul in 1 Cor. 15 : 3-7.

Several women—the exact number is not known—go together at early dawn, between daybreak and sunrise, to the tomb, to anoint the body. They find the grave opened and the body gone. Mary, supposing that the tomb has been rifled by the enemies of the Lord, hastens instantly back to the city for help, tells Peter and John, who forthwith hasten to the sepulchre. She accompanies, or more probably follows them, unable to keep up. That they hastened is evident from John 20 : 4. Meanwhile the angel in the tomb has announced the resurrection of the Lord to the other women, who have gone back into the city to tell the news to the disciples. Peter and John come, find the tomb empty, and depart perplexed. Mary, in greater grief than before, at the helplessness of their situation, their Lord's tomb robbed, and their Lord's body borne away to some dishonored grave, remains weeping, is accosted by some one whom she believes to be the gardener, discovers in him her risen Lord, and hastens to Jerusalem to inform the disciples. This I believe to be the first appearance of Jesus to any of the disciples, and probably the basis of the less full and accurate account of Matt. 28 : 9, 10. The same day Christ appears to the disciples at Emmaus (Luke); and on the evening of that day to the ten at meat; and a week later again, when Thomas is present. The appearances in Galilee (John, ch. 21; Matt. 28 : 16, 17) are later. The commission to the eleven is given perhaps still later, whether in Galilee or Judea is uncertain; I incline to think in Judea, and that it is followed almost immediately by the ascension. That this harmony is in all respects correct I do not assert; it is only hypothetical, but there is nothing in any of the four narratives inconsistent with it. It is at all events clear that there is a substantial accord in the four accounts. They are not irreconcilable, and the discrepancies are in matters of minor and comparatively unimportant details.

2. *Authentication of the Resurrection.* Since the resurrection of Jesus Christ necessarily carries with it the supernatural origin and divine authority of Christianity, it is not strange that from the earliest ages it has been the chief evidence of Christianity in the hands of Christians, and the chief point of attack on the part of unbelievers. The following considerations have led the majority of impartial students of history to consider the resurrection of Jesus Christ as well authenticated as any fact in history. (1.) The early church universally believed in the resurrection of Jesus Christ; it formed the basis of the first apostolic preaching (Acts 2 : 24-32; 3 : 21; 4 : 2, 10; 10 : 39-40; 13 : 30-37; 17 : 31, 32); and it was universally accepted by Christians at the time when Paul wrote the first Epistle to the Corinthians, *i. e.*, within about thirty years after its supposed occurrence. It is incredible that a myth should have grown up, without substantial foundation, in a quarter of a century, in spite of hostility of both Jew and Gentile, and during the lifetime of those who were competent to contradict and dispute the falsehood if it had been false. (2.) This belief is sustained by four narratives which (see above) substantially agree, yet, which are all unmistakably original and independent accounts, neither produced by collusion, nor drawn from a common source. The accounts bear in many places the evident indication of being prepared by eye-witnesses; and of being the natural and even child-like description of events which the narrators themselves could not comprehend. The very seeming contradictions afford incidental evidence of the belief of the narrators. "Nothing can exceed in artlessness and simplicity the four accounts of the first appearance of Jesus after his crucifixion. If these qualities are not discernible here, then we must despair of ever being able to discern their presence anywhere." — (*Furness.*) (3.) This universality of belief must, on any hypothesis, be accounted for. It cannot be accounted for by the ancient Jewish explanation, viz., that the body was stolen and the story of resurrection invented by the disciples (Matt. 28 : 13). This is not only negatived by the precautions which the priests took against fraud (Matt. 27 : 62-66), by the facts that the disciples

were not anticipating a resurrection (see below), and that such a deception could not possibly and did not, in fact, enure in any way to their advantage, but also by the abundant evidence of their honesty in their labors and self-sacrifice, and by the incredibility of the supposition that a number of men could have banded together to promulgate such a system of religion as that of Jesus Christ, embodying such exalted precepts and principles of truth, purity, and love, by means of a deliberately-framed fraud. This hypothesis is now almost, if not quite, universally abandoned, even by infidel scholars. For example, "Only thus much need be acknowledged, that the disciples firmly believed that Jesus had arisen ; this is perfectly sufficient to make their further progress and operations intelligible."—(*Strauss*.) "It is an indisputable fact that in the early morning of the first day of the week following the crucifixion, the grave of Jesus was found empty * * * It is a second fact that the disciples and other members of the Apostolic communion were convinced that Jesus was seen after his crucifixion." —(*Schenkel*.) The honesty of the Apostles is even admitted by the Jewish Rabbinical writings, which accounts for the disappearance of the body by saying that it was removed from the grave by the priests (see note on verses 11-15, above). Nor can this universal belief be explained by the hypothesis that Christ did not really die, but swooned, and was subsequently recovered from his swoon. For his death is as well authenticated as any fact in history. It was made sure of by the enmity of the priests (Matt. 27 : 62, 63), by the spear-thrust of the soldiers (John 19 : 34, 35), by the questioning of Pilate (Mark 15 : 44), these concurrent facts being testified to by independent witnesses ; and the recovery of Jesus from a swoon could not have formed the basis of any belief in a resurrection, without deliberate fraud on the part of his followers, which, as we see, is not regarded as tenable even by infidels. Nor can this belief be accounted for by regarding it with Renan as the production of an enthusiastic imagination and ardent hope in the disciples, in other words as a spiritual fantasy. For they had no such imagination and no such hope. The fact of the resurrection is attested, not by persons predisposed to believe in it, but by skeptical critics hard to be convinced. They were utterly disheartened by his death and had as little expectation of his resurrection as they had before entertained of his crucifixion. The women who came to anoint the body were surprised and grief-stricken to find it gone ; they thought the tomb had been robbed. When they carried back the report of the resurrection to the other disciples "their words seemed to them as idle words, and they believed them not." The two disciples who conversed with the unrecognized Christ on their walk to Emmaus, had given up their faith in the Messiahship, and were thunderstruck at the revelation of his presence. When he appeared to the ten, Thomas refused to accept their testimony. So marked and stubborn was their incredulity, that Christ more than once upbraided them for their unbelief. The reader who is interested to see how little historical basis there is for the latest and perhaps most popular rationalistic theory of the resurrection, namely, that it was the honest figment of a diseased imagination, the unconscious creation of those who "amuse themselves with what is impossible, and, rather than renounce all hope, do violence to every reality," may find it in an examination of the following among other passages, indicating how stolid, prosaic, despairing, unhopeful, and unimaginative were the witnesses who have testified to the resurrection (Mark 16 : 10-14; Luke 24 : 11-20, 21, 25, 32, 37-39 ; John 20 : 9, 11-15, 24, 25). The facts, then, are indisputable, even admitted by rationalistic writers,—Schenkel, Renan, Strauss, and by Rabbinical writers (see Goldstien's *Life of Jesus*),—that the grave of Jesus was found empty early in the morning of the first day of the week following the crucifixion, that it was not opened by connivance of the disciples, that they believed that they saw their risen Lord, conversed with him, touched him, ate with him, that this belief was shared by above five hundred persons who at different times had intercourse with him (1 Cor. 15 : 3-8), that on this belief the whole structure of Christianity, as a divine religion, was rested by the early preachers, at a time when it would have been easy to expose the error, if error there were, and was universally believed in the church, within thirty years after its occurrence. (4.) Only the fact of the resurrection can account for the marvelous change in the spirit and character of the Apostles. While he lived they had no accurate conception of his mission, believed he was about to inaugurate a political Jewish kingdom, were eager for precedence in it, and this even up to the time of his Passion, looked to the last moment for a miraculous deliverance from the Roman soldiers, when this hope was crushed by Christ's surrender, forsook him and fled, and after his crucifixion abandoned all idea of his being the Messiah and returned to their old avocation of fishing (Matt. 16 : 22; 20 : 20-24 ; Luke 19 : 11; 22 : 24-30 ; John 21 : 3). But the resurrection completely transformed them; inspired them with a new conception of Christ's kingdom as for all people, with a new courage to suffer for the sake of their risen Lord and his kingdom, and with a new purpose to preach Christ and him crucified everywhere as a spiritual redemption for sin (Acts 2 : 39; 5 : 41; 10 : 43). Neither fraud nor fiction are competent to account for the moral contrast between the Apostles of the four Gospels and those of the Book of Acts. (5.) A singular and significant testimony to the truth of the resurrection is afforded by the change in the Sabbath-day. Nothing is more difficult to alter than religious ceremonials. No religious ceremonial could be more difficult to alter than a day observed, if not from the creation of the world, certainly for 1500 years. It was changed, not by any express command, for there is none in the N. T., but by the almost universal consent of the church, which could not endure to observe as a day of joy and gladness that on which Christ lay in the tomb, nor forbear to mark as a weekly festival that on which he arose. This fact can be accounted for only by recognizing the universal and ancient character of the belief in the resurrection of Jesus Christ—a belief, for which, as we have seen, it is impossible to account on any hypothesis which denies the substantial truthfulness of the Evangelical accounts.

ANCIENT PATHWAY FROM BETHANY TO JERUSALEM. (From a photograph.)

The view is taken from near the foot of the Mount of Olives; the garden of Gethsemane is in the foreground; in the background, on the left, is the north corner of the east wall of Jerusalem. The path crosses the Cedron near the garden of Gethsemane.